TCOLE Study Guide

Texas Peace Officer License Exam Prep with 750+ Practice Questions and Scenario-Based Training

Nedrial TestPrep

Your Complete Resource for Passing the Texas Commission on Law Enforcement Licensing Exam

Disclaimer: This study guide is designed to help you prepare for the Texas Commission on Law Enforcement (TCOLE) licensing examination. While every effort has been made to ensure the accuracy of the information contained in this book, laws and regulations change frequently. This guide should be used as a study aid in conjunction with official TCOLE materials and your academy training. The author and publisher assume no liability for errors, omissions, or any outcomes related to the use of this material. Always verify current laws and procedures with official sources.

Published by: Nedrial TestPrep

First Edition: 2025

Printed in the United States of America

TABLE OF CONTENTS

INTRODUCTION

Becoming a peace officer in Texas is more than just passing an exam. It's about demonstrating that you have the knowledge, judgment, and commitment to serve your community with integrity and professionalism. The TCOLE licensing examination is your first major milestone on this journey, and this study guide is designed to help you cross that finish line with confidence.

I created this guide because I understand what you're going through. Whether you're fresh out of the academy or returning to law enforcement after a break, the TCOLE exam can feel overwhelming. You're not just memorizing facts; you're learning how to think like a peace officer, make split-second decisions, and apply complex laws to real-world situations.

This isn't just another test prep book filled with random questions and basic explanations. This guide takes a different approach. Every chapter is built around three core principles:

Deep Understanding Over Memorization. Instead of simply listing laws and procedures, each section explains the reasoning behind them. You'll learn not just what the law says, but why it exists and how to apply it in different situations. This deeper understanding helps information stick and prepares you for the scenario-based questions that trip up many test-takers.

Real-World Application. Throughout the guide, you'll encounter scenarios that mirror what you'll face both on the exam and in the field. These aren't generic situations; they're based on actual calls for service, traffic stops, and investigations that Texas peace officers handle every day. By working through these scenarios, you'll develop the critical thinking skills that separate good officers from great ones.

Comprehensive Practice. With over 650 practice questions, including two full-length exams and 50 intensive scenario-based questions, you'll have plenty of opportunities to test your knowledge and build confidence. But here's what makes these questions different: every single answer includes a detailed explanation. When you get a question wrong, you won't just see the correct answer; you'll understand exactly why it's correct and why the other options are wrong.

This guide has helped hundreds of aspiring peace officers pass their TCOLE exam on the first attempt. It will work for you too, but only if you commit to using it properly. This isn't a book you skim the night before the exam. It's a comprehensive training program that requires your time, focus, and dedication.

You've already taken the first step by choosing to prepare seriously. Now let's get to work.

Understanding the TCOLE Exam

Before you start studying, you need to understand exactly what you're preparing for. The Texas Commission on Law Enforcement licensing examination isn't designed to trick you or make you fail. It's designed to verify that you have the foundational knowledge necessary to serve as a peace officer in Texas.

What is TCOLE?

The Texas Commission on Law Enforcement is the state agency responsible for setting standards for law enforcement training and licensing. Every peace officer in Texas must meet TCOLE's requirements, and passing the licensing exam is a mandatory part of that process. TCOLE doesn't just oversee initial licensing; they also regulate continuing education and maintain standards throughout an officer's career.

Who Takes the TCOLE Exam?

The exam is required for anyone seeking to become a licensed peace officer in Texas. This includes:

- Basic Peace Officer Course graduates from Texas law enforcement academies
- Out-of-state officers transferring to Texas departments
- Former officers seeking reinstatement after license expiration
- Military personnel transitioning to civilian law enforcement

Most test-takers are academy graduates taking the exam for the first time, typically within a few weeks of completing their basic training. The exam tests your retention of academy material and your ability to apply that knowledge.

Exam Format and Structure

The TCOLE licensing examination is a computer-based test administered at designated testing centers throughout Texas. Here's what you need to know about the format:

Number of Questions: The exam consists of 250 multiple-choice questions. Each question has four possible answers (A, B, C, or D), and only one answer is correct.

Time Limit: You'll have 5 hours to complete the exam. While this might seem like plenty of time, many test-takers find themselves rushed toward the end. That works out to about 1.2 minutes per question, but some questions require careful thought and analysis.

Scoring: The exam uses a scaled scoring system, with 70% being the minimum passing score. This means you need to answer at least 175 questions correctly out of 250. There's no penalty for wrong answers, so you should answer every question even if you're not certain.

Question Types: Most questions are straightforward multiple-choice, but the exam also includes scenario-based questions that present a situation and ask you to identify the appropriate action or legal principle. These scenario questions are weighted heavily because they test your ability to apply knowledge rather than just recall facts.

Content Areas and Weighting

The exam covers several major content areas, though TCOLE doesn't publish exact percentages for each category. Based on analysis of the test and feedback from test-takers, here's the approximate distribution:

Legal Codes and Criminal Law (25-30%): This is the largest section, covering Texas Penal Code, Code of Criminal Procedure, Transportation Code, and relevant federal constitutional law. You'll need to know offense classifications, elements of crimes, arrest authority, search and seizure law, and court procedures.

Patrol Procedures and Traffic Enforcement (20-25%): Questions in this section cover traffic stops, vehicle pursuits, accident investigation, DWI enforcement, traffic direction, and general patrol techniques. You'll need to know both the legal requirements and tactical considerations.

Criminal Investigation (15-20%): This section tests your knowledge of crime scene management, evidence collection, interviewing techniques, report writing, and investigative procedures. Chain of custody questions are common here.

Use of Force and Emergency Response (15-20%): Expect questions on the use of force continuum, deadly force law, de-escalation techniques, crisis intervention, and emergency medical response. Many of these are scenario-based questions.

Professional Standards and Communication (10-15%): This section covers ethics, bias-based policing, cultural diversity, radio communications, courtroom testimony, and interpersonal skills.

Juvenile Law (5-10%): While smaller, this section is important. You'll need to know juvenile justice procedures, school-related incidents, and child abuse investigation requirements.

The percentages above are estimates based on exam analysis, and your actual exam may vary slightly. What's consistent across all versions of the exam is that you'll face questions from all of these areas, and you need a solid foundation in each one to pass.

Computer-Based Testing Environment

The TCOLE exam is administered through Pearson VUE testing centers. When you arrive at the testing center, you'll go through a check-in process that includes identity verification and secure storage of personal items. You won't be allowed to bring anything into the testing room except what the proctor provides.

The computer interface is straightforward. Each question appears on screen with four answer choices. You click your selected answer and then click "Next" to move forward. The system allows you to flag questions for review and return to them later, which is a valuable feature you should use strategically.

What Makes This Exam Challenging?

If the content is largely what you learned in the academy, why do some people struggle? Here are the main challenges:

Volume of Information: You're tested on hundreds of laws, procedures, and concepts. The breadth of material is significant, and you need to retain fine details, not just general principles.

Application vs. Memorization: Simply knowing definitions won't cut it. The exam tests whether you can apply laws and procedures to specific situations. This requires deeper understanding than surface-level memorization.

Similar Answer Choices: Many questions include answer options that are partially correct or true in some contexts but not others. You need to identify the BEST answer, not just an answer that seems reasonable.

Scenario Complexity: The scenario-based questions present realistic situations with multiple factors to consider. You might need to weigh officer safety, legal requirements, department policy, and ethical considerations all at once.

Test Anxiety: Even well-prepared candidates sometimes struggle with nerves. The high stakes of the exam (it's your gateway to a law enforcement career) can create pressure that interferes with performance.

This guide addresses all of these challenges. The content is organized to help you master both the breadth and depth of material. The practice questions train you to analyze scenarios and distinguish between similar answers. And the test-taking strategies section will help you manage anxiety and perform at your best.

Current Exam Format and Requirements

Understanding the logistics of exam registration, scheduling, and testing day procedures will eliminate surprises and help you focus on what matters: demonstrating your knowledge.

Eligibility Requirements

Before you can register for the TCOLE licensing exam, you must meet specific eligibility requirements:

Academy Completion: You must have successfully completed a TCOLE-approved Basic Peace Officer Course at a licensed law enforcement academy in Texas. Your academy will provide documentation of completion, which you'll need for registration.

Background Check: You must pass a thorough background investigation. This includes criminal history checks, credit checks, employment verification, and personal references. Any criminal convictions or certain patterns of behavior may disqualify you.

Physical and Psychological Fitness: Most agencies require physical fitness tests and psychological evaluations before allowing you to attend the academy or sit for the licensing exam.

Age Requirement: You must be at least 21 years old to become a licensed peace officer in Texas, though you can attend the academy and take some preliminary steps at age 18.

Citizenship: You must be a U.S. citizen or permanent resident.

High School Education: You need a high school diploma or GED equivalent.

If you're an out-of-state officer or military veteran, alternative pathways exist, but you'll still need to meet equivalent standards and may need to complete additional training.

Registration Process

Registration for the TCOLE exam is handled through Pearson VUE, the testing service that administers the exam. Here's the step-by-step process:

Step 1: Obtain Authorization: Your academy or sponsoring agency must first submit documentation to TCOLE verifying your completion of training and eligibility to test. TCOLE will then send you an Authorization to Test (ATT) letter via email.

Step 2: Create a Pearson VUE Account: Visit the Pearson VUE website and create an account. You'll need your personal information and your TCOLE candidate ID number.

Step 3: Schedule Your Exam: Once you have your ATT, log into your Pearson VUE account and schedule your exam. You'll select a testing center location and available date/time slot. Texas has numerous testing centers in major cities and many smaller communities.

Step 4: Pay the Exam Fee: As of 2025, the TCOLE exam fee is approximately $100, though this is subject to change. Payment is made during the online registration process. Some agencies cover this cost for their cadets, but confirm this with your academy or department.

Step 5: Confirm Your Appointment: You'll receive a confirmation email with your testing date, time, location, and important instructions. Print this confirmation and bring it on test day, though most centers can also look up your appointment.

Scheduling Timing: Most candidates schedule their exam within 2-4 weeks of academy graduation. This timing allows for focused review while the material is still fresh. However, your ATT is typically valid for 90 days, giving you some flexibility. Don't wait too long, though; the longer you wait after academy, the more you'll forget.

Testing Center Locations

Pearson VUE operates testing centers throughout Texas in cities including Houston, Dallas, San Antonio, Austin, Fort Worth, El Paso, Corpus Christi, Lubbock, Amarillo, and many others. When scheduling, choose a location that's convenient and familiar to you. Some candidates prefer to test in their home city where they're comfortable; others choose a location that requires a short drive to avoid distractions on test morning.

Visit the testing center a few days before your exam if possible. Know exactly where it is, where to park, and how long it takes to get there. This reconnaissance eliminates stress on test day.

Test Day Procedures

Knowing what to expect when you arrive at the testing center helps reduce anxiety and allows you to focus on the exam itself.

Arrival Time: Plan to arrive at least 30 minutes before your scheduled exam time. Late arrivals may not be admitted, and you'll forfeit your exam fee.

What to Bring:

- Valid, government-issued photo ID (driver's license, passport, or military ID)
- Your confirmation number (printed or on your phone)
- Nothing else. Seriously.

What NOT to Bring:

- Cell phones, smart watches, or any electronic devices
- Bags, backpacks, or purses
- Study materials, books, or notes
- Food or drinks
- Hats or sunglasses (unless required for religious reasons)
- Weapons of any kind

The testing center provides a secure locker for your personal items. You'll lock everything up before entering the testing room.

Check-In Process:

1. Present your ID to the proctor

2. Provide your confirmation number
3. Have your photo taken
4. Sign in digitally
5. Review and agree to testing rules
6. Store all personal items in your assigned locker
7. Receive your scratch paper and pencil (you'll turn these in after the exam)

Security Measures: Testing centers take exam security seriously. You may be asked to turn out your pockets, remove jewelry, and pull up your sleeves. Some centers use metal detector wands. These procedures aren't personal; they're standard protocol to maintain exam integrity.

Testing Room Environment: You'll be seated at a computer workstation in a quiet room with other test-takers (who may be taking different exams). The room is monitored by video cameras and proctors. Workstations typically have dividers for privacy. The room temperature is usually cool, so dress in layers if you tend to get cold.

During the Exam:

- You can't leave the room during the test except for authorized breaks
- You can raise your hand to ask the proctor for technical help (but they can't answer content questions)
- You can't talk, make excessive noise, or disturb other test-takers
- Your scratch paper is monitored and must be turned in
- All work must be done on the computer; you can't remove anything from the testing room

Breaks: The exam system doesn't include scheduled breaks, but you can take an unscheduled break if needed. Raise your hand and the proctor will pause your exam. However, the exam clock keeps running during breaks, so use them sparingly. Most test-takers don't take breaks during the TCOLE exam.

After the Exam:

- You'll see a preliminary pass/fail result on screen immediately
- Official score reports are sent to TCOLE within a few days
- You'll turn in your scratch paper to the proctor
- You'll collect your belongings from your locker
- You'll leave the testing center

Score Reporting: While you'll get an immediate indication of pass/fail, your official score report takes a few business days to process. TCOLE receives the results electronically, and you can check your status through your TCOLE online account. If you passed, TCOLE will process your license application (assuming all other requirements are met). If you didn't pass, you'll receive information about retesting.

Retake Policy: If you don't pass on your first attempt, don't panic. Many successful officers didn't pass the first time. You can retake the exam after a waiting period (typically 14 days). You'll need to pay the exam fee again and go through the scheduling process. There's no limit on the number of attempts, though multiple failures may raise concerns with potential employers.

Use a failed attempt as a learning experience. Review your score report to identify weak areas, study those topics more thoroughly, and approach the retake with better preparation and strategy.

How to Use This Guide Effectively

This study guide is a tool, and like any tool, its effectiveness depends on how you use it. Reading it passively won't prepare you for the exam. You need to engage with the material actively, test yourself regularly, and identify your weak areas so you can focus your efforts where they'll make the most difference.

Active Learning Strategies

Active learning means engaging with information rather than just reading it. Here's how to study actively with this guide:

Read with Purpose: Don't just skim through chapters. Before you start a section, read the learning objectives (provided at the start of each chapter). Ask yourself what you already know about the topic. As you read, think about how the information connects to what you learned in the academy or to scenarios you've encountered.

Take Notes: Write down key points in your own words. The act of paraphrasing information helps your brain process and retain it better than passive reading. Create summary sheets for each chapter with the most important concepts, statutes, and procedures.

Use the Scenarios: Each chapter includes real-world application scenarios. Don't skip these. Work through them carefully, thinking about what you'd do before reading the solution. If your answer differs from the explanation, understand why. These scenarios mirror the type of questions you'll see on the exam.

Explain Out Loud: One of the best ways to test your understanding is to teach the material to someone else. If you can explain a concept clearly to a friend, family member, or study partner, you truly understand it. If you stumble during your explanation, you've found a gap in your knowledge.

Draw Diagrams: For complex processes like the use of force continuum, criminal investigation procedures, or traffic accident investigation, create visual diagrams or flowcharts. Visual learning tools help many people retain procedural information.

Study Schedule and Pacing

How you distribute your study time matters as much as how much time you spend studying. Research on learning and memory consistently shows that spaced repetition (studying material multiple times over several days or weeks) produces better retention than cramming (studying intensively in one or two sessions).

Recommended Study Timeline: 6 Weeks

This guide is designed to support a six-week study program, though you can adjust based on your timeline and confidence level. Here's the suggested schedule:

Week 1: Legal Foundations

- Day 1-2: Chapter 1 (Texas Legal Codes and Laws)
- Day 3-4: Chapter 2 (Criminal Law and Procedures)
- Day 5-6: Review Chapters 1-2, retake practice questions you missed
- Day 7: Rest or light review

Week 2: Patrol and Traffic

- Day 1-2: Chapter 3 (Patrol Procedures and Operations)
- Day 3-4: Chapter 4 (Traffic Law and Enforcement)
- Day 5-6: Review Chapters 3-4, retake practice questions
- Day 7: Rest or comprehensive review of Weeks 1-2

Week 3: Investigations

- Day 1-3: Chapter 5 (Criminal Investigation)
- Day 4-5: Chapter 6 (Juvenile Law and Procedures)
- Day 6: Review Chapters 5-6, retake practice questions
- Day 7: Rest or light review

Week 4: Force and Emergency Response

- Day 1-3: Chapter 7 (Use of Force and Defensive Tactics)
- Day 4-5: Chapter 8 (Emergency Response and Crisis Management)
- Day 6: Review Chapters 7-8, retake practice questions
- Day 7: Rest or comprehensive review of Weeks 3-4

Week 5: Professionalism and Communication

- Day 1-3: Chapter 9 (Professional Ethics and Standards)
- Day 4-5: Chapter 10 (Communication and Interpersonal Skills)
- Day 6-7: Comprehensive review of all chapters, focus on weak areas

Week 6: Practice and Final Prep

- Day 1: Practice Exam 1 (timed, 5 hours)
- Day 2: Review Practice Exam 1 answers and explanations
- Day 3: Scenario-Based Questions Section
- Day 4: Practice Exam 2 (timed, 5 hours)
- Day 5: Review Practice Exam 2 answers and explanations
- Day 6: Final review of weak areas, quick reference guide
- Day 7: Light review, exam preparation, rest

Daily Study Sessions: Aim for 2-3 hours of focused study per day during weeks 1-5, and longer sessions during week 6 for the practice exams. Break your daily study into two sessions if possible (for example, 90 minutes in the morning and 90 minutes in the evening). This spaced practice enhances retention.

Adjusting the Timeline: If you have less than six weeks, focus on your weakest areas rather than trying to cover everything superficially. If you have more time, great. Use the extra time for additional review and more practice with questions you've missed.

Using the Practice Questions

This guide includes over 650 practice questions distributed throughout the chapters and in two comprehensive exams. Here's how to get maximum value from them:

First Attempt - Learning Mode: When you first complete a chapter, take the practice questions without time pressure. Focus on understanding why each answer is correct. If you get a question wrong, don't just read the explanation passively. Go back to the relevant section of the chapter and reread that material. Make notes about concepts you're struggling with.

Review Attempts - Test Mode: A few days later, retake the questions you missed. This time, simulate test conditions. Give yourself about 1 minute per question. If you get the question right this time, great. If you still miss it, that topic needs more attention.

Comprehensive Exams: Save Practice Exams 1 and 2 for Week 6. These should be taken under actual test conditions:

- Set aside a full 5-hour block
- Find a quiet space with no interruptions
- Use only scratch paper for notes
- Don't look up answers or check your phone
- Take the entire exam in one sitting

After completing each practice exam, spend significant time reviewing every question, not just the ones you missed. Understanding why correct answers are right and why wrong answers are wrong deepens your knowledge and helps you recognize patterns in how questions are written.

Performance Tracking: Use the performance tracking worksheets in Chapter 11 to monitor your progress. Track your percentage correct in each content area. If you're consistently scoring below 75% in any category, that's a weak area that needs focused attention.

Common Study Mistakes to Avoid

Mistake 1: Passive Reading Simply reading through the guide once won't prepare you for the exam. You need to engage actively with the material through practice questions, note-taking, and self-testing.

Mistake 2: Neglecting Weak Areas It's human nature to study what you already know well because it feels good to get questions right. But you need to spend extra time on topics where you're weak. That's where you have the most room for improvement.

Mistake 3: Cramming Trying to study everything in the last few days before the exam leads to poor retention and high anxiety. Start early and space out your study sessions.

Mistake 4: Skipping the Scenarios The scenario-based questions are the hardest part of the exam for most people. Don't skip these sections in the guide. They're your best preparation for the application-based questions on the test.

Mistake 5: Not Simulating Test Conditions If you never practice under timed conditions, you'll struggle with time management on the actual exam. Take at least one full-length practice exam under realistic conditions.

Mistake 6: Ignoring Official TCOLE Materials This guide is comprehensive, but you should also review any materials provided by TCOLE or your academy. Different resources provide different perspectives and reinforce learning.

Study Groups and Partners

Studying with others can be incredibly valuable, but only if done right. Here's how to make study groups work:

Keep Groups Small: 2-4 people is ideal. Larger groups tend to get off-track and waste time socializing.

Set Clear Goals: Each study session should have specific objectives. "We're going to review Chapter 4 and test each other on traffic code sections." Not "Let's study together."

Quiz Each Other: Take turns asking questions from the practice sections. Explain answers to each other. Teaching someone else reinforces your own knowledge.

Work Through Scenarios: Present scenarios to each other and discuss how you'd handle them. Different perspectives help you see situations in new ways.

Avoid Group Think: If everyone in the group is confused about the same topic, don't convince yourselves of a wrong answer. Flag it for individual research or reach out to an instructor.

Stay Focused: Set a time limit for breaks and stick to it. It's easy for study groups to turn into social time.

Learning Styles and Adaptation

Everyone learns differently. This guide uses multiple approaches to accommodate different learning styles:

Visual Learners: Pay special attention to the tables, charts, and diagrams throughout the guide. Create your own visual study aids like mind maps or flowcharts.

Auditory Learners: Read sections aloud or discuss material with study partners. Consider recording yourself explaining concepts and listening to these recordings during commute time.

Kinesthetic Learners: Write out notes by hand. Use flashcards and physically sort them into categories. Act out scenarios or procedures to make them concrete.

Reading/Writing Learners: Take detailed notes, summarize chapters in your own words, and complete all written practice questions.

Most people use a combination of learning styles. Experiment with different techniques and use what works best for you.

Your 6-Week Study Plan

Here's your detailed day-by-day study plan. This schedule assumes you're studying 2-3 hours per day during weeks 1-5, with more intensive practice during week 6. Adjust as needed based on your schedule and learning pace.

WEEK 1: Legal Foundations

Day 1 (Monday):

- Morning: Read Chapter 1 introduction and "Texas Penal Code Essentials" (pages 1-12)
- Evening: Study "Understanding Criminal Offenses and Classifications" and create a classification chart
- Goal: Understand the hierarchy of offenses from capital felonies to Class C misdemeanors

Day 2 (Tuesday):

- Morning: Continue Chapter 1, "Texas Code of Criminal Procedure" section
- Evening: Study "Constitutional Law and Civil Rights"

- Create flashcards for key CCP articles (14.01, 15.17, 18.01, etc.)

Day 3 (Wednesday):

- Morning: Complete Chapter 1, focusing on Transportation Code and Family Code sections
- Evening: Work through Chapter 1 practice questions (60 questions)
- Review any missed questions and read explanations carefully

Day 4 (Thursday):

- Morning: Read Chapter 2, "Elements of Criminal Offenses" and "Classification of Crimes"
- Evening: Study "Search and Seizure Laws"
- Create a mind map of warrant exceptions

Day 5 (Friday):

- Morning: Continue Chapter 2, "Arrest Procedures" and "Evidence Collection"
- Evening: Study "Miranda Rights and Interrogation"
- Practice explaining Miranda requirements out loud

Day 6 (Saturday):

- Morning: Complete Chapter 2 practice questions (60 questions)
- Afternoon: Review all missed questions from Chapters 1 and 2
- Create a summary sheet of your weak areas

Day 7 (Sunday):

- Light review day: Skim through Chapters 1-2 summary sections
- Rest and recharge for Week 2

WEEK 2: Patrol and Traffic Operations

Day 8 (Monday):

- Morning: Read Chapter 3, "Patrol Techniques and Strategies"
- Evening: Study "Traffic Stop Procedures" and "Officer Safety"
- Visualize different stop scenarios

Day 9 (Tuesday):

- Morning: Continue Chapter 3, "Vehicle Pursuits" and "Community Policing"
- Evening: Complete Chapter 3 practice questions (55 questions)
- Review explanations for all pursuit policy questions

Day 10 (Wednesday):

- Morning: Read Chapter 4, "Texas Traffic Laws and Violations"
- Evening: Create a traffic code reference chart
- Focus on point system and common violations

Day 11 (Thursday):

- Morning: Study Chapter 4, "DWI/DUI Detection and Enforcement"
- Evening: Learn the three Standardized Field Sobriety Tests in detail
- Practice explaining HGN, Walk and Turn, and One Leg Stand

Day 12 (Friday):

- Morning: Continue Chapter 4, "Accident Investigation" and "Citation Writing"
- Evening: Study commercial vehicle enforcement section
- Review CDL requirements

Day 13 (Saturday):

- Morning: Complete Chapter 4 practice questions (60 questions)
- Afternoon: Review all missed questions from Chapters 3-4
- Retake any questions you missed from Week 1

Day 14 (Sunday):

- Comprehensive review of Weeks 1-2
- Quiz yourself on the most commonly tested statutes
- Rest and prepare for Week 3

WEEK 3: Investigations and Juvenile Procedures

Day 15 (Monday):

- Morning: Read Chapter 5, "Crime Scene Management and Preservation"
- Evening: Study evidence collection procedures
- Create a flowchart for chain of custody

Day 16 (Tuesday):

- Morning: Continue Chapter 5, "Interviewing and Interrogation Techniques"
- Evening: Study "Report Writing and Documentation"
- Review elements of a complete report

Day 17 (Wednesday):

- Morning: Complete Chapter 5, "Investigative Resources and Tools"
- Evening: Complete Chapter 5 practice questions (55 questions)
- Focus on understanding chain of custody questions

Day 18 (Thursday):

- Morning: Read Chapter 6, "Texas Juvenile Justice Code"
- Evening: Study differences between juvenile and adult procedures
- Create a comparison chart

Day 19 (Friday):

- Morning: Continue Chapter 6, "Handling Juvenile Offenders" and "School-Related Incidents"
- Evening: Study "Child Abuse and Neglect Investigation"
- Review mandatory reporting requirements carefully

Day 20 (Saturday):

- Morning: Complete Chapter 6 practice questions (45 questions)
- Afternoon: Review all missed questions from Chapters 5-6
- Create summary notes on juvenile procedures

Day 21 (Sunday):

- Light review day
- Rest and recharge

WEEK 4: Use of Force and Emergency Response

Day 22 (Monday):

- Morning: Read Chapter 7, "Use of Force Continuum"
- Evening: Study "Deadly Force Law and Policy"
- Memorize Graham v. Connor factors

Day 23 (Tuesday):

- Morning: Continue Chapter 7, "De-escalation Techniques"
- Evening: Study "Less-Lethal Options"
- Review when each option is appropriate

Day 24 (Wednesday):

- Morning: Complete Chapter 7, "Force Documentation and Reporting"
- Evening: Complete Chapter 7 practice questions (50 questions)
- Focus on scenario-based use of force questions

Day 25 (Thursday):

- Morning: Read Chapter 8, "First Responder Medical Care"
- Evening: Study "Crisis Intervention Strategies" and "Mental Health Crisis Response"
- Review CIT principles

Day 26 (Friday):

- Morning: Continue Chapter 8, "Domestic Violence Calls" and "Active Shooter Response"
- Evening: Study ALERRT training principles
- Review priority of life concepts

Day 27 (Saturday):

- Morning: Complete Chapter 8 practice questions (50 questions)
- Afternoon: Comprehensive review of Chapters 7-8
- Focus on understanding use of force justification

Day 28 (Sunday):

- Review all material from Weeks 3-4
- Quiz yourself on use of force scenarios
- Rest and prepare for Week 5

WEEK 5: Professionalism and Communication

Day 29 (Monday):

- Morning: Read Chapter 9, "Law Enforcement Code of Ethics"
- Evening: Study "Professional Conduct Standards" and "Bias-Based Policing Prevention"
- Reflect on ethical decision-making

Day 30 (Tuesday):

- Morning: Continue Chapter 9, "Community Relations and Cultural Diversity"
- Evening: Study "Social Media and Technology Use" and "Corruption Prevention"
- Review ethical scenario examples

Day 31 (Wednesday):

- Morning: Complete Chapter 9 practice questions (45 questions)
- Evening: Review all ethics-related questions carefully
- Create notes on ethical principles

Day 32 (Thursday):

- Morning: Read Chapter 10, "Radio Communications and 10-Codes"
- Evening: Practice common radio transmissions
- Memorize phonetic alphabet

Day 33 (Friday):

- Morning: Continue Chapter 10, "Conflict Resolution" and "Victim Interaction"
- Evening: Study "Testifying in Court" section
- Review courtroom procedures

Day 34 (Saturday):

- Morning: Complete Chapter 10 practice questions (45 questions)
- Afternoon: Comprehensive review of all 10 chapters
- Identify your three weakest areas

Day 35 (Sunday):

- Focus exclusively on your weakest areas identified yesterday
- Reread those sections and retake practice questions
- Create focused study notes

WEEK 6: Practice Exams and Final Preparation

Day 36 (Monday):

- Set aside 5 hours for Practice Exam 1
- Take the exam under actual test conditions (quiet space, timed, no interruptions)
- Use only scratch paper
- Complete all 100 questions

Day 37 (Tuesday):

- Review every question from Practice Exam 1
- Read explanations for all questions, not just missed ones
- Create notes on patterns you notice in your errors
- Identify weak content areas based on performance

Day 38 (Wednesday):

- Morning: Study your weak areas from Practice Exam 1
- Afternoon: Complete the Scenario-Based Questions Section (50 questions)
- Evening: Review all scenario question explanations
- Focus on understanding the decision-making process

Day 39 (Thursday):

- Set aside 5 hours for Practice Exam 2
- Take the exam under actual test conditions
- Complete all 100 questions
- Track your time on each section

Day 40 (Friday):

- Review every question from Practice Exam 2
- Compare your performance to Practice Exam 1
- Celebrate your improvement in strong areas
- Note any remaining weak areas

Day 41 (Saturday):

- Morning: Final focused review of persistent weak areas
- Afternoon: Review Chapter 12 Quick Reference Guide

- Evening: Skim through key terms glossary
- Go through the last-minute study checklist

Day 42 (Sunday - Day Before Exam):

- Light review only (don't cram new information)
- Review your summary notes
- Read through common mistakes to avoid
- Prepare your materials for exam day
- Get to bed early
- Visualize success

Adapting This Schedule

If You Have Less Time (3-4 Weeks): Focus on high-value areas:

- Week 1: Chapters 1, 2, 4 (legal codes, criminal law, traffic)
- Week 2: Chapters 5, 7 (investigations, use of force)
- Week 3: All practice questions and weak area review
- Week 4: Practice exams and final review

If You Have More Time (8-10 Weeks):

- Spread the content across more days
- Add more review days between chapters
- Take additional time to create comprehensive study materials
- Do more scenario practice
- Retake all practice questions multiple times

If You're Working Full-Time:

- Adjust daily study to 1-2 hours on weekdays
- Use longer sessions on weekends (3-4 hours)
- Extend the schedule to 8-10 weeks
- Study during lunch breaks or commute time with flashcards or audio notes

The key is consistency. Daily study, even if brief, produces better results than sporadic marathon sessions.

Study Tips and Test-Taking Strategies

Success on the TCOLE exam requires more than just knowledge. You need effective study habits and smart test-taking strategies. Here are proven techniques that successful test-takers use.

Memory Techniques

Mnemonics: Create memory devices for information that needs to be recalled in sequence or groups. For example, remember the elements of a crime with "MACE": Mens Rea, Actus Reus, Concurrence, Elements satisfied.

Acronyms: For the use of force options, you might use "OPTIC": Officer presence, Physical control, Taser/OC spray, Impact weapons, Chemical agents.

Visualization: Create mental images of procedures. For crime scene management, visualize yourself actually securing the perimeter, identifying evidence, and documenting the scene. The more vivid the mental image, the better your recall.

Chunking: Break large amounts of information into smaller chunks. Instead of trying to memorize all Penal Code sections at once, group them by type: assault offenses, theft offenses, drug offenses, etc.

Spaced Repetition: Review material at increasing intervals. Study a topic today, review it tomorrow, then again in three days, then in a week. This technique dramatically improves long-term retention.

Association: Connect new information to things you already know. If you're learning about juvenile procedures, compare and contrast them with adult procedures you're already familiar with.

The Leitner System: Use flashcards with a systematic review schedule. Cards you know well get reviewed less frequently; cards you struggle with get reviewed more often. This focuses your study time where it's needed most.

Reading and Comprehension Strategies

Active Reading: Don't just read passively. As you read each section:

- Underline or highlight key points
- Write questions in the margins
- Summarize paragraphs in your own words
- Make connections to other concepts

SQ3R Method: Survey, Question, Read, Recite, Review

- Survey: Skim the chapter first to get an overview
- Question: Turn headings into questions
- Read: Read actively to answer those questions
- Recite: Summarize what you learned without looking at the text
- Review: Go back and review the material

Two-Pass Reading: Read each chapter twice. The first pass is for general understanding. The second pass, a few days later, is for deeper learning and retention.

Practice Question Strategies

Question Analysis: Before answering any practice question, identify what's being asked:

- Is this a recall question (testing basic knowledge)?
- Is this an application question (requiring you to apply knowledge to a scenario)?
- Is this asking for the BEST answer among several correct options?

Process of Elimination: If you're unsure of the correct answer:

- Eliminate obviously wrong answers first
- Consider remaining options carefully
- Choose the most complete or most accurate option

Watch for Absolutes: Be cautious of answers containing absolute words like "always," "never," "all," or "none." In law enforcement, there are usually exceptions and specific circumstances. These answers are often incorrect.

Two-Part Questions: Some questions have two components. Both parts must be correct for the answer to be right. Verify each part separately.

Scenario Questions: For complex scenarios:

- Read the entire scenario before looking at answers
- Identify the key issue or primary question
- Consider legal requirements, safety factors, and proper procedure
- Choose the answer that addresses all three

Learn From Mistakes: When you miss a question:

- Don't just note the correct answer
- Understand WHY your answer was wrong
- Understand WHY the correct answer is right
- Identify the knowledge gap that caused the error
- Review that topic in the relevant chapter

Test-Taking Strategies for Exam Day

Time Management:

- You have 5 hours for 250 questions (approximately 1.2 minutes per question)
- Don't spend more than 2 minutes on any single question
- Flag difficult questions and move on
- Complete all questions first, then return to flagged ones
- Save 30-45 minutes at the end for reviewing flagged questions

Question-Reading Technique:

- Read the question carefully before looking at answers
- Identify what's specifically being asked
- Look for key words like "except," "not," "best," "first," "most appropriate"
- Read ALL answer choices before selecting one

Answer Selection:

- Choose your answer based on knowledge, not gut feeling
- If two answers seem correct, choose the more complete or legally precise one
- Don't change answers unless you're certain you misread the question
- Your first instinct is usually correct if you've studied well

Managing Difficult Questions:

- If you don't know an answer, use process of elimination
- Make an educated guess rather than leaving it blank (no penalty for wrong answers)
- Flag the question and move on if you're taking too much time
- Don't let one difficult question derail your confidence

Staying Focused:

- Take a deep breath if you feel anxious
- Don't worry about how fast others are working
- Stay in your own space mentally
- If your concentration wavers, close your eyes for 10 seconds and refocus

Avoiding Common Pitfalls:

- Don't rush through questions you think are easy (careless errors cost points)
- Don't overthink questions (the test is straightforward, not trying to trick you)
- Don't panic if you don't know several answers in a row (questions are randomized)
- Don't change a lot of answers during review (usually, your first choice is correct)

The 50/50 Rule for Guessing: If you can eliminate even one wrong answer, your odds improve significantly:

- Four options with no elimination: 25% chance
- Three options (one eliminated): 33% chance
- Two options (two eliminated): 50% chance

Always try to eliminate at least one option before guessing.

Managing Test Anxiety

Before the Exam:

- Prepare thoroughly (the best anxiety reducer is confidence from preparation)
- Visit the testing center beforehand to eliminate unknowns
- Get 7-8 hours of sleep the night before
- Eat a healthy breakfast
- Arrive early to avoid rushing
- Use positive self-talk: "I've prepared well. I know this material. I'm ready."

During the Exam:

- Use breathing techniques if you feel anxious (slow, deep breaths)
- Remember that some anxiety is normal and can enhance performance
- Focus on one question at a time, not the entire exam
- Take a brief mental break if needed (close your eyes for 10 seconds)
- Maintain positive self-talk throughout

Physical Strategies:

- Stay hydrated (drink water before the exam)
- Use the restroom before starting
- Maintain good posture (reduces physical stress)
- Periodically stretch your neck and shoulders
- Blink regularly to avoid eye strain from the computer screen

Cognitive Strategies:

-

- If your mind goes blank on a question, skip it and come back
- Use your scratch paper to work through complex scenarios
- Break complicated questions into smaller parts
- Trust your preparation and knowledge

What If You Start Running Out of Time?

- Don't panic; stay focused
- Quickly answer remaining questions using educated guesses
- Ensure you've answered every question (no blanks)
- If you have only 5 minutes left and 20 questions remaining, quickly read each question and select the most reasonable answer
- Remember: A guess has a 25% chance of being right; a blank answer has 0% chance

What Makes This Guide Different

You might be wondering what sets this study guide apart from others on the market. It's a fair question, and you deserve to know why this guide is worth your time and investment.

Comprehensive Explanations, Not Just Answer Keys

Many study guides provide practice questions with simple answer keys: "1. B, 2. C, 3. A..." That approach tells you what's correct but not why. Every practice question in this guide includes a detailed explanation that:

- Explains why the correct answer is right
- Identifies why the wrong answers are incorrect
- References the specific law, procedure, or principle being tested
- Provides additional context or related information

This approach transforms practice questions from simple assessment tools into powerful learning opportunities.

Real-World Scenarios Throughout

Law enforcement isn't about memorizing statutes in a vacuum. It's about applying knowledge in dynamic, complex situations. This guide integrates realistic scenarios throughout every chapter, not just in a separate section at the end. These scenarios:

- Reflect actual calls for service and situations Texas officers encounter
- Require you to balance multiple factors (legal requirements, officer safety, policy considerations)
- Include the kind of gray-area situations where the "right" answer isn't always obvious
- Prepare you for the scenario-based questions that many test-takers find most challenging

Current and Texas-Specific Content

Some study guides use generic law enforcement content that could apply anywhere. This guide is specifically tailored to Texas law enforcement:

- Texas Penal Code sections and classifications
- Texas Code of Criminal Procedure articles
- Texas Transportation Code provisions
- Texas-specific procedures and terminology
- TCOLE-specific exam format and question styles

All content is current as of 2025, reflecting recent legal updates and policy changes.

Learning Science Applied

This guide incorporates proven learning principles from educational psychology:

- Spaced repetition through the recommended study schedule
- Active recall through practice questions distributed throughout chapters
- Elaborative interrogation through scenario analysis
- Interleaving of topics to enhance retention
- Retrieval practice through multiple testing opportunities

These aren't just buzzwords; they're evidence-based techniques that improve learning outcomes.

Performance Tracking and Adaptive Study

The guide includes performance tracking tools that help you:

- Identify your weak areas across different content domains
- Focus your study time where it will have the most impact
- Monitor your improvement over time
- Build confidence as you see your scores increase

This data-driven approach ensures you're studying efficiently, not just logging hours.

Written by Someone Who Understands the Process

This guide wasn't created by someone who's never worn a badge or taken the TCOLE exam. It's written by professionals who understand both the academic content and the practical realities of law enforcement work. The scenarios are realistic, the advice is practical, and the focus is on helping you not just pass the exam but become a capable, confident peace officer.

Exam Day Preparation Checklist

Use this checklist in the days leading up to your exam and on exam day itself. Proper preparation eliminates unnecessary stress and lets you focus on performing your best.

One Week Before Exam Day: □ Confirm your exam date, time, and location □ Know the testing center address and parking situation □ Plan your route and estimate travel time (add buffer for traffic) □ Arrange time off work if needed □ Inform family/roommates of your exam schedule (minimize distractions) □ Begin adjusting your sleep schedule to be well-rested on exam day

Three Days Before: □ Visit the testing center location if you haven't already (optional but recommended) □ Verify that your ID is current and matches the name on your registration □ Gather your confirmation number and documentation □ Check the weather forecast for exam day □ Plan your exam day outfit (comfortable, layered clothing)

Day Before Exam: □ Complete light review only (no heavy studying or new material) □ Review your summary notes and quick reference guide □ Organize items you'll bring: ID, confirmation number, keys, wallet □ Prepare your exam day outfit (comfortable clothes, layers for temperature control) □ Plan your exam day meals (breakfast and possibly lunch) □ Set multiple alarms for exam day □ Get to bed early (aim for 8 hours of sleep) □ Avoid alcohol and heavy foods □ Use relaxation techniques if needed (deep breathing, meditation, light exercise) □ Visualize success (picture yourself confidently answering questions)

Exam Day Morning: □ Wake up at least 2 hours before you need to leave □ Eat a healthy, substantial breakfast (protein and complex carbs, not too much sugar) □ Avoid excessive caffeine (a normal amount is fine, but don't overdo it) □ Review your quick reference materials if desired (but don't cram) □ Use the restroom before leaving home □ Double-check that you have your ID and confirmation number □ Leave early enough to arrive 30-45 minutes before your scheduled time □ Bring water and a snack for after the exam (you'll be hungry and tired)

At the Testing Center: □ Arrive 30 minutes before your scheduled exam time □ Use the restroom before checking in □ Turn off your cell phone completely □ Check in at the front desk with your ID and confirmation □ Store all personal items in the provided locker □ Listen carefully to proctor instructions □ Ask questions if anything is unclear about the testing procedures □ Take a deep breath and enter the testing room with confidence

During the Exam: □ Read the tutorial screens carefully □ Note the clock and your end time □ Read each question completely before looking at answers □ Use your scratch paper for complex scenarios or calculations □ Flag difficult questions and move on (return to them later) □ Keep a steady pace (don't rush, but don't overthink) □ Take a brief mental break if needed (10 seconds, eyes closed, deep breath) □ Answer every question (no blanks) □ Review flagged questions if time permits □ Submit your exam when complete

After the Exam: □ Collect your belongings from the locker □ Review your preliminary score if provided □ Avoid discussing specific exam content (it's prohibited) □ Celebrate that you completed the exam □ Eat something and rehydrate □ Rest and decompress □ Avoid obsessing over questions you think you missed □ Wait for your official score report

If You Pass: □ Celebrate your achievement □ Wait for TCOLE to process your license application □ Prepare for the next steps in your law enforcement career □ Consider keeping your study materials for future reference

If You Don't Pass: □ Don't be discouraged (many successful officers didn't pass the first time) □ Review your score report to identify weak areas □ Take the required waiting period seriously (don't rush into a retake) □ Use this guide to focus on your weak areas □ Adjust your study approach based on what didn't work □ Schedule your retake when you're truly ready □ Approach the retake with renewed confidence and better preparation

Remember: Passing the TCOLE exam is absolutely achievable with proper preparation. You've made the commitment to study seriously by getting this guide. Now trust the process, put in the work, and walk into that testing center knowing you're prepared to succeed.

Let's begin your journey to becoming a licensed Texas peace officer.

PART I: LEGAL FOUNDATIONS

Chapter 1: Texas Legal Codes and Laws

Learning Objectives

By the end of this chapter, you will be able to:

- Identify and explain the major classifications of offenses under the Texas Penal Code
- Understand the key articles of the Texas Code of Criminal Procedure that govern arrests, searches, and investigations
- Apply Texas Transportation Code provisions to traffic enforcement scenarios
- Recognize Family Code requirements for protective orders and family violence situations
- Explain how constitutional protections affect law enforcement procedures
- Distinguish between different levels of criminal offenses and their legal consequences
- Identify proper legal authority for law enforcement actions in various situations

Why This Chapter Matters

Texas law is the foundation of everything you'll do as a peace officer. Every arrest you make, every search you conduct, every traffic stop you initiate must be grounded in legal authority. Without a solid understanding of Texas legal codes and constitutional law, you can't effectively protect the community or yourself from civil liability.

This chapter covers the most frequently tested legal content on the TCOLE exam. You'll need to know specific statute numbers, understand the elements of common offenses, and be able to apply legal principles to real-world scenarios. This isn't just about memorizing laws; it's about understanding how they work together to guide your decision-making in the field.

Texas Penal Code Essentials

The Texas Penal Code is your primary legal tool as a peace officer. It defines criminal conduct, establishes penalties, and provides the legal framework for prosecution. Understanding the Penal Code isn't just about knowing what's illegal; it's about understanding the elements that must be proven, the defenses that might apply, and the proper classification of offenses.

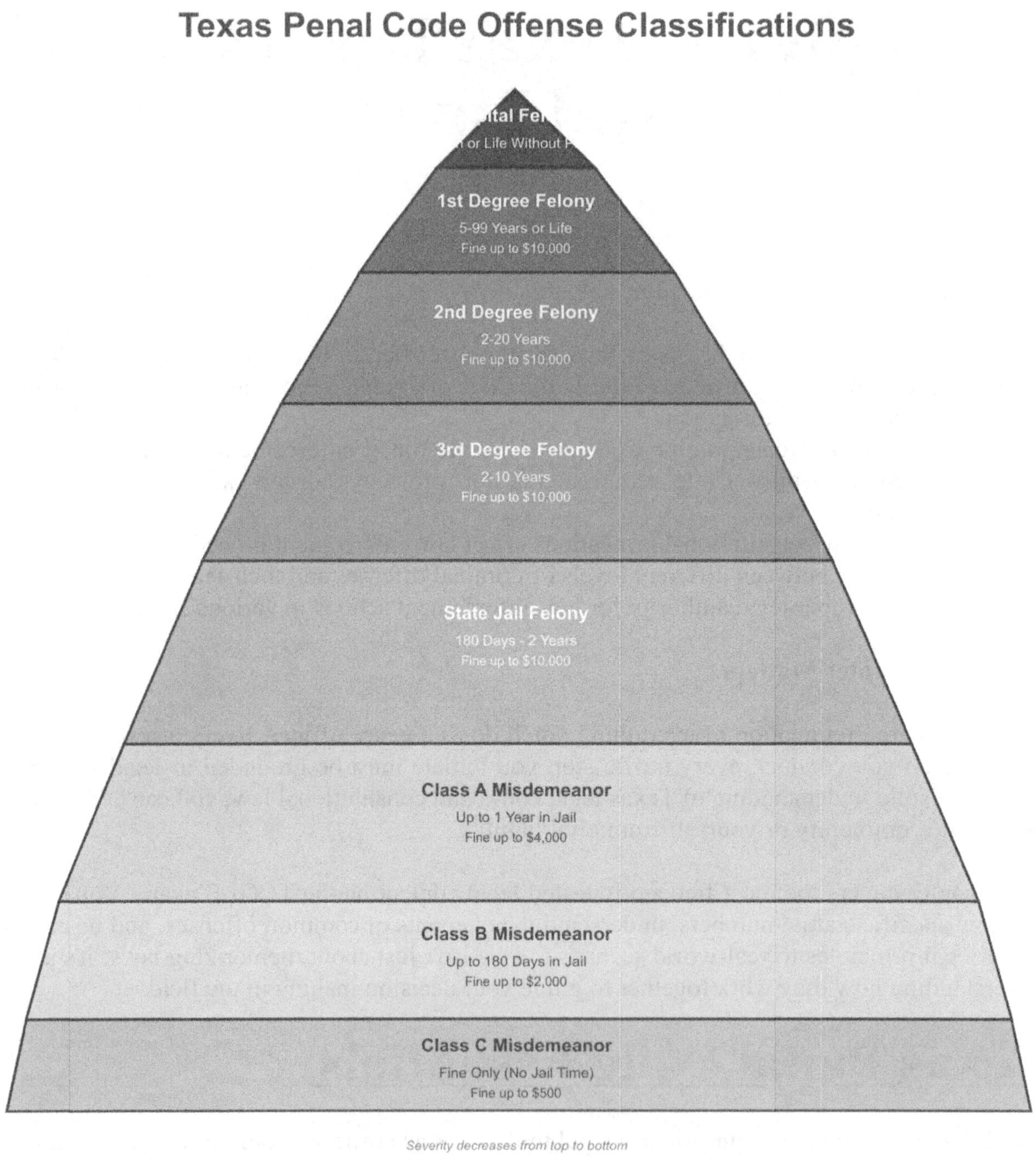

The Structure of the Penal Code

The Texas Penal Code is organized into titles and chapters. Title 1 contains introductory provisions that apply to all offenses. Titles 2 through 11 define specific offenses, grouped by type:

- Title 2: General Principles of Criminal Responsibility
- Title 3: Defenses to Criminal Responsibility
- Title 4: Inchoate Offenses (attempt, conspiracy, solicitation)
- Title 5: Offenses Against the Person
- Title 6: Offenses Against the Family
- Title 7: Offenses Against Property
- Title 8: Offenses Against Public Administration
- Title 9: Offenses Against Public Order and Decency
- Title 10: Offenses Against Public Health, Safety, and Morals
- Title 11: Organized Crime

As a peace officer, you'll work most frequently with Titles 5, 7, 9, and 10.

Felony Classifications

Texas law classifies felonies into five categories, from most to least serious:

Capital Felony: The most serious offense, punishable by death or life imprisonment without parole. Capital murder is the only capital felony in Texas (Penal Code §19.03). Capital murder includes murder committed under specific circumstances such as:

- Murdering a peace officer or firefighter in the line of duty
- Murder committed during certain felonies (kidnapping, burglary, robbery, aggravated sexual assault, arson, obstruction/retaliation, terroristic threat)
- Murder for remuneration (hired killing)
- Murder of multiple victims
- Murder of a child under 10 years old

First Degree Felony: Punishment ranges from 5 to 99 years or life in prison, plus a fine up to $10,000. Examples include:

- Aggravated robbery (Penal Code §29.03)
- Aggravated sexual assault (Penal Code §22.021)
- Murder (Penal Code §19.02)
- Aggravated kidnapping (Penal Code §20.04)

Second Degree Felony: Punishment ranges from 2 to 20 years in prison, plus a fine up to $10,000. Examples include:

- Manslaughter (Penal Code §19.04)
- Aggravated assault (Penal Code §22.02)
- Robbery (Penal Code §29.02)
- Sexual assault (Penal Code §22.011)
- Arson (Penal Code §28.02)

Third Degree Felony: Punishment ranges from 2 to 10 years in prison, plus a fine up to $10,000. Examples include:

- Stalking (Penal Code §42.072)
- Tampering with evidence (Penal Code §37.09)
- Possession of controlled substance (certain amounts)
- Escape (Penal Code §38.06)
- Deadly conduct (Penal Code §22.05)

State Jail Felony: Punishment ranges from 180 days to 2 years in state jail, plus a fine up to $10,000. Examples include:

- Theft of property valued at $2,500 to $30,000 (Penal Code §31.03)
- Burglary of a building (not a habitation) (Penal Code §30.02)
- Forgery (Penal Code §32.21)
- Credit card abuse (Penal Code §32.31)
- Unauthorized use of a vehicle (Penal Code §31.07)

Misdemeanor Classifications

Texas recognizes three classes of misdemeanors:

Class A Misdemeanor: Punishment up to 1 year in county jail and/or a fine up to $4,000. Examples include:

- Assault causing bodily injury (Penal Code §22.01)
- DWI (first offense with no aggravating factors) (Penal Code §49.04)
- Resisting arrest (Penal Code §38.03)
- Theft of property valued at $750 to $2,500 (Penal Code §31.03)
- Criminal mischief causing damage of $750 to $2,500 (Penal Code §28.03)

Class B Misdemeanor: Punishment up to 180 days in county jail and/or a fine up to $2,000. Examples include:

- DWI (first offense with certain aggravating factors or lower BAC) (Penal Code §49.04)
- Possession of marijuana (2 ounces or less) (Health & Safety Code §481.121)
- Terroristic threat (Penal Code §22.07)
- Criminal trespass (Penal Code §30.05)
- Theft of property valued at $100 to $750 (Penal Code §31.03)

Class C Misdemeanor: Punishment is a fine only, up to $500. No jail time. Examples include:

- Theft of property valued under $100 (Penal Code §31.03)
- Assault by contact (Penal Code §22.01)
- Disorderly conduct (Penal Code §42.01)

- Most traffic violations (Transportation Code)

Enhancement of Offenses

Certain factors can enhance (increase) the classification of an offense:

Repeat Offenses: A person with prior convictions may face enhanced penalties. For example:

- Third DWI becomes a third degree felony
- Theft convictions can be enhanced based on prior theft convictions
- Domestic assault can be enhanced from Class A misdemeanor to third degree felony with prior domestic assault convictions

Use of a Deadly Weapon: Many offenses increase by one category if committed with a deadly weapon. For example, assault causing bodily injury is normally a Class A misdemeanor, but assault with a deadly weapon causing bodily injury is aggravated assault, a second degree felony.

Victim Status: Offenses against certain protected classes (peace officers, firefighters, elderly individuals, children, public servants) may be enhanced. For example, assault on a public servant is a third degree felony, compared to Class A misdemeanor for assault on a regular citizen.

Location: Certain offenses are enhanced when committed in specific locations (school zones, drug-free zones, etc.).

Understanding these classifications is critical because they determine your authority to arrest, whether you can issue a citation instead, and how the case will be prosecuted.

Key Penal Code Sections Every Officer Must Know

While you can't memorize the entire Penal Code, certain sections appear repeatedly on the TCOLE exam and in your daily work. Here are the most critical ones:

Penal Code Chapter 1: General Provisions

§1.07 - Definitions: This section defines terms used throughout the Penal Code. You need to know several critical definitions:

"Intentionally" - A person acts intentionally when it is their conscious objective or desire to engage in the conduct or cause the result. This is the highest level of culpable mental state. Example: If someone points a gun at another person and pulls the trigger with the goal of killing them, they act intentionally.

"Knowingly" - A person acts knowingly when they are aware that their conduct is reasonably certain to cause the result. Example: If someone fires a gun into a crowded room, even if they don't specifically want to kill anyone, they knowingly create a substantial risk of death.

"Recklessly" - A person acts recklessly when they are aware of but consciously disregard a substantial and unjustifiable risk. The risk must be of such a nature that its disregard constitutes a gross deviation from the standard of care an ordinary person would exercise. Example: Driving 90 mph through a school zone during dismissal time.

"Criminal Negligence" - A person acts with criminal negligence when they ought to be aware of a substantial and unjustifiable risk, and the failure to perceive it constitutes a gross deviation from the standard of care. Example: Leaving a loaded firearm accessible to small children.

"Bodily Injury" - Physical pain, illness, or any impairment of physical condition. This is a lower threshold than serious bodily injury. A simple bruise or cut can constitute bodily injury.

"Serious Bodily Injury" - Bodily injury that creates a substantial risk of death or that causes death, serious permanent disfigurement, or protracted loss or impairment of any bodily member or organ. Examples include broken bones, significant burns, loss of consciousness, or injuries requiring surgery.

"Deadly Weapon" - Includes firearms and anything manifestly designed, made, or adapted for the purpose of inflicting death or serious bodily injury, or anything that in the manner of its use or intended use is capable of causing death or serious bodily injury. This definition is broader than many people realize. A vehicle used to run someone down is a deadly weapon. A hammer used to strike someone in the head is a deadly weapon. The context of use matters as much as the object itself.

"Reasonable Belief" - A belief that would be held by an ordinary and prudent person in the same circumstances as the actor. This standard appears throughout the Penal Code, particularly in defense provisions.

Understanding these definitions is critical because they appear in virtually every offense definition. The difference between "intentionally," "knowingly," "recklessly," and "with criminal negligence" can mean the difference between a capital felony and a misdemeanor, or between guilt and innocence.

Penal Code Chapter 2: Criminal Responsibility for Conduct of Another

§2.01 - Requirement of Voluntary Act or Omission: A person commits an offense only if they voluntarily engage in conduct, including an act, omission, or possession. This means you can't convict someone for thoughts alone, or for involuntary acts (such as movements during a seizure).

§2.02 - Requirement of Culpability: Unless the statute defining an offense specifies otherwise, a person doesn't commit an offense unless they intentionally, knowingly, recklessly, or with criminal negligence engage in the conduct. This section establishes that criminal offenses generally require both a physical act (actus reus) and a culpable mental state (mens rea).

§7.01 - Parties to Offenses: A person is criminally responsible as a party to an offense if they:

- Act with the kind of culpability required for the offense and cause or aid an innocent or non-responsible person to engage in conduct
- Acting with intent to promote or assist the commission of the offense, they solicit, encourage, direct, aid, or attempt to aid the other person to commit the offense
- Have a legal duty to prevent commission of the offense and intentionally promote its commission by failing to make a reasonable effort to prevent it

This section is crucial for understanding accomplice liability. If you drive the getaway car for a robbery, you're criminally responsible for the robbery even though you never entered the building. If you act as a lookout during a burglary, you're responsible for the burglary. The law treats parties to an offense the same as the principal actor.

§7.02 - Criminal Responsibility for Conduct of Another: This section extends party liability to situations where one person acts through an innocent agent. For example, if you trick a child into delivering drugs by telling them it's candy, you're responsible for the drug delivery even though the child didn't know what they were carrying.

Penal Code Chapter 9: Justification Excluding Criminal Responsibility

Chapter 9 contains the most important defense provisions you'll encounter. These sections explain when the use of force is legally justified.

§9.21 - Public Duty: Conduct is justified when the actor reasonably believes it is required or authorized by law, court order, or process. This section provides the foundation for lawful use of force by peace officers when making arrests or preventing escapes.

§9.22 - Necessity: Conduct is justified if the actor reasonably believes it is immediately necessary to avoid imminent harm, and the desirability and urgency of avoiding the harm clearly outweigh the harm sought to be prevented by the law defining the offense charged. Example: Breaking into a cabin to escape a blizzard when lost in the wilderness.

§9.31 - Self-Defense: A person is justified in using force against another when and to the degree they reasonably believe the force is immediately necessary to protect themselves against the other's use or attempted use of unlawful force. However, the use of force is not justified:

- In response to verbal provocation alone
- To resist an arrest or search being made by a peace officer (even if the arrest is unlawful, as long as the officer is acting under color of their official authority and is using no more force than reasonably necessary)
- If the actor provoked the other's use of unlawful force

Understanding when citizens can't use force to resist arrest is critical for your safety and for explaining to suspects why resisting will result in additional charges.

§9.32 - Deadly Force in Defense of Person: A person is justified in using deadly force against another if they reasonably believe deadly force is immediately necessary to protect themselves against the other's use or attempted use of unlawful deadly force. Additionally, deadly force is justified to prevent:

- Aggravated kidnapping
- Murder
- Sexual assault
- Aggravated sexual assault
- Robbery
- Aggravated robbery

Deadly force is NOT justified if:

- The actor provoked the person against whom force was used
- The actor was attempting to commit, committing, or fleeing after committing a crime
- The actor did not reasonably believe that retreating was impossible (except there is no duty to retreat if the actor was in their own habitation, vehicle, or workplace, or they were a lawful occupant defending against someone who unlawfully entered)

§9.33 - Defense of Third Person: A person is justified in using force or deadly force to protect a third person to the degree they reasonably believe they would be justified in using force or deadly force to protect themselves, if they reasonably believe intervention is immediately necessary and the third person would be justified in using such protection.

§9.41 - Protection of One's Own Property: A person is justified in using force against another when and to the degree they reasonably believe the force is immediately necessary to prevent or terminate the other's trespass on or unlawful interference with their property. However, deadly force is NOT justified merely to protect property.

§9.42 - Deadly Force to Protect Property: Deadly force is justified only to prevent:

- Arson, burglary, robbery, aggravated robbery, theft during the nighttime, or criminal mischief during the nighttime
- When the actor reasonably believes deadly force is immediately necessary to prevent the commission of one of those offenses or to prevent the other who is fleeing after committing one of those offenses from escaping with the property
- And the actor reasonably believes there is no other way to protect or recover the property or the use of force other than deadly force would expose them to a substantial risk of death or serious bodily injury

This section is frequently misunderstood by the public. While Texas does allow deadly force to protect property in limited circumstances, the requirements are strict. You must be able to articulate why you reasonably believed deadly force was the only way to prevent the loss of property and that lesser force would have exposed you to substantial risk.

§9.51 - Arrest and Search: The use of force to effect an arrest or conduct a search is justified if the arrest or search is lawful, or the actor believes the arrest or search is lawful. Before using force, the actor must first inform the person to be arrested of the actor's authority and purpose, or reasonably believes notification is unnecessary or would be useless or dangerous.

The degree of force that is justified is limited to the degree reasonably necessary to effect the arrest or search or to prevent escape.

§9.52 - Prevention of Escape: The use of force to prevent escape is justified when force is justified under §9.51 and the actor reasonably believes force is necessary to prevent the escape and the use of force doesn't create a substantial risk of injury to an uninvolved third party.

§9.53 - Maintaining Security in Correctional Facility: This section justifies the use of force in jails and prisons to maintain security, order, and discipline.

Understanding Justification Defenses in Practice

These justification sections don't give you unlimited authority to use force. Every use of force must be:

- Reasonable under the circumstances
- Immediately necessary
- Proportional to the threat or resistance encountered
- Consistent with your training and department policy

When documenting use of force incidents, you need to articulate the specific facts that made your belief reasonable and the force immediately necessary. "He was resisting" isn't sufficient. You need to describe the specific actions, the threat they posed, why lesser force options were inadequate, and how the force you used was proportional and necessary.

Penal Code Title 5: Offenses Against the Person

Chapter 19: Criminal Homicide

§19.02 - Murder: A person commits murder if they:

- Intentionally or knowingly cause the death of an individual
- Intend to cause serious bodily injury and commit an act clearly dangerous to human life that causes death

- Commit or attempt to commit a felony (other than manslaughter) and in the course of and in furtherance of that felony, or in immediate flight from that felony, commit an act clearly dangerous to human life that causes death

Murder is a first degree felony. The key distinction between murder and capital murder is the presence of aggravating factors that make it a capital offense.

§19.03 - Capital Murder: A person commits capital murder if they commit murder as defined in §19.02 and:

- The person murders a peace officer or fireman who is acting in the lawful discharge of an official duty and who the person knows is a peace officer or fireman
- The person intentionally commits murder during the commission or attempted commission of kidnapping, burglary, robbery, aggravated sexual assault, arson, obstruction or retaliation, or terroristic threat
- The person commits murder for remuneration or promises of remuneration, or employs another to commit murder for remuneration
- The person commits murder while escaping or attempting to escape from a penal institution
- The person, while incarcerated, murders another who is employed in the operation of the penal institution
- The person murders more than one person during the same criminal transaction or under a scheme or course of conduct
- The person murders an individual under 10 years of age
- The person murders an individual under 15 years of age while in the course of committing or attempting to commit certain offenses
- The person murders a judge or justice in retaliation or on account of their service

Capital murder is the only capital felony in Texas and is punishable by death or life imprisonment without parole. Understanding what makes a murder "capital" is critical when investigating homicides and preparing charges.

§19.04 - Manslaughter: A person commits manslaughter if they recklessly cause the death of an individual. Manslaughter is a second degree felony.

The key distinction between murder and manslaughter is the mental state: murder requires intent or knowledge, while manslaughter requires only recklessness. Example: A person driving recklessly at high speed loses control and crashes, killing a passenger. This is manslaughter, not murder, because while the driver recklessly created the risk, they didn't intend to cause death.

§19.05 - Criminally Negligent Homicide: A person commits criminally negligent homicide if they cause the death of an individual by criminal negligence. This is a state jail felony.

This is the lowest level of criminal homicide. Example: A parent leaves a toddler unattended in a hot car and the child dies. The parent didn't intend the death and may not have consciously created the risk, but they failed to perceive a risk that an ordinary person would have recognized.

Chapter 22: Assaultive Offenses

§22.01 - Assault: A person commits assault if they:

- Intentionally, knowingly, or recklessly cause bodily injury to another
- Intentionally or knowingly threaten another with imminent bodily injury
- Intentionally or knowingly cause physical contact with another when they know or reasonably should believe the other will regard the contact as offensive or provocative

Assault is generally a Class A misdemeanor. However, it becomes a third degree felony if committed:

- Against a public servant while lawfully discharging official duty
- Against a family member or household member with a previous domestic assault conviction
- Against a pregnant person (if the actor knew of the pregnancy)
- By someone in a dating relationship or against a family member by impeding breathing or circulation

It's a Class C misdemeanor if it involves only threatening or offensive contact (often called "assault by contact").

Understanding the different levels of assault is crucial because they determine whether you can make a warrantless arrest and how the case will be charged. Assault causing bodily injury to a family member allows warrantless arrest if you have probable cause. Assault by contact doesn't, unless it occurs in your presence.

§22.02 - Aggravated Assault: A person commits aggravated assault if they commit assault as defined in §22.01 and:

- Cause serious bodily injury to another
- Use or exhibit a deadly weapon during the commission of the assault

Aggravated assault is a second degree felony, or a first degree felony if committed:

- Against a public servant lawfully discharging official duty (including peace officers)
- Against a witness or informant in retaliation
- Against a family member or household member
- By a public servant acting under color of office

The distinction between assault and aggravated assault often hinges on whether the injury constitutes "serious bodily injury" or whether a deadly weapon was used. A black eye and bruising are bodily injury (assault). A broken jaw requiring surgery is serious bodily injury (aggravated assault). Hitting someone with your fist is assault causing bodily injury. Hitting someone with a baseball bat is aggravated assault because the bat, in that manner of use, is a deadly weapon.

§22.011 - Sexual Assault: A person commits sexual assault if they intentionally or knowingly:

- Cause the penetration of the anus or sexual organ of another person without that person's consent
- Cause the penetration of the mouth of another person by the sexual organ of the actor without that person's consent
- Cause the sexual organ of another person to contact or penetrate the mouth, anus, or sexual organ of another person without consent

Sexual assault is a second degree felony. The statute defines several circumstances where consent is legally absent, including:

- The actor compels the other person to submit by use of force, violence, or coercion
- The actor knows the other person is unconscious or physically unable to resist
- The actor knows the other person is unaware that the sexual assault is occurring
- The other person has not consented and the actor knows the other person is mentally incapable of appraising the nature of the act
- The other person has not consented and the actor knows the other person is unaware the act is occurring
- The actor is a public servant, clergy, or mental health professional who uses their position to cause the other person to submit
- The actor is an employee of a facility where the other person resides
- The other person is younger than 17 and not the spouse of the actor

Understanding the consent provisions is critical. Even if a person doesn't physically resist, the law recognizes circumstances where legal consent is impossible.

§22.021 - Aggravated Sexual Assault: A person commits aggravated sexual assault if they commit sexual assault as defined in §22.011 and:

- Cause serious bodily injury or attempt to cause death to the victim or another
- Place the victim in fear that death, serious bodily injury, or kidnapping will be imminently inflicted on any person
- By acts or words threaten to cause death, serious bodily injury, or kidnapping of any person
- Use or exhibit a deadly weapon during the commission

- Act in concert with another who engages in sexual assault directed toward the same victim and occurring during the same criminal episode
- Administer a drug or other substance to the victim without the victim's knowledge
- The victim is younger than 14 years
- The victim is an elderly or disabled person

Aggravated sexual assault is a first degree felony with enhanced penalties in certain circumstances. This is one of the most serious felonies you'll investigate, and proper evidence collection and victim care are critical.

§22.05 - Deadly Conduct: A person commits deadly conduct if they:

- Recklessly engage in conduct that places another in imminent danger of serious bodily injury
- Knowingly discharge a firearm at or in the direction of one or more individuals, or a habitation, building, or vehicle, and is reckless as to whether the habitation, building, or vehicle is occupied

Deadly conduct is a Class A misdemeanor, or a third degree felony if the firearm is discharged. This offense often applies when someone fires a gun recklessly (such as into the air in a residential area) or drives recklessly at high speeds through crowded areas.

Penal Code Title 7: Offenses Against Property

Chapter 28: Arson, Criminal Mischief, and Other Property Damage

§28.02 - Arson: A person commits arson if they start a fire or cause an explosion with intent to destroy or damage:

- Any vegetation, fence, or structure on open-space land
- Any building, habitation, or vehicle knowing it is within city limits or insured against damage or destruction, knowing it is subject to a mortgage or security interest, knowing it is located on property belonging to another, or knowing it is subject to a lien that includes personal property, or owned by the actor who intends to defraud or harm an insurer or lienholder
- Knowing the building, habitation, or vehicle is in or on property owned by another

Arson is a second degree felony, or a first degree felony if:

- It's committed with intent to destroy or damage a habitation or place of worship and a person suffers bodily injury or death
- The building is a habitation or place of worship
- It causes bodily injury or death to a person

Arson investigations are complex and often require specialized training and coordination with fire investigators.

§28.03 - Criminal Mischief: A person commits criminal mischief if, without the effective consent of the owner, they:

- Intentionally or knowingly damage or destroy the tangible property of the owner
- Intentionally or knowingly tamper with the tangible property of the owner and cause pecuniary loss or substantial inconvenience
- Intentionally or knowingly make markings (including inscriptions, slogans, drawings, or paintings) on tangible property of the owner

The classification of criminal mischief depends on the amount of pecuniary loss:

- Class C misdemeanor: Less than $100
- Class B misdemeanor: $100 to $750
- Class A misdemeanor: $750 to $2,500
- State jail felony: $2,500 to $30,000
- Third degree felony: $30,000 to $150,000
- Second degree felony: $150,000 to $300,000
- First degree felony: $300,000 or more

Criminal mischief also increases to the next higher category if committed against a public or private elementary or secondary school.

Determining the value of damage is crucial for proper charging. You'll need estimates, repair bills, or replacement costs documented for the investigation.

Chapter 29: Robbery

§29.02 - Robbery: A person commits robbery if, in the course of committing theft and with intent to obtain or maintain control of property, they:

- Intentionally, knowingly, or recklessly cause bodily injury to another
- Intentionally or knowingly threaten or place another in fear of imminent bodily injury or death

Robbery is a second degree felony. The key distinction between theft and robbery is the use of force or threat of force. If someone snatches a purse and runs without any physical contact or threat, that's theft. If they push the victim to the ground in the process, it's robbery.

§29.03 - Aggravated Robbery: A person commits aggravated robbery if they commit robbery and:

- Cause serious bodily injury to another

- Use or exhibit a deadly weapon
- Cause bodily injury to or threaten or place in fear another who is 65 years or older or disabled

Aggravated robbery is a first degree felony. The presence of a weapon (even if unloaded or fake, as long as the victim reasonably believes it's real) elevates robbery to aggravated robbery.

Chapter 30: Burglary and Criminal Trespass

§30.02 - Burglary: A person commits burglary if, without the effective consent of the owner, they:

- Enter a habitation or building (or any portion of a building) not then open to the public, with intent to commit a felony, theft, or assault
- Remain concealed in a building or habitation with intent to commit a felony, theft, or assault
- Enter a building or habitation and commit or attempt to commit a felony, theft, or assault

Burglary is a:

- State jail felony if committed in a building other than a habitation
- Second degree felony if committed in a habitation
- First degree felony if committed in a habitation and the actor intends to commit (or commits or attempts to commit) a felony other than felony theft

The intent to commit a crime inside the structure is what separates burglary from criminal trespass. Someone who enters an unlocked home intending to steal commits burglary even if they don't actually take anything. Someone who enters an unlocked home just to get out of the rain commits criminal trespass.

§30.05 - Criminal Trespass: A person commits criminal trespass if they:

- Enter or remain on property of another without effective consent and had notice that entry was forbidden
- Enter or remain on agricultural land of another without effective consent

Notice can be given by:

- Oral or written communication
- Fencing or other enclosure designed to exclude intruders
- Signs posted indicating entry is forbidden
- Purple paint marks on trees or posts (this is specific to Texas and is commonly used for rural property)

Criminal trespass is a Class B misdemeanor, or a Class A misdemeanor if committed:

- In a habitation or shelter center
- On agricultural land
- Within 100 feet of a school
- With a deadly weapon

Criminal trespass becomes burglary if the person enters with the intent to commit a felony, theft, or assault inside.

Chapter 31: Theft

§31.03 - Theft: A person commits theft if they unlawfully appropriate property with intent to deprive the owner of the property. Appropriation is unlawful if:

- It's without the owner's effective consent
- The property is stolen and the actor appropriates it knowing it was stolen
- Property in the custody of a law enforcement agency was explicitly represented to the actor as stolen, and the actor appropriates it believing it was stolen

The classification depends on the value of property stolen or the type of property:

- Class C misdemeanor: Less than $100
- Class B misdemeanor: $100 to $750
- Class A misdemeanor: $750 to $2,500
- State jail felony: $2,500 to $30,000
- Third degree felony: $30,000 to $150,000 (or certain specific property types like firearms or official ballot boxes)
- Second degree felony: $150,000 to $300,000
- First degree felony: $300,000 or more

Theft also increases to the next category if the stolen property is an official ballot or election record, a firearm, certain livestock, or metal stolen from certain critical infrastructure.

Understanding theft values is essential. Always document the value of stolen property through receipts, owner statements, comparable sales data, or expert appraisals.

§31.07 - Unauthorized Use of a Vehicle: A person commits unauthorized use of a vehicle if they intentionally or knowingly operate another's boat, airplane, or motor-propelled vehicle without the effective consent of the owner. This is a state jail felony.

This offense is often called "joyriding." The key distinction from theft (auto theft) is the intent. If someone takes a vehicle intending to keep it permanently, that's theft. If they take it intending to use it temporarily and return it, that's unauthorized use of a vehicle. In practice, proving intent can be difficult, so both charges may be filed initially.

Penal Code Title 9: Offenses Against Public Order and Decency

§42.01 - Disorderly Conduct: A person commits disorderly conduct if they intentionally or knowingly:

- Use abusive, indecent, profane, or vulgar language in a public place, and the language by its very utterance tends to incite an immediate breach of the peace
- Make an offensive gesture or display in a public place, and the gesture or display tends to incite an immediate breach of the peace
- Create, by chemical means, a noxious and unreasonable odor in a public place
- Abuse or threaten a person in a public place in an obviously offensive manner
- Make unreasonable noise in a public place or near a private residence
- Fight with another in a public place
- Discharge a firearm in a public place (unless doing so in self-defense)
- Display a firearm or other deadly weapon in a public place in a manner calculated to alarm
- Expose their anus or genitals in a public place (not including a mother breastfeeding)

Disorderly conduct is a Class C misdemeanor, except discharge of a firearm which is a Class B misdemeanor.

This is one of the most commonly charged offenses, but it's also frequently challenged in court. The key is that the conduct must occur in a public place and must be objectively offensive or disturbing. Simply being rude or using profanity, by itself, usually doesn't meet the standard unless it's likely to provoke a violent response.

§42.07 - Harassment: A person commits harassment if, with intent to harass, annoy, alarm, abuse, torment, or embarrass another, they:

- Initiate communication and make a comment, request, suggestion, or proposal that is obscene
- Threaten in a manner reasonably likely to alarm the person
- Convey a false report of death or serious bodily injury to a person
- Cause the telephone of another to ring repeatedly or make repeated telephone communications anonymously or in a manner reasonably likely to harass
- Knowingly permit a telephone under their control to be used for prohibited communications
- Send repeated electronic communications in a manner reasonably likely to harass
- Publish on an Internet website repeated electronic communications in a manner reasonably likely to cause emotional distress

Harassment is a Class B misdemeanor, or a Class A misdemeanor if the actor was previously convicted or if the conduct is committed against someone younger than 18 with intent to cause them to commit suicide or engage in conduct causing serious bodily injury.

§46.02 - Unlawful Carrying of Weapons: Texas law regarding weapon carrying has changed significantly in recent years with constitutional carry provisions. However, certain locations and circumstances still prohibit weapon carrying:

- By felons within five years of release from confinement or supervision
- On premises licensed to sell alcohol (51% establishments)
- In schools or educational institutions
- At polling places on election day
- In courts or courthouses
- at racetracks
- In secured areas of airports
- In correctional facilities
- In civil commitment facilities
- At professional sporting events
- By someone who is intoxicated

Understanding current weapon laws is essential because they change frequently through legislation. Always verify the most current version of §46.02 and related sections.

§46.04 - Unlawful Possession of Firearm: A person commits an offense if they possess a firearm:

- After conviction of a felony, before the fifth anniversary of release from confinement or supervision (whichever is later)
- After conviction of certain domestic violence misdemeanors
- Subject to a protective order

This is a third degree felony. Federal law (18 USC §922(g)) also prohibits firearm possession by certain classes of people, and federal prosecution may be pursued in addition to state charges.

Texas Code of Criminal Procedure

While the Penal Code defines what conduct is criminal, the Code of Criminal Procedure (CCP) tells you how to investigate, arrest, and prosecute those crimes. The CCP is your operational manual as a peace officer.

Key CCP Articles Every Officer Must Know

Article 1.04 - Due Process of Law: No citizen of this state shall be deprived of life, liberty, property, privileges, or immunities, except by the due course of the law of the land. This article enshrines due process protections and underlies all criminal procedures.

Article 2.12 - Who Are Peace Officers: This article lists who qualifies as a peace officer in Texas, including:

- Sheriffs, their deputies, and constables
- Marshals and police officers of incorporated cities and towns
- Rangers and officers of the Department of Public Safety
- Investigators of the district attorney's, criminal district attorney's, or county attorney's offices
- Law enforcement agents of the Texas Alcoholic Beverage Commission
- Officers commissioned by the Parks and Wildlife Department
- Numerous other specifically enumerated positions

Understanding who qualifies as a peace officer matters because certain laws apply differently to peace officers than to civilians, and certain crimes (like assault on a public servant) require that the victim be a peace officer acting in official capacity.

Article 2.13 - Duties and Powers: Peace officers have specific duties including:

- Preserve the peace within their jurisdiction
- Execute all lawful process issued to them
- Give notice to suspected violators of the law
- Arrest offenders without warrant when authorized by law
- Prevent or suppress offenses
- Aid persons suffering bodily harm

You have broad authority to maintain peace and order, but that authority must be exercised reasonably and within legal bounds.

Article 14.01 - Warrant of Arrest: A warrant of arrest is a written order from a magistrate directed to a peace officer commanding them to take a person accused of an offense into custody. The warrant must:

- Issue in the name of "The State of Texas"
- Be signed by the magistrate with office title
- Specify the name of the accused (or describe them if name is unknown)
- State the offense charged
- Command that the accused be arrested and brought before the magistrate

A valid warrant gives you authority to arrest regardless of whether the offense was committed in your presence.

Article 14.03 - Arrest Without Warrant: You may arrest without a warrant when:

- An offense is committed in your presence or within your view
- A felony has been committed and you have probable cause to believe the person committed it
- A felony has been committed and you have probable cause to believe the person is about to escape
- You have probable cause to believe the person has committed assault resulting in bodily injury to a family member or household member
- You have probable cause to believe the person has violated a protective order
- The person is found in a suspicious place under circumstances that reasonably show they have committed a felony or are about to commit a felony or breach the peace
- You have probable cause to believe the person has committed certain misdemeanors involving family violence

Understanding the limits of warrantless arrest is critical. You can arrest for any offense committed in your presence. For offenses not committed in your presence, you generally need either a warrant or probable cause that a felony was committed (with specific exceptions for family violence and protective order violations).

Article 14.04 - When Felony Has Been Committed: You may arrest without a warrant when a felony has actually been committed and you have probable cause to believe the person arrested committed it. The key word is "actually" - if no felony actually occurred, even if you reasonably believed one did, the arrest may not be valid under this article.

Article 15.16 - How Warrant Is Executed: When executing an arrest warrant, you must:

- Inform the person of your authority and purpose
- Show the warrant if demanded (though you don't need to have the physical warrant with you if you have knowledge of its existence)
- Use reasonable force if necessary to effect the arrest

Article 15.17 - Arrest Without Warrant for Failure to Appear: You may arrest without a warrant persons who fail to appear as required by written promise, summons, or court order.

Article 15.24 - What Force May Be Used: When arresting someone, you may use the amount of force reasonably necessary to effect the arrest and prevent escape. You cannot use more force than necessary. If the person flees from arrest, you may use force to prevent escape, but deadly force is justified only if:

- The arrest is authorized by warrant and the warrant commands the arrest of the person for a felony
- You reasonably believe the person escaping has committed a felony involving the use or threat of deadly force
- You reasonably believe using deadly force is immediately necessary to prevent escape
- You reasonably believe there is no substantial risk of injury to innocent third parties

This article reflects the Supreme Court's holding in Tennessee v. Garner and sets strict limits on when you can use deadly force to prevent escape.

Article 18.01 - Search Warrant: A search warrant is a written order, issued by a magistrate and directed to a peace officer, commanding them to search for and seize specific items. The warrant must be based on probable cause, supported by oath or affirmation, and particularly describe the place to be searched and the items to be seized.

The requirements for a valid search warrant come from both the Fourth Amendment to the U.S. Constitution and Article 18.01. A search warrant must contain:

- The name of the county and state
- The name or description of the person whose property is to be searched (if known)
- A description of the property or place to be searched
- A description of the items to be seized
- A statement of probable cause
- The signature of the magistrate
- The date and time of issuance

When executing a search warrant, you must generally knock and announce your presence and purpose before entering, unless the warrant specifically authorizes a "no-knock" entry based on circumstances that would create danger or lead to destruction of evidence.

Article 18.02 - Grounds for Issuance: A search warrant may be issued to search for and seize:

- Property acquired by theft or in any other manner that makes its acquisition an offense
- Property specially designed, made, or adapted for or commonly used in the commission of an offense
- Arms and munitions kept or prepared for use in insurrection or riot
- Weapons prohibited by the Penal Code
- Gambling devices or equipment
- Obscene materials possessed for commercial distribution
- Drug paraphernalia
- Controlled substances

- Human remains
- Contraband subject to forfeiture
- Electronic customer data held by a provider of electronic communications service or remote computing service
- Other property or items constituting evidence of an offense or constituting evidence tending to show that a particular person committed an offense

The list is extensive, but the key principle is that you can search for evidence of criminal activity or contraband. You can't obtain a warrant to search for items that aren't connected to criminal activity.

Article 18.021 - Issuance of Search Warrant to Photograph Injured Child: This article allows for warrants to photograph a child who is suspected of being abused or neglected, even without parental consent. This is critical for child abuse investigations where the parent or guardian may be the perpetrator.

Article 27.14 - Waiver of Rights: This article addresses the magistrate's duty to inform an arrested person of their rights. A magistrate must inform someone arrested without a warrant:

- Of the accusation against them
- Of their right to retain counsel
- Of their right to remain silent
- That any statement may be used against them
- Of their right to have an attorney present during questioning
- That if they cannot afford an attorney, one will be appointed
- Of their right to request appointment of counsel and to have reasonable time to communicate with counsel

This requirement is separate from Miranda warnings. Miranda applies during custodial interrogation. Article 27.14 applies when bringing someone before a magistrate after arrest.

Article 38.22 - Confessions: This article governs the admissibility of statements made by accused persons. Key provisions include:

Section 2: A written statement by an accused person is admissible only if it is voluntarily made. Before making a written statement, the person must be warned:

- That they have the right to remain silent and not make any statement
- That any statement may be used against them
- That they have the right to have a lawyer present
- That if they cannot afford a lawyer, one will be appointed

The warnings must be given in writing and must include a statement that the person understands their rights and is willing to make a statement. The person must sign the warning statement.

Section 3: An oral statement made by an accused during custodial interrogation is admissible only if:

- It was electronically recorded
- The recording shows the accused was given the required warnings
- The recording shows the accused knowingly, intelligently, and voluntarily waived their rights
- The recording is accurate and hasn't been altered

There are exceptions for statements made before electronic recording equipment became available or practical, or for exigent circumstances.

Section 5: Nothing in this article precludes admission of a statement that doesn't meet these requirements if it was made spontaneously (not in response to custodial interrogation) or if it was made in open court at a trial, hearing, or grand jury proceeding.

Understanding Article 38.22 is absolutely critical. Statements obtained in violation of this article will be suppressed, potentially destroying your case. Always follow proper procedures for obtaining statements, ensure Miranda warnings are given when required, and document everything.

Article 38.23 - Evidence Not to Be Used: No evidence obtained in violation of the Constitution or laws of Texas or the United States shall be admitted in evidence against the accused on the trial of any criminal case. This is Texas's version of the exclusionary rule. If you conduct an unlawful search, make an unlawful arrest, or obtain a statement in violation of the defendant's rights, any evidence obtained as a result will be suppressed. This rule exists to deter constitutional violations and protect individual rights.

The "fruit of the poisonous tree" doctrine extends this exclusion to evidence derived from the initial illegality. For example, if you conduct an illegal search and find a key, then use that key to lawfully open a storage unit and find drugs, the drugs may be suppressed because they're the "fruit" of the illegal search.

Article 39.14 - Discovery: This article requires the state to provide discovery to the defense, including:

- Written statements of the defendant
- Recorded statements of the defendant
- Witness statements
- Criminal history records of the defendant
- Documents, items, and tangible evidence in the state's possession
- Exculpatory evidence (evidence favorable to the defendant)
- Expert witness reports and credentials

Understanding discovery obligations is important because failure to disclose required information can result in sanctions, exclusion of evidence, or even dismissal of charges. When investigating cases, document everything carefully and maintain proper chain of custody, knowing that the defense will eventually receive access to your reports and evidence.

Article 42.12 - Community Supervision (Probation): This article governs probation in Texas. While you won't typically deal with probation administration, you should understand basic probation terms because you'll frequently encounter people on probation during your duties. Common probation conditions include:

- Reporting regularly to a probation officer
- Maintaining employment or attending school
- Not committing any criminal offenses
- Not possessing firearms
- Submitting to drug testing
- Paying fines, restitution, and court costs
- Completing community service

When you arrest someone who's on probation, notify the probation department because the arrest may result in probation revocation in addition to charges for the new offense.

Article 45.041 - Judgment: This article deals with judgments in justice and municipal courts. It's relevant for understanding how traffic citations and Class C misdemeanor cases are processed. Key points:

- Defendants may enter pleas in person or in writing
- Courts may allow payment plans for fines
- Failure to appear or pay results in additional penalties
- Certain offenses require mandatory court appearances

Article 49.25 - Automobile Insurance: While technically part of the Transportation Code provisions incorporated into the CCP, this article requires officers to determine whether drivers involved in accidents have valid insurance. Failure to maintain insurance is a Class C misdemeanor (first offense) or Class B misdemeanor (subsequent offenses). You must issue citations for failure to maintain insurance when investigating accidents.

Texas Transportation Code

The Transportation Code governs motor vehicle operation, traffic control, vehicle registration, driver licensing, and related matters. As a peace officer, you'll enforce the Transportation Code daily through traffic stops, accident investigations, and DWI enforcement.

Traffic Violations and Enforcement Authority

Understanding Traffic Law Structure

The Transportation Code is organized into subtitles and chapters covering different aspects of transportation regulation. The most relevant chapters for patrol officers include:

Chapter 521: Driver's Licenses and Certificates **Chapter 522:** Commercial Driver's Licenses **Chapter 541:** Definitions and General Provisions **Chapter 542:** General Provisions (rules of the road) **Chapter 543:** Offenses and Penalties **Chapter 544:** Traffic Signs, Signals, and Markings **Chapter 545:** Operation and Movement of Vehicles (the core "rules of the road") **Chapter 546:** Regulation of Vehicle Operation on Highways **Chapter 547:** Vehicle Equipment **Chapter 548:** Compulsory Inspection of Vehicles **Chapter 549:** Financial Responsibility (insurance requirements) **Chapter 550:** Accidents and Accident Reports **Chapter 724:** Implied Consent (DWI chemical testing)

Common Traffic Violations

Speeding (Transportation Code §545.352): A person may not drive at a speed greater than is reasonable and prudent under the circumstances or greater than the posted speed limit. Speed limits vary based on location:

- 30 mph in urban districts (unless otherwise posted)
- 70 mph on numbered highways outside urban districts
- 60 mph on most other roads outside urban districts
- Posted limits in school zones (typically 20 mph when children are present)
- Posted limits in construction zones (fines doubled when workers present)

Speeding violations are classified based on the speed over the limit. Generally, speeding is a Class C misdemeanor punishable by fine. However, speeding in certain zones (school zones, construction zones) or at certain excessive speeds can result in higher fines and more serious charges.

Failure to Maintain Financial Responsibility (Transportation Code §601.191): Every driver must maintain liability insurance coverage. First offense is a Class C misdemeanor with fines from $175 to $350 plus surcharges. Subsequent offenses are Class B misdemeanors with fines from $350 to $1,000. Additionally, the vehicle may be impounded and the driver's license suspended.

When you stop a driver, you must ask for proof of insurance. Acceptable proof includes:

- Insurance policy documents
- Insurance card or certificate
- Electronic display of insurance information on a phone or other device

- Verbal verification from insurance company (during traffic stop with company on phone)

If a driver cannot provide proof, issue a citation. The driver may later show proof to the court to have the charge dismissed (if they actually had insurance), but the citation must be issued at the scene if proof isn't available.

Driving While License Invalid (Transportation Code §521.457): Operating a motor vehicle while license is invalid, suspended, revoked, or denied is a Class C misdemeanor (first offense) or Class B misdemeanor (subsequent offense). If the license is invalid due to a DWI conviction, it's a Class B misdemeanor.

Always verify driver's license status through dispatch before releasing a driver. If the license is invalid, you must not allow them to continue driving. The vehicle must be legally parked or released to a licensed driver.

Failure to Control Speed (Transportation Code §545.351): A person may not drive at a speed that endangers others, considering traffic, weather, road conditions, and other circumstances. This is a separate offense from exceeding the posted speed limit. You can cite someone for failure to control speed even if they're below the speed limit, if their speed is unreasonable for the conditions (such as driving 50 mph on an icy road where the limit is 65 mph).

Following Too Closely (Transportation Code §545.062): A driver shall not follow another vehicle more closely than is reasonable and prudent, having due regard for the speed of the vehicles, traffic, and road conditions. The "reasonable and prudent" standard gives you discretion based on circumstances. Following too closely is a Class C misdemeanor.

Failure to Yield Right of Way (Various Sections): Multiple Transportation Code sections address right of way in different circumstances:

- §545.151: Failure to yield at stop sign
- §545.152: Failure to yield at yield sign
- §545.153: Failure to yield when turning left
- §545.155: Failure to yield to emergency vehicles
- §545.156: Failure to yield to pedestrian in crosswalk

Each is a Class C misdemeanor. These violations are significant because they're frequently contributing factors in traffic accidents.

Disregarding Stop Sign or Red Light (Transportation Code §544.007-§544.010): Failing to stop at a stop sign or red light is a Class C misdemeanor. The vehicle must come to a complete stop before entering the intersection or crosswalk. A "rolling stop" (slowing but not stopping completely) is a violation.

At a red light, the vehicle must stop before entering the crosswalk or intersection. The driver may turn right on red after stopping (unless prohibited by sign) but must yield to traffic and pedestrians. Left turns on red are permitted only from one-way street to one-way street.

Improper Lane Change (Transportation Code §545.060): A driver shall drive as nearly as practical entirely within a single lane and shall not move from the lane unless the movement can be made safely. Unsafe lane changes are Class C misdemeanors and are common contributing factors in accidents.

Failure to Signal (Transportation Code §545.104): A driver shall use turn signals to indicate an intention to turn, change lanes, or start from a parked position. The signal must be given continuously for at least the last 100 feet before turning. This is a Class C misdemeanor.

Texting While Driving (Transportation Code §545.4251): A person may not operate a motor vehicle while using a portable wireless communication device to read, write, or send an electronic message, unless the vehicle is stopped. Exceptions include:

- Using GPS or navigation
- Reporting illegal activity or emergency
- Using hands-free device
- Licensed driver operating commercial vehicle reading electronic data

This is a Class C misdemeanor, punishable by fine up to $99 (first offense) or $100-$200 (subsequent offense). If the violation causes death or serious bodily injury, penalties increase significantly.

Open Container (Texas Penal Code §49.031): While technically in the Penal Code rather than Transportation Code, open container violations are commonly encountered during traffic enforcement. A person commits an offense if they knowingly possess an open container of alcohol in the passenger area of a motor vehicle on a public highway. The driver is responsible if they are aware of the open container. This is a Class C misdemeanor.

Exceptions include:

- Passengers in buses, taxis, or limousines
- Containers in locked glove compartment or trunk
- Passengers in the living quarters of a motorhome

Driving Without Valid License in Possession (Transportation Code §521.025): A person may not operate a motor vehicle unless the person holds a driver's license. This is distinct from driving with an invalid license. If the person has a valid license but simply doesn't have it with them, it's a less serious violation that can be dismissed upon proof of valid license. Always verify through dispatch whether the person is actually licensed.

Reckless Driving (Transportation Code §545.401): A person commits reckless driving if they drive a vehicle in willful or wanton disregard for the safety of persons or property. This is a Class B misdemeanor. The key distinction from other traffic violations is the willful or wanton disregard standard. This typically requires evidence of intentionally dangerous driving such as:

- Excessive speed combined with other dangerous maneuvers
- Street racing
- Intentionally running other vehicles off the road
- Evading or fleeing from police

Racing on Highway (Transportation Code §545.420): A person may not participate in a race, vehicle speed competition, or contest on a highway, or arrange such a race. This is a Class B misdemeanor. Street racing has become increasingly problematic in many Texas cities, and enforcement is a priority.

Traffic Stop Procedures and Legal Authority

Understanding your legal authority during traffic stops is essential for officer safety, proper enforcement, and avoiding civil liability.

Initiating a Traffic Stop

You may initiate a traffic stop when you have reasonable suspicion that a traffic violation has occurred or is occurring. Reasonable suspicion requires specific, articulable facts that would lead a reasonable officer to believe a violation occurred. "I had a hunch" is not reasonable suspicion. "I observed the vehicle weave across the center line three times in one-quarter mile" is reasonable suspicion.

Once you activate your emergency lights to initiate a stop, the driver is legally seized under the Fourth Amendment. The driver must stop as soon as safely possible. Failure to stop is evading detention (Texas Penal Code §38.04), at minimum a Class A misdemeanor, and potentially a state jail felony or higher depending on circumstances.

Duration and Scope of Traffic Stops

The Supreme Court has established that traffic stops must be limited in duration and scope to the purpose of the stop. You may:

- Request driver's license, registration, and proof of insurance
- Run warrant and criminal history checks
- Write a citation or warning
- Ask basic questions related to the traffic violation
- Conduct investigations reasonably related to the traffic violation

You may extend the duration of the stop beyond the time needed for these tasks only if:

- You develop reasonable suspicion of additional criminal activity, or
- The driver voluntarily consents to additional questioning or searches

In Rodriguez v. United States, the Supreme Court held that you cannot extend a traffic stop to conduct a dog sniff unless you have reasonable suspicion of criminal activity beyond the traffic violation. Prolonging a stop without reasonable suspicion violates the Fourth Amendment.

Requesting Occupants to Exit the Vehicle

You may order the driver and all passengers to exit the vehicle during a traffic stop for officer safety reasons. You don't need any additional justification beyond the traffic stop itself. This authority comes from Pennsylvania v. Mimms and Maryland v. Wilson. However, once ordered out, you can't automatically search them unless you have reasonable suspicion they're armed and dangerous (then you can conduct a Terry frisk) or you have probable cause for arrest.

Searching Vehicles During Traffic Stops

Vehicle searches require either:

- Probable cause to believe the vehicle contains contraband or evidence of a crime (automobile exception)
- Consent from the driver or owner
- Search incident to a lawful arrest
- Plain view of contraband or evidence

Simply stopping someone for a traffic violation doesn't give you authority to search the vehicle. The traffic violation alone typically doesn't provide probable cause to search unless it's an offense like transportation of alcohol or drugs where the vehicle itself is instrumentality of the crime.

If you see or smell evidence during the stop that creates probable cause (such as marijuana odor, visible contraband, or drug paraphernalia), you may then search the vehicle under the automobile exception. Document exactly what you observed that created probable cause.

Consent Searches

You may always ask for consent to search a vehicle. Consent must be:

- Voluntary (not coerced)
- Given by someone with authority to consent (owner or driver with control)
- Clear and unambiguous

Best practice is to get written consent using a consent-to-search form. At minimum, document the consent clearly in your report, including the exact words used and circumstances. Consent may be withdrawn at any time, and you must stop searching immediately when consent is withdrawn.

Arrest During Traffic Stops

You may arrest during a traffic stop if:

- You develop probable cause that a felony has been committed
- You observe an offense committed in your presence
- You discover an active warrant
- The driver is driving with invalid license and continues to violate the law

For most Class C misdemeanor traffic violations, you should issue a citation rather than making a custodial arrest. However, you may arrest for Class C misdemeanors if:

- The person refuses to provide identification
- The person refuses to sign the citation
- You reasonably believe the person will not appear in court
- You reasonably believe the person will continue to violate the law

Inventory Searches

If you arrest the driver and impound the vehicle, you may conduct an inventory search according to your department's inventory policy. Inventory searches are administrative (not investigative) and are conducted to:

- Protect the owner's property
- Protect the department from false claims of loss or damage
- Protect officers and others from dangerous items

Inventory searches must follow standardized procedures. You can't use "inventory" as a pretext to search for evidence when you lack probable cause. If your department requires inventorying only closed containers or doesn't require opening the trunk, you must follow that policy.

DWI Detection and Enforcement

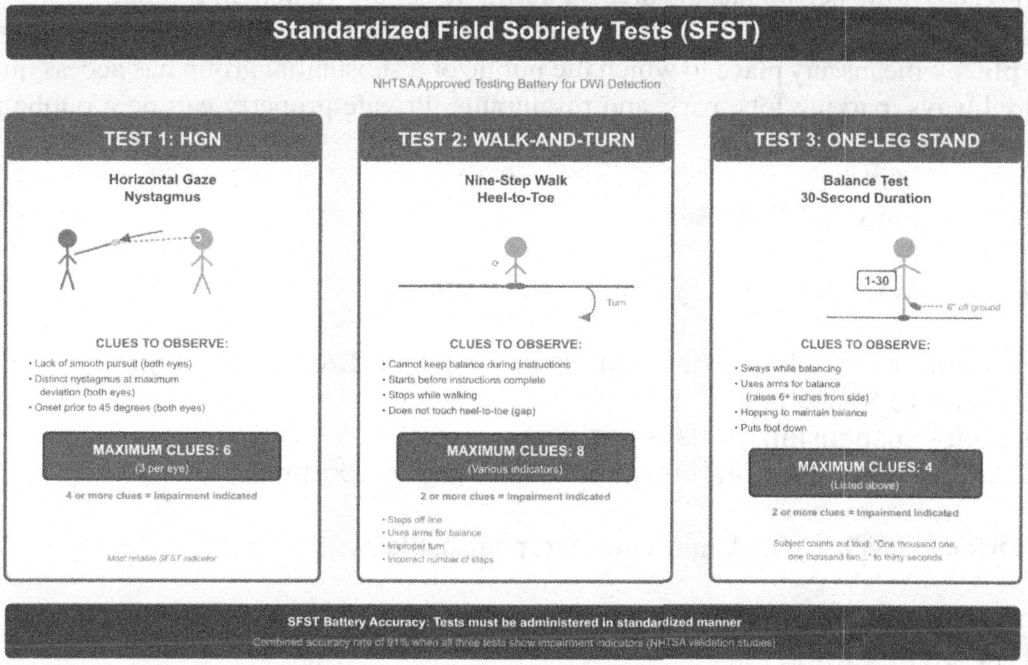

Driving While Intoxicated is one of the most dangerous crimes you'll encounter and one of the most frequently prosecuted. Understanding DWI law and proper enforcement procedures is critical.

DWI Legal Standard (Texas Penal Code §49.04)

A person commits DWI if they are:

- Intoxicated while operating a motor vehicle in a public place, OR
- While operating a motor vehicle in a public place, have an alcohol concentration of 0.08 or more

"Intoxicated" means:

- Not having the normal use of mental or physical faculties by reason of the introduction of alcohol, controlled substance, drug, dangerous drug, or combination, OR
- Having an alcohol concentration of 0.08 or more

This creates two ways to prove DWI:

1. Loss of normal use of faculties (regardless of BAC)
2. BAC of 0.08 or higher (even if faculties don't appear impaired)

"Operating" has been broadly interpreted by Texas courts. You don't need to see someone actually driving. Operating can include sitting in a parked vehicle with the keys in the ignition or within reach, if the person has the present ability to set the vehicle in motion.

"Public place" means any place to which the public or a substantial group has access, including streets, highways, parking lots, bars, and restaurants. Private property can be a public place if the public has general access.

DWI Classifications and Penalties

First Offense DWI: Class B misdemeanor, punishable by:

- 72 hours to 180 days in jail (minimum 6 days if BAC .15 or higher)
- Fine up to $2,000
- License suspension 90 days to 1 year
- Installation of ignition interlock device may be required

Second Offense DWI: Class A misdemeanor, punishable by:

- 30 days to 1 year in jail
- Fine up to $4,000
- License suspension 180 days to 2 years

Third Offense DWI: Third degree felony, punishable by:

- 2 to 10 years in prison
- Fine up to $10,000
- License suspension 180 days to 2 years

DWI with Child Passenger: If a person operates a motor vehicle while intoxicated and the vehicle is occupied by a passenger younger than 15 years, it's a state jail felony regardless of the number of prior DWI convictions. Penalties include 180 days to 2 years in state jail and fine up to $10,000.

Intoxication Assault (Texas Penal Code §49.07): If a person operating a vehicle while intoxicated causes serious bodily injury to another by reason of intoxication, it's a third degree felony (or second degree felony if the victim is a peace officer, firefighter, or emergency medical personnel acting in official capacity).

Intoxication Manslaughter (Texas Penal Code §49.08): If a person operating a vehicle while intoxicated causes the death of another by reason of intoxication, it's a second degree felony (or first degree felony if the victim is a peace officer, firefighter, or emergency medical personnel, or if multiple deaths occur).

Detecting Impaired Drivers

DWI enforcement begins with recognizing the signs of impaired driving. Research by the National Highway Traffic Safety Administration (NHTSA) has identified driving behaviors that correlate with impairment. The most reliable indicators include:

Weaving (70% correlation with DWI):

- Weaving within lane
- Swerving across lane lines
- Drifting across center line

Speed and Braking Problems (60-70% correlation):

- Driving 10+ mph under limit without reason
- Stopping without cause in traffic
- Accelerating or decelerating rapidly without reason
- Varying speed significantly

Vigilance Problems (60-65% correlation):

- Driving in opposing lanes or wrong way on one-way street
- Slow response to traffic signals
- Stopping inappropriately (not at intersection)

Judgment Problems (50-55% correlation):

- Following too closely
- Improper or unsafe lane change
- Illegal or improper turn
- Driving without headlights at night

While these behaviors create reasonable suspicion for a traffic stop, they don't by themselves prove DWI. You need additional evidence from your observations during the stop and field sobriety testing.

Conducting the DWI Investigation

Once you've initiated the traffic stop based on observed driving behavior, your investigation proceeds through several phases:

Phase 1: Initial Contact and Observation

As you approach the vehicle, observe and document:

- Any odor of alcohol or drugs
- The driver's eyes (bloodshot, watery, glassy)

- The driver's face (flushed or pale)
- The driver's speech (slurred, slow, confused)
- The driver's coordination (fumbling with documents, dropping items)
- Any open containers or drug paraphernalia visible
- The driver's clothing (soiled, disheveled, stained)

Ask basic questions and listen to responses:

- Where are you coming from? Where are you going?
- Have you had anything to drink tonight?
- Are you taking any medications?

Pay attention not just to what they say but how they say it. Slurred speech, slow responses, confusion, and repetitive answers indicate impairment.

Many impaired drivers will admit to drinking but minimize the amount: "I just had a couple of beers" or "I had two drinks with dinner three hours ago." Document their exact statements. Later evidence may contradict their claims.

Phase 2: Field Sobriety Tests

If your observations create reasonable suspicion of intoxication, request the driver to perform Standardized Field Sobriety Tests (SFSTs). You should explain that these tests help determine if they're safe to drive.

Note on Consent: Field sobriety tests are voluntary. The driver can refuse without direct legal penalties (though refusal itself may be considered in your probable cause determination and can be mentioned in court). If they refuse, document the refusal and proceed based on your other observations.

NHTSA recognizes three standardized field sobriety tests that have been validated through research:

Horizontal Gaze Nystagmus (HGN): This test detects involuntary jerking of the eyes (nystagmus) which becomes more pronounced under the influence of alcohol. You instruct the subject to follow a pen or your finger with their eyes while keeping their head still. You check for:

1. **Lack of Smooth Pursuit:** The eye doesn't track smoothly but jerks or bounces as it follows the stimulus. You check each eye separately.
2. **Distinct and Sustained Nystagmus at Maximum Deviation:** When the eye is held at maximum deviation (as far to the side as it can move), nystagmus persists for at least four seconds. Check each eye.
3. **Onset of Nystagmus Prior to 45 Degrees:** Nystagmus begins before the eye reaches 45 degrees from center. Check each eye.

Each clue counts as one point, for a maximum of six points (three per eye). Four or more clues indicates a BAC of .08 or above with approximately 77% accuracy.

HGN is the most reliable SFST because it's difficult to fake and isn't affected by nervousness or physical conditions as much as the other tests. However, certain medical conditions, medications, and injuries can cause nystagmus, so you should always ask about these before administering the test.

Walk and Turn (WAT): This divided attention test requires the subject to maintain balance while following instructions and walking a straight line. Proper administration is critical:

Instruction Stage:

- Place the subject on a real or imaginary line
- Instruct them to place right foot ahead of left, heel-to-toe
- Keep arms at sides
- Maintain this position while you give instructions
- Do not begin until told to start

Walking Stage Instructions:

- Take nine heel-to-toe steps along the line
- On the ninth step, keep front foot on the line and turn by taking several small steps with the other foot
- Return nine heel-to-toe steps along the line
- Keep arms at sides, watch feet, count steps out loud, do not stop once started

Scoring (Eight Possible Clues):

1. Cannot keep balance during instructions (steps off line, raises arms, etc.)
2. Starts before instructions are complete
3. Stops while walking
4. Does not touch heel-to-toe (gap of half inch or more)
5. Steps off line
6. Uses arms to balance (raises arms more than six inches from sides)
7. Loses balance on turn or turns incorrectly
8. Takes wrong number of steps

Two or more clues indicates a BAC of .08 or above with approximately 68% accuracy. You should also look for signs that the subject cannot complete the test (stumbles off line, falls, uses arms/body for balance, cannot perform test).

People with back, leg, or inner ear problems, people over 65, and people more than 50 pounds overweight may have difficulty with this test for reasons unrelated to intoxication. Ask about these conditions before administering the test.

One Leg Stand (OLS): This is another divided attention test requiring balance and concentration.

Instructions:

- Stand with feet together, arms at sides
- When told to start, raise one leg (either leg) approximately six inches off ground, foot parallel to ground
- Keep both legs straight, arms at sides
- Look at elevated foot
- Count out loud "one thousand one, one thousand two..." until told to stop
- Continue for 30 seconds

Scoring (Four Possible Clues):

1. Sways while balancing (side-to-side or back-and-forth motion)
2. Uses arms to balance (raises arms six inches or more from sides)
3. Hopping to maintain balance
4. Puts foot down (cannot maintain balance)

Two or more clues indicates a BAC of .08 or above with approximately 65% accuracy. The same physical limitations that affect WAT also affect OLS.

Administering SFSTs Properly

For SFSTs to be admissible and reliable, you must:

- Administer them in standardized manner as trained
- Select appropriate location (level surface, adequate lighting, away from traffic, minimal distractions)
- Demonstrate each test before asking the subject to perform it
- Ask about physical limitations before testing
- Score according to NHTSA guidelines
- Document your observations thoroughly

Non-standardized tests (alphabet recitation, finger-to-nose, finger count, etc.) are not validated and generally shouldn't be used. If you do use them, they should supplement, not replace, the SFSTs.

Phase 3: Chemical Testing

If SFSTs and your other observations establish probable cause for DWI, you should request chemical testing. Texas has an implied consent law (Transportation Code Chapter 724) which means that by operating a motor vehicle in Texas, a person consents to providing a breath or blood sample if arrested for DWI.

Breath Testing: You must read the statutory DIC-24 warning before requesting a breath test. This warning informs the person that:

- Failure to provide a sample will result in license suspension
- Refusal can be used against them in court
- They don't have the right to consult an attorney before deciding whether to provide a sample (though they can consult one if it doesn't interfere with testing)

If the person refuses breath testing, their license will be suspended for 180 days (first refusal) or two years (subsequent refusal). Document the refusal carefully, including your exact words in requesting the test and the suspect's exact words in refusing.

If the person agrees to testing, the test must be administered by a certified breath test operator using an approved device. The device must be in proper working order and calibrated according to regulations. Two tests should be administered, with results within .02 of each other.

Blood Testing: Blood tests are more invasive than breath tests and generally require either:

- Consent (documented carefully)
- A search warrant
- Exigent circumstances (such as the suspect being unconscious or medical treatment interfering with breath testing)

Following the Supreme Court's decision in Missouri v. McNeely, you cannot force a blood draw in DWI cases without a warrant unless exigent circumstances exist. The natural dissipation of alcohol in the bloodstream alone doesn't constitute exigency.

Blood draws must be conducted by qualified medical personnel (physician, registered nurse, licensed vocational nurse, paramedic, or other approved provider) in a sanitary place. The blood sample must be properly preserved and stored to maintain chain of custody.

Mandatory Blood Draw: Transportation Code §724.012 requires you to request a blood specimen if you arrest someone for DWI or intoxication assault/manslaughter and:

- The person was involved in an accident that resulted in death or serious bodily injury, OR
- You reasonably believe a child younger than 15 was a passenger in the vehicle

In these cases, if the person refuses, you must obtain a warrant for the blood draw.

Implied Consent Warnings and Rights

The DIC-24 warning you provide before requesting a breath or blood sample is statutorily required and must be read verbatim. Failure to provide proper warning can result in suppression of test results or license suspension hearing issues. The warning informs the suspect that refusing the test will result in license suspension and that refusal can be used as evidence against them in court.

One critical point that confuses many people: unlike the right to counsel during custodial interrogation, there is no right to consult an attorney before deciding whether to submit to chemical testing. You must inform the suspect of this fact in the DIC-24 warning. The reasoning is that alcohol dissipates quickly from the bloodstream, and allowing unlimited delay for attorney consultation would defeat the purpose of testing.

However, if an attorney is immediately available (already present or quickly contacted by phone), the suspect may speak with them as long as it doesn't unreasonably interfere with the testing process. Document any attorney contact and the timeline involved.

Refusal Consequences

When a person refuses chemical testing after receiving the DIC-24 warning and being arrested for DWI, several consequences follow:

Administrative License Suspension: The Texas Department of Public Safety (DPS) will suspend the person's driver's license for:

- 180 days for first refusal
- 2 years for second or subsequent refusal

This is a separate administrative action from any criminal charges. The person may request an Administrative License Revocation (ALR) hearing within 15 days of receiving the notice of suspension. At the ALR hearing, the issues are limited to whether you had reasonable suspicion to stop, probable cause to arrest, and whether the person refused testing after proper warning.

Admissibility of Refusal: The fact that someone refused testing is admissible in court as evidence of consciousness of guilt. Prosecutors will argue that innocent people don't refuse to prove their innocence. However, defense attorneys often counter that refusal is simply exercising constitutional rights.

Enhanced Penalties: Some prosecutors seek enhanced penalties for refusal cases, arguing that refusal shows deliberate efforts to hide evidence.

No Test Results to Challenge: While refusal eliminates one piece of evidence against the defendant, it also eliminates their ability to argue that test results were inaccurate, improperly obtained, or below the legal limit.

Documenting DWI Arrests

Your DWI report must be thorough and detailed because these cases often go to trial. Document:

Pre-Stop Observations:

- Exact driving behaviors observed (weaving, speeding, braking, etc.)
- Duration of observation
- Traffic and road conditions
- Time and location

Initial Contact:

- Exact time of stop
- Location and conditions (lighting, weather, traffic)
- Odor of alcohol (describe it: faint, moderate, strong)
- Physical appearance (bloodshot eyes, flushed face, disheveled clothing)
- Speech patterns (slurred, slow, confused, normal)
- Behavior (fumbling with documents, dropping items, difficulty following instructions)
- Statements made (document exact words, especially admissions of drinking)

Field Sobriety Tests:

- Which tests were administered
- Instructions given to the suspect
- Demonstrations you performed
- Specific clues observed on each test
- Environmental conditions during testing
- Any factors that might affect performance (injuries, age, weight)

Chemical Testing:

- DIC-24 warning (confirm you read it)
- Suspect's response (consent or refusal, and exact words)
- Testing procedures followed
- Results obtained
- Time of testing
- Who administered test

Arrest Decision:

- Probable cause factors
- Time of arrest
- Miranda warning given
- Transport and booking procedures

Additional Evidence:

- Witness statements
- Video evidence (dashcam, bodycam, booking room video)
- Photographs
- Medical records (if suspect was injured or transported to hospital)

Quality DWI investigations require attention to detail and thorough documentation. Defense attorneys scrutinize every aspect of DWI cases, so your reports must withstand that scrutiny.

Texas Family Code

The Texas Family Code governs domestic relations, including marriage, divorce, parent-child relationships, child protection, and protective orders. As a peace officer, you'll most frequently deal with Family Code provisions related to family violence, protective orders, and child welfare.

Protective Orders and Family Violence

Family Violence Definition (Family Code §71.004)

"Family violence" means an act by a member of a family or household against another member that is intended to result in physical harm, bodily injury, assault, or sexual assault, or that is a threat that reasonably places the member in fear of imminent physical harm, bodily injury, assault, or sexual assault. The act need not result in physical injury to constitute family violence.

Who Qualifies as Family or Household Member (Family Code §71.003):

- Current or former spouses
- Parents of the same child (regardless of marriage)
- Persons related by blood or marriage
- Persons in a dating relationship
- Foster parents and foster children
- Former foster parents and former foster children
- Persons who currently or formerly lived together

Understanding these relationships is critical because it determines whether conduct qualifies as family violence (which has special enforcement provisions) or ordinary assault or harassment.

Dating Relationship: The Family Code specifically includes dating relationships even if the parties have never lived together or married. Courts look at factors including the length of the relationship, nature and frequency of interaction, and whether the relationship includes romantic or intimate aspects. A single date generally doesn't establish a dating relationship, but ongoing romantic involvement does.

Protective Orders (Family Code Chapter 85)

A protective order is a civil court order that prohibits a person from:

- Committing family violence
- Communicating directly with protected parties (except through attorneys)
- Going near the residence, workplace, or school of protected parties
- Possessing firearms
- Other conditions the court deems necessary for safety

Protective orders are issued by district courts or, in some counties, statutory county courts. They may be temporary (ex parte orders issued without the respondent present) or final orders (issued after a hearing where both parties have opportunity to be heard).

Types of Protective Orders:

Ex Parte Protective Orders: These temporary orders are issued based on the applicant's testimony alone, without notice to the respondent. They're designed to provide immediate protection when there's a clear and present danger of family violence. Ex parte orders typically last 20 days or until the hearing for a final order.

When you serve an ex parte protective order, the respondent may be genuinely surprised because they haven't had a hearing yet. Explain that this is a temporary order and they'll have opportunity to present their side at the final hearing. But also make clear that violating the order, even if they disagree with it, is a criminal offense.

Final Protective Orders: These orders are issued after a hearing where both parties have opportunity to present evidence. Final protective orders can last up to two years, or longer in cases involving serious family violence. They can be renewed.

Magistrate's Orders for Emergency Protection (Article 17.292 CCP): These are separate from Family Code protective orders and are issued by magistrates at the time of arrest or initial appearance for certain offenses:

- Family violence offenses
- Sexual assault or abuse
- Stalking
- Trafficking

MOEPs provide immediate protection without requiring the victim to file for a civil protective order. They typically last 31 to 61 days.

Your Duties Regarding Protective Orders:

Service: You may be tasked with serving protective orders on respondents. Service requires physically delivering the order and explaining that violating it is a crime. You must complete an affidavit of service documenting when, where, and how service was accomplished.

Enforcement: When you receive a call involving parties subject to a protective order, your first step is verifying the order's existence and terms. You can check through:

- TCIC/NCIC protective order database
- Direct contact with the issuing court
- Copy of the order held by the protected party

Once you verify the order exists and the respondent has been served, enforcement is straightforward. If the respondent violated the order's terms, you have probable cause for arrest.

Verification of Service: A person cannot be arrested for violating a protective order unless they've been served with it or are present at the hearing where it was issued. Always verify service before making an arrest for protective order violation.

Common Protective Order Provisions:

Most protective orders include some combination of these conditions:

No Contact: The respondent may not communicate directly or indirectly with protected parties. This includes phone calls, text messages, emails, social media contact, messages through third parties, or any other communication. Some orders allow communication through attorneys regarding specific matters like child custody exchanges.

Stay-Away Requirements: The respondent must stay at least a specified distance (commonly 200 yards or 500 feet) from the residence, workplace, or school of protected parties. This can create complications if the parties have children together and need to exchange them for visitation. The order should address this, often by specifying a neutral exchange location.

Firearms Prohibition: Federal and Texas law prohibit persons subject to protective orders from possessing firearms. When you serve a protective order, you must inform the respondent of this prohibition and may need to seize firearms if they're accessible. Document any firearms seized, following your department's property procedures.

Vacate Residence: The court may order the respondent to vacate the family residence, even if they own it. This gives the protected party exclusive use of the residence for the order's duration.

Counseling Requirements: Courts often order respondents to complete family violence or substance abuse counseling as a condition of the protective order.

Child-Related Provisions: If the parties have children together, the order may address custody, visitation, and child support. These provisions can be complex, and you should read them carefully to understand what contact is prohibited versus what's required for child exchanges.

Violation of Protective Order (Penal Code §25.07):

A person commits an offense if they violate a protective order by:

- Committing family violence
- Communicating directly with a protected individual in a threatening or harassing manner
- Communicating a threat through any person to a protected individual
- Coming within a specified distance of a protected place
- Possessing a firearm (if prohibited by the order)

Violation is a Class A misdemeanor for first offense, or a third degree felony if the defendant has a prior conviction for violating a protective order or has violated the order by committing assault, stalking, or certain other offenses.

You may arrest without a warrant for protective order violations if you have probable cause to believe the violation occurred, even if it didn't occur in your presence (Family Code §85.042).

Family Violence Arrests and Procedures

Texas law strongly encourages arrest in family violence situations. Article 14.03(b) CCP specifically authorizes warrantless arrest when you have probable cause to believe a person committed assault resulting in bodily injury to a family or household member, even if the offense didn't occur in your presence.

Primary Aggressor Determination: When responding to family violence calls where both parties claim the other was the aggressor, you must determine who was the primary aggressor. Consider:

- Prior complaints of family violence
- Relative severity of injuries
- Likelihood of future injury
- Whether one party acted in self-defense
- Witness statements
- Apparent motivation (offense vs. defense)

The primary aggressor is not necessarily the person who struck the first blow. It's the person who was the dominant aggressor considering the totality of circumstances. Arrest the primary aggressor, not both parties, unless you cannot determine who was primary.

Victim Safety: When handling family violence calls:

- Separate the parties immediately for officer safety and to prevent further violence
- Interview victim and suspect separately, out of hearing of each other
- Document injuries with photographs (even minor injuries)

- Provide victim with information about protective orders, shelters, and victim services
- Consider safety planning (does victim have a safe place to stay? Can friends or family help?)
- Never minimize the danger or pressure the victim to reconcile

Victim Advocacy: Texas law requires law enforcement agencies to have policies for family violence response, including providing victims with written information about their rights and available resources. You should carry this information and provide it to every family violence victim you encounter.

Why Victims Don't Always Cooperate: Many family violence victims decline to pursue charges or later recant their statements. Understanding why helps you handle these situations appropriately:

- Financial dependence on the abuser
- Fear of retaliation
- Hope that the abuser will change
- Concern about children being removed or custody being affected
- Cultural or religious beliefs about marriage and family
- Immigration status concerns
- Emotional attachment to the abuser (trauma bonding)

These are not reasons to refuse to investigate or make arrests when you have probable cause. Your job is to enforce the law and provide immediate protection, not to convince the victim to prosecute. Document everything thoroughly so prosecutors can pursue the case even if the victim becomes uncooperative.

Evidence-Based Prosecution: Because family violence victims often become uncooperative, prosecutors increasingly pursue "evidence-based prosecution" that doesn't rely solely on victim testimony. Your documentation and evidence collection are critical:

- Photographs of injuries
- Photographs of property damage
- 911 recordings
- Your observations of the scene and parties' demeanor
- Excited utterances and statements made at the scene
- Medical records
- Witness statements
- Prior incidents and protective order violations

Collect this evidence on every family violence call, even if the victim says they don't want to press charges.

Child Welfare and Mandatory Reporting

Child Abuse and Neglect (Family Code Chapter 261)

As a peace officer, you're a mandatory reporter of child abuse and neglect. You must report any reasonable belief that a child has been or may be abused or neglected. The law defines your obligation broadly because children cannot protect themselves, and early intervention can prevent serious harm or death.

Definitions:

Abuse (Family Code §261.001):

- Mental or emotional injury that results in observable impairment of growth, development, or psychological functioning
- Causing or permitting sexual conduct harmful to a child
- Failure to make reasonable effort to prevent sexual conduct harmful to a child
- Physical injury that results in substantial harm, or the genuine threat of substantial harm from physical injury
- Failure to make reasonable effort to prevent an action that results in physical injury resulting in substantial harm

Neglect (Family Code §261.001):

- Placing a child in or failing to remove from a situation that a reasonable person would realize requires judgment or actions beyond the child's maturity, physical condition, or mental abilities and that results in bodily injury or substantial risk of immediate harm
- Failing to seek, obtain, or follow through with medical care resulting in or presenting substantial risk of death, disfigurement, or bodily injury
- Negligent supervision resulting in substantial risk of harm
- The child is a victim of trafficking
- Abandonment without arrangement for adequate care

Mandatory Reporting (Family Code §261.101):

You must make a report not later than 48 hours after you first suspect abuse or neglect. The report must be made to:

- Texas Department of Family and Protective Services (DFPS)
- Texas Youth Commission (for children in TYC custody)
- State agency operating a facility where the child is located

You can make reports through the Texas Abuse Hotline (1-800-252-5400) which operates 24/7. You must provide:

- Your name and contact information
- Child's name, age, and location
- Names and contact information for parents or caretakers
- Nature and extent of injury or condition
- Any other pertinent information

Immunity: You have immunity from civil and criminal liability for reporting in good faith, even if the report is later determined to be unfounded. However, failure to report when required can result in Class A misdemeanor charges against you personally, plus civil liability.

Investigation of Child Abuse:

When investigating suspected child abuse:

Medical Attention: If the child has injuries requiring medical attention, arrange immediate care. Medical personnel can document injuries and provide expert opinions on whether injuries are consistent with the explanation given or suggest abuse.

Interviews: Interview the child separately from parents or caretakers when possible. Use age-appropriate language and questions. Avoid leading questions or repeated questioning that might contaminate the child's memory. Consider requesting a forensic interview by a trained child abuse specialist.

Documentation: Photograph all visible injuries from multiple angles. Include photographs showing the injury in relation to the child's body (context photos). Photograph the scene where abuse allegedly occurred. Document everything in your report, including the child's exact words when describing what happened.

Evidence Collection: Preserve physical evidence including:

- Clothing worn during the incident
- Items used to inflict injury (belts, cords, etc.)
- Bedding or other items with biological evidence (in sexual abuse cases)

Parent Interviews: Interview parents separately. Note any inconsistencies in their explanations for injuries. Be alert for common excuses that don't match injury patterns (falls, accidents, sibling altercations when injuries suggest adult force).

Child Protective Services Coordination: DFPS investigators will become involved once you make a report. Coordinate with them to avoid duplicating interviews and to share information. Their focus is child safety and welfare; yours is criminal investigation. Both roles are important.

Removing Children: In some cases, you may need to take emergency custody of children to protect them from immediate danger (Family Code §262.104). You can do this without a court order if:

- The child is in immediate danger of physical or sexual abuse
- Continuing in the home would expose the child to immediate risk
- There's no time to obtain a court order

When taking emergency custody:

- Document the specific facts creating immediate danger
- Notify DFPS immediately
- Transport the child to a safe location (relative's home, emergency shelter, or DFPS office)
- A court hearing must be held within one business day

Taking children from their parents is an extreme measure used only when necessary to prevent immediate harm. Document your decision-making thoroughly because it will be reviewed by courts and attorneys.

Constitutional Law and Civil Rights

While Texas law provides the framework for most of your day-to-day enforcement activities, the U.S. Constitution establishes fundamental limits on government power that override state law. Understanding constitutional limits is essential for lawful law enforcement and avoiding civil rights violations.

Fourth Amendment and Search/Seizure

The Fourth Amendment protects "the right of the people to be secure in their persons, houses, papers, and effects, against unreasonable searches and seizures." This amendment is the foundation of search and seizure law.

Reasonable Expectation of Privacy

The Fourth Amendment protects places and items where a person has a "reasonable expectation of privacy." To have Fourth Amendment protection, two requirements must be met:

- The person must have an actual, subjective expectation of privacy
- That expectation must be one that society recognizes as reasonable

Places With Privacy Expectations:

- Homes (the strongest protection)
- Hotel rooms (even though temporarily rented)
- Private offices and businesses (though less protection than homes)
- Personal vehicles (though less protection than homes)
- Phone conversations

- Email and electronic communications (with some limitations)
- Enclosed backyards and curtilage

Places Without Privacy Expectations:

- Open fields (even on private property)
- Items in plain view from public locations
- Garbage left for collection
- Information knowingly exposed to third parties (bank records, phone numbers dialed)
- Vehicle exterior and characteristics observable from public areas

Searches

A "search" occurs when government action infringes on a person's reasonable expectation of privacy. Not all investigative techniques constitute searches. For example:

- Looking through a car window from outside is not a search
- Using a flashlight to illuminate interior of car is not a search
- Using drug-sniffing dog to sniff exterior of car is not a search (but extending a traffic stop to conduct the sniff may violate Fourth Amendment)
- Using thermal imaging to detect heat from inside a home IS a search

When a search occurs, it must be reasonable. The Fourth Amendment doesn't prohibit all searches; it prohibits unreasonable searches. A search is reasonable if:

- It's conducted pursuant to a valid warrant based on probable cause, OR
- An exception to the warrant requirement applies

Search Warrant Requirements:

Valid search warrants must be:

- Based on probable cause
- Supported by oath or affirmation
- Issued by a neutral magistrate
- Particularly describing the place to be searched and items to be seized

Probable cause means facts and circumstances that would lead a reasonable person to believe that evidence of a crime will be found in the place to be searched. It's more than mere suspicion but less than proof beyond reasonable doubt.

Particularity requires that the warrant specifically describe what you're looking for and where you'll look. A warrant to search "Joe's house for drugs" is too general. It should specify the address, describe the house, and identify the types of drugs or drug paraphernalia you expect to find.

Warrant Exceptions:

Several well-established exceptions allow warrantless searches:

Consent: If a person with authority to consent voluntarily allows you to search, no warrant is needed. Consent must be:

- Voluntary (not coerced by threat or show of authority)
- Given by someone with authority (owner, resident, or person with shared control over the area)
- Limited to the scope granted (if someone consents to search for a stolen TV, you can't search small containers that couldn't hold a TV)

Consent can be withdrawn at any time, and you must stop searching when consent is withdrawn.

Search Incident to Arrest: When you lawfully arrest someone, you may search:

- The person arrested (full search for weapons and evidence)
- The area within their immediate control (the "grab area" where they could reach for weapons or destroy evidence)
- Vehicles (if the arrestee is unsecured and could access the vehicle, or if you reasonably believe evidence of the offense of arrest might be in the vehicle)

This exception is automatic upon arrest and requires no additional justification. However, the search must be contemporaneous with the arrest (not hours later) and limited in scope to areas the arrestee could access.

Automobile Exception: If you have probable cause to believe a vehicle contains evidence of a crime or contraband, you may search the vehicle without a warrant. The justification is that vehicles are mobile and evidence could be lost if you had to obtain a warrant.

The automobile exception allows you to search:

- The entire vehicle
- All containers within the vehicle that could hold the items you're looking for
- Locked containers (though you should document efforts to obtain keys)

This exception does not require the vehicle to be moving or about to move. Once you have probable cause, the mobility of vehicles generally justifies a warrantless search even if the vehicle is parked and the owner is arrested.

Plain View: If you're lawfully in a position to view an item and immediately recognize it as evidence or contraband, you may seize it without a warrant. Three requirements:

- You must be lawfully in the location where you view the item
- The incriminating nature of the item must be immediately apparent (probable cause)
- You must have lawful access to the item

Example: While conducting a traffic stop, you see a baggie of what appears to be methamphetamine on the passenger seat. You're lawfully positioned at the car window (traffic stop), the incriminating nature is immediately apparent (it looks like meth), and you have lawful access (you can reach through the window or open the door). You may seize the drugs without a warrant.

Exigent Circumstances: Warrantless searches are permitted when emergency circumstances exist:

- Hot pursuit of a fleeing suspect
- Imminent destruction of evidence
- Emergency aid (someone inside needs help)
- Imminent danger to officers or others

The exigency must be real and immediate, not manufactured by police. If you create the exigency through your own conduct (such as knocking on the door and announcing your presence, then claiming you heard evidence being destroyed), courts may find the search unlawful.

Inventory Searches: When you lawfully impound a vehicle or take custody of property, you may conduct an inventory search following standardized procedures. The purpose is administrative (protecting the property and documenting it) rather than investigative. However, evidence discovered during a proper inventory search is admissible.

Seizures

A "seizure" occurs when government action meaningfully interferes with a person's possessory interest in property, or when a reasonable person would not feel free to leave or terminate the encounter with police.

Seizures of Property: Taking property for evidence, forfeiture, or safekeeping constitutes a seizure that must be reasonable. Generally, this requires either:

- A warrant
- An exception to the warrant requirement (such as plain view, search incident to arrest, or exigent circumstances)

Seizures of Persons: There are three types of police-citizen encounters:

Consensual Encounter: No seizure occurs. You approach someone and ask questions, and they're free to refuse to answer and leave. No reasonable suspicion required. However, if your show of authority is such that a reasonable person wouldn't feel free to leave, it becomes a seizure.

Investigative Detention (Terry Stop): A brief seizure for investigation requires reasonable suspicion that criminal activity is afoot. You may:

- Briefly detain the person
- Ask questions
- Request identification
- Conduct a protective frisk if you reasonably believe they're armed

The detention must be brief (generally no more than 15-20 minutes unless circumstances justify longer) and limited in scope to investigating the suspected crime. You cannot conduct a full search without arrest or consent.

Arrest: Taking someone into custody requires probable cause that they committed a crime. Arrests are seizures that must be reasonable under the Fourth Amendment.

Quick Reference: Essential Texas Statutes

This section provides a condensed reference for the statutes you'll encounter most frequently. Use this for quick review, but refer back to the detailed explanations when you need more context.

Texas Penal Code Classifications:

Classification	Punishment	Examples
Capital Felony	Death or life without parole	Capital murder
1st Degree Felony	5-99 years or life, up to $10,000 fine	Murder, aggravated robbery, aggravated sexual assault
2nd Degree Felony	2-20 years, up to $10,000 fine	Manslaughter, robbery, aggravated assault, sexual assault
3rd Degree Felony	2-10 years, up to $10,000 fine	Stalking, tampering with evidence, deadly conduct with firearm

Classification	Punishment	Examples
State Jail Felony	180 days-2 years, up to $10,000 fine	Burglary of building, theft $2,500-$30,000, forgery
Class A Misdemeanor	Up to 1 year jail, up to $4,000 fine	Assault causing bodily injury, DWI (1st), resisting arrest
Class B Misdemeanor	Up to 180 days jail, up to $2,000 fine	DWI (certain circumstances), terroristic threat, criminal trespass
Class C Misdemeanor	Fine up to $500 (no jail)	Assault by contact, theft under $100, most traffic violations

Warrantless Arrest Authority (CCP Art. 14.01-14.04):

You may arrest without warrant when:

- Offense committed in your presence or view
- Felony committed and you have probable cause person committed it
- Felony committed and probable cause person is about to escape
- Probable cause person committed assault with bodily injury against family/household member
- Probable cause person violated protective order
- Person found in suspicious place under circumstances showing felony commission or attempt

Key Use of Force Statutes:

§9.21 - Public Duty (peace officer authority) §9.31 - Self-Defense (citizens) §9.32 - Deadly Force in Defense of Person §9.51 - Force to Effect Arrest or Search §9.52 - Force to Prevent Escape

Family Violence Indicators:

- Current or former spouses
- Parents of same child
- Blood or marriage relatives
- Dating relationship
- Current or former residents of same household
- Foster family relationships

Protective Order Violations (PC §25.07):

- Class A misdemeanor (first offense)
- 3rd degree felony (prior conviction or violation by assault/stalking)

DWI Standards (PC §49.04):

- Intoxicated = Loss of normal use of faculties OR BAC .08+
- Class B misdemeanor (1st offense)
- Class A misdemeanor (2nd offense)
- 3rd degree felony (3rd+ offense)
- State jail felony (child passenger under 15)

Real-World Application: Legal Code Scenarios

The following scenarios test your ability to apply the legal principles you've learned in real-world situations. Work through each scenario carefully, identifying the relevant laws, proper procedures, and appropriate actions. After attempting your answer, read the explanation to understand the reasoning.

Scenario 1: Traffic Stop Search Decision

Situation: You stop a vehicle for speeding (72 mph in a 60 mph zone) at 2:30 AM on a rural highway. The driver, a 28-year-old male, provides a valid license and proof of insurance. As you speak with him, you notice he seems extremely nervous—his hands are shaking, he's sweating despite cool weather, and he's avoiding eye contact. When you ask where he's coming from, he gives a vague answer about "visiting friends." You see nothing illegal in plain view inside the vehicle.

Question: Do you have legal authority to search the vehicle? What are your options?

Your Analysis:

Consider:

- What was your legal authority for the initial stop?
- What additional observations have you made?
- Do those observations create reasonable suspicion or probable cause?
- What can you do within the law, and what would exceed your authority?

Answer and Explanation:

You do NOT have legal authority to search the vehicle based solely on the facts provided. Here's why:

Legal Authority for Stop: The speeding violation gave you reasonable suspicion to conduct the traffic stop. This authority is solid and unquestionable.

Nervous Behavior: While the driver's nervous behavior is notable and might heighten your suspicion, nervousness alone doesn't create probable cause or even reasonable suspicion of criminal activity. Many people are nervous during traffic stops for legitimate reasons—they're getting a ticket, they're worried about being late, or they simply feel uncomfortable with police interaction.

Vague Answers: Similarly, vague responses to questions don't establish probable cause. People have Fourth Amendment rights to be vague or to decline to answer questions altogether during consensual portions of a traffic stop.

No Observable Evidence: You've seen nothing in plain view that would create probable cause. Without probable cause, you cannot search under the automobile exception.

Your Options:

Option 1 - Complete the Traffic Stop: You can complete the purpose of the stop (issue citation or warning for speeding), return documents, and release the driver. You cannot extend the stop beyond the time reasonably necessary to complete these tasks without additional justification.

Option 2 - Request Consent: You may ask the driver for permission to search the vehicle. This request must not unreasonably prolong the stop. If you've already completed the purpose of the stop (issued the citation), you must make clear through your words and actions that the driver is free to leave, and that cooperation with your request to search is completely voluntary. If the driver consents, document the consent carefully. If they refuse, you must let them leave.

Option 3 - Develop Additional Reasonable Suspicion: If, during your lawful questioning related to the traffic stop, you observe or learn facts that create reasonable suspicion of criminal activity (such as detecting marijuana odor, seeing drug paraphernalia, or receiving information that the vehicle matches description of one involved in a crime), you may extend the detention to investigate further. But nervousness and vague answers aren't sufficient.

What You Cannot Do:

- You cannot search without consent, probable cause, or another warrant exception
- You cannot extend the stop beyond what's necessary to complete the traffic citation unless you develop reasonable suspicion of additional criminal activity
- You cannot detain the driver while a drug dog is brought to the scene unless you've completed the stop and the dog is immediately available, or you have reasonable suspicion

Key Legal Principles:

This scenario illustrates Rodriguez v. United States (2015), where the Supreme Court held that you cannot extend a traffic stop to conduct a dog sniff without reasonable suspicion of criminal activity beyond the traffic violation. The case reinforces that traffic stops must be limited in duration to the time reasonably necessary to complete the stop's purpose.

It also illustrates that "hunches" based on nervous behavior, even reasonable hunches, don't satisfy Fourth Amendment standards. You need articulable facts creating reasonable suspicion or probable cause.

Scenario 2: Domestic Violence Response

Situation: You're dispatched to a domestic disturbance at 11:45 PM. Dispatch advises that a neighbor heard yelling and a loud crash. When you arrive, a woman answers the door. She has a visible red mark on her left cheek and her lip is slightly swollen. She states that her husband "just got angry" and that everything is fine now. She doesn't want to press charges. Her husband emerges from the back of the house and states, "She started it. She threw a plate at me and I pushed her away in self-defense. This is none of your business." You observe a broken plate on the kitchen floor and no visible injuries on the husband.

Question: What is your legal authority and responsibility in this situation? Must you arrest someone? If so, whom?

Your Analysis:

Consider:

- What offense has occurred based on the physical evidence?
- Do you have authority to arrest without a warrant?
- What if the victim doesn't want to prosecute?
- How do you determine who was the primary aggressor?

Answer and Explanation:

You have both the legal authority and professional responsibility to make an arrest in this situation. Here's your analysis:

Legal Authority: Article 14.03(b) of the Texas Code of Criminal Procedure authorizes you to arrest without a warrant when you have probable cause to believe a person committed assault resulting in bodily injury against a family or household member, even if the offense didn't occur in your presence. The visible injuries on the wife's face provide probable cause that assault with bodily injury occurred.

Family Violence: The parties are married, which makes them family members under Texas Family Code §71.003. The assault between family members constitutes family violence. This is significant because:

- It triggers your warrantless arrest authority under CCP 14.03(b)

- The offense is enhanced to at least a Class A misdemeanor (potentially higher if there are prior family violence convictions)
- It allows for emergency protective orders

Victim Cooperation Not Required: The victim's statement that she doesn't want to press charges is not legally relevant to your decision to arrest. You don't enforce the law at the victim's discretion. Your role is to:

- Enforce the law based on probable cause
- Protect the victim (who may be minimizing the situation due to fear, financial dependence, or trauma bonding)
- Document evidence for prosecution

Many family violence victims initially refuse to cooperate due to fear of retaliation, financial concerns, or emotional attachment to the abuser. This doesn't diminish the seriousness of the offense or remove your authority to arrest.

Determining Primary Aggressor: Both parties claim the other started the altercation, which is common in domestic situations. You must determine who was the primary aggressor based on:

Physical Evidence:

- The wife has visible injuries (red mark, swollen lip)
- The husband has no visible injuries
- A broken plate suggests thrown object, but injury pattern doesn't match being hit by a plate

Statements:

- The husband admits to pushing her
- Even if she threw a plate first, his response appears to have exceeded reasonable force in self-defense
- "Pushing" that results in facial injuries suggests significant force

Totality of Circumstances:

- The husband's physical advantage (typically)
- The location and type of injuries (facial injuries from a "push" suggest forceful contact)
- The wife's apparent fear or minimization of the situation
- No evidence corroborating that the wife was the aggressor beyond the husband's self-serving statement

Decision: Based on the evidence, the husband is the primary aggressor. His claim of self-defense doesn't justify the level of force that caused her facial injuries. Even if she threw a plate (which isn't confirmed by her statement), his response was disproportionate.

Proper Actions:

1. **Separate the parties** immediately for safety and to prevent further violence or coordination of stories
2. **Document everything:**
    - Photograph the wife's injuries from multiple angles
    - Photograph the scene (broken plate, any other evidence)
    - Document both parties' exact statements
    - Note any other observations (torn clothing, other property damage)
3. **Arrest the husband** for assault causing bodily injury to a family member (Class A misdemeanor at minimum)
4. **Provide victim resources:**
    - Written information about protective orders
    - Shelter and victim services contact information
    - Inform her about the arrest process and potential protective order
    - Safety planning (does she have a safe place to stay?)
5. **Request emergency protective order** from the magistrate when the husband is brought before them for initial appearance
6. **Complete thorough report** including:
    - Dispatch information and response time
    - Scene description and observations
    - Both parties' statements (verbatim when possible)
    - Injury descriptions and photograph reference numbers
    - Witness information (neighbor who called)
    - Your determination of primary aggressor and reasoning

What Not to Do:

- Don't ask the victim if she wants you to arrest her husband (you're enforcing the law, not taking a poll)
- Don't minimize the situation or suggest they "work it out"
- Don't arrest both parties unless you truly cannot determine who was primary aggressor (rare)
- Don't leave without making an arrest when you have probable cause
- Don't fail to document thoroughly, thinking the victim won't cooperate later

Why This Matters:

Family violence escalates over time. Today's shove becomes tomorrow's serious injury or homicide. Your intervention may be the only opportunity this victim has to break the cycle.

Even if she doesn't cooperate with prosecution now, your thorough documentation may save her life in the future when the violence escalates and she finally seeks help.

Scenario 3: Vehicle Search and Consent Issues

Situation: You conduct a traffic stop for a non-functioning brake light at 8:00 PM. The driver is a 19-year-old female who provides her license and registration. While speaking with her, you notice a strong smell of air freshener, which you know is sometimes used to mask marijuana odor. You also see an air freshener hanging from the rearview mirror. When you ask if she has anything illegal in the vehicle, she nervously says "no." You ask if you can search the vehicle and she responds, "I guess so, if you have to."

Question: Is this valid consent to search? What factors should you consider? How should you proceed?

Your Analysis:

Consider:

- What is the legal standard for valid consent?
- Does the air freshener odor create probable cause?
- How do you interpret the driver's response?
- What documentation is necessary?

Answer and Explanation:

This scenario presents a questionable consent situation that requires careful analysis:

Consent Legal Standards:

Valid consent to search requires three elements:

1. **Voluntary** - Given freely without coercion or duress
2. **Intelligent** - The person understands what they're consenting to
3. **Unequivocal** - Clear and definite, not ambiguous

The driver's statement "I guess so, if you have to" fails to clearly meet these standards:

Voluntariness Question: Her phrasing "if you have to" suggests she may believe she's required to consent. This indicates potential confusion about her rights. True voluntary consent occurs when a person knows they can refuse and chooses to allow the search anyway.

Ambiguity: "I guess so" is hesitant and uncertain language, not clear agreement. Courts prefer unambiguous consent like "Yes, you may search" or "I consent to a search."

Probable Cause Analysis:

You must also consider whether you even need consent:

Air Freshener Alone: The presence of air freshener and its smell do NOT create probable cause to search. Many people use air fresheners legitimately. This alone doesn't create a reasonable belief that contraband is present.

Marijuana Odor: If you actually smelled marijuana (not just air freshener), you'd have probable cause to search without consent under the automobile exception. But you didn't smell marijuana - you smelled air freshener and suspected it might be masking something.

Nervous Behavior: Nervousness during a traffic stop is common and doesn't create reasonable suspicion or probable cause.

Proper Approach:

Option 1 - Clarify Consent:

Since the consent statement is ambiguous, you should clarify before searching:

"Ma'am, I want to be clear - you don't have to consent to a search. You have the right to refuse. If you give me permission to search your vehicle, I'll document your consent. Do you voluntarily consent to me searching your vehicle?"

Wait for a clear response. If she says "yes" clearly, you may proceed and should document:

- The question you asked
- Her exact response
- That you explained she could refuse
- The time and location

If she refuses or gives another ambiguous answer, you must respect that. Complete the traffic stop (issue citation for the brake light) and release her.

Option 2 - Complete Traffic Stop Without Search:

If you're uncertain about the consent or uncomfortable with the ambiguity, the safest approach is to complete the traffic stop without searching. You have no probable cause, and the consent is questionable. Issue the citation for the equipment violation and release her.

Documentation Requirements:

If you do obtain clear consent and search, document thoroughly:

- Your observations that led to the consent request (be honest - "I smelled strong air freshener and requested consent to search")
- Your exact words requesting consent
- Her exact response
- That you informed her of her right to refuse
- Whether you found anything during the search

Best practice is to use a written consent-to-search form that the person signs. Many departments require this for all consent searches. At minimum, document the consent in your report and on your bodycam if equipped.

Why This Matters:

Consent searches are frequently challenged in court. Defense attorneys scrutinize the circumstances to argue consent was coerced or involuntary. Ambiguous consent creates reasonable doubt about whether the search was lawful. If you find contraband through an unlawful search, it will be suppressed and the case dismissed.

When consent is unclear, you must decide whether to:

- Clarify and seek unambiguous consent
- Not search and complete the traffic stop
- Develop probable cause through other means (like actually smelling marijuana or seeing contraband)

You cannot search based on hunches, ambiguous consent, or nervous behavior. The Fourth Amendment requires more.

Key Takeaway: When in doubt about consent, clarify or don't search. An unlawful search that yields evidence is worse than no search at all, because the evidence will be suppressed and the guilty person goes free.

Scenario 4: Miranda and Interrogation

Situation: You arrest a suspect for burglary based on a warrant. During transport to jail, before you've read Miranda warnings, the suspect spontaneously states, "I didn't think anyone would be home. I just needed money for rent." You arrive at jail, complete booking, and place the suspect in an interview room. You read Miranda warnings from a card. The suspect states he understands his rights and is willing to talk. During the interview, he admits to the burglary and describes taking a laptop and jewelry. After 45 minutes of questioning, he says "Maybe I should talk to a lawyer." You respond, "Well, you've already told me most of it. You might as well finish explaining what happened." He continues talking and provides additional details about selling the stolen property.

Question: Which statements are admissible in court? Which statements should be suppressed? What errors were made?

Your Analysis:

Consider:

- When are Miranda warnings required?
- What makes a statement admissible or inadmissible?
- How should you respond when a suspect invokes rights?
- What is spontaneous versus interrogated statement?

Answer and Explanation:

This scenario involves multiple statements, each with different admissibility:

Statement 1 - Transport Spontaneous Statement: "I didn't think anyone would be home. I just needed money for rent."

Admissible: This statement is likely admissible even though no Miranda warnings were given. Here's why:

Miranda warnings are required only during "custodial interrogation." Custodial means the person is under arrest or deprived of freedom in a significant way. Interrogation means questioning or actions reasonably likely to elicit an incriminating response.

The suspect was in custody (under arrest), but you didn't interrogate him. He made the statement spontaneously without any prompting. Spontaneous statements that aren't the product of interrogation don't require Miranda warnings.

However, you must be prepared to testify that:

- You didn't ask any questions or make any statements designed to elicit a response
- The statement was truly voluntary and spontaneous
- You didn't create conditions designed to make him want to talk

If you had asked "Why'd you do it?" or made comments like "Breaking into homes is serious business," those could be considered interrogation that requires Miranda warnings.

Statement 2 - Post-Miranda Interview Admission: The initial admission to the burglary and details about the laptop and jewelry.

Admissible: This statement was properly obtained:

- Miranda warnings were given
- The suspect indicated he understood his rights
- He voluntarily waived his rights and agreed to talk
- The questioning occurred after proper waiver

Texas law (Article 38.22 CCP) requires that oral statements during custodial interrogation be electronically recorded to be admissible. Assuming you recorded the interview, this statement meets all requirements.

Statement 3 - After Invocation of Right to Counsel: Additional details about selling the stolen property, made after suspect said "Maybe I should talk to a lawyer."

INADMISSIBLE: This statement should be suppressed, and you made a serious error in how you handled the situation.

When a suspect invokes the right to counsel (or even arguably invokes it with ambiguous language like "Maybe I should talk to a lawyer"), you must:

- Stop questioning immediately
- Not resume questioning unless the suspect initiates further communication
- Not attempt to persuade the suspect to continue talking

The suspect's statement "Maybe I should talk to a lawyer" is an invocation of the right to counsel, even though it's phrased as a question or possibility. Courts interpret any reasonable assertion of rights in the suspect's favor.

Your response - "Well, you've already told me most of it. You might as well finish explaining what happened" - was improper for several reasons:

1. **Continued Interrogation After Invocation:** You were required to stop all questioning when he mentioned wanting a lawyer.
2. **Coercive Persuasion:** Your statement was designed to convince him that invoking his rights was pointless since he'd already incriminated himself. This undermines the voluntariness of any subsequent waiver.
3. **Minimization of Rights:** Suggesting that exercising constitutional rights is futile violates the spirit and purpose of Miranda.

Any statements made after this point are tainted by your improper continuation of interrogation. A court will likely suppress everything said after the suspect mentioned wanting a lawyer.

Proper Procedure:

Here's what should have happened:

During Transport:

- The spontaneous statement is fine to listen to and document
- Don't ask follow-up questions or make comments designed to elicit more information
- If he continues talking spontaneously, you may listen, but be prepared to prove you didn't encourage it

At Jail:

- Advise Miranda rights before any interrogation
- Document the advisement (read from card, time, location, suspect's response)
- If suspect waives rights and agrees to talk, conduct your interview
- Electronically record the entire interview per Texas law

When Rights Are Invoked:

- Stop questioning immediately
- Document the invocation and the time
- Don't attempt to persuade suspect to continue
- Don't resume questioning unless suspect initiates further conversation
- If suspect later initiates conversation, re-advise Miranda before questioning

Correct Response to "Maybe I should talk to a lawyer":

"Okay, we'll stop questioning now. If you want to talk to a lawyer, we can arrange that. I'm going to end this interview." Then leave the interview room or cease all interrogation.

Documentation Requirements:

For all statements to be admissible, document:

- Exact circumstances of each statement
- Whether statement was spontaneous or in response to questioning
- For interrogations, proof that Miranda was given and properly waived
- Electronic recording of custodial interrogation (Texas requirement)
- Any invocation of rights and your response

Consequences of Errors:

The improper continuation of questioning after the suspect invoked his right to counsel will result in:

- Suppression of all statements made after the invocation
- Potential disciplinary action for violating departmental policy
- Possible civil liability for violation of constitutional rights
- Damaged credibility if you testify in future cases

The case isn't necessarily destroyed (you still have the first two statements and other evidence), but you've lost valuable admissions that could have secured a conviction or guilty plea.

Key Takeaway:

Miranda rights exist to protect suspects from coercive interrogation. When a suspect invokes rights (even ambiguously), you must stop immediately. Attempting to talk them out of exercising their rights violates the Constitution and will result in suppression of evidence. Better to lose some statements than to lose the entire case and your credibility.

Scenario 5: Search Incident to Arrest

Situation: You observe a driver run a red light. You initiate a traffic stop. As you approach, you see the driver making furtive movements toward the center console. When you contact the driver, he can't provide proof of insurance and his license shows as suspended. You decide to arrest him for driving with invalid license. After removing him from the vehicle and handcuffing him, you place him in your patrol car. You then return to his vehicle and conduct a thorough search, including opening the center console (where you find a small bag of what appears to be methamphetamine), the glove box, under the seats, and the trunk (where you find a locked box that you pry open, discovering additional drugs and cash).

Question: Which portions of your search were lawful? Which portions exceeded your authority? What should you have done differently?

Your Analysis:

Consider:

- What authority do you have for search incident to arrest?
- How does vehicle search law apply?
- What is the scope of a proper search in this situation?
- What role did the furtive movements play?

Answer and Explanation:

This scenario involves multiple search authorities and limitations. Let's analyze each portion:

The Arrest:

Your arrest for driving with invalid license was lawful. Transportation Code §521.457 makes driving while license invalid an offense, and Article 14.01(b) CCP authorizes arrest for any offense committed in your presence. The arrest provides you with authority to search incident to arrest, but with limitations.

Search Incident to Arrest - General Rule:

When you lawfully arrest someone, you may search:

1. The person arrested (full search of their person and immediately worn clothing)
2. The area within their immediate control (the "grab area")

The purpose is to:

- Find and secure weapons that could endanger you
- Prevent destruction of evidence
- Find evidence of the crime of arrest

Vehicle Search Incident to Arrest - Arizona v. Gant:

The Supreme Court in Arizona v. Gant (2009) limited vehicle searches incident to arrest. You may search a vehicle incident to arrest only if:

Option 1: The arrestee is unsecured and could access the vehicle's interior at the time of the search, OR

Option 2: You reasonably believe evidence of the offense of arrest might be found in the vehicle

In your scenario:

- The driver was secured in your patrol car, so Option 1 doesn't apply
- Driving while license invalid wouldn't have evidence in the vehicle (the offense is simply the act of driving), so Option 2 doesn't apply

Therefore, search incident to arrest does NOT authorize your vehicle search in this case.

Furtive Movements:

The furtive movements you observed created reasonable suspicion that warranted investigating further, but they don't automatically create probable cause to search. Furtive movements might justify:

- Extra caution during the traffic stop
- Asking the driver about the movements
- Conducting a Terry frisk if you reasonably believe he's armed

But without more (such as seeing a weapon or contraband), furtive movements alone don't create probable cause to search.

Proper Analysis of Your Search:

Center Console Search - POTENTIALLY UNLAWFUL:

You had no authority to search the center console based on search incident to arrest (Gant doesn't apply). The furtive movements created reasonable suspicion but not probable cause.

However, you could argue the search was lawful if:

- You were conducting an inventory search before towing the vehicle (but you'd need to follow standardized inventory procedures)
- You had probable cause from observations during the traffic stop (such as seeing contraband or smelling marijuana)

If the search was unlawful, the drugs found in the center console may be suppressed under the exclusionary rule.

Glove Box and Under Seats - SAME ANALYSIS:

Same issue as the center console. Without probable cause or proper inventory procedures, these searches exceeded your authority.

Trunk Search - DEFINITELY UNLAWFUL:

Even if you had authority for search incident to arrest (which you didn't under Gant), that authority doesn't extend to the trunk. The trunk is beyond any possible "grab area" and wouldn't contain evidence of driving with invalid license.

Locked Box in Trunk - DEFINITELY UNLAWFUL:

Even in a lawful search, you generally can't forcibly open locked containers without:

- Probable cause specific to that container
- A search warrant
- Exigent circumstances

Prying open the locked box exceeded any lawful authority you had.

What You Should Have Done:

Here's the proper procedure:

Step 1 - Arrest and Secure:

- Arrest for invalid license (lawful)
- Search the person (lawful search incident to arrest of his person)
- Secure him in patrol car (proper procedure)

Step 2 - Vehicle Disposition:

- Determine what to do with the vehicle (park legally, release to passenger, or tow)
- If towing, conduct inventory search per department policy

Step 3 - Regarding the Furtive Movements:

If the furtive movements created reasonable suspicion he was armed:

- Conduct a Terry frisk of his person for weapons (during initial contact, before placing him in patrol car)
- You might look in the immediate area where he was reaching if you reasonably believe a weapon is there and it poses an immediate threat

But this doesn't justify a full vehicle search.

Step 4 - If You Want to Search:

If you want to search the vehicle beyond what search incident to arrest allows:

- Request consent from the driver (get it clearly documented)
- Develop probable cause (smell marijuana, see contraband, etc.)
- Obtain a search warrant (if you have time and the vehicle is secured)
- Conduct proper inventory search if towing (following standardized procedures)

Inventory Search Option:

If you were towing the vehicle, an inventory search would have been lawful if:

- Your department has a standardized inventory policy
- You follow that policy (don't use "inventory" as pretext for investigative search)
- The purpose is administrative (protect property, protect department from claims)

An inventory search following proper procedures would have allowed you to document and secure items in the passenger compartment and possibly the trunk (depending on policy). If you discovered contraband during a proper inventory, it would be admissible.

Consequences:

Because your search exceeded lawful authority:

- The drugs from the center console, glove box, and trunk may be suppressed
- The locked box search will almost certainly be deemed unlawful
- Any evidence derived from the unlawful search (fruit of the poisonous tree) may also be suppressed
- You could face civil liability for violating Fourth Amendment rights

- The guilty person may go free because of the unlawful search

Key Takeaway:

Search incident to arrest is a useful tool, but it has limits, especially for vehicle searches after Gant. Don't rely on automatic authority to search just because you made an arrest. Consider whether Gant's requirements are met, whether you have probable cause for the automobile exception, or whether an inventory search is appropriate. When in doubt, get a warrant or consent. An unlawful search that finds evidence is worse than no search at all.

Chapter 1: Texas Legal Codes and Laws - Practice Questions

Instructions

This section contains 60 practice questions covering all the material in Chapter 1. These questions mirror the format and difficulty level you'll encounter on the actual TCOLE exam. Some test your recall of specific facts, while others require you to apply legal principles to scenarios.

How to Use These Questions:

First Attempt: Answer all questions without looking at the answers or referring back to the chapter. This simulates test conditions and helps you identify what you actually know versus what you think you know.

Review: After completing all questions, check your answers and read every explanation, even for questions you answered correctly. The explanations often contain additional information that reinforces learning.

Track Your Performance: Note which content areas are giving you trouble. If you miss several questions on a particular topic (such as search and seizure, or family violence), go back and review that section of the chapter before moving forward.

Retake Missed Questions: A few days later, retake any questions you missed. If you get them right the second time, that's great progress. If you still miss them, that topic needs more focused study.

Practice Questions

Question 1: Under the Texas Penal Code, which of the following is the most serious classification of felony?

A) First degree felony B) Capital felony C) Aggravated felony D) Special circumstance felony

Answer: B

Explanation: A capital felony is the most serious offense classification in Texas, punishable by death or life imprisonment without parole. Capital murder under Penal Code §19.03 is the only capital felony in Texas. First degree felonies (option A) are serious but carry a punishment range of 5 to 99 years or life, which is less severe than capital punishment. Options C and D are not actual classifications under Texas law. Understanding the felony classification hierarchy is essential for properly charging offenses and understanding your arrest authority.

Question 2: A person who acts "recklessly" under the Texas Penal Code is someone who:

A) Consciously desires to engage in the conduct or cause the result B) Is aware that their conduct is reasonably certain to cause the result C) Is aware of but consciously disregards a substantial and unjustifiable risk D) Ought to be aware of a substantial and unjustifiable risk but fails to perceive it

Answer: C

Explanation: "Recklessly" means the person is aware of but consciously disregards a substantial and unjustifiable risk that their conduct will cause a particular result. The risk must be of such a nature and degree that its disregard constitutes a gross deviation from the standard of care an ordinary person would exercise. Option A describes "intentionally." Option B describes "knowingly." Option D describes "criminal negligence." These culpable mental states form a hierarchy: intentionally > knowingly > recklessly > criminal negligence. Understanding these distinctions is critical because they determine the level of offense charged. For example, causing death intentionally or knowingly is murder (first degree felony), while causing death recklessly is manslaughter (second degree felony), and causing death with criminal negligence is criminally negligent homicide (state jail felony).

Question 3: Which of the following situations would NOT authorize a warrantless arrest under Article 14.03 of the Texas Code of Criminal Procedure?

A) You observe a driver run a red light B) You have probable cause that a person committed aggravated robbery yesterday C) You have probable cause that a person committed theft (Class B misdemeanor) two days ago D) You have probable cause that a person committed assault causing bodily injury against their spouse an hour ago

Answer: C

Explanation: Article 14.03 CCP authorizes warrantless arrest for offenses committed in your presence or view, and for felonies (even if not committed in your presence) when you have probable cause. It also specifically authorizes warrantless arrest for assault causing bodily injury to a family/household member and protective order violations. Option C describes a Class B misdemeanor (theft) that was not committed in your presence. For this situation, you would need an arrest warrant. You cannot make a warrantless arrest for a misdemeanor that didn't occur in your presence, unless specific statutory authority exists (like family violence). Option A is lawful because the traffic violation occurred in your view. Option B is lawful because aggravated robbery is a first degree felony, and you can arrest for any felony with probable cause even if it didn't occur in your presence. Option D is lawful under the specific family violence exception in Article 14.03(b).

Question 4: Under Texas law, "serious bodily injury" means:

A) Any physical pain, illness, or impairment of physical condition B) Bodily injury that requires medical treatment C) Bodily injury that creates substantial risk of death or causes death, serious permanent disfigurement, or protracted loss or impairment of any bodily member or organ D) Any injury that results in visible bruising or bleeding

Answer: C

Explanation: Texas Penal Code §1.07(a)(46) defines "serious bodily injury" as bodily injury that creates a substantial risk of death or that causes death, serious permanent disfigurement, or protracted loss or impairment of the function of any bodily member or organ. This is a much higher threshold than simple "bodily injury" (option A), which is merely physical pain, illness, or any impairment of physical condition. Options B and D do not match the legal definition. The distinction between "bodily injury" and "serious bodily injury" is critical for charging decisions. For example, assault causing bodily injury is a Class A misdemeanor, but assault causing serious bodily injury is aggravated assault, a second degree felony. Examples of serious bodily injury include: broken bones requiring surgery, loss of consciousness, severe burns, injuries requiring hospitalization, permanent scarring, or loss of use of a body part.

Question 5: A peace officer may use deadly force to prevent escape only if:

A) The suspect is fleeing from any felony arrest B) The officer reasonably believes deadly force is necessary to prevent escape and the person is fleeing from an arrest for a crime involving use or threat of deadly force C) The suspect refuses verbal commands to stop D) The officer has reasonable suspicion the person committed a felony

Answer: B

Explanation: Penal Code §9.52 and Article 15.24 CCP authorize deadly force to prevent escape only under strict circumstances. The officer must reasonably believe deadly force is immediately necessary to prevent escape AND the person must be fleeing from a crime involving the use or threat of deadly force, or the officer must reasonably believe the person poses an imminent threat of death or serious bodily injury. This reflects the U.S. Supreme Court's holding in Tennessee v. Garner (1985), which held that deadly force may not be used to prevent the escape of an apparently unarmed suspected felon unless the officer has probable cause to believe the suspect poses a significant threat of death or serious physical injury to officers or others. Option A is too broad—deadly force is not justified for all felonies. Option C is insufficient—refusal to stop doesn't justify deadly force. Option D uses the wrong standard (reasonable suspicion instead of probable cause) and doesn't address the threat requirement. This is one of the most important use of force rules you'll learn.

Question 6: During a lawful traffic stop, an officer may order passengers to exit the vehicle:

A) Only if the officer has reasonable suspicion that the passengers are armed B) Only if the passengers are suspected of committing a crime C) For officer safety, without any additional justification D) Never, unless the passengers are under arrest

Answer: C

Explanation: Based on Maryland v. Wilson (1997), officers may order passengers to exit a vehicle during a lawful traffic stop for officer safety reasons, without any additional reasonable suspicion or probable cause. This authority extends the holding in Pennsylvania v. Mimms (1977), which established that officers may order drivers to exit vehicles during traffic stops. The Court reasoned that the safety risk to officers during traffic stops justifies this minimal intrusion on passengers' freedom. However, ordering someone out of the vehicle doesn't automatically authorize searching them. If you want to conduct a frisk for weapons, you need reasonable suspicion that the person is armed and dangerous (Terry v. Ohio). This authority is important for officer safety during traffic stops, especially when you observe suspicious behavior or multiple occupants.

Question 7: A person commits assault under Texas Penal Code §22.01 if they:

A) Intentionally, knowingly, or recklessly cause bodily injury to another B) Only if they intentionally cause bodily injury to another C) Negligently cause bodily injury to another D) Accidentally cause bodily injury to another

Answer: A

Explanation: Penal Code §22.01(a)(1) states that a person commits assault if they intentionally, knowingly, OR recklessly cause bodily injury to another. All three mental states satisfy the assault statute. This is different from some other offenses that require only specific mental states. Options B, C, and D are incorrect because they limit or expand the required mental state beyond what the statute requires.

Question 8: Which of the following is TRUE regarding Miranda warnings?

A) They must be given immediately upon arresting someone B) They are required before any custodial interrogation C) They must be given before conducting a traffic stop D) They are only required for felony arrests

Answer: B

Explanation: Miranda warnings are required before custodial interrogation—when a person is in custody AND you're questioning them. They're not required at the moment of arrest if you're not questioning the person (option A), during traffic stops unless the person is under arrest and being questioned (option C), or only for felonies (option D).

Question 9: Under Texas law, which mental state represents the HIGHEST level of culpability?

A) Recklessly B) Knowingly
C) Intentionally D) Criminal negligence

Answer: C

Explanation: The hierarchy of culpable mental states from highest to lowest is: intentionally, knowingly, recklessly, criminal negligence. "Intentionally" means the person's conscious objective or desire was to cause the result, making it the most culpable mental state.

Question 10: A state jail felony in Texas is punishable by:

A) 2 to 10 years in prison B) 180 days to 2 years in state jail C) Up to 1 year in county jail D) 5 to 99 years in prison

Answer: B

Explanation: State jail felonies carry 180 days to 2 years in state jail, plus a fine up to $10,000. Option A describes third degree felonies, option C describes Class A misdemeanors, and option D describes first degree felonies.

Question 11: Family violence under Texas law includes acts between which of the following?

A) Only current spouses B) Only persons who are currently living together C) Current or former spouses, parents of same child, blood or marriage relatives, dating relationships, and current or former household members D) Only persons who are related by blood

Answer: C

Explanation: Family Code §71.003 broadly defines family or household members to include current or former spouses, parents of the same child (regardless of marriage), blood or marriage relatives, dating relationships, and current or former household members. This broad definition ensures protection across various relationship types.

Question 12: An officer may arrest without a warrant for a Class C misdemeanor:

A) Whenever the officer has probable cause B) Only if committed in the officer's presence C) Never, a warrant is always required D) Only for traffic violations

Answer: B

Explanation: Generally, warrantless arrest for misdemeanors requires the offense to be committed in the officer's presence or view (Article 14.01 CCP). Specific exceptions exist for family violence and protective order violations, but the general rule for Class C misdemeanors is that they must occur in your presence.

Question 13: The "automobile exception" to the warrant requirement allows officers to search a vehicle without a warrant when:

A) The vehicle is parked in a public place B) The officer has reasonable suspicion of criminal activity C) The officer has probable cause to believe the vehicle contains evidence or contraband D) The vehicle was involved in a traffic violation

Answer: C

Explanation: The automobile exception requires probable cause that the vehicle contains evidence of a crime or contraband. Mere presence in a public place (option A), reasonable suspicion (option B), or involvement in a traffic violation (option D) are insufficient to justify a warrantless search under this exception.

Question 14: Under Penal Code §9.31, a person is NOT justified in using force against another when:

A) The force is in response to verbal provocation alone B) They reasonably believe force is immediately necessary for self-protection C) Another person is using unlawful force against them D) They are in imminent danger

Answer: A

Explanation: Section 9.31 specifically states that force is NOT justified in response to verbal provocation alone. Words, no matter how offensive or threatening, don't justify physical force. Options B, C, and D describe situations where defensive force may be justified.

Question 15: Which of the following offenses is a capital felony in Texas?

A) Murder of a peace officer acting in official capacity B) Aggravated robbery C) Intoxication manslaughter D) Manslaughter

Answer: A

Explanation: Murder of a peace officer or fireman acting in official capacity is capital murder under §19.03, the only capital felony in Texas. Aggravated robbery is a first degree felony, intoxication manslaughter is a second degree felony, and manslaughter is a second degree felony.

Question 16: A protective order violation under Penal Code §25.07 is classified as:

A) Always a Class A misdemeanor B) A Class A misdemeanor for first offense; third degree felony if prior conviction or violation by assault C) Always a felony D) A Class B misdemeanor

Answer: B

Explanation: First-time protective order violations are Class A misdemeanors. The offense elevates to a third degree felony if the defendant has a prior conviction for violating a protective order OR violated the order by committing assault, stalking, or certain other offenses.

Question 17: Burglary of a habitation under Texas Penal Code §30.02 is:

A) A state jail felony B) A second degree felony C) A first degree felony if done with intent to commit any felony D) Both B and C are correct

Answer: D

Explanation: Burglary of a habitation is generally a second degree felony. It becomes a first degree felony if committed with intent to commit a felony other than felony theft. Burglary of a building (non-habitation) is a state jail felony.

Question 18: During a lawful arrest, an officer may search:

A) The person arrested and any area within their immediate control B) The entire building where the arrest occurs C) Any vehicle in the vicinity D) Any person present at the scene

Answer: A

Explanation: Search incident to arrest is limited to the person arrested and the area within their immediate control (the "grab area"). You cannot automatically search the entire building (option B), nearby vehicles without additional justification (option C), or other people without separate authority (option D).

Question 19: The Horizontal Gaze Nystagmus (HGN) test checks for:

A) The suspect's ability to maintain balance B) Involuntary jerking of the eyes that becomes more pronounced with alcohol consumption C) The suspect's ability to follow verbal instructions D) Physical coordination during walking

Answer: B

Explanation: HGN detects involuntary eye jerking (nystagmus) that alcohol consumption exacerbates. It's the most reliable of the three standardized field sobriety tests. Options A, C, and D describe aspects of the Walk and Turn or One Leg Stand tests.

Question 20: Theft classification under Texas Penal Code §31.03 is determined primarily by:

A) The defendant's criminal history B) The value of property stolen C) Whether the theft occurred during daytime or nighttime D) The method used to commit the theft

Answer: B

Explanation: Theft classification depends primarily on the value of property stolen, ranging from Class C misdemeanor (under $100) to first degree felony ($300,000 or more). While certain types of property can affect classification (firearms, official ballots), value is the primary determinant.

Question 21: Article 38.22 of the Texas Code of Criminal Procedure requires that:

A) All statements by defendants must be in writing B) Oral statements during custodial interrogation must be electronically recorded to be admissible C) Officers must obtain written consent before questioning D) Miranda warnings are only required for felonies

Answer: B

Explanation: Article 38.22 mandates electronic recording of oral statements made during custodial interrogation. The recording must show the defendant was properly warned and voluntarily waived rights. This is a Texas-specific requirement beyond federal Miranda requirements.

Question 22: A person commits aggravated assault under §22.02 if they commit assault and:

A) Use any amount of force B) Cause serious bodily injury OR use or exhibit a deadly weapon C) Only if they cause permanent injury D) Only if a deadly weapon is actually used to injure someone

Answer: B

Explanation: Aggravated assault occurs when assault is committed AND serious bodily injury is caused OR a deadly weapon is used or exhibited. The weapon doesn't need to actually cause injury (exhibiting it is sufficient), and serious bodily injury doesn't require permanent injury, though it must create substantial risk of death or cause serious permanent disfigurement or protracted loss of function.

Question 23: Under Texas Transportation Code, a driver must maintain financial responsibility by:

A) Carrying at least $100,000 in liability insurance B) Having a valid driver's license C) Maintaining minimum liability insurance coverage as required by law D) Only if they have previous traffic violations

Answer: C

Explanation: All drivers must maintain minimum liability insurance coverage (currently $30,000 per person for bodily injury, $60,000 per accident for bodily injury, and $25,000 for property damage). This requirement applies to all drivers regardless of driving history. Failure to maintain insurance is a criminal offense.

Question 24: Consent to search must be:

A) In writing to be valid B) Voluntary, given by someone with authority, and not coerced C) Given only by the vehicle owner D) Obtained before conducting any traffic stop

Answer: B

Explanation: Valid consent must be voluntary (freely given without coercion), given by someone with authority to consent (owner or person with control), and unambiguous. While written consent is best practice, it's not legally required. Consent can be given by a driver with control even if they're not the owner.

Question 25: The exclusionary rule means that:

A) Certain people are excluded from prosecution B) Evidence obtained in violation of the Constitution cannot be used against the defendant C) Officers are excluded from testifying in certain cases D) Defendants can exclude their prior criminal history from trial

Answer: B

Explanation: Article 38.23 CCP and the Fourth Amendment exclusionary rule prohibit use of illegally obtained evidence. This rule deters constitutional violations by removing the incentive to conduct illegal searches. The "fruit of the poisonous tree" doctrine extends this to evidence derived from the initial illegality.

Question 26: A person acts with "criminal negligence" when they:

A) Intentionally ignore a known risk B) Ought to be aware of a substantial and unjustifiable risk but fail to perceive it C) Consciously disregard a known risk D) Make an honest mistake

Answer: B

Explanation: Criminal negligence is the lowest culpable mental state, occurring when a person ought to be aware of but fails to perceive a substantial risk. This differs from recklessness (option C), where the person is aware of the risk but disregards it. Option A describes intentional conduct, and option D doesn't meet criminal negligence standards.

Question 27: During a traffic stop, an officer observes marijuana in plain view on the passenger seat. The officer:

A) Must obtain a warrant before seizing it B) Must obtain consent before seizing it C) May seize it under the plain view doctrine D) Cannot seize it without probable cause

Answer: C

Explanation: The plain view doctrine allows seizure when: (1) the officer is lawfully positioned, (2) the incriminating nature is immediately apparent, and (3) the officer has lawful access. During a lawful traffic stop, seeing marijuana in plain view satisfies all three requirements and creates probable cause to search the vehicle under the automobile exception.

Question 28: Robbery under Texas Penal Code §29.02 differs from theft in that robbery:

A) Involves higher value property B) Includes use of force or threat during the course of committing theft C) Can only occur in commercial establishments D) Must involve a weapon

Answer: B

Explanation: Robbery is theft committed with use of force or threat of force. The key distinction is the force or threat element. Property value doesn't differentiate them (option A), robbery can occur anywhere (option C), and weapons aren't required though their presence makes it aggravated robbery (option D).

Question 29: The "Terry frisk" allows an officer to:

A) Conduct a full search of any person during a traffic stop B) Pat down a person's outer clothing for weapons when reasonable suspicion exists that they're armed C) Search a vehicle without probable cause D) Arrest someone based on reasonable suspicion

Answer: B

Explanation: Terry v. Ohio established that officers with reasonable suspicion a person is armed and dangerous may conduct a limited pat-down of outer clothing for weapons. This is a protective measure, not a full search for evidence. Options A, C, and D exceed Terry authority.

Question 30: Under Texas law, mandatory reporters of child abuse include:

A) Only teachers and doctors B) Only child care workers C) Peace officers, teachers, doctors, nurses, and numerous other professionals D) Anyone who suspects abuse

Answer: C

Explanation: Family Code §261.101 lists numerous mandatory reporters including peace officers, teachers, nurses, doctors, day care employees, and many others. While anyone may report suspected abuse (option D), certain professionals are legally required to report and face criminal penalties for failure to report.

Question 31: Deadly force to protect property under Texas Penal Code §9.42 is justified:

A) To prevent any theft B) To prevent arson, burglary, robbery, theft during nighttime, or criminal mischief during nighttime when other conditions are met C) Whenever someone trespasses on your property D) Only to protect human life, never to protect property

Answer: B

Explanation: Section 9.42 allows deadly force to protect property in limited circumstances: preventing arson, burglary, robbery, theft during nighttime, or criminal mischief during nighttime, AND when the actor reasonably believes deadly force is immediately necessary and no other way exists to protect the property. Option A is too broad, option C doesn't meet the requirements, and option D is incorrect as Texas does allow deadly force for property under specific circumstances.

Question 32: When a suspect invokes their right to counsel during interrogation, the officer must:

A) Continue questioning if the crime is serious B) Stop questioning immediately and not resume unless the suspect initiates further communication C) Finish the current line of questioning then stop D) Obtain supervisor approval before continuing

Answer: B

Explanation: Once a suspect invokes the right to counsel, all interrogation must cease immediately. You cannot resume questioning unless the suspect initiates further communication and re-waives their rights. Options A, C, and D violate Miranda and will result in suppression of statements.

Question 33: The classification of DWI in Texas depends on:

A) Only the blood alcohol concentration B) Number of prior DWI convictions and presence of aggravating factors C) Whether anyone was injured D) The time of day

Answer: B

Explanation: First DWI is typically Class B misdemeanor, second is Class A misdemeanor, third or more is third degree felony. Aggravating factors like child passengers (state jail felony) or causing serious injury (intoxication assault - third degree felony) or death (intoxication manslaughter - second degree felony) elevate the offense.

Question 34: Arizona v. Gant limits vehicle searches incident to arrest by allowing such searches only when:

A) Any arrest is made near a vehicle B) The arrestee is unsecured and could access the vehicle OR evidence of the arrest offense might be in the vehicle C) The officer has reasonable suspicion D) The vehicle is parked illegally

Answer: B

Explanation: Gant restricts vehicle searches incident to arrest to two scenarios: (1) the arrestee is unsecured and could access the vehicle, or (2) the officer reasonably believes evidence of the arrest offense is in the vehicle. Options A, C, and D don't reflect Gant's requirements.

Question 35: A person commits criminal trespass under §30.05 when they:

A) Enter property without permission after receiving notice entry is forbidden B) Enter any property without the owner present C) Walk across property to reach another location D) Park on property without permission

Answer: A

Explanation: Criminal trespass requires entering or remaining on property without effective consent AND having received notice entry is forbidden. Notice can be oral, written, fencing, signs, or purple paint marks. Mere entry without these elements isn't criminal trespass.

Question 36: The primary purpose of field sobriety tests is to:

A) Gather evidence for court B) Help determine if probable cause exists for DWI arrest C) Punish the driver D) Delay the driver

Answer: B

Explanation: Field sobriety tests help officers develop probable cause for DWI arrest by providing standardized, validated observations of impairment. While they also serve as evidence (option A), their primary purpose during the investigation is establishing probable cause.

Question 37: Under Penal Code §9.51, before using force to effect an arrest, an officer must:

A) Always obtain a warrant B) Inform the person of their authority and purpose, unless reasonably believing notification is unnecessary, useless, or dangerous C) Call for backup D) Wait for the person to resist

Answer: B

Explanation: Section 9.51(c) requires officers to inform the person of their authority and purpose before using force, unless notification is reasonably believed unnecessary, useless, or dangerous. This gives the person opportunity to submit peacefully.

Question 38: Sexual assault under Texas Penal Code §22.011 requires:

A) Use of force or violence B) Causing penetration of the anus or sexual organ without the other person's consent C) Physical injury to the victim D) A stranger victim relationship

Answer: B

Explanation: Sexual assault is defined as causing sexual penetration without consent. Force isn't required if other circumstances negate consent (unconsciousness, mental incapacity, age under 17, position of authority). Physical injury isn't required, and the relationship between parties doesn't determine whether the offense occurred.

Question 39: The Rodriguez v. United States decision holds that:

A) All traffic stops must last less than 20 minutes B) Officers can extend traffic stops indefinitely for investigations C) Traffic stops cannot be extended beyond the time reasonably necessary to complete the stop's mission without reasonable suspicion of additional criminal activity D) Drug dogs can be used on all traffic stops

Answer: C

Explanation: Rodriguez established that extending a traffic stop to conduct a dog sniff or other investigation unrelated to the stop violates the Fourth Amendment unless reasonable suspicion of additional criminal activity exists. The stop's duration must be limited to its purpose.

Question 40: Arson under Texas Penal Code §28.02 is:

A) Always a first degree felony B) A second degree felony, or first degree if involving a habitation, place of worship, or causing bodily injury or death C) Only a crime if someone is injured D) A Class A misdemeanor

Answer: B

Explanation: Arson is generally a second degree felony. It elevates to first degree if the damaged property is a habitation or place of worship, or if the offense causes bodily injury or death. The seriousness reflects the danger arson poses to human life.

Question 41: An inventory search of a vehicle is lawful when:

A) The officer wants to search for evidence but lacks probable cause B) The vehicle is lawfully impounded and the search follows standardized department procedures C) Any vehicle is parked in a public place D) The officer has reasonable suspicion

Answer: B

Explanation: Inventory searches must follow standardized procedures and serve administrative purposes (protecting property, preventing false claims). They can't be pretextual searches for evidence when probable cause is lacking. Lawful impoundment and policy compliance are required.

Question 42: Disorderly conduct under Penal Code §42.01 requires that the conduct:

A) Occur in any location B) Occur in a public place or near a private residence C) Result in someone being injured D) Be directed at a peace officer

Answer: B

Explanation: Disorderly conduct must occur in a public place (for most subsections) or near a private residence (for noise complaints). Private conduct not observable by the public generally doesn't constitute disorderly conduct. The offense is about public disturbance.

Question 43: When responding to a domestic violence call, the officer should:

A) Arrest both parties if both claim the other was the aggressor B) Let the victim decide whether to make an arrest C) Determine the primary aggressor based on totality of circumstances and arrest that person D) Issue citations to both parties and let the court sort it out

Answer: C

Explanation: Officers must determine who was the primary aggressor by considering injury severity, prior complaints, self-defense claims, and other factors. Arresting both parties (dual arrest) is inappropriate unless you truly cannot determine the primary aggressor. The victim's wishes don't control your enforcement decision.

Question 44: The legal standard for a valid search warrant is:

A) Reasonable suspicion B) Probable cause C) Beyond a reasonable doubt D) Preponderance of the evidence

Answer: B

Explanation: The Fourth Amendment requires probable cause for search warrants. This means facts and circumstances leading a reasonable person to believe evidence of a crime will be found in the place to be searched. It's more than reasonable suspicion but less than proof beyond reasonable doubt.

Question 45: A peace officer's duty to report suspected child abuse must occur:

A) Within 24 hours B) Within 48 hours C) Within 72 hours D) Within 1 week

Answer: B

Explanation: Family Code §261.101 requires mandatory reporters to make a report not later than 48 hours after first suspecting abuse or neglect. The report goes to the Texas Department of Family and Protective Services through the abuse hotline. Failure to report is a Class A misdemeanor.

Question 46: Driving while license invalid under Transportation Code §521.457 is classified as:

A) Always a Class C misdemeanor B) Class C misdemeanor for first offense; Class B for subsequent offenses C) A felony if the suspension was DWI-related D) Not a criminal offense

Answer: B

Explanation: First offense DWLI is Class C misdemeanor. Subsequent offenses are Class B misdemeanors. If the license is invalid specifically due to DWI conviction, it's automatically Class B misdemeanor even on first offense.

Question 47: The "plain view" doctrine allows seizure of evidence when:

A) The officer is anywhere and sees evidence B) The officer is lawfully positioned, the incriminating nature is immediately apparent, and the officer has lawful access C) The officer has reasonable suspicion D) The evidence is in a vehicle

Answer: B

Explanation: Plain view requires three elements: lawful positioning, immediately apparent incriminating nature (probable cause), and lawful access to seize. All three must be present. Simply seeing something from an unlawful position doesn't justify seizure.

Question 48: Aggravated robbery under Penal Code §29.03 becomes a first degree felony when:

A) The stolen property exceeds $2,500 B) The offense is committed during daytime C) It's robbery committed with serious bodily injury, use of a deadly weapon, or victim is elderly or disabled D) The robbery occurs in a business

Answer: C

Explanation: Aggravated robbery (already serious) is always a first degree felony. It occurs when robbery is committed AND serious bodily injury is caused, a deadly weapon is used/exhibited, or the victim is 65+ or disabled. Property value doesn't affect robbery classification.

Question 49: Manslaughter under Penal Code §19.04 requires that death be caused:

A) Intentionally B) Knowingly C) Recklessly D) Negligently

Answer: C

Explanation: Manslaughter is recklessly causing another's death. This distinguishes it from murder (intentionally or knowingly causing death) and criminally negligent homicide (negligently causing death). The mental state determines the offense level and classification.

Question 50: Emergency removal of a child from a dangerous situation under Family Code §262.104:

A) Always requires a court order first B) Can be done without court order if child is in immediate danger, but requires court hearing within one business day C) Can only be done by CPS workers D) Requires parental consent

Answer: B

Explanation: Peace officers may take emergency custody without court order when a child faces immediate danger and there's no time for court process. However, a hearing must be held within one business day to review the removal. This balances child safety with parental rights.

Question 51: The Fourth Amendment protects people from:

A) All government searches B) Unreasonable searches and seizures C) Any police contact D) Traffic stops

Answer: B

Explanation: The Fourth Amendment prohibits "unreasonable" searches and seizures, not all searches. Searches conducted with warrants based on probable cause, or falling under established exceptions, are reasonable. The key is reasonableness, not prohibition of all searches.

Question 52: In Tennessee v. Garner, the Supreme Court held that:

A) Deadly force can be used to prevent any felony escape B) Deadly force to prevent escape requires the fleeing person pose a significant threat of death or serious physical injury C) Deadly force can never be used to prevent escape D) Only federal officers can use deadly force

Answer: B

Explanation: Garner prohibits using deadly force to prevent escape of apparently unarmed, non-dangerous suspects. Deadly force is justified only when the officer has probable cause to believe the suspect poses significant threat of death or serious physical injury to officers or others.

Question 53: Theft of property valued between $2,500 and $30,000 is classified as:

A) Class A misdemeanor B) Class B misdemeanor C) State jail felony D) Third degree felony

Answer: C

Explanation: Theft in the $2,500-$30,000 range is a state jail felony. Below $2,500 is misdemeanor (with breakpoints at $100 and $750). Above $30,000, it increases through third, second, and first degree felonies at higher amounts.

Question 54: A magistrate's order for emergency protection (MOEP) under Article 17.292 CCP:

A) Is the same as a Family Code protective order B) Is issued at arrest or magistrate warning for certain offenses and provides immediate temporary protection C) Requires the victim to file an application D) Only applies in family violence cases

Answer: B

Explanation: MOEPs are issued by magistrates at arrest or initial appearance for qualifying offenses (family violence, sexual assault, stalking, trafficking). They provide immediate protection (typically 31-61 days) without requiring victim to file a separate application. They're distinct from civil protective orders.

Question 55: The standard for a valid "Terry stop" (investigative detention) is:

A) Probable cause B) Reasonable suspicion of criminal activity C) Beyond reasonable doubt D) Preponderance of evidence

Answer: B

Explanation: Terry v. Ohio established that brief investigative detentions require reasonable suspicion—specific articulable facts suggesting criminal activity. This is lower than probable cause (required for arrest) but higher than mere hunches or generalizations.

Question 56: Article 14.01(b) CCP authorizes warrantless arrest when:

A) Any offense occurs B) An offense is committed in the officer's presence or within view C) The officer has reasonable suspicion D) The officer obtains consent

Answer: B

Explanation: Article 14.01(b) authorizes warrantless arrest for offenses committed in the officer's presence or view. For offenses not in your presence, you generally need a warrant unless specific exceptions apply (felonies, family violence, protective order violations).

Question 57: Unauthorized use of a vehicle under Penal Code §31.07 differs from theft of a vehicle in:

A) The value of the vehicle B) The intent—temporary use vs. permanent deprivation C) Whether the vehicle was locked D) The time of day

Answer: B

Explanation: Unauthorized use involves taking a vehicle intending to temporarily use and return it. Theft involves intent to permanently deprive the owner. Proving intent can be difficult, so both charges may initially be filed. Unauthorized use of a vehicle is a state jail felony.

Question 58: A "deadly weapon" under Texas Penal Code §1.07 includes:

A) Only firearms B) Firearms and anything designed, made, or adapted for inflicting death or serious bodily injury C) Firearms, items designed for harm, AND anything that in its manner of use is capable of causing death or serious bodily injury D) Only items specifically listed in the statute

Answer: C

Explanation: The definition includes three categories: (1) firearms, (2) items manifestly designed/made/adapted for causing death or serious bodily injury, and (3) anything that in its manner of use or intended use is capable of causing death or serious bodily injury. A hammer used to strike someone's head is a deadly weapon under category 3.

Question 59: When booking a defendant arrested for DWI, the defendant must:

A) Be taken immediately to trial B) Appear before a magistrate who advises them of their rights under Article 27.14 CCP C) Post bond within 24 hours or be released D) Submit to additional chemical testing

Answer: B

Explanation: Article 27.14 requires that persons arrested without warrant be taken before a magistrate who must inform them of the accusation, their right to counsel, right to remain silent, right to have counsel present during questioning, and right to appointed counsel if indigent. This is separate from Miranda warnings.

Question 60: Under Texas Family Code, who qualifies as a "family or household member" for family violence purposes?

A) Only people currently married or living together B) Only blood relatives C) Current or former spouses, parents of same child, relatives by blood or marriage, dating relationships, and current or former household members D) Only people related by blood or currently married

Answer: C

Explanation: Family Code §71.003 broadly defines family/household members to include: current or former spouses, parents of same child (regardless of marital status), relatives by blood or marriage, persons in dating relationships, current or former household members, and foster relationships. This expansive definition ensures comprehensive protection against family violence across various relationship types.

Scoring Your Practice Questions

Count the number of questions you answered correctly:

57-60 correct (95-100%): Excellent! You have a strong grasp of Texas legal codes and laws. Continue to review areas where you had any uncertainty, and move forward to the next chapter with confidence.

51-56 correct (85-94%): Very Good! You understand most of the material well. Review the questions you missed carefully, focusing on why the correct answer is right and why your answer was wrong. Pay special attention to any content area where you missed multiple questions.

45-50 correct (75-84%): Good! You're on the right track, but need more focused study. Go back to the sections of the chapter corresponding to questions you missed. Create summary notes or flashcards for topics giving you trouble. Retake these questions in a few days.

39-44 correct (65-74%): Fair. You understand some concepts but have significant gaps. Don't get discouraged—this is why you're studying! Review the entire chapter again, taking detailed notes. Focus especially on areas where you missed questions. Work through the scenarios again. Retake all questions after thorough review.

Below 39 correct (less than 65%): Needs Improvement. You need substantial additional study of this material before moving forward. Chapter 1 contains foundation material that appears throughout the exam and your career. Review the chapter section by section, taking detailed notes. Use the scenarios to understand application. Consider creating a study group or seeking additional resources. Retake all questions after comprehensive review.

Remember: Missing questions now, during practice, is good! It shows you what you need to study more. The goal is to learn from mistakes now so you don't make them on the actual exam. Every question you miss is a learning opportunity that makes you better prepared for test day.

Study Tip: For questions you missed, don't just memorize the correct answer. Understand the underlying principle. Ask yourself:

- Why is this answer correct?
- What principle or law does this test?
- How would I recognize a similar question on the exam?
- What related concepts should I review?

This deeper analysis ensures genuine understanding, not just memorization, which is exactly what the TCOLE exam tests.

CHAPTER 2: CRIMINAL LAW AND PROCEDURES

Learning Objectives

By the end of this chapter, you will be able to:

- Identify and explain the essential elements that must be present for a crime to occur
- Distinguish between different types of criminal intent (mens rea) and criminal acts (actus reus)
- Apply search and seizure laws correctly in field situations
- Understand when warrants are required and when exceptions apply
- Execute lawful arrests based on proper legal authority
- Recognize and articulate probable cause in various circumstances
- Properly collect, document, and preserve evidence while maintaining chain of custody
- Administer Miranda warnings correctly and conduct lawful interrogations
- Identify when custodial interrogation rules apply

Why This Chapter Matters

Criminal procedure isn't just legal theory—it's the roadmap you'll follow every single day as a peace officer. Understanding criminal procedure protects you from civil liability, ensures your cases hold up in court, and safeguards constitutional rights while allowing you to do your job effectively. Every arrest you make, every piece of evidence you collect, and every statement you obtain must follow proper procedures. Get it right, and justice is served. Get it wrong, and guilty people go free while you face potential lawsuits and disciplinary action.

This chapter builds directly on Chapter 1's legal foundation. Where Chapter 1 focused on what the law says, Chapter 2 focuses on how you apply it. You'll learn the mechanics of criminal investigation and prosecution from the officer's perspective—the procedures that transform probable cause into convictions.

Elements of Criminal Offenses

Every crime consists of essential elements that must all be proven beyond a reasonable doubt for a conviction. Understanding these elements helps you investigate thoroughly, recognize when a crime has occurred, and articulate probable cause for arrest.

The Building Blocks of Crime

Think of a crime like a puzzle. All the pieces must fit together perfectly, or you don't have a complete picture. Missing even one essential element means no crime occurred, no matter how suspicious or harmful the conduct might seem.

The Three Core Components:

1. Actus Reus (Criminal Act) The physical act, conduct, or omission that constitutes the crime. This is the "what happened" of criminal law. Criminal law doesn't punish thoughts or intentions alone—there must be some voluntary act or, in limited circumstances, a failure to act when there's a legal duty to do so.

2. Mens Rea (Criminal Intent) The mental state or intent accompanying the criminal act. This is the "what was the person thinking" element. Different crimes require different levels of intent, and the required mental state often determines how serious the offense is.

3. Concurrence The criminal act and criminal intent must occur together. You must have the required mental state at the time you commit the act. Having intent before or after the act, without it existing during the act, doesn't satisfy concurrence.

Some crimes also require additional elements like:

- **Causation:** The defendant's conduct caused the result (important in homicide and assault cases)
- **Harm:** Actual damage or injury occurred (in crimes like theft or criminal mischief)
- **Attendant Circumstances:** Specific conditions that must exist (like the victim being a peace officer in assault on a public servant)

Let's examine each component in detail.

Mens Rea and Actus Reus Explained

Understanding Actus Reus (The Criminal Act)

Actus reus is the physical component of crime—the action or inaction that the law prohibits. For an act to constitute actus reus, it must be:

Voluntary: The defendant must have control over their actions. Involuntary movements (like reflexes, convulsions during a seizure, or actions while unconscious) don't constitute voluntary acts for criminal purposes.

Example: If someone has an epileptic seizure while driving and crashes into another vehicle, they haven't committed a voluntary act. Their body moved, but they had no control. However, if they knew they were prone to seizures and chose to drive anyway without taking prescribed medication, that knowing choice to drive might be the voluntary act supporting a criminal negligence charge.

Affirmative Act vs. Omission:

Most crimes require an affirmative act—you must do something prohibited. But sometimes criminal liability arises from failing to act when you have a legal duty to act.

Legal duties to act arise from:

- Statutory requirements (mandatory reporting of child abuse)
- Special relationships (parent-child, where parent has duty to provide care)
- Contractual obligations (lifeguard at a pool)
- Voluntary assumption of care (if you begin rescuing someone, you can't abandon them in worse condition)
- Creation of peril (if you create a dangerous situation, you have duty to address it)

Example: A parent who fails to feed their child, causing the child to suffer malnutrition, can be prosecuted for injury to a child through omission. The parent had a legal duty to provide care, and their failure to act satisfies the actus reus requirement.

Single Acts vs. Continuing Acts:

Some crimes consist of a single act (punching someone), while others involve continuing conduct (possessing illegal drugs over time). Understanding this distinction matters for statute of limitations purposes and for determining when crimes occur in your jurisdiction.

Understanding Mens Rea (The Criminal Intent)

Mens rea is the mental state accompanying the criminal act. Texas law recognizes four levels of culpable mental states, arranged from most to least culpable:

1. INTENTIONALLY (Highest Culpability)

A person acts intentionally when it is their conscious objective or desire to engage in the conduct or cause the result.

Key characteristics:

- The person wants the result to occur
- Purpose and desire drive the action

- This is the most culpable mental state

Example: John points a gun at Mary and pulls the trigger with the goal of killing her. John acts intentionally because his conscious objective is to cause Mary's death.

Practical Application: When investigating potential intentional crimes, look for evidence of:

- Planning or premeditation
- Statements showing desire for the outcome
- Actions specifically designed to cause the result
- Lack of alternative explanations for the conduct

2. KNOWINGLY (High Culpability)

A person acts knowingly when they are aware that their conduct is reasonably certain to cause the result, even if causing that result isn't their conscious objective.

Key characteristics:

- Awareness that the result is practically certain
- May not desire the result but knows it will happen
- Certainty of outcome, not mere possibility

Example: John fires a gun into a crowded room. He doesn't specifically want to kill anyone, but he knows firing into a crowd will almost certainly kill or seriously injure someone. John acts knowingly even though killing wasn't his specific objective.

Practical Application: The distinction between intentionally and knowingly often matters less for charging decisions because many statutes authorize prosecution for either mental state. However, it can matter for sentencing and for explaining the defendant's mindset to juries.

3. RECKLESSLY (Moderate Culpability)

A person acts recklessly when they are aware of but consciously disregard a substantial and unjustifiable risk that the result will occur. The risk must be of such a nature and degree that its disregard constitutes a gross deviation from the standard of care an ordinary person would exercise under similar circumstances.

Key characteristics:

- Awareness of the risk
- Conscious disregard of that risk
- The risk is substantial and unjustifiable
- Gross deviation from reasonable care

Example: John drives 90 mph through a residential neighborhood during school dismissal time. He's aware this creates substantial risk of killing or injuring children but does it anyway. He doesn't want to hurt anyone and doesn't think he actually will, but he consciously disregards the obvious risk. If he strikes and kills a child, he acted recklessly.

Practical Application: Recklessness requires proof the person was actually aware of the risk. This distinguishes it from criminal negligence. Look for evidence showing:

- The person recognized the danger
- They chose to act despite that recognition
- Their behavior deviated grossly from what reasonable people do

4. CRIMINAL NEGLIGENCE (Lowest Culpability)

A person acts with criminal negligence when they ought to be aware of a substantial and unjustifiable risk but fail to perceive it. The failure to perceive the risk must constitute a gross deviation from the standard of care an ordinary person would exercise.

Key characteristics:

- Should have been aware of the risk but wasn't
- Failure to perceive risk is gross deviation from reasonable care
- This is still culpable because reasonable people would have recognized the danger

Example: John leaves his loaded handgun on the coffee table where his three-year-old child can reach it. He doesn't think about the danger—it simply doesn't occur to him that the child might find and fire the weapon. When the child shoots and kills a sibling, John acted with criminal negligence. He should have recognized the risk even though he didn't actually think about it.

Practical Application: Criminal negligence is harder to prove than recklessness because you must show the person should have known, not that they did know. Look for situations where:

- The risk was obvious to reasonable people
- The defendant failed to take basic precautions
- Their failure represents gross deviation from normal care

The Hierarchy and Why It Matters

These mental states form a hierarchy that affects both the classification of offenses and your charging decisions:

INTENTIONALLY = KNOWINGLY > RECKLESSLY > CRIMINAL NEGLIGENCE

Example - Causing Death:

- Intentionally or knowingly causing death = Murder (1st degree felony)
- Recklessly causing death = Manslaughter (2nd degree felony)
- With criminal negligence causing death = Criminally Negligent Homicide (state jail felony)

The same act (causing someone's death) results in dramatically different charges based solely on the person's mental state. This is why thoroughly investigating the defendant's mindset is as important as documenting the physical acts.

Default Mental State:

If a statute defining an offense doesn't specify a required mental state, you must prove the person acted intentionally, knowingly, recklessly, or with criminal negligence (Penal Code §6.02(b)). However, most statutes specify which mental state is required.

Transferring Intent:

If someone intends to harm one person but accidentally harms another, their intent transfers to the actual victim. If John shoots at Mary but misses and kills Bill, John's intent to kill Mary transfers to Bill. This prevents defendants from avoiding liability because they harmed the "wrong" person.

Proving Mental State

You can't read minds, so how do you prove mental state? Through circumstantial evidence:

Direct Evidence of Intent (Rare):

- Confessions or admissions
- Statements showing purpose ("I'm going to kill him")
- Journals, texts, or emails expressing intent

Circumstantial Evidence (Common):

- The nature of the act itself (pointing a gun at someone's head and firing shows intent to kill)
- Planning and preparation
- Defendant's statements before, during, or after the crime
- The relationship between defendant and victim
- Prior threats or similar incidents
- The specific method used
- Actions taken to conceal the crime or flee

Example: You respond to a shooting. The victim survives with a gunshot wound to the leg. The shooter claims the gun "just went off" accidentally. Your investigation reveals:

- The shooter sent threatening texts to the victim earlier that day
- Multiple witnesses heard the shooter say "I'm going to shoot you" before firing
- The shooter fled the scene and tried to hide the gun
- The shooter previously assaulted this victim

This circumstantial evidence proves intentional assault with a deadly weapon, not an accident. The mental state becomes clear from the surrounding circumstances even without a confession.

Classification of Crimes

Understanding how crimes are classified helps you make proper charging decisions, know your arrest authority, determine bond amounts, and understand case processing procedures.

Felonies vs. Misdemeanors vs. Infractions

FELONIES: Most Serious Offenses

Felonies are the most serious category of criminal offenses, punishable by confinement in state prison or state jail. Texas recognizes five levels of felonies:

Capital Felony:

- Death or life without parole
- Only capital murder qualifies
- Extremely rare prosecutions

First Degree Felony:

- 5 to 99 years or life in prison
- Fine up to $10,000
- Examples: murder, aggravated robbery, aggravated sexual assault

Second Degree Felony:

- 2 to 20 years in prison
- Fine up to $10,000
- Examples: manslaughter, robbery, sexual assault, arson

Third Degree Felony:

- 2 to 10 years in prison
- Fine up to $10,000
- Examples: stalking, deadly conduct with firearm, tampering with evidence

State Jail Felony:

- 180 days to 2 years in state jail (not state prison)
- Fine up to $10,000
- Examples: burglary of building, theft $2,500-$30,000, forgery, POCS small amounts

Arrest Authority: You may arrest for any felony based on probable cause, even if the offense didn't occur in your presence and you don't have a warrant (Article 14.03 CCP).

MISDEMEANORS: Less Serious Offenses

Misdemeanors are punishable by confinement in county jail (not state prison) and/or fines. Texas has three classes:

Class A Misdemeanor:

- Up to 1 year in county jail
- Fine up to $4,000
- Examples: assault causing bodily injury, DWI (1st), theft $750-$2,500, resisting arrest

Class B Misdemeanor:

- Up to 180 days in county jail
- Fine up to $2,000
- Examples: DWI (with certain factors), POCS 2 oz or less, terroristic threat, criminal trespass, theft $100-$750

Class C Misdemeanor:

- Fine only, up to $500
- No jail time possible
- Examples: theft under $100, assault by contact, disorderly conduct, most traffic violations

Arrest Authority for Misdemeanors:

You may arrest for misdemeanors only if:

- The offense occurs in your presence or view, OR
- Specific statutory authority exists (family violence assault, protective order violations)

For Class C misdemeanors, you typically issue citations rather than making custodial arrests unless:

- The person refuses to identify themselves
- You reasonably believe they won't appear in court
- They refuse to sign the citation
- You believe they'll continue violating the law

INFRACTIONS: Non-Criminal Violations

Some jurisdictions recognize "infractions" or "violations" as non-criminal offenses. Texas doesn't formally use this category, but many Class C misdemeanors function similarly—they're minor offenses with fine-only punishment.

The key distinction: even Class C misdemeanors are crimes that result in criminal records, while true infractions in some states don't. In Texas, speeding tickets and other traffic violations are Class C misdemeanors and technically criminal convictions, though they're often not treated as seriously as other criminal offenses.

Why Classification Matters

1. Your Arrest Authority

- Felonies: May arrest with probable cause anytime
- Misdemeanors: Generally must occur in your presence (with exceptions)
- Class C: Usually cite and release rather than arrest

2. Bond and Release Decisions

- Felonies: Higher bonds, more restrictions
- Misdemeanors: Lower bonds or personal recognizance release
- Class C: Often released on citation with court date

3. Case Processing

- Felonies: Grand jury indictment required for prosecution
- Misdemeanors: Information filed by prosecutor
- Class C: Can be prosecuted on citation alone

4. Statute of Limitations

- Felonies: Varies by offense (no limitation for murder, 10 years for theft, etc.)
- Misdemeanors: Generally 2 years
- Class C: Generally 2 years

5. Penalties and Records

- Felony convictions have lasting impacts: loss of voting rights, firearm possession, professional licenses
- Misdemeanor convictions create criminal records but fewer collateral consequences
- Class C convictions are still criminal records despite fine-only punishment

Enhancement of Offenses

Many offenses can be enhanced (increased in severity) based on specific factors:

Repeat Offenders: Third DWI becomes third degree felony. Multiple theft convictions enhance future thefts. Domestic violence assault with prior domestic violence conviction becomes third degree felony.

Use of Deadly Weapons: Assault (Class A misdemeanor) + deadly weapon = aggravated assault (2nd degree felony)

Protected Victims: Assault on public servant = 3rd degree felony. Assault on elderly or disabled = enhanced classification.

Special Locations: Drug offenses in school zones carry enhanced penalties. Criminal mischief against schools is enhanced.

Understanding these enhancement factors helps you charge cases correctly and advise prosecutors about potential enhancements.

Search and Seizure Laws

The Fourth Amendment's prohibition against unreasonable searches and seizures is the most important constitutional limit on your authority as a peace officer. Understanding search and seizure law protects both constitutional rights and the admissibility of evidence you collect.

The Fourth Amendment Framework

"The right of the people to be secure in their persons, houses, papers, and effects, against unreasonable searches and seizures, shall not be violated, and no Warrants shall issue, but upon probable cause, supported by Oath or affirmation, and particularly describing the place to be searched, and the persons or things to be seized."

This single sentence creates the entire framework for search and seizure law. Let's break it down:

Key Principle 1: The Amendment prohibits UNREASONABLE searches and seizures, not all searches.

Reasonable searches are constitutionally permissible. A search is reasonable if:

- It's conducted pursuant to a valid warrant based on probable cause, OR
- A recognized exception to the warrant requirement applies

Key Principle 2: Warrants require probable cause, oath or affirmation, and particularity.

When warrants are required, they must meet strict standards to be valid.

Key Principle 3: This applies to "persons, houses, papers, and effects."

The Fourth Amendment protects people and their property from unreasonable intrusions by government.

What Constitutes a "Search"?

Not every investigative technique constitutes a search requiring Fourth Amendment protections. A "search" occurs when government action infringes on a person's reasonable expectation of privacy.

The Two-Part Test (Katz v. United States):

1. Subjective Expectation: Did the person have an actual expectation of privacy? **2. Objective Reasonableness:** Is that expectation one that society recognizes as reasonable?

Both elements must be present.

Activities That ARE Searches:

- Entering a home without consent
- Opening closed containers
- Looking through windows into areas not visible from public spaces
- Using drug-sniffing dogs on private property (like a home's front porch)
- Using thermal imaging to detect heat patterns inside a home
- Reading someone's text messages or emails
- GPS tracking of vehicles over extended periods

Activities That Are NOT Searches:

- Observing things in plain view from public areas
- Looking through a car's windows from outside

- Using drug-sniffing dogs in public areas (like sniffing vehicle exterior during lawful traffic stop, though extending the stop for this purpose may violate Fourth Amendment)
- Observing property from aircraft flying in public airspace
- Examining garbage left at the curb for collection
- Obtaining information from third parties (bank records, phone records showing numbers dialed)

Why This Matters:

If an activity isn't a search, the Fourth Amendment doesn't apply. You don't need probable cause or a warrant to do things that aren't searches. But if it is a search, you need either a warrant or an exception.

What Constitutes a "Seizure"?

Seizures of Property:

Property is seized when government meaningfully interferes with a person's possessory interest in that property. Taking evidence, impounding vehicles, or holding property for investigation all constitute seizures requiring reasonableness under the Fourth Amendment.

Seizures of Persons:

A person is seized when, based on the totality of circumstances, a reasonable person would not feel free to leave or terminate the encounter with police.

Three Types of Police-Citizen Encounters:

1. Consensual Encounter (No Seizure)

You approach someone and begin talking. They're free to refuse to answer and free to leave. No Fourth Amendment protections apply because there's no seizure.

Characteristics:

- No show of authority
- Police merely request cooperation
- Reasonable person would feel free to leave
- No reasonable suspicion required

Example: You see someone sitting on a park bench and walk up saying, "Hi, do you mind if I ask you a few questions?" They can say "no" and walk away. This is consensual.

2. Investigative Detention / Terry Stop (Seizure)

You briefly detain someone based on reasonable suspicion of criminal activity. This is a seizure, but it's reasonable under the Fourth Amendment if you have reasonable suspicion.

Characteristics:

- Reasonable suspicion of criminal activity required
- Brief duration (generally 15-20 minutes max)
- Limited scope (investigation of suspected crime)
- May include protective frisk if reasonable suspicion person is armed

Example: You observe someone matching the description of a burglary suspect in the area where a burglary just occurred. You may briefly detain them to investigate. You may ask for identification and ask questions about their presence in the area.

3. Arrest (Seizure)

You take someone into custody. This is a significant seizure requiring probable cause that they committed a crime.

Characteristics:

- Probable cause required
- Can involve significant restriction of freedom
- Authorizes search incident to arrest
- Must be based on specific facts, not hunches

Example: After investigating the person matching the burglary description, you learn they're carrying property stolen in the burglary and they can't explain lawful possession. You now have probable cause to arrest.

Determining When a Seizure Occurs:

Courts look at the totality of circumstances from the perspective of a reasonable person. Factors include:

- Number of officers present
- Display of weapons
- Physical touching
- Use of commanding language
- Blocking the person's path
- Activating emergency lights
- Duration of encounter

The question is always: Would a reasonable person feel free to leave or terminate the encounter?

Warrant Requirements and Exceptions

The general rule is that searches require warrants based on probable cause. However, numerous exceptions allow warrantless searches in specific circumstances. Understanding when warrants are required and when exceptions apply is critical for lawful evidence collection.

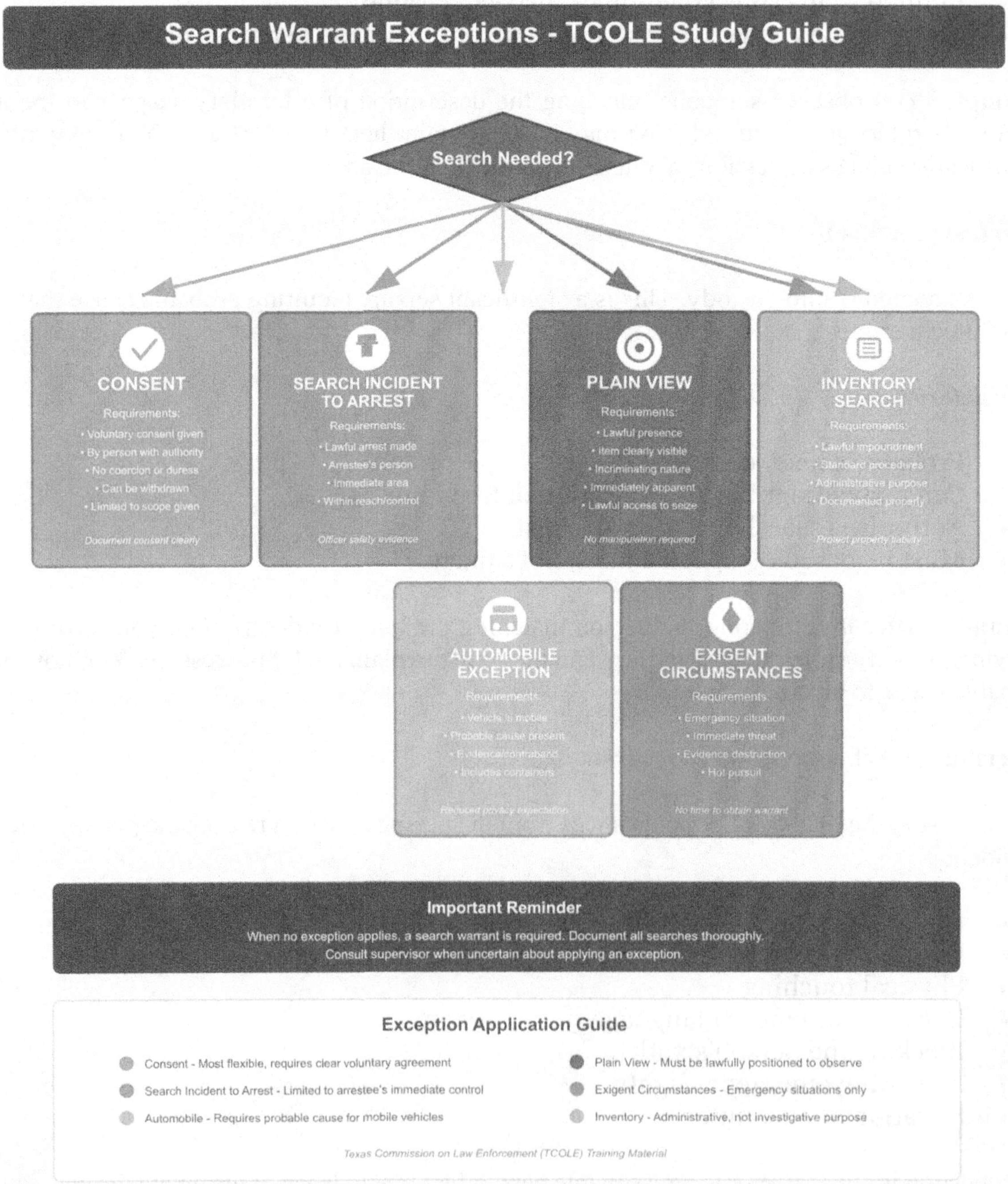

Search Warrant Requirements

Valid search warrants must satisfy constitutional and statutory requirements:

1. Probable Cause

The affidavit supporting the warrant must establish probable cause—facts and circumstances that would lead a reasonable person to believe evidence of a crime will be found in the place to be searched.

Sources of probable cause:

- Your personal observations
- Victim statements
- Witness statements
- Reliable confidential informant information
- Surveillance results
- Records and documents
- Expert opinions

Probable cause is a flexible standard:

- More than mere suspicion or speculation
- Less than proof beyond reasonable doubt
- Based on totality of circumstances
- Focuses on probability, not certainty

2. Oath or Affirmation

You must swear or affirm under penalty of perjury that the facts in your affidavit are true. This requirement ensures accountability and deters false information.

3. Neutral Magistrate

Warrants must be issued by neutral, detached magistrates—judges who aren't involved in the investigation and have no personal interest in the outcome.

4. Particularity

The warrant must particularly describe:

- The place to be searched (address, description, any specific areas)
- The items to be seized (specific enough that executing officers know what to look for)

Why particularity matters:

General warrants allowing police to search wherever they want for whatever they want are prohibited. Particularity prevents "fishing expeditions" and protects privacy by limiting the scope of authorized searches.

Example of Proper Particularity:

"2546 Elm Street, a single-story brick residence with white trim and the numbers '2546' on the front door, specifically including all rooms, outbuildings, and vehicles on the premises, for the following items: cocaine and other controlled substances, drug paraphernalia including scales and packaging materials, currency, and records related to drug distribution including cell phones, computers, and ledgers."

Example of Insufficient Particularity:

"John Doe's house, for evidence of crimes."

This fails to adequately describe the location or the items sought.

Executing Search Warrants

Once you have a valid warrant, proper execution is essential:

Knock and Announce:

Before entering to execute a search warrant, you must generally knock, announce your identity as police, announce your purpose, and give occupants reasonable time to answer (typically 15-30 seconds).

No-Knock Warrants:

The magistrate may authorize no-knock entry if you establish in your affidavit that:

- Knocking would be dangerous
- Knocking would lead to destruction of evidence
- Knocking would be futile (nobody home, occupants aware of police presence)

Timing:

Search warrants typically must be executed during daytime unless nighttime execution is specifically authorized based on necessity.

Scope of Search:

You may search anywhere the items described in the warrant could reasonably be located. If you're looking for stolen televisions, you can't search small dresser drawers. If you're looking for drugs, you can search small containers.

Detention During Search:

You may detain occupants present during execution of a search warrant for officer safety and to maintain the integrity of the search.

Seizure of Items Not Listed:

If you discover evidence of crimes not listed in the warrant but it's in plain view during the lawful search, you may seize it under the plain view doctrine.

Warrant Exceptions: When Warrants Aren't Required

The Supreme Court has recognized several exceptions to the warrant requirement. These exceptions allow warrantless searches in specific circumstances where obtaining a warrant is impractical or unnecessary.

1. CONSENT

If someone with authority voluntarily consents to a search, no warrant is needed.

Requirements for Valid Consent:

- **Voluntary:** Not the result of duress, coercion, or threats
- **Authority:** Given by someone with actual or apparent authority over the area searched
- **Scope:** Limited to what was authorized

Who Can Consent:

- Owner of property
- Resident with shared control (roommate can consent to search of common areas)
- Person with apparent authority (someone who appears to have authority even if they don't)
- Parent can consent to search child's room in parent's home (with some limitations for adult children)

Who Cannot Consent:

- Guests generally can't consent to search of host's home
- Landlords can't consent to search of tenant's rented premises

- Vehicle passengers generally can't consent to search (unless they have control)

Scope Limitations:

If you ask to search for a stolen television and receive consent, you can search areas where a TV might be. You can't search small dresser drawers where a TV couldn't fit. If you discover evidence of another crime in plain view during the authorized search, you may seize it.

Withdrawal of Consent:

Consent can be withdrawn at any time. When someone says "stop searching" or "I want you to leave," you must stop immediately. Anything found after consent is withdrawn will be suppressed.

Best Practices:

- Get written consent on a consent-to-search form
- Document the voluntariness (was force used? Were weapons displayed? Did you make threats?)
- Record the exact words of consent
- Document the scope of consent
- Note if consent was limited to certain areas

2. SEARCH INCIDENT TO LAWFUL ARREST

When you lawfully arrest someone, you may search their person and the area within their immediate control without a warrant.

Justifications:

- Officer safety (finding weapons)
- Preventing destruction of evidence
- Finding evidence of the crime of arrest

Scope for Person:

Full search of the arrested person's body and clothing, including pockets, bags they're carrying, and items immediately on their person.

Scope for Area:

The "grab area"—the area within the person's immediate reach where they could grab a weapon or destroy evidence. This area "freezes" at the moment of arrest. Once the person is secured and removed from the area, you can't search areas they could have reached before being secured.

Vehicle Searches Incident to Arrest (Arizona v. Gant):

You may search a vehicle incident to arrest only if:

- The arrestee is unsecured and could access the vehicle's interior at the time of the search, OR
- You reasonably believe evidence of the offense of arrest might be found in the vehicle

Example: You arrest someone for DWI. You may search the vehicle for evidence of DWI (alcohol containers, drugs) because it's reasonable to believe evidence of DWI might be in the vehicle.

Example: You arrest someone for driving with invalid license. You may NOT search the vehicle incident to arrest because evidence of that offense (the license status) wouldn't be in the vehicle.

3. AUTOMOBILE EXCEPTION

If you have probable cause to believe a vehicle contains evidence or contraband, you may search it without a warrant.

Justifications:

- Vehicles are mobile and could be driven away
- Reduced expectation of privacy in vehicles (they're visible from public areas, heavily regulated)

Requirements:

- Probable cause that the vehicle contains evidence or contraband
- The vehicle is mobile (even if currently parked)

Scope:

You may search anywhere in the vehicle where the evidence or contraband could be located, including:

- Passenger compartment
- Trunk
- Closed containers
- Locked compartments (though document efforts to obtain keys)

Duration:

The automobile exception doesn't expire quickly. If you have probable cause but can't search immediately, you may impound the vehicle and search later.

Example: You stop a vehicle for speeding and smell marijuana. This creates probable cause that the vehicle contains marijuana. You may search the entire vehicle under the automobile exception.

4. PLAIN VIEW DOCTRINE

If you're lawfully positioned and see evidence or contraband in plain view, you may seize it without a warrant.

Requirements:

- **Lawful positioning:** You must have a right to be where you are
- **Immediately apparent:** The incriminating nature must be immediately obvious (you must have probable cause the item is evidence or contraband)
- **Lawful access:** You must be able to lawfully access the item to seize it

Example: During a lawful traffic stop, you see a baggie of white powder on the passenger seat that appears to be cocaine. All three requirements are met:

- You're lawfully positioned (conducting traffic stop)
- Incriminating nature is immediately apparent (looks like cocaine)
- You have lawful access (can reach through window or open door)

Example of What Doesn't Work: You're walking down the sidewalk and see through a window into someone's home where drugs are visible on a table. The incriminating nature is immediately apparent, but you don't have lawful access. You can't enter the home without a warrant or consent. However, you now have probable cause to seek a warrant.

5. EXIGENT CIRCUMSTANCES

Warrantless searches are justified when emergency circumstances exist that make obtaining a warrant impractical.

Types of Exigent Circumstances:

Hot Pursuit: You're chasing a fleeing felon and they enter a building. You may enter to apprehend them without waiting for a warrant.

Imminent Destruction of Evidence: You have probable cause evidence exists and it will be destroyed if you take time to get a warrant.

Emergency Aid: Someone inside needs immediate help (screams, signs of violence, medical emergency).

Danger to Officers or Others: The situation poses imminent danger that requires immediate action.

Important Limitation:

You can't create the exigency through your own actions. If you knock on someone's door, they open it, and you hear toilets flushing, you can't claim exigent circumstances that you created by knocking.

Example: You're investigating a noise complaint at an apartment. When someone opens the door, you see an injured person lying on the floor bleeding. You may enter under exigent circumstances to provide aid.

6. INVENTORY SEARCHES

When you lawfully impound property (vehicles or personal belongings), you may conduct inventory searches following standardized procedures.

Purpose:

- Protect owner's property
- Protect department from false claims of loss
- Protect officers from danger

Requirements:

- Lawful impoundment
- Standardized department procedures
- Administrative purpose (not investigative pretext)

Scope:

Follow your department's inventory policy. If policy requires inventorying closed containers, you may open them. If policy doesn't require it, you shouldn't.

Example: You arrest a driver and impound their vehicle. Following department policy, you inventory the contents, opening the glove box and center console. You discover drugs. The evidence is admissible because you followed proper inventory procedures.

7. STOP AND FRISK (TERRY FRISK)

During a lawful Terry stop, if you have reasonable suspicion the person is armed and dangerous, you may conduct a protective pat-down of their outer clothing for weapons.

Justification:

Officer safety during legitimate investigations.

Requirements:

- Lawful Terry stop (reasonable suspicion of criminal activity)
- Additional reasonable suspicion the person is armed and dangerous

Scope:

Pat-down of outer clothing for weapons only. This is not a full search. If you feel something that's immediately recognizable as contraband (like a bag of drugs), you may seize it under plain feel doctrine.

What You Cannot Do:

Manipulate objects to determine what they are. In Minnesota v. Dickerson, the Court held that when an officer felt a small lump in a pocket during a frisk, squeezed it, manipulated it, and determined it was crack cocaine, the seizure was unlawful. The officer exceeded the scope of a protective frisk.

Example: You stop someone matching description of an armed robbery suspect. You have reasonable suspicion they're armed (based on the robbery report). You may pat down their outer clothing for weapons. If you feel what's immediately recognizable as a gun, you may remove it.

8. BORDER SEARCHES

At international borders and their functional equivalents (international airports), searches can be conducted without warrants or probable cause. The government's interest in controlling what enters the country creates an exception to normal Fourth Amendment protections.

9. SCHOOL SEARCHES

School officials can search students based on reasonable suspicion rather than probable cause. However, when you as a law enforcement officer conduct searches in schools, you're generally held to the higher probable cause standard unless you're acting at the school's request to maintain order.

Protective Sweeps

During arrest in a home, you may conduct a "protective sweep"—a quick, cursory visual inspection of areas where someone could hide and pose danger. This is limited to ensuring officer safety and doesn't authorize a full search.

Requirements:

- Lawful arrest in a home
- Reasonable belief someone else may be present who poses danger
- Limited to quick visual inspection
- Only areas where person could hide

Scope: You can look in closets, behind doors, and in rooms adjacent to the arrest, but you can't open drawers, cabinets, or containers.

Arrest Procedures and Legal Authority

Making arrests is one of your core functions as a peace officer. Understanding when you have authority to arrest, what procedures you must follow, and how to execute arrests safely and lawfully is essential.

What Constitutes an Arrest?

An arrest occurs when you take someone into custody in a manner that a reasonable person wouldn't feel free to leave. Arrests are seizures under the Fourth Amendment requiring probable cause.

Factors indicating arrest:

- Telling the person they're under arrest
- Using handcuffs
- Placing person in patrol car
- Transporting to jail
- Duration of detention beyond brief Terry stop
- Level of force or show of authority used

Arrest vs. Detention:

The line between Terry stops and arrests can blur. Courts look at the totality of circumstances:

- **Terry Stop:** Brief, limited scope, reasonable suspicion
- **Arrest:** Longer duration, broader scope, probable cause required

If your detention becomes too lengthy or intrusive, it may be deemed an arrest requiring probable cause even if you call it a "detention."

Arrest Authority: When You Can Arrest

WITH WARRANT (Article 14.01 CCP):

A valid arrest warrant gives you clear authority to arrest. The warrant must:

- Be issued in the name of "The State of Texas"
- State the name of the accused or describe them
- State the offense charged
- Be signed by the magistrate
- Command that the accused be arrested

When executing warrants:

- You don't need to have the physical warrant with you if you have knowledge it exists
- You must inform the person of your authority and purpose
- You must show the warrant if demanded
- You may use reasonable force to effect arrest

WITHOUT WARRANT (Article 14.03 CCP):

You may arrest without warrant when:

1. Offense committed in your presence or view

- You directly observe any offense occurring
- This includes felonies, misdemeanors, and Class C misdemeanors
- "Presence" includes what you perceive through any of your senses (sight, smell, hearing)

Example: You see someone punch another person. You may arrest for assault even though you don't have a warrant. The offense occurred in your view.

2. Felony has been committed and probable cause

- You have probable cause to believe a felony occurred
- You have probable cause to believe this person committed it
- The felony must have actually occurred (if no felony occurred, the arrest may be invalid even if you reasonably believed one had)

Example: A store reports a robbery that occurred 30 minutes ago. Witnesses describe the suspect. You locate someone matching the description nearby with property from the robbery. You have probable cause to arrest for robbery even though you didn't witness it.

3. Felony committed and about to escape

- A felony has been committed
- You have probable cause this person committed it
- They're about to escape (fleeing, about to board plane, etc.)

4. Family violence assault (Article 14.03(b))

- Probable cause to believe assault causing bodily injury to family/household member
- Even if offense didn't occur in your presence
- This specific exception allows warrantless arrest for what would normally require a warrant

Example: You respond to a domestic violence call. The victim has visible injuries and tells you her husband struck her an hour ago. You have authority to arrest the husband even though the assault didn't occur in your presence.

5. Protective order violation

- Probable cause to believe the person violated a protective order
- Even if violation didn't occur in your presence

6. Suspicious circumstances indicating felony

- Person found in suspicious place
- Circumstances reasonably show felony commission or attempt
- This is rarely used and requires strong articulable facts

Probable Cause Standards

Probable cause is the cornerstone of arrest authority. Understanding what constitutes probable cause protects you from false arrest liability and ensures your arrests survive court scrutiny.

Definition:

Probable cause exists when facts and circumstances within your knowledge are sufficient to warrant a reasonable person to believe a particular person has committed or is committing a crime.

Key characteristics:

- Based on totality of circumstances
- More than reasonable suspicion or "mere hunch"
- Less than proof beyond reasonable doubt
- Focuses on probability, not certainty
- Must be particularized to the individual arrested

Building Probable Cause:

Probable cause comes from combining facts and circumstances:

Direct Observations:

- You witness the crime
- You see evidence of crime
- You observe suspicious conduct combined with other facts

Victim/Witness Statements:

- Reliable victim identification
- Multiple consistent witness accounts
- Detailed descriptions

Physical Evidence:

- Property matching stolen items
- Contraband in plain view
- Physical evidence connecting suspect to crime

Circumstantial Evidence:

- Suspect's presence at crime scene
- Possession of proceeds of crime
- Flight from police
- Inconsistent or false explanations
- Prior relationship with victim

Information from Others:

- Fellow officers' observations
- Dispatch information
- Records checks
- Reliable informant information

Informant Information:

Informant tips can contribute to probable cause, but courts scrutinize them carefully. Consider:

- The informant's reliability and track record
- Basis of knowledge (firsthand observation vs. hearsay)
- Corroboration of details
- Level of detail provided
- Whether informant has reason to lie

Anonymous tips alone rarely create probable cause unless significantly corroborated.

Example of Sufficient Probable Cause:

You respond to a burglary in progress call. Dispatch provides suspect description: white male, 20s, blue jacket, jeans. You arrive and see someone matching that description running from the area carrying a laptop. The victim confirms their laptop was stolen and identifies the person you detained as the one they saw in their house. You have probable cause from:

- Dispatch information (in-progress burglary)
- Your observations (matching description, fleeing area, carrying laptop)
- Victim statement (identification and confirmation laptop was stolen)

Example of Insufficient Probable Cause:

You receive an anonymous tip that "someone at 123 Main Street has drugs." You go to that address and see several people outside. One person sees you and walks away quickly. This alone isn't probable cause. You have:

- Unreliable source (anonymous tip)
- No corroboration
- Legal conduct (walking away isn't illegal)

Executing Arrests

Once you have legal authority to arrest, proper execution is critical for safety and legality.

Before Making Physical Arrest:

1. Assess the situation:

- Is the suspect armed?
- Are other people present who might interfere?
- What's the safest way to approach?
- Do you need backup?

2. Plan your approach:

- Position yourself advantageously
- Maintain reactionary gap
- Control suspect's movement options
- Be ready for resistance

3. Issue commands:

- Identify yourself as police
- Give clear, direct commands
- Tell the person they're under arrest
- Instruct them how to comply

During the Arrest:

Use of Force:

Use only the force reasonably necessary to effect the arrest. The force continuum guides your response:

- Officer presence
- Verbal commands
- Empty hand control (soft)
- Empty hand control (hard)
- Less-lethal weapons (OC spray, Taser)
- Deadly force (only when justified)

Your force must be objectively reasonable based on:

- Severity of crime
- Whether suspect poses immediate threat
- Whether suspect is actively resisting or attempting to evade
- Other circumstances known to you

Searching the Arrestee:

Conduct a full search incident to arrest:

- Check for weapons first (immediate safety concern)
- Remove all items from pockets
- Check waistband, socks, shoes
- Be thorough but professional
- Opposite gender searches require special considerations (follow your department policy)

Handcuffing:

Standard practice is to handcuff arrested persons with hands behind back, palms out, double-locked. This prevents escape and injury while protecting your safety.

Miranda Warnings:

You must advise Miranda rights before custodial interrogation. You don't need to Mirandize immediately upon arrest if you're not questioning the person. However, best practice is to advise rights shortly after arrest.

After Arrest:

1. Transport safely:

- Search prisoner and vehicle before transport
- Secure prisoner properly
- Monitor prisoner during transport
- Maintain professional demeanor

2. Booking procedures:

- Complete required paperwork
- Document personal property
- Take photographs and fingerprints
- Conduct booking search (more thorough than field search)

3. Magistrate appearance:

- Arrange for the arrested person to appear before magistrate
- Magistrate will advise rights under Article 27.14 CCP
- Magistrate will set bond or release conditions

4. Documentation:

- Complete arrest report thoroughly
- Document probable cause clearly
- Include all relevant facts
- Note any statements made by arrestee
- Photograph any injuries (to officer or arrestee)

Arrest in Special Circumstances

Arrest at Residence:

When arresting someone at a residence, Fourth Amendment protections are strongest. You need either:

- Arrest warrant (preferred)
- Consent to enter from resident
- Exigent circumstances justifying warrantless entry

You can't enter a home to make a routine arrest without warrant or consent, even if you have probable cause for the arrest (Payton v. New York).

Exceptions:

- Hot pursuit of fleeing felon
- Preventing imminent destruction of evidence
- Emergency aid
- Preventing escape of dangerous person

Arrest at Third Party's Home:

To enter a third party's home to arrest someone, you need:

- Arrest warrant for the suspect
- Search warrant for the third party's residence
- Consent from the resident
- Exigent circumstances

Arrest of Juveniles:

Special considerations apply when arresting juveniles (persons under 17):

- Authority is to "take into custody" rather than "arrest"
- Must notify parents/guardians promptly
- May be released to parents rather than detained
- Different processing procedures apply
- More restrictions on interrogation

Arrest of Out-of-State Residents:

People arrested on out-of-state warrants may face extradition proceedings. The arresting process is similar, but additional procedures govern their return to the requesting state.

Evidence Collection and Chain of Custody

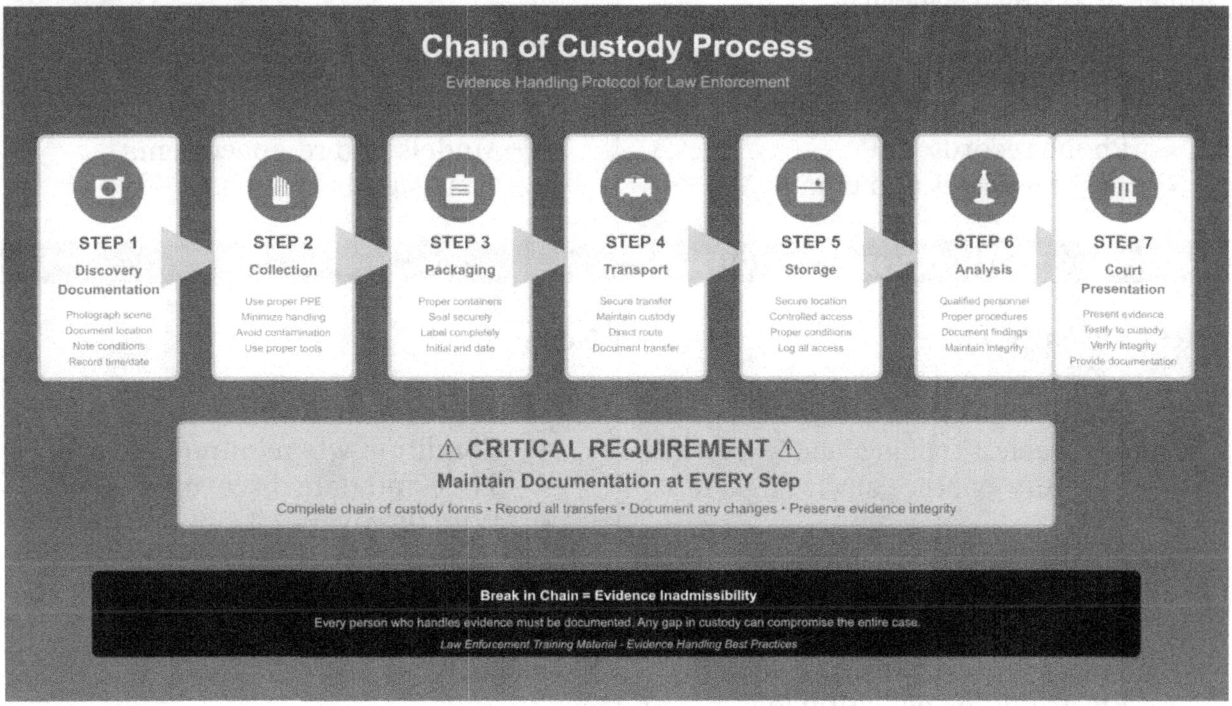

Collecting and preserving evidence properly is as important as finding it. Evidence that's contaminated, lost, or improperly documented will be excluded from court, potentially destroying your case.

Types of Evidence

Understanding evidence types helps you recognize what's valuable and how to collect it properly.

Physical Evidence:

Tangible objects that prove or disprove facts:

- Weapons used in crimes
- Stolen property
- Drugs and contraband
- Blood, DNA, fingerprints
- Documents, photographs
- Clothing with trace evidence
- Tools used in burglaries
- Electronic devices

Testimonial Evidence:

Statements from people with relevant knowledge:

- Victim statements
- Witness testimony
- Expert opinions
- Confessions and admissions

- Your observations and actions

Documentary Evidence:

Written or recorded materials:

- Business records
- Medical records
- Phone records
- Text messages and emails
- Videos and photographs
- Computer files

Demonstrative Evidence:

Materials created to explain or illustrate facts:

- Diagrams and maps
- Models and re-enactments
- Charts and timelines

Evidence Collection Principles

1. RECOGNIZE IT

You must recognize that something has evidentiary value. Training and experience help you identify evidence others might miss:

- Fingerprints on surfaces
- DNA on clothing or weapons
- Tool marks on doors or windows
- Trace evidence (fibers, hair, soil)
- Electronic evidence on phones or computers
- Documents showing motive or planning

2. DOCUMENT IT

Before collecting anything, document it thoroughly:

Photography:

- Overall scene photos showing context
- Medium-range photos showing relationships between items
- Close-up photos of individual items
- Photos with and without scales/rulers
- Multiple angles of important evidence

Notes:

- Exact location where found
- Condition when found
- Time and date discovered
- Who discovered it
- Environmental conditions
- Relationship to other evidence

Sketches/Diagrams:

- Scale drawings of crime scenes
- Measurements showing distances
- Item locations marked clearly

Video:

- Walk-through of scene
- Narration explaining what's shown
- Supplement to photos, not replacement

3. COLLECT IT

Use proper techniques for each evidence type:

General Principles:

- Wear gloves to avoid contamination
- Use clean tools for each item
- Prevent cross-contamination

- Collect sufficient quantity for testing
- Maintain evidence in condition as found when possible

Specific Evidence Types:

Firearms:

- Don't handle with cloth through trigger guard (damages trigger evidence)
- Clear weapon only if absolutely necessary for safety
- Note condition (loaded, safety on/off)
- Secure properly to prevent alteration

Ammunition:

- Handle carefully to preserve fingerprints
- Keep separate from firearms
- Note caliber and quantity

Bloodstains:

- Air dry wet blood before packaging
- Don't use plastic bags for biological evidence (promotes mold)
- Use paper bags or envelopes
- Collect control samples from unstained areas nearby

DNA Evidence:

- Avoid touching areas where DNA might be
- Air dry before packaging
- Use paper, not plastic
- Collect elimination samples from victims and consensual partners

Drugs:

- Field test carefully (follow safety protocols)
- Photograph in place before collection
- Weigh carefully (weight affects charges)
- Submit representative samples if large quantities

Digital Evidence:

- Don't turn on devices that are off
- Don't access files yourself
- Photograph screens before touching
- Preserve battery power
- Consider Faraday bags to prevent remote wiping

Documents:

- Handle minimally to preserve prints
- Use gloves or tools
- Protect from damage
- Photograph before collecting if fragile

4. PACKAGE IT

Proper packaging preserves evidence integrity:

General Packaging Rules:

- Use appropriate containers (paper bags for most biological evidence, plastic for most inorganic evidence)
- Seal containers securely
- Label immediately and completely
- Keep different items separated
- Maintain condition (refrigerate perishables, keep moisture away from documents)

Labels Must Include:

- Case number
- Your name and ID number
- Date and time collected
- Location where found
- Description of item
- Your signature or initials

5. TRANSPORT IT

Get evidence to proper storage safely:

- Maintain security and control
- Prevent contamination or damage
- Follow special handling requirements (refrigeration, hazmat protocols)
- Document transport in reports

6. STORE IT

Evidence must be stored securely:

- Limited access (only authorized personnel)
- Climate controlled as needed
- Organized for easy retrieval
- Protected from damage, contamination, tampering

Preserving Evidence Integrity

The Chain of Custody:

Chain of custody is the documented, unbroken trail of evidence handling from collection to presentation in court. Every person who handles evidence must be documented.

Why Chain of Custody Matters:

Courts require proof that evidence presented at trial is the same evidence collected at the scene and hasn't been tampered with, substituted, or contaminated. Broken chain of custody can result in evidence being excluded.

Documenting Chain of Custody:

Every time evidence changes hands, document:

- Who released it
- Who received it
- Date and time of transfer
- Purpose of transfer
- Condition of evidence
- How it was secured

Example of Chain of Custody:

1. **You collect a knife at a crime scene:**
    - Document in report: "At 1430 hours, I collected a kitchen knife from the living room floor. Item tagged as Evidence #1."

    - Package in paper bag, seal, label, initial seal
2. **You transport it to evidence room:**
    - Sign evidence into property system: "At 1550 hours, submitted Evidence #1 to Property Officer Johnson."
    - Property Officer Johnson signs receipt acknowledging receipt
3. **Crime lab analyzes it:**
    - Property Officer releases to lab: Documents date, time, analyst receiving it
    - Lab analyst documents receiving it, analyzing it, returning it
4. **You retrieve it for trial:**
    - Document checking it out from property
    - Transport to court
    - Present in court

At trial, you'll testify:

- When and where you found it
- What you did with it
- How you marked it
- Where you stored it
- That the knife in court is the same knife you recovered

Any unexplained gaps in documentation create doubt about evidence integrity.

Maintaining Integrity:

Prevent Contamination:

- Change gloves between handling different items
- Use clean tools
- Keep evidence separated
- Avoid coughing, sneezing on evidence

Prevent Tampering:

- Seal packages securely
- Use tamper-evident tape
- Initial seals
- Store in secure locations
- Limit access

Prevent Degradation:

- Follow storage requirements (refrigeration, etc.)
- Protect from environmental damage

- Handle minimally
- Document condition changes

Common Evidence Collection Errors

1. Contamination

Mixing evidence from different sources or introducing foreign material destroys evidentiary value.

Example: Placing multiple bloody items in the same bag causes cross-contamination. DNA testing may become impossible or inconclusive.

Prevention: Use separate, clean packaging for each item.

2. Broken Chain of Custody

Failing to document every transfer or storage creates gaps that defense attorneys exploit.

Example: You collect evidence but don't log it into property for three days. What happened to it during those three days? Can you prove it wasn't altered?

Prevention: Document everything immediately and completely.

3. Improper Packaging

Wrong packaging materials cause damage or degradation.

Example: Placing wet bloodstained clothing in plastic bag causes mold growth, destroying DNA evidence.

Prevention: Air dry biological evidence before packaging in paper.

4. Insufficient Documentation

Failing to photograph or note evidence location makes it challengeable.

Example: You recover a gun but don't photograph where it was found or measure its distance from the victim. Defense claims you moved it or it was never there.

Prevention: Photograph everything in place before collecting. Measure and document locations.

5. Inadequate Collection

Taking insufficient samples prevents proper testing.

Example: You collect only a tiny bloodstain but lab needs more for complete DNA profile.

Prevention: Collect adequate quantities when possible. Consult with lab if unsure.

Miranda Rights and Interrogation

Miranda warnings protect Fifth Amendment rights against self-incrimination. Understanding when Miranda applies and how to properly administer warnings is critical for obtaining admissible statements.

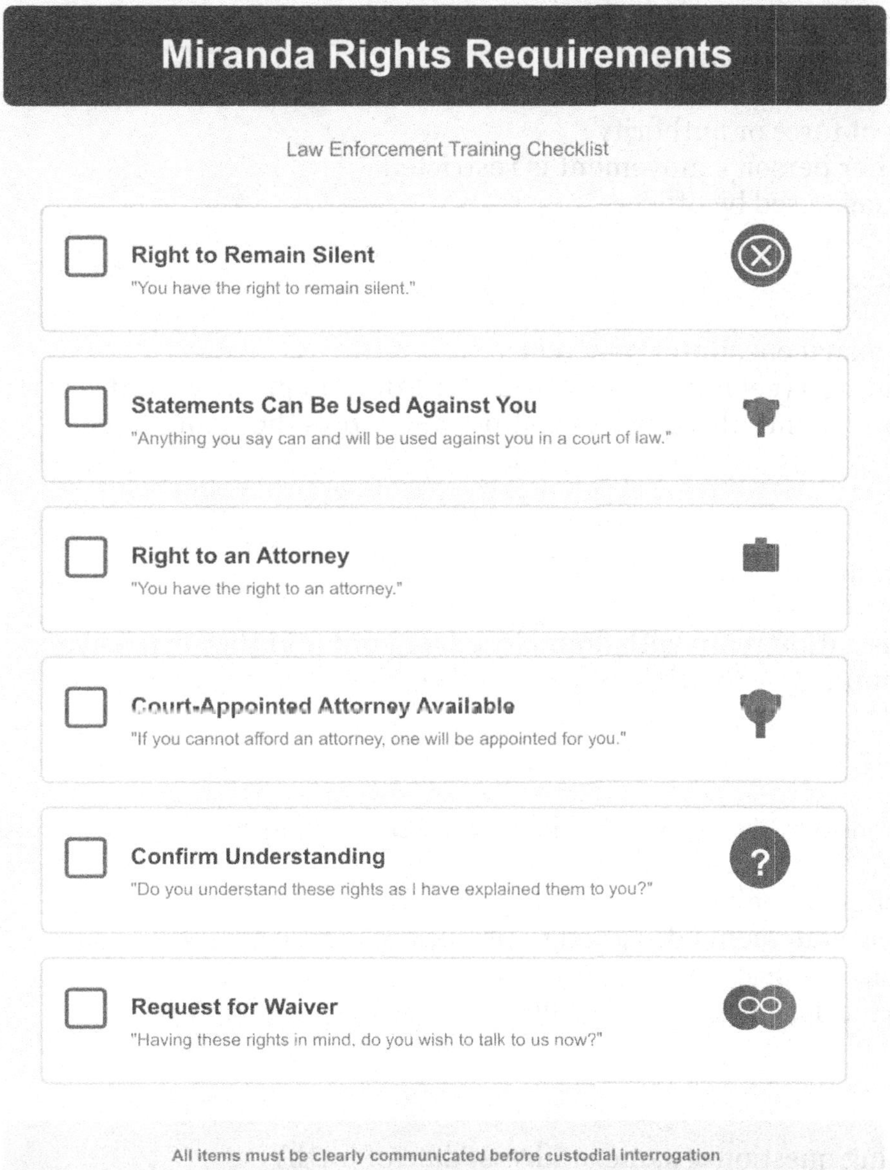

When Miranda Warnings Are Required

Miranda warnings are required only during "custodial interrogation":

CUSTODY + INTERROGATION = MIRANDA REQUIRED

Custody:

A person is in custody when a reasonable person in their situation wouldn't feel free to leave or terminate the encounter. Consider:

- Whether person is under arrest
- Location (police station, their home, public place)
- Duration of encounter
- Number of officers
- Show of force or authority
- Whether person's movement is restricted
- Language used by officers

Not in custody:

- Consensual encounter on street
- Traffic stop (generally not custody for Miranda purposes unless arrest occurs)
- Person voluntarily comes to station and knows they can leave

In custody:

- Under arrest
- In patrol car
- Interrogation room with door closed and not told they can leave
- Surrounded by multiple officers blocking exit

Interrogation:

Words or actions by police reasonably likely to elicit incriminating response. This includes:

- Direct questioning
- Making statements designed to prompt response
- Playing one suspect off against another
- Confronting suspect with evidence to provoke explanation

Not interrogation:

- Booking questions (name, address, date of birth)
- Public safety questions ("Where's the gun?")

- Spontaneous statements by suspect
- General conversation not designed to elicit admissions

The Miranda Warnings

The required warnings come directly from Miranda v. Arizona (1966):

You must advise the person:

1. You have the right to remain silent.

Anything you say can and will be used against you in court.

2. You have the right to an attorney.

You have the right to have an attorney present during questioning.

3. If you cannot afford an attorney, one will be appointed for you.

4. Do you understand these rights?

5. Having these rights in mind, do you wish to talk to us now?

Proper Administration:

- Read from Miranda card to ensure accurate wording
- Speak clearly
- Ensure the person understands (consider language barriers, mental capacity, intoxication)
- Get affirmative acknowledgment they understand
- Document the warning (written waiver form is best, or note exact words in report)
- Record the entire exchange if possible (Texas law requires recording)

Understanding and Waiver

For statements to be admissible after Miranda warnings, you must show the person:

1. Understood their rights

Not just that you said the words, but that they comprehended them. Consider:

- Education level
- Mental capacity
- Language comprehension

- Intoxication level
- Age (juveniles may not fully understand)

If there's doubt about understanding, don't proceed with interrogation.

2. Knowingly and voluntarily waived their rights

Waiver must be:

- **Knowing:** Made with understanding of what's being given up
- **Intelligent:** Made with awareness of consequences
- **Voluntary:** Free from coercion, threats, or promises

Written Waiver:

Best practice is obtaining written waiver where the person signs a form acknowledging:

- They were advised of their rights
- They understand those rights
- They're willing to answer questions without a lawyer present

Verbal Waiver:

Verbal waiver is valid but less provable. Document exact words:

- Officer: "Do you understand these rights?"
- Suspect: "Yes."
- Officer: "Having these rights in mind, are you willing to talk to me without a lawyer?"
- Suspect: "Yeah, I'll talk."

Implied Waiver:

Courts are skeptical of implied waiver. Simply beginning to answer questions after being warned may not constitute valid waiver. Get affirmative agreement to waive.

Invoking Miranda Rights

Once properly warned, suspects can invoke their rights at any time.

Two Ways to Invoke:

1. Right to Remain Silent:

"I don't want to answer questions." "I'm not saying anything." "I don't want to talk."

Effect: You must stop questioning. You may attempt to re-initiate questioning after significant time passes if you re-advise Miranda and the person waives again.

2. Right to Counsel:

"I want a lawyer." "I think I should talk to an attorney." "Maybe I need a lawyer."

Effect: ALL questioning must cease immediately. You may not re-initiate questioning unless the suspect initiates further communication and validly waives rights again.

Ambiguous Invocations:

Courts interpret any reasonable assertion of rights in suspect's favor:

- "Maybe I should talk to a lawyer" = invocation
- "Do I need a lawyer?" = probably invocation
- "I think I'm done talking" = invocation of right to silence

When in doubt, treat it as an invocation and stop questioning.

What You Cannot Do After Invocation:

- Continue current line of questioning
- Switch to different topic
- Attempt to persuade suspect to talk
- Make statements designed to elicit response
- Have different officer try questioning
- Minimize importance of lawyer

Example of Improper Continuation:

Suspect: "I want a lawyer." Officer: "Well, getting a lawyer will just take longer. Why don't you tell me your side first, then get a lawyer?"

This violates Miranda. Any statements obtained after this will be suppressed.

Proper Response to Invocation:

Suspect: "I want a lawyer." Officer: "Okay, we're done questioning. I'll arrange for you to contact an attorney."

End all interrogation immediately.

Custodial Interrogation Rules

Texas Requirements (Article 38.22 CCP):

Texas law imposes additional requirements beyond Miranda:

Electronic Recording Requirement:

Oral statements made during custodial interrogation must be electronically recorded to be admissible. The recording must show:

- The time the statement was made
- Advisement of Miranda rights
- Suspect's acknowledgment of understanding
- Voluntary waiver of rights
- The complete statement
- No evidence of tampering or editing

Exceptions to Recording Requirement:

- Statement isn't made during custodial interrogation
- Recording wasn't feasible due to equipment failure (document why)
- Suspect refused to make statement with recording (document refusal)
- Exigent circumstances made recording impossible
- Statement made in court or grand jury

Written Statements:

Written statements by suspects require:

- Miranda warnings given in writing
- Suspect reads and signs the warning form
- Statement is voluntary
- Suspect signs the statement

Exceptions:

Article 38.22 doesn't apply to:

- Spontaneous statements (not in response to interrogation)
- Res gestae statements (part of the event itself)
- Statements made in open court
- Non-custodial statements

Conducting Effective Interrogations

Once you've properly administered Miranda and obtained waiver, effective interrogation techniques help you get truthful statements:

Preparation:

- Review all evidence before questioning
- Develop questioning strategy
- Prepare questions and topics
- Anticipate defenses or explanations
- Set up recording equipment

Building Rapport:

- Use appropriate tone (professional but not hostile)
- Show respect even while being direct
- Listen actively
- Don't interrupt constantly

Questioning Techniques:

Open-Ended Questions:

- "Tell me what happened."
- "Explain your relationship with the victim."
- Let suspect talk

Specific Questions:

- "Where were you at 10 PM?"
- "What did you do with the gun?"
- Pin down details

Confrontation:

- Present evidence contradicting suspect's story
- Point out inconsistencies
- But don't lie about evidence (creates problems for prosecution)

Obtaining Details:

- Crime scene details only the perpetrator would know
- Specific sequence of events
- Motive and intent
- Location of evidence or proceeds

Documentation:

- Record everything (audio/video)
- Take notes during interrogation
- Memorialize key admissions immediately
- Have suspect repeat important admissions on recording

Avoid:

- Threats or promises
- Physical coercion
- Lengthy interrogations without breaks
- Lying about what the law allows
- Minimizing seriousness to point of implying no consequences

Common Miranda Errors

1. Failing to Advise Before Custodial Interrogation

Starting to question arrested person without Miranda warning.

Result: Statements suppressed.

Prevention: Miranda should be one of your first actions after arrest if you plan to question.

2. Continuing After Invocation

Suspect says "I want a lawyer" and you keep questioning.

Result: All subsequent statements suppressed.

Prevention: Stop immediately when rights invoked.

3. Coercive Waiver

Threatening consequences for invoking rights or promising leniency for waiving them.

Result: Waiver invalid, statements suppressed.

Prevention: Let suspect make free choice without threats or promises.

4. Failure to Record (Texas)

Not electronically recording custodial interrogation.

Result: Oral statements inadmissible under Article 38.22.

Prevention: Always record custodial interrogations. If equipment fails, document why.

5. Questioning Outside Your Jurisdiction

Assuming another state's Miranda requirements match Texas.

Result: Potential suppression if that state has different requirements.

Prevention: When working with out-of-state agencies, follow the strictest requirements.

This thorough understanding of criminal procedures provides the foundation you need for lawful, effective law enforcement. In the next section, we'll apply these principles to real-world scenarios that test your ability to make quick, legally sound decisions in the field.

Real-World Application: Criminal Procedure Scenarios

These scenarios challenge you to apply the criminal procedure principles you've learned. Work through each carefully, considering all relevant factors before reading the explanation.

Scenario 1: The Questionable Vehicle Search

Situation: At 2:15 AM, you stop a vehicle for failure to signal a lane change. The driver provides license and insurance but seems extremely nervous. While speaking with him, you notice the smell of air freshener and observe fast food bags and clothes scattered throughout the vehicle. When you ask where he's traveling, he gives vague answers. You request consent to search, and he responds, "I guess you're going to search anyway, right?" You proceed to search the vehicle and find methamphetamine in the glove box.

Questions to Consider:

- Was the consent valid?
- Did you have probable cause to search without consent?
- Will the evidence be admissible?
- What should you have done differently?

Analysis and Answer:

Consent Validity Issue:

The driver's response—"I guess you're going to search anyway, right?"—is not valid consent. Valid consent must be:

- **Voluntary:** Freely given without coercion
- **Unequivocal:** Clear and definite

This response suggests the driver believed he had no choice, indicating the consent wasn't truly voluntary. The phrasing "I guess you're going to search anyway" implies resignation to perceived inevitability rather than genuine permission.

Probable Cause Analysis:

Let's examine whether you had probable cause to search without consent:

- **Nervousness:** Common during traffic stops; insufficient alone
- **Air freshener smell:** Not probable cause (many people use air freshener legitimately)
- **Messy vehicle:** Not indicative of criminal activity
- **Vague answers:** Suspicious but not probable cause
- **Late hour:** Legal to drive at night

None of these factors, individually or combined, create probable cause to believe the vehicle contains contraband. You had reasonable suspicion at most, which justifies the traffic stop but not a search.

Admissibility:

The methamphetamine will likely be suppressed because:

- Consent was not clearly voluntary
- No probable cause existed for warrantless search
- No other warrant exception applied

Proper Procedure:

Here's what you should have done:

Option 1 - Clarify Consent: "Sir, I want to be clear—you have the right to refuse a search. I'm asking for your permission, but you can say no. If you give me permission to search your vehicle, I need you to tell me clearly. Do you consent to a search of your vehicle?"

Wait for unambiguous response. If he says "yes" clearly, document it thoroughly and proceed. If he refuses or gives another ambiguous answer, you cannot search without probable cause.

Option 2 - Complete the Traffic Stop: Issue the citation for failure to signal and release him. Without probable cause or clear consent, you have no authority to search.

Option 3 - Develop Probable Cause: If during your lawful activities (issuing citation, checking for warrants), you observe something creating probable cause (marijuana odor, visible contraband, drug paraphernalia), then you may search under the automobile exception.

Key Takeaway: Ambiguous consent isn't consent. When a person's response suggests they feel compelled rather than agreeing voluntarily, you don't have valid consent. Either clarify until you get clear consent or refusal, or don't search. A suppressed methamphetamine case is worse than no search at all.

Scenario 2: Miranda Timing and Invocation

Situation: You arrest a suspect for aggravated robbery. During transport to jail, before Miranda warnings, he spontaneously says, "I didn't mean to hurt anybody. I just needed the money." At the jail, you read Miranda warnings. He says he understands and agrees to talk. During the interview, he describes the robbery in detail. After 30 minutes, he says, "This is making me uncomfortable. Should I have a lawyer?" You respond, "That's up to you, but you're doing fine. We're almost done anyway." He continues answering questions and admits where he hid the stolen property.

Questions to Consider:

- Is the transport statement admissible?
- Was the Miranda warning properly administered?
- Did the suspect invoke his right to counsel?
- Are the post-invocation statements admissible?
- What should you have done when he mentioned a lawyer?

Analysis and Answer:

Statement 1 - Transport Statement:

ADMISSIBLE. This spontaneous statement made during transport is admissible despite the lack of Miranda warnings because:

- The statement was spontaneous, not in response to interrogation
- You didn't question him or do anything designed to elicit a response
- Miranda only applies to custodial interrogation
- Spontaneous statements don't require warnings

You must be prepared to testify that you said nothing to prompt this statement and didn't create conditions designed to make him want to talk.

Statement 2 - Initial Interview Admissions:

ADMISSIBLE. After proper Miranda warnings and valid waiver, these statements were properly obtained:

- Miranda was administered at the jail
- Suspect indicated understanding
- Suspect voluntarily waived rights
- Interview was recorded (as required by Texas law)

Statement 3 - Post-Invocation Statements:

INADMISSIBLE. Everything said after "Should I have a lawyer?" must be suppressed. Here's why:

Invocation Occurred:

"Should I have a lawyer?" is an invocation of the right to counsel. Courts interpret any reasonable assertion of the right to counsel in the suspect's favor. Even when phrased as a question or possibility, statements like "Should I have a lawyer?" or "Maybe I need a lawyer" constitute invocations.

Your Response Was Improper:

Your response—"That's up to you, but you're doing fine. We're almost done anyway"—violated Miranda in multiple ways:

- You continued the interrogation after invocation
- You minimized the importance of counsel
- You suggested invoking rights was unnecessary

- You implied cooperation without counsel was preferable

Correct Response:

The moment he said "Should I have a lawyer?" you should have:

- Immediately stopped all questioning
- Said something like: "If you want to speak with an attorney, we'll stop questioning now and arrange for you to contact one."
- Ended the interview
- Left the room or ceased all questioning

Cannot Resume Unless Suspect Re-Initiates:

Once counsel is invoked, you cannot resume questioning unless:

- The suspect initiates further communication (not in response to your prompting)
- The suspect validly waives rights again after re-advisement

Your encouragement to continue talking and minimization of the lawyer's importance prevents any subsequent waiver from being voluntary.

Impact on the Case:

You still have:

- The spontaneous transport statement (admissible)
- The initial post-Miranda admissions (admissible)
- Other evidence from the robbery investigation

But you've lost:

- Admission about where stolen property is hidden
- Any other details he provided after invoking counsel

Key Takeaway: When a suspect mentions wanting a lawyer—even tentatively—all questioning must cease immediately. You cannot talk them out of exercising their rights. Respecting this rule may cost you some admissions, but violating it will cost you all subsequent statements and possibly your credibility.

Scenario 3: Search Incident to Arrest Boundaries

Situation: You respond to a domestic disturbance call. Upon arrival, you determine the male party committed assault causing bodily injury to his girlfriend. You arrest him in the living room of their shared apartment. After handcuffing him, you:

1. Search his person (finding car keys and a wallet)
2. Search the couch where he was sitting (finding nothing)
3. Walk through the apartment "for safety" and look in the bedroom, bathroom, and kitchen
4. Open the bedroom closet and find a handgun on the shelf
5. Open a dresser drawer in the bedroom and find what appears to be cocaine
6. Place the arrested person in your patrol car
7. Return to the apartment and search the kitchen cabinets, finding marijuana

Questions to Consider:

- Which searches were lawful?
- Which exceeded your authority?
- What warrant exceptions apply?
- Which evidence will be admissible?

Analysis and Answer:

Let's analyze each search:

Search #1 - Person (LAWFUL):

Searching the arrested person is authorized as search incident to arrest. You have full authority to search his clothing, pockets, and items immediately on his person. This protects officer safety and prevents destruction of evidence.

Search #2 - Couch (LAWFUL):

The immediate area where he was sitting at the time of arrest (the "grab area") may be searched incident to arrest. The couch falls within this grab area—he could have reached it to grab a weapon or destroy evidence.

Search #3 - Walking Through Apartment:

POTENTIALLY LAWFUL as a protective sweep IF you had reasonable suspicion someone else was present who might pose a danger. A protective sweep allows a quick visual inspection of places where someone could hide.

Requirements for valid protective sweep:

- Reasonable belief someone else might be present
- Articulable safety concerns
- Limited to quick visual inspection
- Only areas where person could hide
- No opening of containers or drawers

If the girlfriend was present and cooperative, or you had no reason to believe others were there, this exceeds protective sweep authority.

Search #4 - Bedroom Closet (QUESTIONABLE):

Opening the closet during a protective sweep is permissible IF you could articulate why you reasonably believed someone might be hiding there. However, looking on a shelf (rather than just checking if someone's hiding inside) exceeds protective sweep scope.

The handgun might be admissible if it was in plain view when you opened the closet to check for people. If you had to search the shelf to find it, it exceeds protective sweep authority.

Search #5 - Dresser Drawer (UNLAWFUL):

Opening a dresser drawer clearly exceeds any lawful authority:

- Not within grab area (he's already secured)
- Not within protective sweep scope (people don't hide in dresser drawers)
- No consent obtained
- No probable cause for search warrant exception
- No other warrant exception applies

The cocaine will be suppressed.

Search #6-7 - Kitchen Search After Securing Suspect (UNLAWFUL):

Once the suspect is secured in your patrol car, you have no authority to continue searching:

- Search incident to arrest no longer applies (he can't access the apartment)
- Protective sweep is complete (you've verified no one else is there)
- You left and returned specifically to search more
- No consent, warrant, or other exception

The marijuana will be suppressed.

What You Should Have Done:

Lawful Actions:

1. Search the arrested person thoroughly
2. Search the immediate grab area (couch)
3. If safety concerns exist, conduct quick protective sweep (look for people only)
4. Secure the scene
5. Remove the arrestee

If You Want to Search Further:

- Obtain consent from a resident with authority (the girlfriend if she has equal control of the apartment)
- Get a search warrant based on probable cause
- Articulate exigent circumstances (like specific knowledge drugs were about to be destroyed)

Admissible Evidence:

- Items found on his person: YES
- Items from couch: YES
- Handgun from closet: MAYBE (depends on whether protective sweep was justified and whether gun was in plain view)
- Cocaine from dresser: NO
- Marijuana from kitchen: NO

Key Takeaway: Search incident to arrest and protective sweeps are limited doctrines. Once the arrestee is secured and you've ensured no threats exist, your warrantless search authority ends. If you want to search more thoroughly, get consent or a warrant. Don't assume that making an arrest in a home gives you carte blanche to search the entire residence.

Scenario 4: Probable Cause Development

Situation: At 11:30 PM, you observe a vehicle parked in a closed business parking lot with its engine running. You approach to conduct a welfare check. The driver appears startled when you knock on the window. You see an open beer can in the cup holder. You ask the driver to step out. He stumbles slightly and you smell alcohol. You ask if he's been drinking, and he says "just a couple beers." You notice his speech is slightly slurred. You ask him to perform field sobriety tests. He performs poorly on the HGN test (all six clues), moderately on Walk and Turn (three clues), and poorly on One Leg Stand (three clues).

Questions to Consider:

- When did you develop reasonable suspicion?
- When did you develop probable cause?
- Was your request for FSTs lawful?
- Do you have authority to arrest?
- What charges are supported?

Analysis and Answer:

Timeline of Suspicion and Probable Cause:

Initial Contact (No Seizure): Walking up to a parked vehicle for a welfare check is a consensual encounter. No reasonable suspicion required.

Reasonable Suspicion Develops (Justifies Detention): When you observe:

- Open alcohol container (violation of open container law)
- Driver's startled reaction combined with open container

You now have reasonable suspicion of criminal activity (open container violation at minimum). This justifies detaining the driver to investigate further.

Probable Cause Develops (Justifies Arrest): As you gather more information, probable cause for DWI develops:

Evidence accumulating:

1. Open beer can (consumption suggested)
2. Stumbling when exiting vehicle (physical manifestation of intoxication)
3. Odor of alcohol (confirms consumption)
4. Admission to drinking ("just a couple beers")
5. Slurred speech (additional impairment indicator)
6. Poor performance on HGN (6/6 clues = highly correlated with .08+ BAC)
7. Poor performance on Walk and Turn (3/8 clues = significant)
8. Poor performance on One Leg Stand (3/4 clues = significant)

By the conclusion of field sobriety tests, you have probable cause that the driver:

- Is intoxicated (loss of normal use of faculties based on multiple indicators)
- Operated a vehicle while intoxicated (vehicle running, in driver's seat, in parking lot)

Lawfulness of FST Request:

Your request for field sobriety tests was lawful because:

- You had reasonable suspicion of DWI
- FSTs are investigative tools used during lawful detentions
- They're voluntary (driver could refuse, though refusal can be considered)
- They help establish probable cause for arrest

Operating a Motor Vehicle:

Defense attorneys will argue the driver wasn't "operating" because the vehicle was parked. However, Texas courts have held that "operating" includes:

- Having the engine running
- Being in the driver's seat
- Having present ability to set the vehicle in motion

The driver meets all three criteria. The vehicle was running, he was in the driver's seat, and he could have driven away. This constitutes operation.

Public Place:

The parking lot of a closed business is a public place because it's accessible to the public during business hours and not secured. This satisfies the "public place" element of DWI.

Arrest Authority:

You have probable cause to arrest for:

- **DWI (§49.04):** Intoxicated while operating a motor vehicle in a public place (Class B misdemeanor)
- **Open Container (§49.031):** Knowingly possessing open container in vehicle on public highway (Class C misdemeanor)

Chemical Testing:

After arrest for DWI, you should:

- Transport to jail or testing facility
- Read DIC-24 statutory warning
- Request breath or blood test
- Document consent or refusal
- Arrange testing if consent obtained

Proper Documentation:

Your report must thoroughly document:

- Initial observations justifying welfare check
- Open container observation
- Physical indicators of intoxication (stumbling, odor, slurred speech)
- Driver's admissions
- Field sobriety test performance (detailed observations for each test)
- Decision to arrest based on totality of circumstances

Potential Defenses:

Anticipate these defenses:

- "I wasn't driving, just sitting there" (Counter: vehicle was running, you were in driver's seat)
- "The beer wasn't mine" (Counter: you were in possession and admitted drinking)
- "I wasn't planning to drive" (Counter: vehicle was running and you were in control)

Key Takeaway: Probable cause develops incrementally through accumulation of facts. No single indicator creates probable cause for DWI, but the totality of circumstances—multiple physical indicators, poor FST performance, and admissions—builds a strong case. Document each observation thoroughly because DWI cases often go to trial, and your probable cause determination will be scrutinized.

Scenario 5: Chain of Custody Challenge

Situation: You respond to a burglary report. The victim states their prescription Oxycodone was stolen from the bathroom. You locate the suspect nearby based on victim's description. The suspect has a pill bottle in his pocket containing white pills. You seize the bottle at 3:15 PM and place it in your patrol car. You complete the investigation, write your report, and go off-shift at 11:00 PM. You forget to submit the pill bottle to evidence. The next day at 3:00 PM (approximately 24 hours after seizure), you remember and submit the bottle to property. The pills are later tested and confirmed to be Oxycodone. At trial, six months later, the defense challenges chain of custody.

Questions to Consider:

- Is the chain of custody broken?
- What problems exist with your evidence handling?
- How will you explain the 24-hour gap?
- Will the evidence be admissible?
- How could this have been prevented?

Analysis and Answer:

Chain of Custody Problem:

You have a serious chain of custody gap. The 24-hour period when the pills were in your possession without proper documentation creates doubt about evidence integrity.

Issues with Your Handling:

1. Delayed Submission: Evidence should be submitted as soon as practical after collection, ideally at the end of your shift. The 24-hour delay is unexplained and problematic.

2. Lack of Security: Where were the pills during those 24 hours?

- In your patrol car? (Accessible to others?)
- In your personal vehicle? (No security)
- At your home? (Completely improper)

3. No Documentation: Your report doesn't reflect what happened to the evidence between seizure and submission because you didn't know you'd forget to submit it.

4. Broken Chain: You cannot account for the pills' location and security for 24 hours. During that time:

- Could someone have accessed them?
- Could they have been tampered with?
- Could they have been substituted?
- Were they exposed to conditions affecting integrity?

Defense Attorney's Arguments:

"Officer, you testified you seized these pills at 3:15 PM on March 1st, correct?" "Yes."

"And you submitted them to evidence at 3:00 PM on March 2nd?" "Yes."

"That's 24 hours later. Where were the pills during that time?" "In my patrol car."

"Who else had access to your patrol car?" "Other officers during shift briefings, anyone near the parking lot..."

"So you can't say with certainty that these pills are the same pills you seized, can you?" "They're sealed in the evidence bag I placed them in."

"But you can't account for every minute of those 24 hours, can you? Someone could have opened that bag, removed some pills, added different pills, and resealed it?" "I suppose that's theoretically possible, but—"

"No further questions."

Admissibility:

The evidence may still be admissible, but it's significantly weakened:

- The court will consider the totality of circumstances
- Your credible testimony about maintaining possession may be sufficient
- The sealed evidence bag with your signature provides some assurance
- Testing results matching the victim's prescription supports authenticity

However, the defense has created reasonable doubt about whether these are actually the pills seized from the suspect. Even if admitted, the jury may doubt the evidence's reliability.

How to Explain the Gap:

Your testimony must be honest: "I made an error. I intended to submit the evidence at end of shift but forgot. The pills remained in my locked patrol car in the station parking lot until I remembered and submitted them the following day. I maintained the seal I placed on the evidence bag. While I cannot account for every minute, I can testify that I secured the evidence properly and submitted the same pills I seized."

This honest explanation is better than trying to hide or minimize the mistake.

How to Prevent This:

Best Practices:

1. **Submit evidence immediately** after completing investigation or at end of shift
2. **Create reminders** (note in patrol car, set phone alarm)
3. **Check vehicle** before going off-shift for any evidence
4. **Complete chain of custody forms** immediately when submitting
5. **Photograph evidence** at time of seizure with your name card and date/time
6. **Never take evidence home** or to unauthorized locations
7. **Follow department policy** for evidence handling religiously

If You Must Delay Submission:

- Document reason for delay immediately
- Secure evidence in temporary storage (if available)
- Note in report where evidence is being held
- Ensure multiple people know you have evidence (supervisor, partner)
- Submit as soon as possible

Impact on Case:

Despite the chain of custody issues, you might still obtain a conviction because:

- Suspect's possession of victim's prescription medication is very incriminating
- Testing confirms pills are Oxycodone
- Your testimony about seizure and submission is credible
- No evidence of actual tampering exists

But you've made the prosecutor's job harder and created vulnerability the defense will exploit.

Key Takeaway: Chain of custody isn't just paperwork—it's proof that evidence is authentic and untampered. Any gap in documentation creates doubt. Handle evidence as if you'll have to explain every minute of its custody in court, because you might. Submit evidence promptly and document everything. An unbroken chain of custody is as important as collecting the evidence in the first place.

These scenarios demonstrate that criminal procedure isn't just theoretical—it's the framework for every investigation you conduct. Understanding these principles and applying them correctly protects constitutional rights, ensures evidence admissibility, and results in successful prosecutions. When you cut corners or ignore procedures, guilty people go free and you face liability.

Now let's test your knowledge with practice questions covering all of Chapter 2's material.

Practice Questions

Instructions: Answer all 60 questions. Check your answers and read all explanations, even for questions you answered correctly. Track your performance by content area to identify weak spots needing additional study.

Question 1: The requirement that a criminal act and criminal intent occur together is called:

A) Actus reus B) Mens rea C) Concurrence D) Causation

Answer: C

Explanation: Concurrence requires that the criminal act (actus reus) and criminal intent (mens rea) exist at the same moment. You can't have the intent before the act, perform the act, and then claim they occurred together. They must be concurrent.

Question 2: A person acts "knowingly" under Texas law when:

A) They desire to cause the result B) They are aware their conduct is reasonably certain to cause the result C) They consciously disregard a substantial risk D) They should be aware of a risk but fail to perceive it

Answer: B

Explanation: "Knowingly" means awareness that conduct is reasonably certain to cause the result. Option A describes "intentionally," option C describes "recklessly," and option D describes "criminal negligence."

Question 3: Which of the following is NOT an element required for most crimes?

A) Actus reus (criminal act) B) Mens rea (criminal intent) C) Motive D) Concurrence

Answer: C

Explanation: Motive (the reason why someone commits a crime) is not required to prove guilt, though it may be relevant for investigation and prosecution strategy. The essential elements are actus reus, mens rea, and concurrence.

Question 4: A "search" under the Fourth Amendment occurs when:

A) Any police officer looks at anything B) Government action infringes on a reasonable expectation of privacy C) An officer enters any building D) A citizen reports suspicious activity

Answer: B

Explanation: Under Katz v. United States, a search occurs when government action infringes on an expectation of privacy that society recognizes as reasonable. Not all police observations constitute searches.

Question 5: The "automobile exception" to the warrant requirement requires:

A) Reasonable suspicion B) Probable cause that the vehicle contains evidence or contraband C) The vehicle to be moving D) Consent from the driver

Answer: B

Explanation: The automobile exception requires probable cause to believe the vehicle contains evidence of a crime or contraband. The vehicle need not be moving—even parked vehicles may be searched under this exception if probable cause exists.

Question 6: After lawfully arresting someone, an officer may search:

A) The entire building where the arrest occurred B) Any vehicle in the vicinity C) The person arrested and the area within their immediate control D) Anyone present at the scene

Answer: C

Explanation: Search incident to arrest is limited to the person arrested and the grab area—the area within their immediate control where they could reach for weapons or destroy evidence.

Question 7: Miranda warnings are required before:

A) Any arrest B) Any questioning C) Custodial interrogation D) Issuing traffic citations

Answer: C

Explanation: Miranda warnings are required only when both custody and interrogation exist. Not all arrests or questioning require Miranda—only custodial interrogation (questioning someone who isn't free to leave).

Question 8: A person invokes their right to counsel by saying "I think I need a lawyer." The officer must:

A) Continue questioning about the current topic B) Stop all questioning immediately C) Switch to a different topic D) Explain that getting a lawyer will take longer

Answer: B

Explanation: Any reasonable assertion of the right to counsel must be honored immediately. All questioning must cease. You cannot continue questioning, switch topics, or attempt to dissuade the person from exercising their rights.

Question 9: Probable cause for arrest is best defined as:

A) Proof beyond a reasonable doubt B) More likely than not C) Facts and circumstances sufficient to warrant a reasonable person to believe a crime has been committed D) Any suspicion of criminal activity

Answer: C

Explanation: Probable cause requires facts and circumstances leading a reasonable person to believe a particular person committed a crime. It's more than suspicion but less than proof beyond reasonable doubt.

Question 10: Which of the following statements made by a suspect does NOT require Miranda warnings?

A) Statement made during custodial interrogation B) Spontaneous statement made without questioning C) Response to questions while under arrest D) Statement made during booking interrogation

Answer: B

Explanation: Spontaneous statements made without police interrogation don't require Miranda warnings. Miranda only applies to custodial interrogation—when the person is in custody AND being questioned.

Question 11: A "Terry frisk" allows an officer to:

A) Conduct a full search for evidence B) Pat down outer clothing for weapons when reasonable suspicion exists that the person is armed C) Search any containers the person is carrying D) Automatically search anyone stopped for investigation

Answer: B

Explanation: Terry v. Ohio allows limited pat-down of outer clothing for weapons when reasonable suspicion exists that a person is armed and dangerous. It's not a full search and doesn't authorize opening containers.

Question 12: Chain of custody refers to:

A) The order in which suspects are arrested B) The documented trail of evidence handling from collection to court C) The hierarchy of police command D) The sequence of crimes committed

Answer: B

Explanation: Chain of custody is the documented, unbroken record of everyone who handled evidence and when, where, and why transfers occurred. It proves evidence integrity and authenticity.

Question 13: Under Arizona v. Gant, vehicle searches incident to arrest are limited to situations where:

A) Any arrest is made near a vehicle B) The arrestee is unsecured and could access the vehicle OR evidence of the arrest offense might be in the vehicle C) The officer has reasonable suspicion D) The vehicle was used in the commission of any crime

Answer: B

Explanation: Gant restricts vehicle searches incident to arrest to two scenarios: the arrestee is unsecured and could access the vehicle's interior, or the officer reasonably believes evidence of the offense of arrest might be found in the vehicle.

Question 14: Valid consent to search must be:

A) In writing B) Given only by the owner C) Voluntary, given by someone with authority, and not coerced D) Obtained before any investigation begins

Answer: C

Explanation: Valid consent must be voluntary (freely given), from someone with actual or apparent authority, and not the product of duress or coercion. Written consent is best practice but not legally required.

Question 15: The "plain view" doctrine allows seizure of evidence when:

A) Any officer sees anything illegal B) The officer is lawfully positioned, the incriminating nature is immediately apparent, and the officer has lawful access C) A citizen points out evidence D) Evidence is visible from any location

Answer: B

Explanation: Plain view requires three elements: lawful positioning, immediately apparent incriminating nature (probable cause), and lawful access to seize the item.

Question 16: The lowest level of culpable mental state under Texas law is:

A) Recklessly B) Negligently C) Criminal negligence D) Accident

Answer: C

Explanation: The hierarchy from highest to lowest culpability is: intentionally, knowingly, recklessly, criminal negligence. "Accident" isn't a culpable mental state.

Question 17: Article 38.22 of the Texas Code of Criminal Procedure requires that:

A) All arrests must be documented B) Oral statements during custodial interrogation must be electronically recorded C) All suspects must be fingerprinted D) Miranda warnings must be given in writing

Answer: B

Explanation: Article 38.22 mandates electronic recording of oral statements made during custodial interrogation, showing advisement of rights, waiver, and the complete statement.

Question 18: A protective sweep during an arrest in a home:

A) Authorizes a complete search of the residence B) Allows a quick visual inspection of areas where someone could hide if you have reasonable belief someone else may be present C) Requires a search warrant D) Is never permitted

Answer: B

Explanation: Protective sweeps allow quick, cursory visual inspection of areas where people could hide to ensure officer safety, but only if you have reasonable belief someone else might be present who could pose danger.

Question 19: Exigent circumstances that justify warrantless entry include:

A) Desire to prevent any crime B) Hot pursuit, imminent destruction of evidence, emergency aid, or preventing escape of dangerous person C) Any investigation of a felony D) Convenience of the officers

Answer: B

Explanation: Recognized exigent circumstances include hot pursuit of fleeing felon, imminent destruction of evidence, emergency aid to someone in danger, and preventing escape of a dangerous person.

Question 20: When can an officer arrest for a misdemeanor without a warrant?

A) Never B) Only with supervisor approval C) When the offense occurs in the officer's presence or view, or specific statutory authority exists D) Anytime there's probable cause

Answer: C

Explanation: Generally, warrantless misdemeanor arrests require the offense to occur in the officer's presence/view. Specific exceptions exist for family violence assault and protective order violations.

Question 21: The purpose of field sobriety tests is to:

A) Punish drunk drivers B) Help establish probable cause for DWI arrest C) Replace chemical testing D) Delay the investigation

Answer: B

Explanation: Field sobriety tests help officers develop probable cause for DWI arrest by providing standardized, validated observations of impairment. They're investigative tools, not punishment or substitutes for chemical testing.

Question 22: Evidence obtained in violation of the Fourth Amendment:

A) Can still be used if it proves guilt B) Must be excluded under the exclusionary rule C) Can be used only in misdemeanor cases D) Is admissible if obtained in good faith

Answer: B

Explanation: Article 38.23 CCP and the Fourth Amendment exclusionary rule require suppression of evidence obtained through constitutional violations. The "good faith" exception has limited application and doesn't override clear violations.

Question 23: An inventory search is lawful when:

A) An officer wants to search but lacks probable cause B) The property is lawfully impounded and the search follows standardized procedures C) Any vehicle is in a public place D) The officer has reasonable suspicion

Answer: B

Explanation: Inventory searches must follow standardized department procedures and serve administrative purposes (protecting property, preventing false claims). They can't be pretextual searches for evidence.

Question 24: Consent to search can be withdrawn:

A) Never, once given B) Only with an attorney present C) At any time, and the officer must stop immediately D) Only if written consent was given

Answer: C

Explanation: Consent can be withdrawn at any time by clearly indicating the person wants the search to stop. Officers must cease searching immediately upon withdrawal of consent.

Question 25: Causation in criminal law means:

A) The defendant had a motive B) The defendant's conduct caused the prohibited result C) The defendant planned the crime D) Multiple people were involved

Answer: B

Explanation: Causation requires that the defendant's conduct actually caused the harmful result. This is particularly important in crimes like homicide and assault where the defendant's actions must have caused the death or injury.

Question 26: A person acts "recklessly" when they:

A) Desire to cause the result B) Know the result will occur C) Are aware of but consciously disregard a substantial and unjustifiable risk D) Should be aware of a risk but fail to perceive it

Answer: C

Explanation: Recklessness requires awareness of a substantial risk and conscious disregard of that risk. The person must know the risk exists and choose to ignore it.

Question 27: Which statement about warrantless arrests is TRUE?

A) Officers can never arrest without a warrant B) Officers may arrest for any felony with probable cause, even without witnessing it C) All misdemeanor arrests require warrants D) Only violent crimes allow warrantless arrest

Answer: B

Explanation: Article 14.03 CCP authorizes warrantless arrest for any felony when the officer has probable cause, even if the officer didn't witness the offense. Specific exceptions also exist for certain misdemeanors like family violence.

Question 28: The "knock and announce" rule before executing a search warrant:

A) Is never required B) Requires officers to knock, announce their identity and purpose, and wait a reasonable time before entering C) Only applies to residential searches D) Can be ignored if the officers are in a hurry

Answer: B

Explanation: Before executing a search warrant, officers must generally knock, announce their identity and purpose, and give occupants reasonable time to answer (typically 15-30 seconds) unless the warrant specifically authorizes no-knock entry.

Question 29: If a suspect asks "Should I have a lawyer?" during interrogation, the officer must:

A) Explain the pros and cons of having a lawyer B) Continue questioning but note the question in the report C) Stop all questioning immediately D) Only stop if the suspect explicitly says "I want a lawyer"

Answer: C

Explanation: Courts interpret any reasonable assertion of the right to counsel in the suspect's favor. "Should I have a lawyer?" constitutes invocation of the right to counsel, requiring immediate cessation of all questioning.

Question 30: Search incident to lawful arrest allows officers to search:

A) The entire building where the arrest occurs B) Any vehicles parked nearby C) The arrested person and the area within their immediate control D) All persons present at the scene

Answer: C

Explanation: Search incident to arrest is limited to the person arrested and the area within their immediate control (the "grab area") where they could reach for weapons or destroy evidence at the time of arrest.

Question 31: Probable cause for a search warrant must be:

A) Proven beyond a reasonable doubt B) Based on facts and circumstances leading a reasonable person to believe evidence will be found C) Based solely on an officer's hunch D) Established only by eyewitness testimony

Answer: B

Explanation: Probable cause requires facts and circumstances that would lead a reasonable person to believe evidence of a crime will be found in the place to be searched. It's more than suspicion but less than proof beyond reasonable doubt.

Question 32: The exclusionary rule means:

A) Certain suspects are excluded from prosecution B) Evidence obtained illegally cannot be used against the defendant C) Some crimes cannot be prosecuted D) Officers are excluded from testifying

Answer: B

Explanation: The exclusionary rule (Article 38.23 CCP and Fourth Amendment) prohibits use of evidence obtained through constitutional violations. This deters illegal searches and protects constitutional rights.

Question 33: When must Miranda warnings be given?

A) Upon any arrest B) Before any questioning C) Before custodial interrogation D) Only for felony investigations

Answer: C

Explanation: Miranda warnings are required only before custodial interrogation—when a person is in custody AND being questioned. Not all arrests or questioning require Miranda.

Question 34: An officer may conduct a Terry frisk when:

A) Any person is stopped B) The officer has reasonable suspicion the person is armed and dangerous C) The officer has probable cause of any crime D) The person refuses to answer questions

Answer: B

Explanation: Terry frisks require reasonable suspicion that the person is armed and dangerous. It's a protective measure for officer safety during lawful investigative stops.

Question 35: Chain of custody documentation must include:

A) Only who collected the evidence B) Every person who handled evidence, when, where, and why C) Just the final location of evidence D) Only the officer's badge number

Answer: B

Explanation: Chain of custody requires complete documentation of every person who handled evidence, the date and time of each transfer, the purpose, and how the evidence was secured. Any gap creates doubt about evidence integrity.

Question 36: The "automobile exception" exists because:

A) All vehicles are presumed to contain contraband B) Vehicles are mobile and have reduced expectation of privacy C) Officers don't have time to get warrants D) Vehicle owners have no Fourth Amendment rights

Answer: B

Explanation: The automobile exception recognizes that vehicles are inherently mobile (could be driven away) and that occupants have reduced expectation of privacy compared to homes.

Question 37: Valid consent to search requires:

A) Written documentation in all cases B) Consent from any person present C) Voluntary consent from someone with actual or apparent authority D) Supervisor approval

Answer: C

Explanation: Valid consent must be voluntary (freely given without coercion) and from someone with actual or apparent authority over the area to be searched. Written consent is best practice but not legally required.

Question 38: After a suspect invokes the right to remain silent:

A) All questioning must stop permanently B) Questioning must stop, but may resume after significant time if suspect is re-advised of rights C) The officer can continue with different questions D) Only that specific topic cannot be discussed

Answer: B

Explanation: When the right to remain silent is invoked, questioning must stop. However, unlike invocation of right to counsel, officers may attempt to re-initiate questioning after significant time has passed if they re-advise Miranda and obtain valid waiver.

Question 39: A protective sweep during an arrest in a home allows:

A) Full search of all rooms B) Quick visual inspection of areas where someone could hide, if reasonable belief exists someone else may be present C) Opening all containers and drawers D) Unlimited time to search

Answer: B

Explanation: Protective sweeps allow quick, cursory visual inspection of places where people could hide to ensure officer safety, but only if there's reasonable belief someone else may be present who could pose danger.

Question 40: Article 38.22 CCP requires:

A) All suspects must be fingerprinted B) Oral statements during custodial interrogation must be electronically recorded C) Written reports for all arrests D) Video recording of all traffic stops

Answer: B

Explanation: Article 38.22 is a Texas-specific requirement that oral statements made during custodial interrogation must be electronically recorded, showing Miranda advisement, waiver, and the complete statement.

Question 41: Exigent circumstances justifying warrantless entry include:

A) Any investigation B) Hot pursuit, imminent destruction of evidence, emergency aid, or preventing escape C) Convenience of officers D) Suspicion of criminal activity

Answer: B

Explanation: Recognized exigent circumstances include hot pursuit of fleeing felon, imminent destruction of evidence, emergency aid to someone in danger, and preventing escape of a dangerous person.

Question 42: The plain view doctrine requires:

A) Officers to be anywhere they want B) Lawful positioning, immediately apparent incriminating nature, and lawful access C) Only that officers can see the evidence D) Probable cause for arrest

Answer: B

Explanation: Plain view requires three elements: the officer must be lawfully positioned, the incriminating nature must be immediately apparent (probable cause), and the officer must have lawful access to seize the item.

Question 43: Inventory searches must:

A) Be used as pretext to search for evidence B) Follow standardized department procedures for administrative purposes C) Be conducted on all vehicles D) Require probable cause

Answer: B

Explanation: Inventory searches must follow standardized procedures and serve administrative purposes (protecting property, preventing false claims). They cannot be pretextual searches for evidence when probable cause is lacking.

Question 44: A person acts "intentionally" when:

A) They are aware conduct is reasonably certain to cause the result B) It is their conscious objective or desire to cause the result C) They consciously disregard a risk D) They should be aware of a risk

Answer: B

Explanation: "Intentionally" is the highest culpable mental state, occurring when it's the person's conscious objective or desire to engage in the conduct or cause the result.

Question 45: The "grab area" in search incident to arrest refers to:

A) Where the officer stands B) The area within the arrestee's immediate control at the time of arrest C) The entire building D) Any vehicle nearby

Answer: B

Explanation: The "grab area" is the area within the arrestee's immediate control where they could reach for weapons or destroy evidence. This area "freezes" at the moment of arrest.

Question 46: For a search warrant to be valid, it must:

A) Be signed by any officer B) Be based on probable cause, supported by oath, issued by neutral magistrate, and particularly describe the place and items C) Authorize unlimited searching D) Never expire

Answer: B

Explanation: Valid search warrants require probable cause, oath or affirmation, issuance by a neutral magistrate, and particular description of the place to be searched and items to be seized (Fourth Amendment requirements).

Question 47: When evidence integrity is questioned due to broken chain of custody:

A) The evidence is automatically admissible B) The evidence may be excluded or given less weight C) Only the officer who broke the chain faces consequences D) The case must be dismissed

Answer: B

Explanation: Broken chain of custody creates doubt about evidence integrity and authenticity. Courts may exclude the evidence or allow the jury to give it less weight. The case isn't automatically dismissed, but the evidence is weakened.

Question 48: A spontaneous statement by an arrested person made without questioning:

A) Always requires Miranda warnings B) Doesn't require Miranda warnings because there's no interrogation C) Can never be used in court D) Requires immediate re-arrest

Answer: B

Explanation: Spontaneous statements made without police interrogation don't require Miranda warnings. Miranda only applies to custodial interrogation, not voluntary statements.

Question 49: Reasonable suspicion for a Terry stop requires:

A) Proof beyond reasonable doubt B) Specific articulable facts suggesting criminal activity C) Just a hunch D) Probable cause

Answer: B

Explanation: Terry stops require reasonable suspicion—specific articulable facts that would lead a reasonable officer to believe criminal activity is occurring or about to occur. It's more than a hunch but less than probable cause.

Question 50: The primary purpose of the exclusionary rule is to:

A) Let guilty people go free B) Deter constitutional violations and protect individual rights C) Make prosecutions harder D) Punish police officers

Answer: B

Explanation: The exclusionary rule exists to deter constitutional violations by removing the incentive to conduct illegal searches. It protects Fourth Amendment rights by making illegally obtained evidence inadmissible.

Question 51: A person who ought to be aware of a substantial risk but fails to perceive it acts with:

A) Intent B) Knowledge C) Recklessness D) Criminal negligence

Answer: D

Explanation: Criminal negligence occurs when a person ought to be aware of but fails to perceive a substantial and unjustifiable risk. This differs from recklessness, where the person is actually aware of the risk.

Question 52: After obtaining valid consent to search, if the person says "stop searching," the officer must:

A) Continue until the search is complete B) Stop immediately—consent can be withdrawn at any time C) Finish the current area being searched D) Get supervisor approval to continue

Answer: B

Explanation: Consent can be withdrawn at any time. When a person clearly indicates they want the search to stop, officers must cease immediately. Any evidence found after withdrawal may be suppressed.

Question 53: Arizona v. Gant limits vehicle searches incident to arrest to situations where:

A) Any arrest occurs near a vehicle B) The arrestee is unsecured and could access the vehicle OR evidence of the arrest offense might be in the vehicle C) The vehicle owner gives consent D) The vehicle contains visible contraband

Answer: B

Explanation: Gant requires either that the arrestee is unsecured and could access the vehicle's interior, or that the officer reasonably believes evidence of the offense of arrest might be found in the vehicle.

Question 54: Probable cause is best described as:

A) Absolute certainty B) More than mere suspicion but less than proof beyond reasonable doubt C) Any hunch or feeling D) Witness testimony alone

Answer: B

Explanation: Probable cause is a flexible standard falling between reasonable suspicion and proof beyond reasonable doubt. It requires facts and circumstances sufficient to warrant a reasonable belief that a crime occurred.

Question 55: The fruit of the poisonous tree doctrine means:

A) Outdoor evidence cannot be used B) Evidence derived from an initial illegality is also tainted and may be excluded C) Only the initially seized evidence is excluded D) Evidence found near trees is inadmissible

Answer: B

Explanation: The fruit of the poisonous tree doctrine extends the exclusionary rule to evidence derived from the initial constitutional violation. If the original seizure was illegal, evidence discovered as a result of that illegality is also tainted.

Question 56: When can an officer search a vehicle without a warrant under search incident to arrest?

A) Whenever anyone is arrested near a vehicle B) Only when the arrestee is unsecured and could access the vehicle, or evidence of the arrest offense might be in the vehicle (Gant requirements) C) For any arrest regardless of circumstances D) Never without a warrant

Answer: B

Explanation: Arizona v. Gant restricts vehicle searches incident to arrest. The arrestee must be unsecured and able to access the vehicle, or the officer must reasonably believe evidence of the arrest offense is in the vehicle.

Question 57: The concurrence requirement means:

A) Multiple officers must agree B) The criminal act and criminal intent must exist at the same time C) Witnesses must corroborate the crime D) The prosecutor must approve charges

Answer: B

Explanation: Concurrence requires that actus reus (criminal act) and mens rea (criminal intent) occur together. You can't have intent before the act and then commit the act separately—they must be concurrent.

Question 58: Which is NOT required for the plain view doctrine?

A) Lawful positioning of the officer B) Immediately apparent incriminating nature C) Lawful access to the item D) Written permission from a supervisor

Answer: D

Explanation: Plain view requires three elements: lawful positioning, immediately apparent incriminating nature (probable cause), and lawful access. Supervisor permission is not required.

Question 59: An inventory search is justified when:

A) An officer wants to search but lacks probable cause B) Property is lawfully impounded and the search follows standardized procedures for administrative purposes C) Any vehicle is parked illegally D) The officer has reasonable suspicion

Answer: B

Explanation: Inventory searches must be conducted following standardized department procedures for administrative purposes (protecting property, preventing false claims), not as a pretext for an investigative search.

Question 60: The purpose of Miranda warnings is to:

A) Make prosecutions harder B) Protect Fifth Amendment rights against self-incrimination during custodial interrogation C) Inform suspects of all possible charges D) Delay arrests

Answer: B

Explanation: Miranda warnings protect Fifth Amendment rights against self-incrimination by ensuring suspects know they have the right to remain silent and to have counsel present during custodial interrogation.

Scoring Your Practice Questions

Count your correct answers:

57-60 correct (95-100%): Outstanding! You've mastered the criminal procedure material. Your understanding of search and seizure, arrest authority, evidence handling, and Miranda principles is excellent. Review any questions you missed to ensure complete understanding, then confidently move to Chapter 3.

51-56 correct (85-94%): Excellent work! You have a strong grasp of criminal procedures. Focus on the specific areas where you missed questions—whether it's search warrant exceptions, chain of custody, or Miranda requirements. Review those sections carefully, then retake the missed questions.

45-50 correct (75-84%): Good progress! You understand the core concepts but need to strengthen specific areas. Identify patterns in your missed questions (Are they mostly about searches? Miranda? Evidence handling?). Review those sections thoroughly with additional notes. Practice applying the concepts to scenarios before moving forward.

39-44 correct (65-74%): You're developing understanding but have significant gaps. Don't get discouraged—criminal procedure is complex! Review the entire chapter systematically, focusing especially on topics where you missed multiple questions. Work through the scenarios again, thinking about how the principles apply. Create summary sheets for key concepts like warrant exceptions and Miranda requirements.

Below 39 correct (less than 65%): You need substantial additional study before moving forward. Criminal procedure is foundational material that appears throughout law enforcement work and the exam. Review Chapter 2 section by section, taking detailed notes. Focus on understanding WHY procedures exist, not just memorizing rules. Use the scenarios to see how principles apply in practice. Consider creating flashcards for key concepts and finding a study partner for discussion.

Moving Forward

Criminal procedure isn't just about passing the exam—it's about protecting constitutional rights while effectively enforcing the law. Every search you conduct, every arrest you make, and every statement you obtain must follow proper procedures. Understanding these principles protects you from civil liability, ensures your cases hold up in court, and demonstrates your professionalism.

Key Concepts to Solidify Before Moving On:

- **Search and Seizure:** When warrants are required, what exceptions exist, how to properly execute searches
- **Arrest Authority:** When you can arrest with and without warrants, probable cause standards
- **Miranda Rights:** When warnings are required, how to properly administer them, what happens when rights are invoked
- **Evidence Handling:** Proper collection, documentation, chain of custody, preventing contamination
- **Mental States:** Understanding intentionally, knowingly, recklessly, and criminal negligence

If you're scoring below 85%, spend additional time reviewing before proceeding. These procedures form the foundation of everything you'll do as a peace officer. Getting them right is essential.

When you're confident in this material, you're ready to move to **Chapter 3: Patrol Procedures and Operations**, where you'll learn how to apply these legal principles in the field during routine patrol activities, traffic stops, and emergency response.

Study Reminder: The TCOLE exam tests not just your ability to recall facts, but your ability to apply principles to realistic situations. As you study Chapter 3, continue thinking about how criminal procedure rules apply to patrol operations. The connections between chapters strengthen your overall understanding and exam performance.

PART II: PATROL AND TRAFFIC OPERATIONS

CHAPTER 3: PATROL PROCEDURES AND OPERATIONS

Learning Objectives

By the end of this chapter, you will be able to: identify and apply effective patrol techniques; distinguish between proactive and reactive policing strategies; conduct safe traffic stops using proper procedures; recognize high-risk situations requiring specialized tactics; understand vehicle pursuit policies and termination criteria; apply officer safety principles and tactical awareness; implement community policing strategies; and properly prioritize and respond to calls for service.

Why This Chapter Matters: Patrol is the backbone of law enforcement. How you conduct patrol, interact with the community, and respond to calls determines your effectiveness and safety. This chapter translates legal authority into practical field operations. Poor patrol techniques endanger you and the public. Effective patrol prevents crime, builds community trust, and ensures your survival.

Patrol Techniques and Strategies

Proactive vs. Reactive Policing

Reactive Policing is responding to crimes after they occur. You receive a call, respond, investigate, and take action. This is necessary but limits crime prevention. You're always behind the curve, responding to problems rather than preventing them.

Proactive Policing involves actively working to prevent crime before it happens through: **Visible Presence** - marked patrol creates deterrent effect. Criminals avoid areas with heavy police presence. Your visibility alone prevents crimes. Park in high-crime areas, conduct foot patrols in business districts, and maintain visibility during peak crime hours. **Directed Patrol** - concentrating resources in high-crime areas during peak times based on crime analysis data. If burglaries occur between 2-4 PM in a specific neighborhood, patrol that area during those hours. **Field Interviews** - conducting consensual contacts with people in high-crime areas. Ask about their presence, activities, and gather intelligence. This isn't harassment; it's legitimate community engagement that yields valuable information. **Problem-Oriented Policing** - identifying underlying causes of recurring problems and developing solutions. If frequent calls involve juveniles loitering at a convenience store, work with the business to address the root cause rather than just responding to calls.

Effective Patrol Combines Both: You can't only be proactive—calls for service require reactive response. Balance proactive work during downtime with reactive response when needed. Between calls, conduct proactive patrol in high-crime areas. When calls come in, respond promptly and professionally.

Patrol Observation Skills

Effective patrol requires constant observation and awareness. Most officers drive through their beats seeing nothing. Skilled officers notice everything: **People** - who's where, doing what, at what time. Notice patterns. The same vehicle parked on different streets over several days may indicate surveillance for burglaries. Someone repeatedly looking into car windows may be a thief. People who avoid eye contact or suddenly change direction when they see you may warrant attention. **Vehicles** - suspicious vehicles include those driving slowly through neighborhoods, vehicles with occupants watching businesses, cars with mismatched or covered plates, vehicles heavily loaded and riding low (stolen property), and cars parked in unusual locations at odd hours. **Property** - look for open windows or doors in businesses after hours, property staged near buildings (preparation for theft), discarded items that might be evidence, graffiti (indicates gang activity), and damage to property suggesting recent crimes.

ALERT Framework for Patrol Observation: **A**ssess your surroundings constantly. **L**ook for anomalies—things that don't fit normal patterns. **E**valuate whether observations warrant further investigation. **R**espond appropriately based on your evaluation. **T**rack and document significant observations for future reference.

Beat Familiarity

Know your patrol area intimately: **Geography** - street layouts, dead ends, access points, escape routes criminals might use. **Businesses** - operating hours, owners, employees, normal activity patterns. Know when businesses should be closed, who typically parks where, and what vehicles belong. **Residents** - who lives where, their vehicles, normal routines. This helps identify when something's wrong. **Crime Patterns** - where crimes occur, when they occur, common methods used, likely suspects. **Problem Locations** - bars that generate fights, apartments with drug activity, intersections with frequent accidents, areas where juveniles congregate.

The better you know your beat, the more effective you are. You'll recognize when something's out of place, identify suspects more quickly, and prevent crimes through strategic positioning.

Patrol Patterns

Random Patrol involves unpredictable movement throughout your beat, preventing criminals from timing your patterns. Vary your routes, speeds, and times in different areas. **Zone Defense** means staying primarily in assigned area rather than crossing entire jurisdiction, ensuring all areas receive coverage while maintaining response time standards. **Split-Force Patrol** uses some units for call response while others conduct proactive patrol in high-crime areas, balancing reactive and proactive needs. **Foot Patrol** in business districts and apartment complexes allows closer community contact, better observation, and access to areas vehicles can't reach. While slower for response, foot patrol builds relationships and gathers intelligence vehicles miss.

Traffic Stop Procedures

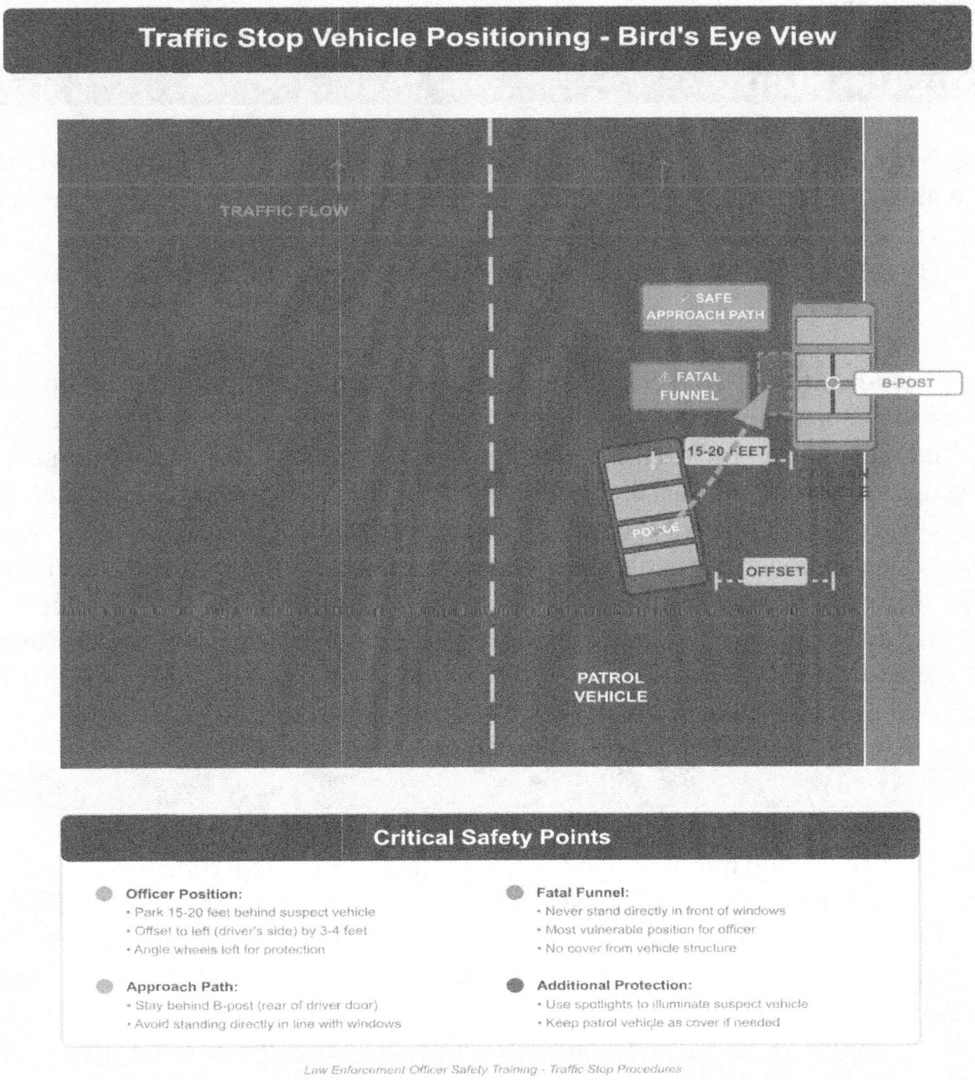

Traffic stops are among the most common and dangerous activities you'll perform. Proper procedures protect your safety and ensure legal compliance.

Pre-Stop Assessment

Before activating your lights: **Observe the Violation** - ensure you have legal basis for the stop. Document the specific violation (speeding, lane violation, equipment failure, etc.). **Assess Conditions** - traffic flow, weather, road conditions, lighting. Is this location safe for a stop? **Choose Stop Location** - look ahead for safe area with shoulder space, good lighting if possible, and low traffic. Sometimes follow the vehicle until reaching a better location. **Notify Dispatch** - provide location, vehicle description, license plate, and reason for stop before activating lights. This creates a record and ensures help knows your location if needed. **Observe Driver Behavior** - note any suspicious actions when you activate lights. Does the driver flee? Make furtive movements? Take excessive time to stop? These observations establish reasonable suspicion for further investigation.

Executing the Stop

Positioning Your Vehicle: Park offset to the left (driver's side) of the violator's vehicle, 15-20 feet back, at an angle. This provides cover from passing traffic, gives you observation angle into the stopped vehicle, and protects you if the vehicle is struck from behind. Turn your steering wheel left so if struck, your vehicle angles away from you rather than crushing you against the violator's car.

Approach Considerations: Driver's Side Approach (standard) provides direct contact with driver and most occupants visible. Approach from the rear of your vehicle to the rear of their vehicle, staying outside the traffic lane when possible. Keep the B-post (rear door post) between you and occupants as you approach. This limits their angle to attack you. Watch hands and observe occupants continuously. **Passenger Side Approach** (tactical) is used when traffic makes driver's side approach too dangerous, you suspect occupants may ambush on driver's side, or you want different tactical advantage. Cross behind both vehicles quickly, approach along passenger side, and maintain awareness of traffic danger. **Stay Behind the B-Post:** Position yourself at the rear door post, not directly at the driver's window. This limits the driver's ability to shoot you and provides better view of the entire vehicle interior.

Initial Contact

Contact the Driver: "Good morning, I'm Officer [Name] with [Department]. The reason for the stop is [specific violation]. I need to see your driver's license, registration, and proof of insurance." **Observe Continuously:** Watch the driver's hands at all times. Note passenger behavior, observe interior of vehicle (plain view contraband, weapons, furtive movements), smell for alcohol, marijuana, or other odors suggesting criminal activity, and listen to the driver's speech (slurred, confused, normal). **Request Documents Safely:** Have the driver place hands on steering wheel. Ask where their license and registration are located before allowing them to reach for them. Watch as they retrieve documents—ensure they're not reaching for weapons.

High-Risk vs. Low-Risk Stops

Low-Risk Stops are routine traffic violations with no indication of danger: single occupant or family, normal behavior during stop, no criminal history indicators, daylight hours in good visibility, and no contraband visible. Use standard procedures: one-officer approach, casual but professional demeanor, and routine document check.

High-Risk Stops involve known felons, stolen vehicles, armed suspects, or other serious threats: vehicle matching description in violent crime, occupants known to be armed and dangerous, driver/passengers displaying weapons, multiple occupants acting suspiciously, or vehicle fleeing before stopping. **High-Risk Stop Procedures:** Wait for backup before initiating stop when possible. Notify dispatch of high-risk nature. Use PA system for commands—don't approach vehicle. Order occupants out one at a time with hands visible. Maintain position behind cover (engine block, door). Have each occupant walk backward toward you. Handcuff and secure each person before ordering next person out. Clear vehicle only after all occupants are secured. Multiple officers provide cover throughout.

Never approach a high-risk vehicle alone. Your safety takes precedence over expediency. Wait for backup.

Officer Safety During Stops

The Fatal Funnel: The area directly in front of the stopped vehicle's windows is the "fatal funnel." Anyone inside has clear line of fire at you. Minimize time spent directly in front of windows. Approach from rear angles and position yourself at the B-post, not the driver's window. **Hands Kill:** Watch the driver's and all occupants' hands constantly. Hands kill you, not people. If you can see their hands, they can't harm you with them. If hands disappear from view, create distance and issue commands to show hands. **Tactical Positioning:** Stand slightly behind the driver so they must turn to see you. This gives you reaction time advantage and better view of the vehicle interior. Keep your weapon side away from the vehicle to prevent grabbing. **Background Awareness:** Maintain awareness of traffic passing behind you. Positions yourself so you can see approaching vehicles peripherally. Many officers are struck by passing vehicles during stops.

Post-Stop Actions

Return Documents: After completing citation or warning, return documents and explain the citation or warning clearly. Provide court information if issuing citation. Answer questions professionally. **Watch Them Leave:** Don't return to your vehicle until they've driven away safely. Maintain observation in case they make furtive movements, toss contraband, or commit additional violations. **Document the Stop:** Note date, time, location, reason for stop, observations, actions taken, and any relevant information for later reference. If the stop led to arrest or search, document thoroughly.

Vehicle Pursuits and Emergency Response

Pursuits are inherently dangerous. Many departments have restricted pursuit policies because risks often outweigh benefits. Understanding pursuit policies and making sound decisions protects everyone.

When to Initiate Pursuit

Permissible Reasons: Most policies authorize pursuit only for: violent felonies (murder, robbery, sexual assault, aggravated assault), felonies involving serious bodily injury or death, DWI where the driver poses immediate danger, or suspects known to be violent and dangerous. **Generally Prohibited:** Most policies prohibit pursuit for: misdemeanors, traffic violations, property crimes without violence, and non-violent felonies when suspect identity is known.

Decision Factors: Crime Severity - does the offense justify the risks of pursuit? Pursuing a shoplifter isn't worth potential crashes. **Public Safety Risk** - what's the danger of pursuit versus the danger of letting the suspect escape? Heavy traffic, pedestrians, school zones, and weather conditions increase risk. **Vehicle Conditions** - what's the condition of your vehicle and the suspect's vehicle? Don't pursue a sports car in your patrol car on winding mountain roads. **Officer Experience** - are you trained and experienced in pursuit driving? **Alternative Methods** - can you identify the suspect and apprehend later rather than pursuing now?

Pursuit Policies and Termination Criteria

Your Department Policy Controls: Know your department's pursuit policy intimately. Violating policy can result in discipline, civil liability, and criminal charges if someone is injured. Policies typically require: supervisor notification and authorization, continuous evaluation of risk versus benefit, and immediate termination when risks exceed benefits.

Mandatory Termination Conditions: Terminate immediately when: supervisor orders termination, road/weather conditions make pursuit too dangerous, traffic density creates substantial risk to public, you lose sight of suspect vehicle for extended period, suspect's identity is known and apprehension can occur later, or vehicle or equipment failure occurs.

Communications During Pursuit: Continuously broadcast: your location and direction, suspect vehicle description, traffic and road conditions, speeds, suspect actions (running lights, wrong way, etc.), and any factors suggesting termination is needed. **Role of Supervisor:** Supervisors monitor pursuit, order additional units or discontinue pursuit, coordinate with other agencies if pursuit leaves your jurisdiction, and arrange for spike strips or other intervention if appropriate. **Role of Other Units:** Only units authorized by supervisor should join pursuit. Other units stage ahead to take over if pursuit enters their area, block intersections to protect public, or deploy intervention devices. Excessive units increase danger without adding benefit.

Emergency Response Driving

When responding to emergencies with lights and sirens: **Proceed with Due Regard:** Emergency vehicles aren't exempt from obeying traffic laws—they must proceed with "due regard" for safety. You can exceed speed limits, proceed through red lights, and disregard certain traffic controls, but only when it's safe and you use appropriate warning devices. **Right of Way:** Emergency vehicles have right of way when using lights and sirens, but other drivers must yield—they don't always. Never assume vehicles will move. Slow at intersections even with green lights. **Intersection Clearing:** The most dangerous part of emergency response. Slow substantially at every intersection, ensure all lanes yield, and proceed carefully. Most emergency vehicle crashes occur at intersections. **Maintain Control:** Emergency driving requires smooth, controlled inputs. Jerky steering, abrupt braking, and excessive speed cause loss of control. Arrive safely even if slightly slower.

Officer Safety and Tactical Awareness

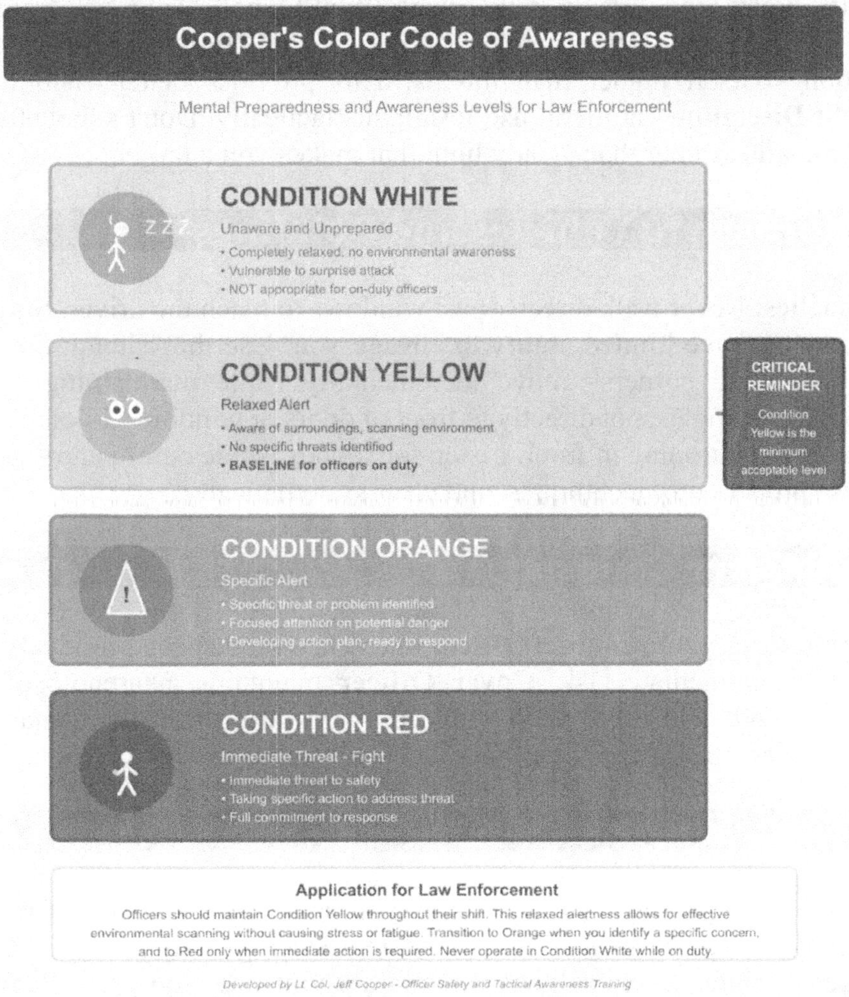

Survival isn't luck—it's mindset, training, and constant awareness. Officers die because they become complacent, fail to recognize threats, or position themselves poorly.

Threat Assessment and Positioning

Cooper's Color Code of Awareness: Condition White - unaware, relaxed, no vigilance. Never acceptable for officers on duty. **Condition Yellow** - relaxed alertness, aware of surroundings, scanning for threats. This is your baseline state on duty. **Condition Orange** - specific alert, potential threat identified, focused attention on threat. Enter this when you observe suspicious behavior or potentially dangerous situations. **Condition Red** - immediate threat, prepare to act. When someone presents weapon, attacks, or poses immediate danger.

Tactical Positioning Principles: Cover vs. Concealment - Cover stops bullets (engine blocks, concrete walls, heavy trees). Concealment hides you but doesn't stop bullets (car doors, wooden fences, bushes). Always seek cover, not just concealment. **Distance Creates Time** - maintain reactionary gap. You need distance to react to threats. At contact distance (arm's reach), you can't react to sudden attacks. Maintain at least 6-10 feet from suspects when possible. **Angles and Movement** - don't stand directly in doorways (fatal funnel). Approach from angles. Move after using cover—don't stay static where threats expect you. **High Ground Advantage** - when possible, position yourself higher than threats. This provides better visibility and tactical advantage. **Light Discipline** - at night, use flashlights tactically. Don't silhouette yourself. Use momentary illumination rather than steady light that makes you a target.

Tactical Approach to Vehicles and Buildings

Vehicle Approaches: Never walk directly past windows to reach the driver. Stay behind the B-post where occupants have limited ability to engage you. Use the "slicing the pie" technique when approaching blind corners—move incrementally while maintaining cover. **Building Entry:** Approach from angles, not directly in front of doors or windows. Look through windows from the side before positioning in front. Listen for sounds inside before entry. If making entry, have backup, use proper entry techniques, and clear systematically.

Contact and Cover Concept

When two officers are present: **Contact Officer** interacts with suspects, conducts investigations, and focuses on the immediate task. **Cover Officer** maintains awareness of surroundings, watches suspects' hands and other people, and provides protection for contact officer. Both officers don't interview the same person simultaneously—one covers while one contacts.

Common Tactical Errors

Fixation - focusing so intently on one thing you miss other threats. The person you're handcuffing might not be the threat—their friend approaching from behind is. **Complacency** - routine stops aren't routine. Every call has potential for violence. Stay alert. **Poor Positioning** -

standing in doorways, trapping yourself with no escape route, getting too close to suspects, exposing yourself needlessly. **Inadequate Use of Cover** - failing to use available cover or choosing concealment over cover. **Ignoring Hands** - if you can't see their hands, you're in danger. Never proceed when hands are hidden.

Community Policing Principles

Effective policing requires community support. You can't arrest your way out of crime problems. Building community trust makes your job easier and more effective.

Building Community Trust

Legitimacy Through Action: Communities support police they view as legitimate—fair, respectful, and trustworthy. You build legitimacy through: **Procedural Justice** - treating people fairly in interactions, giving them voice and opportunity to explain, showing respect regardless of circumstance, and making neutral, unbiased decisions. **Fair and Impartial Policing** - enforcing laws consistently without bias, treating all community members respectfully, and avoiding assumptions based on race, ethnicity, or appearance. **Transparency** - explaining your actions, being honest about mistakes, and maintaining accountability.

Every Interaction Matters: Every contact with community members builds or destroys trust. Traffic stops, street contacts, investigation interviews—all shape public perception. Treat everyone with respect and professionalism. Explain your actions when appropriate. Listen to community concerns. Rudeness, disrespect, or bias in one interaction affects the entire department's relationship with the community.

Community Engagement

Proactive Contact: Don't only interact with community members during enforcement. Attend community meetings, visit schools and talk with students, stop and talk with residents during patrol (consensual, friendly conversations), participate in community events, and work with neighborhood associations. **Problem-Solving Partnerships:** Identify persistent problems and work with community members to solve them. If a park has drug activity, work with neighbors to increase lighting, schedule regular patrol presence, and connect users with treatment resources. **Information Sharing:** Communities have information you need. Build relationships so people trust you enough to share intelligence. If residents see you as adversarial, they won't call with tips. If they trust you, they become your eyes and ears.

Calls for Service Management

Priority Assessment and Response

Priority Classification Systems: Priority 1 - immediate life-threatening emergencies requiring emergency response: in-progress violent crimes, officer needs assistance, person with weapon, serious injury accidents, armed robberies in progress. **Priority 2** - serious but not immediately life-threatening: injury accidents without serious injury, disturbances without weapons, thefts in progress, suspicious persons with weapons reported. **Priority 3** - routine calls requiring response but not urgent: cold thefts, minor traffic accidents, disturbances resolved, vandalism reports, routine follow-ups. **Priority 4** - administrative or delayed response appropriate: report pick-ups, informational calls, non-emergency assistance requests.

Response Procedures: For Priority 1 calls: respond immediately with lights/sirens, notify dispatch you're responding, request additional units if needed, and prepare mentally for potential conflict. For Priority 2-3 calls: respond promptly without emergency equipment unless situation escalates, gather information from dispatch en route, and assess whether immediate or delayed response is more appropriate. For Priority 4 calls: handle when time permits between higher priorities, consider telephone report options, or schedule appointment with complainant.

Information Gathering En Route

While responding, obtain as much information as possible from dispatch: exact location, nature of call, description of suspects/vehicles, weapons information, complainant information, prior history at location, and ongoing updates if available. This information helps you prepare and position yourself tactically upon arrival.

Arrival Procedures

Approach Safely: Don't park directly in front of the location—park short or past to maintain cover and observation angles. Observe before exiting—look for suspects leaving, weapons visible, or other threats. Note vehicles present and people in the area. **Coordinate with Backup:** If waiting for backup on high-risk calls, stage out of sight until backup arrives, then coordinate approach and assignments.

Real-World Application: Patrol Scenarios

Scenario 1: Suspicious Vehicle

Situation: During routine patrol at 3:00 AM, you observe a vehicle slowly driving through a residential neighborhood with lights off. The vehicle stops in front of a house, a person exits and walks to the side of the house, then returns quickly to the vehicle. The vehicle drives away slowly, still without lights.

Questions: Do you have reasonable suspicion for a stop? What's your approach? What might this indicate?

Analysis: You have reasonable suspicion based on: late hour in residential area, driving without headlights (traffic violation), behavior consistent with burglary (checking house, quick return to vehicle), and totality suggesting criminal activity.

Proper Actions: Notify dispatch of location, vehicle description, and your observations. Initiate traffic stop for no headlights violation. Request backup given suspicious circumstances. Conduct high-awareness approach—this could be burglars or scouts. Upon contact, observe for burglary tools, stolen property, or other contraband in plain view. Ask questions about their presence in the area. Check for outstanding warrants. If probable cause develops for burglary, arrest and search. If only the traffic violation, issue citation but document observations in case burglaries are reported in that area later.

Scenario 2: Domestic Disturbance Call

Situation: Dispatched to domestic disturbance, neighbors reporting yelling and sounds of items breaking. En route, dispatch updates that a female caller states her boyfriend is "destroying the apartment" and "threatening her." Dispatch doesn't know if weapons are involved.

Analysis: This is Priority 1—domestic violence with threats.

Proper Actions: Request backup immediately, respond code if backup isn't immediately available, gather all available information from dispatch en route, and stage near location if backup isn't on scene yet—don't make entry alone. Upon arrival with backup: park away from the door, approach from angles (don't stand in front of door), listen at door for sounds of ongoing violence, knock and announce loudly, separate parties immediately upon entry, assess for injuries and threats, determine primary aggressor, make arrest based on probable cause for assault/family violence, provide victim with resources and protective order information, document thoroughly with photos of injuries and property damage, and request emergency protective order.

Practice Questions (55 questions)

Question 1: Proactive policing is best defined as: A) Responding to calls after crimes occur B) Working to prevent crime before it happens through visible presence and directed patrol C) Only investigating serious felonies D) Waiting for community complaints

Answer: B **Explanation:** Proactive policing actively prevents crime through visible patrol, directed presence in high-crime areas, field interviews, and problem-solving rather than merely responding after crimes occur.

Question 2: During a traffic stop, an officer should position their patrol vehicle: A) Directly behind the stopped vehicle B) Offset to the left, 15-20 feet back, at an angle C) In front of the stopped vehicle D) Parallel to the stopped vehicle

Answer: B **Explanation:** Offset positioning protects from passing traffic, provides cover, gives observation angle into the vehicle, and prevents crushing if your vehicle is struck from behind.

Question 3: The "B-post" positioning during traffic stops refers to: A) Standing at the driver's window B) Standing at the rear door post between you and occupants C) Positioning at the front of the vehicle D) Standing at the passenger side

Answer: B **Explanation:** The B-post (rear door post) position limits occupants' angle to attack you, provides better view of the interior, and offers tactical advantage over standing directly at the driver's window.

Question 4: High-risk traffic stops should: A) Be handled by a single officer to avoid confusion B) Involve backup, use of PA system for commands, and not approaching the vehicle C) Be conducted the same as routine stops D) Never be attempted

Answer: B **Explanation:** High-risk stops require backup, commands via PA system to maintain distance and cover, ordering occupants out one at a time, and never approaching the vehicle until all occupants are secured.

Question 5: Vehicle pursuits should generally be initiated for: A) Any traffic violation B) All felonies regardless of circumstances C) Violent felonies or when the suspect poses serious danger to public D) Misdemeanors if the suspect flees

Answer: C **Explanation:** Most pursuit policies limit pursuits to violent felonies or situations where the danger of allowing escape exceeds the risks of pursuit. Property crimes and misdemeanors typically don't justify pursuit risks.

Question 6: Mandatory pursuit termination is required when: A) The suspect speeds up B) Supervisor orders termination or risks exceed benefits C) Another officer wants to take over D) The pursuit lasts more than 5 minutes

Answer: B **Explanation:** Pursuits must be terminated when supervisors order it, road/weather conditions create excessive danger, risks exceed benefits of apprehension, or other specified policy conditions exist.

Question 7: Cooper's Color Code "Condition Yellow" means: A) Unaware and relaxed B) Relaxed alertness with awareness of surroundings—the baseline state for officers on duty C) Specific threat identified D) Immediate danger present

Answer: B **Explanation:** Condition Yellow is relaxed alertness where you're aware of surroundings and scanning for threats. This should be every officer's baseline state while on duty.

Question 8: The difference between cover and concealment is: A) There is no difference B) Cover stops bullets; concealment only hides you C) Concealment stops bullets; cover only hides you D) Both provide equal protection

Answer: B **Explanation:** Cover (engine blocks, concrete, heavy barriers) stops bullets. Concealment (car doors, bushes, wooden fences) hides you but doesn't stop bullets. Always seek cover over concealment.

Question 9: The "contact and cover" concept means: A) Both officers interview the same person B) One officer makes contact while the other maintains awareness and provides security C) Officers take turns talking D) One officer stays in the patrol car

Answer: B **Explanation:** The contact officer interacts with suspects while the cover officer maintains situational awareness, watches hands and surroundings, and provides protection. This division of duties enhances safety.

Question 10: Community policing emphasizes: A) Aggressive enforcement only B) Building partnerships with community to identify and solve problems collaboratively C) Avoiding contact with community members D) Only responding to calls for service

Answer: B **Explanation:** Community policing builds partnerships with community members to identify problems, develop solutions collaboratively, and address underlying causes of crime rather than just responding to incidents.

Question 11: Procedural justice in policing includes: A) Treating people unfairly based on assumptions B) Treating people fairly, giving them voice, showing respect, and making neutral decisions C) Only being polite to people who cooperate D) Avoiding explanations of police actions

Answer: B **Explanation:** Procedural justice requires treating people fairly, giving them opportunity to explain, showing respect regardless of circumstances, and making neutral, unbiased decisions. This builds legitimacy and community trust.

Question 12: Priority 1 calls include: A) Cold theft reports B) In-progress violent crimes, officer needs assistance, and immediate life-threatening emergencies C) Routine traffic stops D) Administrative tasks

Answer: B **Explanation:** Priority 1 calls are immediate life-threatening emergencies requiring emergency response: in-progress violent crimes, officer assistance calls, armed persons, and serious injury accidents.

Question 13: When approaching a suspicious vehicle during a traffic stop, officers should: A) Walk directly to the driver's window B) Watch hands continuously and stay outside the "fatal funnel" C) Ignore the passengers D) Stand directly in front of the window

Answer: B **Explanation:** Always watch hands (hands kill), stay outside the fatal funnel (area directly in front of windows), and maintain tactical positioning that gives you reaction time advantage.

Question 14: Beat familiarity helps officers: A) Take longer routes B) Recognize when something is out of place and identify suspicious activity quickly C) Avoid certain areas D) Spend less time patrolling

Answer: B **Explanation:** Knowing your beat's geography, residents, businesses, and normal patterns allows you to quickly recognize anomalies and suspicious activity, making your patrol more effective.

Question 15: Emergency response driving with lights and sirens requires: A) Ignoring all traffic laws B) Proceeding with due regard for safety—slowing at intersections and ensuring clear right of way C) Driving as fast as possible D) Assuming all vehicles will yield

Answer: B **Explanation:** Emergency vehicles must proceed with "due regard" for safety. While you can exceed limits and proceed through red lights, you must slow at intersections, ensure vehicles yield, and maintain control.

Question 16: The "fatal funnel" refers to: A) A tornado warning B) The area directly in front of windows where occupants have clear line of fire C) A pursuit maneuver D) A type of traffic pattern

Answer: B **Explanation:** The fatal funnel is the area directly in front of vehicle or building windows where anyone inside has clear line of fire at you. Minimize time spent in this exposed area.

Question 17: Reactive policing is characterized by: A) Preventing crimes before they occur B) Responding to crimes after they've been committed C) Community engagement D) Directed patrol

Answer: B **Explanation:** Reactive policing responds to crimes after they occur—answering calls, investigating completed crimes, and taking enforcement action. While necessary, it's less effective than proactive prevention.

Question 18: During vehicle pursuits, the pursuing officer must continuously communicate: A) Nothing—radio silence is best B) Location, direction, speeds, traffic conditions, and factors affecting safety C) Only their location D) Personal opinions about the suspect

Answer: B **Explanation:** Continuous communication about location, direction, speeds, traffic/road conditions, and risk factors allows supervisors to evaluate the pursuit and make termination decisions.

Question 19: Random patrol patterns help: A) Waste gas B) Prevent criminals from timing your presence and planning crimes around your routine C) Confuse dispatchers D) Make response times longer

Answer: B **Explanation:** Varying your routes, times, and patterns prevents criminals from predicting your location and timing crimes for when you're absent from areas.

Question 20: The primary purpose of field interviews is to: A) Harass citizens B) Gather intelligence, deter crime through presence, and identify suspicious activity C) Meet quotas D) Generate revenue

Answer: B **Explanation:** Field interviews (consensual contacts) gather intelligence about area activity, deter crime through police presence, and help identify suspicious persons or activity before crimes occur.

Question 21: Foot patrol is valuable because: A) It's faster than vehicle patrol B) It builds community relationships, allows closer observation, and accesses areas vehicles cannot C) It requires less training D) It eliminates need for vehicles

Answer: B **Explanation:** Foot patrol enables closer community contact, better observation of details vehicles miss, access to areas vehicles can't reach, and relationship-building that generates intelligence and trust.

Question 22: When executing a traffic stop at night, officers should: A) Use spotlight to illuminate vehicle interior before approaching B) Turn off all lights for surprise C) Immediately approach in darkness D) Wait for daylight

Answer: A **Explanation:** Use your spotlight and takedown lights to illuminate the vehicle interior, allowing you to observe occupants' actions and identify threats before approaching.

Question 23: The reactionary gap refers to: A) Time between crimes B) Distance needed to react to sudden threats—maintain at least 6-10 feet from suspects C) Space between patrol vehicles D) Gap in your schedule

Answer: B **Explanation:** The reactionary gap is the distance you need to react to threats. At contact distance (arm's reach), you can't react to attacks. Maintain 6-10 feet when possible.

Question 24: Problem-oriented policing involves: A) Only making arrests B) Identifying underlying causes of recurring problems and developing long-term solutions C) Ignoring minor issues D) Transferring problems to other shifts

Answer: B **Explanation:** Problem-oriented policing identifies root causes of recurring issues and develops solutions addressing those causes rather than just repeatedly responding to symptoms.

Question 25: After completing a traffic stop, officers should: A) Immediately return to patrol B) Watch the vehicle leave and document the stop in case later issues arise C) Ignore the vehicle once documents are returned D) Follow the vehicle to ensure compliance

Answer: B **Explanation:** Watch the vehicle leave to observe any furtive movements, contraband disposal, or additional violations. Document the stop for future reference, especially if it led to warnings or observations requiring follow-up.

Question 26: Tactical approach to buildings requires: A) Walking directly to the front door B) Approaching from angles, using cover, and listening before entry C) Running to the door for speed D) Announcing your presence from the street

Answer: B **Explanation:** Approach from angles (not directly in front of doors/windows), use available cover, look and listen before positioning in exposed areas, and plan your entry tactically.

Question 27: Directed patrol means: A) Random driving B) Concentrating resources in high-crime areas during peak times based on data analysis C) Following specific routes only D) Avoiding certain neighborhoods

Answer: B **Explanation:** Directed patrol uses crime analysis data to deploy resources where and when crimes are most likely, focusing prevention efforts on high-probability targets rather than random patrol.

Question 28: When multiple officers respond to a call, the contact and cover roles mean: A) All officers interview simultaneously B) One officer makes contact while another maintains awareness of surroundings and threats C) Officers take turns every few minutes D) The senior officer always makes contact

Answer: B **Explanation:** Contact officer focuses on the interaction while cover officer maintains situational awareness, watches hands, monitors other people, and provides security. This division enhances safety and effectiveness.

Question 29: Procedural justice builds community trust through: A) Aggressive enforcement only B) Fair treatment, respectful interactions, giving voice to citizens, and neutral decision-making C) Avoiding enforcement in certain communities D) Only helping people who request it

Answer: B **Explanation:** Procedural justice emphasizes treating people fairly, showing respect regardless of outcome, giving them opportunity to be heard, and making decisions based on facts rather than bias. This builds perceived legitimacy.

Question 30: The primary danger during emergency response driving occurs: A) On straightaways B) At intersections where other vehicles may not yield C) In parking lots D) During acceleration

Answer: B **Explanation:** Most emergency vehicle crashes occur at intersections. Other drivers may not hear sirens, may panic, or may not see you. Always slow substantially at intersections and ensure all lanes yield.

Question 31: During a traffic stop, if you observe the driver making furtive movements toward the console: A) Ignore it and continue with routine procedures B) Note it as creating reasonable suspicion warranting heightened awareness and possible further investigation C) Immediately draw your weapon D) Return to your vehicle and wait

Answer: B **Explanation:** Furtive movements create reasonable suspicion warranting heightened awareness. Approach cautiously, watch hands continuously, and be prepared for threats. This doesn't automatically justify search but does heighten your alertness.

Question 32: Beat familiarization includes knowing: A) Only major streets B) Street layouts, businesses, residents, crime patterns, and problem locations C) Where to get coffee D) Only high-crime areas

Answer: B **Explanation:** Thorough beat knowledge includes geography (streets, access points, escape routes), businesses and their hours, residents and their routines, crime patterns and hot spots, and problem locations requiring attention.

Question 33: When should you terminate a vehicle pursuit? A) Never—always continue until capture B) When supervisor orders termination or risks exceed benefits of apprehension C) Only if you run out of gas D) After exactly 5 minutes

Answer: B **Explanation:** Terminate when ordered by supervisors, when road/weather/traffic conditions create excessive danger, when risks exceed benefits, when you lose sight for extended periods, or when suspect identity is known for later apprehension.

Question 34: The purpose of using a spotlight during nighttime traffic stops is to: A) Blind the driver B) Illuminate the vehicle interior to observe occupants and identify threats before approach C) Annoy the driver D) Signal other units

Answer: B **Explanation:** Spotlights and takedown lights illuminate vehicle interior, allowing you to observe occupant actions, count occupants, see hands, and identify weapons or contraband before you're in danger zone.

Question 35: Community policing differs from traditional policing by: A) Not enforcing laws B) Building partnerships with community to collaboratively identify and solve problems C) Only responding to calls D) Avoiding community contact

Answer: B **Explanation:** Community policing emphasizes partnerships with community members to identify underlying problems, develop collaborative solutions, and address root causes rather than just responding to symptoms through enforcement.

Question 36: Priority 2 calls typically include: A) In-progress violent crimes B) Serious but not immediately life-threatening situations like injury accidents and disturbances without weapons C) Administrative tasks D) Officer needs assistance

Answer: B **Explanation:** Priority 2 calls are serious but not immediately life-threatening: injury accidents without serious injury, disturbances without weapons, thefts in progress, or suspicious persons where weapons were reported but aren't currently visible.

Question 37: The "slicing the pie" technique refers to: A) Dividing patrol areas B) Moving incrementally around corners while maintaining cover to gradually clear blind spots C) Sharing overtime hours D) A pursuit maneuver

Answer: B **Explanation:** "Slicing the pie" means moving incrementally around corners or obstacles while maintaining maximum cover, gradually exposing small areas to observation rather than rushing into unknown spaces.

Question 38: Fixation during tactical situations means: A) Properly focusing on threats B) Concentrating so intently on one thing you miss other threats or important information C) Maintaining eye contact D) Staring at suspects

Answer: B **Explanation:** Fixation—focusing so intently on one element (person you're handcuffing, door you're watching) that you miss other threats—is a dangerous tactical error. Maintain broad awareness.

Question 39: When responding to calls for service, officers should gather what information en route? A) Nothing—wait until arrival B) Exact location, nature of call, suspect descriptions, weapons information, and prior history at location C) Only the address D) Just the type of call

Answer: B **Explanation:** Gather maximum information from dispatch: precise location, call nature, suspect/vehicle descriptions, weapons reported, complainant info, prior calls to that location, and ongoing updates. This prepares you tactically.

Question 40: Passenger-side approach during traffic stops is appropriate when: A) You want to confuse the driver B) Traffic makes driver-side approach too dangerous or tactical considerations warrant different approach C) You're lazy D) It's always preferred

Answer: B **Explanation:** Passenger-side approach is used when heavy traffic makes driver-side approach dangerous, you suspect driver-side ambush, or tactical considerations favor different angle. Cross behind both vehicles quickly and maintain traffic awareness.

Question 41: Proactive contacts with community members should: A) Only occur during enforcement B) Include attending meetings, visiting schools, and casual conversations during patrol to build relationships C) Be avoided to maintain authority D) Only happen if citizens request it

Answer: B **Explanation:** Proactive community engagement includes attending meetings, visiting schools, casual conversations during patrol, participating in events, and regular positive contact that builds relationships and trust beyond enforcement.

Question 42: The most important factor to watch during any citizen contact is: A) The person's clothing B) The person's hands—hands kill, not people C) Their facial expressions D) Their vehicle

Answer: B **Explanation:** Always watch hands. Hands kill you, not people. If you can see their hands, they can't harm you with them. If hands disappear, create distance and command them to show hands immediately.

Question 43: Random patrol helps prevent crime by: A) Wasting fuel B) Making your presence unpredictable so criminals can't time their activities around your patterns C) Confusing supervisors D) Avoiding high-crime areas

Answer: B **Explanation:** Varying routes, times, and patterns prevents criminals from predicting when you'll be absent from specific areas. Predictable patterns allow criminals to time their activities around your routine.

Question 44: During building approaches, officers should avoid: A) Using cover B) Standing directly in doorways or in front of windows (the fatal funnel) C) Looking before entering D) Waiting for backup when needed

Answer: B **Explanation:** Never stand directly in doorways or in front of windows where people inside have clear line of fire. Approach from angles, use cover, and minimize exposure in fatal funnels.

Question 45: Fair and impartial policing requires: A) Treating wealthy people better B) Enforcing laws consistently without bias based on race, ethnicity, or appearance C) Only enforcing certain laws D) Making assumptions about people

Answer: B **Explanation:** Fair and impartial policing means enforcing laws consistently, treating all community members respectfully regardless of demographics, avoiding bias-based decisions, and basing actions on behavior and evidence rather than stereotypes.

Question 46: Cooper's Condition Red indicates: A) Time to go home B) Immediate threat present requiring action C) Everything is normal D) Lunch break

Answer: B **Explanation:** Condition Red means immediate threat exists—someone presents a weapon, attacks, or poses immediate danger. You must be prepared to act decisively to protect yourself or others.

Question 47: Problem-oriented policing addresses: A) Only immediate crimes B) Underlying causes of recurring problems through analysis and collaborative solutions C) Individual incidents only D) Administrative issues

Answer: B **Explanation:** Problem-oriented policing analyzes recurring issues to identify root causes, then develops solutions addressing those causes through community partnerships rather than just responding to incidents repeatedly.

Question 48: When arriving at a call for service, officers should: A) Park directly in front and rush to the door B) Park tactically away from the location, observe before exiting, and assess for threats C) Block the street D) Announce arrival by honking

Answer: B **Explanation:** Park offset from the location (maintaining cover and observation angles), observe before exiting (look for suspects leaving, weapons visible, or threats), assess the scene, and approach tactically.

Question 49: High-risk stop procedures include: A) Approaching the vehicle alone B) Using PA system for commands, waiting for backup, not approaching until occupants are secured C) Standing in front of the vehicle D) Rushing the approach

Answer: B **Explanation:** High-risk stops require backup, PA commands to maintain distance, ordering occupants out one at a time with hands visible, maintaining cover positions, and not approaching the vehicle until all occupants are secured.

Question 50: Distance creates reaction time because: A) It makes you run faster B) Greater distance gives you more time to recognize and react to threats C) Suspects can't see you from far away D) It looks more professional

Answer: B **Explanation:** Distance equals time. The reactionary gap (6-10 feet minimum) gives you time to recognize threats and respond. At contact distance (arm's reach), you can't react to sudden attacks.

Question 51: Traffic stops are dangerous because: A) They're routine and boring B) They involve unknown occupants, potential weapons, unpredictable behavior, and exposure to traffic C) They take too long D) Violators are always cooperative

Answer: B **Explanation:** Traffic stops are inherently dangerous due to unknown occupants who may be armed or wanted, unpredictable behavior, potential for ambush, and exposure to passing traffic. Never treat them as routine.

Question 52: Foot patrol benefits include: A) Faster response times B) Closer community contact, better observation of details, and access to areas vehicles cannot reach C) Less physical exertion D) No citizen contact required

Answer: B **Explanation:** Foot patrol enables intimate community contact building trust, detailed observation vehicles miss, access to walkways and alleys vehicles can't reach, and intelligence gathering through conversations.

Question 53: When backup is en route to a high-risk call, you should: A) Enter immediately alone B) Stage out of sight until backup arrives, then coordinate approach C) Cancel backup and handle it yourself D) Leave the area

Answer: B **Explanation:** For high-risk calls requiring backup, stage nearby but out of sight until backup arrives, then coordinate approach, assignments, and tactics before making entry. Don't compromise safety by acting alone.

Question 54: The primary purpose of communication during pursuits is to: A) Entertain other units B) Allow supervisors to monitor pursuit and make termination decisions based on risk factors C) Prove you're working D) Fill radio time

Answer: B **Explanation:** Continuous communication about location, speeds, traffic conditions, and risk factors allows supervisors to evaluate whether risks exceed benefits and make informed decisions about continuation or termination.

Question 55: Every interaction with community members is important because: A) It wastes time B) Each contact builds or destroys trust affecting the entire department's community relationship C) Supervisors are always watching D) You might get complaints

Answer: B **Explanation:** Every interaction—traffic stops, street contacts, investigations—shapes community perception of police legitimacy and trustworthiness. One disrespectful interaction can damage relationships that took years to build. Treat everyone with respect and professionalism.

Scoring Your Practice Questions

52-55 correct (95-100%): Outstanding! Your grasp of patrol procedures, officer safety, and community policing principles is excellent. You understand both the tactical and community relations aspects of patrol work. Review any missed questions, then advance to Chapter 4 with confidence.

47-51 correct (85-94%): Excellent work! You have strong understanding of patrol operations. Focus on areas where you missed questions—whether traffic stops, tactical positioning, or community engagement. Review those sections and retake missed questions before proceeding.

41-46 correct (75-84%): Good progress! You understand core patrol concepts but need to strengthen specific areas. Identify patterns in missed questions (Are they mostly about traffic stops? Officer safety? Community policing?). Review those sections thoroughly and work through scenarios again.

35-40 correct (65-74%): You're developing understanding but have significant gaps. Review Chapter 3 systematically, focusing on topics where you missed multiple questions. Work through the scenarios carefully, thinking about how procedures protect both officers and citizens. Create summary notes for key concepts.

Below 35 correct (less than 65%): You need substantial additional study. Patrol procedures form the foundation of daily law enforcement work. Review Chapter 3 section by section, taking detailed notes on traffic stop procedures, officer safety principles, and community policing. Consider creating flashcards for key procedures and practicing scenario analysis with a study partner.

Chapter 3 Summary: Key Takeaways

Patrol Effectiveness requires: Combining proactive (prevention-focused) and reactive (response-focused) approaches. Know your beat intimately—geography, residents, businesses, crime patterns. Maintain constant awareness and observation skills. Vary patrol patterns to remain unpredictable.

Traffic Stop Safety depends on: Proper vehicle positioning (offset left, 15-20 feet back, angled). Tactical approach staying outside fatal funnel. B-post positioning for contact. Continuous observation of hands and occupants. Recognizing and appropriately handling high-risk situations. Never treating stops as routine—every stop has potential for danger.

Officer Safety principles include: Maintaining appropriate awareness level (Condition Yellow baseline). Understanding difference between cover (stops bullets) and concealment (hides only). Maintaining reactionary gap distance from suspects. Using contact and cover with multiple officers. Watching hands constantly—hands kill, not people. Avoiding tactical errors like fixation, complacency, and poor positioning.

Vehicle Pursuits require: Understanding when pursuit is justified (violent felonies, serious danger). Continuously evaluating risks versus benefits. Following department policy religiously. Terminating when ordered or risks exceed benefits. Maintaining communication throughout. Recognizing that preservation of life outweighs property crime apprehension.

Community Policing emphasizes: Building partnerships and trust through procedural justice. Fair, respectful treatment of all community members. Proactive engagement beyond enforcement contacts. Collaborative problem-solving addressing root causes. Recognizing that community support makes enforcement more effective.

Emergency Response demands: Proceeding with due regard for safety despite exemptions. Slowing substantially at intersections—most crashes occur there. Ensuring vehicles yield before proceeding. Maintaining control despite urgency. Recognizing that arriving safely is more important than arriving quickly.

These principles aren't just exam topics—they're survival skills and professional standards. Master them now, practice them throughout your career, and you'll be an effective, respected officer who goes home safely every shift.

CHAPTER 4: TRAFFIC LAW AND ENFORCEMENT

Learning Objectives

By the end of this chapter, you will: identify common Texas traffic violations and their classifications; understand the point system for driver's license suspensions; demonstrate proper DWI detection techniques including standardized field sobriety tests; apply implied consent laws correctly; manage and investigate traffic accidents; direct traffic during emergencies; enforce commercial vehicle regulations; and prepare proper citations and court documentation.

Why This Chapter Matters: Traffic enforcement is your most frequent law enforcement activity. You'll conduct thousands of traffic stops in your career. Each stop has potential for discovering serious crimes—outstanding warrants, DWI, drugs, weapons, or stolen vehicles. Proper traffic enforcement prevents accidents, saves lives, and disrupts criminal activity. Understanding traffic law and enforcement procedures keeps you safe, ensures legal compliance, and makes you an effective officer.

Texas Traffic Laws and Violations

Common Violations and Point Systems

Moving Violations are infractions occurring while the vehicle is in motion. These violations add points to the driver's license and can result in suspension if too many points accumulate.

Speeding (Transportation Code §545.352): Operating a vehicle at a speed greater than reasonable and prudent under circumstances or exceeding posted limits. **Penalties:** Class C misdemeanor, fine up to $200 (can increase in construction zones or school zones when workers/children present). **Points:** 2 points for typical speeding violation. **Speed Limits:** 30 mph in urban districts unless posted otherwise; 70 mph on numbered highways outside urban districts; 60 mph on most other roads outside urban; school zones typically 20 mph when children present; posted limits in construction zones with doubled fines when workers present.

Failure to Control Speed (§545.351): Driving at a speed endangering others considering traffic, weather, and road conditions. This violation applies even if the driver is below the posted limit when conditions require slower speed. **Example:** Driving 50 mph on icy roads where posted limit is 65 mph. **Points:** 2 points.

Running Red Light/Stop Sign (§544.007-§544.010): Failing to stop at red traffic signal or stop sign before entering intersection or crosswalk. Vehicle must come to complete stop—"rolling stops" are violations. **Points:** 3 points. This is a significant violation often contributing to serious accidents.

Improper Lane Change (§545.060): Changing lanes when movement cannot be made safely or failing to signal. Drivers must drive as nearly as practical within a single lane and signal before lane changes. **Points:** 2 points. Common cause of side-swipe collisions.

Following Too Closely (§545.062): Following another vehicle more closely than reasonable and prudent considering speed, traffic, and road conditions. No specific distance is defined—it's based on circumstances. **Points:** 2 points.

Failure to Yield Right of Way (§545.151-156): Various sections address yielding at stop signs, yield signs, when turning left, to emergency vehicles, and to pedestrians in crosswalks. **Points:** 3 points. Often contributes to intersection collisions.

Texting While Driving (§545.4251): Using portable wireless device to read, write, or send electronic messages while operating motor vehicle unless vehicle is stopped. **Exceptions:** GPS/navigation use, reporting illegal activity or emergencies, using hands-free devices, licensed drivers operating commercial vehicles reading electronic data. **Penalties:** Class C misdemeanor; $25-$99 first offense, $100-$200 subsequent offenses. If violation causes death or serious bodily injury, penalties increase substantially. **Points:** No points assessed but violation remains on record.

Open Container (Penal Code §49.031): Knowingly possessing open container of alcohol in passenger area of motor vehicle on public highway. **Exceptions:** Passengers in buses, taxis, limousines, or containers in locked glove compartment or trunk. **Penalties:** Class C misdemeanor, fine up to $500. **Points:** No points but creates probable cause for DWI investigation.

No Driver's License (§521.021): Operating vehicle without valid license. Distinguish between not having license with you (Class C misdemeanor, dismissible with proof of valid license) and not having valid license at all (Class C misdemeanor first offense, Class B subsequent offenses). **Points:** Varies based on circumstances.

Driving While License Invalid (DWLI) (§521.457): Operating vehicle while license is suspended, revoked, or denied. **Classifications:** Class C misdemeanor first offense ($100-$500 fine); Class B misdemeanor subsequent offenses (up to 180 days jail, up to $2,000 fine); Class B if invalid due to DWI conviction. **Points:** No points but license suspension extends.

Failure to Maintain Financial Responsibility (§601.191): Operating vehicle without required liability insurance. **Penalties:** Class C misdemeanor first offense ($175-$350 plus surcharges), Class B subsequent offenses ($350-$1,000). License suspension and vehicle impoundment possible. **Proof of Insurance:** Valid insurance card, electronic display on phone, or verbal verification from insurance company. If driver cannot provide proof, issue citation even if they claim to have insurance—they can show proof to court later for dismissal if actually insured.

Equipment Violations include defective lights (headlights, brake lights, turn signals), defective brakes, expired inspection sticker, expired registration, excessive window tint, modified exhaust systems, and unsafe loads. Most equipment violations are Class C misdemeanors punishable by fine only. Many can be dismissed if corrected and proof provided to court.

Driver's License Point System

Texas uses a point system where convictions for moving violations add points to the driver's record. Accumulating too many points results in license suspension.

Point Values: Most moving violations: 2 points. Serious violations (running red lights, passing school bus, etc.): 3 points. Points remain on record for 3 years from conviction date.

Suspension Thresholds: 4 points in 12 months: Warning letter and possible surcharges. 6 points in 3 years: License suspension. 7 points in 3 years: License suspension (if at least two violations in 12 months). Points for violations committed as minors carry same values but more severe consequences including license suspension at lower thresholds.

Driver Responsibility Program Surcharges: Certain serious violations trigger annual surcharges in addition to fines: DWI conviction: $1,000-$2,000 annually for 3 years. Driving without insurance: $250 annually for 3 years. Accumulating 6 points: $100 annually plus $25 per point above 6. Failure to pay surcharges results in license suspension until paid.

DWI/DUI Detection and Enforcement

Recognizing Impaired Drivers

Pre-Stop Indicators: NHTSA research identifies driving behaviors correlating with impairment. **Weaving/Swerving (70% correlation):** Weaving within lane, swerving, drifting, or crossing lane lines. **Speed Problems (60-70%):** Driving 10+ mph below limit without reason, stopping without cause, varying speed, accelerating/decelerating for no reason. **Vigilance Problems (60-65%):** Driving in wrong lane or wrong way, slow response to signals, stopping inappropriately. **Judgment Problems (50-55%):** Following too closely, improper turns, driving without lights at night, illegal or unsafe lane changes.

Initial Contact Observations: Odor: Alcohol odor (faint, moderate, strong) or marijuana. Note: Odor of alcohol alone doesn't prove intoxication but supports investigation. **Eyes:** Bloodshot, watery, glassy, difficulty focusing. **Face:** Flushed or pale. **Speech:** Slurred, slow, confused, repetitive. **Motor Skills:** Fumbling with documents, dropping items, difficulty following instructions. **Attitude:** Overly friendly, combative, confused, or inappropriately relaxed about being stopped.

Standardized Field Sobriety Tests

NHTSA recognizes three validated tests: Horizontal Gaze Nystagmus (HGN), Walk and Turn (WAT), and One Leg Stand (OLS). These tests must be administered in standardized manner to be reliable.

Horizontal Gaze Nystagmus (HGN): Tests involuntary eye jerking (nystagmus) that alcohol consumption exacerbates. **Administration:** Hold stimulus (pen or finger) 12-15 inches from suspect's nose, slightly above eye level. Check for equal tracking, equal pupil size, and resting nystagmus before starting. Move stimulus smoothly—approximately 2 seconds from center to maximum deviation. **Six Clues (3 per eye):** (1) **Lack of Smooth Pursuit:** Eye doesn't track smoothly but jerks or bounces. Check each eye separately. (2) **Distinct Nystagmus at Maximum Deviation:** Eye held at maximum deviation shows distinct, sustained nystagmus for at least 4 seconds. (3) **Onset of Nystagmus Prior to 45 Degrees:** Nystagmus begins before eye reaches 45 degrees from center. **Scoring:** Each clue = 1 point. 4+ clues indicates BAC .08+ with 77% accuracy. **Important:** HGN is most reliable SFST but certain medical conditions, medications, and injuries can cause nystagmus. Ask about these before testing. Document suspect's responses.

Walk and Turn (WAT): Divided attention test requiring balance while following instructions. **Instruction Stage:** Place suspect on real or imaginary line. Instruct: place right foot ahead of left, heel-to-toe; keep arms at sides; maintain position while receiving instructions; don't begin until told. Give walking instructions while they maintain position (this tests ability to divide attention). **Walking Stage:** Take 9 heel-to-toe steps along line; on 9th step, keep front foot on line and turn using small steps with other foot; return 9 heel-to-toe steps. Keep arms at sides, watch feet, count steps aloud, don't stop. **Eight Clues:** (1) Cannot keep balance during instructions; (2) Starts before instructions complete; (3) Stops while walking; (4) Doesn't touch heel-to-toe (gap ½ inch or more); (5) Steps off line; (6) Uses arms for balance (raises 6+ inches from sides); (7) Loses balance on turn or turns incorrectly; (8) Takes wrong number of steps. **Scoring:** 2+ clues indicates BAC .08+ with 68% accuracy. **Limitations:** People with back/leg/inner ear problems, those over 65, and those more than 50 pounds overweight may have difficulty for reasons unrelated to intoxication. Ask about limitations before testing.

One Leg Stand (OLS): Another divided attention test. **Instructions:** Stand with feet together, arms at sides. When told to start: raise one leg (either leg) approximately 6 inches off ground with foot parallel to ground; keep both legs straight, arms at sides; look at elevated foot; count out loud "one thousand one, one thousand two..." until told to stop (30 seconds). **Four Clues:** (1) Sways while balancing; (2) Uses arms to balance (raises 6+ inches from sides); (3) Hopping to maintain balance; (4) Puts foot down. **Scoring:** 2+ clues indicates BAC .08+ with 65% accuracy. Same physical limitations affecting WAT also affect OLS.

Proper Administration Critical: SFSTs must be administered exactly as trained for results to be reliable and admissible. **Environmental Conditions:** Conduct on level surface with adequate lighting away from traffic and distractions. **Demonstrations:** Demonstrate each test before asking suspect to perform. **Instructions:** Give clear, complete instructions. Don't add or omit instructions. **Observation:** Watch carefully and note all clues observed. **Documentation:** Document specific observations for each test, not just pass/fail conclusions. **Video Recording:** Record SFSTs when possible for evidence and to show proper administration.

Implied Consent Laws

Implied Consent (Transportation Code Chapter 724): By operating motor vehicle in Texas, person consents to providing breath or blood sample if arrested for DWI or BWI (boating while intoxicated). Refusal has consequences but isn't a crime.

DIC-24 Statutory Warning: Before requesting chemical test, you must read the DIC-24 warning advising the person: refusal to provide sample will result in license suspension; refusal can be used against them in court; they don't have right to consult attorney before deciding whether to provide sample (though if attorney immediately available and consultation doesn't interfere with testing, brief consultation permitted).

Breath Testing: Person arrested for DWI should be offered breath test. Two samples should be obtained with results within .02 of each other. Test must be administered by certified breath test operator using approved device in proper working order. **Document:** Time of arrest, time warnings given, person's response (consent or refusal), time of testing, results obtained, operator name and certification number.

Blood Testing: More invasive than breath, requires consent or warrant except in specified circumstances. **Consent:** If person consents, document consent thoroughly (written consent form preferred). Person can withdraw consent anytime before sample taken. **Warrant:** If person refuses or can't consent (unconscious), obtain search warrant based on probable cause for DWI. **Mandatory Blood Draw (§724.012):** Must request blood specimen when arrested for DWI/intoxication assault/intoxication manslaughter AND: accident resulted in death or serious bodily injury, OR you reasonably believe child under 15 was passenger. If person refuses mandatory blood draw, obtain warrant.

Blood Draw Procedures: Must be conducted by qualified medical personnel (physician, registered nurse, licensed vocational nurse, paramedic) in sanitary environment. Sample must be properly preserved and stored. Maintain chain of custody. Medical personnel can't be compelled to draw blood if contrary to their judgment.

Refusal Consequences: Administrative license suspension: 180 days first refusal, 2 years subsequent refusals. ALR hearing available if requested within 15 days. Refusal admissible as evidence of consciousness of guilt. No test results to challenge (but also no evidence of specific BAC). Prosecution can proceed based on loss of normal use of faculties even without test results.

Chemical Test Results: Breath/blood test showing .08+ BAC proves intoxication per se—no need to show loss of normal use of faculties. Results below .08 don't prevent prosecution if evidence shows loss of normal use. Results above .15 enhance penalties (6-day minimum jail on first offense DWI).

Accident Investigation Procedures

Crash Scene Management

Initial Response Priorities: (1) **Safety:** Protect scene from additional collisions. Position vehicles with emergency lights to warn traffic. Consider calling fire department for additional scene protection. (2) **Life Safety:** Check for injuries. Request EMS if needed. Render first aid within your training. (3) **Investigation:** Preserve evidence. Identify witnesses. Document scene. (4) **Traffic Flow:** Clear roadway as soon as safely possible to restore traffic flow.

Scene Protection: Park patrol vehicle to protect scene and investigators. Use emergency lights, flares, or cones as appropriate. Consider traffic volume, road design, visibility, and weather. For major accidents on highways, request additional units for extended scene protection. On curves or hills where approaching traffic can't see scene, position unit with lights visible well before scene.

Emergency Medical Response: Check all vehicles for occupants (including trunk—some accidents involve kidnapping or human trafficking victims). Assess injuries and request appropriate EMS response. Render basic first aid if trained. Don't move injured persons unless immediate danger exists (fire, additional collision risk). Document injuries photographically when appropriate.

Evidence Preservation: Don't allow vehicles to be moved until: scene is documented, measurements taken, positions recorded, photographs obtained. **Exception:** Move vehicles if necessary for safety or to restore traffic flow on major roadways, but document original positions first (photographs, measurements, chalk marks). Preserve physical evidence: skid marks, gouge marks, debris, fluid spills, damaged property. Mark or photograph before weather or traffic destroys evidence.

Witness Identification: Identify all persons at scene including drivers, passengers, pedestrians, and uninvolved witnesses. Obtain contact information: full names, addresses, phone numbers, driver's license numbers. Interview witnesses separately to get independent accounts. Document exact statements using quotation marks when possible. Get written statements when feasible.

Accident Documentation

Photography: Photograph scene from multiple angles before anything is moved. Include: overall scene showing vehicle positions and roadway; each vehicle's damage from all angles; skid marks, debris, and other physical evidence; road conditions, traffic controls, and visibility limitations; injuries to occupants (with consent when possible); license plates and VIN numbers of all vehicles.

Measurements: Measure and document: vehicle positions relative to fixed objects (curbs, signs, trees); length of skid marks or tire marks; gouge marks or scrape marks; distance debris traveled;

point of impact location. Use triangulation method when possible: measure from fixed objects to create precise positions. Rough sketches at scene; final diagrams drawn later using measurements.

Vehicle Inspections: Document for each vehicle: make, model, year, color, VIN, license plate; damage (all sides, pre-existing damage noted); mechanical condition (brakes, lights, steering, tires); evidence of impairment (alcohol containers, drug paraphernalia); occupant positions (driver, passengers); safety equipment use (seatbelts, child seats, airbag deployment).

Driver/Witness Interviews: Interview all drivers and passengers separately. Obtain: narrative of events from their perspective; direction of travel and estimated speed; actions before collision (braking, steering); what they saw, heard, or felt; where they were going and where they came from; any distractions or impairments; injuries sustained. Observe for DWI indicators during interviews: odor of alcohol, slurred speech, bloodshot eyes, admissions of drinking, medications affecting driving.

Traffic Crash Report: Complete required state crash report for all accidents meeting reporting thresholds: death or injury, or damage apparently exceeding $1,000. Report must include: date, time, location; roadway and weather conditions; vehicle information; driver/passenger information; narrative describing what happened; diagram showing vehicle positions and movements; contributing factors (speeding, failure to yield, DWI, etc.); enforcement action taken (citations, arrests).

Determining Fault: Analyze physical evidence, statements, and circumstances to determine who violated traffic law causing accident. Consider: right of way violations, speeding, following too closely, improper turns, DWI, distracted driving, mechanical failures. Document specific violations observed or determined through investigation. Issue citations when appropriate. **Note:** You don't determine "fault" for insurance purposes—you identify traffic law violations that caused the accident.

Commercial Vehicle Accidents: Commercial vehicles (trucks with CDL drivers, buses, taxis) have additional requirements. Federal Motor Carrier Safety Regulations (FMCSR) may apply. Serious accidents require notification to Texas Department of Public Safety commercial vehicle enforcement. Driver may be required to submit to drug/alcohol testing even without DWI suspicion. Check driver's CDL, medical certificate, logbook, vehicle inspection records, and cargo securement.

Traffic Direction and Control

Emergency Traffic Management

When to Direct Traffic: Power outages affecting signals, accidents blocking roadways, special events with heavy traffic, evacuations or emergencies, malfunctioning traffic signals. Goal: Keep traffic moving safely while preventing additional accidents.

Positioning: Stand where you're visible to all approaching traffic. Use high-visibility vest or reflective gear. Consider lighting conditions—don't stand in shadows where you can't be seen. Position near center of intersection but not in path of turning vehicles. Keep escape route available in case vehicle doesn't stop. Never turn your back to traffic.

Hand Signals (Daytime): Stop: Face traffic, arm extended straight up or straight out toward traffic, palm facing traffic. Maintain steady position. **Proceed:** Face perpendicular to traffic, arm extended pointing in direction traffic should go, wave traffic forward with beckoning motion. **Slow:** Face traffic, arm extended down at angle, palm facing down, move arm up and down slowly. Signals must be clear, deliberate, and maintained until traffic complies.

Baton or Flashlight Signals (Nighttime): Use illuminated baton or flashlight to make signals visible. Same motions as daytime but with lighted device. Red or orange lights most visible at night. White flashlights work but aren't as visible from distance.

Communication: Make eye contact with drivers to ensure they see and understand your signals. Point at specific vehicles when needed to clarify who should proceed. Don't assume drivers will obey—watch for compliance and be ready to react if they don't stop. Use whistle if needed to get attention but don't rely on it exclusively.

Intersection Control: Establish pattern and stick to it—consistency prevents confusion. Typically: allow one direction to proceed completely before stopping them and starting other direction. For four-way intersections, proceed clockwise around intersection. Watch for pedestrians and ensure they cross safely. Don't allow too many vehicles into intersection—they must be able to clear before next direction proceeds.

Accident Scene Traffic Control: Funnel traffic around scene using cones, flares, or signals. Create single lane if needed. Alternate directions if only one lane passable. Use other officers or fire personnel to control both ends. Establish safe speed for passing scene—signal drivers to slow down. Watch for rubbernecking causing secondary accidents.

Special Considerations: School buses: Allow bus to complete loading/unloading before directing traffic. Emergency vehicles: Stop all traffic and clear path for emergency vehicles regardless of normal pattern. Large trucks: Need wider turning radius—ensure adequate clearance. Pedestrians: Give priority to pedestrians at crosswalks. Direct vehicles to stop until pedestrians clear.

Duration: Direct traffic only as long as necessary. For signal malfunctions, continue until signal repaired or electrical dept installs stop signs. For accidents, clear scene and restore normal flow ASAP. If extended traffic control needed, request relief officers to rotate assignments—directing traffic is physically demanding.

Officer Safety: Wear high-visibility equipment. Maintain awareness of all traffic—don't fixate on one direction. Watch for impaired or distracted drivers. Stay alert for drivers who don't see or obey you. Have escape route planned. If weather makes directing traffic too dangerous (ice, heavy rain limiting visibility), request equipment (electronic signs, additional officers) rather than endangering yourself.

Commercial Vehicle Enforcement

CDL Requirements and Inspections

Commercial Driver's License Required: CDL required to operate: vehicle with GVWR (gross vehicle weight rating) 26,001+ lbs; vehicle towing trailer with GVWR 10,001+ lbs when combined weight exceeds 26,001 lbs; vehicle designed to transport 16+ people including driver; vehicle transporting hazardous materials requiring placards.

CDL Classes: Class A: Combination vehicles (truck and trailer) with combined GVWR 26,001+ lbs and trailer GVWR 10,001+ lbs. Most semi-trucks require Class A. **Class B:** Single vehicles GVWR 26,001+ lbs or towing trailer GVWR 10,000 lbs or less. Includes large straight trucks, buses, dump trucks. **Class C:** Vehicles not meeting Class A or B definitions but designed to transport 16+ people or hazardous materials requiring placards.

Endorsements: H: Hazardous materials. **N:** Tank vehicles. **P:** Passenger vehicles. **S:** School bus. **T:** Double/triple trailers. **X:** Combination of tank and hazardous materials. Drivers must have appropriate endorsements for vehicles/cargo they're operating. Operating without required endorsement is violation.

Medical Certification: CDL holders must maintain current medical certificate (DOT physical). Drivers must carry medical certificate or have it on file with DPS. Certificate valid for up to 2 years depending on driver's health conditions. Operating without valid medical certificate is serious violation potentially affecting CDL status.

Hours of Service: Federal regulations limit driving hours to prevent fatigue-related accidents. **11-Hour Driving Limit:** May drive maximum 11 hours after 10 consecutive hours off duty. **14-Hour Limit:** May not drive beyond 14th consecutive hour after coming on duty (even if took breaks). **Rest Breaks:** 30-minute break required after 8 cumulative hours driving. **60/70 Hour Limit:** May not drive after 60/70 hours on duty in 7/8 consecutive days. **Logbook:** Drivers must maintain accurate logbook (paper or electronic) documenting duty status. Falsifying logbooks is federal violation.

Vehicle Inspection Reports: Drivers must complete pre-trip inspection and post-trip inspection reports. Reports must document defects affecting safety. Vehicles with serious defects cannot be operated until repaired. Drivers carry previous day's inspection report. You can inspect logbook and inspection reports during traffic stops.

Cargo Securement: Load must be properly secured to prevent shifting or falling. Specific regulations govern securing different cargo types (logs, machinery, vehicles, etc.). Unsecured or poorly secured loads create hazards for other motorists.

Basic Inspection During Traffic Stops: Check driver's CDL class matches vehicle operated, endorsements present if required, medical certificate current, logbook up-to-date and accurate, vehicle registration and insurance, obvious vehicle defects (lights, brakes, tires), cargo securement (visible from exterior), and placards match cargo if hazardous materials. For serious violations or crashes, request DPS commercial vehicle inspector for detailed Level I-III inspection.

Common Commercial Vehicle Violations: Operating without proper CDL class/endorsements, operating without valid medical certificate, hours of service violations (driving beyond limits), logbook violations (inaccurate, missing entries), overweight violations, unsafe vehicle conditions (brakes, tires, lights), improper cargo securement, and violations of hazmat transportation rules.

Commercial Vehicle Out-of-Service Orders: If you identify serious safety violations, you can place vehicle out-of-service meaning it cannot be operated until violations corrected. Common OOS violations: brake defects, tire defects, steering problems, lighting violations, hazmat violations, driver hours violations, and driver impairment or medical issues. Document OOS order thoroughly and notify commercial vehicle enforcement division.

Citation Writing and Court Procedures

Proper Documentation Standards

Purpose of Citations: Written promise to appear in court in lieu of custodial arrest for Class C misdemeanors and most other offenses not requiring arrest. Serves as charging document. Must contain specific information to be valid.

Required Information: Defendant's name, address, date of birth, driver's license number; officer's name, badge/ID number; date, time, location of violation (specific as possible); specific violation (cite statute number and description); court information (where and when to appear); signature of defendant (if refuses, note refusal—you can still issue citation); officer signature.

Charging Language: Must specify exactly what law was violated and how. Wrong: "Traffic violation." Correct: "Failed to obey steady red traffic signal in violation of Transportation Code

Section 544.007." Wrong: "Speeding." Correct: "Operating vehicle at speed in excess of posted limit—65 in 55 mph zone—in violation of Transportation Code Section 545.352."

Location Description: Be specific enough that court can establish jurisdiction. Include street names or highway numbers, direction of travel, nearest cross street or mile marker, city or county. Wrong: "Main Street." Correct: "South Main Street at intersection with 5th Avenue, northbound, in Dallas, Dallas County, Texas."

Narrative: Some citations have space for brief narrative. Use it to document key facts: specific behavior observed, reason for stop, relevant circumstances, driver's statements (if any), and any other information supporting the charge. Keep narrative factual, concise, and professional.

Multiple Violations: If driver commits multiple violations, you can issue multiple citations or choose most serious violation. Consider: Was separate bad act committed for each violation? What serves justice and traffic safety best? Department policy regarding multiple citations. Document all violations in your notes even if citing only one—prosecutor may amend charges or add violations later.

Physical vs. Electronic Citations: Many departments use electronic citation systems (tablets or in-car computers). Benefits: automatic population of fields, legibility, faster processing, direct transmission to court. Whether paper or electronic, ensure all required fields completed accurately. Incomplete citations may be dismissed.

Defendant Signature: Explain to defendant that signing citation is NOT admission of guilt—it's promise to appear in court or pay fine by specified date. If defendant refuses to sign, note refusal on citation. Citation remains valid without signature but you must document refusal. If defendant refuses to sign AND refuses to provide identification AND you have no other means to identify them, you may arrest to establish identity.

Copies: Provide defendant with copy of citation. Retain officer copy for your records. Forward court copy per department procedure. Keep copies organized by date until dispositions received.

Court Preparation: When defendant contests citation and requests trial, you'll receive subpoena or notice to appear. Prepare by: reviewing your notes from the stop; reviewing video (if available); refreshing memory on specific facts; bringing documentation (citation copy, notes, any photographs); arriving early and checking in with prosecutor; and dressing in proper uniform.

Courtroom Testimony: When called to testify: address judge as "Your Honor"; testify based on your direct observations and documentation; stick to facts—don't speculate or offer opinions beyond expertise; remain professional regardless of defense attorney tactics; explain technical terms in plain language for jury understanding; admit if you don't remember specific detail rather than guessing; and refer to notes if allowed by court.

Common Defense Arguments: "The officer was mistaken about what I did." (Stick to your observations—testimony based on what you saw. Admit if conditions affected your view.) "My speedometer showed I wasn't speeding." (Explain radar/lidar calibration and accuracy. Note speedometer isn't calibrated to law enforcement standards.) "The officer targeted me." (Explain traffic enforcement basis—observed violation, not profiling.) "I had to speed/run red light because of emergency." (Defendant can present necessity defense but must establish legal requirements.)

Case Disposition: After trial or plea, case disposition entered. Track dispositions to ensure accuracy. If defendant found guilty, conviction creates arrest authority if they fail to pay fine or appear for additional proceedings. Dispositions also tracked for your performance records.

Real-World Application: Traffic Enforcement Scenarios

Scenario 1: Speeding Stop DWI Development

Situation: 11:30 PM, you clock vehicle at 82 mph in 65 mph zone on highway. Initiate stop. Driver slow to stop, pulls into parking lot rather than shoulder. Approach driver's side. Smell moderate alcohol odor. Driver's speech slightly slurred. He admits "I had a few drinks at dinner." Eyes bloodshot. He fumbles dropping license twice before handing it to you.

Analysis: Started as routine speeding stop but observations create reasonable suspicion of DWI. **Proper Actions:** Note all impairment indicators: slow to stop (delayed reaction), alcohol odor (moderate), slurred speech, bloodshot eyes, fumbling (motor skill impairment), admission to drinking. Ask driver to exit vehicle for field sobriety tests. Look for open containers in plain view during approach. Administer SFSTs (HGN, WAT, OLS) following proper procedures. Based on totality (speeding, impairment indicators, poor SFST performance), establish probable cause for DWI arrest. Arrest driver, read implied consent warning, request breath or blood test. Issue citation for speeding in addition to DWI arrest. Arrange for vehicle to be legally parked or towed. Document everything thoroughly: observations, statements, SFST results, arrest basis.

Scenario 2: Accident Investigation—Fault Determination

Situation: Two-vehicle accident at intersection with four-way stop. Driver A says she stopped then proceeded. Driver B struck her vehicle. Driver B says he stopped completely and Driver A ran the stop sign. Both have minor injuries. No independent witnesses. No video available.

Analysis: Conflicting statements with no independent verification. **Investigation:** Document skid marks (if any) showing who braked where. Examine damage location and severity to determine angles and speeds. Note final positions relative to intersection. Check road for stop sign visibility and condition. Interview both drivers about their versions in detail: where they were going, exact movements, when they first saw other vehicle, braking and avoidance efforts.

Check for driver impairment (DWI indicators). Look for distractions (phones, passengers). Examine vehicles for pre-impact braking (locked wheels indicate braking before impact). Check for defective brakes. Examine other physical evidence (debris pattern, gouges, scrapes).

Fault Determination: Based on damage locations: if Driver A's vehicle struck on passenger side and Driver B's vehicle struck on front, suggests Driver B entered intersection while Driver A was already there—Driver B likely ran stop. If Driver A's front struck Driver B's driver side, suggests Driver A failed to yield right of way—Driver A likely at fault. Document your reasoning based on physical evidence and statements. Issue citation to driver who violated traffic law causing accident. **In Report:** Explain how physical evidence supports your conclusion. Don't state "Driver B is at fault"—instead state "Driver B failed to stop at stop sign in violation of TRC 544.010, causing collision with Driver A's vehicle which had already entered intersection."

Practice Questions (60 questions)

Question 1: A driver operating vehicle at 85 mph in a 70 mph zone commits: A) Felony B) Class C misdemeanor with 2 points C) Class B misdemeanor D) No violation if under 90 mph

Answer: B **Explanation:** Speeding violations are Class C misdemeanors assessed 2 points on driver's license. Excessive speed alone doesn't elevate to higher classification unless other factors present.

Question 2: The implied consent law in Texas means: A) All drivers must consent to searches B) By operating a vehicle, drivers consent to providing breath/blood sample if arrested for DWI C) Police can take blood without any authorization D) Drivers must consent to vehicle searches

Answer: B **Explanation:** Implied consent (Transportation Code Chapter 724) means operating vehicle in Texas constitutes consent to chemical testing if arrested for DWI. Refusal has administrative consequences.

Question 3: On the Horizontal Gaze Nystagmus test, how many total clues can be observed? A) 3 B) 4 C) 6 (3 per eye) D) 8

Answer: C **Explanation:** HGN has 6 possible clues total—3 per eye: lack of smooth pursuit, distinct nystagmus at maximum deviation, and onset prior to 45 degrees. Four or more clues indicates BAC .08+ with 77% accuracy.

Question 4: A driver refuses to provide a breath sample after being arrested for DWI. The consequence is: A) Immediate jail time B) Administrative license suspension—180 days first refusal, 2 years subsequent C) Automatic felony charge D) No consequence

Answer: B **Explanation:** Refusing chemical testing results in administrative license suspension separate from criminal charges. First refusal: 180 days suspension. Subsequent refusal: 2 years suspension. Refusal is also admissible evidence.

Question 5: During accident investigation, the first priority is: A) Determining fault B) Writing citations C) Safety—protecting scene and providing medical aid D) Taking photographs

Answer: C **Explanation:** Scene safety and life safety are always first priorities. Protect scene from additional collisions, check for injuries, request EMS, render first aid. Investigation comes after ensuring safety.

Question 6: Walk and Turn test has how many possible clues? A) 4 B) 6 C) 8 D) 10

Answer: C **Explanation:** WAT has 8 clues: can't balance during instructions, starts too soon, stops while walking, doesn't touch heel-to-toe, steps off line, uses arms, improper turn, wrong number of steps. Two or more clues indicates impairment.

Question 7: Texting while driving in Texas is: A) Legal B) Class C misdemeanor with no points but remains on record C) Felony D) Only illegal for minors

Answer: B **Explanation:** Texting while driving (reading, writing, sending electronic messages) is Class C misdemeanor. $25-99 first offense, $100-200 subsequent. No points assessed but conviction recorded. Exceptions: GPS, emergency reporting, hands-free devices.

Question 8: An officer directing traffic should position themselves: A) With their back to traffic B) Where visible to all approaching traffic with escape route available C) Directly in path of turning vehicles D) In the shadows

Answer: B **Explanation:** Stand where all approaching traffic can see you, wear high-visibility equipment, maintain awareness of all directions, keep escape route available. Never turn back to traffic or stand where you can't be seen.

Question 9: A Commercial Driver's License (CDL) is required to operate: A) Any truck B) Vehicle with GVWR 26,001+ lbs, or vehicle transporting 16+ people, or placarded hazmat C) Only semi-trucks D) Vehicles over 10,000 lbs

Answer: B **Explanation:** CDL required for vehicles with GVWR 26,001+ lbs, combination vehicles meeting weight thresholds, vehicles transporting 16+ people including driver, or vehicles transporting placarded hazardous materials.

Question 10: When writing a citation, the officer must include: A) Only the driver's name B) Defendant info, officer info, date/time/location, specific violation with statute, court info, and signatures C) Just the violation D) Only the fine amount

Answer: B **Explanation:** Citations must contain all required information: defendant identification, officer information, precise date/time/location, specific violation and statute number, court information, and both signatures (or notation of refusal).

Question 11: One Leg Stand test has how many clues? A) 2 B) 3 C) 4 D) 6

Answer: C **Explanation:** OLS has 4 clues: sways while balancing, uses arms to balance, hopping, puts foot down. Two or more clues indicates BAC .08+ with 65% accuracy.

Question 12: Driving While License Invalid (DWLI) is classified as: A) Not a crime B) Class C first offense, Class B subsequent offenses (or Class B if invalid due to DWI) C) Always a felony D) Traffic infraction only

Answer: B **Explanation:** DWLI is Class C misdemeanor first offense, Class B subsequent offenses or if license invalid due to DWI conviction. More serious than simply not having license with you.

Question 13: During field sobriety tests, if a person has back or leg problems: A) You cannot test them B) Note the limitations, as they may affect test performance for reasons unrelated to intoxication C) Ignore the conditions D) Automatically arrest them

Answer: B **Explanation:** People with back, leg, or inner ear problems, those over 65, or more than 50 pounds overweight may have difficulty with WAT and OLS for medical reasons. Ask about limitations and document them before testing.

Question 14: The point system in Texas results in license suspension at: A) 3 points B) 4 points in 12 months or 6 points in 3 years C) 10 points D) 5 points

Answer: B **Explanation:** Four points in 12 months triggers warning and possible surcharges. Six points in 3 years or 7 points in 3 years (with at least two violations in 12 months) results in license suspension.

Question 15: Open container law prohibits: A) Any alcohol in vehicle B) Knowingly possessing open container of alcohol in passenger area of vehicle on public highway C) Only applies to drivers D) Drinking anywhere

Answer: B **Explanation:** Penal Code §49.031 prohibits possessing open alcohol container in passenger area of vehicle on public highway. Exceptions: buses, taxis, limousines, or containers in locked glove compartment/trunk.

Question 16: Accident reports are required when: A) Any accident occurs B) Death, injury, or damage apparently exceeding $1,000 C) Only for fatal accidents D) Never required

Answer: B **Explanation:** State crash reports required for accidents involving death, injury, or property damage apparently exceeding $1,000. Report documents circumstances, participants, and factors contributing to collision.

Question 17: The DIC-24 warning must be given: A) During every traffic stop B) Before requesting chemical testing after DWI arrest C) Only if the person asks D) Never required

Answer: B **Explanation:** DIC-24 statutory warning must be read before requesting breath or blood test from person arrested for DWI. Warning advises of consequences of refusal and rights regarding attorney consultation.

Question 18: Commercial vehicle drivers must maintain: A) Only their CDL B) CDL with proper class/endorsements, current medical certificate, accurate logbook, and inspection reports C) Just insurance D) Only registration

Answer: B **Explanation:** Commercial drivers must maintain proper CDL class and endorsements, current DOT medical certificate, accurate hours-of-service logbook, vehicle inspection reports, and comply with all federal motor carrier safety regulations.

Question 19: When positioning patrol vehicle at accident scene, officers should: A) Park directly in front B) Position vehicle with emergency lights to warn and protect scene from additional collisions C) Block all lanes D) Park far away from scene

Answer: B **Explanation:** Position patrol vehicle to protect scene using emergency lights to warn approaching traffic. Consider traffic volume, visibility, and road design. Goal is preventing additional collisions while allowing investigation.

Question 20: Following too closely violations result in: A) No points B) 2 points C) 3 points D) License suspension

Answer: B **Explanation:** Following too closely (Transportation Code §545.062) is 2-point violation. Must maintain reasonable and prudent distance based on speed, traffic, and conditions.

Question 21: Blood testing for DWI requires: A) No authorization B) Consent, warrant, or exigent circumstances (or mandatory blood draw situations) C) Always requires warrant D) Cannot be done

Answer: B **Explanation:** Blood draws require consent (documented thoroughly), search warrant based on probable cause, or qualify as mandatory blood draw situations (serious injury/death or child passenger). Exigent circumstances rarely justify warrantless blood draws per Missouri v. McNeely.

Question 22: Speeding violations carry how many points? A) No points B) 1 point C) 2 points D) 5 points

Answer: C **Explanation:** Speeding violations (Transportation Code §545.352) are assessed 2 points on driver's license and remain on record for 3 years from conviction date.

Question 23: When testifying in court about traffic citation, officers should: A) Guess if they don't remember B) Testify based on direct observations and documentation, admit if don't remember specific details C) Argue with defense attorney D) Make up details

Answer: B **Explanation:** Testify based on what you directly observed and documented. Refer to notes if allowed. Admit if you don't remember specific detail rather than speculating. Remain professional regardless of defense tactics.

Question 24: Hours of service regulations limit commercial drivers to: A) Unlimited driving B) 11 hours driving after 10 consecutive hours off, and 14-hour on-duty limit C) 20 hours driving D) 8 hours driving

Answer: B **Explanation:** Federal hours-of-service rules limit commercial drivers to maximum 11 hours driving after 10 consecutive hours off duty, and cannot drive beyond 14th consecutive hour after coming on duty, regardless of breaks taken.

Question 25: Running red light violations result in: A) Warning only B) 3 points C) 1 point D) License suspension

Answer: B **Explanation:** Running red traffic signals (Transportation Code §544.007) results in 3 points—more serious than standard 2-point violations due to high accident risk at intersections.

Question 26: At accident scenes, vehicles should not be moved until: A) Tow truck arrives B) Scene documented through photos and measurements, unless necessary for safety or traffic flow C) Police chief arrives D) Insurance companies notified

Answer: B **Explanation:** Preserve vehicle positions until scene photographed, measured, and documented. Exception: move if necessary for safety or to restore traffic flow on major roadways, but document original positions first.

Question 27: Failure to maintain financial responsibility (no insurance) penalties include: A) Warning B) Class C first offense ($175-350 plus surcharges), Class B subsequent offenses C) No penalty D) Verbal warning only

Answer: B **Explanation:** No insurance is Class C misdemeanor first offense with $175-350 fine plus surcharges, Class B subsequent offenses with $350-1,000 fine. License suspension and vehicle impoundment also possible.

Question 28: During HGN test, onset of nystagmus prior to 45 degrees means: A) Person is sober B) One clue per eye indicating possible impairment C) Test is invalid D) Nothing significant

Answer: B **Explanation:** When nystagmus begins before eye reaches 45 degrees from center, this counts as one clue per eye. This is one of three clues checked on each eye during HGN testing.

Question 29: CDL endorsement "H" is required for: A) Heavy trucks B) Hazardous materials C) High-speed vehicles D) Hauling trailers

Answer: B **Explanation:** "H" endorsement required for transporting hazardous materials requiring placards. Other endorsements: N (tank), P (passenger), S (school bus), T (double/triple trailers), X (tank + hazmat combination).

Question 30: Citation signatures mean: A) Admission of guilt B) Promise to appear in court or pay fine by specified date—NOT admission of guilt C) Automatic conviction D) Agreement to plead guilty

Answer: B **Explanation:** Defendant signature is promise to appear or resolve citation, not admission of guilt. If defendant refuses to sign, note refusal—citation remains valid but must document refusal clearly.

Question 31: Accident fault determination is based on: A) Insurance company decisions B) Physical evidence, statements, and identifying traffic law violations that caused the accident C) Who has better insurance D) Random selection

Answer: B **Explanation:** Determine who violated traffic law causing accident based on physical evidence (damage, skid marks, debris), statements from participants, and witness accounts. Issue citations for violations identified through investigation.

Question 32: Walk and Turn test requires the person to take: A) 5 steps B) 7 steps C) 9 steps each direction D) As many as they want

Answer: C **Explanation:** WAT requires 9 heel-to-toe steps along line in one direction, turn keeping front foot on line using small steps, return 9 heel-to-toe steps. Wrong number of steps is one of eight possible clues.

Question 33: Commercial vehicle out-of-service orders mean: A) Vehicle parked for the day B) Vehicle cannot be operated until serious safety violations corrected C) Driver gets rest break D) Vehicle needs oil change

Answer: B **Explanation:** OOS orders prohibit operating vehicle until serious safety defects corrected. Common OOS violations: brake/tire/steering defects, lighting violations, hours violations, driver impairment. Must be documented and commercial enforcement notified.

Question 34: Traffic direction hand signals must be: A) Quick and random B) Clear, deliberate, maintained until traffic complies, with eye contact when possible C) Confusing to test drivers D) Given while looking away

Answer: B **Explanation:** Signals must be clear and deliberate: Stop (arm extended up or out, palm to traffic), Proceed (arm pointing direction, beckoning motion), Slow (arm down at angle, palm down, up/down motion). Maintain until traffic complies. Make eye contact.

Question 35: Implied consent law consequences for refusal include: A) No consequences B) Administrative license suspension and refusal admissible as evidence C) Automatic conviction D) Immediate jail time

Answer: B **Explanation:** Refusal results in administrative license suspension (180 days first, 2 years subsequent) separate from criminal charges. Refusal is admissible evidence of consciousness of guilt. ALR hearing available if requested within 15 days.

Question 36: When interviewing drivers after accidents, officers should: A) Interview everyone together B) Interview each driver and passenger separately to get independent accounts C) Not interview anyone D) Only interview the driver at fault

Answer: B **Explanation:** Interview all drivers and passengers separately to obtain independent, uninfluenced accounts. Document exact statements. Compare versions to determine consistency and identify contradictions. Separate interviews prevent coordination of stories.

Question 37: Equipment violations such as defective brake lights are: A) Felonies B) Class C misdemeanors, often dismissible if corrected and proof provided C) Not violations D) Warnings only

Answer: B **Explanation:** Most equipment violations (defective lights, brakes, expired inspection, etc.) are Class C misdemeanors. Many courts dismiss if defendant provides proof of correction ("fix-it tickets").

Question 38: Medical certification for CDL holders: A) Not required B) Required—current DOT physical valid up to 2 years depending on health conditions C) Optional D) Only for school bus drivers

Answer: B **Explanation:** CDL holders must maintain current medical certificate (DOT physical). Certificate valid up to 2 years based on driver's health. Drivers must carry certificate or have it on file with DPS. Operating without valid medical certificate is serious violation.

Question 39: One Leg Stand test requires the person to: A) Stand on both feet B) Raise one leg approximately 6 inches, keep both legs straight, count out loud for 30 seconds C) Jump on one foot D) Run in place

Answer: B **Explanation:** OLS requires person to stand on one leg (either leg) raised approximately 6 inches off ground, both legs straight, arms at sides, looking at elevated foot, counting "one thousand one, one thousand two..." for 30 seconds. Four possible clues assessed.

Question 40: Multiple traffic violations during single stop can result in: A) Only one citation allowed B) Multiple citations for each separate violation, or officer discretion to cite most serious C) Automatic arrest D) Verbal warning only

Answer: B **Explanation:** Officers may issue multiple citations for separate violations during one stop, or use discretion to cite most serious violation. Consider whether separate bad acts occurred, what serves justice, and department policy on multiple citations.

Question 41: Accident scene photography should include: A) Only damaged vehicles B) Overall scene, vehicle damage from all angles, skid marks, debris, road conditions, injuries (with consent), license plates C) Just one photo D) No photos necessary

Answer: B **Explanation:** Photograph comprehensively: overall scene showing positions, each vehicle's damage from multiple angles, skid/gouge marks, debris patterns, road/weather conditions, visibility limitations, injuries, license plates, VINs. Photos document scene before anything moved.

Question 42: Failure to yield right of way violations result in: A) No points B) 2 points C) 3 points D) 1 point

Answer: C **Explanation:** Failure to yield right of way (Transportation Code §545.151-156) results in 3 points due to high accident risk at intersections. Includes failure to yield at stop signs, yield signs, when turning left, to emergency vehicles, to pedestrians.

Question 43: Logbooks for commercial drivers must document: A) Only mileage B) Duty status showing on-duty time, driving time, off-duty time, and sleeper berth time C) Just fuel purchases D) Maintenance only

Answer: B **Explanation:** Logbooks (paper or electronic) must accurately document driver's duty status: on-duty time, driving time, off-duty time, sleeper berth time. Used to verify compliance with hours-of-service regulations. Falsifying logbooks is federal violation.

Question 44: When defendant contests traffic citation and requests trial: A) Case automatically dismissed B) Officer receives subpoena, prepares by reviewing notes/video, appears in court to testify C) Police chief handles it D) No hearing occurs

Answer: B **Explanation:** When defendant requests trial, officer receives notice to appear. Prepare by reviewing notes, video, and documentation. Arrive early, check in with prosecutor, testify based on observations and documentation, remain professional.

Question 45: Improper lane change violations result in: A) Warning only B) 2 points C) 5 points D) No penalty

Answer: B **Explanation:** Improper lane change (Transportation Code §545.060) results in 2 points. Violations include changing lanes unsafely or failing to signal. Common cause of side-swipe collisions.

Question 46: Cargo securement on commercial vehicles must: A) Be loose B) Properly secure load to prevent shifting or falling per federal regulations C) Not matter D) Only for certain cargo

Answer: B **Explanation:** Cargo must be properly secured per federal regulations to prevent shifting or falling. Specific rules govern different cargo types (logs, machinery, vehicles, etc.). Unsecured loads create hazards and are violations.

Question 47: Class A CDL is required for: A) Any truck B) Combination vehicles with combined GVWR 26,001+ lbs and trailer GVWR 10,001+ lbs C) Passenger vehicles only D) Small trucks

Answer: B **Explanation:** Class A CDL required for combination vehicles (truck and trailer) with combined GVWR 26,001+ pounds and towed unit GVWR 10,001+ pounds. Most semi-trucks require Class A.

Question 48: At four-way intersections, hand signals for traffic direction should: A) Be random B) Establish consistent pattern, typically proceeding clockwise around intersection C) Change constantly D) Not be used

Answer: B **Explanation:** Establish and maintain consistent pattern to prevent confusion. Typically proceed clockwise around intersection, allowing one direction to completely clear before starting next. Watch for pedestrians and don't overload intersection.

Question 49: Citation location description must include: A) Just street name B) Specific location with street names, direction of travel, nearest cross street, city and county C) General area D) No location needed

Answer: B **Explanation:** Location must be specific enough to establish court jurisdiction: street names or highway numbers, direction of travel, nearest cross street or mile marker, city or county. Poor location descriptions may result in dismissal.

Question 50: Mandatory blood draw situations include arrests for DWI when: A) Driver is rude B) Accident resulted in death/serious bodily injury OR child under 15 was passenger C) Any accident occurs D) Officer prefers blood test

Answer: B **Explanation:** Transportation Code §724.012 requires requesting blood specimen when arrested for DWI/intoxication assault/manslaughter AND accident resulted in death or serious bodily injury, OR you reasonably believe child under 15 was passenger.

Question 51: Standardized Field Sobriety Tests must be: A) Modified for each person B) Administered in standardized manner as trained for reliability and admissibility C) Skipped if driver seems sober D) Done while sitting

Answer: B **Explanation:** SFSTs must be administered exactly as trained following NHTSA standards. Deviating from standardized procedures affects reliability and may make results inadmissible. Proper administration requires appropriate conditions, clear instructions, and accurate observation.

Question 52: School zone speeding violations: A) Same as regular speeding B) Enhanced penalties when children present—fines increase significantly C) Not enforced D) Always dismissed

Answer: B **Explanation:** Speeding in school zones when children present carries enhanced penalties. Posted limits (typically 20 mph) strictly enforced during school hours. Fines substantially higher than regular speeding violations.

Question 53: When commercial driver is involved in accident, they may be required to: A) Nothing additional B) Submit to drug/alcohol testing even without DWI suspicion per federal regulations C) Pay higher fines D) Surrender license

Answer: B **Explanation:** Federal Motor Carrier Safety Regulations may require commercial drivers involved in serious accidents to submit to drug/alcohol testing regardless of suspicion of impairment. This is separate from DWI investigation procedures.

Question 54: Traffic crash reports must include: A) Only vehicle descriptions B) Date, time, location, conditions, participant info, narrative, diagram, contributing factors, enforcement action C) Just names D) Police opinion only

Answer: B **Explanation:** Complete crash reports include all relevant information: when/where accident occurred, road/weather conditions, vehicle and participant details, narrative describing events, diagram showing positions/movements, contributing factors identified, and enforcement actions taken.

Question 55: Pre-trip inspection reports for commercial vehicles: A) Not required B) Must be completed by driver documenting vehicle condition and any safety defects C) Optional D) Only monthly

Answer: B **Explanation:** Commercial drivers must complete pre-trip and post-trip inspection reports documenting vehicle condition. Must note any defects affecting safety. Vehicles with serious defects cannot be operated until repaired. Driver carries previous day's inspection report.

Question 56: Walk and Turn test, the person must: A) Take breaks whenever needed B) Not stop while walking—stopping is one of eight clues C) Run the test D) Use arms freely

Answer: B **Explanation:** Person must not stop while walking during WAT—stopping is one of eight clues. Other clues: can't balance during instructions, starts early, doesn't touch heel-to-toe, steps off line, uses arms, improper turn, wrong number of steps.

Question 57: When directing traffic, officers should wear: A) Regular uniform only B) High-visibility vest or reflective gear to ensure visibility to all traffic C) Dark clothing D) Whatever is available

Answer: B **Explanation:** Always wear high visibility equipment when directing traffic: reflective vest, bright colors, reflective striping. Must be visible to all approaching traffic in all lighting conditions. Safety depends on being seen.

Question 58: HGN test checks for: A) Balance B) Involuntary eye jerking (nystagmus) that alcohol consumption exacerbates C) Strength D) Vision clarity

Answer: B **Explanation:** HGN tests for involuntary eye jerking (nystagmus) that becomes more pronounced with alcohol consumption. Most reliable of three SFSTs with 77% accuracy when 4+ clues observed. Three clues checked per eye.

Question 59: Citations must specify: A) General violation B) Exact violation with statute number and description of specific conduct observed C) Just a number D) Officer's opinion

Answer: B **Explanation:** Citations must specify exact violation committed: statute number and clear description of specific conduct observed. Must be precise enough for defendant to understand charge and court to establish elements. Poor charging language may result in dismissal.

Question 60: Witness statements at accident scenes should: A) Be group discussions B) Be obtained separately from each witness to get independent, uninfluenced accounts C) Not be documented D) Only from drivers

Answer: B **Explanation:** Interview all witnesses separately to obtain independent accounts uninfluenced by others. Document exact statements, get written statements when possible, obtain contact information. Separate interviews prevent coordination and provide more reliable information for determining what occurred.

Scoring Your Practice Questions

57-60 correct (95-100%): Outstanding! Your understanding of traffic law, DWI enforcement, accident investigation, and traffic control is excellent. You've mastered the material and are ready to apply it effectively in the field. Review any missed questions for complete understanding, then proceed confidently to Chapter 5.

51-56 correct (85-94%): Excellent work! You have strong grasp of traffic enforcement procedures. Focus on areas where you missed questions—whether SFST administration, citation requirements, or commercial vehicle enforcement. Review those sections, then move forward.

45-50 correct (75-84%): Good progress! You understand core traffic enforcement concepts but need to strengthen specific areas. Review sections where you missed multiple questions. Focus on SFST procedures, point system details, or accident investigation techniques as needed.

39-44 correct (65-74%): You're developing understanding but have gaps. Review Chapter 4 systematically, paying special attention to topics with multiple missed questions. Work through scenarios again and create summary notes for SFSTs, citation requirements, and accident procedures.

Below 39 correct (less than 65%): Substantial additional study needed. Traffic enforcement is critical daily work. Review Chapter 4 thoroughly, taking detailed notes. Focus on understanding WHY procedures exist (legal basis, safety reasons, evidentiary requirements). Create flashcards for SFST procedures, point values, and CDL requirements. Practice scenario analysis before proceeding.

Chapter Summary

Traffic enforcement combines legal knowledge, investigative skills, and officer safety tactics. Master these core concepts: **DWI Detection:** Recognize driving indicators, conduct proper SFSTs following standardized procedures, understand implied consent laws and consequences, properly document observations for prosecution. **Traffic Law:** Know common violations and point values, understand classification and penalties, recognize when arrest authority exists versus cite-and-release, apply laws consistently and fairly. **Accident Investigation:** Prioritize safety, document thoroughly through photos and measurements, identify violations causing accidents, provide clear narratives explaining determinations. **Commercial Enforcement:** Understand CDL requirements and endorsements, recognize hours-of-service violations, identify serious safety defects warranting OOS orders, coordinate with specialized enforcement. **Citation Writing:** Include all required information, specify exact violations with statutes, document thoroughly for court proceedings, testify professionally based on observations. **Traffic Control:** Position safely with visibility, use clear hand signals maintained until compliance, establish consistent patterns, prioritize safety over speed.

Every traffic stop is an opportunity for officer safety application, criminal interdiction, and community interaction. Approach each professionally, maintain vigilance, document thoroughly, and apply laws fairly. Your traffic enforcement work prevents accidents, saves lives, and disrupts criminal activity while building or damaging community trust based on how you conduct yourself.

Continue building your expertise with Chapter 5: Criminal Investigation, where you'll learn crime scene management, evidence collection, interviewing techniques, and case development procedures that transform investigations into successful prosecutions.

PART III: INVESTIGATIONS AND SPECIALIZED PROCEDURES

CHAPTER 5: CRIMINAL INVESTIGATION

Learning Objectives

By the end of this chapter, you will: secure and preserve crime scenes properly; collect and document physical evidence maintaining chain of custody; conduct effective interviews and interrogations; write clear, complete reports that support prosecution; utilize investigative databases and resources; and develop cases from initial response through closure. These skills transform crime scenes into courtroom convictions.

Why This Chapter Matters: Investigation is where cases are won or lost. Poor crime scene management destroys evidence. Contaminated evidence gets suppressed. Incomplete reports result in dismissals. Ineffective interviews miss critical information. This chapter teaches you to investigate systematically, document thoroughly, and build prosecutable cases. Your investigative skills directly determine whether victims get justice.

Crime Scene Management and Preservation

Securing and Documenting Scenes

First Responder Responsibilities: You're often first at crime scenes. Your initial actions determine investigation success or failure. **Immediate Actions:** (1) **Safety First:** Assess threats before entering. Suspect still present? Other victims? Hazards? Request backup if needed. Don't rush into danger. (2) **Emergency Aid:** Check for injured persons. Render first aid. Request EMS. Life safety takes precedence over evidence preservation, but minimize scene disturbance when providing aid. (3) **Apprehend Suspects:** If suspect is present and can be safely apprehended, do so. If suspect fled, broadcast description immediately. Establish perimeter to contain suspect if still in area. (4) **Secure the Scene:** Prevent unauthorized entry. Scene security begins immediately and continues until investigation completes.

Scene Security: Establish Perimeter: Use crime scene tape, vehicles, officers, or barriers to create boundary around scene. Start large—easier to reduce perimeter than expand after contamination occurs. Perimeter should include: all areas where evidence might be located;

entry/exit routes suspect may have used; areas where evidence may have been discarded during flight. **Access Control:** One entry/exit point for authorized personnel. Log everyone entering scene: name, badge number, time in, time out, purpose for entry. Only essential personnel enter—investigators, crime scene technicians, supervisors, medical examiner. No spectators, unnecessary officers, media, or victims' families inside perimeter. **Protect Evidence:** Before investigators arrive, protect evidence from weather, foot traffic, and contamination. Cover bloodstains in rain. Place cones around tire tracks. Shield evidence from wind. Document evidence locations before protection measures applied.

Initial Documentation: Observations: Note everything upon arrival: condition of scene (doors/windows open or closed, lights on or off, signs of struggle); people present or leaving; vehicles in area; weather conditions; unusual smells, sounds, or sights; time of arrival and conditions observed. Document through notes, photos on phone, and body camera footage. **Witnesses:** Identify everyone at scene. Separate witnesses—don't let them discuss what happened. Obtain brief preliminary statements: what did they see/hear, when did it happen, where were they located? Get contact information. More detailed interviews conducted later. **Broadcast Information:** Provide dispatch with suspect descriptions, vehicles, direction of travel. Include clothing descriptions, distinguishing features, weapons. Other units can't apprehend suspects without good descriptions.

Common Scene Security Errors: Contamination: Walking through scene before documentation. Touching items unnecessarily. Allowing too many people inside perimeter. Each person who enters potentially destroys evidence. **Inadequate Perimeter:** Setting perimeter too small, then discovering evidence outside boundary after contamination occurred. Start large. **Poor Documentation:** Failing to photograph scene before securing it. Moving items without documenting original positions. Not logging personnel entry. **Lack of Protection:** Allowing evidence to be destroyed by weather, traffic, or animals because protection wasn't provided while waiting for investigators.

Crime Scene Processing

Photography: Document everything before anything is moved or collected. **Overall Photographs:** Show entire scene from multiple angles. Establish context—how rooms relate, where evidence is located relative to other items. Use wide-angle views. **Medium-Range Photographs:** Show relationships between pieces of evidence. How far is the weapon from the body? Where is broken glass relative to the point of entry? Include reference points (furniture, doors, windows). **Close-Up Photographs:** Individual items of evidence. Take multiple photos: with scale/ruler showing size; without scale; from multiple angles. Close-ups should show details: serial numbers on weapons; patterns on shoe prints; texture of bloodstains; damage to property. **Use Scales:** Include ruler or scale in close-up photos to show true size. Take one photo with scale, one without (so scale doesn't obscure evidence). **Lighting:** Use flash for dark areas. Use natural light when possible. Take photos from same angles with different lighting if needed to show details. **360-Degree Documentation:** Photograph entire scene from all angles. Don't assume you know what's important—document everything. You can't go back after scene is released.

Sketches and Diagrams: Photos show what scene looks like but don't accurately show distances and spatial relationships. Sketches provide: overhead view showing layout; measurements between objects; scale representation of scene. **Rough Sketch:** Created at scene with measurements noted. Doesn't need to be artistic—accuracy matters more than appearance. **Finished Diagram:** Created later using rough sketch measurements. Drawn to scale, neat, labeled clearly. May be computer-generated. **Measuring Techniques:** Use tape measures for accuracy. Triangulation method: measure from two fixed points to evidence location. This allows precise reconstruction. Coordinate method: establish baseline, measure perpendicular distances from baseline. Measure all relevant distances: evidence to evidence; evidence to doors/windows; evidence to body; dimensions of rooms.

Evidence Collection: Follow proper procedures for each evidence type. **General Principles:** Photograph before collection. Document exact location. Use clean tools and gloves. Prevent cross-contamination. Package appropriately. Label immediately. Maintain chain of custody. **Biological Evidence (blood, DNA, bodily fluids):** Allow wet blood to air dry before packaging. Use paper bags or envelopes—never plastic (promotes mold growth). Collect control samples from unstained areas nearby. Swab bloodstains with distilled water on sterile swabs. Collect entire items when possible (bloody clothing, weapons). Refrigerate if not air-dried. Document everything collected. **Firearms and Ammunition:** Clear weapons only if absolutely necessary for safety. Note condition: loaded/unloaded, hammer position, safety on/off. Don't handle by inserting object through trigger guard (destroys trigger evidence). Handle by grips if necessary, but better to let firearms examiner handle. Secure in gun box. Document serial number, make, model, caliber. **Fingerprints:** Dust visible surfaces with appropriate powder (black on light surfaces, light on dark surfaces). Photograph prints before lifting. Lift prints using tape or lifting cards. Mark orientation (top, bottom). Document which surface prints came from. Some surfaces require chemical processing by lab. **Trace Evidence (fibers, hair, glass, paint):** Use tape lifts for fibers and hair. Package glass carefully to preserve fracture patterns. Scrape paint samples. Use tweezers or forceps—never fingers. Package separately to prevent cross-contamination. **Digital Evidence:** Don't turn on devices that are off. Don't access files yourself—specialized forensic examination needed. Photograph screens showing relevant information. Preserve battery power. Consider Faraday bags to prevent remote wiping. Document make, model, serial numbers, condition. **Documents:** Handle minimally to preserve fingerprints. Photograph in place before collection. Use gloves or tools. Protect from damage. Package in protective sleeves or folders. Maintain readable condition.

Chain of Custody: Document every time evidence transfers from one person to another. Every break creates doubt about evidence integrity. **Information Required:** Who collected evidence; date and time collected; where collected; description of evidence; how evidence was secured; who received evidence; date and time transferred; purpose of transfer; condition of evidence. Use standardized forms. Initial seals on packages. Log evidence into property system immediately. Maintain continuous documentation from collection to court presentation.

Interviewing and Interrogation Techniques

Building Rapport and Detecting Deception

Interview vs. Interrogation: Interview: Conversation with witnesses, victims, or persons who may have information. Goal is gathering information. Non-accusatory. Conversational tone. **Interrogation:** Questioning of suspects when you have probable cause they committed the crime. Goal is obtaining admission or confession. More confrontational. Structured approach.

Effective Interviewing: Preparation: Review all available information before interview. Know what questions you need answered. Understand the case facts. Identify inconsistencies or gaps. **Environment:** Private location without distractions. Comfortable temperature. Remove barriers between you and interviewee when possible. Minimize intimidation for witnesses/victims. **Rapport Building:** Introduce yourself and explain your role. Express empathy for what they've experienced. Use active listening—let them talk without constant interruption. Show genuine interest in their account. Use open body language. Maintain appropriate eye contact. **Open-Ended Questions:** "Tell me what happened." "Describe what you saw." "Explain your relationship with the victim." Let them provide narrative in their own words without leading. **Specific Questions:** After narrative, clarify details with specific questions. "What time did you see this?" "What was he wearing?" "Which direction did he go?" Pin down specifics. **Active Listening:** Focus on what they're saying, not just waiting to ask next question. Note inconsistencies or important details. Ask follow-up questions based on their answers. Reflect back what you heard: "So you're saying you arrived at 10 PM?" **Cognitive Interview Technique:** Ask witness to recall everything (even details seeming unimportant); reconstruct circumstances (weather, lighting, sounds, smells); recall from different perspectives (what would someone else have seen?); reverse order (start from end, work backward). This technique enhances memory recall.

Detecting Deception: No single indicator proves deception—look for clusters of behaviors suggesting dishonesty. **Verbal Indicators:** Inconsistencies in story; lack of detail where detail should exist; overly rehearsed or scripted responses; evasive answers that don't address question; changing story when pressed; significant delays before answering simple questions; referencing time periods rather than events ("around 10 o'clock" vs. "when I arrived home"); distancing language ("that person" instead of using victim's name). **Non-Verbal Indicators:** Avoiding eye contact or excessive eye contact; fidgeting, touching face, covering mouth; closed body language (crossed arms, turning away); change in baseline behavior when certain topics raised; nervous laughter or inappropriate affect; physical distance or barriers created. **Baseline Establishment:** Observe normal behavior during non-threatening conversation. Note how they typically respond, their usual eye contact, normal fidgeting level. Changes from baseline when discussing critical topics may indicate deception.

Interrogation Techniques: Used with suspects when probable cause exists. **Preparation:** Know the evidence. Understand exactly what you can prove. Identify weaknesses in suspect's likely explanations. Plan questioning strategy. **Theme Development:** Provide moral justification or minimization that makes admitting easier. "Anyone would have been angry in that situation." "This wasn't planned—it just happened in the moment." Theme isn't promising leniency—it's providing psychological justification. **Confrontation:** Present evidence directly. "We have video showing you at the store." "Your fingerprints were on the weapon." "Three witnesses place you at the scene." Watch their response—denial, explanation, or admission? **Alternative Questions:** Offer two explanations—one more socially acceptable than the other. "Did you plan this for weeks, or did it just happen in the moment?" "Was this about the money, or were you trying to teach him a lesson?" Suspect often chooses lesser alternative, which is still admission. **Handling Denials:** Don't let suspect repeatedly deny—interrupts interrogation flow. Acknowledge denial then refocus. "I understand you're saying that, but let's talk about the evidence." **Building Evidence:** Present evidence incrementally. Don't reveal everything immediately. As suspect provides explanation, introduce evidence contradicting it. Each contradiction weakens credibility.

Legal Requirements: Miranda warnings required for custodial interrogation. Must be given before questioning someone in custody. Interrogation must stop if suspect invokes right to counsel. Document Miranda advisement and waiver. Record interrogation electronically per Texas law. Interrogation must be voluntary—no threats, no promises of leniency, no coercion. False confessions occur—ensure suspect's statements are consistent with evidence and contain details only perpetrator would know.

Vulnerable Populations: Juveniles: Simplified language, shorter sessions, parent/guardian present, extra caution about suggestibility, documented protections. **Mentally Ill/Disabled:** Assess capacity to understand rights, simplify language, document capacity issues, consider appropriateness of interrogation. **Non-English Speakers:** Qualified interpreter required, not family members or friends, ensure Miranda and questions accurately translated, document interpreter credentials.

Report Writing and Documentation

Clear, Concise, and Complete Reports

Purpose of Reports: Your report is your case. Prosecutors, judges, juries, defense attorneys, and supervisors all read it. Reports must: document what occurred; establish elements of offenses; preserve information for trial (months or years later); provide information for other investigations; demonstrate professionalism and thoroughness. Poor reports result in: dismissed cases; suppressed evidence; lost trials; disciplinary action; civil liability.

The Three Cs: Clear, Concise, Complete: Clear: Easily understood by anyone reading it. Use simple language. Define technical terms. Organize logically. Use proper grammar and spelling. **Concise:** Include all important information but eliminate unnecessary words. Every sentence should add value. Don't ramble. Get to the point. **Complete:** Include all relevant facts. Answer who, what, when, where, why, how. Don't leave gaps requiring reader to guess or assume.

Report Organization: Heading Information: Case number, date, time, location, type of offense, reporting officer, assisting officers, supervisor. Ensure accuracy—wrong case number or date creates problems. **Narrative:** Tell the story chronologically. What happened first, second, third? Use paragraphs to separate topics or time periods. **Subject-Verb-Object Structure:** "I observed the suspect running from the store." Not "The suspect was observed by me running from the store." Active voice is clearer and more direct than passive voice. **First Person:** "I arrived at the scene at 1430 hours." Not "Officer Smith arrived at the scene." You're writing about your actions and observations—use first person. **Past Tense:** Events already occurred. "I saw the vehicle," not "I see the vehicle." **Specific Details:** Include times, measurements, descriptions, exact locations. "I arrived at 1430 hours" not "I arrived in the afternoon." "The suspect wore a red t-shirt with Nike logo" not "The suspect wore a red shirt." "The vehicle traveled approximately 80 mph" not "The vehicle traveled fast." **Objective vs. Subjective:** State facts objectively. "The driver smelled of alcohol, had bloodshot eyes, and failed field sobriety tests" not "The driver was drunk." "The victim had bruising on her face and a swollen lip" not "The victim was brutally beaten."

What to Include: Initial Information: How you became aware of the incident (dispatch, flagged down, observation). Date, time, location. Weather and lighting conditions if relevant. **Actions Taken:** What you did upon arrival. Who you contacted. Where you went. What you observed. Use chronological order. **Observations:** Everything you saw, heard, smelled, or otherwise perceived. Describe crime scene conditions. Note evidence located. Document injuries. **Statements:** What people told you. Use quotation marks for exact words when possible. "The witness stated, 'I saw him punch her three times.'" Distinguish between paraphrased and direct quotes. **Evidence:** What you collected and where you found it. How it was packaged and where it was stored. Reference evidence numbers. **Identification:** How suspects, witnesses, or victims were identified. Confirm spellings of names. Include birthdates, addresses, phone numbers. **Charges:** What charges you filed and the specific statutes. Explain probable cause for arrests. **Follow-Up:** What additional investigation is needed. What you requested from others (warrants, lab analysis, interviews).

Common Report Writing Errors: Vague Language: "Several people," "a while ago," "near the door." Be specific. "Three witnesses," "approximately 10 minutes ago," "five feet from the north door." **Opinions Without Basis:** "The suspect was lying" without explaining indicators of deception. "The victim deserved it" (never appropriate). State facts that support conclusions. **Assumptions:** Don't assume reader knows context. Explain who people are. "J. Smith (store manager)" not just "Smith." **Spelling Errors:** Use spell check. Proofread. Names must be spelled correctly. Professional reports don't contain typos. **Missing Information:** Forgetting to include how case was resolved, whether arrests were made, what evidence was collected. Review before submitting. **Inconsistencies:** Times or descriptions that don't match other parts of report. Ensure all details consistent throughout. **Judgmental Language:** "The stupid suspect," "the victim wouldn't cooperate." Remain professional and objective always.

Special Report Types: Supplemental Reports: Additional information added after initial report. Clearly mark as supplement. Reference original case number. Explain what new information is being added. **Use of Force Reports:** Document decisions to use force. Describe threat, options considered, force used, effects observed, medical treatment provided. Explain reasonableness under circumstances. **Search Warrant Affidavits:** Establish probable cause for search warrant. Include training and experience, facts establishing offense occurred, facts connecting evidence to location, reliability of information sources. Must be detailed and specific.

Report Review: Before submitting: Read it yourself looking for errors. Check that all questions are answered. Verify names, dates, times, locations. Ensure narrative flows logically. Confirm all evidence documented. Review grammar and spelling. Have partner review if possible. Submit timely per department policy.

Physical Evidence Collection

Types of Evidence and Collection Methods

Evidence Categories: Direct Evidence: Proves fact without inference. Eyewitness testimony, video recording, confession. If believed, conclusively establishes fact. **Circumstantial Evidence:** Requires inference to connect to fact. Fingerprints at scene suggest presence but don't directly prove person committed crime. DNA on weapon connects person to weapon but doesn't prove they used it. Circumstantial evidence is not weaker than direct—it's simply different. Multiple pieces of circumstantial evidence can be more compelling than single piece of direct evidence.

Biological Evidence: Includes blood, semen, saliva, hair, skin cells, bodily fluids. **Collection:** Wear gloves. Prevent cross-contamination. Air dry wet items before packaging. Use paper packaging, not plastic. Collect control samples from unstained areas. Document exact locations. Swab dried stains with distilled water on sterile swabs. Collect entire item when possible. Refrigerate if cannot air dry. **Value:** DNA identification, blood typing, connecting suspects to scenes/victims, excluding innocent persons. **DNA Analysis:** Highly discriminating—can identify individuals with statistical certainty. Requires proper collection and storage. Contaminated samples produce unreliable results. Chain of custody critical.

Latent Prints: Fingerprints, palm prints, footprints left on surfaces. **Collection:** Photograph before processing. Dust with appropriate powder. Lift with tape or cards. Mark orientation. Document surface prints came from. Some surfaces require chemical processing (porous materials like paper). **Value:** Positive identification. No two people have same fingerprints. Finding suspect's prints on weapon, entry point, or stolen item connects them to crime. **Limitations:** Many surfaces don't retain usable prints. Prints may be partial or smudged. Environmental conditions affect quality.

Firearms Evidence: Weapons, ammunition, cartridge cases, bullets. **Collection:** Clear weapon only if necessary. Note condition. Don't insert objects through trigger guard. Handle minimally.

Preserve for fingerprints and DNA. Secure properly. Document serial numbers. Collect all related ammunition. **Firearms Examination:** Ballistics comparison—matching bullets and casings to weapons. Serial number restoration. Functionality testing. Distance determination. Gunshot residue analysis. **Cartridge Cases and Bullets:** Can be matched to specific firearm. Location where found indicates shooting positions. Number of cartridges indicates number of shots.

Tool Marks: Impressions left by tools on surfaces (pry bars on doors, bolt cutters on chains). **Collection:** Photograph with scale. Cast impressions if possible. Collect entire item if feasible. If not, photograph from multiple angles with proper lighting. Never fit suspect tool into mark (may damage). **Comparison:** Tool mark examiners can match marks to specific tools. Unique characteristics created during manufacturing and through use create individual patterns.

Impression Evidence: Tire tracks, shoe prints, tool marks. **Collection:** Photograph with scale. Cast using dental stone or similar material. Collect loose items (shoes, tires) for comparison. **Value:** Connects suspects to scenes. Pattern evidence can identify specific shoes or tires. Wear patterns individualize items.

Trace Evidence: Small materials transferred during crimes: fibers, hair, glass, paint, soil, gunshot residue. **Locard's Exchange Principle:** Every contact leaves a trace. Perpetrators take trace evidence from scene; leave trace evidence behind. **Collection:** Use tape lifts for fibers/hair. Carefully package glass fragments. Scrape paint samples. Collect soil samples. Vacuum trace evidence from clothing/vehicles. Prevent cross-contamination. **Value:** Links suspects to victims or scenes. Transferred fibers from victim's clothing on suspect's clothing. Glass fragments on suspect's shoes matching broken window.

Digital Evidence: Phones, computers, tablets, storage devices, GPS units, security cameras. **Collection:** Don't turn on powered-off devices. Don't access files. Photograph screens. Preserve battery power. Faraday bags prevent remote access. Document make, model, serial numbers. Maintain chain of custody. **Forensic Examination:** Specialists extract data: text messages, call logs, emails, photos, videos, internet history, GPS locations, deleted files. **Value:** Proves communications between suspects, establishes timeline, shows planning, reveals locations, provides evidence of crimes (child pornography, threats, fraud).

Documentary Evidence: Papers, receipts, notes, checks, contracts. **Collection:** Handle minimally for prints. Photograph in place. Protect from damage. Package appropriately. **Value:** Shows motive, proves transactions, establishes relationships, demonstrates planning, provides handwriting for comparison.

Investigative Resources and Tools

Databases and Inter-Agency Resources

Criminal Databases: TCIC (Texas Crime Information Center): State database containing warrants, wanted persons, stolen property, criminal histories, protective orders, gang information, vehicle registration, driver license status. Accessible through patrol computers and dispatch. Check suspects, witnesses, vehicles routinely. **NCIC (National Crime Information Center):** Federal database similar to TCIC but nationwide. Contains information from all states. Check for out-of-state warrants, stolen vehicles from other states, missing persons, sex offender registry. **Restrictions:** Criminal justice purposes only. Unauthorized access is crime. Information is confidential. Cannot share with unauthorized persons.

Specialized Databases: CODIS (Combined DNA Index System): DNA database. Submit evidence DNA for comparison against known offenders and unsolved cases. Can link cases through DNA even without suspect identified. **AFIS (Automated Fingerprint Identification System):** Fingerprint database. Submit latent prints from scenes for comparison. Can identify suspects when prints match database entries. **NIBIN (National Integrated Ballistic Information Network):** Ballistics database. Submit bullets and cartridge cases for comparison. Links shootings through firearm evidence even when weapon not recovered.

Information Sharing: Regional Intelligence Centers: Share information about crimes, suspects, trends across jurisdictions. Many areas have fusion centers coordinating multi-agency efforts. **Case Management Systems:** Track cases, share information among investigators, document follow-up actions, generate reports. **Inter-Agency Communication:** Cases often span jurisdictions. Coordinate with other departments. Share information about suspects, vehicles, methods. Request assistance when needed. Offer assistance when asked.

Investigative Techniques: Surveillance: Physical observation of suspects or locations. Labor-intensive but effective. Document observations thoroughly. Follow legal restrictions on privacy expectations. **Undercover Operations:** Infiltrating criminal organizations or conducting controlled buys. Specialized training required. Coordinate with narcotics units. **Informants:** Develop sources providing inside information. Maintain confidentiality. Document reliability. Corroborate information when possible. **Social Media:** Often contains valuable evidence. Suspects post incriminating photos, videos, locations, statements. Obtain through legal process (warrants) when necessary. **Financial Records:** Follow the money. Bank records, credit cards, asset purchases show criminal proceeds. Require warrants or subpoenas.

Follow-up Investigation Procedures

Case Development and Closure

Initial vs. Follow-Up: Patrol officers handle initial response. Investigators conduct follow-up. But patrol officers often do preliminary investigation affecting case outcome. **Patrol's Role:** Secure scene. Collect perishable evidence. Identify witnesses. Obtain preliminary statements. Document thoroughly. **Investigator's Role:** In-depth interviews. Evidence analysis. Case development. Warrant service. Suspect apprehension. Court preparation.

Case Assignment: Factors determining follow-up: **Solvability:** Are there leads? Identified suspects? Witnesses? Evidence? Cases with strong leads get priority. **Seriousness:** Violent crimes prioritized over property crimes. Severity affects resources allocated. **Victim Cooperation:** If victim won't cooperate, prosecution difficult. May affect priority. **Workload:** Limited investigators mean case management decisions necessary.

Follow-Up Actions: Evidence Submission: Send evidence to lab for analysis. Fingerprints to AFIS. DNA to lab. Digital devices to forensic examiners. Track submissions and follow up on results. **Additional Interviews:** Re-interview witnesses for details. Interview new witnesses identified. Interview suspects after information developed. **Records Checks:** Obtain phone records through warrants. Financial records. Employment records. Vehicle registration. Any records relevant to investigation. **Warrant Preparation:** Search warrants for residences, vehicles, phones. Arrest warrants when probable cause develops. **Suspect Identification:** Photo lineups shown to witnesses. Develop suspect lists through informants, database checks, modus operandi comparison. **Scene Re-examination:** Return to scene for additional investigation. Different lighting conditions may reveal evidence. Canvass neighborhood again.

Case Status: Active: Ongoing investigation with leads being pursued. Regular activity documented. **Suspended:** Investigation suspended due to lack of leads. Can be reactivated if new information develops. Not closed—can be reopened without re-filing. **Cleared by Arrest:** Suspect arrested and charged. Case proceeds to prosecution. **Cleared by Exception:** Case solved but arrest not possible (suspect dead, prosecution declined, victim refuses to cooperate). **Unfounded:** Investigation determined crime didn't occur. False report or mistake.

Prosecution Coordination: Early Communication: Contact prosecutor early in major cases. Discuss evidence needed. Legal issues. Search warrant review. **Evidence Presentation:** Provide organized case file. Clear reports. Evidence inventory. Witness list with contact information. **Court Preparation:** Be available for consultation. Review case before testimony. Update prosecutor on developments. Respond promptly to requests. **Victim/Witness Coordination:** Keep victims informed. Prepare witnesses for court. Arrange victim advocates when appropriate.

Case Closure: Documentation should include: all investigation conducted; evidence collected and analyzed; witnesses interviewed; suspects identified and their status; basis for case status determination; recommendations for prosecution. Closed cases may be reopened if new evidence develops. Maintain thorough documentation for future reference.

Real-World Application: Investigation Scenarios

Scenario 1: Residential Burglary—Evidence Collection

Situation: Dispatched to burglary report. Homeowner returned from vacation, found rear door pried open. Bedroom ransacked. Jewelry and electronics missing. Fresh pry marks on door frame. Possible fingerprints on jewelry box. No witnesses.

Proper Investigation: Secure scene—ensure suspect not still inside. Walk-through with victim identifying taken items and areas disturbed—but don't let victim contaminate evidence. Photograph: pry marks on door; ransacked rooms; areas where items were taken from; tool marks; any surfaces potentially containing prints. Collect evidence: process jewelry box for fingerprints; photograph and cast pry marks; collect tool mark impressions if possible. Obtain from victim: list of stolen items with descriptions, serial numbers, values; receipts for items if available; names of people with access to home; victim's activities and timeline. Canvass neighborhood: did neighbors see vehicles, people, activity during timeframe? Check for security cameras in area. Enter stolen property into TCIC. Search pawn shops for items. Examine method—does it match other burglaries (same entry point, items targeted, time of day)? Could be series. Check for DNA on pry bar if located or surfaces touched. Submit fingerprints to AFIS. Follow up on any hits. **Solvability Factors:** Physical evidence (prints, tool marks), pawn shop recovery of items, similar burglary pattern linking cases, informant information.

Scenario 2: Assault Investigation—Conflicting Statements

Situation: Bar fight. Two subjects injured. Both claim other started fight. Multiple witnesses with varying accounts. Some say Subject A threw first punch. Others say Subject B started it. Video surveillance system present but owner hasn't provided footage yet.

Investigation: Separate all parties immediately. Interview each separately before they coordinate stories. Document injuries photographically. Get medical treatment information. Obtain detailed statements from each: where were you, what led to altercation, who struck first, self-defense claims, alcohol consumption. Interview witnesses separately: independent accounts more reliable than group consensus; document exactly what each saw; note positions they were viewing from; some may have only seen part of fight. Obtain surveillance video: view before relying on statements; video may resolve conflicts; preserve original; make working copy. Compare physical evidence to statements: injuries consistent with accounts? Damage to property match descriptions? Determine aggressor based on: totality of witness accounts; video evidence; injury patterns; who had opportunity to leave but chose to escalate. Decide on charges: mutual combat (both charged), one primary aggressor (charge that person), insufficient evidence (no charges but document investigation). Consider alcohol as factor but not excuse. **Key Point:** Video evidence often resolves conflicting accounts. Physical evidence (injuries, property damage) may corroborate or contradict statements.

Practice Questions (55 questions)

Question 1: First priority upon arriving at crime scene is: A) Collecting evidence B) Interviewing witnesses C) Safety assessment—checking for threats and providing emergency aid D) Taking photographs

Answer: C **Explanation:** Safety always first. Assess for suspects, threats, and injured persons. Render aid, request EMS, apprehend suspects if safe. Investigation comes after safety secured.

Question 2: Crime scene perimeter should be: A) As small as possible B) Established large initially—easier to reduce than expand after contamination C) Only around body in homicides D) Not necessary

Answer: B **Explanation:** Start with large perimeter including all potential evidence areas, entry/exit routes, possible discard areas. Easier to reduce perimeter than expand after people have walked through and contaminated areas outside initial boundary.

Question 3: Chain of custody documentation must include: A) Just who collected evidence B) Every person handling evidence, when, where, why, and condition of evidence at each transfer C) Only final location D) Nothing if evidence photographed

Answer: B **Explanation:** Complete chain of custody documents every transfer: who collected, who received, dates/times, purpose, condition, how secured. Any gap creates doubt about integrity.

Question 4: Biological evidence (blood, DNA) should be packaged in: A) Plastic bags B) Paper bags or envelopes after air drying C) Any container D) No packaging needed

Answer: B **Explanation:** Paper allows air circulation preventing mold growth. Air dry wet blood before packaging. Never use plastic for biological evidence—promotes bacterial growth destroying DNA.

Question 5: The difference between interview and interrogation is: A) No difference B) Interview is non-accusatory gathering of information; interrogation is questioning suspects with probable cause C) Interviews are formal; interrogations are casual D) Only suspects are interviewed

Answer: B **Explanation:** Interviews gather information from witnesses/victims non-accusatorily. Interrogations question suspects when probable cause exists, seeking admissions. Different techniques and legal requirements apply.

Question 6: Miranda warnings are required during interrogation of: A) All witnesses B) Suspects in custody being questioned C) Victims D) Anyone at crime scene

Answer: B **Explanation:** Miranda required for custodial interrogation—questioning person in custody who isn't free to leave. Not required for witnesses, victims, or non-custodial conversations.

Question 7: When collecting fingerprints, you should: A) Lift first, then photograph B) Photograph before lifting, document surface, mark orientation C) Only lift visible prints D) Skip if smudged

Answer: B **Explanation:** Photograph prints before lifting to document original appearance. Document which surface prints came from and orientation (top/bottom). Lifting may damage print so photo preserves original.

Question 8: Reports should be written in: A) Third person, future tense B) First person, past tense using clear, specific language C) Second person, present tense D) Passive voice always

Answer: B **Explanation:** Use first person ("I observed"), past tense (events already occurred), active voice, clear specific language. "I saw the suspect run" not "The suspect was seen running by this officer."

Question 9: Cognitive interview technique includes: A) Rapid questioning B) Asking witness to recall everything, reconstruct circumstances, recall from different perspectives, reverse order C) Leading questions D) Limiting details

Answer: B **Explanation:** Cognitive interviewing enhances recall by: asking for all details even seemingly unimportant; reconstructing circumstances (weather, sounds, smells); recalling from other perspectives; reversing chronological order.

Question 10: Digital evidence collection requires: A) Turning on all devices B) Not powering on devices that are off, photographing screens, preserving battery, maintaining chain of custody C) Immediately searching files D) Deleting irrelevant data

Answer: B **Explanation:** Don't power on devices that are off. Don't access files yourself—specialized forensic examination needed. Photograph visible screens. Preserve battery. Consider Faraday bags. Document thoroughly.

Question 11: Crime scene photographs should include: A) Only close-ups of evidence B) Overall views, medium-range showing relationships, and close-ups with scales C) Just one photo per scene D) Only damaged property

Answer: B **Explanation:** Three-level photography: overall showing entire scene context, medium-range showing evidence relationships, close-ups of individual items with and without scales. Multiple angles document thoroughly.

Question 12: When interviewing witnesses, officers should: A) Interview all together B) Separate witnesses and interview individually to prevent influence and coordination C) Rush through quickly D) Only talk to victims

Answer: B **Explanation:** Interview witnesses separately to get independent, uninfluenced accounts. Group discussions lead to coordination of stories and contamination of memories. Document each person's individual observations.

Question 13: Locard's Exchange Principle states: A) Money must be exchanged B) Every contact leaves a trace—perpetrators take evidence from scene and leave evidence behind C) Evidence doesn't matter D) Only fingerprints count

Answer: B **Explanation:** Locard's principle: every contact between persons, or between person and object, results in exchange of materials. This forms basis of trace evidence examination—transferred fibers, hair, glass, soil connect suspects to scenes.

Question 14: Active listening during interviews means: A) Interrupting constantly B) Focusing on what person is saying, asking follow-up questions, reflecting understanding C) Thinking about next question D) Looking at phone

Answer: B **Explanation:** Active listening requires full attention to speaker, noting details and inconsistencies, asking relevant follow-up questions based on answers received, reflecting back what you heard to confirm understanding.

Question 15: TCIC database contains: A) Only warrants B) Warrants, wanted persons, stolen property, criminal histories, protective orders, vehicle/license info C) Just criminal histories D) Social media posts

Answer: B **Explanation:** TCIC (Texas Crime Information Center) contains warrants, wanted persons, stolen property, criminal histories, protective orders, gang information, vehicle registration, driver license status. Check suspects, vehicles, and property routinely.

Question 16: Firearms should be collected by: A) Inserting object through trigger guard B) Handling minimally, not inserting anything through trigger guard, documenting condition, preserving for prints/DNA C) Immediately unloading D) Anyone can handle

Answer: B **Explanation:** Don't insert objects through trigger guard—destroys trigger evidence. Handle minimally. Note condition (loaded/unloaded, hammer position). Preserve for fingerprints and DNA. Clear only if necessary for safety.

Question 17: Reports must be: A) Vague and general B) Clear, concise, complete with specific details and objective facts C) Opinion-based D) Written in third person future tense

Answer: B **Explanation:** The three Cs: Clear (easily understood), Concise (no unnecessary words), Complete (all relevant facts). Use specific details, objective language, first person past tense, active voice.

Question 18: Deception indicators include: A) Single behavior proves lying B) Clusters of verbal and non-verbal behaviors suggesting dishonesty C) Eye contact always means truth D) Fidgeting always means guilt

Answer: B **Explanation:** No single indicator proves deception. Look for clusters: inconsistencies, lack of detail, evasive answers, changes from baseline behavior, nervous behaviors when discussing critical topics. Consider context and baseline.

Question 19: Crime scene sketches should include: A) Artistic drawings only B) Measurements, scale, overhead view, item locations relative to fixed objects C) No measurements needed D) Only rough approximations

Answer: B **Explanation:** Sketches provide overhead view with accurate measurements showing distances between objects and from fixed reference points. Use triangulation or coordinate methods. Rough sketch at scene; finished diagram later using measurements.

Question 20: CODIS database is used for: A) Fingerprints B) DNA—comparing evidence DNA to known offenders and linking cases C) Ballistics D) Criminal histories

Answer: B **Explanation:** CODIS (Combined DNA Index System) compares DNA from evidence to database of known offenders and unsolved cases. Can identify suspects and link crimes through DNA even when suspect unknown.

Question 21: Trace evidence includes: A) Only fingerprints B) Fibers, hair, glass, paint, soil, gunshot residue—small materials transferred during crimes C) Large items only D) Just blood

Answer: B **Explanation:** Trace evidence includes small materials transferred during contact: fibers from clothing, hair, glass fragments, paint chips, soil, gunshot residue. Collect using tape lifts, careful packaging, preventing cross-contamination.

Question 22: Open-ended questions in interviews: A) Yes/no questions B) "Tell me what happened" "Describe what you saw"—allow narrative responses C) Leading questions D) Multiple choice

Answer: B **Explanation:** Open-ended questions allow person to provide narrative in own words without leading: "Tell me what happened," "Describe what you saw," "Explain the situation." Follow with specific questions to clarify details.

Question 23: Case status "cleared by arrest" means: A) Case dismissed B) Suspect arrested and charged—case proceeds to prosecution C) No charges filed D) Investigation continues

Answer: B **Explanation:** Cleared by arrest indicates suspect has been arrested and charged with offense. Case moves forward to prosecution. This is desired outcome for solved cases when suspect is identified and apprehended.

Question 24: Tool mark evidence can: A) Never be matched B) Be matched to specific tools through unique characteristics C) Only show tool type D) Be ignored

Answer: B **Explanation:** Tool marks can be matched to specific tools. Manufacturing processes and use create unique characteristics. Examiners compare marks from scene to marks made by suspect tool. Never fit suspect tool into mark—may damage evidence.

Question 25: When processing crime scene for fingerprints: A) Skip if surface looks clean B) Photograph prints before lifting, use appropriate powder, mark orientation, document surface C) Lift then photograph D) Only visible prints matter

Answer: B **Explanation:** Photograph before lifting (lifting may damage). Use appropriate powder (black on light surfaces, light on dark). Mark orientation. Document which surface. Some surfaces require chemical processing by lab.

Question 26: Theme development during interrogation: A) Accusing suspect directly B) Providing moral justification or minimization making admission psychologically easier C) Promising leniency D) Threatening suspect

Answer: B **Explanation:** Theme development provides psychological justification: "Anyone would be angry in that situation," "This just happened in the moment." Not promising leniency—providing face-saving explanation making admission easier.

Question 27: AFIS is used for: A) DNA analysis B) Automated Fingerprint Identification System—comparing latent prints from scenes to database C) Ballistics D) Document examination

Answer: B **Explanation:** AFIS (Automated Fingerprint Identification System) compares fingerprints from crime scenes to database of known prints. Can identify suspects when prints match database entries even when suspect unknown.

Question 28: Report writing should avoid: A) Specific times B) Vague language, opinions without basis, assumptions, judgmental language C) First person D) Past tense

Answer: B **Explanation:** Avoid vague language ("several people"), unsupported opinions ("suspect was lying"), assumptions (explaining what you didn't observe), judgmental language ("stupid suspect"). Use specific facts, objective descriptions.

Question 29: Circumstantial evidence: A) Is weaker than direct evidence B) Requires inference to connect to fact—fingerprints, DNA, trace evidence C) Cannot convict D) Is inadmissible

Answer: B **Explanation:** Circumstantial evidence requires inference: fingerprints suggest presence, DNA connects to item. Not weaker than direct evidence—different. Multiple circumstantial pieces often more compelling than single direct evidence.

Question 30: Digital evidence requires: A) Immediate file access B) Specialized forensic examination—don't access files yourself C) Deletion of irrelevant data D) Powering on all devices

Answer: B **Explanation:** Digital evidence requires specialized forensic examination. Don't turn on devices. Don't access files yourself—may alter evidence. Specialists extract: messages, photos, internet history, GPS data, deleted files.

Question 31: Crime scene entry log should document: A) Just names B) Name, badge number, time in, time out, purpose for each person entering scene C) Only investigators D) Nothing needed

Answer: B **Explanation:** Log everyone entering scene: name, badge/ID number, time entered, time exited, purpose. Limits contamination, tracks who had access, documents scene security. Only essential personnel should enter.

Question 32: Cognitive interview asks witness to: A) Answer yes/no only B) Recall everything, reconstruct circumstances, use different perspectives, reverse chronological order C) Guess at details D) Keep answers brief

Answer: B **Explanation:** Cognitive interview enhances recall: recall everything even details seeming unimportant; reconstruct circumstances (weather, lighting, sounds); recall from different perspectives; reverse order (start from end). Improves memory retrieval.

Question 33: Ballistics evidence analysis can: A) Only identify gun type B) Match bullets and cartridge cases to specific firearms C) Never be used D) Show nothing useful

Answer: B **Explanation:** Ballistics examination matches bullets and cartridge cases to specific firearms through unique markings created by barrel rifling and firing pin. Can link shootings to weapons even when gun not recovered. NIBIN database links cases.

Question 34: Biological evidence packaging requires: A) Plastic bags always B) Air drying then paper packaging to prevent bacterial growth C) No special requirements D) Wet storage

Answer: B **Explanation:** Air dry biological evidence before packaging. Use paper bags or envelopes—never plastic which promotes bacterial growth and mold destroying DNA. Refrigerate if cannot air dry. Prevents contamination and degradation.

Question 35: When testifying in court about reports: A) Make up forgotten details B) Refer to notes/reports if allowed, admit if don't remember, testify based on documentation C) Argue with attorneys D) Guess at answers

Answer: B **Explanation:** Testify based on observations and documentation. Refer to notes if court allows. Admit if you don't remember specific detail rather than speculating. Remain professional. Explain technical terms clearly.

Question 36: Impression evidence includes: A) Only fingerprints B) Tire tracks, shoe prints, tool marks—can connect suspects to scenes C) Just photographs D) Nothing physical

Answer: B **Explanation:** Impression evidence: tire tracks, shoe prints, tool marks. Photograph with scales. Cast using dental stone. Pattern evidence can identify specific shoes or tires. Wear patterns individualize items connecting suspects to scenes.

Question 37: Surveillance as investigative technique: A) Never useful B) Physical observation of suspects/locations—labor-intensive but effective C) Illegal always D) Only for federal cases

Answer: B **Explanation:** Surveillance involves observing suspects or locations. Labor-intensive requiring multiple officers and shifts. Effective for gathering intelligence, documenting activities, identifying associates. Follow legal restrictions on privacy expectations.

Question 38: Case solvability factors include: A) Only confession B) Identified suspects, witnesses, physical evidence, leads to pursue C) Just victim cooperation D) Nothing matters

Answer: B **Explanation:** Solvability factors determine follow-up priority: identified suspects, cooperative witnesses, physical evidence (DNA, prints, video), clear leads. Cases with strong solvability factors get resources. Limited investigators require case management decisions.

Question 39: Documentary evidence should be: A) Handled frequently B) Handled minimally preserving fingerprints, photographed in place, protected from damage C) Folded for storage D) Ignored

Answer: B **Explanation:** Handle documents minimally to preserve fingerprints. Photograph in place before collection. Use gloves or tools. Protect from damage. Package in protective sleeves. Documents show motive, prove transactions, provide handwriting samples.

Question 40: Miranda requirements during interrogation: A) Never needed B) Required for custodial interrogation—must cease if suspect invokes rights C) Optional D) Only for felonies

Answer: B **Explanation:** Miranda warnings required before custodial interrogation. Must stop all questioning if suspect invokes right to counsel. Record interrogation per Texas law. Must be voluntary without threats or promises. Document advisement and waiver.

Question 41: Scene contamination prevention requires: A) Unlimited access B) Establishing perimeter, limiting access, protecting evidence, logging entries C) No controls D) Public viewing

Answer: B **Explanation:** Prevent contamination by: establishing large perimeter initially; limiting access to essential personnel only; protecting evidence from weather and traffic; logging everyone who enters; using proper PPE; documenting before moving anything.

Question 42: Alternative questions during interrogation: A) Yes/no only B) Offering two explanations—one more socially acceptable—suspect often chooses lesser but both are admissions C) Open-ended only D) No questions

Answer: B **Explanation:** Alternative questioning: "Did you plan this for weeks, or did it just happen in the moment?" "Was it about money, or teaching a lesson?" Suspect often chooses lesser alternative feeling better, but both are admissions.

Question 43: Follow-up investigation typically involves: A) No additional work B) Evidence submission to labs, additional interviews, records checks, warrant preparation C) Just writing reports D) Closing case immediately

Answer: B **Explanation:** Follow-up includes: submitting evidence to labs (fingerprints, DNA, digital forensics); conducting detailed interviews; obtaining records through warrants/subpoenas; preparing search and arrest warrants; identifying suspects through databases and lineups.

Question 44: Victim cooperation affects: A) Nothing B) Case priority and prosecution viability—uncooperative victims make prosecution difficult C) Only sentencing D) Evidence collection

Answer: B **Explanation:** Victim cooperation significant factor. Uncooperative victims make prosecution difficult—key witness unavailable. May affect case priority. However, evidence-based prosecution possible using: physical evidence, 911 recordings, witness statements, photos, medical records.

Question 45: Crime scene processing order: A) Collect evidence, then photograph B) Photograph overall, medium, close-up before collecting; document locations; collect systematically C) Random collection D) Take one photo only

Answer: B **Explanation:** Systematic order: overall photography establishing context; medium-range showing relationships; close-ups with scales; sketch with measurements; then collect evidence documenting each item's location. Never disturb before documentation complete.

Question 46: Rapport building with interviewees: A) Be aggressive immediately B) Show empathy, listen actively, express genuine interest, use open body language C) Ignore their concerns D) Rush interview

Answer: B **Explanation:** Build rapport through: introducing yourself and explaining role; expressing empathy for their experience; active listening without constant interruption; genuine interest; appropriate eye contact; open body language. People share more when comfortable.

Question 47: Physical evidence value includes: A) Nothing useful B) Connecting suspects to scenes/victims, corroborating statements, excluding innocents, proving elements C) Only for serious crimes D) Cannot be used

Answer: B **Explanation:** Physical evidence: connects suspects to crimes; corroborates or contradicts statements; excludes innocent persons; proves offense elements; provides objective facts independent of testimony. Critical for successful prosecution.

Question 48: NIBIN database is used for: A) DNA B) Ballistics—linking shootings through bullets and cartridge cases C) Fingerprints D) Vehicle identification

Answer: B **Explanation:** NIBIN (National Integrated Ballistic Information Network) compares bullets and cartridge cases from shootings. Links cases through firearm evidence even when weapon not recovered. Submit ballistics evidence for comparison.

Question 49: Report completeness requires: A) Brief mention only B) Answering who, what, when, where, why, how with all relevant facts C) Officer opinions mainly D) Minimal details

Answer: B **Explanation:** Complete reports answer: who was involved; what happened; when it occurred (specific times); where it occurred (exact location); why it happened (if known); how it occurred (sequence of events). Include all relevant facts without gaps.

Question 50: Latent prints can be: A) Only visible prints matter B) Developed on surfaces using powder, chemicals, or other methods revealing invisible prints C) Never found D) Ignored if not visible

Answer: B **Explanation:** Latent (hidden) prints can be developed using: fingerprint powder for non-porous surfaces; chemical processing for porous surfaces (paper, cardboard); alternate light sources; superglue fuming. Many surfaces retain prints invisible to naked eye.

Question 51: Interrogation must be: A) Coerced for effectiveness B) Voluntary without threats, promises, or coercion—involuntary statements suppressed C) Unlimited in duration D) Without documentation

Answer: B **Explanation:** Interrogation must be voluntary. No threats, no promises of leniency, no physical coercion, no psychological torture. Involuntary confessions are suppressed. False confessions occur—ensure statements match evidence and contain details only perpetrator would know.

Question 52: Social media evidence: A) Cannot be used B) Often contains valuable evidence—photos, videos, locations, statements—obtain through legal process C) Never admissible D) Requires no warrants

Answer: B **Explanation:** Social media frequently contains evidence: incriminating photos/videos, location data, statements, associations. Obtain through legal process (search warrants, subpoenas) when necessary. Document as found. Authenticate for court.

Question 53: Cleared by exception means: A) Case unsolved B) Case solved but arrest not possible—suspect dead, prosecution declined, victim refuses cooperation C) Arrest made D) Case unfounded

Answer: B **Explanation:** Cleared by exception: investigation determined who committed crime but arrest/prosecution not possible. Reasons include: suspect deceased, prosecutor declines charges, victim refuses to cooperate, extradition denied. Not closed—remains cleared exception.

Question 54: Witness credibility assessment considers: A) Nothing relevant B) Consistency of statements, position to observe, corroboration, bias, demeanor C) Only appearance D) Just first impression

Answer: B **Explanation:** Assess credibility through: consistency across multiple tellings; position/ability to observe; corroboration from other evidence; potential bias or motive to lie; demeanor during interview; specific details versus vague accounts; admission of uncertainty about details.

Question 55: Case file organization for prosecution should include: A) Random papers B) Organized reports, evidence inventory, witness list with contacts, clear documentation C) Just arrest warrant D) No organization needed

Answer: B **Explanation:** Provide prosecutor with organized case file: clear reports; evidence inventory with descriptions and locations; witness list with contact information; relevant records obtained; photos and diagrams; timeline of events; legal issues identified. Organization facilitates prosecution.

Scoring Your Practice Questions

52-55 correct (95-100%): Outstanding! Your mastery of crime scene management, evidence collection, interviewing techniques, and report writing is excellent. You understand how to conduct thorough investigations that support successful prosecutions. Review any missed questions, then move confidently to Chapter 6.

47-51 correct (85-94%): Excellent work! You have strong investigative knowledge. Focus on areas where you missed questions—whether evidence collection techniques, interviewing strategies, or report writing standards. Review those sections and proceed forward.

41-46 correct (75-84%): Good progress! You grasp core investigative concepts but need strengthening in specific areas. Identify patterns in missed questions. Review relevant sections focusing on proper procedures, documentation requirements, and evidence handling.

35-40 correct (65-74%): You're developing understanding but have gaps. Review Chapter 5 systematically. Focus on crime scene management, chain of custody, interviewing techniques, and report writing. Create summary notes for evidence types and collection methods.

Below 35 correct (less than 65%): Substantial additional study needed. Investigation skills are fundamental to successful law enforcement. Review thoroughly, taking detailed notes. Focus on understanding WHY procedures exist—legal requirements, evidence preservation, prosecution support. Practice scenario analysis before proceeding.

Chapter Summary

Effective investigation transforms crime scenes into convictions through:

Crime Scene Management: Secure scenes immediately establishing large perimeter. Limit access logging all entries. Document everything before disturbing. Protect evidence from contamination and weather.

Evidence Collection: Photograph before collecting (overall, medium, close-up with scales). Use proper techniques for each evidence type. Package appropriately maintaining chain of custody. Document every transfer preventing gaps.

Interviewing: Build rapport showing empathy and active listening. Use open-ended questions for narratives, then specific questions for details. Interview witnesses separately. Detect deception through behavioral clusters, not single indicators.

Interrogation: Use structured approach with theme development and alternative questions. Obtain voluntary statements after proper Miranda advisement. Record per Texas law. Ensure admissions match evidence.

Report Writing: Clear, concise, complete reports using specific details and objective language. First person, past tense, active voice. Answer who, what, when, where, why, how. Avoid vague language, unsupported opinions, assumptions.

Resources: Utilize TCIC/NCIC for warrant checks and stolen property. Submit evidence to CODIS (DNA), AFIS (fingerprints), NIBIN (ballistics). Coordinate with other agencies sharing information.

Follow-Up: Submit evidence for analysis. Conduct additional interviews. Obtain records through legal process. Prepare warrants. Identify suspects through databases and informants. Develop cases systematically.

Your investigative skills directly determine justice outcomes. Poor scene management destroys evidence. Inadequate documentation results in dismissals. Effective investigation, thorough documentation, and proper evidence handling ensure victims get justice and guilty parties face consequences.

CHAPTER 6: JUVENILE LAW AND PROCEDURES

Learning Objectives

By the end of this chapter, you will: understand Texas juvenile justice system differences from adult system; identify age of criminal responsibility and jurisdiction; recognize juvenile rights and special protections; properly handle juvenile offenders distinguishing custody from arrest; manage school-related incidents appropriately; fulfill mandatory reporting requirements for child abuse; and utilize diversion programs as alternatives to formal processing.

Why This Chapter Matters: Juveniles require different handling than adults. The juvenile justice system emphasizes rehabilitation over punishment. Mishandling juveniles violates their rights and jeopardizes cases. Understanding juvenile law protects children's welfare while maintaining public safety. Your interactions with juveniles shape their future—positive intervention can redirect lives away from crime.

Texas Juvenile Justice Code

Age of Criminal Responsibility

Juvenile Jurisdiction: Texas Family Code Title 3 governs juvenile justice. **Age Range:** Persons age 10-16 at time of conduct fall under juvenile court jurisdiction. Children under 10 cannot be prosecuted for any offense—they lack criminal responsibility. Age 17+ are adults for criminal purposes (though civil law considers 18 the age of majority).

Determining Age: Age at time of alleged conduct determines jurisdiction, not age at arrest or prosecution. If a 16-year-old commits burglary then turns 17 before arrest, they're still processed as juvenile because they were 16 when the offense occurred. Verify birthdate through reliable sources: driver's license, birth certificate, parent verification, school records. Document age determination in reports.

Transfer to Adult Court (Certification): Juveniles age 14+ charged with certain serious offenses may be transferred to adult court through certification hearing. **Automatic Transfer:** At age 18, jurisdiction automatically transfers to adult criminal court for any pending juvenile matters. **Discretionary Transfer:** Prosecutor may seek transfer for juveniles 14+ accused of capital felonies, first-degree felonies, or aggravated controlled substance felonies. Court considers: seriousness of offense, sophistication and maturity of juvenile, prior record, prospects for rehabilitation, protection of public. Certified juveniles face adult penalties including prison and permanent criminal records.

Status Offenses: Conduct illegal only because person is juvenile: truancy (skipping school), running away from home, curfew violations, tobacco/alcohol possession by minor, insubordination to parents. These are not crimes—they're status offenses handled through juvenile courts but don't result in delinquency adjudications. Officers typically refer status offenders to juvenile probation or diversion programs rather than formal processing.

Juvenile Rights and Protections

Constitutional Rights: Juveniles possess same constitutional rights as adults with additional protections: **Fourth Amendment:** Protection from unreasonable searches and seizures. **Fifth Amendment:** Right against self-incrimination. Miranda warnings required. **Sixth Amendment:** Right to counsel. **Fourteenth Amendment:** Due process rights.

Additional Juvenile Protections: Miranda Plus: When taking juveniles into custody and interrogating, standard Miranda warnings must be given. However, courts scrutinize juvenile confessions more closely. Consider juvenile's age, education, experience with system, presence of parent/attorney, length of interrogation. Younger juveniles may not fully understand rights despite

being read warnings. **Right to Attorney:** Juveniles have right to attorney at all stages. Parents may retain counsel. If indigent, court appoints attorney. Don't interrogate juvenile without considering need for parental or attorney presence. **Parental Notification:** Must notify parents promptly when taking juvenile into custody (except in limited circumstances like abuse investigations where parent is suspect). **Confidentiality:** Juvenile records are confidential and sealed. Media cannot publish juvenile identities in most cases. Fingerprints and photographs handled differently than adults.

School Searches: Different standards apply to school searches. School officials may search students based on reasonable suspicion (lower than probable cause required for police). When you conduct searches on school grounds as law enforcement (not assisting school officials with school discipline), you're held to probable cause standard. Coordinate with school administrators understanding respective roles.

Handling Juvenile Offenders

Custody vs. Arrest Distinctions

Legal Terminology: For juveniles, use "take into custody" rather than "arrest." While functionally similar to arrest, the distinction emphasizes juvenile system's focus on rehabilitation rather than punishment. **Taking into Custody:** Authorized when: juvenile committed delinquent conduct (would be crime if adult) or conduct indicating need for supervision (status offense), or juvenile violates probation conditions.

Authority to Take into Custody: Police may take juveniles into custody without warrant when: offense committed in officer's presence, probable cause exists juvenile committed felony, probable cause exists juvenile committed misdemeanor and won't appear for court if released, or juvenile violates probation. Similar to adult arrest authority but uses different terminology reflecting rehabilitative focus.

Processing Differences from Adults: No Booking Photos Posted: Juvenile photos not publicly distributed unless specific circumstances (violent offender at large). **Limited Fingerprinting:** Juveniles fingerprinted only for specific serious offenses. **Sealed Records:** Records confidential and generally sealed upon reaching adulthood if successfully complete probation. **Different Facilities:** Juveniles cannot be held in adult jails except under narrow circumstances and with strict separation requirements.

Miranda for Juveniles: Standard Miranda warnings required but courts examine validity more closely considering: juvenile's age and education level, prior experience with justice system, length and nature of questioning, whether parent or attorney present, whether juvenile appeared to understand rights, any special vulnerabilities (mental disability, intoxication). Best practice: Have parent or attorney present during interrogation when possible. Keep interrogation brief and age-appropriate. Document juvenile's apparent understanding of rights. Use simple language explaining rights.

Detention Decisions: After taking juvenile into custody, you have options: **Release to Parents:** For minor offenses with cooperative parents and low flight risk. Obtain parent signature promising to bring juvenile to court. **Detention:** For serious offenses, repeat offenders, or when release would endanger public. Juveniles held in juvenile detention facilities, not adult jails. **Citation/Summons:** For less serious offenses, issue citation requiring appearance before juvenile court. Release to parents with court date.

Fingerprinting and Photographing: Juveniles are NOT routinely fingerprinted and photographed like adults. Restrictions apply: **Fingerprinting Authorized:** Only for felonies and specific serious misdemeanors listed in Family Code §58.002. **Photograph Restrictions:** Extremely limited circumstances. Generally prohibited. **Purpose:** When authorized, prints submitted to state for background check purposes but handled differently than adult prints.

School-Related Incidents

School Resource Officers (SROs): Many officers are assigned to schools as SROs. This unique position requires balancing law enforcement duties with educational environment needs. **Primary Responsibilities:** Provide security and immediate response to threats; serve as law enforcement liaison; build positive relationships with students; educate about law enforcement and safety; mentor at-risk youth; investigate crimes occurring on campus.

Roles and Limitations: Law Enforcement vs. School Discipline: Distinguish between criminal matters (your responsibility) and school discipline (administrator's responsibility). Don't involve yourself in purely school discipline issues (dress code violations, tardiness, disrespect to teachers) unless they escalate to criminal conduct. **Criminal Conduct on Campus:** You handle criminal offenses: assaults, drug possession/sales, weapons possession, thefts, vandalism, terroristic threats, sexual assault. **School Discipline:** Administrators handle rule violations not rising to criminal conduct: truancy, dress code, academic dishonesty (unless rises to forgery), minor disruptions.

Searches on School Property: Complex area requiring careful analysis of your role: **School Official Conducting Search:** School officials (principals, teachers, administrators) may search students based on reasonable suspicion—lower standard than probable cause. Doesn't require warrant. Searches must be reasonable in scope. **SRO Assisting School Officials:** If you're acting at school's request for school discipline purposes, courts may apply reasonable suspicion standard. **SRO Conducting Independent Investigation:** If you're conducting independent criminal investigation, you're held to probable cause standard and may need warrant. **Best Practice:** Understand whether you're acting as law enforcement or assisting school with discipline before conducting searches. Document the basis for your involvement.

Common School Incidents: Fights/Assaults: Determine if mutual combat (both charged with assault) or one-sided attack (charge aggressor). Consider assault on school grounds as potential enhancement. Document injuries. Obtain witness statements from students and staff. **Drug Offenses:** Possession on school grounds creates drug-free zone considerations enhancing penalties. Follow proper evidence collection for controlled substances. Notify specialized units if distribution suspected. **Weapons:** Firearms on school property are serious felonies (Gun-Free School Zones Act). Even juveniles face federal prosecution. Knives and other weapons violate state law and school policy. Secure weapons safely. **Threats:** Terroristic threat charges appropriate for threatening school violence. Social media threats taken seriously post-Columbine. Investigate thoroughly even if seem like "jokes." Threats disrupt schools and traumatize students. **Sexual Offenses:** Sexual assault and harassment occur in schools. Obtain statements from victim, witnesses, and suspect separately. Involve specialized investigators. Notify parents (except when parent is suspect). Consider Title IX implications alongside criminal investigation.

Parental Notification: When juveniles are involved in school incidents, notification protocols vary: **Minor School Discipline:** School handles parent notification. **Criminal Conduct:** You notify parents when taking juvenile into custody or when their involvement needed for investigation. **Child Abuse Situations:** If parent is suspect, notify CPS rather than parent initially.

Child Abuse and Neglect Investigation

Mandatory Reporting Requirements

Mandatory Reporters: Texas Family Code §261.101 requires certain professionals to report suspected child abuse or neglect. Peace officers are mandatory reporters. **When to Report:** Must report when you have cause to believe child's physical or mental health or welfare has been adversely affected by abuse or neglect. "Cause to believe" is lower standard than probable cause—reasonable suspicion suffices. Don't need certainty to report. When in doubt, report. **Time Frame:** Must report no later than 48 hours after first suspecting abuse or neglect. Sooner is better—call immediately when safe to do so. **How to Report:** Texas Abuse Hotline: 1-800-252-5400 (24/7). Online reporting also available. Provide: your name and contact information, child's name and location, parents' names, nature and extent of injury or condition, any other pertinent information.

Types of Abuse: Physical Abuse: Injury to child caused by other than accidental means. Includes hitting, kicking, burning, shaking, biting. Red flags: injuries inconsistent with explanation, pattern injuries (belt marks, hand prints), injuries in various stages of healing, delay in seeking medical treatment, multiple injuries. **Sexual Abuse:** Sexual conduct harmful to child's mental, emotional, or physical welfare. Includes inappropriate touching, exposure, exploitation, penetration. May involve family members (incest) or others. Children rarely lie about sexual abuse—believe and investigate. **Emotional/Mental Abuse:** Observable impairment of emotional or mental functioning. Hardest to prove but devastating effects. Includes severe criticism, rejection, isolation, terrorizing. Often accompanies other abuse types. **Neglect:** Failure to provide for child's basic needs. Includes inadequate food, clothing, shelter, medical care, supervision. Consider family resources—poverty alone isn't neglect, but failure to utilize available resources may be.

Indicators of Abuse: Physical Indicators: Unexplained injuries, injuries in various healing stages, pattern injuries, injuries to unusual areas (inner thighs, back, buttocks), burns with distinctive patterns, fractures especially in young children, head injuries, malnourishment, poor hygiene, inadequate clothing for weather. **Behavioral Indicators:** Withdrawal, aggression, sexualized behavior inappropriate for age, fear of specific people, reluctance to go home, dramatic behavior changes, regression (thumb-sucking, bed-wetting in previously trained children), running away, substance abuse, self-harm, suicidal ideation.

Investigation Procedures: Child Interview: Conduct in safe, comfortable environment. Use age-appropriate language. Avoid leading questions. Ask open-ended questions: "Tell me what happened." Document exact words used. Consider forensic interview by trained specialist—children's advocacy centers have professionals skilled in child interviews. Don't repeatedly interview—can be traumatizing and may contaminate statements. **Parent/Caretaker Interview:** Separate from child. Obtain explanation for injuries or conditions. Note demeanor, defensiveness, cooperation level. Ask about child's behaviors, development, medical history. Don't confront accusatorily unless making arrest—may cause parent to flee with child. **Medical Examination:** Arrange medical evaluation documenting injuries. Medical professionals can distinguish accidental from intentional injuries. Sexual abuse cases require specialized sexual assault examination. Medical records crucial evidence. **Scene Documentation:** Photograph injuries from multiple angles. With scale for size reference. Include context photos showing body location. Photograph living conditions if neglect suspected. Document unsanitary conditions, lack of food, dangerous situations, inadequate sleeping arrangements. **CPS Coordination:** Child Protective Services investigates abuse/neglect focusing on child safety and family services. You investigate criminal aspects. Coordinate to avoid duplicating interviews and share information efficiently. CPS has authority to remove children from dangerous situations. You have authority to arrest perpetrators.

Emergency Removal: Family Code §262.104 authorizes officers to take emergency custody of children without court order when: child is in immediate danger from physical or sexual abuse, and continuing in home exposes child to immediate risk, and no time exists to obtain court order. **When Removing:** Take child to safe place: relative's home, emergency shelter, or CPS office. Notify CPS immediately. Court hearing must occur within one business day to review removal. Document specific facts creating immediate danger justifying removal. Balance child safety against family integrity—removal is serious intervention reserved for genuine emergencies.

Referral and Diversion Programs

Alternatives to Formal Processing

Philosophy: Juvenile justice emphasizes rehabilitation. Not every juvenile offense requires formal court processing. Diversion programs provide alternatives addressing underlying problems while holding juveniles accountable. **Benefits of Diversion:** Avoids formal record, reduces system burden, addresses root causes (family dysfunction, substance abuse, mental health), maintains family structure, faster resolution than court processing, lower recidivism rates for minor offenses.

Diversion Options: Warning and Release: For very minor first offenses with cooperative parents. Document warning in report. May involve parent conference explaining seriousness. **Probation Department Referral:** Informal probation without court involvement. Juvenile meets with probation officer, completes requirements (community service, counseling, restitution), upon completion matter closed without formal adjudication. **First Offender Programs:** Structured programs for first-time offenders teaching consequences, requiring community service, involving parent participation. Successful completion prevents formal record. **Teen Court/Youth Court:** Peer jury of teenagers hears case, determines appropriate sanctions, juvenile serves on future juries as part of sanction. Addresses accountability through peer pressure. **Mediation/Restorative Justice:** Victim and juvenile meet with mediator. Juvenile hears impact of actions, makes amends, victim gets closure. Focuses on repairing harm rather than punishment.

When Diversion Appropriate: Consider diversion for: minor offenses (theft under $50, minor vandalism, trespassing, disorderly conduct), first-time offenders with no delinquency history, juvenile and parents cooperative, victim supports alternative resolution (if applicable), underlying issues amenable to intervention (family problems, peer pressure, impulsivity). **When Formal Processing Required:** Serious offenses (violence, sexual offenses, significant property crimes), repeat offenders showing pattern, juvenile uncooperative or absconding risk, parents uninvolved or unable to supervise, victim demands prosecution, public safety concerns.

Referral Process: Discuss diversion possibility with juvenile, parents, and victim when appropriate. Explain requirements and consequences of non-completion. Obtain cooperation commitment. Complete referral paperwork per department procedure. Follow up on compliance. If juvenile fails to complete diversion successfully, proceed with formal charges. Document diversion attempts showing good-faith effort at rehabilitation before court involvement.

Real-World Application: Juvenile Justice Scenarios

Scenario 1: School Fight—Determining Charges

Situation: SRO, you witness two students fighting in hallway. Both trading punches. Both have minor injuries (bloody noses, bruising). Teachers separate them. Both claim other started fight. Both are 15 years old. No weapons involved. No prior incidents with either student.

Analysis: This is mutual combat—both actively fighting rather than one defending against attack. **Proper Actions:** Separate immediately. Ensure no weapons. Check for injuries requiring medical attention. Interview both students separately obtaining statements about what led to fight. Interview witnesses (other students, teachers) about who started altercation and whether self-defense claims valid. Photograph injuries on both students. Determine primary aggressor or if truly mutual combat. **Charging Decisions:** Both could be charged with assault (Class A misdemeanor—bodily injury to another). However, consider diversion: First offense for both? Minor injuries? Underlying dispute resolvable? School consequences (suspension)? Alternative: Issue citations, release to parents, refer to diversion program. Formal charges may not be necessary if school consequences adequate and juveniles learn from experience. **Coordination with School:** School administrators handle discipline (suspension, alternative placement). You handle criminal aspects. Don't duplicate punishments—work together for appropriate consequences. **Documentation:** Complete report documenting fight circumstances, injuries, statements, your determination about charges or diversion. Even if diverting, document thoroughly in case juveniles don't complete diversion successfully.

Scenario 2: Child Abuse Report—Suspicious Injuries

Situation: Dispatched to hospital for possible child abuse. 4-year-old brought by mother with broken arm. Doctor suspects abuse—injury inconsistent with mother's explanation (claims child fell off couch). X-rays show old fractures in various healing stages. Child appears fearful, withdrawn. Mother's boyfriend has access to child and history of violence.

Analysis: Multiple red flags: injury inconsistent with explanation, pattern of injuries in various healing stages (suggests ongoing abuse), child's fearful behavior, presence of person with violence history. **Proper Investigation:** Interview mother separately from boyfriend and child. Obtain her explanation for current injury and old fractures. Note demeanor and cooperation level. Interview boyfriend separately. Obtain his explanation and whereabouts during injury.

Observe interactions with mother and child. Interview child using age-appropriate questions. Don't lead or suggest answers. Consider forensic interview specialist. Document exact words used. Consult with medical staff. Doctors can distinguish accidental from intentional injuries. Get written medical opinion about whether injuries consistent with explanation. Photograph all visible injuries (current and old if visible). Document with scale. Review CPS history. Have there been prior reports? Coordinate with CPS. They'll investigate family situation and child safety. You investigate criminal aspects. **Decision Point:** Based on medical evidence, inconsistent explanations, injury pattern, determine whether probable cause exists for injury to child charges. Consider who likely perpetrator—mother, boyfriend, or both? If removing child for safety, document immediate danger justifying emergency custody. Place with relative if possible; otherwise CPS assumes custody. If arresting perpetrator, charge with injury to child (felony based on serious bodily injury). **Follow-Up:** This investigation continues beyond initial response. Additional interviews, CPS findings, medical records, and child's statements develop case. Document everything thoroughly—child abuse cases face intense scrutiny in court.

Practice Questions (45 questions)

Question 1: In Texas, juvenile court jurisdiction includes persons aged: A) Under 18 at time of offense B) 10-16 at time of conduct C) Under 21 D) 10-17

Answer: B **Explanation:** Texas juvenile courts have jurisdiction over persons age 10-16 at time of alleged conduct. Children under 10 cannot be prosecuted. Age 17+ are adults for criminal purposes. Age at time of offense determines jurisdiction.

Question 2: The key difference between taking a juvenile into custody and adult arrest is: A) No difference at all B) Juveniles receive additional protections and terminology emphasizes rehabilitation C) Juveniles cannot be detained D) Different Miranda warnings

Answer: B **Explanation:** While functionally similar, juvenile custody emphasizes rehabilitation. Additional protections include confidential records, limited fingerprinting, parental notification, sealed records upon successful completion. Terminology reflects rehabilitative rather than punitive focus.

Question 3: Mandatory reporters of child abuse must report: A) Only when certain abuse occurred B) Within 48 hours when they have cause to believe child has been abused or neglected C) Within 1 week D) Only for physical abuse

Answer: B **Explanation:** Mandatory reporters must report no later than 48 hours after first suspecting abuse or neglect. "Cause to believe" is lower standard than probable cause—reasonable suspicion suffices. When in doubt, report. Call Texas Abuse Hotline: 1-800-252-5400.

Question 4: Status offenses are: A) Serious crimes B) Conduct illegal only because person is juvenile—truancy, running away, curfew violations C) Adult crimes D) Always result in detention

Answer: B **Explanation:** Status offenses are acts illegal only for juveniles: truancy, running away, curfew violations, tobacco/alcohol possession by minor. Not criminal offenses—handled through juvenile court but don't result in delinquency adjudications. Typically referred to diversion.

Question 5: When juveniles are taken into custody, officers must: A) Immediately place in adult jail B) Notify parents promptly except in limited circumstances like abuse cases where parent is suspect C) Never notify parents D) Wait 24 hours before notifying

Answer: B **Explanation:** Must notify parents promptly when taking juvenile into custody. Exception: when investigating abuse and parent is suspect, notify CPS instead. Parents have right to know child's location and situation.

Question 6: School resource officers should: A) Handle all school discipline B) Distinguish between criminal matters (law enforcement responsibility) and school discipline (administrator responsibility) C) Ignore criminal conduct on campus D) Arrest for dress code violations

Answer: B **Explanation:** SROs must distinguish criminal conduct (assaults, drugs, weapons—law enforcement handles) from school discipline (tardiness, dress code, disrespect—administrators handle). Don't involve yourself in purely disciplinary matters unless they escalate to criminal conduct.

Question 7: Diversion programs for juveniles: A) Are never appropriate B) Provide alternatives to formal processing emphasizing rehabilitation for minor offenses C) Only for violent crimes D) Require court involvement

Answer: B **Explanation:** Diversion programs offer alternatives for minor offenses and first-time offenders: warnings, informal probation, first offender programs, teen court, mediation. Emphasize rehabilitation, address root causes, avoid formal records. Not appropriate for serious or repeat offenses.

Question 8: Juveniles' Miranda rights: A) Same as adults with no differences B) Same constitutional rights but courts scrutinize confessions more closely considering age, education, comprehension C) Don't apply to juveniles D) Only apply for felonies

Answer: B **Explanation:** Juveniles have same Miranda rights but courts examine validity more closely: age, education, prior system experience, interrogation length, parent/attorney presence, apparent understanding. Best practice: have parent/attorney present, keep interrogations brief, use simple language.

Question 9: Emergency removal of child from home without court order is authorized when: A) Convenient for investigation B) Child in immediate danger from abuse and no time to obtain court order C) Parent requests it D) Always prohibited

Answer: B **Explanation:** Family Code §262.104 allows emergency custody when child is in immediate danger from physical/sexual abuse, continuing in home exposes to immediate risk, and no time for court order. Court hearing must occur within one business day. Document specific facts justifying removal.

Question 10: Juvenile records are: A) Public information B) Confidential and generally sealed upon reaching adulthood if successfully complete probation C) Published in newspapers D) Same as adult records

Answer: B **Explanation:** Juvenile records are confidential. Media cannot publish juvenile identities in most cases. Records generally sealed upon reaching adulthood if juvenile successfully completes probation. Emphasizes rehabilitation and second chances rather than permanent stigma.

Question 11: School searches by school officials require: A) Probable cause and warrant B) Reasonable suspicion—lower standard than probable cause C) No justification D) Parental permission

Answer: B **Explanation:** School officials may search students based on reasonable suspicion (lower than probable cause). Search must be reasonable in scope. When law enforcement conducts independent criminal investigation on campus, probable cause standard applies.

Question 12: Certification (transfer to adult court) may occur for juveniles: A) Of any age for any offense B) Age 14+ charged with certain serious offenses after hearing considering factors C) Automatically at age 16 D) Never allowed

Answer: B **Explanation:** Juveniles age 14+ charged with capital felonies, first-degree felonies, or aggravated controlled substance felonies may be certified to adult court. Court considers: offense seriousness, juvenile's sophistication/maturity, prior record, rehabilitation prospects, public protection.

Question 13: When investigating child abuse, officers should: A) Interview child and parent together B) Interview child separately using age-appropriate questions, avoid leading, consider forensic interview specialist C) Not interview the child D) Repeatedly question until story changes

Answer: B **Explanation:** Interview child separately in safe environment using age-appropriate language. Avoid leading questions. Ask open-ended questions. Document exact words. Consider forensic interview by trained specialist at children's advocacy center. Don't repeatedly interview—traumatizing and contaminates statements.

Question 14: Juveniles may be fingerprinted: A) For all offenses like adults B) Only for felonies and specific serious misdemeanors listed in Family Code C) Never D) At officer's discretion

Answer: B **Explanation:** Juveniles NOT routinely fingerprinted like adults. Fingerprinting authorized only for felonies and specific serious misdemeanors listed in Family Code §58.002. Prints handled differently than adult prints, emphasizing confidentiality.

Question 15: Indicators of physical child abuse include: A) Only broken bones B) Unexplained injuries, injuries in various healing stages, pattern injuries, injuries inconsistent with explanation C) Just bruises D) No visible signs

Answer: B **Explanation:** Physical abuse indicators: unexplained injuries, injuries in various healing stages suggesting ongoing abuse, pattern injuries (belt marks, hand prints), injuries inconsistent with explanation, burns with distinctive patterns, fractures especially in young children, injuries to unusual body areas.

Question 16: First-time juvenile offenders for minor offenses should: A) Always be formally charged B) Be considered for diversion programs addressing underlying issues without formal record C) Be ignored D) Automatically face detention

Answer: B **Explanation:** Consider diversion for minor first offenses: warnings, informal probation, first offender programs, teen court, mediation. Addresses root causes while holding juveniles accountable without formal record. Reserve formal processing for serious offenses or repeat offenders.

Question 17: When taking juveniles into custody, detention decisions include: A) Must detain all juveniles B) Release to parents, detention in juvenile facility for serious offenses, or citation with court date C) Place in adult jail D) No options available

Answer: B **Explanation:** Options: release to parents for minor offenses with low flight risk; detention in juvenile facility for serious offenses or repeat offenders; citation requiring court appearance. Juveniles cannot be held in adult jails except narrow circumstances with strict separation requirements.

Question 18: Child neglect includes: A) Only physical abuse B) Failure to provide basic needs—food, shelter, medical care, supervision C) Just poverty D) Normal parenting

Answer: B **Explanation:** Neglect is failure to provide child's basic needs: inadequate food, clothing, shelter, medical care, supervision. Consider family resources—poverty alone isn't neglect, but failure to utilize available resources may be. Can be as harmful as physical abuse.

Question 19: Teen court/youth court programs involve: A) Adult judges only B) Peer jury of teenagers hearing case and determining sanctions with juvenile serving on future juries C) No consequences D) Automatic criminal record

Answer: B **Explanation:** Teen court uses peer juries of teenagers to hear cases, determine appropriate sanctions. Juveniles serve on future juries as part of their sanction. Addresses accountability through peer pressure. Effective for first-time offenders teaching consequences without formal record.

Question 20: Sexual abuse of children: A) Always involves penetration B) Includes inappropriate touching, exposure, exploitation—children rarely lie about sexual abuse C) Never happens in families D) Easy to prove

Answer: B **Explanation:** Sexual abuse includes any sexual conduct harmful to child: inappropriate touching, exposure, exploitation, penetration. May involve family members (incest) or others. Children rarely fabricate sexual abuse—believe and investigate thoroughly. Requires specialized examination and interview techniques.

Question 21: Juvenile interrogations should: A) Last as long as needed B) Be brief, age-appropriate, with parent/attorney present when possible, documenting understanding of rights C) Occur without Miranda D) Use complex language

Answer: B **Explanation:** Best practices: keep interrogations brief; use age-appropriate simple language; have parent/attorney present when possible; document juvenile's apparent understanding of rights; consider age, education, maturity when evaluating waiver validity; courts scrutinize juvenile confessions closely.

Question 22: School-related incidents requiring law enforcement: A) All discipline problems B) Criminal conduct—assaults, drugs, weapons, threats, sexual offenses C) Tardiness D) Dress code violations

Answer: B **Explanation:** Law enforcement handles criminal conduct: assaults, drug possession/sales, weapons, thefts, vandalism, terroristic threats, sexual assault. School administrators handle rule violations not criminal: truancy, dress code, academic issues, minor disruptions.

Question 23: CPS (Child Protective Services) role differs from law enforcement because: A) No difference B) CPS investigates child safety and family services while law enforcement investigates criminal aspects C) CPS arrests perpetrators D) Law enforcement removes children

Answer: B **Explanation:** CPS investigates abuse/neglect focusing on child safety and family services. Has authority to remove children from dangerous situations. Law enforcement investigates criminal aspects and arrests perpetrators. Coordinate to avoid duplicating interviews and efficiently share information.

Question 24: Emotional/mental abuse of children: A) Doesn't exist B) Causes observable impairment through severe criticism, rejection, isolation, terrorizing C) Is not as serious as other abuse D) Cannot be investigated

Answer: B **Explanation:** Emotional/mental abuse causes observable impairment of emotional or mental functioning. Includes severe criticism, rejection, isolation, terrorizing. Hardest to prove but devastating effects. Often accompanies other abuse types. Can be as damaging as physical abuse.

Question 25: Restorative justice programs: A) Focus only on punishment B) Bring victim and juvenile together with mediator to repair harm and provide closure C) Ignore victims D) Are ineffective

Answer: B **Explanation:** Restorative justice uses mediation bringing victim and juvenile together. Juvenile hears impact of actions, makes amends, victim gets closure. Focuses on repairing harm rather than punishment. Effective for appropriate offenses when victim willing to participate.

Question 26: Age 17 in Texas means: A) Still juvenile B) Adult for criminal purposes facing adult charges and penalties C) Immune from prosecution D) Special category

Answer: B **Explanation:** At age 17, individuals are adults for criminal purposes in Texas (though civil law considers 18 age of majority). Face adult criminal charges, adult court, adult penalties including prison. Age at time of offense determines jurisdiction.

Question 27: Behavioral indicators of child abuse include: A) Only physical symptoms B) Withdrawal, aggression, inappropriate sexualized behavior, fear of specific people, behavior changes C) Normal childhood behavior D) No observable signs

Answer: B **Explanation:** Behavioral indicators: withdrawal, aggression, sexualized behavior inappropriate for age, fear of specific people, reluctance to go home, dramatic behavior changes, regression, running away, substance abuse, self-harm, suicidal ideation. Consider context and combinations of behaviors.

Question 28: Formal juvenile court processing is appropriate for: A) All offenses B) Serious offenses, repeat offenders, uncooperative juveniles, public safety concerns C) First-time minor offenses D) Never appropriate

Answer: B **Explanation:** Formal processing required for: serious offenses (violence, sexual offenses, significant property crimes), repeat offenders showing pattern, uncooperative juveniles or absconding risks, uninvolved parents unable to supervise, victim demands prosecution, public safety concerns.

Question 29: When child abuse is suspected, officers must: A) Wait for certainty B) Report when they have cause to believe abuse occurred—reasonable suspicion standard C) Only report confirmed cases D) Investigate fully before reporting

Answer: B **Explanation:** Must report when you have cause to believe child's welfare adversely affected by abuse/neglect. "Cause to believe" is lower than probable cause—reasonable suspicion suffices. Don't need certainty. When in doubt, report. Investigation can occur after reporting.

Question 30: Juvenile confidentiality means: A) Nothing is confidential B) Records sealed, media cannot publish identities, fingerprints/photos restricted C) Everything is public D) Only applies to some juveniles

Answer: B **Explanation:** Juvenile records are confidential and sealed. Media generally cannot publish juvenile identities. Fingerprints and photographs restricted to specific serious offenses. Emphasizes rehabilitation and second chances. Records generally sealed upon reaching adulthood if probation completed successfully.

Question 31: School searches by SROs acting in law enforcement capacity require: A) No justification B) Probable cause when conducting independent criminal investigation C) Just reasonable suspicion always D) Parental permission

Answer: B **Explanation:** When SRO conducts independent criminal investigation (not assisting school with discipline), probable cause standard applies. If assisting school officials with school discipline, courts may apply reasonable suspicion standard. Understand your role before conducting searches.

Question 32: Referral to diversion programs should occur: A) For all offenses B) When minor offense, first-time offender, cooperative juvenile/parents, victim supports alternative C) Only for violent crimes D) Never appropriate

Answer: B **Explanation:** Consider diversion for: minor offenses, first-time offenders with no delinquency history, cooperative juveniles and parents, victim supports alternative (if applicable), underlying issues amenable to intervention. Reserve formal processing for serious offenses or repeat offenders.

Question 33: Medical examination in child abuse cases: A) Not necessary B) Crucial for documenting injuries and distinguishing accidental from intentional injuries C) Only for sexual abuse D) Can be skipped

Answer: B **Explanation:** Medical examination documents injuries, distinguishes accidental from intentional trauma, provides expert opinions, creates crucial evidence. Sexual abuse requires specialized sexual assault examination. Medical professionals trained to identify abuse patterns.

Question 34: Juvenile court hearings are: A) Public like adult trials B) Generally closed to protect juvenile confidentiality C) Always open D) Held in adult courts

Answer: B **Explanation:** Juvenile hearings generally closed to public protecting confidentiality. Emphasis on rehabilitation rather than public shaming. Records sealed. Media restricted from publishing juvenile identities in most cases. Different from public adult criminal proceedings.

Question 35: When investigating school threats, officers should: A) Ignore if seem like jokes B) Take all threats seriously, investigate thoroughly, consider social media threats equally serious C) Only investigate direct threats D) Wait for actual violence

Answer: B **Explanation:** All school threats require thorough investigation even if seem like "jokes." Post-Columbine era demands serious response. Social media threats taken equally seriously. Threats disrupt schools, traumatize students, require appropriate charges (terroristic threat) when warranted.

Question 36: Children under age 10 in Texas: A) Can be prosecuted for crimes B) Cannot be prosecuted for any offense—lack criminal responsibility C) Only prosecuted for felonies D) Same as adults

Answer: B **Explanation:** Children under age 10 cannot be prosecuted for any offense in Texas. They lack criminal responsibility under law. May be referred to family services or mental health resources if serious behavioral issues exist, but no criminal prosecution possible.

Question 37: Pattern injuries on children suggest: A) Accidental causes B) Ongoing abuse with distinctive marks like belt marks, hand prints, or ligature marks C) Normal childhood injuries D) No concern

Answer: B **Explanation:** Pattern injuries indicate abuse: belt marks showing buckle imprint, hand prints from slapping, ligature marks from restraints, loop marks from cords. Distinctive patterns distinguish intentional from accidental injuries. Multiple pattern injuries especially concerning.

Question 38: Informal probation for juveniles: A) Requires court involvement B) Diverts from formal system—juvenile meets with probation officer, completes requirements, upon success matter closed without formal adjudication C) Results in criminal record D) Not available in Texas

Answer: B **Explanation:** Informal probation diverts juveniles from formal court processing. Juvenile works with probation officer completing requirements: community service, counseling, restitution. Upon successful completion, matter closed without formal delinquency adjudication. No formal record created.

Question 39: When multiple injuries in various healing stages are observed: A) All accidental B) Strong indicator of ongoing abuse requiring thorough investigation C) Not concerning D) Normal for active children

Answer: B **Explanation:** Injuries in various healing stages (fresh, days old, weeks old) strongly suggest ongoing abuse rather than single accident. Indicates pattern of repeated trauma. Requires thorough investigation, medical evaluation, and protective intervention.

Question 40: Juvenile probation violation results in: A) Automatic adult charges B) Consequences including extension of probation, additional conditions, or detention C) No consequences D) Immediate release

Answer: B **Explanation:** Probation violations result in consequences: probation extension, additional conditions (more community service, stricter supervision), short-term detention, or formal charges for new offenses committed. Severity depends on violation nature and juvenile's overall compliance.

Question 41: School officials' authority to search differs from law enforcement because: A) No difference B) School officials may use reasonable suspicion standard for school discipline purposes C) School officials need warrants D) School officials cannot search

Answer: B **Explanation:** School officials conducting searches for school discipline purposes use reasonable suspicion standard (lower than probable cause). Searches must be reasonable in scope. This differs from law enforcement's probable cause requirement for criminal investigations.

Question 42: Warning and release for juveniles is appropriate when: A) All circumstances B) Very minor first offense with cooperative parents and low risk C) Serious crimes D) Never appropriate

Answer: B **Explanation:** Warning and release appropriate for very minor first offenses (minor trespassing, low-value shoplifting) with cooperative parents able to supervise, low flight risk, and victim doesn't demand prosecution. Document warning thoroughly in case future contact occurs.

Question 43: Child advocacy centers provide: A) Criminal prosecution B) Specialized forensic interviews by trained professionals skilled in child-appropriate questioning C) Only therapy D) Arrest services

Answer: B **Explanation:** Child advocacy centers have professionals trained in forensic interviewing of children using age-appropriate techniques. Minimize trauma of multiple interviews. Provide coordinated investigation environment with CPS, law enforcement, prosecution, and medical professionals working together.

Question 44: Juveniles certified to adult court face: A) Juvenile consequences B) Adult penalties including prison and permanent criminal records C) No consequences D) Automatic dismissal

Answer: B **Explanation:** Juveniles certified (transferred) to adult court face adult criminal penalties including prison sentences (not juvenile detention), permanent criminal records (not sealed), and adult court proceedings. Reserved for serious offenses by older juveniles where rehabilitation prospects deemed poor.

Question 45: Texas Abuse Hotline is: A) Not available 24/7 B) 1-800-252-5400, available 24/7 for reporting suspected child abuse or neglect C) Only for emergencies D) Closed on weekends

Answer: B **Explanation:** Texas Abuse Hotline operates 24/7 at 1-800-252-5400 for reporting suspected child abuse or neglect. Mandatory reporters must call within 48 hours of suspecting abuse. Online reporting also available. Hotline staff assess reports and dispatch CPS investigators.

Scoring Your Practice Questions

43-45 correct (95-100%): Outstanding! You've mastered juvenile law and procedures. Your understanding of juvenile system differences, mandatory reporting requirements, diversion programs, and child protection procedures is excellent. You recognize how to balance enforcement with rehabilitation. Review any missed questions and proceed confidently to Chapter 7.

38-42 correct (85-94%): Excellent work! You have strong grasp of juvenile justice principles. Focus on any areas where you missed questions—whether custody procedures, school incidents, or child abuse investigation. Review those sections and move forward with solid understanding.

34-37 correct (75-84%): Good progress! You understand core juvenile law concepts but need strengthening in specific areas. Identify patterns in missed questions. Review sections on age jurisdictions, diversion programs, or mandatory reporting as needed. Work through scenarios again.

29-33 correct (65-74%): You're developing understanding but have significant gaps. Review Chapter 6 systematically. Focus on how juvenile system differs from adult system, mandatory reporting obligations, and proper handling of juvenile offenders. Create summary notes for key differences and requirements.

Below 29 correct (less than 65%): Substantial additional study needed. Juvenile law has unique requirements you'll use frequently. Review thoroughly focusing on: age jurisdictions, custody vs. arrest distinctions, mandatory reporting requirements, diversion options, child abuse indicators. Understand philosophy of rehabilitation over punishment guiding juvenile justice.

Chapter Summary

Juvenile law emphasizes rehabilitation over punishment, requiring different approaches than adult criminal justice. **Key Concepts: Jurisdiction:** Age 10-16 at time of conduct determines juvenile court jurisdiction. Under 10 cannot be prosecuted. Age 17+ are adults criminally. Age at offense determines jurisdiction, not age at arrest. **Rights and Protections:** Juveniles have same constitutional rights plus additional protections: confidential records, limited fingerprinting, parental notification, sealed records upon successful completion. Courts scrutinize juvenile confessions closely considering age, understanding, circumstances. **Handling Juveniles:** Use "custody" not "arrest" terminology. Notify parents promptly except when parent is suspect. Options include: release to parents, detention in juvenile facilities (never adult jails without strict separation), or citations with court dates. **Diversion Programs:** Emphasize rehabilitation through alternatives to formal processing: warnings, informal probation, first offender programs, teen court, mediation. Reserve formal processing for serious offenses, repeat offenders, or public safety concerns. **Mandatory Reporting:** Peace officers must report suspected child abuse/neglect within 48 hours when cause to believe abuse occurred. "Cause to believe" is lower than probable cause. When in doubt, report. Call Texas Abuse Hotline 1-800-252-5400. **Child Abuse Investigation:** Recognize indicators: unexplained injuries, injuries in various healing stages, pattern injuries, inconsistent explanations, behavioral changes. Interview child separately using age-appropriate questions. Coordinate with CPS. Document thoroughly. Emergency removal authorized when immediate danger exists. **School Resource Officers:** Distinguish criminal conduct (law enforcement handles) from school discipline (administrators handle). Understand search standards: school officials use reasonable suspicion for discipline; SROs conducting criminal investigations need probable cause. Build positive relationships while maintaining safety. **Status Offenses:** Truancy, running away, curfew violations are illegal only for juveniles. Not criminal offenses. Handle through diversion and family intervention rather than formal delinquency proceedings.

Effective juvenile work requires understanding developmental differences, balancing accountability with rehabilitation, protecting children's welfare while maintaining public safety. Every interaction shapes juvenile futures—positive intervention redirects lives. Your approach determines whether juveniles become productive citizens or career criminals. Handle with care, fairness, and commitment to rehabilitation.

CHAPTER 7: USE OF FORCE AND DEFENSIVE TACTICS

The decision to use force is the most consequential choice you'll make as a peace officer. Use too little force, and you or others may be injured or killed. Use excessive force, and you violate constitutional rights, face criminal prosecution, civil liability, and destroy community trust. Getting use of force right requires understanding the legal framework, developing tactical skills, mastering de-escalation techniques, and knowing when and how to apply force appropriately. This chapter provides the knowledge foundation for making sound use of force decisions that protect life while respecting rights. Every use of force will be scrutinized—by supervisors, prosecutors, juries, and the public. Your ability to articulate why force was necessary, reasonable, and proportional determines whether you're viewed as a professional acting lawfully or an officer who violated someone's rights. Master these principles now, because in the field, you won't have time to reference a textbook. Your training, understanding of law, and judgment are all you'll have in those critical seconds when force decisions must be made.

Use of Force Continuum

The use of force continuum is a model guiding your force decisions based on subject resistance and threat level. While not a rigid formula requiring you to try each level sequentially, it provides a framework for selecting appropriate force responses. Modern policing emphasizes de-escalation at every level, using the minimum force necessary to achieve lawful objectives while protecting everyone's safety.

Understanding Force Levels

Officer Presence (Level 1): Your mere presence in uniform often prevents or stops resistance. Most people comply when they see police. This is the least intrusive use of authority and should always be your starting point. Professional demeanor, confident bearing, and proper positioning demonstrate authority without physical contact. Many situations resolve through presence alone—subjects who were arguing stop when you arrive, people disperse when you tell them to leave, suspects surrender when confronted. Effective use of presence requires: professional appearance (clean uniform, good grooming, proper equipment), confident demeanor (calm, controlled, authoritative voice), tactical positioning (maintaining distance and angles), and visible commitment to handle the situation.

Verbal Direction (Level 2): Commands and instructions directing subject behavior. Use clear, direct language stating exactly what you want: "Stop," "Show me your hands," "Step out of the vehicle," "Place your hands behind your back." Effective verbal direction: Uses simple, direct commands. Speaks firmly but not aggressively. Repeats commands when necessary. Escalates tone appropriately if ignored. Explains consequences of non-compliance when appropriate. Example: "Sir, place your hands on the vehicle. If you don't comply, I'll use force to gain compliance. Place your hands on the vehicle now." This gives the subject opportunity to comply before physical force becomes necessary.

Empty Hand Control - Soft (Level 3): Physical techniques with low probability of injury, used to guide or direct subject movement without pain compliance. Includes: Escort holds (guiding subject by arm), Joint manipulation without pain (directing through biomechanics), Pressure point control that guides without pain, Come-along holds for cooperative subjects. Soft empty hand techniques are appropriate when: Subject is passively resistant (not following directions but not aggressive), You need to move or position subject, Verbal commands haven't achieved compliance, and Subject isn't aggressive or threatening.

Empty Hand Control - Hard (Level 4): Physical techniques with higher probability of injury, using pain compliance, takedowns, or strikes to overcome resistance. Includes: Pain compliance techniques (joint locks, pressure points applied with pain), Takedowns (forcing subject to ground), Strikes (punches, kicks, knee strikes), Defensive tactics (blocks, counters). Hard empty hand techniques are appropriate when: Subject actively resists (pulling away, fighting, tensing up), Subject is aggressive but not presenting deadly force threat, Soft techniques have failed or would be ineffective, and You need to overcome resistance to effect arrest or prevent harm.

Less-Lethal Weapons (Level 5): Tools designed to incapacitate without causing death or serious bodily injury, though serious injury or death can occur in some circumstances. Includes: OC spray (oleoresin capsicum/pepper spray), Conducted energy weapons (Tasers, stun guns), Impact weapons (batons, flashlights used as weapons), Bean bag rounds or rubber projectiles. Less-lethal weapons are appropriate when: Empty hand techniques have failed or would be ineffective, Subject presents active resistance or aggression, You need to maintain distance from subject, Multiple subjects require control, and Deadly force isn't justified but significant resistance exists. Important: "Less-lethal" doesn't mean "non-lethal." These weapons can cause serious injury or death under certain circumstances (pre-existing conditions, vulnerable impact areas, prolonged exposure). They're "less likely" to cause death than firearms but aren't risk-free.

Deadly Force (Level 6): Force reasonably likely to cause death or serious bodily injury, including: Firearms, Impact weapons used against head/neck/spine, Chokeholds or neck restraints (prohibited in many jurisdictions), Vehicles used as weapons, Any force directed at vulnerable areas with serious injury potential. Deadly force is the absolute last resort, justified only when: You or others face imminent threat of death or serious bodily injury, Subject is using or threatening deadly force, Subject presents imminent threat through actions (armed, attacking, attempting to access weapons), and Lesser force options are ineffective or would increase danger.

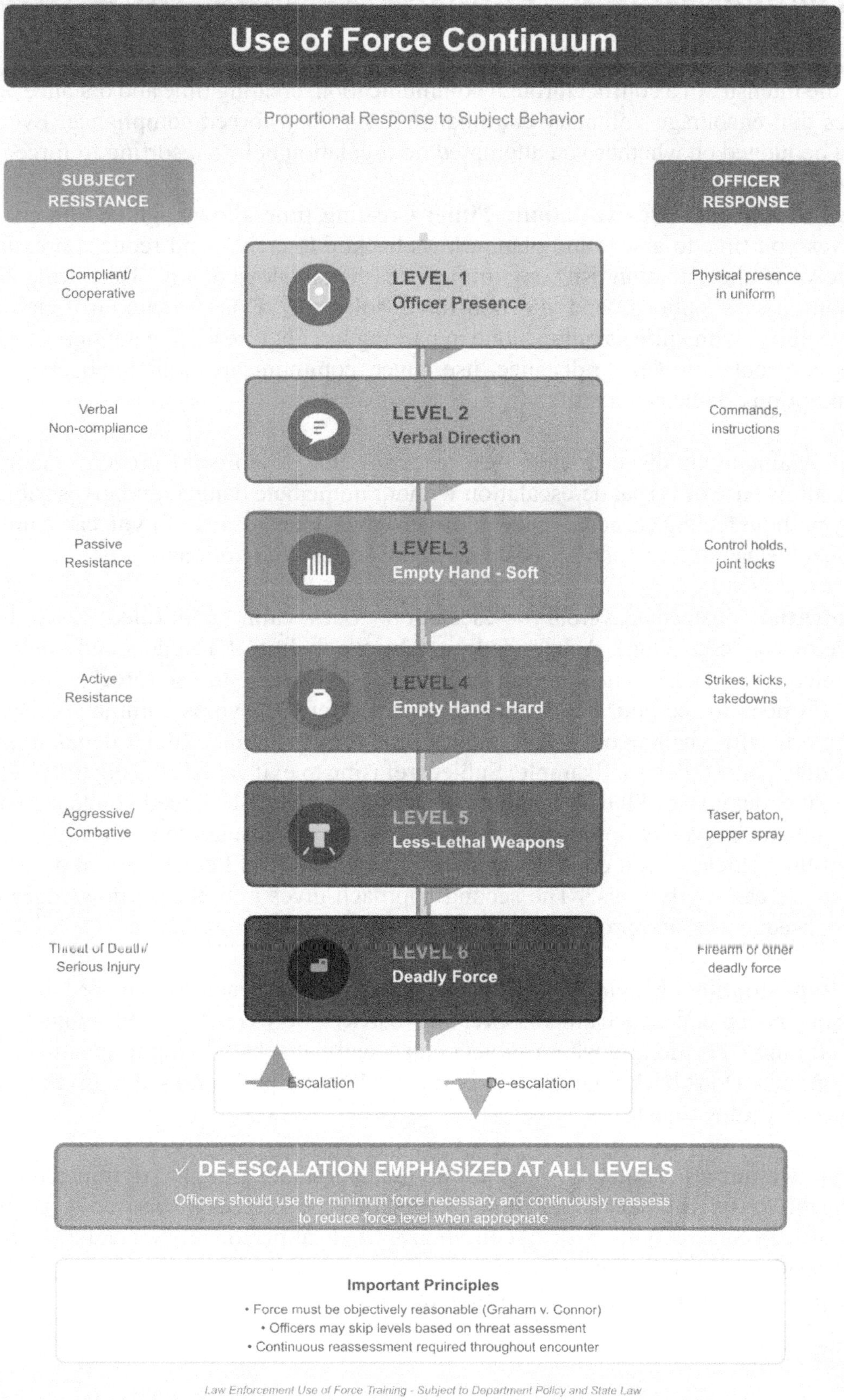

Use of Force Continuum
Proportional Response to Subject Behavior
SUBJECT RESISTANCE
OFFICER RESPONSE
Compliant/ Cooperative
LEVEL 1
Officer Presence
Physical presence in uniform
Verbal Non-compliance
LEVEL 2
Verbal Direction
Commands, instructions
Passive Resistance
LEVEL 3
Empty Hand - Soft
Control holds, joint locks
Active Resistance
LEVEL 4
Empty Hand - Hard
Strikes, kicks, takedowns
Aggressive/ Combative
LEVEL 5
Less-Lethal Weapons
Taser, baton, pepper spray
Threat of Death/ Serious Injury
LEVEL 6
Deadly Force
Firearm or other deadly force
Escalation
De-escalation
✓ DE-ESCALATION EMPHASIZED AT ALL LEVELS
Officers should use the minimum force necessary and continuously reassess to reduce force level when appropriate
Important Principles
• Force must be objectively reasonable (Graham v. Connor)
• Officers may skip levels based on threat assessment
• Continuous reassessment required throughout encounter
Law Enforcement Use of Force Training - Subject to Department Policy and State Law

De-escalation as the First Option

Modern policing emphasizes de-escalation whenever safe and feasible. De-escalation means reducing the intensity of a conflict through communication, creating time and distance, and using techniques that encourage voluntary compliance rather than forced compliance. Every use of force will be judged on whether you attempted de-escalation before resorting to force.

Principles of Effective De-escalation: Time: Creating time allows agitated people to calm down, gives you time to assess and plan, allows backup to arrive, and reduces pressure to act immediately. If the situation isn't an immediate threat, slow down. Take time to gather information, assess options, and try non-force solutions. Don't create artificial urgency. Example: Subject with knife standing alone in parking lot, not threatening anyone. Don't rush in and force confrontation. Create distance, use cover, communicate, wait for backup, consider less-lethal options. Time is your ally.

Distance: Maintaining distance provides reaction time to threats, prevents subject from attacking, allows use of verbal de-escalation without immediate danger, and gives subject space to comply without feeling cornered. Don't close distance unnecessarily. If you can communicate from 20 feet instead of 5 feet, do so. Distance equals safety and options.

Communication: Effective verbal de-escalation: Uses calm, controlled voice tone (not aggressive or condescending), Acknowledges subject's feelings ("I understand you're upset"), Offers choices ("You can come with me voluntarily, or I'll have to use force"), Explains what you need ("I need to see your hands for everyone's safety"), Avoids commands that escalate (racial slurs, insults, challenges to ego), Gives time for compliance (don't demand immediate action if safety permits delay). Example: Subject refusing to exit vehicle during traffic stop. Poor approach: "Get out now or I'll drag you out!" Better approach: "Sir, I need you to step out of the vehicle. I understand you're upset about the stop, and we can discuss that, but right now I need you to exit the vehicle. If you don't, I'll have to remove you, and I don't want to do that. Please step out so we can resolve this." The second approach gives options, acknowledges feelings, explains consequences, and provides opportunity for voluntary compliance.

Tactical Repositioning: Moving to positions that increase safety and reduce need for immediate force: Using cover and concealment, Creating barriers between you and subject (vehicles, fences, buildings), Positioning where subject can't easily attack, Moving to positions that limit subject's options. Don't back yourself into corners. Maintain positioning that gives you tactical advantage and escape routes.

Requesting Resources: Sometimes the best de-escalation is getting the right person on scene: Mental health crisis = Crisis Intervention Team officer, Language barrier = Translator or bilingual officer, Subject with medical condition = Medical personnel, Specialized situations = SWAT, negotiators, supervisors. There's no shame in asking for help. Getting appropriate resources prevents escalation and improves outcomes.

When De-escalation Isn't Appropriate: While de-escalation is preferred, some situations require immediate action: Imminent threat of death or serious bodily injury, Active violence in progress, Subject attacking you or others, No safe opportunity to create time or distance, Ongoing threats to public safety. In these situations, waiting or attempting de-escalation increases danger. Act immediately with appropriate force to stop the threat.

Graham v. Connor Standards

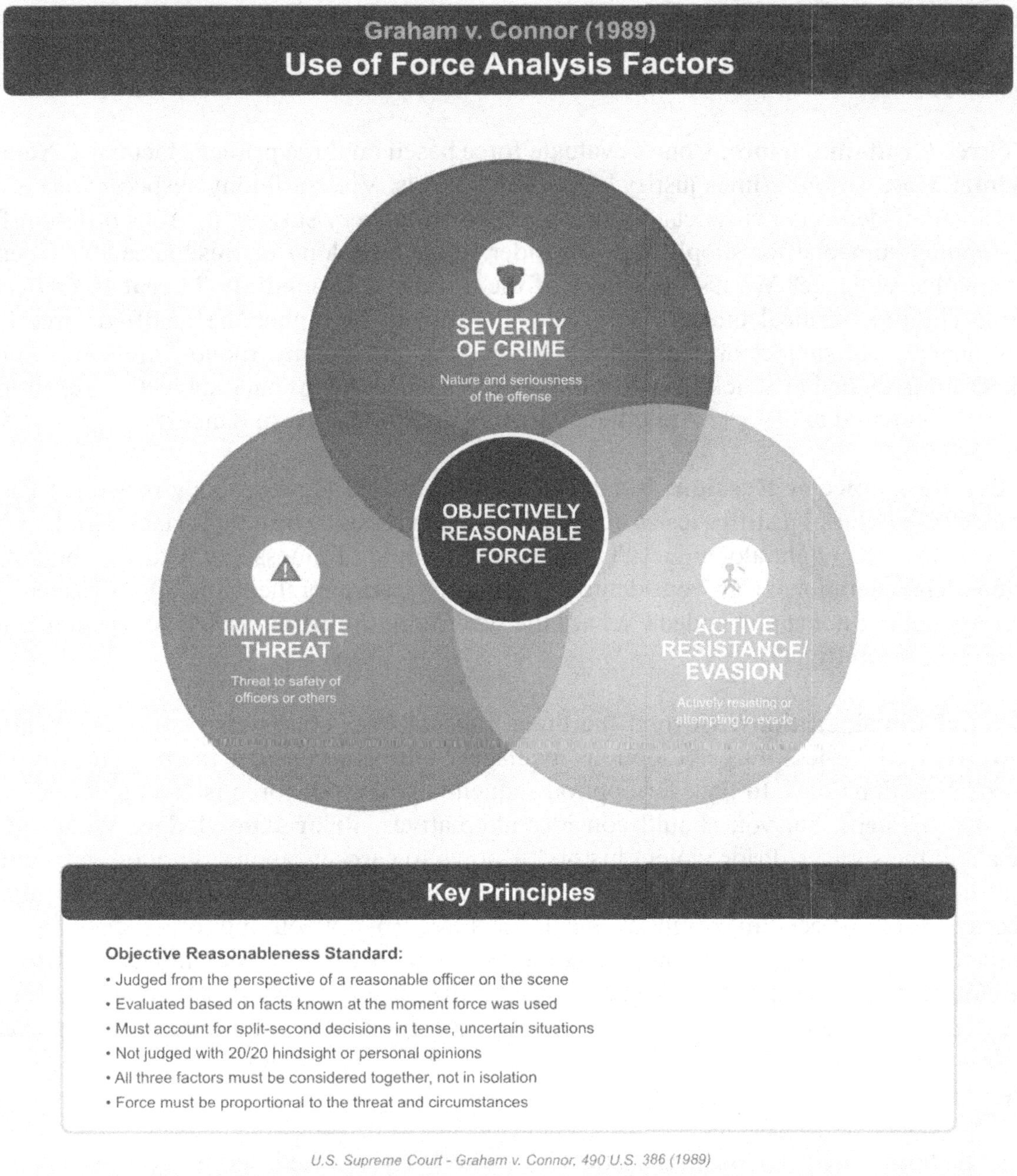

The Supreme Court case Graham v. Connor (1989) established the legal standard for evaluating use of force. All your force decisions will be judged by Graham factors. Understanding this case is essential for legal use of force.

The Reasonable Officer Standard: Force must be "objectively reasonable" based on the totality of circumstances. What does this mean? **Objective:** Judged from perspective of a reasonable officer on scene, not with 20/20 hindsight. Courts don't second-guess split-second decisions with calm deliberation after the fact. The question is: "Would a reasonable officer in the same situation, knowing what this officer knew at the time, use the same force?" **Not Subjective:** Your personal feelings, intent, or motivation don't matter. Even if you acted with bad intent, if the force was objectively reasonable under the circumstances, it's lawful. Conversely, good intent doesn't excuse unreasonable force.

The Three Graham Factors: Courts evaluate force based on three primary factors: **1. Severity of Crime:** More serious crimes justify higher force levels. Violent felony suspects pose greater danger than misdemeanor suspects. Stopping an armed robbery suspect justifies different force than stopping someone for shoplifting. Consider: Is this a felony or misdemeanor? Does the crime involve violence? What's the nature of the threat? **2. Immediate Threat to Officer or Others:** The most critical factor. The greater the threat, the higher the justified force level. Courts analyze: Is subject armed? Is subject making threatening movements? Has subject attacked or threatened to attack? Could subject access weapons? What's subject's size, strength, skill level compared to officer? Are others (citizens, other officers) in danger?

3. Active Resistance or Evasion: Is subject resisting arrest? How are they resisting? Passive resistance (going limp) justifies less force than active aggression (fighting, attacking). Is subject attempting to flee? Flight alone doesn't justify deadly force (Tennessee v. Garner), but creates additional considerations: Can you identify suspect for later apprehension? Does suspect pose danger to public if not apprehended? What's the severity of the crime? Is use of less-lethal force appropriate to stop flight?

Additional Considerations: Beyond the three main factors, courts also consider: **Available Alternatives:** Were less intrusive options available? Did you consider them? Why were they rejected? You don't have to try every option sequentially (use of force isn't a ladder you must climb step-by-step), but you should consider alternatives. **Prior Knowledge:** What did you know about the subject? Prior violent history? Known to carry weapons? Previous encounters? Mental health issues? This information affects reasonableness of your response. **Number of Officers:** More officers may reduce need for force (overwhelming presence encourages compliance). But in rapidly evolving situations, you may act before backup arrives. **Duration of Encounter:** How long did the situation last? Split-second decisions are judged differently than extended encounters where you had time to assess and plan. **Training and Experience:** Your training affects what's considered "reasonable" for you. Tactics you were trained to use are more defensible than improvisation.

What Graham Doesn't Consider: The Court explicitly rejected certain factors: **Intent or Motivation:** Your subjective intent (anger, fear, malice) is irrelevant. Only the objective reasonableness of force matters. This protects officers who act properly under stress and prevents wrongdoers from escaping liability by claiming good intent. **20/20 Hindsight:** Courts can't second-guess with information learned afterward. Decisions are judged based on what you reasonably believed at the time. If subject's gun turns out to be a replica, but you reasonably believed it was real, your use of force is still reasonable.

Applying Graham: When using force, consciously consider: Severity of crime (violent felony? misdemeanor?), Immediate threat level (armed? attacking? how dangerous?), Resistance/evasion (complying? resisting? fleeing?). Articulate these factors in your report. Courts will evaluate your force based on Graham, so your documentation should address Graham factors explicitly.

Deadly Force Law and Policy

Deadly force is force reasonably likely to cause death or serious bodily injury. The legal standard for deadly force is strict, and violations result in criminal prosecution and civil liability.

Legal Authority for Deadly Force

Texas Penal Code §9.51 - Force to Effect Arrest: Peace officers may use force to effect arrests or prevent escapes when they reasonably believe force is immediately necessary. However, deadly force has additional requirements.

Deadly Force Requirements (Penal Code §9.52): You may use deadly force to prevent escape only when: You're making a lawful arrest or preventing escape after lawful arrest, and You reasonably believe deadly force is immediately necessary to prevent escape, and The person is fleeing from arrest/custody for a felony, and You reasonably believe person has committed or attempted to commit a crime involving infliction or threat of serious bodily injury, and You reasonably believe there's substantial risk person will cause serious bodily injury if not immediately apprehended.

Tennessee v. Garner Application: Federal constitutional standard (Tennessee v. Garner, 1985) prohibits deadly force to prevent escape unless: Officer has probable cause to believe suspect poses significant threat of death or serious physical injury to officers or others, or Suspect committed crime involving infliction or threatened use of deadly force, and There's no other way to prevent escape. Texas law generally aligns with Garner, but Garner provides the constitutional floor—the minimum protection. Texas can't authorize deadly force that violates Garner.

Deadly Force to Protect Life: You may use deadly force when: You or another person is in imminent danger of death or serious bodily injury, and Deadly force is immediately necessary to prevent the harm, and A reasonable officer in your position would believe deadly force is necessary. Key word: **Imminent**. The threat must be immediate and unavoidable. Future threats, past attacks that have ended, or speculative dangers don't justify deadly force. The threat must be happening now or about to happen immediately.

Evaluating Deadly Force Situations

The Reasonable Belief Standard: Your decision is judged on what you reasonably believed based on the circumstances you faced, not perfect information. If someone points what appears to be a real gun at you, your use of deadly force is reasonable even if the "gun" later proves to be a replica. You're not required to wait until shot to determine if the weapon is real.

Indicators of Deadly Force Threats: Weapons: Firearms (real or replica if reasonably believed real), Knives or edged weapons, Impact weapons (baseball bats, pipes, hammers), Vehicles used as weapons, Improvised weapons capable of serious injury. **Actions:** Drawing or displaying weapons, Pointing weapons at you or others, Making movements toward weapons, Aggressive actions with deadly force potential (attacking with weapon, attempting to run you over), Attacking in manner capable of serious injury (striking head/neck, choking, beating). **Subject Factors:** Size/strength disparity (much larger/stronger than you), Multiple subjects attacking, Demonstrated capability to inflict serious injury, Violent behavior or statements indicating intent, Known history of violence, Mental state suggesting lack of self-preservation.

21-Foot Rule (Tueller Drill): An attacker with knife at 21 feet can reach you in approximately 1.5 seconds—less time than it takes most officers to draw and fire accurately. This isn't a bright-line rule authorizing deadly force automatically at 21 feet, but it illustrates the danger posed by edged weapons at what seems like a safe distance. Courts consider: Distance between you and threat, Available cover or barriers, Your ability to create distance, Whether backup is present, Subject's movements (advancing? stationary?).

Proportionality Principle: While deadly force doesn't need to be precisely proportional to threat (you don't need to match force level exactly), gross disproportionality may indicate unreasonableness. Example: Subject throws a rock from 50 feet away. While a rock could potentially cause serious injury, shooting them from that distance when you could easily take cover may be considered disproportionate. Better response: Take cover, issue commands, use less-lethal force if available.

After Deadly Force Use

Immediate Actions: Secure the scene and any weapons, Provide or request medical aid for all injured persons (even the subject you shot—you have duty to preserve life once threat is neutralized), Separate officers involved in shooting (prevents appearance of collusion on statements), Notify supervisor immediately, Preserve evidence (don't disturb scene, collect witness information), Don't discuss specifics with anyone except investigators and attorneys.

Your Rights After Deadly Force: You have rights after using deadly force: Right to consult attorney before detailed interview, Reasonable time to recover from physiological stress before interview, Right to have union representative or attorney present during interview, Right to review evidence before final statement (in some jurisdictions). Don't waive these rights hastily. Deadly force incidents are criminal investigations initially—you're a subject until cleared. While you must provide basic information (where scene is, where evidence is, general description of what occurred), detailed interrogation can wait until you've had time to process the event and consult counsel.

Administrative Investigation: Your agency will conduct administrative review examining: Was force within policy? Was force objectively reasonable? Were alternatives available? What training or policy changes are needed? This is separate from criminal investigation. Even if criminally cleared, you may face administrative consequences if you violated policy.

Criminal Investigation: District attorney or grand jury will review for potential criminal charges. They'll examine: Was use of force justified under law? Was it objectively reasonable under Graham? Did officer act in good faith? Does evidence support officer's account? Most officer-involved shootings where force was reasonable result in no criminal charges. But the investigation is thorough and stressful.

Civil Liability: Even if criminally and administratively cleared, you may face civil lawsuit. Subject or family may claim excessive force, violation of civil rights, or wrongful death. Civil standard is "preponderance of evidence" (more likely than not), lower than "beyond reasonable doubt" for criminal. Qualified immunity protects you from civil liability if your actions were objectively reasonable and didn't violate clearly established law. Document everything thoroughly to protect yourself.

De-escalation Techniques

While we discussed de-escalation as part of the force continuum, specific techniques warrant detailed examination.

Verbal De-escalation Strategies

Active Listening: Show you're hearing the person: Maintain appropriate eye contact, Acknowledge what they're saying ("I hear that you're upset"), Don't interrupt constantly, Paraphrase to confirm understanding ("So you're saying..."), Validate feelings without necessarily agreeing with actions ("I understand you're frustrated"). Example: Subject yelling about unfair treatment. "I understand you feel this is unfair. Let me explain what's happening and why. But I need you to calm down so we can talk about this." You've acknowledged feelings while maintaining control.

Empathetic Communication: Expressing understanding without condoning behavior: "I understand this is stressful," "I know this isn't the situation you wanted," "I can see you're having a difficult day." This reduces defensiveness and builds rapport. But don't fake empathy—people detect insincerity immediately.

Offering Choices: Giving subjects controlled options increases compliance: "You can come with me voluntarily, or I'll have to place you in handcuffs. Which do you prefer?" "You can calm down and we'll talk, or you'll be arrested for disorderly conduct. Your choice." This frames compliance as their decision, not your imposition. But choices must be real—don't offer options you can't deliver.

Tactical Communication: Using language that de-escalates: **Use "I" statements:** "I need you to..." rather than "You need to..." **Explain reasons:** "I'm asking for your ID because I need to verify who you are for my report." **Avoid challenges:** Don't say "You're going to comply or else." This triggers defiance. **Use calm, controlled voice:** Don't match their volume. Stay calm. **Give time to comply:** "I need you to step back. I'll give you a moment to do that." **Avoid absolutes:** "Always," "never," and similar absolute statements escalate conflicts.

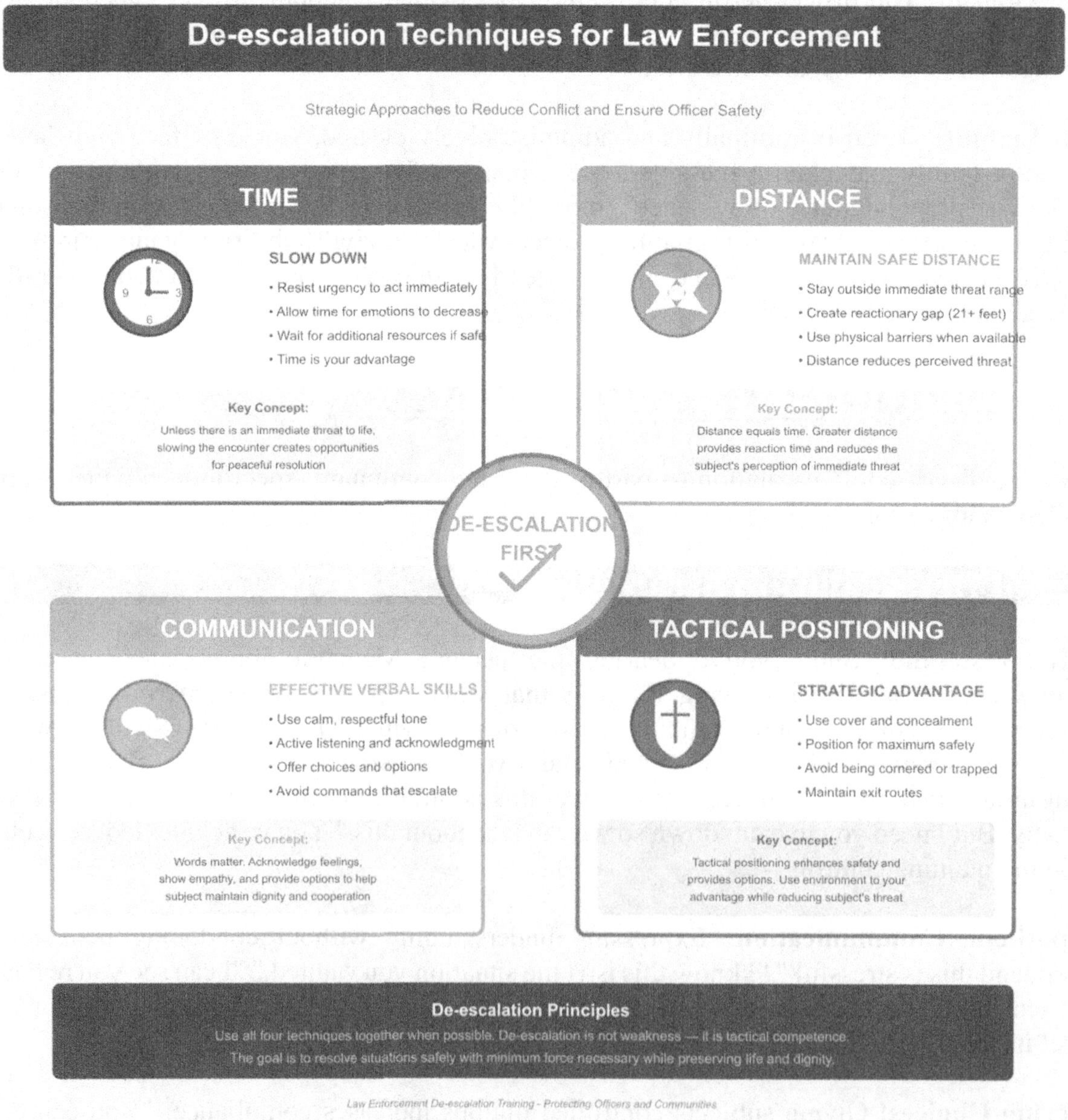

Crisis Intervention Techniques

Recognizing Crisis Situations: Signs someone is in crisis: Confused or irrational speech, Extreme emotional distress, Inability to follow simple directions, Statements about harming self or others, Disorganized thinking, Unusual behavior for that person. Crises require different approach than criminal behavior. Person in mental health crisis isn't thinking rationally. Traditional police commands and threats may escalate rather than resolve the situation.

CIT Approach (Crisis Intervention Team): If you're CIT trained, apply those principles: Slow down—there's usually no need to rush, Keep safe distance, Speak calmly and non-threateningly, Avoid sudden movements, Listen more than you talk, Be patient—crisis resolution takes time, Consider involving mental health professionals. The goal in crisis situations is connection and calm, not compliance and control.

Distance and Time as De-escalation Tools

Creating Tactical Distance: Distance provides options: Time to assess and plan, Opportunity for verbal resolution, Ability to use less-lethal force if needed, Protection from sudden attacks, Space for subject to calm without feeling threatened. If subject isn't immediate threat, don't rush in. Hold position, use cover, communicate. Let time work for you.

Slowing Things Down: Many situations improve simply by not rushing: Allow subject time to process and comply, Give backup time to arrive, Let subject's anger dissipate, Allow alcohol/drugs to wear off, Create opportunity for mental health intervention. Officers often create urgency where none exists. If subject is contained and not threatening anyone, there's no requirement to force immediate resolution.

Arrest and Control Procedures

Approach and Positioning

Safe Approach Principles: Never approach directly in front of subject—gives them clear target and attack angle. Approach from angles or rear when possible. Maintain reactionary gap (6-10 feet minimum) until ready to make physical contact. Use cover when available. Keep your weapon side away from subject to prevent access. Watch hands continuously—hands kill, not people. Have partner provide cover while you make contact if multiple officers present.

Command Presence: Your demeanor affects subject response: Confident posture (stand tall, shoulders back), Calm voice tone (firm but not aggressive), Direct eye contact (when culturally appropriate), Clear, simple commands ("Place your hands behind your back"), Professional bearing (no nervousness or hesitation). Subjects comply more readily when you project competence and authority.

Handcuffing Techniques

Verbal Commands Before Handcuffing: Tell subject exactly what you want and what will happen: "I'm going to place you in handcuffs. Turn around and place your hands behind your back with palms facing out." "Interlock your fingers behind your back." "Do not resist or pull away." Clear directions reduce resistance and confusion.

Safe Handcuffing Procedures: For Standing Position: Position subject facing away from you, Have them interlock fingers behind back with palms out, Maintain control of one hand while applying first cuff, Secure first cuff (check tightness—one finger should fit), Control subject during transition to second hand, Apply second cuff, Double-lock both cuffs (prevents tightening), Check fit again (too tight causes injury; too loose allows escape).

For Prone Position: Subject lying face-down on ground, Gain control of one arm at a time, Pull arm behind back and apply cuff, Control subject while securing second arm, Once both cuffs applied, double-lock them, Maintain control throughout. **For Kneeling Position:** Subject kneeling with hands visible, Approach from rear, Verbal commands to interlock fingers behind head, Pull one arm down and cuff, Maintain control while cuffing second arm.

Common Handcuffing Errors: Too Loose: Subject can slip hands out. Check tightness—cuffs should be snug but not cutting circulation. **Too Tight:** Causes nerve damage, injury, pain complaints, and potential liability. One finger should fit between cuff and wrist. **Not Double-Locked:** Cuffs can tighten during movement, causing injury and liability. Always double-lock. **Poor Control:** Failing to maintain control during application allows subject to resist, attack, or flee. **Wrong Position:** Handcuffs palms-in (toward body) instead of palms-out makes escape easier.

Subject Control Techniques

Escort Holds: When moving compliant but handcuffed subjects: Grip upper arm firmly above elbow, Walk slightly behind and to side, Maintain control without causing pain, Guide direction of movement, Be prepared for sudden resistance.

Come-Along Holds: For mildly resistant subjects: Control joints (wrist, elbow, shoulder), Apply biomechanical advantage (leverage through joint manipulation), Use minimal pain necessary for compliance, Release when compliance achieved, Transition to cuffs once controlled.

Ground Control: When you've taken subject to ground: Control both arms, Use body weight for control (not punishment), Don't kneel on neck/spine/head, Maintain control while minimizing injury risk, Cuff as quickly as possible, Monitor breathing throughout.

Multiple Subject Control: When controlling multiple people: Handcuff most dangerous/resistant first, Position others where you can observe them, Use additional officers for security, Separate subjects (prevents group resistance), Prioritize officer safety over speed.

Less-Lethal Options

OC Spray (Pepper Spray)

What It Is: Oleoresin capsicum (OC) is inflammatory agent derived from peppers. It causes: Immediate burning sensation in eyes, nose, throat, Temporary blindness from involuntary eye closure, Respiratory distress and coughing, Skin irritation and burning, Disorientation and discomfort. Effects typically last 30-45 minutes, sometimes longer.

When to Use OC: Appropriate for: Active resistance requiring physical force, Aggressive subjects where distance is needed, Multiple subjects requiring control, Subjects too large/strong for empty hand control, Situations where impact weapons would cause excessive injury. **Not Appropriate for:** Passive resistance alone, Subjects with known respiratory problems (if alternatives exist), Enclosed spaces with poor ventilation (affects everyone), Situations where cross-contamination affects innocents.

Application Techniques: Stream: Directed spray for outdoor use, good range (10-15 feet), less cross-contamination. **Cone/Fog:** Wide dispersal pattern, good for multiple subjects, higher cross-contamination risk. **Application Points:** Aim for face/eyes, Use short bursts (1-2 seconds), Re-assess and re-apply if needed, Create distance after application.

After Effects and Care: After using OC: Subject will be in significant discomfort—this is expected and temporary, Provide fresh air (remove from enclosed space), Don't rub eyes—makes it worse, Flush with cool water when practical, Monitor breathing—most complaints are discomfort, not actual respiratory distress, Seek medical evaluation if breathing problems persist, Document use in report, Photograph subject for documentation.

Cross-Contamination: You'll likely be affected by OC you deploy: Anticipate reduced vision and breathing difficulty, Try to position upwind when deploying, Have water available for decontamination, Consider this in tactical planning.

Conducted Energy Weapons (Tasers)

How They Work: CEWs deliver electrical pulse disrupting voluntary muscle control: Probes deliver charge, Subject loses neuromuscular control, Incapacitation lasts 5 seconds per trigger pull, Subject can't voluntarily move during cycle. This is not "pain compliance"—subject physically can't control muscles during electrical cycle.

When to Use CEW: Appropriate for: Active resistance or aggression, Subject armed with less-lethal weapons (knife, club) at distance, Multiple subjects where control is needed, Large/strong subjects difficult to control by hand, Situations requiring subject incapacitation rather than pain compliance. **Not Appropriate for:** Passive resistance alone (though this depends on specific circumstances and policy), Subjects on elevated surfaces (fall risk), Subjects near water or flammable liquids, Pregnant women (if alternatives exist), Elderly or medically fragile (if alternatives exist).

Application Guidelines: Aim for center mass (large muscle groups in torso), Avoid face, neck, groin, female breasts when possible (though center mass is priority), Ensure good probe spread (at least 12 inches apart for best effect), Be prepared for subject to fall—protect head from impact, Have backup plan if CEW fails (they fail more often than people think), Approach and handcuff immediately after cycle.

Medical Considerations: CEWs have caused deaths in rare cases, typically involving: Pre-existing heart conditions, Drug intoxication (especially stimulants), Excited delirium, Prolonged or repeated applications, Other contributing factors. Always monitor subject after CEW use: Check for breathing problems, Check pulse, Look for injuries from fall, Request medical evaluation if subject complains of chest pain, has pre-existing heart conditions, or was shocked repeatedly, Document all applications (how many cycles, where probes struck).

Drive-Stun Mode: Contact stun without probes: Less effective than probe deployment (causes pain but not incapacitation), Use when probes already deployed and subject still resists, Use when distance doesn't allow probe deployment, Not recommended as primary technique—probe mode is more effective.

Impact Weapons

Types: Batons: Straight batons, Collapsible batons (ASP), PR-24/side-handle batons. **Improvised:** Flashlights used as impact weapons (common in practice).

Target Areas: Approved Targets (Non-Lethal Intent): Large muscle groups: thighs, upper arms, shins, calves, Muscle areas that cause pain and dysfunction but low risk of serious injury. **Prohibited/Deadly Force Targets:** Head, neck, spine, groin, kidneys, Strikes to these areas can cause death or serious injury—only justified when deadly force is justified.

When to Use Impact Weapons: Appropriate for: Active aggression requiring hard control, Multiple subjects, Subject armed with less-lethal weapon, Empty hand control ineffective or too dangerous, Creating distance from aggressive subject. **Strikes vs. Blocks:** Impact weapons can be used defensively (blocking attacks) without same justification required for strikes. Blocking an attack is force justified by the attack itself.

After Using Impact Weapons: Assess for injuries, Document strikes (location, number, reason), Photograph injuries, Request medical evaluation (even if subject refuses, document the offer), Be prepared to articulate why impact weapon was necessary.

Force Documentation and Reporting

Every use of force must be thoroughly documented. Your report may be reviewed by supervisors, prosecutors, defense attorneys, civil attorneys, judges, juries, and the media. Quality documentation protects you and your department.

What Requires Force Documentation

Any Physical Force Beyond Handcuffing: Empty hand control (soft or hard), Takedowns, Pain compliance, Strikes, OC spray, CEW/Taser, Impact weapons, Deadly force, K-9 deployments, Any force resulting in injury or complaint of injury.

What Generally Doesn't Require Separate Force Report: Routine handcuffing of compliant subject, Escort holds for compliant subjects, Verbal commands only (though document in regular report). When in doubt, document. Over-documentation is better than under-documentation.

Elements of Force Reports

Subject Description and Behavior: Physical description (size, build, apparent fitness level), Mental state (calm, agitated, enraged, confused), Intoxication indicators (alcohol, drugs), Behavior before force (aggressive actions, threats, resistance level), Specific actions requiring force (attacked me, reached for weapon, fled, actively resisted).

Your Response: Pre-Force Actions: Verbal commands given, Warnings about force, De-escalation attempts, Why de-escalation failed or wasn't appropriate, Time given for compliance. **Force Used:** Specific technique (not just "I used force"), Duration of force application, Number of strikes/applications, Target areas, Why that force level was necessary, Why lesser force was inadequate. **Post-Force Actions:** When force stopped and why, Medical attention provided, Subject condition after force, Additional officers involved, Witness information.

Graham v. Connor Factors: Explicitly address in your report: **Crime Severity:** What offense was subject suspected of? Felony? Misdemeanor? Violent? **Immediate Threat:** What threat did subject pose? Armed? Attacking? Making threatening movements? Size/strength advantage? **Resistance/Evasion:** How was subject resisting? Passive? Active? Aggressive? Attempting escape?

Your Perception and Belief: What you reasonably believed at the time: "I believed subject was reaching for a weapon based on his movements toward his waistband," "I believed subject posed immediate threat of serious bodily injury based on his size advantage and aggressive actions," "I believed lesser force would be ineffective based on subject's violent resistance." Your reasonable belief at the time is what matters, not perfect information revealed later.

Writing Effective Force Reports

Be Specific: Poor: "Subject resisted and I used force to gain compliance." Better: "Subject pulled away when I attempted to handcuff him, jerked his right arm free, and made a fist. I used a wrist lock on his right arm and delivered one knee strike to his right thigh (common peroneal area) to overcome resistance. Subject then complied and was handcuffed without further resistance."

Be Objective: Describe what happened, not conclusions. Poor: "Subject was obviously trying to attack me." Better: "Subject clenched fists, assumed fighting stance, and moved toward me stating 'I'm going to (expletive) you up.'"

Be Honest: If you made errors, document them honestly: "In hindsight, I could have created more distance before force became necessary," "My baton strike inadvertently hit subject's head rather than intended target (upper arm)." Honesty is more defensible than trying to hide mistakes.

Common Documentation Mistakes

Vague Language: "I used force to gain control." This tells reviewers nothing. What force? Why was it needed? What happened? **Passive Voice:** "Force was used" obscures who did what. Use active voice: "I applied a wrist lock." **Conclusions Without Facts:** "Subject was obviously going to attack." How do you know? What did you observe? "Subject clenched fists, assumed fighting stance, and stepped toward me with raised hands." **Minimizing Force:** Describing serious force casually makes you look unprofessional and raises suspicion you're hiding something. Be direct and factual. **Exaggerating Threat:** Inflating danger to justify force backfires when evidence contradicts your account. Describe facts, not hyperbole.

Photographs and Evidence

Document visually: **Officer Injuries:** Even minor injuries (scratches, redness, pain). These corroborate your account of resistance or attack. **Subject Injuries:** Document all injuries from your force. Don't hide injuries—they're expected from force and must be documented. **Scene:** Photograph the location showing distances, positions, obstacles, and other relevant factors. **Weapons/Evidence:** Document any weapons, contraband, or evidence related to the incident.

Supervisor Review Process

Your force report goes through review: **Immediate Supervisor:** Reviews for completeness, reasonableness, policy compliance. May require additional information or clarification. **Use of Force Review Board:** Many departments have boards that review all force incidents. They examine patterns, training needs, and policy compliance. **Command Staff:** Higher-level review for serious force (OIS, serious injury, controversial incidents). **Legal Review:** Department attorneys may review for liability issues. **Be Responsive:** If supervisors ask for clarification or additional information, provide it promptly and completely. They're not attacking you—they're ensuring proper documentation.

Real-World Application: Use of Force Scenarios

Scenario 1: Armed Subject with Knife

Situation: You respond to a disturbance call at a convenience store. Dispatch advises a male subject is "acting crazy" and "destroying property." Upon arrival, you observe through the window a male subject holding a large kitchen knife, pacing erratically inside the store. The clerk has fled outside. The subject sees you and yells incoherently, waving the knife. He's approximately 20 feet from the door.

Questions: What's your immediate response? Can you use deadly force now? What de-escalation options exist? What if he charges toward you with the knife?

Analysis: Immediate Threat Assessment: Subject is armed with deadly weapon (knife), displaying erratic behavior suggesting mental crisis or intoxication, currently contained in store with no hostages, not immediately threatening anyone outside. **Initial Response:** Take cover position with good observation angle. Request backup and supervisor. Consider Crisis Intervention Team officer if available. Establish containment—don't allow escape. Request less-lethal options (Taser, beanbag shotgun) if available. Begin communication attempts.

Can You Use Deadly Force Now? Not yet. Subject isn't presenting imminent threat to you or others at this moment. He's 20 feet away, inside building, not advancing. Deadly force requires imminent threat. He has a weapon and could quickly become threat, but imminent means immediate—happening now or about to happen immediately. **De-escalation Options:** Maintain distance and cover. Use calm, non-threatening voice. "Sir, I'm here to help. Can you tell me what's going on?" Avoid commands that might escalate ("Drop the knife or I'll shoot"). Try to establish rapport. Look for signs of mental health crisis vs. criminal behavior. Consider: "Sir, you seem upset. What's bothering you? Let's talk about this. Nobody needs to get hurt."

If He Charges: If subject charges toward you with knife: Distance matters—remember 21-foot rule. At 20 feet, he can reach you in approximately 1.5 seconds. Your response options: **Best Option if Available:** Taser or other less-lethal while maintaining distance and cover. If subject keeps advancing after less-lethal fails, transition to deadly force. **If Only Deadly Force Available:** Issue commands ("Stop! Drop the knife!"). Create distance if possible (retreat while maintaining sight). If he continues advancing and closes to danger distance with knife raised, deadly force is justified. You have imminent threat of death/serious bodily injury from edged weapon.

Documentation: Your report must articulate: Subject was armed with deadly weapon (kitchen knife approximately 8-inch blade). You attempted de-escalation (specific commands and time spent). Subject's actions created imminent threat (charged at you with knife from X feet, closed distance rapidly, raised knife in threatening manner). Why deadly force was immediately necessary (no time to retreat, less-lethal failed or unavailable, reasonable belief of imminent serious bodily injury). Graham factors (violent crime—aggravated assault; immediate threat—armed with deadly weapon attacking; active resistance—charging with weapon).

Key Takeaway: Mental health crisis doesn't eliminate use of force authority, but it changes approach. Try de-escalation first when safe. But if subject with deadly weapon presents imminent threat, mental illness doesn't require you to accept injury or death. The standard remains objective reasonableness, not perfect de-escalation.

Scenario 2: Resisting Arrest

Situation: You stop a vehicle for speeding. The driver provides false name and date of birth. When you determine the actual identity and discover active warrants, you inform him he's under arrest. He says "I'm not going to jail" and tenses up when you reach for his arm. He's approximately 6'2", 220 pounds, athletic build. You're 5'10", 180 pounds. Your backup is 3 minutes away.

Questions: What force is justified now? Should you wait for backup? What if he actively fights? What if he flees on foot?

Analysis: Current Situation: Subject knows he's under arrest. Subject is tensing (preparing to resist). Subject has size/strength advantage. You're alone. **Options: Wait for Backup:** Safest option if subject isn't immediate flight risk. Maintain distance, keep hand on weapon, issue verbal commands: "Sir, you're under arrest. I understand you don't want to go to jail, but you have warrants. Don't make this worse by resisting. Keep your hands where I can see them and don't move until my backup arrives." Waiting for backup isn't cowardice—it's smart tactics. Two officers have overwhelming advantage.

If You Proceed Alone: Higher risk but sometimes necessary: Give clear commands: "Place your hands behind your back." Be ready for resistance. If he tenses or pulls away: Empty hand control techniques (wrist locks, come-alongs) are appropriate. OC spray if he actively resists. Takedown if he fights. Strikes to large muscle groups if he's aggressively fighting. Document that he tensed up and resisted, requiring escalated force to overcome resistance and effect lawful arrest.

If He Actively Fights: Punching, kicking, or grappling: Use hard empty hand control (strikes, takedowns). Target large muscle groups. Continue until he's controlled enough to handcuff. Request emergency backup immediately. After control, request medical evaluation even if no apparent injury.

If He Flees on Foot: Fleeing alone doesn't justify deadly force (Tennessee v. Garner). Your options: Pursue on foot if safe and you can maintain visual. Call for backup and establish perimeter. Deploy K-9 if available. Use Taser if he's close enough and you can safely deploy.

Do NOT use deadly force just because he's fleeing from warrant arrest—he's not presenting deadly force threat.

Documentation: Your report addresses: Subject's physical advantages (size, build, apparent strength). Your reasonable concern about safety given size disparity. Subject's statement and actions showing intent to resist ("I'm not going to jail," tensing up). Specific resistance encountered (pulled away, struck at you, etc.). Force used and why it was reasonable (wrist lock failed due to strength advantage, used OC spray to gain compliance, delivered two strikes to right thigh to overcome resistance). Graham factors (arrest warrants; actively resisting; size advantage created safety concern).

Key Takeaway: Size and strength matter in force analysis. Officers aren't required to fight suspects on equal terms. Disparity of force (subject much larger/stronger) justifies higher force level. Waiting for backup is tactically sound and defensible—you're not required to take on a larger opponent alone if time permits waiting.

Scenario 3: Domestic Violence with Weapon

Situation: Dispatched to domestic violence in progress. Caller states her boyfriend is "drunk and destroying things." En route, dispatch updates that male subject "has a gun and is threatening to shoot her and himself." You arrive with your partner. Through the window you see female subject cowering in corner while male subject paces with what appears to be a handgun.

Questions: What's your tactical approach? Can you make entry without warrant? When can you use deadly force? What if subject points gun at his own head instead of you?

Analysis: Exigent Circumstances: You have exigent circumstances justifying warrantless entry: Imminent threat to person inside (victim at gunpoint). Risk subject will harm victim or himself. No time to obtain warrant. Emergency aid exception applies.

Tactical Approach: Don't rush in blindly: Establish positions with cover. Multiple entry points if possible (front and back). Quick coordination with partner on entry assignments. Less-lethal options ready if available (but armed subject may require deadly force response). Clear communication before entry.

Making Entry: Knock and announce if tactically sound (may not be—could provoke shooting). Forced entry if necessary to prevent imminent harm. Move to address immediate threat (subject with gun). Protect victim from crossfire concerns.

Deadly Force Justification: You can use deadly force when: Subject points gun at victim or you. Subject makes movements suggesting he's about to shoot. Subject refuses commands to drop weapon and presents imminent threat. Standard: Reasonable officer would believe deadly force immediately necessary to prevent death or serious bodily injury.

If Subject Points Gun at Own Head: This complicates things. Generally, you can't use deadly force to prevent suicide—he's only threatening himself, not you or others. But tactical reality differs: If he's also threatening the victim, deadly force may still be justified to protect her. If he's highly erratic, he could swing gun toward you at any moment—maintain tactical distance and cover. Consider less-lethal options if available and safe. Request mental health professionals/negotiators. The moment he points gun at you or victim, deadly force is justified.

After Deadly Force: If you must shoot: Provide medical aid immediately to both subject and victim. Secure all weapons. Preserve evidence. Notify supervisor immediately of officer-involved shooting. Separate officers involved (prevents appearance of collusion). Request medical evaluation for victim. Document victim's statements immediately (excited utterances are admissible and crucial evidence). Prepare for extensive investigation—domestic violence shootings are heavily scrutinized.

Documentation Priorities: Victim statements about threats and violence (documented immediately—she may recant later). Your observations through window before entry (what you saw that created reasonable belief of imminent danger). Exigent circumstances justifying entry (threat to victim's life). Subject's actions with weapon (where pointed, movements, statements). Commands given ("Drop the gun!"). Why deadly force was necessary (subject pointed gun at victim/you, refused commands, posed imminent threat). Graham factors (violent felony—aggravated assault with deadly weapon; immediate threat to life; subject armed and refusing to comply).

Key Takeaway: Domestic violence with weapons creates high-risk situations requiring tactical entry and potential deadly force. Exigent circumstances justify warrantless entry when imminent danger exists. But suicide threats complicate things—you generally can't use deadly force solely to prevent self-harm unless subject also threatens others or could quickly turn weapon on you.

Practice Questions (50 questions)

Question 1: The use of force continuum serves to: A) Require officers to try each level of force sequentially B) Provide framework for selecting appropriate force based on subject resistance and threat C) Guarantee officer safety D) Eliminate all force from policing

Answer: B **Explanation:** The force continuum is a framework guiding force decisions based on subject behavior, not a rigid ladder requiring sequential escalation. Officers select appropriate force based on circumstances.

Question 2: De-escalation should be attempted: A) Never—it shows weakness B) Only after force fails C) Whenever safe and feasible before resorting to force D) Only with mentally ill subjects

Answer: C **Explanation:** Modern policing emphasizes de-escalation as first option whenever it can be done safely. This doesn't mean you must de-escalate in all situations—immediate threats require immediate action.

Question 3: Graham v. Connor established that use of force must be: A) Minimal in all cases B) Objectively reasonable based on totality of circumstances C) Approved by supervisor first D) Equal to force used by subject

Answer: B **Explanation:** Graham requires force be objectively reasonable from perspective of reasonable officer on scene, considering totality of circumstances, not with 20/20 hindsight.

Question 4: The three primary Graham v. Connor factors are: A) Time, distance, cover B) Severity of crime, immediate threat, active resistance or evasion C) Subject's age, race, gender D) Officer's intent, training, experience

Answer: B **Explanation:** Graham's three main factors are: severity of crime at issue, whether suspect poses immediate threat to safety, and whether suspect is actively resisting or attempting to evade arrest.

Question 5: Deadly force may be used to prevent escape when: A) Any felony suspect flees B) Suspect poses significant threat of death or serious injury and committed violent felony C) You're angry about the chase D) Any time you want during pursuit

Answer: B **Explanation:** Tennessee v. Garner and Texas law prohibit deadly force to prevent escape unless suspect poses significant threat of death/serious injury to officers or public and committed crime involving deadly force.

Question 6: "Objectively reasonable" force means: A) What you personally thought was right B) What reasonable officer in same situation would believe, not judged by hindsight C) Perfect force decision with no mistakes D) Minimal force in all situations

Answer: B **Explanation:** Force is judged from perspective of reasonable officer on scene with information available at that moment, not by 20/20 hindsight or what's learned afterward.

Question 7: The 21-foot rule illustrates: A) Minimum distance for all stops B) Danger posed by edged weapons—attacker can close 21 feet in time it takes most officers to draw and fire C) Required distance for deadly force D) Maximum distance for OC spray

Answer: B **Explanation:** The Tueller drill demonstrates that attacker with knife at 21 feet can reach officer in approximately 1.5 seconds—less time than drawing and accurately firing. This illustrates danger of edged weapons, not automatic deadly force authorization.

Question 8: De-escalation techniques include: A) Aggressive commands and immediate force B) Time, distance, communication, and tactical repositioning C) Ignoring threats D) Only working with mentally ill

Answer: B **Explanation:** Effective de-escalation uses time (slowing things down), distance (maintaining safe space), communication (calm verbal techniques), and tactical positioning to resolve situations without force.

Question 9: Empty hand control—soft includes: A) Punching and kicking B) Escort holds and joint manipulation without pain C) Strikes to head D) Choking

Answer: B **Explanation:** Soft empty hand control uses low probability of injury techniques like escort holds and biomechanical guidance without pain compliance for passive resistance.

Question 10: Empty hand control—hard may include: A) Only verbal commands B) Pain compliance, takedowns, and strikes to overcome active resistance C) Deadly force D) Nothing physical

Answer: B **Explanation:** Hard empty hand control uses higher force techniques with greater injury probability—pain compliance, takedowns, strikes—to overcome active resistance or aggression.

Question 11: OC spray (pepper spray) is appropriate for: A) Passive resistance only B) Active resistance requiring physical control at distance C) Deadly force situations D) Punishment after arrest

Answer: B **Explanation:** OC spray is appropriate for active resistance where maintaining distance is advantageous or where subject's size/strength makes empty hand control difficult.

Question 12: Conducted energy weapons (Tasers) work by: A) Causing pain only B) Disrupting voluntary muscle control through electrical pulse C) Burning the subject D) Scaring subjects into compliance

Answer: B **Explanation:** CEWs deliver electrical charge disrupting neuromuscular control. This is incapacitation, not pain compliance—subject physically can't control muscles during cycle.

Question 13: Impact weapons should target: A) Head and neck B) Large muscle groups like thighs and upper arms C) Groin area D) Spine

Answer: B **Explanation:** Impact weapons should target large muscle groups (thighs, calves, upper arms) that cause dysfunction without high risk of serious injury. Head, neck, spine are deadly force targets.

Question 14: After using force, officers must: A) Hide any injuries B) Document thoroughly including Graham factors, subject behavior, and force used C) Destroy evidence D) Blame the subject

Answer: B **Explanation:** Thorough documentation is required including what happened, why force was necessary, what force was used, Graham factors, de-escalation attempts, and outcomes.

Question 15: "Immediate threat" in Graham analysis means: A) Any potential future danger B) Subject poses threat right now or imminently through actions or capabilities C) Subject has criminal history D) Subject looks dangerous

Answer: B **Explanation:** Immediate threat focuses on current circumstances—is subject armed, attacking, capable of causing serious harm right now? Future or speculative threats don't justify force.

Question 16: Handcuffs should be applied: A) As tightly as possible B) Palms facing out, double-locked, tight enough to prevent escape but not cutting circulation C) Loosely to avoid complaints D) Only on violent suspects

Answer: B **Explanation:** Proper handcuffing: palms facing out (prevents escape), double-locked (prevents tightening), snug but not too tight (one finger should fit between cuff and wrist).

Question 17: Less-lethal weapons are: A) Completely safe with no risk B) Designed to incapacitate without death but can cause serious injury or death in some circumstances C) Always preferable to any other force D) Never appropriate

Answer: B **Explanation:** "Less-lethal" means less likely to cause death than firearms, not "non-lethal." These weapons can cause serious injury or death under certain circumstances (pre-existing conditions, vulnerable areas, prolonged use).

Question 18: When documenting force, you should: A) Use vague language B) Be specific about subject actions, your observations, force used, and why it was necessary C) Minimize your force description D) Exaggerate the threat

Answer: B **Explanation:** Effective force documentation uses specific descriptions of subject behavior, your observations and perceptions, exact force used, why it was necessary, and Graham factors.

Question 19: The purpose of double-locking handcuffs is to: A) Make them look professional B) Prevent cuffs from tightening during movement and causing injury C) Impress other officers D) Slow down booking process

Answer: B **Explanation:** Double-locking prevents handcuffs from continuing to tighten during movement, which would cause pain, nerve damage, and potential liability.

Question 20: "Active resistance" in Graham analysis refers to: A) Passive non-compliance B) Subject physically resisting through pulling away, fighting, or fleeing C) Verbal resistance only D) Thinking about resisting

Answer: B **Explanation:** Active resistance means physical resistance—pulling away, fighting, tensing up, striking at officers, or fleeing. This is distinct from passive resistance (going limp, not moving).

Question 21: Deadly force is defined as: A) Any force that hurts B) Force reasonably likely to cause death or serious bodily injury C) Only using firearms D) Force approved by supervisor

Answer: B **Explanation:** Deadly force is force reasonably likely to cause death or serious bodily injury, including firearms, strikes to vital areas, chokeholds, vehicles as weapons, etc.

Question 22: An officer may use deadly force when: A) Angry at suspect B) There's imminent threat of death or serious bodily injury to officer or others C) Supervisor approves D) Subject is rude

Answer: B **Explanation:** Deadly force is justified only when officer reasonably believes there's imminent threat of death or serious bodily injury to themselves or others, and force is immediately necessary.

Question 23: After using deadly force, an officer should: A) Leave immediately B) Provide medical aid, secure scene, notify supervisor, preserve evidence C) Discuss details with all other officers D) Clean up evidence

Answer: B **Explanation:** After deadly force: render medical aid to all injured, secure scene and weapons, notify supervisor immediately, preserve evidence, separate involved officers, and document thoroughly.

Question 24: Command presence helps reduce need for force by: A) Intimidating citizens B) Projecting confidence and authority that encourages voluntary compliance C) Making officers look tough D) Scaring everyone

Answer: B **Explanation:** Professional appearance, confident demeanor, calm voice, and clear commands project authority that encourages compliance without physical force.

Question 25: Verbal de-escalation is most effective when: A) Yelling at subjects B) Using calm tone, acknowledging feelings, offering choices, and giving time to comply C) Making threats D) Challenging subject's ego

Answer: B **Explanation:** Effective verbal de-escalation uses calm voice, acknowledges subject's emotions, offers controlled choices, explains what's needed, and provides time for voluntary compliance.

Question 26: Distance in tactical situations provides: A) Nothing useful B) Reaction time to threats, ability to use verbal de-escalation, and tactical options C) Weakness D) Cowardice

Answer: B **Explanation:** Distance equals time and options. Greater distance provides reaction time to threats, space for verbal de-escalation, and ability to use various force options if needed.

Question 27: When can officers use deadly force to prevent escape? A) Whenever anyone flees B) Only when fleeing felon poses significant threat of death/serious injury and committed violent crime C) Never D) Whenever they want

Answer: B **Explanation:** Deadly force to prevent escape requires suspect pose significant threat of death/serious injury, have committed crime involving deadly force, and no other way to prevent escape (Tennessee v. Garner).

Question 28: OC spray should NOT be used: A) For active resistance B) In enclosed spaces with poor ventilation where innocents will be affected C) When distance is needed D) For large/strong subjects

Answer: B **Explanation:** OC spray in enclosed spaces affects everyone present. While sometimes necessary, avoid using it where cross-contamination will incapacitate innocents or other officers.

Question 29: Crisis Intervention Techniques emphasize: A) Immediate force B) Slowing down, maintaining distance, calm communication, and involving mental health professionals C) Ignoring the person D) Aggressive commands

Answer: B **Explanation:** CIT approach recognizes mental health crises require different tactics—slow down, maintain distance, use calm non-threatening communication, be patient, consider mental health resources.

Question 30: Subject control techniques include: A) Unnecessary pain B) Escort holds, come-along holds, and ground control that maintain control while minimizing injury C) Strikes to head D) Choking

Answer: B **Explanation:** Subject control uses techniques like escort holds, come-alongs, and ground control that maintain physical control over resisting subjects while minimizing unnecessary injury.

Question 31: The primary factor in use of force decisions should be: A) Officer's anger B) Objective reasonableness based on totality of circumstances C) Subject's race D) Time of day

Answer: B **Explanation:** Force decisions must be objectively reasonable based on totality of circumstances, considering Graham factors, not subjective feelings, bias, or irrelevant factors.

Question 32: Proportionality in use of force means: A) Force must exactly match suspect's force B) Force should be reasonable in relation to threat, though not required to be precisely equal C) Always use minimal force D) Never use more force than suspect

Answer: B **Explanation:** Proportionality means force should be reasonable relative to threat, though you're not required to match force exactly. Gross disproportionality may indicate unreasonable force.

Question 33: When should de-escalation NOT be attempted? A) Never—always de-escalate B) When imminent threat requires immediate action to prevent death/serious injury C) With all subjects D) During daytime

Answer: B **Explanation:** While de-escalation is preferred, immediate threats to life (active violence, attacks in progress) require immediate action. You're not required to de-escalate when doing so increases danger.

Question 34: Force reports should address: A) Only what helps your case B) Graham factors, subject behavior, force used, why it was necessary, and de-escalation attempts C) Minimal information D) Only supervisor requests

Answer: B **Explanation:** Comprehensive force reports document subject behavior, your observations and beliefs, Graham factors, de-escalation attempts, force used and why necessary, and outcomes.

Question 35: An officer's subjective intent when using force: A) Is the only thing that matters B) Is irrelevant—only objective reasonableness matters under Graham C) Determines legality completely D) Is more important than actions

Answer: B **Explanation:** Graham explicitly rejects subjective intent. Force is judged on objective reasonableness, not officer's personal feelings, motivation, or intent.

Question 36: Less-lethal weapons should be used: A) For all situations B) When active resistance/aggression exists and empty hand techniques are ineffective or inappropriate C) As punishment D) Only on violent felons

Answer: B **Explanation:** Less-lethal weapons are appropriate for active resistance or aggression where empty hand control is ineffective, dangerous, or inappropriate, and deadly force isn't justified.

Question 37: After deploying OC spray, officers should: A) Leave immediately B) Provide fresh air, flush with water when practical, monitor breathing, request medical evaluation C) Ignore the subject D) Apply more spray

Answer: B **Explanation:** After OC use: provide fresh air, flush with cool water when practical, monitor breathing (most complaints are discomfort, not actual respiratory distress), request medical evaluation, document use.

Question 38: Impact weapon strikes to the head are: A) Always appropriate B) Deadly force justified only when deadly force threat exists C) Preferred targets D) Never allowed

Answer: B **Explanation:** Strikes to head, neck, spine with impact weapons are deadly force, justified only when deadly force criteria are met (imminent threat of death/serious bodily injury).

Question 39: Tactical repositioning during confrontations helps by: A) Looking cowardly B) Using cover, creating distance, improving tactical advantage, and limiting subject's options C) Confusing everyone D) Wasting time

Answer: B **Explanation:** Tactical repositioning improves your position through cover/concealment, distance, barriers between you and subject, positions limiting subject's attack options, and positions providing escape routes.

Question 40: The "reactionary gap" refers to: A) Time between shifts B) Distance needed to react to sudden threats—minimum 6-10 feet from subjects C) Gaps in training D) Space between officers

Answer: B **Explanation:** Reactionary gap is distance needed to perceive and react to threats. At contact distance (arm's reach), you can't react to attacks. Maintain 6-10 feet when possible.

Question 41: Force is objectively reasonable when: A) You feel it's right B) Reasonable officer in same situation, with same information, would believe it necessary C) Supervisor approves afterward D) Everyone agrees

Answer: B **Explanation:** Objective reasonableness asks whether reasonable officer facing same circumstances with same information would view force as necessary, not whether perfect decision was made with hindsight.

Question 42: When multiple officers respond, contact and cover roles mean: A) All officers engage simultaneously B) One officer makes contact while others maintain awareness and provide security C) Officers take turns D) Everyone does the same thing

Answer: B **Explanation:** Contact officer interacts with subject while cover officer(s) maintain situational awareness, watch for threats, monitor other people, and provide security.

Question 43: Qualified immunity protects officers from civil liability when: A) They do anything they want B) Their actions were objectively reasonable and didn't violate clearly established law C) They have good intentions D) Supervisors approve

Answer: B **Explanation:** Qualified immunity shields officers from civil liability when actions were objectively reasonable and didn't violate clearly established constitutional rights known to reasonable officer.

Question 44: CEW (Taser) should NOT be used on: A) Actively resisting subjects B) Subjects on elevated surfaces where fall would cause serious injury, if alternatives exist C) Subjects with weapons D) Large subjects

Answer: B **Explanation:** CEWs cause complete loss of muscle control and falling. On elevated surfaces (roofs, stairs, balconies), falls can cause serious injury or death. Avoid if alternatives exist.

Question 45: "Severity of crime" in Graham analysis considers: A) Only if it's a felony or misdemeanor B) Whether crime involves violence, danger to others, and seriousness of offense C) Subject's criminal history D) Time of day

Answer: B **Explanation:** Severity analysis considers whether crime is violent or nonviolent, danger posed to public, seriousness of offense. Violent felonies justify higher force than property misdemeanors.

Question 46: Active listening during de-escalation includes: A) Interrupting constantly B) Maintaining eye contact, acknowledging what they're saying, and showing you're hearing them C) Ignoring the person D) Arguing

Answer: B **Explanation:** Active listening shows you're hearing the person through eye contact, acknowledging their statements, paraphrasing to confirm understanding, and validating feelings without necessarily agreeing.

Question 47: Drive-stun mode on CEWs: A) Is most effective method B) Causes pain but not incapacitation like probe mode does C) Should be primary technique D) Is always preferred

Answer: B **Explanation:** Drive-stun (contact without probes) causes pain but doesn't incapacitate like probe deployment. It's less effective and generally used only when probes already deployed or distance prevents probe use.

Question 48: Force documentation photographs should include: A) Only officer injuries B) Officer injuries, subject injuries, scene showing distances/positions, and any weapons or evidence C) Nothing—photos aren't needed D) Only what helps your case

Answer: B **Explanation:** Document all injuries (officer and subject), scene showing layout and distances, weapons or evidence, and anything relevant to understanding what occurred and why force was necessary.

Question 49: Time as a de-escalation tool means: A) Taking as long as you want B) Slowing things down when safe to do so, creating opportunity for calm and resolution C) Rushing situations D) Ignoring urgency

Answer: B **Explanation:** Creating time (when situation permits) allows agitated people to calm down, gives you time to assess and plan, allows backup/resources to arrive, and reduces pressure for immediate force.

Question 50: After any use of force, officers should: A) Celebrate B) Assess for injuries, provide medical care, document thoroughly, and report to supervisors C) Hide what happened D) Blame others

Answer: B **Explanation:** After force: assess all parties for injuries, provide or request medical care, document thoroughly and objectively, notify supervisor, preserve evidence, and complete required reports.

Scoring Your Practice Questions

48-50 correct (96-100%): Outstanding! Your understanding of use of force law, de-escalation, and tactical applications is excellent. You grasp both legal requirements and practical application. Review any missed questions to ensure complete understanding.

43-47 correct (86-94%): Excellent work! You have strong grasp of use of force principles. Focus on areas where you missed questions—whether deadly force standards, less-lethal options, or documentation. Review those sections carefully.

38-42 correct (76-84%): Good progress! You understand core concepts but need to strengthen specific areas. Identify patterns in missed questions. Review those topics thoroughly, focusing on Graham standards, de-escalation requirements, and proper force application.

33-37 correct (66-74%): You're developing understanding but have significant gaps. Review Chapter 7 systematically. Focus on Graham v. Connor factors, deadly force requirements, and when each force level is appropriate. Work through scenarios multiple times.

Below 33 correct (less than 66%): You need substantial additional study. Use of force is critical—mistakes cost lives, freedom, and careers. Review Chapter 7 section by section. Master Graham factors, understand force continuum, study de-escalation techniques. Create summary notes and review scenarios repeatedly.

CHAPTER 8: EMERGENCY RESPONSE AND CRISIS MANAGEMENT

You're often the first person to arrive when life hangs in the balance. Heart attacks, shootings, car accidents, mental health crises, domestic violence escalations, hostage situations, and active shooters—you'll face them all. Your actions in those critical first minutes determine whether people live or die. This chapter prepares you for the most challenging calls you'll encounter. Emergency response isn't just about enforcement—it's about saving lives, managing chaos, and making split-second decisions under extreme stress. The techniques you'll learn here go beyond basic academy training. You'll understand how to provide life-saving medical care, recognize and respond to mental health crises, assess lethality in domestic violence situations, manage hostage and barricaded subjects, and respond to active shooters using proven tactics. These are the calls that test everything you've learned. They're also the calls where your training, judgment, and courage make the difference between tragedy and survival.

First Responder Medical Care

You're not a paramedic, but you're often first on scene when someone is dying. Basic medical knowledge saves lives while EMS is en route. Your department requires Basic Life Support certification, but understanding when and how to apply that training in tactical situations is different from classroom practice.

Basic Life Support and Trauma Care

The ABCs of Emergency Care: Airway: Is the airway open and clear? Unconscious victims may have airway obstructions from tongue, blood, vomit, or objects. Open airway by tilting head back (if no spinal injury suspected) or jaw thrust maneuver (if spinal injury possible). Clear visible obstructions with fingers (careful—don't push objects deeper). Consider recovery position for unconscious breathing victims (on side to prevent aspiration). **Breathing:** Is the person breathing? Look for chest rise, listen for breath sounds, feel for air movement. If not breathing, begin rescue breathing after opening airway. Provide one breath every 5-6 seconds for adults. Watch for chest rise to confirm effective breaths. **Circulation:** Is there a pulse? Check carotid (neck) or femoral (groin) arteries. If no pulse, begin CPR immediately. Compressions are priority—"push hard, push fast" on center of chest at 100-120 compressions per minute. Depth: at least 2 inches for adults. Continue until EMS arrives or person recovers.

Severe Bleeding Control: Uncontrolled bleeding kills within minutes. Your priority after neutralizing threats is stopping hemorrhage. **Direct Pressure:** Apply firm, direct pressure to wound using gauze, cloth, or your gloved hand. Don't remove first layer if it soaks through—

add more material on top. Maintain pressure for several minutes (usually 5-10) until bleeding slows. **Pressure Points:** If direct pressure fails, apply pressure to arteries supplying the wounded area: Arm wounds = brachial artery (inside of upper arm), Leg wounds = femoral artery (groin area), Head wounds = temporal artery (side of head). **Tourniquets:** For life-threatening extremity bleeding that direct pressure can't control: Apply tourniquet 2-3 inches above wound (between wound and heart). Tighten until bleeding stops completely. Note time of application (write on victim or tourniquet). Don't remove once applied—let EMS handle that. Modern tourniquets are safe and effective—don't hesitate to use them for severe arterial bleeding. Combat experience proves tourniquets save lives.

Treating Shock: Shock is insufficient blood flow to organs and tissues. It kills even if injuries aren't immediately fatal. **Signs of Shock:** Rapid, weak pulse, Rapid, shallow breathing, Pale, cool, clammy skin, Altered mental status (confused, anxious, unresponsive), Nausea or vomiting, Weakness or fatigue. **Treatment:** Control bleeding (main cause of traumatic shock), Keep victim lying down, Elevate legs 12 inches if no spinal injury or head trauma suspected, Maintain body temperature (cover with blanket but don't overheat), Provide reassurance and monitor continuously, Do NOT give food or water (risk of vomiting/aspiration).

Chest Wounds: Penetrating chest wounds (gunshots, stabbings) can cause collapsed lung (pneumothorax) or tension pneumothorax (air trapped in chest cavity). **Open Chest Wound (Sucking Chest Wound):** Seal wound with occlusive dressing (non-porous material). Use commercial chest seals if available. If not, plastic wrapper, petroleum gauze, or even gloved hand works temporarily. Tape on three sides (top and both sides), leaving bottom open. This creates one-way valve allowing air out but not in. Monitor breathing continuously. **Signs of Tension Pneumothorax:** Severe breathing difficulty, Distended neck veins, Decreased breath sounds on affected side, Rapid deterioration. If commercial chest seal or improvised seal causes worsening (suggesting tension pneumothorax), briefly lift one corner to release trapped air, then reseal. This is temporary measure until EMS arrives with equipment to decompress chest.

Head Injuries: Head trauma requires different treatment than other injuries. **DO:** Maintain airway, Control bleeding with direct pressure (but don't apply pressure to depressed skull fractures), Keep victim still (suspect spinal injury), Monitor consciousness level, Position victim carefully (if vomiting likely, recovery position; if increased intracranial pressure suspected, elevate head 30 degrees). **DON'T:** Remove impaled objects from head, Give food or water, Allow victim to sleep without periodic checks, Apply pressure to obvious skull depressions.

Spinal Injuries: Suspect spinal injury when: Fall from height, Motor vehicle accident, Diving accident, Unconscious trauma victim, Victim complains of back/neck pain or numbness/tingling. **Treatment:** Minimize movement (in-line stabilization of head/neck), Don't remove helmets unless airway compromise, Only move victim if immediate danger exists (fire, gunfire, explosion risk), If must move, maintain in-line spinal alignment. Remember: Your scene safety comes first. If you're under fire, you can't help anyone. Once tactical situation is secure, medical care becomes priority.

Tactical Combat Casualty Care (TCCC) Principles: Law enforcement adopted these military principles: **Care Under Fire:** Return fire and neutralize threat first. You can't treat casualties while being shot at. Move casualties to cover if possible while maintaining tactical advantage. Consider dragging versus carrying (dragging is faster, keeps you lower). **Tactical Field Care:** Once immediate threat is neutralized: Control major bleeding (tourniquets for extremity hemorrhage), Secure airway if needed, Seal chest wounds, Prevent shock, Prepare for evacuation. **Evacuation Care:** During transport to hospital, continue monitoring and treating: Reassess tourniquets (note times, don't remove), Monitor airway and breathing, Check and control bleeding, Treat for shock.

Medical Equipment and Supplies

Your patrol car should contain: **Basic Trauma Kit:** Tourniquets (at least one, preferably two), Hemostatic gauze (QuikClot, Celox), Chest seals (Hyfin, Asherman), Israeli bandages or pressure dressings, Gloves (multiple pairs), Trauma shears, Nasopharyngeal airway, CPR mask or shield. **Many officers carry individual first aid kits (IFAKs) on their person.** In gunfights or explosions, you may be separated from your vehicle. An IFAK on your belt or vest provides immediate access to life-saving equipment.

Scene Safety and Exposure Control: Universal precautions apply to every scene: **Assume all body fluids are infectious.** Wear gloves for all patient contact. Change gloves between patients. Eye protection if splash risk exists. Wash hands thoroughly after any exposure. Report exposure incidents immediately (needle sticks, blood contact with open wounds, mucous membrane exposure).

Crisis Intervention Strategies

Crisis situations differ from criminal situations. People in crisis aren't thinking rationally. Traditional policing tactics often escalate rather than resolve these situations. Understanding crisis dynamics and applying specialized techniques reduces violence and connects people with needed resources.

Recognizing Mental Health Crises

Common Mental Health Crisis Indicators: Behavioral Signs: Confusion or disorganized thinking, Inability to follow simple directions, Talking to people who aren't there (hallucinations), Hearing voices (auditory hallucinations), Extreme mood swings, Paranoia or delusions ("They're watching me," "You're trying to harm me"), Inappropriate emotional responses (laughing at serious topics, crying without apparent reason), Repetitive movements or speech. **Verbal Indicators:** Statements about self-harm or suicide, Grandiose claims ("I'm God," "I control the universe"), Persecution themes ("Everyone is against me"), Disorganized or incoherent speech, Responding to stimuli others don't perceive.

Common Mental Health Conditions You'll Encounter: Schizophrenia and Psychotic Disorders: May involve hallucinations, delusions, disorganized thinking. Person may appear to be responding to internal stimuli. May believe things that aren't true (delusions) and act on those beliefs. Often not dangerous but may become aggressive if they perceive threats (real or imagined). **Bipolar Disorder:** Extreme mood swings from depression to mania. During manic episodes: excessive energy, rapid speech, poor judgment, impulsive behavior, may go days without sleep. During depressive episodes: extreme sadness, hopelessness, low energy, may contemplate suicide. **Severe Depression:** Profound sadness, hopelessness, withdrawal. High suicide risk. May express desire to die or give away possessions. May have made plans for suicide. **Anxiety Disorders/Panic Attacks:** Extreme fear or anxiety, rapid breathing, chest pain, feeling of losing control. May appear to be having medical emergency. Usually not dangerous but person is terrified. **Dementia:** Confusion, memory loss, disorientation. Common in elderly. May become combative when confused or frightened. Often wanders and gets lost.

Crisis vs. Crime: Key distinction: Is this person choosing criminal behavior or are they in crisis? **Criminal Behavior:** Deliberate choices, Goal-oriented actions, Attempts to hide or escape, Responds to incentives and consequences, Generally rational decision-making process. **Crisis Behavior:** Driven by symptoms beyond person's control, Not goal-oriented (may be responding to internal stimuli), Often doesn't try to hide, Doesn't respond rationally to incentives/consequences, Impaired judgment due to mental state. This distinction matters because it determines your approach. Criminals respond to show of force and consequences. People in crisis often escalate when confronted with traditional policing tactics.

Mental Health Crisis Response - CIT Techniques and Resources

Crisis Intervention Team (CIT) training provides tools for responding to mental health situations. Even if you're not CIT-trained, these principles apply:

The CIT Approach: Slow Down: Most mental health crises aren't emergencies requiring immediate action. Slowing down reduces pressure and allows time for calm. Unless person is actively violent or someone is in immediate danger, take your time. **Create Distance:** Maintain safe distance (15-25 feet if possible). This gives person space and you safety. Avoid crowding—it increases anxiety. **Lower Your Voice:** Speak calmly and quietly. Match person's volume or speak slightly quieter. Loud voices escalate agitation. **Use Simple Language:** Short, clear sentences. "I'm here to help. My name is Officer Smith. Can you tell me your name?" Avoid complex explanations or commands. **Listen More Than You Talk:** Let person speak. Don't interrupt. Show you're listening through body language and acknowledgment. **Avoid Sudden Movements:** Move slowly and deliberately. Announce your movements: "I'm going to move over here." Sudden movements may be perceived as threats.

Building Rapport: Introduce Yourself: "Hi, I'm Officer Smith. What's your name?" Personal introduction humanizes the interaction. **Acknowledge Their Experience:** "I can see you're having a difficult time." "This must be really frustrating." You're not agreeing with delusions, but you're acknowledging their distress is real to them. **Offer Help:** "I want to help. Can you tell me what's going on?" "What do you need right now?" Frame yourself as helper, not adversary. **Don't Argue with Delusions:** If someone says "The FBI implanted a chip in my brain," don't argue. Say something like "That sounds really scary. I can see why that would upset you." Arguing reinforces their perception of threat. **Validate Feelings:** "I understand you're upset." "That does sound confusing." You're not validating the delusion, but the emotion is real.

Safety Considerations: While using CIT techniques, maintain officer safety: **Watch Hands:** People in crisis can still be violent. Watch hands continuously. **Maintain Distance:** Your reactionary gap still applies. **Use Cover:** Position yourself with cover available. **Have Backup:** Request additional officers. More officers allows containment and gives you time to use CIT techniques. **Remove Weapons:** If weapons are present, focus on safely securing them. **Consider Less-Lethal:** Have Taser or other less-lethal options ready if person becomes violent.

When to Transition from CIT to Force: CIT doesn't mean accepting danger. Transition to traditional tactics when: Person becomes violent or attacks, Person presents deadly force threat, Person is actively harming self or others, Attempts at de-escalation fail and danger increases, Tactical situation requires immediate action. You can attempt CIT techniques while maintaining tactical readiness. Have less-lethal and lethal options immediately available.

Connecting with Resources: Mental Health Professionals: Many departments have mental health liaisons or co-responders. Request them if available. Hospitals have psychiatric crisis teams. Consider transport to mental health facility rather than jail when appropriate. **Emergency Detention:** Texas law (Health & Safety Code Chapter 573) allows peace officers to detain persons with mental illness who pose imminent danger to self or others for psychiatric evaluation. This is civil detention, not arrest. Complete required paperwork. Transport to mental health facility. **Mobile Crisis Outreach Teams:** Many areas have mobile crisis units—mental health professionals who respond to calls with or instead of police. Know what's available in your jurisdiction.

Common Mistakes in Mental Health Calls: Rushing: Taking too long feels uncomfortable, but rushing escalates situations. Give it time. **Too Many Officers:** Overwhelming presence scares people in crisis. Limit officers making contact. **Aggressive Posture:** Standing over person, hands on weapons, aggressive stance—all escalate. Stay calm, open posture. **Commands Instead of Requests:** "Come here now!" escalates. "Would you mind coming over here so we can talk?" works better. **Taking Things Personally:** Person in crisis may say insulting things. It's the illness talking, not personal attack. Don't react emotionally.

Domestic Violence Calls

Domestic violence calls are among the most dangerous you'll handle. Emotions run high, alcohol or drugs are often involved, weapons may be present, and dynamics are volatile. These calls require tactical awareness, careful assessment, and thorough investigation.

Lethality Assessment and Victim Safety

Lethality Factors: Certain factors dramatically increase risk of domestic violence homicide: **Weapons Access:** Does abuser have access to firearms? Gun presence increases homicide risk sevenfold. Has abuser threatened victim with weapon? **Escalating Violence:** Is violence increasing in frequency or severity? Strangulation attempts (one of strongest predictors of eventual homicide)? Has violence moved beyond slapping/pushing to punching, kicking, or choking? **Separation:** Is victim trying to leave? Most domestic violence homicides occur when victim leaves or threatens to leave. Abuser may feel losing control and resort to violence. **Obsessive Behavior:** Extreme jealousy, monitoring victim's activities, isolating victim from friends/family, constant contact requirements—all indicate dangerous control issues. **Threats to Kill:** Direct threats: "I'll kill you if you leave." Indirect threats: "If I can't have you, nobody will." Any threats must be taken seriously. **Depression or Suicide Threats:** Abuser who's depressed or suicidal may decide to kill victim and then self ("murder-suicide"). **Substance Abuse:** Alcohol and drugs lower inhibitions and increase violence. **Violation of Protective Orders:** Shows abuser doesn't respect legal consequences and will continue pursuing victim despite orders.

Conducting Lethality Assessment: Many departments use standardized lethality assessment tools (like Maryland Network Against Domestic Violence Lethality Assessment Program). Even without formal tool, assess these factors during every domestic violence call: Ask victim directly about these risk factors. Document responses thoroughly. If multiple high-risk factors present, consider immediate safety planning. Connect victim with domestic violence advocates immediately (many departments have on-call advocates). Strongly encourage victim to seek shelter and protective order.

Immediate Victim Safety: During Your Response: Separate parties immediately upon arrival. Interview victim privately, away from abuser (different rooms, outside, in your patrol car). Assess injuries and document thoroughly (photographs from multiple angles). Ask about children—are they safe? Were they present during violence? Provide victim with information about protective orders, shelters, and victim services (written information in multiple languages if possible). Help victim develop safety plan if they're staying in the home. **Safety Planning:** If victim won't leave or can't leave immediately: Identify safe room with lock and window for escape. Keep phone charged and accessible. Have important documents in safe place (birth certificates, Social Security cards, financial documents). Prepare bag with essentials, keep at friend's house. Tell trusted friends/neighbors about situation, develop code word to signal danger. Know shelter locations and hotline numbers. Consider protective order.

Children in Domestic Violence Situations: Children present during domestic violence suffer trauma even if not directly harmed. Texas law recognizes exposure to family violence as child abuse in some circumstances. Document whether children were present. Note children's emotional state and any statements they make. Consider whether CPS notification is required. Ensure children's immediate safety.

Hostage and Barricaded Subjects

Hostage situations and barricaded subjects require specialized responses. Your role as patrol officer is usually containment and establishing command structure for specialized units.

Containment and Negotiation

Hostage vs. Barricaded Subject: Hostage Situation: Subject is holding one or more persons against their will, using them as bargaining chips or shields. Life safety for hostages is paramount. Negotiations focus on hostage release. Tactical interventions carry extreme risk to hostages. Time usually favors police—hostage-takers rarely harm hostages initially. **Barricaded Subject:** Subject has fortified position but no hostages. Subject may be wanted suspect barricading to avoid arrest, person in crisis who's isolated themselves, armed subject refusing to surrender. Less immediate danger than hostage situation, but still requires careful handling.

Initial Response—Patrol Officer Role: Establish Perimeter: Create inner perimeter (containment—no one in or out) and outer perimeter (crowd/traffic control). Position officers with good observation points and cover. Ensure subject can't escape undetected. **Gather Intelligence:** Who's inside? How many hostages? Description of hostage-taker? Weapons present? Building layout? Entry/exit points? Prior criminal history? Mental health history? Family contacts? **Evacuate Bystanders:** Clear area of uninvolved persons. Don't let media or crowd gather in danger zone. Establish safe zone for staging. **Request Resources:** Supervisor, SWAT/tactical team, Hostage negotiators, EMS (stage nearby but out of danger), Mental health professionals if crisis situation. **Establish Command Post:** Unified command location away from immediate danger. Coordinate arriving resources. Brief command staff on situation.

Do Not: Enter Alone: Patrol officers almost never make entry on barricaded subjects or hostage situations. You're not trained or equipped for hostage rescue. Wait for specialized units. **Rush the Situation:** Time usually favors police. Subject who's contained and not actively harming hostages can wait for negotiators and tactical team. **Negotiate Without Training:** Untrained negotiations can escalate situations. Basic communication to maintain status quo is acceptable ("Are you okay in there?" "Is anyone hurt?"). But complex negotiations require trained negotiators. **Allow Media Access:** Media presence complicates situations. Establish media staging area far from scene.

Supporting Negotiators: Once negotiators arrive, patrol officers support by: Maintaining perimeter security, Gathering additional intelligence, Coordinating with tactical team for contingency plans, Clearing areas for safe routes if surrender occurs, Remaining ready for dynamic entry if negotiations fail. **When Negotiations Fail:** Some situations can't be resolved through negotiations: Active harm to hostages, Subject setting fires or creating other immediate dangers, Significant time passed with no progress and intelligence suggests subject won't surrender, Negotiations break down and subject presents imminent threat. In these cases, tactical team makes entry. Patrol officers support by: Securing outer perimeter, Maintaining evacuation areas, Providing fire suppression support, Securing surrender subjects or victims upon exit.

Active Shooter Response

Active shooter events demand immediate action. Victims are dying every second you wait. The active shooter response has evolved dramatically—you can't wait for SWAT. Patrol officers must engage immediately.

ALERRT Training Principles

Advanced Law Enforcement Rapid Response Training (ALERRT) provides nationally-recognized active shooter response protocols. These principles guide response:

Immediate Action vs. Delayed Response: Old Model (Columbine): Establish perimeter, wait for SWAT, begin negotiations. Result: Victims bled out while police waited outside. This model is obsolete. **Current Model (ALERRT):** First officers on scene immediately enter and engage shooter. Form contact teams with available officers (even solo entry if necessary). Move toward sound of gunfire. Engage and neutralize threat quickly. Stop the killing, then stop the dying (render medical aid once threat is neutralized). **Priority of Life:** ALERRT establishes priority for active shooter situations: 1. Hostages/victims, 2. Uninvolved citizens, 3. Police officers, 4. Suspect. This means you accept risk to save hostages and citizens. But you can't save anyone if you're killed. Balance aggressive action with sound tactics.

Solo Officer Response: If you're first on scene and shooter is actively killing: Enter immediately. Don't wait for backup. Move toward sound of gunfire. Engage shooter as quickly as possible. Use speed, surprise, and violence of action. Every second you wait, more people die. **This is the hardest thing you'll ever do:** Running toward gunfire alone contradicts every survival instinct. But active shooter doctrine is clear—immediate action saves lives. Your training and courage make the difference between mass casualty event and limited casualties.

Contact Team Formation: As additional officers arrive, form contact teams: **Two-Officer Team:** Ideal minimum for room clearing. One covers, one moves. Faster than solo, safer than solo, still rapid response. **Three-Four Officer Team:** Allows better coverage and multiple angles. Faster room clearing. More firepower if confronting determined shooter. **Larger Teams:** Diminishing returns after four officers. More officers create coordination difficulties in dynamic environment. Additional officers should form rescue teams or secure perimeter.

Movement and Clearing: Move with Purpose: Fast walking, not running. Maintain weapon ready positions. Communicate quietly. Stay oriented (know where teammates are). **Threshold Evaluation:** At doorways and corners: Quick peek to assess, Decide whether to bypass or clear based on information, Move decisively once committed. **Room Clearing:** Fundamentals apply: Slice the pie, Use angles and cover, Clear corners systematically, Don't silhouette in doorways, Communicate with team. **Following Sound:** Move toward gunfire quickly. Sound indicates where victims are being killed and where shooter is located. Accept risk of moving toward danger—that's your mission.

Engaging the Shooter: Immediate Action: When you encounter the shooter: Engage immediately with accurate fire. Don't issue commands first if shooter is actively firing. Your priority is stopping the killing. Multiple officers should coordinate fire, but don't delay engagement waiting for perfect setup. Shoot to stop the threat—center mass, multiple rounds, assess and continue firing until threat stops. **After Shooter is Down:** Secure weapons, Handcuff if possible (even if appears dead), Don't assume they're dead or only one shooter exists, Continue clearing until building is secure, Request EMS for shooter once secured (your duty doesn't end because they're the bad guy).

Rescue Teams: After threat is neutralized or by-passed, rescue teams: Evacuate victims from danger areas, Provide immediate medical care, Direct walking wounded to safe areas, Extract seriously wounded for EMS, Mark cleared rooms.

Victim Considerations: Understand victim behavior in active shooter events: **Denial:** Many victims freeze or deny danger initially. They need clear, direct commands: "Run! Get out now!" "Hide in this room and lock the door!" **Panic:** Some victims panic and make poor decisions. You may need to physically direct them. Stay calm—your demeanor affects victims. **Hostility:** Victims are terrified. They may not immediately recognize you as police. Announce yourself clearly and repeatedly: "Police! We're here to help!" Some victims may be hostile or uncooperative due to stress. Don't take it personally.

Communication: Tactical communication during active shooter: Radio traffic will be heavy—keep transmissions brief and essential. Provide: Location of shooter (last known), Number of shooters (if known), Description of shooter(s), Casualties (approximate numbers), Your location and actions. Receive: Additional responding units locations, Intelligence from other sources (school officials, security, etc.), Command decisions about perimeter or evacuation.

Post-Engagement: After shooter is neutralized: Remain alert for additional threats (secondary devices, second shooter), Begin emergency medical care, Establish casualty collection point, Coordinate with EMS for triage and transport, Preserve evidence as much as possible (but life safety is priority), Prepare for long investigation and after-action review. **Mental Health After Active Shooter:** You'll likely experience stress reactions after active shooter events—this is normal. Seeing numerous casualties, especially children, affects everyone. Use available support services: Critical Incident Stress Debriefing, Employee Assistance Programs, Peer support, Professional counseling. There's no shame in seeking help. These events are traumatic for everyone involved.

Real-World Application: Emergency Response Scenarios

Scenario 1: Gunshot Victim Under Fire

Situation: Dispatched to shots fired. En route, dispatch updates that multiple callers report active shooting. You arrive and see victim lying in street bleeding from apparent gunshot wounds. You hear additional shots in the distance. The victim is conscious and crying for help.

Questions: What are your priorities? How do you approach? When do you provide medical care?

Analysis: Tactical Situation: Active shooting ongoing (you hear shots), Victim in open area (street) exposed to fire, Unknown shooter location, Other victims possible. **Priorities (TCCC Principles):** 1. Return fire/neutralize threat (you can't treat casualties while being shot at), 2. Move casualties to cover if possible, 3. Provide medical care once tactically feasible.

Approach: Don't drive directly to victim—you'll create another casualty (you). Park in covered position away from victim. Assess whether you can reach victim safely. If shooter location unknown and shots ongoing, reaching victim may be suicide. Consider: Can you approach from covered angle? Can you use vehicle for mobile cover? Is smoke/obscuration available? Where are additional officers?

Decision Matrix: If You Can Safely Reach Victim: Move quickly to victim using cover. Grab victim and drag to cover (don't attempt to carry—dragging is faster and keeps you lower). Once in cover, begin medical treatment (control bleeding, assess injuries, prepare for evacuation). Continue monitoring for threats. **If You Cannot Safely Reach Victim:** Establish position with cover and good observation. Try to locate shooter. Request backup and provide intel on situation. Wait for additional units before attempting rescue. Coordinate with other officers to provide cover fire while one unit extracts victim.

Medical Care: Once in covered position: Control severe bleeding (tourniquets for extremity arterial bleeding, direct pressure for other wounds), Assess airway/breathing, Treat for shock, Prepare for evacuation once scene secure. **Key Principle:** You can't help anyone if you become a casualty. Sometimes the tactical situation requires waiting for additional resources rather than immediately rushing to victim's aid. This is agonizing but necessary—one dead victim is tragic; one dead victim plus one dead officer is worse.

Scenario 2: Mental Health Crisis with Weapon

Situation: Called to "welfare check" on elderly male. Family reports he hasn't answered phone in two days and "hasn't been himself lately." You arrive and knock. Male opens door partially, holding handgun at his side. He appears disheveled and confused. He says "Go away. Leave me alone. I don't want to hurt anyone." You can see inside—the house is in disarray.

Analysis: Situation Assessment: Mental health crisis likely (family reports behavior change, confusion, disheveled appearance). Armed with handgun but not pointing at you. States he doesn't want to hurt anyone. No immediate attack. Appears more fearful than aggressive.

Immediate Actions: Create Distance: Back away from door to create tactical distance. Don't reach for weapon or make sudden movements—may be perceived as threat. Move to covered position. **Call for Backup:** Request additional officers, supervisor, and CIT-trained officer if available. Consider mental health crisis professional. **Contain:** Establish perimeter (prevent him from leaving, prevent others from entering). Evacuate neighbors if risk exists.

De-escalation Approach: Use CIT techniques: Keep distance, Speak calmly and introduce yourself again: "Sir, I'm Officer Smith. I'm here because your family is worried about you. Are you okay?" Let him talk. Don't rush him. Acknowledge his feelings: "I understand you want to be left alone. Your family is worried. Can you tell me what's going on?" Avoid commands about the gun initially—mentioning it may escalate. Instead, focus on building rapport. Offer help: "How can I help you? What do you need?"

If He Closes Door: If he closes door without threatening anyone: Don't force entry immediately (no imminent danger). Maintain perimeter. Continue attempting communication through door. Consider phone contact (have family provide number). Request mental health professional to assist. Time usually helps—he may calm down and come out.

If He Points Gun: If he raises gun and points it at you or others: Take cover immediately, Consider deadly force if presenting imminent deadly threat, Announce: "Put the gun down!" but don't give up cover to continue negotiations, Coordinate with other officers for crossfire if deadly force necessary. **Ideal Outcome:** With patient CIT approach, many of these situations resolve peacefully: He agrees to put gun down, You or mental health professional continues talking him through crisis, He eventually comes out and agrees to voluntary or involuntary mental health transport, No one hurt, person gets needed help.

Key Takeaway: Mental health crisis doesn't eliminate use of force authority when weapons present. But approach matters. Traditional aggressive tactics escalate mentally ill armed subjects. CIT techniques combined with tactical awareness resolve many situations peacefully.

Practice Questions (50 questions)

Question 1: The ABCs of emergency medical care stand for: A) Alert, Breathing, Circulation B) Airway, Breathing, Circulation C) Assess, Bandage, Control D) Ambulance, Backup, Clear

Answer: B **Explanation:** ABCs are Airway (is it open?), Breathing (is person breathing?), Circulation (is there pulse?). This is the foundational assessment sequence for emergency medical care.

Question 2: For severe extremity bleeding that direct pressure doesn't control, you should: A) Give up B) Apply tourniquet 2-3 inches above wound and tighten until bleeding stops C) Ignore it D) Wait for EMS without doing anything

Answer: B **Explanation:** Tourniquets save lives from severe arterial bleeding. Apply 2-3 inches above wound (between wound and heart), tighten until bleeding stops completely, note time, don't remove.

Question 3: When treating shock, you should: A) Give victim water B) Control bleeding, keep victim lying down, elevate legs if no spinal injury, maintain temperature C) Make victim stand up D) Apply heat to increase blood flow

Answer: B **Explanation:** Shock treatment: control bleeding (main cause), keep victim lying down, elevate legs 12 inches (if no spinal/head injury), maintain body temperature. Don't give food/water.

Question 4: Open chest wounds (sucking chest wounds) should be treated by: A) Leaving them open B) Sealing with occlusive dressing taped on three sides, creating one-way valve C) Packing tightly with gauze D) Ignoring them

Answer: B **Explanation:** Seal open chest wounds with non-porous material taped on three sides (top and both sides), leaving bottom open. This creates one-way valve allowing air out but not in.

Question 5: CIT (Crisis Intervention Team) approach to mental health crises emphasizes: A) Immediate force B) Slowing down, creating distance, calm communication, and involving mental health professionals C) Aggressive commands D) Ignoring the situation

Answer: B **Explanation:** CIT emphasizes slowing down (most aren't emergencies requiring immediate action), creating distance, using calm communication, listening more than talking, and involving mental health resources.

Question 6: When responding to someone experiencing hallucinations, you should: A) Argue about whether hallucinations are real B) Acknowledge their distress without reinforcing delusions, and focus on their feelings C) Mock them D) Force them to admit hallucinations aren't real

Answer: B **Explanation:** Don't argue with delusions/hallucinations. Acknowledge their distress is real to them ("That sounds scary"), validate their feelings, but don't reinforce the delusions as reality.

Question 7: Lethality factors in domestic violence include: A) Only physical injuries B) Weapons access, strangulation attempts, threats to kill, separation/leaving, obsessive behavior C) Arguments only D) Nothing specific

Answer: B **Explanation:** High lethality indicators: weapons (especially firearms), strangulation attempts, threats to kill, victim trying to leave, extreme jealousy/obsession, depression/suicide threats, protective order violations.

Question 8: When arriving at a domestic violence call, you should immediately: A) Leave both parties together B) Separate parties, interview victim privately, assess injuries, document thoroughly C) Ignore the victim D) Talk to both together

Answer: B **Explanation:** Immediately separate parties for safety and honest disclosure. Interview victim privately (away from abuser), assess and photograph injuries, provide resources, help develop safety plan.

Question 9: In an active shooter situation, the current response model requires: A) Establish perimeter and wait for SWAT B) First officers immediately enter and engage shooter to stop the killing C) Negotiate with shooter D) Evacuate building first

Answer: B **Explanation:** ALERRT training requires immediate action—first officers enter and move toward gunfire, form contact teams, engage shooter quickly. Every second of delay means more victims die.

Question 10: ALERRT Priority of Life in active shooter situations is: A) Officers first B) Hostages/victims, uninvolved citizens, officers, suspect C) Everyone equally D) Suspect first

Answer: B **Explanation:** Priority: 1) Hostages/victims, 2) Uninvolved citizens, 3) Officers, 4) Suspect. Officers accept risk to save innocents, but can't save anyone if killed.

Question 11: Tactical Combat Casualty Care (TCCC) "Care Under Fire" phase means: A) Provide medical care while being shot at B) Return fire and neutralize threat first—you can't treat casualties while under fire C) Ignore casualties D) Call for ambulance only

Answer: B **Explanation:** Care Under Fire: neutralize threat first, move casualties to cover if possible while maintaining tactical advantage. Can't help anyone while being shot at.

Question 12: When encountering someone in mental health crisis, you should avoid: A) Calm communication B) Rushing, using too many officers, aggressive posture, commands instead of requests C) Listening D) Offering help

Answer: B **Explanation:** Common mistakes that escalate: rushing (give it time), too many officers (overwhelming), aggressive posture, commands instead of requests, taking insults personally.

Question 13: A tourniquet applied for severe bleeding should be: A) Removed after 5 minutes B) Left in place with time noted—let EMS remove it C) Applied loosely D) Not used under any circumstances

Answer: B **Explanation:** Once tourniquet is applied, don't remove it (can cause shock from sudden blood flow). Note time applied, let EMS handle removal. Modern tourniquets are safe and effective.

Question 14: For a barricaded subject with no hostages, patrol officers should: A) Make immediate entry alone B) Establish perimeter, gather intelligence, request specialized units, contain situation C) Leave the scene D) Negotiate without training

Answer: B **Explanation:** Patrol role: establish inner/outer perimeter, gather intelligence, evacuate bystanders, request SWAT/negotiators, establish command post. Don't enter alone—wait for specialized units.

Question 15: An officer's immediate response to an active shooter should be: A) Wait for SWAT B) Establish perimeter only C) Enter immediately and move toward gunfire to engage shooter D) Interview witnesses first

Answer: C **Explanation:** Immediate action: enter immediately, move toward gunfire, engage shooter quickly. Solo entry if necessary. Every second of delay costs lives.

Question 16: Signs of shock include: A) Increased blood pressure only B) Rapid weak pulse, pale/cool/clammy skin, altered mental status, rapid shallow breathing C) Fever D) Increased appetite

Answer: B **Explanation:** Shock indicators: rapid weak pulse, rapid shallow breathing, pale/cool/clammy skin, altered mental status (confused/anxious), nausea, weakness. Treat immediately.

Question 17: When building rapport with someone in mental health crisis, you should: A) Argue with their delusions B) Introduce yourself, acknowledge their distress, offer help, validate feelings without reinforcing delusions C) Force them to be rational D) Mock their beliefs

Answer: B **Explanation:** Build rapport: introduce yourself personally, acknowledge their distress ("I can see you're upset"), offer help, validate feelings without agreeing with delusions.

Question 18: Strangulation attempts in domestic violence are significant because: A) They're minor injuries B) They're one of strongest predictors of eventual domestic homicide C) They don't matter D) They're always accidental

Answer: B **Explanation:** Strangulation attempts are extremely serious indicators of lethality—strong predictor subject will eventually kill victim. Document thoroughly, treat as high-risk situation.

Question 19: In hostage situations, time usually: A) Favors the hostage-taker B) Favors police—hostage-takers rarely harm hostages initially, giving negotiators opportunity C) Doesn't matter D) Should be minimized

Answer: B **Explanation:** Time usually favors police in hostage situations. Initial emotion/adrenaline fades, hostage-taker may become more rational, negotiators build rapport. Don't rush unless active harm occurring.

Question 20: CPR compressions should be performed: A) Slowly and gently B) At 100-120 compressions per minute, at least 2 inches deep on center of chest C) Only if pulse is present D) On the stomach

Answer: B **Explanation:** Effective CPR: 100-120 compressions per minute (push hard, push fast), at least 2 inches deep for adults, center of chest, continue until EMS arrives or person recovers.

Question 21: When responding to mental health crisis, the CIT principle of "slowing down" means: A) Taking hours to respond B) Most crises aren't emergencies—taking time reduces pressure and allows for calm resolution C) Ignoring urgent situations D) Delaying all responses

Answer: B **Explanation:** Most mental health crises aren't immediate emergencies requiring instant action. Slowing down reduces pressure on everyone, allows time for calm, enables better outcomes. Rush only if imminent danger exists.

Question 22: Emergency detention for mental health evaluation in Texas requires: A) Nothing specific B) Reasonable belief person has mental illness and poses imminent danger to self or others C) Family request only D) Crime commission

Answer: B **Explanation:** Health & Safety Code Chapter 573 allows detention when officer reasonably believes person has mental illness and poses imminent danger to self/others. Civil detention, not arrest.

Question 23: After using deadly force, an officer should: A) Leave the scene B) Provide medical aid to all injured, secure scene, notify supervisor, preserve evidence, separate involved officers C) Discuss details with everyone D) Destroy evidence

Answer: B **Explanation:** Post-deadly force: render medical aid (even to suspect), secure scene and weapons, notify supervisor immediately, preserve evidence, separate involved officers to prevent collusion appearance.

Question 24: A two-officer contact team in active shooter response should: A) Wait for more officers B) Enter immediately, with one covering while one moves, moving toward gunfire C) Establish perimeter only D) Wait for negotiators

Answer: B **Explanation:** Two-officer team is ideal minimum—one covers while one moves. Safer than solo, still rapid response. Enter immediately and move toward gunfire to engage shooter.

Question 25: When someone in crisis says "The government is watching me through cameras," you should: A) Argue it's not true B) Acknowledge their fear without reinforcing delusion: "That sounds scary. I can see why that upsets you" C) Agree with them D) Laugh at them

Answer: B **Explanation:** Don't argue with delusions (reinforces perception you're threat). Acknowledge their distress is real to them, validate feelings, but don't reinforce delusion as reality.

Question 26: Hemostatic gauze (QuikClot, Celox) is used for: A) Minor cuts B) Severe bleeding that direct pressure doesn't adequately control C) Broken bones D) Burns

Answer: B **Explanation:** Hemostatic gauze helps blood clot faster for severe bleeding. Pack directly into wound, apply pressure. Used when direct pressure alone isn't controlling hemorrhage.

Question 27: When victims are evacuated during active shooter event, officers should: A) Let them wander B) Direct them to safe areas, provide clear commands, extract seriously wounded, mark cleared rooms C) Ignore them D) Search them for weapons first

Answer: B **Explanation:** Rescue teams evacuate victims to safe areas, give clear direct commands ("Run! Get out!"), provide immediate medical care, extract seriously wounded, mark cleared rooms.

Question 28: Domestic violence safety planning for victims who won't leave includes: A) Nothing—force them to leave B) Identify safe room, keep phone accessible, prepare escape bag, tell trusted contacts, know shelter locations C) Ignore their decision D) Blame them

Answer: B **Explanation:** Safety plan: identify safe room with lock/window, keep charged phone accessible, have documents/essentials ready, tell trusted friends/neighbors, know shelter locations and hotline numbers.

Question 29: In active shooter situations, officers should move: A) Very slowly B) With purpose—fast walking while maintaining weapon ready, not running C) Crawling D) Running at full speed

Answer: B **Explanation:** Move with purpose: fast walking (not running—maintains control and accuracy), weapon ready, quiet communication, stay oriented to team positions.

Question 30: Signs of mental health crisis include: A) Normal rational behavior only B) Confusion, inability to follow directions, hallucinations, paranoia, extreme mood swings, disorganized thinking C) Perfect clarity D) Nothing observable

Answer: B **Explanation:** Crisis indicators: confusion/disorganized thinking, can't follow simple directions, hallucinations (visual/auditory), paranoia, extreme mood swings, inappropriate emotional responses.

Question 31: When containing a barricaded subject, you should: A) Let them leave B) Establish inner perimeter (containment) and outer perimeter (crowd control), prevent escape C) Announce your weakness D) Give up

Answer: B **Explanation:** Establish two perimeters: inner (containment—no one in/out), outer (crowd/traffic control). Ensure subject can't escape undetected while waiting for specialized units.

Question 32: Universal precautions when providing medical care mean: A) Only protecting yourself sometimes B) Assume all body fluids are infectious, wear gloves for all patient contact, wash hands after exposure C) Never using protection D) Only gloves for known diseases

Answer: B **Explanation:** Universal precautions: assume all body fluids infectious, wear gloves for all patient contact, change gloves between patients, eye protection if splash risk, wash hands thoroughly.

Question 33: Active shooter doctrine prioritizes: A) Evidence preservation B) Stop the killing, stop the dying—engage shooter immediately, then render medical aid C) Interviewing witnesses D) Establishing perimeter only

Answer: B **Explanation:** Priority: stop the killing (engage shooter immediately), then stop the dying (render medical aid once threat neutralized). Speed saves lives—victims are dying every second.

Question 34: Victim behavior during active shooter events often includes: A) Perfect rational responses B) Denial, panic, freezing, or hostility due to extreme stress C) Immediate cooperation D) Calm assessment

Answer: B **Explanation:** Victims experience denial (freeze/deny danger), panic (poor decisions), freezing, hostility toward police (due to fear). Give clear direct commands, stay calm, announce yourself repeatedly.

Question 35: For head injuries, you should: A) Apply pressure to obvious skull depressions B) Maintain airway, control bleeding with direct pressure (not on depressions), keep victim still C) Give food and water D) Remove impaled objects

Answer: B **Explanation:** Head injury care: maintain airway, control bleeding with direct pressure (avoid obvious skull depressions), keep victim still (suspect spinal injury), monitor consciousness, don't remove impaled objects.

Question 36: When forming contact teams for active shooter response, the ideal number is: A) One officer only B) Two to four officers—more provides diminishing returns C) Twenty officers D) Zero officers

Answer: B **Explanation:** Ideal: 2-4 officers. Two is minimum for safer clearing. Four allows better coverage. More than four creates coordination problems in dynamic environment.

Question 37: CIT techniques combined with tactical awareness means: A) Giving up officer safety B) Using de-escalation while maintaining reactionary gap, having less-lethal/lethal options ready C) Ignoring threats D) Never using force

Answer: B **Explanation:** CIT doesn't mean accepting danger. Use de-escalation techniques while maintaining distance, cover, readiness. Have less-lethal and lethal options immediately available if situation deteriorates.

Question 38: Lethality assessment in domestic violence should be conducted: A) Never B) On every domestic violence call, documenting risk factors thoroughly C) Only on serious injuries D) Only when victim requests

Answer: B **Explanation:** Assess lethality every domestic violence call. Document risk factors: weapons access, strangulation, threats, separation, obsession, depression, protective order violations. High risk requires immediate safety planning.

Question 39: After securing an active shooter, officers should: A) Celebrate B) Remain alert for additional threats, begin medical care, establish casualty collection point C) Leave immediately D) Relax

Answer: B **Explanation:** After shooter down: remain alert (secondary devices? second shooter?), begin emergency medical care, establish casualty collection point, coordinate with EMS, preserve evidence where possible.

Question 40: Mental health crisis differs from criminal behavior in that crisis: A) Is always criminal B) Is driven by symptoms beyond person's control, not goal-oriented, doesn't respond rationally C) Is always safe D) Requires immediate force

Answer: B **Explanation:** Crisis behavior: driven by symptoms beyond control, not goal-oriented, doesn't respond to normal incentives/consequences, impaired judgment. Criminal behavior: deliberate choices, goal-oriented, responds to consequences.

Question 41: Chest seals should be applied: A) With all four sides taped B) With three sides taped, leaving bottom open to create one-way valve C) Loosely D) Never

Answer: B **Explanation:** Tape chest seals on three sides (top and both sides), leaving bottom open. Creates one-way valve—allows air out but not in, preventing tension pneumothorax.

Question 42: When rescue teams extract victims during active shooter event, priority is: A) Perfect evidence preservation B) Saving lives—extract seriously wounded for EMS, direct walking wounded to safety C) Interviewing everyone D) Taking reports

Answer: B **Explanation:** Life safety is priority. Extract seriously wounded for EMS, direct walking wounded to safe areas, provide immediate medical care. Evidence preservation is secondary to saving lives.

Question 43: Domestic violence calls are dangerous because: A) They're routine B) High emotions, alcohol/drugs often present, weapons may be accessible, volatile dynamics C) They're always minor D) No risk exists

Answer: B **Explanation:** Domestic calls are extremely dangerous: high emotions, alcohol/drugs common, weapons often accessible, intimate partner violence is volatile, history of violence may exist.

Question 44: Solo officer response to active shooter requires: A) Waiting for backup B) Entering immediately and engaging shooter despite being alone C) Establishing perimeter D) Calling supervisor for permission

Answer: B **Explanation:** Solo officer must enter immediately if shooter actively killing. Don't wait for backup. Move toward gunfire, engage quickly. Every second matters—more victims die while waiting.

Question 45: Recovery position for unconscious breathing victim means: A) Face down B) On side to prevent aspiration of vomit C) Sitting up D) Standing

Answer: B **Explanation:** Recovery position: on side with head tilted back to maintain airway and prevent aspiration if vomiting. Used for unconscious but breathing victims without suspected spinal injury.

Question 46: When negotiators arrive at hostage/barricaded subject scene, patrol officers should: A) Leave B) Maintain perimeter security, gather intelligence, coordinate with tactical team, remain ready C) Begin negotiations themselves D) Enter the building

Answer: B **Explanation:** Support negotiators by: maintaining perimeter, gathering additional intelligence, coordinating with tactical team, clearing safe routes for surrender, remaining ready if negotiations fail.

Question 47: In mental health crisis, the phrase "validate feelings" means: A) Agree with delusions B) Acknowledge their emotions are real to them without reinforcing delusions C) Mock them D) Argue

Answer: B **Explanation:** Validation acknowledges their distress is real ("I understand you're upset") without agreeing delusions are real. You're validating emotion, not the delusional content.

Question 48: When providing medical care at scene, officer safety requires: A) Ignoring threats B) Neutralizing tactical threats first—can't help anyone if you're shot C) Never treating casualties D) Rushing into danger

Answer: B **Explanation:** Tactical situation comes first. Neutralize threats before treating casualties (TCCC Care Under Fire principle). Can't help anyone if you become casualty. Once secure, medical care becomes priority.

Question 49: Pressure points for bleeding control include: A) Random locations B) Brachial artery (inside upper arm) for arm wounds, femoral artery (groin) for leg wounds C) Toes D) Ears

Answer: B **Explanation:** Major pressure points: brachial artery (inside upper arm) for arm hemorrhage, femoral artery (groin) for leg hemorrhage, temporal artery (side of head) for head wounds.

Question 50: After any emergency response incident, officers should: A) Ignore stress effects B) Recognize stress reactions are normal, use available support services, seek counseling if needed C) Tough it out alone D) Self-medicate

Answer: B **Explanation:** Emergency incidents cause stress reactions—normal response to abnormal events. Use Critical Incident Stress Debriefing, Employee Assistance, peer support, professional counseling. No shame in seeking help.

Scoring and Moving Forward

48-50 correct (96-100%): Outstanding mastery! You've shown excellent understanding of emergency medical care, crisis intervention, domestic violence response, and active shooter tactics. Your knowledge will save lives in the field. You're ready to handle the most challenging calls with confidence. Review any missed questions to achieve perfect understanding, then advance knowing you've mastered critical lifesaving skills.

43-47 correct (86-94%): Strong performance! You grasp the core concepts of emergency response and crisis management. Your understanding of tactical medicine, mental health crisis intervention, and active shooter response is solid. Focus on any areas where you missed questions—perhaps medical procedures, CIT techniques, or ALERRT principles. Review those specific topics, then test yourself again. You're nearly there!

38-42 correct (76-84%): Good foundation with room for growth. You understand many emergency response concepts but need to strengthen specific areas. Identify patterns in your missed questions. Are they about medical care? Mental health crises? Active shooter response? Focus your review on those topics. Work through the scenarios again, visualizing yourself in those situations. This chapter covers lifesaving skills—master them through focused study and you'll be ready.

33-37 correct (66-74%): You're building understanding but significant gaps remain. Don't be discouraged—emergency response is complex and high-stakes. Review Chapter 8 systematically, section by section. Focus especially on: ABCs of medical care and severe bleeding control, CIT de-escalation principles, lethality assessment in domestic violence, ALERRT active shooter response. Create summary notes for each topic. Practice explaining concepts out loud. Visualize yourself applying these skills. When you're consistently scoring 85%+, you'll be ready to move forward.

Below 33 correct (less than 66%): You need substantial additional study before proceeding. Emergency response skills save lives—yours and others'. These aren't just test topics; they're survival skills you'll use in the most critical moments of your career. Commit to mastering this material: Review each section slowly, taking detailed notes. Focus on understanding WHY procedures exist, not just WHAT to do. Work through scenarios multiple times. Consider creating flashcards for medical procedures and crisis intervention techniques. Study with a partner who can quiz you. Don't move forward until you're scoring at least 85% consistently. These skills are too important to rush.

Your Journey Through Critical Skills

You've now completed two of the most demanding chapters in this guide. Chapter 7 (Use of Force) and Chapter 8 (Emergency Response) cover the highest-stakes decisions you'll make as an officer. These aren't just exam topics—they're life-and-death skills that will define critical moments throughout your career.

Every officer who's worked the streets has stories about these moments: The domestic violence call that turned deadly. The mental health crisis resolved peacefully through patient communication. The active shooter engagement that saved dozens of lives. The gunshot victim whose life was saved by quick medical action. You'll have these moments too. The training you're absorbing now determines whether those stories end in tragedy or triumph.

What You've Mastered:

- Life-saving medical skills for trauma situations
- De-escalation techniques for mental health crises
- Domestic violence lethality assessment and victim safety
- Hostage/barricaded subject containment principles
- Active shooter immediate action response (ALERRT)

These skills build on everything you've learned in previous chapters. Use of force decisions (Chapter 7) combine with crisis intervention (Chapter 8). Criminal procedure knowledge (Chapter 2) applies to domestic violence investigations. Officer safety tactics (Chapter 3) integrate with active shooter response. Legal authority (Chapter 1) underlies emergency detentions. Everything connects.

Preparing for What's Next

The remaining chapters build on this foundation. You've learned the law, procedures, patrol operations, traffic enforcement, investigations, juvenile justice, use of force, and emergency response. Now you'll explore professional ethics, communication skills, and comprehensive scenario-based practice that ties everything together.

But before moving forward, ensure you've truly mastered Chapters 7 and 8. These chapters deserve extra attention because they cover the most consequential decisions of your career. Review them one more time. Work through the scenarios again. Visualize yourself in those situations. Ask yourself: "What would I do? Why? What does the law require? What do tactics demand? How do I balance competing priorities?"

When you can answer those questions confidently and consistently score 85%+ on practice questions, you're ready to advance. If not, invest more time here. The investment pays dividends throughout your career and might save your life or someone else's.

You're over halfway through this guide. You've covered the hardest material. The finish line is visible. Keep pushing forward with the same dedication you've shown so far. Success on the TCOLE exam and success in your law enforcement career are both within reach. Trust your preparation, believe in your abilities, and continue building on the strong foundation you're creating.

PART V: PROFESSIONALISM AND COMMUNICATION

CHAPTER 9: PROFESSIONAL ETHICS AND STANDARDS

Your badge represents more than legal authority—it represents trust. Communities grant you extraordinary power: the authority to deprive liberty, use force, even take life. In exchange, they expect integrity, fairness, and ethical conduct. This chapter isn't about abstract philosophy. It's about the daily ethical decisions that define your character and career. Every interaction tests your ethics. The traffic stop where nobody's watching. The drunk driver who offers you money. The colleague who cuts corners. The citizen who challenges your authority. How you respond in these moments determines whether you're a professional or just someone wearing a uniform. Professional ethics aren't situational or negotiable. They're the foundation of legitimate policing. Without ethics, you're just another person with a gun. With ethics, you're a guardian of justice who maintains community trust while enforcing the law fairly. This chapter provides the framework for making sound ethical decisions, maintaining professional standards, preventing corruption, and building the character required for this demanding profession.

Law Enforcement Code of Ethics

Every Texas peace officer swears an oath and commits to the Law Enforcement Code of Ethics. These aren't mere words—they're binding commitments that guide your conduct throughout your career.

Core Values and Oath of Office

The Peace Officer's Oath: When you're commissioned as a Texas peace officer, you take this oath: "I do solemnly swear (or affirm) that I will faithfully execute the duties of a peace officer and will to the best of my ability preserve, protect, and defend the Constitution and laws of the United States and of the State of Texas, so help me God." This oath creates legal and moral obligations. You've sworn to: **Faithfully execute duties** - not selectively, not based on personal preferences, but faithfully according to law and policy. **Preserve, protect, defend the Constitution** - constitutional rights aren't suggestions. They're your primary duty to uphold. **Serve to the best of your ability** - mediocrity isn't acceptable. You committed to excellence.

Law Enforcement Code of Ethics: As a law enforcement officer, my fundamental duty is to serve mankind; to safeguard lives and property; to protect the innocent against deception, the weak against oppression or intimidation, and the peaceful against violence or disorder; and to respect the Constitutional rights of all to liberty, equality and justice. I will keep my private life unsullied as an example to all; maintain courageous calm in the face of danger, scorn, or ridicule; develop self-restraint; and be constantly mindful of the welfare of others. Honest in thought and deed in both my personal and official life, I will be exemplary in obeying the laws of the land and the regulations of my department. Whatever I see or hear of a confidential nature or that is confided to me in my official capacity will be kept ever secret unless revelation is necessary in the performance of my duty. I will never act officiously or permit personal feelings, prejudices, animosities or friendships to influence my decisions. With no compromise for crime and with relentless prosecution of criminals, I will enforce the law courteously and appropriately without fear or favor, malice or ill will, never employing unnecessary force or violence and never accepting gratuities. I recognize the badge of my office as a symbol of public faith, and I accept it as a public trust to be held so long as I am true to the ethics of the police service. I will constantly strive to achieve these objectives and ideals, dedicating myself before God to my chosen profession.

Core Values: Most departments adopt core values reflecting the Code of Ethics. Common values include: **Integrity** - doing what's right even when nobody's watching. Your character matters more than your reputation. **Courage** - physical courage (facing danger) and moral courage (standing up for what's right even when it costs you). **Accountability** - accepting responsibility for your actions and decisions. **Respect** - treating all people with dignity regardless of circumstances. **Service** - putting community needs above personal convenience. **Excellence** - commitment to continuous improvement and professional development.

Professional Conduct Standards

On-Duty Expectations: Professional conduct on duty includes obvious requirements (don't commit crimes, follow policy, obey lawful orders) and subtler ones many officers miss: **Appearance** - clean uniform, proper grooming, functional equipment. You represent your department; look professional. Sloppy appearance suggests sloppy work. **Attitude** - professional demeanor even when tired, frustrated, or dealing with difficult people. Citizens see one interaction with police; their impression of law enforcement comes from you. **Punctuality** - arriving on time, being where you're supposed to be. Chronic tardiness shows disrespect for colleagues who cover your calls. **Effort** - giving full effort throughout shift. Lazy officers endanger themselves, their partners, and the public. **Competence** - maintaining skills through training, practice, and study. Perishable skills deteriorate without practice; lives depend on your competence.

Off-Duty Expectations: The badge doesn't come off when you change clothes. Your off-duty conduct impacts your on-duty effectiveness and department reputation: **Legal Compliance** - obviously, don't break laws off-duty. Criminal conduct off-duty ends careers. But go beyond minimum—avoid even questionable activities that might appear improper. **Social Media Responsibility** - what you post reflects on your department. Racist comments, excessive partying photos, anti-authority statements—all create problems. Assume everything you post online will appear on the front page of the newspaper. **Association** - who you associate with off-duty matters. Hanging out with known criminals, frequenting establishments with illegal activity, maintaining friendships with people engaging in criminal behavior—all compromise your integrity and create conflicts. **Financial Responsibility** - excessive debt, bankruptcy, financial problems create temptation for corruption. Maintain financial stability. **Domestic**

Conduct - domestic violence by police officers is inexcusable and typically results in termination. Departments expect you to model healthy relationships.

Common Conduct Violations: Understanding common violations helps you avoid them: **Excessive Force** - using more force than reasonably necessary. Often results from anger, frustration, or lack of self-control rather than tactical necessity. **False Reports** - lying in reports, omitting material facts, exaggerating to justify actions. This destroys credibility and constitutes criminal conduct. **Discourtesy** - rudeness, condescension, verbal abuse of citizens. Unprofessional behavior damages community relations and violates ethical standards. **Insubordination** - refusing lawful orders, disrespecting supervisors, undermining authority. Chain of command exists for good reason. **Neglect of Duty** - sleeping on duty, failing to respond to calls, avoiding work. You're paid to serve; do your job. **Fraternization** - inappropriate relationships with subordinates, citizens during investigations, or other problematic associations. Maintain professional boundaries. **Misuse of Authority** - using your position for personal gain, intimidating people for non-law enforcement purposes, abusing access to databases. Your authority is for official business only.

Bias-Based Policing Prevention

Bias-based policing destroys community trust, violates civil rights, and undermines legitimate law enforcement. Understanding and preventing bias is essential for professional policing.

Fair and Impartial Law Enforcement

What is Bias-Based Policing? Bias-based policing occurs when law enforcement decisions are based on race, ethnicity, national origin, religion, sexual orientation, gender identity, or other protected characteristics rather than on behavior or legitimate law enforcement criteria. **Examples:** Stopping vehicles primarily because of driver's race ("driving while Black/Brown"). Conducting consent searches disproportionately based on ethnicity. Assuming people of certain backgrounds are involved in criminal activity. Treating people differently during contacts based on appearance or accent. Using slurs or derogatory language based on protected characteristics.

Why It's Wrong: Beyond obvious moral and legal problems: **Violates Constitutional Rights** - Equal Protection Clause prohibits discrimination. Courts have repeatedly struck down policies and practices that disproportionately target groups without legitimate law enforcement justification. **Destroys Community Trust** - communities subjected to biased policing stop cooperating with law enforcement. Witnesses won't come forward, victims won't report crimes, and community members view police as oppressors rather than protectors. **Ineffective Policing** - bias-based decisions ignore actual criminal behavior in favor of stereotypes. Real criminals go undetected while innocent people are harassed. **Legal Liability** - officers and departments face civil rights lawsuits, consent decrees, and federal intervention. **Career Consequences** - bias-based policing ends careers through termination, criminal prosecution, and loss of certification.

Implicit Bias: Everyone has implicit biases—unconscious attitudes and stereotypes affecting our perceptions and actions. Research shows even people who consciously reject stereotypes may still harbor implicit biases. **Recognizing Your Biases:** Acknowledge that you have biases. Denial doesn't eliminate them; awareness helps you manage them. Examine your assumptions. When you think "this person looks suspicious," ask yourself why. Is it behavior or appearance/demographics? Consider whether you'd make the same decision about someone of different race/ethnicity in identical circumstances. Seek feedback from colleagues and supervisors about your decision patterns.

Preventing Biased Policing: Base Decisions on Behavior - stop vehicles for actual traffic violations, not driver characteristics. Conduct field interviews based on suspicious behavior, not appearance. Make arrests based on probable cause, not stereotypes. **Articulate Specific Facts** - document specific, articulable facts justifying your actions. "I stopped him because he's Hispanic" is bias. "I stopped the vehicle for failing to signal lane change" is legitimate. "The area has high drug activity and he looks suspicious" is problematic. "He was loitering in a high-drug area, made quick hand-to-hand exchange consistent with drug transaction, and fled when he saw me" is legitimate. **Treat Everyone with Respect** - regardless of race, ethnicity, appearance, or attitude. Professional courtesy isn't conditional. **Monitor Your Language** - avoid slurs, stereotypes, and derogatory terms. This includes "jokes" with colleagues—they reveal and reinforce biases. **Self-Monitor Patterns** - periodically review your stops, searches, and arrests. Do you stop minority drivers disproportionately? Do you request consent searches more frequently from certain groups? Patterns reveal biases you might not consciously recognize.

Procedural Justice and Legitimacy: Research shows people care as much about how they're treated as the outcome. Procedural justice builds legitimacy: **Voice** - give people opportunity to explain their perspective. Listen to their side. **Respect** - treat everyone with dignity regardless of circumstances. **Neutrality** - make decisions based on facts and law, not personal biases or relationships. **Trustworthy Motives** - demonstrate you're acting in good faith to do your job fairly. People who perceive police as legitimate are more likely to comply voluntarily, cooperate with investigations, and support law enforcement. Procedural justice builds that legitimacy.

Community Relations and Cultural Diversity

Effective policing requires understanding and respecting the diverse communities you serve. Cultural competency isn't political correctness—it's professional necessity.

Cultural Competency Skills

Understanding Cultural Diversity: Texas is remarkably diverse: Multiple racial and ethnic groups (Hispanic/Latino, Black/African American, Asian, Middle Eastern, etc.), Religious diversity (Christian denominations, Judaism, Islam, Hinduism, Buddhism, etc.), Linguistic diversity (Spanish, Vietnamese, Arabic, Chinese, etc.), LGBTQ+ community members, People with disabilities, Economic diversity from poverty to wealth, Urban, suburban, and rural communities.

Each group has cultural norms, communication styles, and experiences with law enforcement that affect interactions. Understanding these differences helps you communicate effectively and avoid unnecessary conflicts.

Cultural Competency Principles: Awareness - recognize your own cultural background and how it shapes your worldview. Your "normal" isn't universal. **Knowledge** - learn about cultures present in your community. Understand religious practices, communication norms, family structures, historical experiences with law enforcement. **Skills** - apply cultural knowledge to adapt your approach. This doesn't mean abandoning law enforcement standards, but recognizing that communication style and approach may need adjustment. **Humility** - acknowledge you can't know everything about every culture. Be willing to ask questions respectfully and learn from community members.

Common Cultural Considerations: Personal Space - varies by culture. Some cultures comfortable with close proximity; others prefer greater distance. Watch for discomfort and adjust. **Eye Contact** - in some cultures, direct eye contact shows respect and honesty. In others, it's disrespectful or aggressive, especially with authority figures. Don't automatically interpret averted eyes as deception or disrespect. **Family Structure** - who makes decisions varies. In some cultures, eldest male speaks for family; in others, decisions are collective. Respect family dynamics while ensuring everyone's rights are protected. **Language Barriers** - limited English proficiency doesn't indicate lack of intelligence or legal status. Use interpreters when needed. Speak clearly and simply (not loudly—that doesn't help). Avoid idioms and slang. **Religious Practices** - understand that religious items (hijabs, turbans, religious symbols) are important. Handle with respect if search is necessary. Religious observances may affect scheduling for interviews or court appearances. **Immigration Status Concerns** - undocumented immigrants fear deportation. This fear makes them reluctant to report crimes or cooperate with investigations. Focus on your law enforcement mission, not immigration status (unless it's relevant to your specific case).

Building Cultural Competence: Community Engagement - attend community events, visit cultural centers, participate in cultural celebrations. This builds relationships and understanding. **Training** - participate in cultural competency training offered by your department. Seek additional education about communities you serve. **Language Skills** - learning even basic phrases in common languages shows respect and facilitates communication. Many departments offer language classes. **Listen and Learn** - when community members explain their perspective, listen without defensiveness. You might learn something that makes you more effective.

Avoiding Cultural Pitfalls: Stereotyping - don't assume all members of a group are identical. Individuals within cultures vary widely. **Tokenism** - don't treat one interaction or one community member as representative of entire group. **Performative Diversity** - genuine cultural competency isn't about appearing "woke" or checking boxes. It's about respectful, effective policing. **Abandoning Standards** - cultural competency doesn't mean lowering standards or ignoring law violations. It means understanding cultural context while maintaining professional standards.

Social Media and Technology Use

Digital technology presents new ethical challenges. Your online presence affects your career and department reputation.

Professional Digital Presence

Social Media Risks: Social media creates numerous problems for law enforcement: **Public Scrutiny** - what you post is public and permanent. Screenshots exist forever. Posts you delete may already be saved and shared. **Department Representation** - citizens don't distinguish between you as individual and you as officer. Your posts reflect on your department. **Investigative Compromise** - defense attorneys search social media for impeachment material. Posts showing bias, excessive drinking, questionable judgment, or inconsistent statements will be used against you in court. **Operational Security** - posting locations, schedules, tactical information, or photos of equipment compromises safety. Criminals monitor law enforcement social media. **Association Issues** - friend lists, likes, comments, and tags may show associations with criminals or problematic individuals.

Social Media Guidelines: Assume Everything is Public - even "private" accounts and closed groups leak. Post as if your supervisor, defense attorney, and local news will see it (because they might). **Avoid Discussing Work** - don't post about cases, arrests, uses of force, or department issues. Confidential information stays confidential. Even general complaints about work create problems. **No Bias or Offensive Content** - racist, sexist, homophobic, or otherwise offensive posts end careers. "It was just a joke" doesn't save you. **Limit Personal Information** - avoid posting home address, family member names, children's schools, or other information criminals could exploit. **Separate Professional and Personal** - consider maintaining separate accounts. Professional accounts for community engagement should be clearly identified as official and appropriate. Personal accounts should be kept truly personal with strong privacy settings. **Think Before Posting** - before posting anything, ask: "Would I be comfortable with this appearing in court? On the news? In a disciplinary hearing?" If not, don't post it.

Department Use of Social Media: Many departments maintain official social media accounts for community engagement, crime prevention, and public information. If you're authorized to post for your department: **Follow Policy** - departments have social media policies. Know and follow them. **Stay Professional** - official accounts require even higher standards than personal accounts. **Verify Information** - ensure information is accurate before posting. Corrections damage credibility. **Avoid Arguments** - don't engage in online arguments with critics. Professional responses to legitimate questions are appropriate; fights are not. **Protect Investigations** - don't compromise cases by releasing information prematurely.

Technology Misuse: Beyond social media, technology creates other ethical issues: **Database Misuse** - accessing criminal justice databases for non-law enforcement purposes (checking on friends, dating interests, family members, etc.) is typically criminal. Access is logged and audited. People lose jobs and face prosecution for unauthorized access. **Digital Evidence Handling** - photographing crime scenes or evidence with personal phones creates chain of custody and privacy problems. Use department-issued equipment. **Recording and Surveillance** - recording conversations, using surveillance equipment, or tracking devices requires legal authority. Unauthorized surveillance violates law and policy. **Department Equipment** - personal use of department computers, vehicles, or equipment may violate policy. Using department resources for personal gain (side businesses, personal errands during duty) is theft.

Stress Management and Officer Wellness

Law enforcement is inherently stressful. Managing that stress is essential for career longevity, personal health, and professional performance.

Recognizing and Managing Stress

Sources of Law Enforcement Stress: Operational Stress - danger, violence, traumatic scenes, life-and-death decisions, unpredictable situations. **Organizational Stress** - shift work, mandatory overtime, bureaucracy, perceived lack of support from administration, internal investigations. **Public Scrutiny** - media criticism, complaints, protests, lawsuits, public distrust. **Personal Life Impact** - irregular schedule affects family time, relationships strained by work stress, difficulty separating work from home life, financial pressures from moderate pay and family needs.

Physical Effects of Stress: Chronic stress causes real physical problems: cardiovascular disease (heart attacks, high blood pressure), gastrointestinal problems, sleep disorders, chronic pain, weakened immune system, accelerated aging. Law enforcement has higher rates of these conditions than general population.

Psychological Effects: Stress also affects mental health: anxiety, depression, PTSD from traumatic incidents, substance abuse (alcohol, prescription drugs), emotional numbness or detachment, irritability and anger, relationship problems, burnout and cynicism.

Warning Signs: Recognize stress in yourself and others: **Physical:** Fatigue, headaches, muscle tension, changes in appetite, sleep problems. **Emotional:** Irritability, mood swings, feeling overwhelmed, difficulty concentrating, loss of motivation. **Behavioral:** Social withdrawal, increased alcohol use, missing work, reduced performance, conflicts with colleagues or family.

Stress Management Strategies: Physical Health: Regular exercise reduces stress hormones and improves mood. Aim for 30 minutes daily. Adequate sleep (7-9 hours) is essential. Shift work makes this difficult, but prioritize sleep hygiene. Healthy diet provides energy and improves stress resilience. Limit caffeine and alcohol. **Mental Health:** Maintain relationships outside law enforcement. Non-cop friends provide perspective and balance. Pursue hobbies and interests unrelated to work. You need identity beyond the badge. Practice relaxation techniques: deep breathing, meditation, progressive muscle relaxation. Take vacation time. Unused vacation increases burnout. Use it to recharge. **Professional Strategies:** Compartmentalization - develop ability to leave work stress at work. Create rituals (changing clothes, exercise) to transition from work mode to home mode. Debrief after difficult calls with colleagues. Talking through traumatic incidents helps process them. Seek peer support. Fellow officers understand the stress in ways civilians can't. Use Employee Assistance Programs (EAP). Confidential counseling is available. There's no shame in using it.

When to Seek Professional Help: Some stress requires professional intervention. Seek help if: Stress significantly impacts your functioning, You're having thoughts of self-harm or suicide, You're using alcohol or drugs to cope, You're experiencing symptoms of PTSD (nightmares, flashbacks, hypervigilance beyond normal officer alertness), Your relationships are severely damaged, You're having difficulty performing your job. **Resources Available:** Most departments offer: Employee Assistance Programs (EAP) with confidential counseling, Peer support teams of officers trained to help colleagues, Critical Incident Stress Debriefing after traumatic events, Chaplain services, Health insurance covering mental health treatment.

Reducing Stigma: Historical stigma around mental health in law enforcement is decreasing, but remains an obstacle. Understand that: Seeking help is strength, not weakness. Acknowledging you need assistance shows self-awareness and courage. Mental health is health. You wouldn't ignore a broken leg; don't ignore psychological injury. Early intervention prevents problems from worsening. Addressing stress early is easier than recovering from burnout, addiction, or PTSD. Your family and career benefit when you maintain your mental health.

Corruption Prevention and Integrity

Corruption destroys careers, ruins departments, and devastates community trust. Understanding how corruption develops helps you avoid it.

Ethical Decision-Making Models

The Slippery Slope: Corruption rarely starts with major crimes. It begins with small ethical compromises that progressively escalate: **Stage 1:** Minor rule violations (extending break, using department phone for personal calls, minor property misuse). Rationalization: "Everyone does it. It's no big deal." **Stage 2:** Accepting minor gratuities (free meals, discounts, small gifts). Rationalization: "I'm not doing anything wrong. People are just being nice." **Stage 3:** Showing favor to people who provide benefits (extra patrol at their businesses, overlooking minor violations). Rationalization: "I'm still doing my job. I just help people who help me." **Stage 4:** Active solicitation (expecting/demanding free items, gifts, or money). Rationalization: "I deserve this. I protect them; they should show appreciation." **Stage 5:** Serious corruption (taking bribes, stealing, protecting criminals, committing crimes). Rationalization: "I'm in too deep. I have to protect myself."

Each stage makes the next easier. The officer who accepts free coffee today may accept bribes tomorrow. Avoid the first step.

Common Forms of Corruption: Gratuities - accepting free or discounted goods/services. Seems minor but creates obligation. **Bribery** - accepting money or valuables to influence official action. This is straightforward criminal conduct. **Theft** - stealing from crime scenes, evidence, arrestees, or department. **Protection Rackets** - providing protection to criminals (warning of raids, not enforcing laws, destroying evidence) in exchange for money. **Brutality for Hire** - using excessive force on behalf of someone who pays you. **Evidence Manipulation** - planting evidence, destroying exculpatory evidence, falsifying reports. **Personal Misconduct** - using position to facilitate personal crimes (sexual assault using authority, stealing through abuse of position).

The Noble Cause Corruption: Some corruption stems from good intentions perverted by means: **Scenario:** You know someone is a drug dealer but lack evidence for arrest. You plant drugs to "get him off the streets." You're convinced he's guilty and you're protecting the community. **Why It's Still Corruption:** Due process matters. Constitutional rights protect everyone, including criminals. Shortcuts undermine the entire justice system. Once you plant evidence on a "bad guy," it's easier to plant it on an innocent person. You've become the criminal.

Rationalization Patterns: Corrupt officers rationalize their behavior: "I'm underpaid. I deserve this" (compensation rationalization). "Everyone does it" (normalization). "I'm just taking from bad guys" (victim derogation). "I still do my job well" (minimization). "The system is broken anyway" (system blame). "I need to protect my family" (necessity). Recognize these patterns in your thinking. They're warning signs.

Maintaining Integrity: Know Your Values - define your ethical boundaries now. Decide what you'll never compromise. When temptation comes, you'll have preset limits. **Avoid Temptation** - don't put yourself in situations where corruption is easy. Refuse gifts. Decline invitations from people who might want favors. Keep professional distance from subjects and witnesses. **Report Misconduct** - seeing colleagues engage in corruption creates moral injury and ethical crisis. Your obligation is to report misconduct. This is difficult but necessary. **Use Ethical Decision-Making:** When facing ethical dilemmas, ask: Is this legal? Is it consistent with policy? Would I be comfortable if this became public? Would I want my children to know I did this? What would happen if everyone did this? If you're asking whether something is ethical, it probably isn't.

Reporting Misconduct: When you witness misconduct by colleagues: **Document What You Saw** - write down facts, dates, times, witnesses. **Report Through Proper Channels** - supervisor, internal affairs, or designated reporting mechanism per policy. **Expect Resistance** - reporting colleagues is extremely difficult. You may face ostracism, retaliation, or career consequences. But you swore an oath to uphold the law, not protect corrupt officers.

Whistleblower Protections - most jurisdictions have whistleblower protections prohibiting retaliation. Know your rights. **Your Obligation** - covering for corrupt officers makes you complicit. Your silence enables their misconduct. You have duty to report.

Real-World Application: Ethics Scenarios

Scenario 1: The Free Meal

You stop at a restaurant for lunch. When the check comes, the owner says "No charge, officer. We appreciate what you do." You've eaten there before and paid. The owner seems genuine and friendly.

Analysis: This appears innocent but creates ethical problems: **Gratuity:** Free meals are gratuities—something of value given because of your position. **Obligation:** Accepting creates sense of obligation. Will you patrol this restaurant more? Overlook violations? **Slippery Slope:** Accepting small gratuities makes larger ones easier to accept. **Department Policy:** Most departments prohibit accepting gratuities of any value. **Public Perception:** Citizens seeing you get free meals (while they pay) believe you're receiving benefits others don't, undermining trust. **Proper Response:** "I appreciate the gesture, but I need to pay. Department policy doesn't allow us to accept free meals." If owner insists, explain: "I understand you're being kind, but accepting would put me in a difficult position. I'd really prefer to pay." Pay full price plus good tip (to show appreciation for their support without compromising ethics).

Scenario 2: Family Member Arrest

You stop a vehicle for DWI. During investigation, you discover the driver is your spouse's sibling—your brother-in-law. He's clearly intoxicated (failed field sobriety tests, strong alcohol odor, admitted to drinking). He begs you not to arrest him, saying it will cost him his job and embarrass the family.

Analysis: This tests your integrity directly: **Clear Violation:** He committed DWI. You have probable cause and duty to arrest. **Conflict of Interest:** Your personal relationship creates conflict between duty and family loyalty. **Equal Treatment:** You've arrested others for identical conduct. Treating family differently is corruption. **Consequences:** Letting him go: Violates oath and duty, Creates liability if he crashes and hurts someone, Constitutes official oppression (using authority to benefit someone), Compromises your integrity and career. **Proper Response:** Arrest him according to policy and procedure. Request another officer complete processing to avoid appearance of favoritism or cover-up. Document decision thoroughly: "During investigation, I determined subject was my brother-in-law. To avoid conflict of interest, I requested Officer Smith complete the arrest and booking. I remained on scene to ensure proper procedures were followed." **After the Arrest:** Expect family tension. This is difficult but necessary. You can explain: "I care about you, but I have a duty to enforce the law equally.

Letting you go would violate my oath and possibly cost me my career. I couldn't live with myself if you drove drunk and killed someone because I let you go."

Scenario 3: Witness Attraction

You're investigating a burglary. The victim is attractive and friendly. During the investigation, they express interest in you and suggest meeting for coffee after you're done with the report. You're single and interested.

Analysis: Personal relationships with victims/witnesses create ethical and practical problems: **Professional Boundaries:** Your role is investigator, not potential romantic partner. Mixing these roles is inappropriate. **Power Dynamics:** You hold position of authority in the investigation. Victim may feel pressured to accept your attention or may believe favorable treatment depends on their response. **Investigation Compromise:** Dating victim compromises your objectivity and creates defense attorney ammunition to challenge your credibility. **Department Policy:** Most departments prohibit relationships with subjects of investigations. **Proper Response:** "I'm flattered, but department policy doesn't allow me to have personal relationships with people involved in cases I'm working. I need to maintain professional boundaries." After the case is closed, if you're still interested, you could contact them (after ensuring no ongoing investigations or court proceedings). But the safer approach is simply maintaining professional distance.

Practice Questions (45 questions)

Question 1: The Law Enforcement Code of Ethics requires officers to: A) Enforce laws based on personal beliefs B) Serve mankind, respect constitutional rights, maintain integrity, and enforce law impartially C) Only help people they like D) Accept rewards for good work

Answer: B **Explanation:** The Code requires serving humanity, respecting constitutional rights of all, maintaining personal and professional integrity, and enforcing law courteously without favor, prejudice, or accepting gratuities.

Question 2: Bias-based policing occurs when: A) Officers enforce traffic laws B) Law enforcement decisions are based on race, ethnicity, religion, or other protected characteristics rather than behavior C) Officers use reasonable suspicion D) Criminals are arrested

Answer: B **Explanation:** Bias-based policing makes law enforcement decisions based on protected characteristics (race, ethnicity, religion, etc.) rather than behavior, criminal conduct, or legitimate law enforcement factors.

Question 3: An officer may accept: A) Free meals from restaurants B) Discounts because of their position C) Nothing of value due to their position beyond their authorized salary and benefits D) Gifts from grateful citizens

Answer: C **Explanation:** Professional ethics and most department policies prohibit accepting anything of value (meals, discounts, gifts) because of your position. This prevents obligations and corruption.

Question 4: Procedural justice in policing includes: A) Treating people unfairly B) Giving people voice, treating them respectfully, making neutral decisions, demonstrating trustworthy motives C) Making biased decisions D) Ignoring citizen input

Answer: B **Explanation:** Procedural justice requires giving people opportunity to be heard, treating them respectfully, making neutral unbiased decisions, and demonstrating you're acting in good faith.

Question 5: Cultural competency means: A) Lowering enforcement standards B) Understanding and respecting cultural diversity while maintaining professional standards C) Only working with people from your culture D) Ignoring cultural differences

Answer: B **Explanation:** Cultural competency means understanding cultural differences, adapting communication appropriately, and respecting diversity while maintaining professional law enforcement standards.

Question 6: On social media, officers should: A) Post whatever they want B) Assume everything is public, avoid discussing work, post no bias or offensive content C) Share case details D) Friend everyone

Answer: B **Explanation:** Social media requires assuming all posts are public/permanent, avoiding work discussions, posting no offensive content, protecting operational security, and maintaining professional standards.

Question 7: The "slippery slope" of corruption typically begins with: A) Major crimes immediately B) Small ethical compromises that progressively escalate to serious misconduct C) Nothing—officers are either corrupt or honest D) Accepting bribes first

Answer: B **Explanation:** Corruption usually starts with minor violations (rule breaking, small gratuities) that progressively escalate through stages to serious corruption. Each compromise makes the next easier.

Question 8: When facing ethical dilemmas, officers should ask: A) Will I get caught? B) Is it legal? Does it follow policy? Would I be comfortable if this became public? C) What benefits me most? D) Nothing—just act

Answer: B **Explanation:** Ethical decision-making requires asking: Is it legal? Consistent with policy? Would I be comfortable if public? Would I want my family to know? What if everyone did this?

Question 9: Officers should report colleague misconduct because: A) It's optional B) They swore an oath to uphold the law and covering for corruption makes them complicit C) It's good for their career D) Never—protect colleagues always

Answer: B **Explanation:** Officers have duty to report misconduct. Covering for corrupt colleagues makes you complicit, violates your oath, and enables continued misconduct harmful to everyone.

Question 10: Implicit bias refers to: A) Conscious discrimination B) Unconscious attitudes and stereotypes that affect perceptions and actions C) Having no biases D) Political views

Answer: B **Explanation:** Implicit biases are unconscious attitudes and stereotypes affecting our perceptions and decisions. Everyone has them; awareness helps manage them to prevent biased actions.

Question 11: Noble cause corruption occurs when: A) Officers commit crimes with good intentions like planting evidence on known criminals B) Officers follow the law C) Officers maintain integrity D) Officers report misconduct

Answer: A **Explanation:** Noble cause corruption uses illegal means (planting evidence, falsifying reports, constitutional violations) for "good" ends (convicting guilty people). Good intentions don't justify illegal methods.

Question 12: Stress management for officers should include: A) Ignoring stress B) Regular exercise, adequate sleep, healthy relationships, hobbies, and seeking help when needed C) Using alcohol to cope D) Never taking vacation

Answer: B **Explanation:** Effective stress management: physical health (exercise, sleep, nutrition), mental health (relationships, hobbies, relaxation), professional strategies (compartmentalization, peer support), and seeking professional help when needed.

Question 13: Officers should seek professional help for stress when: A) Never—handle it alone B) Stress significantly impacts functioning, having thoughts of self-harm, using substances to cope, experiencing PTSD symptoms C) Only after career is destroyed D) It's not necessary

Answer: B **Explanation:** Seek professional help when stress significantly impacts your life, you have self-harm thoughts, you're using substances to cope, experiencing PTSD symptoms, or job performance suffers.

Question 14: Department database access is: A) Unlimited for all purposes B) Only for legitimate law enforcement purposes—unauthorized access is typically criminal C) For checking on friends and family D) Not monitored

Answer: B **Explanation:** Criminal justice databases may only be accessed for legitimate law enforcement purposes. Unauthorized access (checking friends, dates, family) is typically criminal and results in termination and prosecution.

Question 15: When a family member commits a crime in your presence, you should: A) Let them go B) Arrest them according to policy and procedure to maintain integrity and equal treatment C) Warn them to leave D) Cover it up

Answer: B **Explanation:** Duty to enforce law equally applies to everyone, including family. Preferential treatment is corruption. Arrest according to procedure; request another officer complete processing to avoid conflict appearance.

Question 16: Off-duty conduct matters because: A) It doesn't—only on-duty counts B) Your conduct on and off duty reflects on the badge and impacts your effectiveness and department reputation C) Privacy is absolute D) No one will find out

Answer: B **Explanation:** Off-duty conduct affects on-duty credibility and department reputation. The badge doesn't come off. Criminal conduct, embarrassing behavior, and questionable associations all create problems.

Question 17: Treating people with respect during enforcement means: A) Letting them go B) Being professional and courteous regardless of circumstances while enforcing the law C) Being friends with criminals D) Not enforcing laws

Answer: B **Explanation:** Respect means professional, courteous treatment regardless of circumstances. You can arrest someone and still treat them with dignity. Enforcement and respect aren't mutually exclusive.

Question 18: Evidence of bias in policing includes: A) Enforcing traffic laws B) Stopping minority drivers disproportionately without traffic violations, conducting searches based on race C) Using probable cause D) Making arrests for crimes

Answer: B **Explanation:** Bias indicators include disproportionate stops/searches of minorities without legitimate law enforcement justification, decisions based on demographics rather than behavior, and patterns showing disparate treatment.

Question 19: An officer witnesses a colleague use excessive force. The officer should: A) Ignore it to protect the colleague B) Document what was observed and report through proper channels C) Cover for the colleague D) Only report if someone complains

Answer: B **Explanation:** Officers have duty to report misconduct witnessed. Document facts objectively and report through proper channels (supervisor, internal affairs). Covering for misconduct makes you complicit.

Question 20: Professional boundaries with victims/witnesses mean: A) Dating them is fine B) Maintaining appropriate professional distance and avoiding personal relationships during investigations C) Befriending everyone D) Getting personally involved

Answer: B **Explanation:** Maintain professional boundaries. Personal relationships with victims/witnesses compromise investigations, create power dynamic issues, violate policy, and damage credibility.

Question 21: Financial problems in officers are concerning because: A) They don't matter B) Excessive debt creates temptation for corruption and compromises integrity C) They're private matters only D) Everyone has debt

Answer: B **Explanation:** Financial instability increases corruption vulnerability. Desperate officers may accept bribes, steal, or abuse position for financial gain. Departments expect financial responsibility to reduce this risk.

Question 22: When stopping someone of different cultural background, officers should: A) Treat them with suspicion B) Apply same professional standards while being aware of cultural communication differences C) Ignore cultural factors completely D) Assume they're criminals

Answer: B **Explanation:** Maintain professional standards while recognizing cultural differences in communication style, personal space, eye contact, etc. Cultural competency improves communication without lowering enforcement standards.

Question 23: Language barriers should be handled by: A) Yelling louder B) Using interpreters, speaking clearly and simply, avoiding idioms, being patient C) Giving up D) Assuming lack of intelligence

Answer: B **Explanation:** For limited English proficiency: use qualified interpreters, speak clearly (not loudly), avoid slang/idioms, be patient. Language barriers don't indicate intelligence or legal status.

Question 24: Officers experiencing PTSD symptoms should: A) Ignore them B) Seek professional help through EAP, counseling, or mental health services C) Self-medicate with alcohol D) Tough it out alone

Answer: B **Explanation:** PTSD symptoms (nightmares, flashbacks, hypervigilance beyond normal alertness) require professional treatment. Use EAP, counseling, or mental health services. Early intervention prevents worsening.

Question 25: Compartmentalization as stress management means: A) Ignoring problems B) Developing ability to leave work stress at work through transition rituals C) Bringing work home D) Never processing stress

Answer: B **Explanation:** Compartmentalization means separating work and personal life. Use transition rituals (changing clothes, exercise, commute decompression) to shift from work mode to home mode, leaving work stress at work.

Question 26: The purpose of the Law Enforcement Code of Ethics is to: A) Decorate walls B) Establish professional standards and ethical commitments binding all officers C) Suggest optional guidelines D) Create paperwork

Answer: B **Explanation:** The Code establishes binding professional standards and ethical commitments: serving humanity, respecting rights, maintaining integrity, enforcing law impartially. It's not optional or decorative.

Question 27: Posting about work cases on social media: A) Is encouraged B) Violates confidentiality and may compromise investigations C) Is fine if the account is private D) Helps solve cases

Answer: B **Explanation:** Never post about cases, arrests, or work incidents on social media. This violates confidentiality, compromises investigations, creates defense attorney ammunition, and violates policy.

Question 28: Organizational stress in law enforcement comes from: A) Physical danger only B) Shift work, mandatory overtime, bureaucracy, perceived lack of support, internal investigations C) Easy schedules D) Perfect support systems

Answer: B **Explanation:** Organizational stress sources include irregular shifts, mandatory overtime, bureaucracy, perceived lack of administrative support, internal investigations, and organizational politics beyond operational dangers.

Question 29: Taking your oath of office means you committed to: A) Selective enforcement B) Faithfully executing duties, upholding the Constitution, serving to the best of your ability C) Doing minimum required D) Following only convenient laws

Answer: B **Explanation:** The oath commits you to faithfully execute all duties (not selectively), uphold the Constitution (primary duty), and serve to the best of your ability (excellence, not mediocrity).

Question 30: Personal relationships between officers and subordinates are: A) Encouraged B) Prohibited due to power dynamics, favoritism concerns, and policy violations C) Required for good morale D) Nobody's business

Answer: B **Explanation:** Relationships between supervisors and subordinates create power dynamic problems, favoritism accusations, morale issues, and typically violate policy. Maintain professional boundaries throughout chain of command.

Question 31: When asked to violate policy by a supervisor, an officer should: A) Always comply B) Respectfully decline, document the order, and report through appropriate channels C) Quit immediately D) Follow illegal orders

Answer: B **Explanation:** Respectfully decline unlawful or unethical orders. Document what was requested. Report through proper channels. You're responsible for your own actions; "I was ordered to" doesn't excuse misconduct.

Question 32: Criticism from media or public should be handled by: A) Responding with anger B) Maintaining professionalism, providing factual information when appropriate, not engaging in online arguments C) Insulting critics D) Ignoring all criticism

Answer: B **Explanation:** Respond to legitimate criticism professionally with factual information when appropriate. Don't engage in online arguments. Some criticism is unfair but professionalism matters. Let actions speak.

Question 33: Burnout in law enforcement is characterized by: A) High energy and motivation B) Emotional exhaustion, cynicism, reduced performance, loss of motivation C) Perfect job satisfaction D) Increased productivity

Answer: B **Explanation:** Burnout symptoms include emotional exhaustion, cynicism about work/public, reduced job performance, loss of motivation, physical/mental health problems. Address through stress management and professional help.

Question 34: Officers should refuse gifts because: A) They're rude B) Gifts create obligations, compromise independence, and create appearance of favoritism C) Gifts are illegal for anyone D) They're not valuable enough

Answer: B **Explanation:** Refusing gifts prevents obligations to donors, maintains independence in law enforcement decisions, avoids favoritism appearance, and upholds ethical standards. Even small gifts compromise integrity.

Question 35: Proper response to religious items during searches: A) Mock them B) Handle with respect while conducting necessary searches C) Refuse to search D) Destroy them

Answer: B **Explanation:** Treat religious items (hijabs, turbans, religious symbols, texts) with respect during necessary searches. Cultural/religious competency requires respecting beliefs while maintaining professional duties.

Question 36: Off-duty association with known criminals: A) Is fine if you're friends B) Compromises integrity, creates conflicts, and violates most department policies C) Is encouraged D) Doesn't matter

Answer: B **Explanation:** Associating with known criminals off-duty creates integrity questions, conflicts of interest, compromise situations, and typically violates policy. Maintain appropriate distance from criminal element.

Question 37: Peer support in law enforcement: A) Shows weakness B) Provides valuable stress management through shared understanding of job stresses C) Is unnecessary D) Should be avoided

Answer: B **Explanation:** Peer support is valuable—fellow officers understand unique stresses in ways civilians can't. Trained peer support teams, informal debriefing with colleagues, and shared experiences help process stress.

Question 38: Department equipment should be used: A) For personal business anytime B) Only for official law enforcement purposes per policy C) To run side businesses D) However you want

Answer: B **Explanation:** Department equipment (vehicles, computers, phones) is for official business only. Personal use may violate policy. Using department resources for personal gain constitutes theft.

Question 39: When facing ethical dilemma about evidence, ask: A) Will I get caught? B) Is this legal? Does it serve justice? Would I want this done if I were the defendant? C) What benefits me? D) Nothing

Answer: B **Explanation:** Ethical evidence decisions require asking: Is this legal? Does it serve justice (not just conviction)? Would I want this treatment if I were accused? What if everyone did this?

Question 40: Regular exercise helps manage stress by: A) Making you tired B) Reducing stress hormones, improving mood, increasing energy, promoting better sleep C) Wasting time D) Nothing

Answer: B **Explanation:** Exercise reduces cortisol (stress hormone), releases endorphins (mood improvers), increases energy, promotes better sleep, and provides healthy stress outlet. Aim for 30 minutes daily.

Question 41: Critical Incident Stress Debriefing: A) Is punishment B) Helps officers process traumatic incidents and reduce PTSD risk C) Is only for weak officers D) Makes things worse

Answer: B **Explanation:** CISD helps process traumatic incidents through structured discussion, normalizes stress reactions, reduces PTSD risk, and provides support. It's professional intervention, not weakness indicator.

Question 42: Evidence-planting to convict someone you "know" is guilty: A) Is acceptable if they're bad B) Is noble cause corruption that violates rights and undermines justice system C) Is good police work D) Is encouraged

Answer: B **Explanation:** Planting evidence is corruption even with "good" intentions (convicting guilty person). Due process matters for everyone. Once you plant evidence on "bad guy," easier to do to innocent person.

Question 43: Appropriate social media posting includes: A) Case details B) General community engagement without discussing work or posting offensive content C) Offensive jokes D) Evidence photos

Answer: B **Explanation:** Appropriate posts: general community engagement, positive department events, crime prevention tips (approved content). Avoid: case details, offensive content, work complaints, confidential information.

Question 44: Vacation time should be: A) Never used B) Used regularly to recharge and prevent burnout C) Accumulated forever D) Considered weakness

Answer: B **Explanation:** Use vacation time regularly. It's not weakness—it's necessary stress management. Unused vacation increases burnout risk. Regular breaks help maintain long-term career sustainability and mental health.

Question 45: Professional ethics in law enforcement are: A) Optional guidelines B) Foundational commitments that build trust, ensure fair treatment, and maintain legitimacy C) Only relevant if caught D) Suggestions for new officers

Answer: B **Explanation:** Professional ethics are foundational—not optional. They build community trust, ensure fair treatment, maintain police legitimacy, protect constitutional rights, and define the profession. Ethics separate professionals from armed individuals.

Evaluating Your Progress

Take a moment to assess your understanding. Count your correct answers and read the interpretation below. Remember, practice questions aren't just about scoring—they're about identifying gaps in your knowledge so you can focus your study where it's needed most.

43-45 correct (96-100%): Outstanding mastery! You've demonstrated excellent understanding of professional ethics, bias prevention, cultural competency, stress management, and corruption prevention. Your grasp of these principles will serve you throughout your career. These aren't just exam topics—they're the values that will define you as an officer. You understand that integrity isn't negotiable and professionalism isn't situational. Review any missed questions to achieve perfect understanding, then move forward with confidence knowing you've internalized the ethical foundation of law enforcement.

39-42 correct (87-93%): Strong ethical foundation! You understand core professional standards and ethical principles. Your knowledge of bias prevention, cultural competency, and corruption prevention is solid. Focus on any specific areas where you missed questions—perhaps stress management techniques, social media guidelines, or specific ethical scenarios. Review those topics carefully, thinking about how you'd apply them in real situations. You're nearly there. A little more study and you'll have complete mastery.

34-38 correct (76-84%): Good foundation with room for growth. You grasp many ethical principles but need to strengthen specific areas. This is actually good news—you've identified exactly where to focus your efforts. Look at your missed questions. Are they clustered in certain topics? Bias-based policing? Stress management? Corruption prevention? Social media guidelines? Focus your review on those specific areas. Work through the ethics scenarios again, really visualizing yourself in those situations. What would you do? Why? Ethics aren't abstract—they're daily decisions. Make them concrete through scenario practice.

29-33 correct (64-75%): You're building understanding but significant gaps remain. Don't be discouraged—ethics is challenging because it requires both knowledge and judgment. Here's your action plan: Review Chapter 9 section by section, taking notes on key principles. For each concept, ask yourself "How would this apply in a real situation?" Work through all five ethics scenarios slowly, thinking about the competing interests and proper responses. Create a personal code of ethics—write down your non-negotiable values. When you know what you stand for, ethical decisions become clearer. Study with a partner who can present ethical dilemmas for you to work through. Practice explaining why certain actions are right or wrong. When you can articulate the reasoning, you've internalized the principles.

Below 29 correct (less than 64%): You need substantial additional study, and that's okay. Ethics and professionalism form the character foundation of law enforcement. These principles are worth the extra time and effort. Here's how to master this material: **Step 1:** Read Chapter 9 again, but differently this time. Don't just read—reflect. After each section, close the book and think about what you just read. How does it apply to you? What challenges might you face? **Step 2:** Create a study guide in your own words. Write out the Law Enforcement Code of Ethics and explain what each phrase means to you. Define bias-based policing and list three ways to prevent it. Describe five stress management techniques and commit to using them. **Step 3:** Work through every ethics scenario multiple times. First, write your initial response. Then read the explanation. Finally, write what you learned. This process builds judgment through reflection. **Step 4:** Talk to officers (family, friends, mentors) about ethical challenges they've faced. Real-world perspective helps you understand that these aren't just textbook issues—they're daily realities. **Step 5:** Study with intention. Dedicate focused time to ethics. When you're consistently scoring 85%+, you're ready to move forward.

Building Your Professional Character

You've now worked through nine chapters covering law, procedures, tactics, use of force, emergency response, and ethics. Each chapter builds on the previous ones, creating a comprehensive foundation for your law enforcement career.

But Chapter 9 is different. The previous chapters taught you what to know and what to do. This chapter taught you who to be. Ethics, professionalism, integrity—these qualities define you as an officer more than any tactical skill or legal knowledge ever will. You can be tactically perfect and legally correct while still being a terrible officer if you lack integrity. Conversely, strong ethical character overcomes many technical mistakes and builds a career of respect and trust.

Here's the reality: You will face ethical challenges. The free meal. The colleague who cuts corners. The citizen who offers money to avoid arrest. The supervisor who pressures you to overlook something. The use of force that nobody witnessed. The evidence that could help your case if you just "misremembered" what you saw. These moments are coming. The question isn't whether you'll face ethical tests—it's whether you'll pass them.

Your preparation now determines your responses then. The officer who thinks about ethics for the first time when facing temptation often makes the wrong choice. The officer who's reflected on their values, studied ethical decision-making, and committed to integrity beforehand usually makes the right choice. You're doing that preparation now. You're not just studying for an exam—you're building the character that will sustain a career of integrity.

What you've learned in this chapter:

- The Law Enforcement Code of Ethics and oath commitments that bind you
- Professional conduct standards both on and off duty
- How to recognize and prevent bias-based policing
- Cultural competency skills for diverse communities
- Social media and technology responsibilities
- Stress management and officer wellness strategies
- Corruption patterns and how to maintain integrity
- Ethical decision-making frameworks for difficult situations

These aren't separate topics—they're interconnected. Cultural competency prevents bias. Stress management supports good judgment. Understanding corruption's slippery slope helps you avoid the first compromise. Professional conduct builds trust that supports difficult enforcement. Ethics aren't a chapter in a book. They're the foundation of everything you do.

Preparing for the Remaining Chapters

You're approaching the finish line. Three more chapters remain: Chapter 10 covers communication and interpersonal skills—how you interact with citizens, testify in court, resolve conflicts, and work with other agencies. Chapter 11 provides comprehensive practice exams integrating everything you've learned. Chapter 12 offers final review materials and preparation strategies for exam day.

Each remaining chapter builds on this ethical foundation. Good communication without ethics is manipulation. Effective testimony without integrity is meaningless. Professional collaboration without trust is impossible. The principles you've studied in Chapter 9 will appear throughout your remaining preparation and throughout your career.

Before moving to Chapter 10, take time to reflect: What kind of officer do you want to be? What values will you never compromise? What will you do when facing pressure to cut corners or cover for colleagues? Write down your answers. These commitments, made now in private reflection, will guide you through public challenges later.

You've worked hard to reach this point. You've absorbed thousands of facts, learned countless procedures, and studied complex legal principles. Now you've added the ethical framework that gives all that knowledge meaning and purpose. You're not just preparing to pass an exam—you're preparing to serve with honor, integrity, and professionalism that will make your community safer and your badge meaningful.

Moving Forward with Purpose

The TCOLE exam tests whether you have the knowledge to be a peace officer. But knowledge without character is dangerous. This chapter tested whether you understand the ethical principles that make knowledge valuable. Based on your performance on these practice questions and your reflection on the scenarios, you know whether you've mastered this material.

If you're scoring consistently above 85%, you're ready to advance. If not, invest more time here. Ethics aren't just another chapter to check off—they're the core of who you'll be as an officer.

When you're ready, Chapter 10 awaits. You'll learn communication skills that allow you to de-escalate conflicts, build rapport with diverse communities, testify effectively, and work collaboratively with other agencies. These skills, built on the ethical foundation you've established in Chapter 9, will make you an effective, respected officer.

You've come far. Keep pushing forward. Success isn't just about passing the TCOLE exam—though you will pass if you continue working with this dedication. Success is about becoming the kind of officer communities need: knowledgeable, skilled, ethical, and committed to serving with integrity. You're building that foundation now, one chapter at a time.

CHAPTER 10: COMMUNICATION AND INTERPERSONAL SKILLS

Communication isn't just talking—it's the foundation of everything you do as a peace officer. You'll use communication to calm volatile situations, gather information from witnesses, explain arrests to suspects, coordinate with other officers, testify in court, and build community trust. Poor communication escalates conflicts, loses evidence, destroys cases in court, and damages your department's relationship with the community. Excellent communication resolves conflicts without force, builds rapport that generates intelligence, creates clear documentation that wins prosecutions, and establishes you as a professional. This chapter teaches you the communication skills that separate adequate officers from exceptional ones. You'll learn radio procedures that keep everyone safe, verbal techniques that de-escalate violence, interview methods that uncover truth, courtroom testimony that convicts criminals, and interpersonal skills that build community partnerships. Master these skills now, because in the field, your words are as important as your actions—sometimes more so.

Radio Communications and 10-Codes

Radio is your lifeline. It summons backup when you need help, coordinates multi-unit responses, tracks officer locations for safety, and documents your activities for legal purposes. Poor radio discipline confuses everyone and endangers officers. Professional radio communication ensures everyone understands what's happening and where you are.

Clear and Effective Radio Traffic

Radio Discipline Principles: Be Clear and Concise: Say what you need in minimum words. Radio channels are shared resources. Long transmissions prevent others from using the channel. Poor: "Hey dispatch, this is Unit 245, I'm currently located at the intersection of Main Street and 5th Avenue, and I've got a vehicle stopped here for speeding, and I need you to run the license plate for me when you get a chance." Better: "245, traffic stop Main and 5th, run plate ABC-1234." **Use Proper Format:** Unit identifier first (who you are), then information. This ensures everyone knows who's talking. Format: "[Your Unit], [Information/Request]." Example: "245, 10-23" (Unit 245 arriving at scene). **Speak Clearly:** Enunciate words clearly. Speak at moderate pace—not rushed, not slow. Poor radio technique: mumbling, speaking too fast, using casual slang. Professional technique: clear pronunciation, moderate pace, proper radio terminology. **Control Your Breathing:** Key the mic, take a breath, then speak. Don't breathe heavily into the mic or speak while gasping. **Wait for Clear Channel:** Listen before transmitting. Don't step on other transmissions. If you accidentally interrupt, say "Unit [X], disregard, go ahead with your traffic."

Priority of Transmissions: Certain transmissions take absolute priority: **Emergency Traffic:** Officer needs immediate assistance, in-progress dangerous situations, pursuits, officer-involved shootings. All other traffic stops immediately. Example: "All units, emergency traffic, 245 needs assistance, officer down, Main and 5th." **Urgent Traffic:** Serious situations requiring quick response but not immediate life-threatening: felonies in progress, injury accidents, disturbances with weapons. Takes priority over routine traffic. **Routine Traffic:** Normal communications, status updates, non-emergency requests. Wait for clear channel and don't interrupt higher priority transmissions.

Common Radio Procedures: Checking Available: "245, available." Tells dispatch you're ready for calls. **Responding to Call:** "245, copy, en route to [location]." Acknowledges assignment and confirms you're responding. **Arriving on Scene:** "245, 10-23." You've arrived. This is critical for officer safety—supervisor and other units know you're on scene. **Checking Status:** "Dispatch, status of backup to my location?" Asking for information about requested assistance. **Requesting Assistance:** "245, need backup, traffic stop getting uncooperative, Main and 5th." Clear statement of need and location. **Emergency Assistance:** "245, 10-33, officer needs assistance, Main and 5th, subject armed with knife!" Emergency code, what's happening, exact location. **Clearing Scene:** "245, 10-24, no report needed" or "245, 10-24, report to follow." Indicates you're clearing scene and whether documentation is needed.

Phonetic Alphabet Usage

When spelling names, addresses, or license plates, use phonetic alphabet to prevent confusion. Letters like B/D/E/T or M/N sound similar over radio. Phonetics eliminate ambiguity.

Standard NATO Phonetic Alphabet: A = Alpha, B = Bravo, C = Charlie, D = Delta, E = Echo, F = Foxtrot, G = Golf, H = Hotel, I = India, J = Juliet, K = Kilo, L = Lima, M = Mike, N = November, O = Oscar, P = Papa, Q = Quebec, R = Romeo, S = Sierra, T = Tango, U = Uniform, V = Victor, W = Whiskey, X = X-ray, Y = Yankee, Z = Zulu.

Practical Application: Spelling "SMITH": "Sierra-Mike-India-Tango-Hotel." License plate "ABC-123": "Alpha-Bravo-Charlie-1-2-3" or "Adam-Boy-Charles-1-2-3" (some departments use different phonetics). This ensures accuracy. Instead of mishearing "B" as "D," phonetics make it clear. **Numbers:** Most numbers are spoken individually. "123" = "one-two-three" not "one hundred twenty-three." Exception: Addresses may be spoken in groups based on local custom. "1234 Main Street" might be "twelve thirty-four Main" or "one-two-three-four Main"—know your department's practice.

10-Codes

10-codes are shorthand for common radio transmissions. They save time and reduce radio traffic. However, codes vary by department and region. Learn YOUR department's codes—don't assume codes from TV or other departments match yours.

Common 10-Codes (Examples—Your Department May Differ): 10-4: Acknowledgment/OK. "I understand." 10-6: Busy/Stand by. 10-7: Out of service. (Off duty or unavailable for calls). 10-8: In service. (Available for calls). 10-9: Repeat/Say again. (Didn't understand transmission). 10-15: Prisoner in custody. 10-20: Location. "What's your 10-20?" = "Where are you?" 10-23: Arrived at scene. 10-24: Assignment completed. 10-27: Driver's license check. 10-28: Vehicle registration check. 10-29: Warrant check. 10-33: Emergency traffic/Officer needs assistance. 10-50: Traffic accident. 10-78: Need assistance (non-emergency). 10-97: Arrived at scene. 10-98: Assignment completed.

Plain English Trend: Many departments are moving away from 10-codes toward plain English for clarity, especially during multi-agency responses where codes differ. Example: Instead of "10-50," say "Traffic accident at Main and 5th." Be ready to adapt based on your department's policy and the situation. Multi-agency incidents (mutual aid, joint operations) should use plain English to avoid confusion.

Verbal and Non-Verbal Communication

Communication is more than words. Your tone, body language, facial expressions, and positioning all send messages. Understanding and controlling these elements makes you more effective at every task—calming subjects, interviewing witnesses, de-escalating violence, and projecting authority.

Active Listening and Body Language

Active Listening Techniques: Give Full Attention: Stop what you're doing and focus on the speaker. Put away your phone, turn toward them, make appropriate eye contact. Divided attention tells people they don't matter. **Maintain Appropriate Eye Contact:** Shows engagement and respect. But be culturally aware—some cultures consider direct eye contact disrespectful. **Don't Interrupt:** Let people finish thoughts before responding. Interrupting frustrates speakers and causes them to shut down or become defensive. **Acknowledge Understanding:** Nod, say "I understand," "I hear you," or "Go on." This encourages continued communication. **Paraphrase and Reflect:** Repeat back what you heard in your own words: "So what you're saying is..." This confirms understanding and shows you're listening. **Ask Clarifying Questions:** "Can you tell me more about that?" "What happened next?" "Where exactly were you when you saw this?" **Watch for Non-Verbal Cues:** Body language, facial expressions, tone of voice often reveal more than words.

Reading Body Language: Defensive Postures: Arms crossed, body turned away, backing up = person feels threatened, uncomfortable, or defensive. Response: Give space, lower your voice, use non-threatening posture yourself. **Aggressive Postures:** Clenched fists, jaw tension, aggressive gestures, invading space, chest out = potential violence brewing. Response: Create distance, maintain reactionary gap, prepare for conflict, use de-escalation language, request backup. **Deceptive Indicators:** Avoiding eye contact, fidgeting, touching face/nose, defensive gestures, inconsistent statements. Response: Note for investigation, ask clarifying questions, don't confront directly yet (people get defensive when accused of lying). **Emotional Distress:** Crying, shaking, rapid breathing, inability to focus = trauma, crisis, or extreme stress. Response: Use empathy, speak calmly, give time to collect themselves, offer water or seat, consider victim services. **Cultural Considerations:** Body language varies across cultures. What's respectful in one culture may be offensive in another. Eye contact, personal space, gestures—all have cultural nuances. Be aware of your community's demographics and cultural norms.

Your Body Language: What you communicate non-verbally matters as much as what you say. **Professional Posture:** Stand straight, shoulders back, confident but not aggressive. Slouching looks unprofessional. Overly aggressive stance escalates tensions. **Open Stance:** Don't cross arms (looks defensive or closed-off). Keep hands visible and relaxed. Open posture says "I'm approachable and listening." **Appropriate Distance:** Respect personal space (typically 3-4 feet for casual conversation, more for tense situations). Invading space feels threatening and escalates conflicts. **Calm Demeanor:** Even when you feel stress or fear, project calm confidence. Your demeanor affects others' responses. If you appear panicked, others panic. If you're calm, situations calm. **Facial Expressions:** Maintain neutral or slightly empathetic expressions. Scowling escalates conflicts. Smiling inappropriately (during serious situations) seems dismissive. Match your expression to the situation appropriately.

Conflict Resolution Skills

Conflicts are inevitable in law enforcement. How you handle them determines whether situations escalate to violence or resolve peacefully.

Conflict Resolution Framework: Identify the Issue: What's the actual problem? Often people argue about surface issues while deeper concerns drive the conflict. Example: Two neighbors arguing over parking might really be fighting over longstanding disrespect. Ask questions to understand root causes. **Listen to All Parties:** Give everyone chance to explain their perspective without interruption. People want to feel heard. Even if you can't solve their problem, listening reduces frustration. **Acknowledge Feelings:** "I understand you're upset about this." "I can see why that would frustrate you." Validation doesn't mean agreement—it means recognizing their emotions are real. **Identify Common Ground:** Find areas of agreement: "You both want this resolved peacefully." "Everyone here wants to feel safe in their home." Common ground builds cooperation. **Generate Solutions:** Ask parties what they want: "What would resolve this for you?" Sometimes solutions are simple—parties just needed a mediator. Other times solutions require creative thinking or referrals to other resources. **Implement Agreement:** If parties reach agreement, make it clear: "So you both agree to..." Document agreements in your report in case future problems arise.

When You Can't Resolve Conflicts: Not every conflict can be resolved on scene. Some require: Court intervention (civil disputes, restraining orders, landlord-tenant issues), Social services (family disputes, mental health issues, substance abuse), Time (people need to cool down before rational discussion). In these cases: Explain what resources are available. Provide contact information for appropriate agencies. Document the situation thoroughly. Ensure immediate safety (separate parties if needed, issue warnings about criminal behavior). Make clear what will result in arrest (threats, violence, property damage).

De-escalation Through Communication

We discussed de-escalation in Chapter 7, but specific verbal techniques warrant detailed examination because communication is your primary de-escalation tool.

Verbal De-escalation Strategies: Use Calm, Controlled Voice: Volume, tone, and pace affect responses. Speaking loudly or rapidly increases agitation. Calm, moderate volume and slow pace encourage calm responses. Match your voice to the response you want. **Acknowledge Emotions:** "I can see you're upset." "I understand this is frustrating." People escalate when they feel unheard. Acknowledging emotions often reduces intensity. **Offer Choices:** "You can calm down and we'll talk, or you'll be arrested for disorderly conduct. Your choice." Framing compliance as their decision (not your imposition) increases cooperation. But choices must be real—don't offer options you can't deliver. **Explain Your Actions:** "I'm asking for your ID because I need to verify who you are for my report." Explanations reduce defensiveness. When people understand reasons, they're more cooperative. **Use "I" Statements:** "I need you to step back" rather than "You need to step back." This frames requests as your needs rather than demands about them, reducing defensiveness. **Avoid Challenges to Ego:** Don't say "You're going to comply or else" or use language that forces them to prove toughness. Give face-saving options. **Give Time:** "I'll give you a moment to think about it." Pressure creates resistance. Time allows people to de-escalate internally and make better choices. **Set Clear Boundaries:** "I'm willing to talk with you, but if you continue yelling I'll have to end this conversation." Be clear about what's acceptable and what's not. **Stay Professional:** No matter how rude, insulting, or offensive the other person is, maintain professionalism. Don't take insults personally. Losing composure escalates situations and damages your professionalism.

De-escalation Language Pitfalls: Commands That Escalate: "Calm down!" (Never works. People don't calm down when told to). "Shut up!" (Obviously escalates). "Stop resisting!" (While necessary for legal documentation, it doesn't de-escalate). **Threats:** "I'm going to arrest you!" (Sometimes necessary but often escalates). "You're going to jail!" (Increases desperation and resistance). Better: "If this continues, I'll have no choice but to arrest you. I don't want to do that." **Sarcasm and Mockery:** Never use sarcasm, mockery, or condescension. They escalate conflicts and look terrible in court or on video. **Absolute Statements:** "You always do this." "You never comply." Absolutes trigger defensiveness. **Arguing:** Don't argue with subjects about facts, law, or their opinions. State what you need clearly and move forward. Arguing is ineffective and escalates situations.

Victim and Witness Interaction

How you interact with victims and witnesses determines the quality of information you gather and whether they cooperate with prosecution. Victims deserve compassionate treatment. Witnesses need encouragement to come forward and testify.

Trauma-Informed Interviewing

Victims of crime—especially violent crime—experience trauma. Trauma affects memory, behavior, and ability to communicate. Understanding trauma improves your ability to gather information while treating victims compassionately.

Effects of Trauma on Memory and Behavior: Memory Fragmentation: Traumatic memories form differently than normal memories. Victims may remember vivid details (smells, sounds, specific moments) while forgetting seemingly important facts (timeline, how they got somewhere, sequence of events). This doesn't mean they're lying—it's how traumatic memory works. **Emotional Numbness:** Some victims appear calm or emotionless after trauma. This confuses officers who expect crying or visible distress. Emotional numbness is a common trauma response—the brain's protective mechanism. Don't interpret calm demeanor as indicating the crime wasn't serious. **Inability to Recall:** Victims sometimes can't immediately recall details. Memory returns over time as trauma subsides. Pushing too hard for immediate details can traumatize further and actually impair memory formation. **Shame and Self-Blame:** Many victims (especially sexual assault and domestic violence victims) feel shame or blame themselves. They may minimize the crime, refuse to cooperate, or recant later. This reflects trauma and fear, not dishonesty. **Fear of Not Being Believed:** Past negative experiences with police or society's tendency to doubt victims makes many fearful of reporting. Your response determines whether they trust the system.

Trauma-Informed Interview Techniques: Believe the Victim: Start from a position of belief. You can investigate and verify facts later, but initially, convey that you believe their account. Example: "I believe you, and I'm here to help." This simple statement opens communication. **Provide Safety:** Before detailed interview, ensure victim feels safe. Get them away from the scene if possible. Separate them from suspect. Ask: "Are you safe now? What do you need to feel safe?" **Explain the Process:** Reduce fear by explaining what happens next: "I'm going to ask you some questions about what happened. This helps me investigate and document what occurred. If you need to take a break at any time, just tell me. There's no rush." **Ask Open-Ended Questions:** "Can you tell me what happened?" Let them tell their story in their own words and sequence. Don't interrupt with specific questions yet. **Don't Judge:** No matter what circumstances led to the crime, don't express judgment. Victims who were drinking, using drugs, engaged in sex work, or made poor decisions still deserve justice. Judgment stops cooperation. **Be Patient with Inconsistencies:** Expect memory issues and inconsistencies. Ask clarifying questions gently: "Earlier you said X, but now you're saying Y. Can you help me understand?" (Not: "You're contradicting yourself!") **Allow Breaks:** Trauma interviews are emotionally exhausting. Offer breaks, water, restroom access, time to compose themselves. **Document Carefully:** Document exact words when possible. Note emotional state, injuries, demeanor. Take photographs of injuries (with consent). **Provide Resources:** Give information about victim services, counseling, protective orders, shelters. Victims need resources, not just criminal justice response. **Follow Up:** Some victims can't provide full statements immediately. Offer follow-up interview: "I understand this is difficult. We can talk more later when you're ready. Here's my card—call me anytime."

Interviewing Witnesses

Witnesses provide crucial evidence but often hesitate to get involved. Your interviewing skills determine whether witnesses provide useful information and whether they'll testify later.

Building Rapport: Introduce Yourself: "I'm Officer [Name] with [Department]. I need to ask you some questions about what you saw." Clear identification and purpose. **Thank Them:** "Thank you for staying to talk with me. Your information is important." Appreciation encourages cooperation. **Explain Importance:** "What you saw could help solve this crime and bring justice. Your information matters." People want to feel their cooperation makes a difference. **Be Respectful:** Even if witnesses seem unhelpful or difficult, maintain respect. You may need them to testify later.

Effective Witness Interviewing: Separate Witnesses: Interview separately to prevent collaboration or contamination of accounts. Don't allow witnesses to discuss what they saw before giving statements. **Start with Open-Ended Questions:** "Tell me what you saw." Let them provide narrative before asking specific questions. **Move to Specific Questions:** After narrative, ask specifics: "You said you saw a man running. Can you describe him?" "What time was this?" "Where were you standing?" "How far away?" **Avoid Leading Questions:** Don't suggest answers: "The man was wearing a red shirt, wasn't he?" Instead ask: "What was he wearing?" **Document Exact Words:** When witnesses describe important details, quote them directly in your report: Witness stated he saw "a tall white male, maybe 6 feet, wearing blue jeans and dark hoodie, running eastbound on Main Street." **Test Reliability:** Ask questions that test observation ability: "How well could you see from where you were?" "Was it light or dark?" "How long did you observe?" "Were you wearing glasses?" "Do you need glasses?" This information helps assess reliability for court. **Get Complete Contact Information:** Name, address, phone numbers (multiple if possible), email. You'll need to reach them for follow-up and trial. Verify contact information—wrong numbers prevent finding witnesses later. **Ask About Other Witnesses:** "Did anyone else see this?" Witnesses often know of other witnesses you haven't identified.

Reluctant Witnesses: Some witnesses don't want to get involved: Fear of retaliation. Don't want to testify in court. Immigration concerns. Distrust of police. Past negative experiences. Don't want to "snitch." **Addressing Reluctance: Acknowledge Concerns:** "I understand you're concerned about safety. Let me explain how we protect witnesses." **Explain Protections:** What protections exist (confidentiality, witness protection programs for serious cases, prosecutors working with them). **Stress Importance:** "Without witnesses like you, criminals get away with hurting people. Your testimony could prevent future victims." **Be Honest:** Don't promise things you can't deliver. If their name will be in reports, say so. If they'll have to testify, explain that. Honesty builds trust even when the answer isn't what they want. **Follow Up:** Give them time to think: "Here's my card. Think about it and call me. This community needs people like you who are willing to stand up and do the right thing."

Testifying in Court

Testifying is a critical skill. You can conduct a perfect investigation, but if you can't effectively communicate in court, the case fails. Court testimony determines whether criminals are convicted or walk free.

Courtroom Demeanor and Procedures

Preparing for Trial: Review Your Reports: Days or weeks before trial, review every report, note, and document. Refresh your memory. You won't be allowed to read reports extensively on the stand, but thorough pre-trial review ensures you remember details. **Review Evidence:** Look at photographs, videos, physical evidence. Make sure you remember what each item is and its significance. **Meet with Prosecutor:** The prosecutor will prepare you. Discuss your testimony, anticipated questions, potential problems. This isn't coaching to lie—it's preparation to present truth effectively. **Dress Appropriately:** Full uniform (clean and pressed) or professional business attire (suit and tie). Appearance affects credibility. **Arrive Early:** Get to court at least 30 minutes before scheduled time. Testifying while rushed and flustered looks bad.

Courtroom Conduct: Professional Demeanor: Maintain serious, professional bearing. No joking, laughing, or casual conversation in courtroom. **Respect for Court:** Stand when judge enters. Address judge as "Your Honor." Address attorneys as "Sir" or "Ma'am" unless they specify otherwise. **Body Language:** Sit upright in witness chair. Don't slouch. Keep hands visible (on armrests or in lap—don't fidget). Face the attorney asking questions, but occasionally turn toward jury when answering (they're evaluating you). **Voice:** Speak clearly and loudly enough for everyone to hear. Courtrooms have poor acoustics. Project your voice. Don't mumble or speak too quietly.

Testifying Effectively

Answering Questions: Listen to the Entire Question: Don't anticipate and answer before question is complete. Listen carefully to what's being asked. **Pause Before Answering:** Take a breath, formulate your answer, then speak. Pausing looks thoughtful and gives prosecutor time to object if needed. **Answer Only What's Asked:** Don't volunteer information beyond the question. If asked "What time did you arrive?" answer "2:30 PM," not "2:30 PM and when I got there I saw three suspects and a white vehicle and..." **Be Direct and Concise:** Yes or no questions get yes or no answers. Don't elaborate unless asked. When explanation is needed, be concise. **Speak in Plain English:** Avoid jargon and police codes. Jury doesn't understand 10-codes or police terminology. Say "I checked if he had any warrants" not "I ran a 10-29." **Use Facts, Not Opinions:** State what you observed, not conclusions: "Subject had slurred speech, bloodshot eyes, and odor of alcohol" not "Subject was drunk." **Admit When You Don't Know:** If you don't know or don't remember, say so: "I don't recall" or "I don't know." Don't guess or make up answers. Honesty about uncertainty is more credible than fake confidence. **Don't Argue:** Defense attorneys may try to make you defensive or argumentative. Stay calm and professional. Answer questions politely even if attorney is aggressive or insulting.

Cross-Examination: Expect Aggressive Questioning: Defense attorney's job is to create doubt. They'll question your memory, procedures, and credibility. Don't take it personally. **Stay Calm:** No matter how confrontational the questions, remain professional. Getting defensive or angry damages your credibility. **Don't Volunteer Information:** Cross-examination is not the time to help the prosecutor. Answer only what's asked. **Admit Mistakes:** If you made errors in investigation, admit them honestly: "Yes, I should have photographed that." Trying to cover mistakes looks dishonest and makes small errors seem significant. **It's Okay to Pause:** Take time to think before answering difficult questions. Pausing doesn't make you look uncertain—it makes you look thoughtful.

Common Testimony Mistakes: Overconfidence: Acting like you remember everything perfectly when you don't. Confidence is good; cockiness damages credibility. **Inconsistency:** Contradicting your reports or previous testimony. Review reports thoroughly to avoid inconsistencies. **Defensiveness:** Getting defensive when questioned about procedures or decisions. Stay professional. **Exaggeration:** Inflating facts to help the case. Stick to truth. Exaggeration gets exposed and destroys your credibility. **Jargon:** Using police terminology jury doesn't understand. Speak plainly. **Volunteering:** Offering information beyond what's asked. Answer the question—nothing more.

After Testifying: Don't Discuss: Don't discuss your testimony with other witnesses still waiting to testify. This can be interpreted as witness coaching. **Stay Composed:** If you're dismissed after testimony, leave courtroom calmly and professionally. Don't react to verdict if you're present.

Inter-Agency Cooperation

Modern policing requires working with multiple agencies. Cases cross jurisdictions. Major incidents involve multiple departments. Federal agencies investigate crimes with local impact. Your ability to cooperate with other agencies determines success in complex investigations.

Working with Multiple Jurisdictions

Common Multi-Agency Situations: Mutual Aid: Assisting neighboring departments during major incidents, disasters, or when they're overwhelmed. **Task Forces:** Drug task forces, gang task forces, human trafficking units often combine personnel from multiple agencies. **Major Investigations:** Serious crimes (homicides, organized crime, terrorism) may involve local, state, and federal agencies. **Pursuits:** Vehicle pursuits often cross jurisdictional boundaries requiring coordination. **Regional Specialized Units:** SWAT, bomb squads, crisis negotiation teams often serve multiple jurisdictions.

Inter-Agency Cooperation Principles: Understand Jurisdictional Authority: Know where your authority ends and another agency's begins. City officers have primary jurisdiction in city limits. County sheriff deputies have county-wide authority. State troopers focus on highways and state crimes. Federal agencies handle federal offenses. Don't exceed your authority or step on another agency's jurisdiction without proper coordination. **Establish Clear Command:**

Multi-agency scenes need clear command structure. Who's in charge? Typically the agency with primary jurisdiction leads. Don't have turf battles—focus on mission accomplishment. **Communicate Clearly:** Different agencies may use different radio systems, 10-codes, or terminology. Use plain English when working inter-agency to avoid confusion. **Respect Other Agencies:** Don't trash-talk other departments. Professional courtesy and mutual respect make cooperation work. **Share Information:** Don't hoard information or intelligence. Share promptly with all involved agencies. Cases succeed through collaboration, not competition. **Document Cooperation:** In reports, note which agencies responded and what roles they played. This creates clear record and ensures proper credit.

Federal-Local Cooperation: Federal agencies (FBI, DEA, ATF, Secret Service, HSI, etc.) sometimes investigate crimes with local impact: Drug trafficking, Human trafficking, Organized crime, Public corruption, Terrorism, Bank robbery, Counterfeiting, Cybercrime. **Working with Federal Agencies:** Federal agents have nationwide jurisdiction but often need local knowledge and assistance. You know the area, local criminals, community dynamics. They bring resources, expertise, and federal prosecution power. Good cooperation: Share intelligence about local criminals and patterns. Assist with surveillance, arrests, searches. Provide local knowledge about geography and people. Respect their investigative techniques and federal rules. **Maintaining Local Cases:** Sometimes federal agencies adopt local cases for federal prosecution (stronger penalties, better resources). This can be good (serious criminals face serious charges) or frustrating (you lose "your" case). Focus on what's best for justice, not agency credit. If federal prosecution means better outcome, support it.

Multi-Jurisdictional Task Forces: Task forces combine personnel from multiple agencies for specific missions (drugs, gangs, human trafficking). Benefits: Pooled resources, Shared intelligence, Combined expertise, Unified approach to regional problems. Challenges: Different policies and procedures, Chain of command issues, Credit and arrest statistics, Budget and equipment sharing. **Success in Task Forces:** Check your ego at the door. It's not about who gets credit. Follow task force protocols even if they differ from your department's. Build relationships with officers from other agencies. Share information freely. Stay flexible—task forces require adaptability.

Real-World Application: Communication Scenarios

Scenario 1: Angry Motorist on Traffic Stop

Situation: You stop a driver for speeding (72 in a 60 zone). When you approach, the driver immediately starts yelling: "This is ridiculous! I wasn't speeding! You cops just want to harass people! I know my rights! I'm going to report you!" His face is red, he's pointing his finger at you, and his voice is loud and aggressive.

What's Your Response: Poor Response: "Sir, you need to calm down right now! If you don't stop yelling I'm going to cite you for disorderly conduct!" This escalates the situation, challenges his ego, and likely results in increased resistance or even violence. Better Response: Use de-escalation communication: "Sir, I understand you're upset. Let me explain why I stopped you. I clocked you at 72 in a 60 zone on my radar. I need to see your license and insurance. Once I have that, I'll explain the process and you'll have the opportunity to contest this in court if you disagree." This: Acknowledges his emotion ("I understand you're upset"). Explains your action (radar, speed). States what you need clearly (license, insurance). Provides information (court process if he wants to contest). Remains calm and professional. If he continues yelling, maintain calm: "Sir, I'm willing to talk with you, but I need you to lower your voice. If you can't do that, I'll complete this stop, issue the citation, and you can address your concerns through the proper channels." Setting clear boundaries while remaining professional often de-escalates angry people. Most calm down once they realize yelling won't change the outcome.

Scenario 2: Traumatized Sexual Assault Victim

Situation: You respond to sexual assault report. The victim is a 24-year-old female who appears calm but detached. She provides basic information but seems reluctant to discuss details. She keeps apologizing and saying "Maybe I shouldn't have been drinking" and "I should have just left earlier."

What's Your Approach: Trauma-informed response essential: "I want you to know that what happened to you is not your fault. No matter what circumstances led to this, sexual assault is a crime and you didn't deserve it. I believe you, and I'm here to help." This directly addresses self-blame and establishes support. For the interview: "I need to ask you some questions about what happened. I know this is difficult. If you need to take a break at any time, just let me know. There's no rush." Start with open-ended questions: "Can you tell me what happened?" Let her tell the story in her sequence. Don't interrupt with specific questions yet. When she provides inconsistent information or can't remember details: "It's okay if you don't remember everything. Traumatic experiences affect memory. Just tell me what you do remember." Be patient with emotional responses. If she starts crying, pause, offer tissues, give time to compose herself. Don't push for details she's not ready to give. Provide resources: "I'm going to give you information about victim services. They have counselors who specialize in helping sexual assault survivors. They can help you process this and provide support." Document carefully and sensitively. Describe her emotional state, injuries (if any), and statements without judgment. Never document opinions like "victim seemed credible" or "victim's account seemed questionable." Stick to facts.

Scenario 3: Cross-Examination in Court

Situation: You're testifying in DWI trial. During cross-examination, defense attorney asks: "Officer, you testified the defendant had slurred speech, correct?" You: "Yes." Attorney: "But you didn't have the defendant recite the alphabet or count backwards, did you?" You: "No, I did not." Attorney: "So you don't really know if his speech was impaired from alcohol or if that's just how he normally talks, do you?" How do you respond?

Effective Response: "I conducted multiple sobriety tests including HGN, Walk and Turn, and One Leg Stand, all of which indicated intoxication. Combined with the odor of alcohol, his admission to drinking, and his poor performance on all tests, I had probable cause to believe he was intoxicated. The slurred speech was one of multiple indicators, not the only basis for my conclusion." This: Doesn't get defensive. Provides complete picture (multiple indicators, not just speech). Uses facts and observations. Stays professional. Doesn't argue with attorney. Alternative if attorney persists: "I've conducted hundreds of DWI investigations and field sobriety tests. Based on my training and experience, the combination of indicators I observed were consistent with alcohol intoxication, and the totality of circumstances gave me probable cause for arrest." This references your training and experience without being defensive or confrontational.

Practice Questions (45 questions)

Question 1: When transmitting on radio, officers should: A) Speak as quickly as possible B) Use unit identifier first, speak clearly at moderate pace, and be concise C) Use slang and casual language D) Transmit without checking if channel is clear

Answer: B **Explanation:** Professional radio communication requires identifying yourself first, speaking clearly at moderate pace, being concise to keep channels clear, and ensuring the channel is available before transmitting.

Question 2: The NATO phonetic alphabet is used to: A) Confuse criminals B) Prevent confusion when spelling names, addresses, or license plates over radio C) Sound professional D) Waste time

Answer: B **Explanation:** Phonetic alphabet prevents confusion between similar-sounding letters (B/D/E/T, M/N) by using distinct words (Bravo/Delta/Echo/Tango, Mike/November).

Question 3: Active listening includes: A) Interrupting frequently B) Giving full attention, maintaining eye contact, acknowledging understanding, and paraphrasing C) Looking at your phone while people talk D) Arguing with everything said

Answer: B **Explanation:** Active listening demonstrates engagement through full attention, appropriate eye contact, verbal acknowledgments, paraphrasing to confirm understanding, and allowing speakers to finish thoughts.

Question 4: Crossed arms and body turned away indicate: A) Confidence B) Defensive or uncomfortable feelings C) Aggression D) Cooperation

Answer: B **Explanation:** Defensive body language like crossed arms and turned-away posture indicates the person feels threatened, uncomfortable, or defensive. Adjust your approach to reduce perceived threat.

Question 5: Clenched fists and aggressive gestures suggest: A) Relaxation B) Potential violence brewing—prepare for conflict and create distance C) Cooperation D) Confusion

Answer: B **Explanation:** Aggressive postures (clenched fists, jaw tension, aggressive gestures, invading space) signal potential violence. Create distance, maintain reactionary gap, prepare for conflict, and request backup.

Question 6: When de-escalating through verbal communication, officers should: A) Yell commands loudly B) Use calm controlled voice, acknowledge emotions, offer choices, and give time to comply C) Challenge the person's ego D) Make threats immediately

Answer: B **Explanation:** Effective verbal de-escalation uses calm tone, acknowledges feelings, offers controlled choices, explains actions, and provides time for voluntary compliance rather than forcing immediate confrontation.

Question 7: Telling someone to "calm down" typically: A) Calms them immediately B) Never works and often escalates the situation C) Is highly effective D) Shows empathy

Answer: B **Explanation:** "Calm down!" rarely works because it dismisses the person's emotions and feels condescending. Instead, acknowledge feelings: "I can see you're upset. Let's talk about this."

Question 8: Trauma affects memory by: A) Making everything perfectly clear B) Causing fragmentation—vivid details of some moments while forgetting seemingly important facts C) Preventing any recall D) Having no effect

Answer: B **Explanation:** Traumatic memories form differently than normal memories. Victims may remember vivid sensory details while forgetting timelines or sequences. This doesn't indicate lying—it's how trauma affects memory formation.

Question 9: When interviewing trauma victims, officers should: A) Push hard for immediate complete details B) Believe the victim, provide safety, explain process, ask open-ended questions, and be patient C) Express doubt about inconsistencies D) Rush through the interview

Answer: B **Explanation:** Trauma-informed interviewing starts with belief, ensures safety, explains what will happen, uses open-ended questions, remains patient with inconsistencies, allows breaks, and provides resources.

Question 10: Witnesses should be interviewed: A) All together so they can corroborate stories B) Separately to prevent contamination of accounts C) Only if they volunteer information D) With leading questions to confirm your theory

Answer: B **Explanation:** Interview witnesses separately before they discuss observations with each other. This prevents contamination and ensures independent accounts for comparison.

Question 11: When testifying in court, officers should: A) Memorize scripted answers B) Listen to complete question, pause, answer only what's asked, and speak clearly in plain English C) Volunteer extra information to help prosecutor D) Argue with defense attorney

Answer: B **Explanation:** Effective testimony involves listening carefully, pausing before answering, responding only to the question asked, using plain English (not jargon), and maintaining professional demeanor even during aggressive cross-examination.

Question 12: If asked a question on the stand that you don't know the answer to, you should: A) Guess B) Admit honestly "I don't know" or "I don't recall" C) Make something up D) Avoid answering

Answer: B **Explanation:** Honesty about what you don't know is more credible than guessing or faking knowledge. Simply state "I don't recall" or "I don't know" when you truly don't remember or know.

Question 13: During cross-examination, defense attorneys may: A) Always be friendly B) Use aggressive questioning to create doubt—stay calm and professional C) Never challenge your testimony D) Help you remember details

Answer: B **Explanation:** Defense attorneys' job is creating reasonable doubt. They may use aggressive questioning, challenge your memory and procedures, or attempt to make you defensive. Stay calm and professional regardless of their tactics.

Question 14: Body language communicates: A) Nothing important B) As much or more than words through posture, gestures, facial expressions, and positioning C) Only what you intend D) Less than verbal communication

Answer: B **Explanation:** Non-verbal communication through body language, facial expressions, tone, and positioning often conveys more than words. Understanding and controlling your body language improves effectiveness.

Question 15: Appropriate professional posture includes: A) Slouching to appear casual B) Standing straight with shoulders back—confident but not aggressive C) Crossing arms defensively D) Invading personal space

Answer: B **Explanation:** Professional posture involves standing straight with shoulders back, projecting confidence without aggression. Slouching looks unprofessional; overly aggressive stance escalates tensions.

Question 16: When working with multiple jurisdictions, officers should: A) Fight over who's in charge B) Use plain English, establish clear command, respect other agencies, and share information C) Hoard intelligence D) Ignore other departments

Answer: B **Explanation:** Multi-agency cooperation requires clear command structure, plain English communication (different agencies have different codes), professional respect, and information sharing for mission success.

Question 17: The purpose of conflict resolution in policing is to: A) Always make everyone happy B) Identify issues, listen to parties, acknowledge feelings, find common ground, and generate solutions when possible C) Take sides D) Avoid all conflicts

Answer: B **Explanation:** Conflict resolution involves identifying root issues, listening to all parties, acknowledging emotions, finding common ground, and working toward solutions when possible, though not all conflicts can be resolved on scene.

Question 18: "I" statements in de-escalation: A) Sound weak B) Frame requests as your needs rather than demands, reducing defensiveness C) Don't work D) Should never be used

Answer: B **Explanation:** "I need you to step back" frames the request as your need rather than a demand about them ("You need to step back"), which reduces defensiveness and increases compliance.

Question 19: Providing victims with resources means: A) Just investigating the crime B) Giving information about victim services, counseling, protective orders, and support services C) Telling them to figure it out themselves D) Only helping if they ask

Answer: B **Explanation:** Comprehensive victim response includes providing information about victim services, counseling, protective orders, shelters, and other resources beyond just criminal investigation.

Question 20: Open-ended questions: A) Require yes/no answers B) Allow subjects to explain in their own words—"Tell me what happened" C) Suggest answers D) Should never be used

Answer: B **Explanation:** Open-ended questions ("Tell me what happened," "Can you describe...") let people provide narratives in their own words and sequence, revealing more information than yes/no questions.

Question 21: When addressing reluctant witnesses, officers should: A) Threaten them with obstruction charges B) Acknowledge concerns, explain protections, stress importance, be honest about process C) Give up immediately D) Promise things you can't deliver

Answer: B **Explanation:** Address reluctance by acknowledging concerns (safety, retaliation), explaining available protections, stressing the importance of their testimony, and being honest about what the process involves.

Question 22: Professional courtroom attire means: A) Casual clothes B) Clean pressed uniform or professional business attire (suit and tie) C) Whatever you wore on duty D) Jeans and t-shirt

Answer: B **Explanation:** Court appearance requires full dress uniform (clean and pressed) or professional business attire (suit and tie). Appearance affects credibility with judge and jury.

Question 23: Sarcasm and mockery during citizen contacts: A) Show authority B) Always escalate conflicts and look terrible in court or on video—never use them C) De-escalate situations D) Are professional

Answer: B **Explanation:** Sarcasm, mockery, and condescension always escalate conflicts, damage your professionalism, and look terrible when videos are reviewed by supervisors, courts, or the public. Never use them.

Question 24: Federal-local cooperation works best when: A) Everyone fights for credit B) Agencies share intelligence, assist with local knowledge, respect expertise, and focus on mission over credit C) Local agencies refuse to help D) Federal agents work alone

Answer: B **Explanation:** Successful federal-local cooperation involves sharing intelligence, locals providing area knowledge, respecting each other's expertise and resources, and focusing on successful outcomes rather than credit.

Question 25: Emergency radio traffic: A) Is same priority as routine calls B) Takes absolute priority—all other traffic stops for officer needs assistance, officer-involved shootings, pursuits C) Should be ignored D) Can wait

Answer: B **Explanation:** Emergency traffic (officer needs assistance, officer down, pursuits, shootings) takes absolute priority. All other radio traffic stops immediately to keep the channel clear for coordination.

Question 26: When someone appears emotionally numb after trauma, this means: A) They're lying about what happened B) It's a common trauma response—emotional numbness is protective mechanism C) The crime wasn't serious D) They don't care

Answer: B **Explanation:** Emotional numbness or flat affect after trauma is common protective response. Don't interpret calm demeanor as indicating crime wasn't serious or person is lying.

Question 27: Allowing interview breaks for trauma victims: A) Wastes time B) Is necessary—trauma interviews are emotionally exhausting and breaks improve information quality C) Shows weakness D) Isn't needed

Answer: B **Explanation:** Trauma interviews are exhausting. Offering breaks, water, restroom access, and time to compose themselves shows compassion and often results in better information as victims collect themselves.

Question 28: Leading questions in interviews: A) Are preferred B) Suggest answers and should be avoided—"What was he wearing?" not "He wore red, right?" C) Always work well D) Are required

Answer: B **Explanation:** Leading questions suggest answers ("The man was wearing a red shirt, wasn't he?") and contaminate testimony. Use open questions: "What was he wearing?" Let witnesses provide information without suggestion.

Question 29: When reviewing reports before trial testimony, officers should: A) Just wing it B) Thoroughly review all reports, notes, and evidence to refresh memory C) Only read them on the witness stand D) Ignore them completely

Answer: B **Explanation:** Days before trial, thoroughly review all reports, notes, photographs, and evidence to refresh memory. You can't extensively read reports on the stand, so pre-trial review is essential.

Question 30: Arguing with defense attorneys during cross-examination: A) Shows you're right B) Damages your credibility—stay calm and professional regardless of attorney's tactics C) Is expected D) Helps your case

Answer: B **Explanation:** Never argue with defense attorneys no matter how confrontational their questions. Getting defensive or argumentative damages credibility. Answer professionally even when challenged aggressively.

Question 31: Radio 10-codes: A) Are universal across all departments B) Vary by department and region—know YOUR department's codes C) Should always be used D) Are no longer used anywhere

Answer: B **Explanation:** 10-codes vary significantly between departments and regions. Learn your department's specific codes. Many departments use plain English for clarity, especially during multi-agency operations.

Question 32: Explaining your actions during citizen contacts: A) Shows weakness B) Reduces defensiveness—"I'm asking for ID because I need to verify identity for my report" C) Isn't necessary D) Makes you look uncertain

Answer: B **Explanation:** Explaining reasons for your requests reduces defensiveness and increases cooperation. When people understand why you're asking, they're more likely to comply voluntarily.

Question 33: Validating emotions means: A) Agreeing with everything B) Acknowledging feelings are real without necessarily agreeing—"I understand you're upset" C) Dismissing concerns D) Taking sides

Answer: B **Explanation:** Validation acknowledges emotions are real ("I understand you're frustrated") without necessarily agreeing with the person's position or actions. This reduces defensiveness and builds rapport.

Question 34: Task force success requires: A) Fighting over jurisdiction B) Checking ego, following task force protocols, building relationships, and sharing information freely C) Competing with other agencies D) Hoarding intelligence

Answer: B **Explanation:** Multi-agency task forces succeed when members check egos, follow unified protocols, build relationships across agencies, and share information freely rather than competing for credit.

Question 35: Witness reliability can be assessed by: A) Their appearance B) Asking about observation conditions—lighting, distance, vision, how long they observed C) Their personality D) Whether you like them

Answer: B **Explanation:** Test reliability by asking about observation conditions: how well could they see, distance, lighting, duration of observation, whether they need glasses. This helps assess testimony weight.

Question 36: Professional radio discipline includes: A) Long rambling transmissions B) Checking channel is clear, being concise, speaking clearly, using proper format C) Interrupting others frequently D) Using unclear language

Answer: B **Explanation:** Radio discipline means checking the channel is clear before transmitting, being concise (radio is shared resource), speaking clearly at moderate pace, and using proper format (unit ID first).

Question 37: When victims recant or become uncooperative: A) Drop the case immediately B) This is common in trauma cases—document thoroughly because evidence-based prosecution may continue C) Blame the victim D) Stop investigating

Answer: B **Explanation:** Many victims become uncooperative due to fear, dependence, or trauma bonding. Thorough documentation (photos, 911 calls, statements, injuries) allows evidence-based prosecution without relying solely on victim testimony.

Question 38: Testimony should use: A) Police jargon and codes B) Plain English the jury understands—"I checked for warrants" not "I ran a 10-29" C) Technical terminology D) Abbreviations

Answer: B **Explanation:** Speak in plain English juries understand. Avoid jargon, 10-codes, and police terminology. Say "I checked if he had warrants" instead of "I ran a 10-29 and got a hit."

Question 39: Paraphrasing during interviews: A) Wastes time B) Confirms understanding—"So what you're saying is..." ensures accurate comprehension C) Insults the speaker D) Should never be done

Answer: B **Explanation:** Paraphrasing ("So what you're saying is...") confirms you understood correctly, shows you're listening actively, and gives the speaker chance to clarify any misunderstandings.

Question 40: Acknowledging witness concerns about testifying: A) Shows weakness B) Builds trust—address safety concerns, explain protections, stress importance honestly C) Isn't necessary D) Discourages cooperation

Answer: B **Explanation:** Many witnesses fear retaliation or court process. Acknowledging concerns, explaining available protections, and honestly discussing what's involved builds trust even when you can't eliminate all concerns.

Question 41: Personal space during interactions: A) Doesn't matter B) Should be respected—typically 3-4 feet for conversation, more in tense situations C) Should always be invaded to show authority D) Is only important for victims

Answer: B **Explanation:** Respect personal space (typically 3-4 feet for casual conversation, more when tensions are high). Invading space feels threatening and escalates conflicts.

Question 42: Multi-agency command structure: A) Should be unclear to keep everyone flexible B) Must be clearly established—typically agency with primary jurisdiction leads C) Doesn't matter who's in charge D) Should involve constant power struggles

Answer: B **Explanation:** Multi-agency operations require clear command structure. Typically the agency with primary jurisdiction leads. Establish this immediately to prevent confusion and turf battles.

Question 43: When admitting mistakes during testimony: A) Never admit errors—deny everything B) Admit honestly—"Yes, I should have..." Honesty is more credible than covering mistakes C) Blame others D) Change your story

Answer: B **Explanation:** Admit mistakes honestly. Trying to cover errors makes small mistakes seem significant and damages overall credibility. "Yes, I should have photographed that" is better than defensive denial.

Question 44: Offering choices during de-escalation: A) Shows weakness B) Frames compliance as their decision, increasing cooperation—"You can calm down and we'll talk, or..." C) Never works D) Should be avoided

Answer: B **Explanation:** Offering controlled choices ("You can comply voluntarily, or I'll have to use force. Your choice.") frames compliance as their decision rather than your imposition, increasing cooperation.

Question 45: Cross-contamination of witness accounts: A) Improves accuracy B) Should be prevented—interview separately before witnesses discuss what they saw C) Doesn't matter D) Helps investigation

Answer: B **Explanation:** Prevent cross-contamination by interviewing witnesses separately before they discuss observations. This ensures independent accounts that can be compared for consistency and reliability.

Scoring Your Practice Questions

43-45 correct (96-100%): Outstanding! Your grasp of communication principles is excellent. You understand radio procedures, de-escalation techniques, trauma-informed interviewing, courtroom testimony, and inter-agency cooperation. These skills will make you an effective officer who builds community trust while successfully investigating cases.

39-42 correct (87-95%): Excellent work! You have strong communication skills foundation. Review areas where you missed questions—whether radio procedures, victim interviewing, or courtroom testimony. These skills improve with practice, so continue working on them.

34-38 correct (76-84%): Good progress! You understand core communication concepts but need strengthening in specific areas. Focus on weak areas—perhaps trauma-informed interviewing or courtroom testimony. Practice these skills through role-playing and scenario work.

29-33 correct (64-73%): You're developing understanding but have significant gaps. Communication skills are critical for every aspect of policing. Review Chapter 10 systematically. Practice active listening, de-escalation language, and interview techniques. Consider finding a study partner for role-playing scenarios.

Below 29 correct (less than 64%): You need substantial additional study. Communication failures cause more problems than any other skill deficit—escalating conflicts, losing evidence, destroying cases, and damaging community relations. Review Chapter 10 section by section. Focus on understanding WHY techniques work, not just memorizing them. Practice extensively.

Chapter Summary: Communication Excellence

Effective communication is the foundation of professional law enforcement. Every skill in this chapter matters daily: **Radio communication** keeps you and other officers safe by ensuring clear coordination and location tracking. Poor radio discipline confuses everyone and endangers officers. **Verbal de-escalation** resolves conflicts without force, preventing injuries and use of force complaints. Your words can calm situations that might otherwise require physical intervention. **Active listening and body language** build rapport, gather better information, and project professional authority. Understanding non-verbal communication helps you read situations and control your own messaging. **Trauma-informed interviewing** shows compassion while gathering crucial evidence. Understanding how trauma affects victims improves information quality and demonstrates professionalism. **Courtroom testimony** determines whether criminals are convicted. Your investigation means nothing if you can't effectively communicate in court. Clear, honest, professional testimony wins cases. **Inter-agency cooperation** solves complex crimes that cross jurisdictions. Checking your ego and working collaboratively accomplishes missions that no single agency could handle alone.

Communication skills separate adequate officers from exceptional ones. Master these skills through conscious practice. Every citizen contact is an opportunity to practice active listening. Every radio transmission is chance to improve clarity. Every difficult person is an opportunity to refine de-escalation skills. The best officers aren't necessarily the strongest or fastest—they're the ones who can talk people down, gather complete information through skilled interviewing, and present cases convincingly in court. Commit to excellence in communication. Your effectiveness, safety, and career success depend on it.

PART VI: COMPREHENSIVE ASSESSMENT

CHAPTER 11: PRACTICE EXAMS AND SCENARIO-BASED TRAINING

You've studied the material, worked through practice questions, and absorbed concepts from ten comprehensive chapters. Now it's time to test yourself under conditions that mirror the actual TCOLE exam. This chapter provides two full-length 100-question practice exams, 50 intensive scenario-based questions, and performance tracking tools that show exactly where you stand and what needs more work. Think of these practice exams as dress rehearsals for the real performance. Athletes don't show up on game day without practicing under game conditions. Musicians don't perform concerts without full rehearsals. You shouldn't take the TCOLE exam without experiencing what it feels like to answer 250 questions under time pressure. These practice exams give you that experience in a safe environment where mistakes are learning opportunities, not career obstacles. Your performance on these exams will tell you whether you're ready for the real test or need additional focused study. Be honest with yourself. If you're not scoring at least 80% on these practice exams, you're not ready for the TCOLE exam. Use these results to guide your final preparation, focusing your remaining study time on weak areas these exams reveal.

How to Use These Practice Exams

These aren't just random questions to complete casually while watching TV. These are diagnostic tools and preparation instruments that, used properly, significantly increase your chances of passing the TCOLE exam on your first attempt.

Practice Exam 1: Comprehensive Review (100 Questions) covers all topics from Chapters 1-10 at similar difficulty to the actual TCOLE exam. Questions are distributed proportionally across content areas: Legal Codes and Criminal Law (30 questions), Patrol and Traffic (25 questions), Investigations and Specialized Procedures (20 questions), Use of Force and Emergency Response (15 questions), Professionalism and Communication (10 questions). This distribution mirrors the actual exam's emphasis on legal knowledge and patrol operations.

Practice Exam 2: Advanced Assessment (100 Questions) increases difficulty slightly, presenting more complex scenarios and questions requiring deeper analysis. This exam challenges you beyond the minimum passing standard. If you can score well on Exam 2, you'll be confident and well-prepared for anything the actual exam presents.

Scenario-Based Questions (50 Questions) focus exclusively on application scenarios requiring you to analyze situations and apply knowledge to realistic field situations. These questions are harder than simple recall questions and mirror the TCOLE exam's increasing emphasis on scenario-based testing.

Simulating Test Conditions

To get maximum benefit from these practice exams, simulate actual testing conditions as closely as possible:

Schedule Properly: Block out 2.5 hours for each 100-question exam (matching the actual exam's pace of approximately 1.5 minutes per question). Take the exam when you're alert and focused, not exhausted after a 12-hour shift. Morning or early afternoon works best for most people.

Find a Quiet Space: No distractions. No TV, music, phone notifications, or interruptions. Tell family or roommates you're unavailable. The actual testing center is quiet—practice in similar conditions.

Use Only Scratch Paper: Don't reference study materials, notes, or previous chapters. You won't have these during the actual exam. Use blank paper for any notes or calculations, just as you'll receive scratch paper at the testing center.

Take the Full Exam in One Sitting: Don't break it into sections. The actual exam requires sustained concentration for hours. Practice maintaining focus for the entire duration. Mental stamina is as important as knowledge.

Time Yourself: Set a timer for 2.5 hours. When time expires, stop immediately even if you haven't finished. This shows whether you're working at appropriate pace. If you don't finish, you need to practice faster decision-making.

No Checking Answers Until Complete: Don't peek at answer keys during the exam. Mark difficult questions and move on, just as you would on the actual test. Return to them if time permits.

Track Your Performance: Use the Performance Tracking Worksheets (provided at the end of this chapter) to analyze results by content area. This identifies weak areas requiring additional study before the actual exam.

How to Approach Each Question

Read Carefully: Read the entire question before looking at answer choices. Identify what's being asked. Watch for key words like "EXCEPT," "NOT," "BEST," "FIRST," or "MOST APPROPRIATE."

Eliminate Wrong Answers: If you're uncertain, eliminate obviously wrong answers first. This improves your odds significantly. Even eliminating one option increases your success probability from 25% to 33%.

Choose the BEST Answer: Many questions have multiple partially correct answers. Choose the most complete or most legally accurate option. The TCOLE exam asks for the BEST answer, not just any answer that seems reasonable.

Don't Overthink: Your first instinct is usually correct if you've studied well. Don't talk yourself out of right answers by overanalyzing. Simple questions have simple answers.

Manage Your Time: Aim for approximately 1.5 minutes per question. If you're spending more than 2 minutes on a question, mark it and move on. Return to difficult questions after completing the easier ones.

Answer Every Question: There's no penalty for wrong answers on the TCOLE exam. If you don't know an answer, make an educated guess. A 25% guess is better than a 0% blank.

After Completing Each Exam

Score Honestly: Count your correct answers. Don't give yourself partial credit or make excuses for mistakes. Either you got it right or you didn't.

Calculate Your Percentage: Divide correct answers by total questions (100) and multiply by 100. The TCOLE passing score is 70%. If you're scoring below 80% on these practice exams, you need more preparation before taking the actual exam.

Analyze Your Performance by Content Area: Use the Performance Tracking Worksheet to identify weak areas. If you missed multiple questions on search and seizure, that's a red flag requiring focused review. Don't just retake the exam—study your weak areas first.

Review ALL Explanations: Don't just review questions you missed. Read explanations for every question, including those you answered correctly. Sometimes you get questions right for wrong reasons, or explanations provide additional insight that deepens understanding.

Identify Patterns: Are you missing application questions while getting recall questions right? Are certain content areas consistently problematic? Do you make mistakes because you misread questions or because you don't know the material? Identifying patterns helps focus remaining study time.

Wait Before Retaking: Don't retake the same exam immediately. You'll remember answers rather than truly testing your knowledge. Wait at least 3-5 days between attempts, during which you should review weak areas identified by your first attempt.

Practice Exam 1: Comprehensive Review (100 Questions)

Instructions: Answer all 100 questions. Allow yourself 2.5 hours (150 minutes) to complete this exam. Work in a quiet space without distractions or study materials. Mark difficult questions and return to them if time permits. After completing all questions, use the answer key to score your performance and read all explanations.

Question 1: Under Texas Penal Code, which mental state represents the highest level of culpability? A) Recklessly B) Knowingly C) Intentionally D) Criminal negligence

Question 2: An officer may arrest without a warrant for a misdemeanor: A) Anytime with probable cause B) Only when the offense occurs in the officer's presence or view (with specific exceptions) C) Never without a warrant D) Only for violent misdemeanors

Question 3: The Fourth Amendment prohibits: A) All searches B) Unreasonable searches and seizures C) Any police contact with citizens D) All arrests

Question 4: Miranda warnings are required before: A) Any arrest B) Custodial interrogation C) Traffic stops D) All citizen contacts

Question 5: Valid consent to search requires: A) Written documentation in all cases B) Voluntary consent from someone with authority, not coerced C) Approval from a supervisor D) A warrant

Question 6: The "automobile exception" to the warrant requirement requires: A) Reasonable suspicion B) Probable cause that the vehicle contains evidence or contraband C) The vehicle to be moving D) Driver consent

Question 7: Arizona v. Gant limits vehicle searches incident to arrest to situations where: A) Any arrest occurs near a vehicle B) The arrestee is unsecured and could access the vehicle OR evidence of arrest offense might be in vehicle C) The officer has reasonable suspicion D) The vehicle was used in any crime

Question 8: Probable cause is best defined as: A) Beyond reasonable doubt B) Facts and circumstances sufficient to warrant reasonable person to believe crime was committed C) Any suspicion D) Officer's intuition

Question 9: Chain of custody refers to: A) Sequence of arrests B) Documented trail of evidence handling from collection to court C) Order of police authority D) Suspect custody procedures

Question 10: Deadly force may be used to prevent escape when: A) Any suspect flees B) Fleeing felon poses significant threat of death/serious injury and committed violent crime C) The officer is frustrated D) Anytime during a pursuit

Question 11: The "plain view" doctrine allows seizure when: A) Officers see anything from anywhere B) Officer is lawfully positioned, incriminating nature immediately apparent, and has lawful access C) Citizens report evidence D) Evidence is visible from any location

Question 12: A "Terry stop" requires: A) Probable cause B) Reasonable suspicion of criminal activity C) Proof beyond reasonable doubt D) No justification

Question 13: Graham v. Connor established that use of force must be: A) Minimal always B) Objectively reasonable based on totality of circumstances C) Approved by supervisor D) Equal to suspect's force

Question 14: The three primary Graham factors are: A) Time, distance, cover B) Severity of crime, immediate threat, active resistance/evasion C) Age, race, gender D) Intent, training, experience

Question 15: Proactive policing is characterized by: A) Waiting for calls B) Working to prevent crime through visible presence and directed patrol C) Only investigating serious crimes D) Avoiding community contact

Question 16: During traffic stops, officers should position patrol vehicles: A) Directly behind the stopped vehicle B) Offset left, 15-20 feet back, at an angle C) In front of the vehicle D) Parallel to the vehicle

Question 17: The "B-post" position during traffic stops refers to: A) Standing at driver's window B) Positioning at rear door post between officer and occupants C) Front of vehicle D) Passenger side

Question 18: Vehicle pursuits should generally be initiated for: A) Any traffic violation B) Violent felonies or when suspect poses serious danger C) All felonies D) Misdemeanors if suspect flees

Question 19: Cooper's Color Code "Condition Yellow" means: A) Unaware B) Relaxed alertness with awareness of surroundings—baseline for officers on duty C) Specific threat identified D) Immediate danger

Question 20: Cover differs from concealment in that: A) No difference exists B) Cover stops bullets; concealment only hides C) Concealment stops bullets; cover only hides D) Both provide equal protection

Question 21: Community policing emphasizes: A) Aggressive enforcement only B) Building partnerships to identify and solve problems collaboratively C) Avoiding community contact D) Only responding to calls

Question 22: Priority 1 calls include: A) Cold theft reports B) In-progress violent crimes and immediate life-threatening emergencies C) Routine traffic stops D) Administrative tasks

Question 23: Texas classifies felonies into how many levels? A) Three B) Four C) Five (Capital, First, Second, Third, State Jail) D) Six

Question 24: A Class A misdemeanor is punishable by: A) Up to 6 months jail B) Up to 1 year jail and/or fine up to $4,000 C) Fine only D) 2 years minimum

Question 25: DWI requires proof that a person operated a vehicle while: A) Tired B) Intoxicated (loss of normal use of faculties OR BAC .08+) C) Angry D) Only if BAC is .15 or higher

Question 26: The horizontal gaze nystagmus (HGN) test checks for: A) Balance B) Involuntary eye jerking that alcohol exacerbates C) Vision clarity D) Verbal ability

Question 27: Field sobriety tests help officers: A) Punish suspects B) Develop probable cause for DWI arrest C) Replace chemical testing D) Delay suspects

Question 28: Implied consent laws mean: A) Everyone consents to all searches B) Operating a vehicle implies consent to chemical testing if arrested for DWI C) Officers don't need warrants D) Consent is always assumed

Question 29: Refusing chemical testing after DWI arrest results in: A) No consequences B) License suspension (180 days first refusal, 2 years subsequent) C) Immediate jail D) Fine only

Question 30: Crime scene preservation requires: A) Letting everyone enter B) Securing perimeter, documenting before disturbing, maintaining chain of custody C) Cleaning immediately D) Ignoring evidence

Question 31: Miranda must be given: A) Upon arrest always B) Before custodial interrogation C) Before traffic stops D) Never

Question 32: Spontaneous statements without police questioning: A) Always require Miranda B) Don't require Miranda—no interrogation occurred C) Can never be used D) Require warrants

Question 33: When a suspect invokes right to counsel: A) Questioning can continue B) All questioning must stop immediately C) Only that topic cannot be discussed D) Officer can persuade them to talk

Question 34: Article 38.22 CCP requires: A) All arrests in writing B) Oral statements during custodial interrogation be electronically recorded C) Miranda in Spanish D) Video of all traffic stops

Question 35: Search incident to arrest allows searching: A) Entire building B) Person arrested and area within immediate control C) All vehicles nearby D) Everyone present

Question 36: Exigent circumstances justifying warrantless entry include: A) Convenience B) Hot pursuit, imminent destruction of evidence, emergency aid, preventing escape C) Any investigation D) Suspicion only

Question 37: Inventory searches must: A) Be pretext for evidence searches B) Follow standardized procedures for administrative purposes C) Be conducted on all vehicles D) Require probable cause

Question 38: A person acts "knowingly" when: A) They desire the result B) They are aware conduct is reasonably certain to cause the result C) They consciously disregard a risk D) They should be aware of risk

Question 39: Burglary of a habitation is: A) State jail felony B) Second degree felony (first degree if intent to commit felony other than theft) C) Class A misdemeanor D) Capital felony

Question 40: Theft classification depends primarily on: A) Criminal history B) Value of property stolen C) Time of day D) Method used

Question 41: Assault causing bodily injury is: A) Class C misdemeanor B) Class A misdemeanor (may be enhanced based on victim or circumstances) C) First degree felony D) Not a crime

Question 42: Aggravated assault includes assault plus: A) Any injury B) Serious bodily injury OR use/exhibition of deadly weapon C) Only permanent injury D) Weapon actually causing injury

Question 43: Capital murder differs from murder by: A) Amount of planning B) Presence of specific aggravating factors (killing peace officer, during certain felonies, multiple victims, etc.) C) Victim's age only D) Time of day

Question 44: Manslaughter requires: A) Intent to kill B) Recklessly causing death C) Accidentally causing death D) Planning the death

Question 45: Family violence includes acts between: A) Only spouses B) Current/former spouses, parents of same child, blood/marriage relatives, dating relationships, household members C) Only blood relatives D) Only married couples

Question 46: Protective order violations are: A) Always Class A misdemeanors B) Class A misdemeanor (first offense); third degree felony if prior conviction or violation by assault C) Not criminal D) Capital felonies

Question 47: Child abuse must be reported: A) Within 72 hours B) Within 48 hours by mandatory reporters including peace officers C) Only if convenient D) Only by CPS

Question 48: Traffic stops should NOT exceed: A) Exactly 5 minutes B) Time reasonably necessary to complete stop's purpose without reasonable suspicion of additional criminal activity C) 30 minutes always D) However long officer wants

Question 49: High-risk traffic stops require: A) Single officer approach B) Backup, PA system commands, not approaching vehicle until occupants secured C) Same procedures as routine stops D) No special procedures

Question 50: Emergency response driving requires: A) Ignoring all traffic laws B) Proceeding with due regard for safety, slowing at intersections, ensuring clear right-of-way C) Maximum speed always D) Assuming all yield

Question 51: Directed patrol means: A) Random driving B) Concentrating resources in high-crime areas during peak times based on crime data C) Following set routes only D) Avoiding certain areas

Question 52: Beat familiarization helps officers: A) Waste time B) Recognize anomalies and suspicious activity quickly C) Avoid work D) Drive longer routes

Question 53: Foot patrol is valuable for: A) Speed B) Community relationships, close observation, accessing areas vehicles cannot C) Less training D) Avoiding citizens

Question 54: Problem-oriented policing involves: A) Only making arrests B) Identifying root causes of recurring problems and developing solutions C) Ignoring minor issues D) Transferring problems to other shifts

Question 55: Criminal trespass requires: A) Entry to any property B) Entry or remaining on property without consent after receiving notice entry forbidden C) Walking across property D) Parking without permission

Question 56: Open container violations involve: A) Any container B) Knowingly possessing open alcohol container in vehicle passenger area on public highway C) Closed containers D) Only drunk driving

Question 57: Criminal mischief classification depends on: A) Time of day B) Amount of pecuniary loss caused C) Type of property only D) Intent only

Question 58: Robbery differs from theft by: A) Property value B) Use of force or threat during commission of theft C) Location D) Time of day

Question 59: Driving while license invalid (DWLI) is: A) Not criminal B) Class C misdemeanor (first offense); Class B (subsequent or DWI-related suspension) C) Always a felony D) Capital offense

Question 60: Disorderly conduct requires: A) Private behavior B) Conduct in public place or near private residence that disturbs peace C) Polite behavior D) Victim injury

Question 61: Use of force continuum serves to: A) Require sequential force escalation B) Provide framework for selecting appropriate force based on resistance/threat C) Eliminate all force D) Guarantee safety

Question 62: De-escalation should be attempted: A) Never B) Whenever safe and feasible before resorting to force C) Only with mentally ill D) After force fails

Question 63: OC spray is appropriate for: A) Passive resistance only B) Active resistance requiring control at distance C) Deadly force situations D) Punishment

Question 64: Conducted energy weapons (Tasers) work by: A) Pain only B) Disrupting voluntary muscle control through electrical pulse C) Burning D) Scaring suspects

Question 65: Impact weapons should target: A) Head and neck B) Large muscle groups (thighs, upper arms) C) Groin D) Spine

Question 66: Deadly force is justified when: A) Officer is angry B) Imminent threat of death/serious bodily injury to officer or others exists C) Suspect is rude D) Supervisor approves

Question 67: After using deadly force, officers must: A) Leave immediately B) Provide medical aid, secure scene, notify supervisor, preserve evidence C) Destroy evidence D) Discuss details with everyone

Question 68: The "21-foot rule" illustrates: A) Traffic stop distance B) Danger of edged weapons—attacker can close 21 feet in time to draw and fire C) Required distance for deadly force D) OC spray maximum range

Question 69: Handcuffs should be applied: A) As tightly as possible B) Palms out, double-locked, snug but not cutting circulation C) Loosely D) Only on violent suspects

Question 70: Less-lethal weapons are: A) Completely safe B) Designed to incapacitate without death but can cause serious injury in some circumstances C) Always preferable D) Never appropriate

Question 71: Force reports must address: A) Only helpful information B) Graham factors, subject behavior, force used, why necessary, de-escalation attempts C) Minimal information D) Only supervisor requests

Question 72: Qualified immunity protects officers when: A) They do anything B) Actions were objectively reasonable and didn't violate clearly established law C) They have good intentions D) Supervisors approve

Question 73: Active resistance means: A) Verbal complaints B) Physical resistance through pulling away, fighting, or fleeing C) Thinking about resisting D) Passive non-compliance

Question 74: Command presence helps reduce force by: A) Intimidation B) Projecting confidence and authority encouraging voluntary compliance C) Looking tough D) Scaring everyone

Question 75: Distance in tactical situations provides: A) Nothing B) Reaction time to threats and tactical options C) Weakness D) Cowardice

Question 76: Crisis intervention techniques emphasize: A) Immediate force B) Slowing down, maintaining distance, calm communication, involving mental health professionals C) Ignoring the person D) Aggressive commands

Question 77: Juvenile procedures differ from adult procedures in: A) No differences B) Juveniles have enhanced protections, different terminology (custody vs. arrest), rehabilitation focus C) Juveniles have fewer rights D) Same exact procedures

Question 78: Age of criminal responsibility in Texas is: A) 12 years old B) 10-17 years (with exceptions) C) 18 years old D) 21 years old

Question 79: School resource officers must: A) Arrest all students B) Balance law enforcement with educational environment, understanding school policies C) Ignore crimes on campus D) Never interact with students

Question 80: Mandatory reporting of child abuse applies to: A) Only teachers B) Peace officers and numerous other professionals—failure to report is criminal C) Only CPS workers D) No one—it's voluntary

Question 81: Radio communications should be: A) Lengthy and detailed B) Clear, concise, and professional using proper codes/procedures C) Casual and informal D) Rarely used

Question 82: The phonetic alphabet is used to: A) Show off B) Ensure clear communication of letters/numbers avoiding confusion C) Waste time D) Confuse people

Question 83: Testifying in court requires: A) Lying to help prosecution B) Truthful, direct answers based on personal knowledge and observation C) Exaggerating to convict D) Guessing

Question 84: Professional ethics require: A) Loyalty to other officers above all B) Integrity, honesty, fairness, and accountability even when difficult C) Ignoring misconduct D) Personal gain

Question 85: Bias-based policing means: A) Fair enforcement B) Making decisions based on race, ethnicity, or demographics rather than behavior C) Following policy D) Constitutional policing

Question 86: Cultural competency in policing involves: A) Ignoring differences B) Understanding and respecting diverse cultures while enforcing law fairly C) Treating everyone differently D) Avoiding certain communities

Question 87: Officer wellness and stress management are important because: A) They're not important B) Chronic stress affects judgment, health, relationships, and public safety C) Officers don't experience stress D) Weakness to admit stress

Question 88: Corruption prevention requires: A) Ignoring ethical violations B) Strong personal integrity, accountability, and reporting misconduct C) Covering for partners D) Personal gain

Question 89: Crime scene documentation should include: A) Minimal notes B) Photographs, sketches, measurements, detailed notes of observations C) Officer's theories only D) Nothing—memory is sufficient

Question 90: Interviewing witnesses requires: A) Leading questions B) Open-ended questions, active listening, documenting exact statements C) Threatening witnesses D) Ignoring statements

Question 91: Report writing should be: A) Vague and general B) Clear, concise, complete, accurate, and objective C) Subjective opinions D) Minimal effort

Question 92: Evidence collection requires: A) Touching everything B) Using gloves, proper packaging, maintaining chain of custody, preventing contamination C) Ignoring procedures D) Losing evidence

Question 93: Victim-centered approaches mean: A) Ignoring victims B) Treating victims with respect, providing resources, minimizing re-traumatization C) Blaming victims D) Avoiding victims

Question 94: Inter-agency cooperation requires: A) Competing with other agencies B) Professional communication, information sharing, coordinated response C) Refusing to work together D) Ignoring other jurisdictions

Question 95: Emergency medical response by officers includes: A) Waiting for ambulance always B) Providing basic life support, controlling bleeding, preventing shock, requesting medical help C) Ignoring injuries D) Medical treatment beyond training

Question 96: Active shooter response priorities are: A) Establish perimeter and wait B) Stop the killing, stop the dying, contact/cover advancing to threat C) Evacuate building before entry D) Wait for SWAT

Question 97: Domestic violence calls require: A) Minimal response B) Determining primary aggressor, making arrest when probable cause exists, providing victim resources C) Leaving it for family to resolve D) Arresting both parties always

Question 98: Mental health crisis calls benefit from: A) Immediate force B) CIT techniques, de-escalation, mental health professional involvement, patience C) Ignoring the person D) Aggressive commands

Question 99: Hostage situations require: A) Immediate assault B) Containment, negotiation, specialized units, patience C) Rushing in alone D) Ignoring the situation

Question 100: Traffic accident investigation requires: A) Minimal documentation B) Scene preservation, witness interviews, measurements, determining causation, proper documentation C) Guessing what happened D) Leaving immediately

Practice Exam 1: Answer Key

1. C | 2. B | 3. B | 4. B | 5. B | 6. B | 7. B | 8. B | 9. B | 10. B
2. B | 12. B | 13. B | 14. B | 15. B | 16. B | 17. B | 18. B | 19. B | 20. B
3. B | 22. B | 23. C | 24. B | 25. B | 26. B | 27. B | 28. B | 29. B | 30. B
4. B | 32. B | 33. B | 34. B | 35. B | 36. B | 37. B | 38. B | 39. B | 40. B
5. B | 42. B | 43. B | 44. B | 45. B | 46. B | 47. B | 48. B | 49. B | 50. B
6. B | 52. B | 53. B | 54. B | 55. B | 56. B | 57. B | 58. B | 59. B | 60. B
7. B | 62. B | 63. B | 64. B | 65. B | 66. B | 67. B | 68. B | 69. B | 70. B
8. B | 72. B | 73. B | 74. B | 75. B | 76. B | 77. B | 78. B | 79. B | 80. B
9. B | 82. B | 83. B | 84. B | 85. B | 86. B | 87. B | 88. B | 89. B | 90. B
10. B | 92. B | 93. B | 94. B | 95. B | 96. B | 97. B | 98. B | 99. B | 100. B

Scoring:

- 90-100 correct (90-100%): Excellent! You're well-prepared.
- 80-89 correct (80-89%): Good! Review missed questions and weak areas.
- 70-79 correct (70-79%): Passing range but needs improvement. Focus study on weak areas.
- Below 70 correct (Below 70%): Not ready yet. Intensive review needed before exam.

Performance Tracking Worksheet

Track your scores by content area:

Content Area	Exam 1 Score	Exam 2 Score	Scenarios Score	Needs Review?
Legal Codes & Criminal Law	__/30	__/30	__/15	□ Yes □ No
Patrol & Traffic	__/25	__/25	__/12	□ Yes □ No
Investigations	__/20	__/20	__/10	□ Yes □ No
Use of Force	__/15	__/15	__/8	□ Yes □ No
Professionalism	__/10	__/10	__/5	□ Yes □ No
TOTAL	__/100	__/100	__/50	

Areas scoring below 75% need focused review before taking the TCOLE exam.

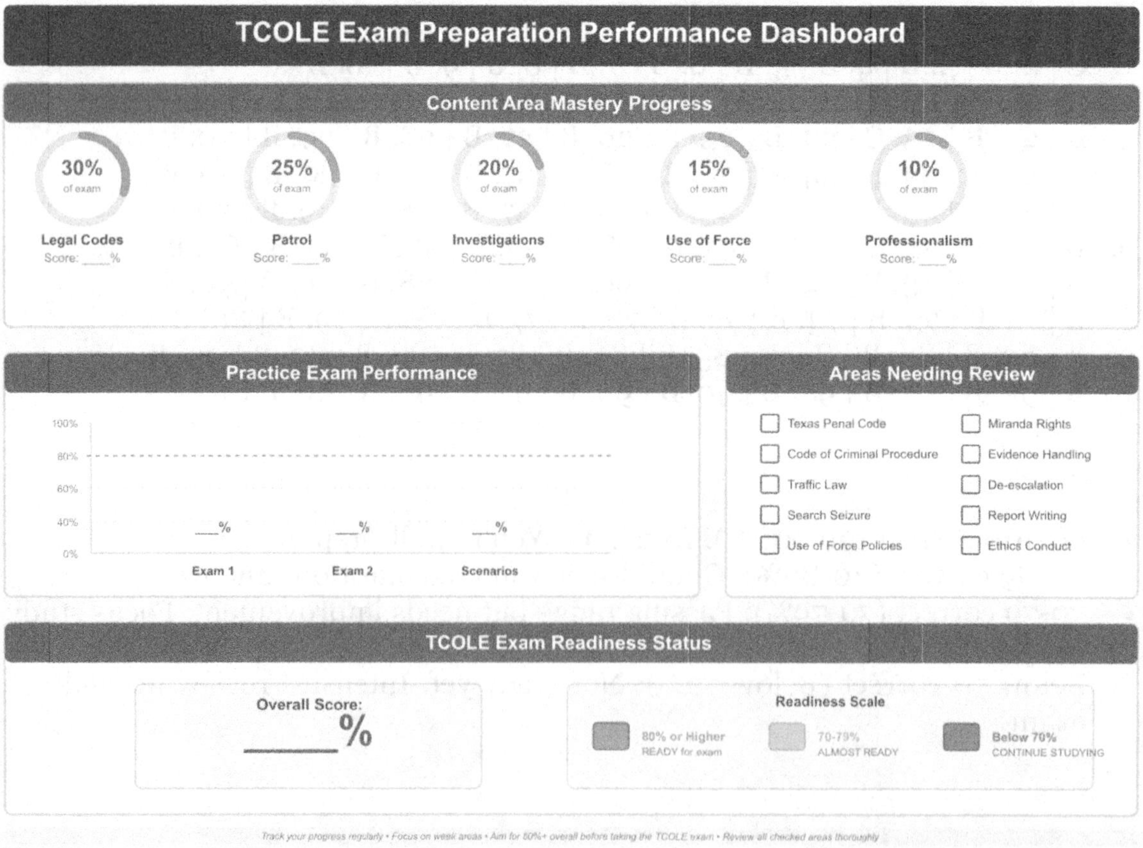

Practice Exam 2: Advanced Assessment (100 Questions)

Welcome to Practice Exam 2. You've completed the first comprehensive review exam, and now it's time to push yourself further. This exam is deliberately more challenging, featuring complex scenarios, nuanced questions, and situations requiring deeper analysis. Think of this as your final dress rehearsal before the actual performance. If you struggled with Exam 1, take time to review your weak areas before attempting this exam. If you scored well on Exam 1, use this exam to confirm your readiness and identify any remaining gaps. Remember: difficulty breeds competence. By practicing with harder material than you'll face on the actual exam, you build confidence and skill that makes the real test feel manageable. Take this exam seriously. Set aside the full 2.5 hours, eliminate distractions, and approach it as if it were the actual TCOLE exam. Your performance here will tell you whether you're truly ready or need additional focused preparation. Let's begin.

Question 1: An officer stops a vehicle for a broken taillight at 2 AM. During the stop, the driver appears nervous, provides inconsistent answers about his destination, and the officer detects faint marijuana odor. The officer has the driver exit and conducts a pat-down, finding nothing. The officer then searches the vehicle without consent and finds methamphetamine under the driver's seat. Which statement is most accurate regarding this search?

A) The search was lawful under the automobile exception based on marijuana odor creating probable cause B) The search was unlawful because nervousness and inconsistent answers don't create probable cause, and faint marijuana odor alone may not create probable cause for vehicle search in current legal environment C) The search was lawful as search incident to arrest D) The search was lawful because it occurred at night

Answer: B **Explanation:** While this is a complex scenario, nervousness and inconsistent answers create reasonable suspicion at most, not probable cause. Faint marijuana odor is increasingly problematic as probable cause given legal hemp and changing marijuana laws. Without clear probable cause or consent, the search likely violates Fourth Amendment. The methamphetamine may be suppressed.

Question 2: During a domestic violence investigation, the victim initially tells you her boyfriend struck her twice in the face, causing the visible injuries. After you arrest the boyfriend, the victim recants, stating she fell and the boyfriend didn't touch her. What should you do?

A) Release the boyfriend immediately—victim changed her story B) Continue with the arrest based on initial statement, physical evidence, and totality of circumstances; document both statements and reasons for arrest C) Arrest the victim for filing false report D) Let them resolve it themselves

Answer: B **Explanation:** Victim recantation is common in domestic violence cases due to fear, financial dependence, or emotional attachment. Your arrest decision is based on probable cause from initial statements, physical evidence (injuries inconsistent with fall), and circumstances. Document both statements thoroughly but proceed with arrest. Prosecutors handle charging decisions and can pursue evidence-based prosecution.

Question 3: You respond to a call of a male subject threatening suicide with a handgun. Upon arrival, you see through the window that he's sitting on a couch with gun pointed at his own head, crying. No one else is in the residence. He's not threatening anyone else. Can you make warrantless entry, and if so, on what basis?

A) No—suicide threats don't justify entry B) Yes—under emergency aid exception to provide assistance to someone in imminent danger of harming himself C) No—you need a warrant for all entries D) Yes—but only if he threatens to shoot you

Answer: B **Explanation:** The emergency aid exception permits warrantless entry when someone inside faces imminent danger requiring immediate assistance, including suicide attempts. While you generally can't use deadly force to prevent suicide (he's only threatening himself), you can enter to provide aid, de-escalate, and prevent the suicide. This is distinct from deadly force authority.

Question 4: During a traffic stop, you ask the driver for consent to search the vehicle. He responds, "Why? Do you think I have something?" You say, "I'm just asking. Do I have your permission?" He says, "I guess I don't have a choice, do I?" and shrugs. You search and find drugs. Is this valid consent?

A) Yes—he consented by shrugging B) No—his response suggests he felt he had no choice, indicating consent wasn't truly voluntary C) Yes—asking questions isn't refusing consent D) Yes—he didn't explicitly say no

Answer: B **Explanation:** "I guess I don't have a choice" strongly suggests the person believes consent isn't voluntary but rather compelled. Valid consent must be freely given. This ambiguous, resigned response doesn't meet the voluntary consent standard. Courts would likely suppress the evidence. Officers should clarify consent by explicitly stating the person can refuse.

Question 5: You're investigating a burglary and interview a witness who describes the suspect in detail, including distinctive tattoos and clothing. Two blocks away, you encounter someone matching that exact description walking away from the burglary scene 10 minutes after the crime. Do you have probable cause to arrest?

A) No—matching description alone isn't probable cause B) Yes—specific description matching suspect, proximity to scene, timing, and direction of travel create probable cause C) No—you need eyewitness identification first D) Yes—but only for detention, not arrest

Answer: B **Explanation:** Totality of circumstances creates probable cause: detailed specific description (not generic), close proximity to fresh crime scene, timing (10 minutes after), walking away from scene. These factors together create reasonable belief this person committed the burglary. You can arrest with probable cause even without eyewitness confrontation, though getting witness identification strengthens the case.

Question 6: You're dispatched to a call of "person with a gun" at a convenience store. Upon arrival, you observe through the window a male subject holding what appears to be a handgun, pointing it at the clerk. The clerk has his hands raised. You have a clear shot through the window. Can you use deadly force immediately?

A) Yes—he's threatening someone with deadly weapon B) No—you should yell commands through the window first C) Maybe—it depends on whether you can clearly see he's actually threatening the clerk with what reasonably appears to be a deadly weapon and deadly force is immediately necessary to prevent death or serious bodily injury D) No—you must enter and give warnings first

Answer: C **Explanation:** This tests understanding of when deadly force is immediately necessary. If subject is actively threatening clerk with apparent deadly weapon and you reasonably believe deadly force is immediately necessary to prevent death/serious injury, deadly force may be justified. However, if possible to issue commands that might result in surrender without increasing danger to clerk, that's preferable. The key is "immediately necessary"—can you wait or issue commands without increasing danger? Answer C recognizes the complexity rather than giving simplistic yes/no.

Question 7: You arrest a suspect for aggravated robbery. You properly administer Miranda warnings. The suspect says, "I understand my rights and I'll talk." Fifteen minutes into the interview, he says, "Maybe I shouldn't say anything else." You respond, "That's your decision, but you've already told me most of it. You might as well finish." He continues talking and provides additional incriminating information. Are his post-invocation statements admissible?

A) Yes—he voluntarily continued talking B) No—"Maybe I shouldn't say anything else" is invocation of right to remain silent, and your response improperly encouraged him to continue, tainting subsequent statements C) Yes—he didn't clearly invoke his rights D) Yes—you didn't force him to talk

Answer: B **Explanation:** "Maybe I shouldn't say anything else" is invocation of the right to remain silent. All questioning must stop. Your response—"You've already told me most of it, might as well finish"—improperly minimized his rights and encouraged continued waiver. This taints subsequent statements. When someone invokes (even tentatively), stop immediately. Don't persuade them to continue.

Question 8: You're conducting a traffic stop. The driver produces a license showing he's 45 years old. However, you notice the photo appears to be of someone much younger. The birthdate on the license would make the holder 45, but the person in front of you appears to be in his mid-20s. What's your best course of action?

A) Ignore it—license looks official B) Detain the person, investigate further (ask biographical questions, check for warrants under both the name on license and suspected actual identity), and potentially arrest for presenting false identification C) Let them go—you can't prove anything D) Seize the license but let them drive away

Answer: B **Explanation:** Discrepancy between photo and current appearance suggests fraudulent use of someone else's license or altered ID. You have reasonable suspicion to extend detention to investigate. Ask biographical questions (mother's maiden name, address history, schools attended), check warrants under both identities, consider requesting additional identification. If investigation confirms false identity, arrest for presenting false identification to peace officer and potentially identity theft.

Question 9: You're executing a search warrant for drugs at a residence. While searching a bedroom, you find a locked safe. The warrant describes "cocaine, marijuana, drug paraphernalia, scales, packaging materials, currency, and records of drug sales." Can you open the safe?

A) No—warrant doesn't specifically mention safes B) Yes—safe could contain items described in warrant (drugs, currency, records), so searching it is within warrant's scope C) No—you need separate warrant for safe D) Only if you can open it without damaging it

Answer: B **Explanation:** The scope of warrant is determined by what you're looking for. If a safe could reasonably contain items described in warrant (drugs, currency, records can all fit in safes), you may search it. You don't need warrant to specifically list every container. However, you should document efforts to get keys/combination before forcing entry if practical.

Question 10: During a vehicle pursuit, you're traveling 85 mph on a residential street chasing a suspect who stole a car. Children are visible playing near the street, and traffic is moderate. Your supervisor orders you to terminate the pursuit. You believe you're about to catch the suspect. What should you do?

A) Continue pursuit—you're close to catching him B) Terminate immediately per supervisor's order—pursuits require supervisor authorization and supervisors can order termination C) Slow down slightly but continue D) Ignore supervisor—you know better

Answer: B **Explanation:** When supervisors order pursuit termination, you must comply immediately. Supervisors monitor pursuits, weigh risks versus benefits, and have authority to order termination. Continuing after termination order violates policy and creates liability. Risks (children present, residential area, traffic) clearly exceed benefits (property crime—auto theft). Terminate and investigate suspect's identity for later apprehension.

Question 11: You're interviewing a child abuse victim, age 6. The child describes abuse in detail but uses terminology and descriptions that seem unusually adult or sophisticated. What should you consider?

A) The child is lying—kids don't talk like that B) Possible coaching by an adult or previous forensic interview training; document exact language used and consider forensic interview specialist C) Nothing unusual—just proceed normally D) The child watches too much TV

Answer: B **Explanation:** Unusual sophistication in language may indicate coaching (parent coaching child to make false allegations), previous forensic interviews (child repeating language learned from trained interviewers), or exposure to adult conversations about the abuse. Document child's exact words, note the sophisticated terminology, and strongly consider involving forensic interview specialists trained in child interviews. Don't make assumptions, but be aware of indicators requiring additional scrutiny.

Question 12: You observe a vehicle traveling 55 mph in a 60 mph zone at 3 AM, driving perfectly within lane lines. The only unusual factor is the late hour. Do you have reasonable suspicion to stop the vehicle?

A) Yes—driving late at night is suspicious B) No—absent specific articulable facts suggesting criminal activity, merely driving legally at an unusual hour doesn't create reasonable suspicion C) Yes—most drunk drivers are out at this hour D) Yes—you can stop anyone at any time

Answer: B **Explanation:** Reasonable suspicion requires specific, articulable facts suggesting criminal activity. Driving legally at an unusual hour, without more, doesn't create reasonable suspicion. Many people work night shifts or have legitimate reasons to drive late. Generalized suspicion about time of day isn't sufficient. You need observable driving behavior, equipment violations, or other specific facts creating suspicion.

Question 13: During a search incident to arrest, you handcuff the suspect and place him in your patrol car. You then return to his vehicle and search the passenger compartment and trunk, finding drugs in the trunk. Is this search lawful?

A) Yes—search incident to arrest authorizes vehicle searches B) No—under Arizona v. Gant, once arrestee is secured and cannot access vehicle, search incident to arrest no longer applies unless you reasonably believe evidence of arrest offense is in vehicle C) Yes—arrestees lose all Fourth Amendment rights D) Yes—the trunk is part of the vehicle

Answer: B **Explanation:** Gant requires either that arrestee is unsecured and can access vehicle, or officer reasonably believes evidence of arrest offense is in vehicle. Once suspect is secured in patrol car, search incident to arrest no longer justifies vehicle search unless evidence of arrest crime might be in vehicle. Trunk search is especially problematic—arrestee could never have accessed trunk anyway.

Question 14: You're testifying in court about your use of force during an arrest. The defense attorney asks, "Isn't it true you were angry at my client when you struck him?" You were frustrated during the incident. What's the best response?

A) "No, I wasn't angry" (lie to protect yourself) B) "I was focused on safely effecting the arrest. The force I used was objectively reasonable based on his resistance, not based on emotion" C) "Yes, I was angry and he deserved what he got" D) Refuse to answer the question

Answer: B **Explanation:** Under Graham v. Connor, your subjective feelings are legally irrelevant—only objective reasonableness matters. Acknowledge the attempt to focus on improper factors while redirecting to the proper legal standard. You're testifying about objective facts and reasonable force, not your emotions. Lying (Option A) destroys your credibility. Admitting anger without context (Option C) is problematic. Option B addresses the question honestly while refocusing on proper legal analysis.

Question 15: You respond to a domestic violence call. The male states the female attacked him first, and he only pushed her away in self-defense. The female has minor scratches; the male has no visible injuries. Both claim the other was the aggressor. What factors should determine who you arrest?

A) Always arrest the male in domestic situations B) Evaluate totality: injury severity/type, prior domestic violence history, relative size/strength, who appears afraid, evidence at scene, witness statements, and apparent defensive versus offensive injuries C) Arrest both D) Arrest neither—let them work it out

Answer: B **Explanation:** Primary aggressor determination requires evaluating totality of circumstances: Who has injuries and what type (defensive scratches versus offensive injuries)? Who has prior domestic violence history? Size/strength disparity? Who appears afraid? What does evidence show? Are there witnesses? Injuries consistent with claimed events? Default assumptions based on gender violate fair policing principles. Base your decision on evidence and circumstances, not stereotypes.

Question 16: You're pursuing a vehicle that ran a red light (Class C misdemeanor). The chase reaches residential areas with children present, speeds exceed 70 mph, and the pursuit has lasted 8 minutes. Your department policy prohibits pursuit for Class C misdemeanors. What should you do?

A) Continue—you've invested too much time to stop now B) Terminate immediately—policy prohibits pursuit for Class C misdemeanors, and risks clearly exceed benefits C) Slow down but maintain visual contact D) Continue until supervisor tells you to stop

Answer: B **Explanation:** This tests whether you'll follow policy even when you don't want to. Department policy prohibits pursuit for Class C misdemeanors specifically because risks (injury, death, property damage) exceed benefits (apprehending misdemeanant). Children present, high speeds, residential area, and duration all increase danger. Terminate, document vehicle/suspect description, investigate license plate for later citation/arrest warrant. Your "investment" of time doesn't justify violating policy and creating danger.

Question 17: During a DWI investigation, the suspect performs poorly on FSTs and you develop probable cause for arrest. The suspect requests to speak with an attorney before deciding whether to submit to chemical testing. What should you tell him?

A) "You have the right to contact an attorney" B) "You don't have right to attorney before deciding on chemical testing; refusal to test will result in license suspension" C) "Call whoever you want" D) "Attorneys aren't allowed to be present"

Answer: B **Explanation:** Under implied consent and Texas law, suspects do NOT have right to consult attorney before deciding whether to submit to chemical testing. The DIC-24 warning explicitly states this. Alcohol dissipates over time, and allowing unlimited attorney consultation would defeat testing's purpose. If attorney is immediately available (already present, quick phone call), suspect may speak briefly, but you're not required to delay testing for attorney consultation.

Question 18: You arrest a suspect for burglary. During booking search, you find a small notebook containing what appears to be a list of names, addresses, and notations like "jewelry box in master bedroom" and "unlocked window on side." What should you do with this notebook?

A) Throw it away—it's just a notebook B) Seize it as evidence of criminal activity (burglary target list), document in property, photograph pages, include in investigation report C) Return it to suspect D) Ignore it

Answer: B **Explanation:** The notebook appears to be evidence of burglary planning—targets, entry methods, valuable locations. This is critical evidence potentially connecting suspect to multiple burglaries. Seize it, document as evidence, photograph all pages (in case original is lost or destroyed), note where found, and include detailed description in reports. This could solve multiple cases and establish pattern/planning showing intent.

Question 19: You're interviewing a witness to an assault. The witness provides a detailed description and says, "I think I might know who did it, but I'm not sure I should say. He's my neighbor and I don't want trouble." What's your best approach?

A) Threaten to arrest him for obstruction B) Acknowledge his concerns while explaining the importance of the information; reassure him about safety measures if needed; document his reluctance and reasons C) Tell him his concerns don't matter D) Leave without getting the information

Answer: B **Explanation:** Witnesses often fear retaliation. Acknowledge concerns (shows empathy), explain why information is important (helps him see his role in justice), discuss safety measures if legitimate threats exist, and document his reluctance/reasons in your report (explains any later recantation). Threats (Option A) destroy cooperation and are unprofessional. Dismissing concerns (Option C) ends cooperation. Leaving without trying (Option D) fails investigation. Build rapport and help witness feel comfortable providing information.

Question 20: You're dispatched to a mental health facility for an escaped patient described as "violent and off medication." You locate the subject walking down the street. He's not threatening anyone, but he's talking to himself and appears confused. When you approach, he doesn't respond to your commands but continues walking. What's your initial approach?

A) Immediately use force to stop him B) Maintain safe distance, use calm non-threatening communication, request Crisis Intervention Team officer or mental health professional, avoid escalating with aggressive commands C) Let him go—he's not committing a crime D) Tackle him immediately

Answer: B **Explanation:** Mental health crises require different approach than criminal behavior. Subject may not understand commands due to mental state, not defiance. Aggressive commands may escalate situation. Use CIT techniques: maintain distance for safety, speak calmly and non-threateningly, request specialized resources (CIT officer, mental health professional), be patient. If he's not immediate danger to self/others, slow approach is appropriate. Force should be last resort after de-escalation attempts, not first response.

Question 21: You stop a vehicle for speeding. The driver provides license from another state showing address in that state. When you ask what brings him to Texas, he says "just visiting." However, you notice Texas vehicle registration and insurance card in the name of someone with different last name. What additional investigation is appropriate?

A) None—speeding is the only issue B) Ask about vehicle ownership, relationship to registered owner, length of time in Texas; this information relevant to proper vehicle operation and possible unauthorized use of vehicle C) Search the vehicle immediately D) Arrest him for theft

Answer: B **Explanation:** Discrepancies between driver information and vehicle registration warrant explanation. Possible issues: borrowed vehicle (legal with owner permission), stolen vehicle, unlicensed driver using another's registration, or out-of-state resident living in Texas without proper registration (violation of Texas law requiring registration within 30 days of establishing residency). Ask clarifying questions. If explanations are suspicious or evasive, investigate further. If reasonable, complete traffic stop normally.

Question 22: During a search warrant execution, you find large amounts of cash ($47,000) in various denominations bundled with rubber bands, along with scales and plastic bags, but you find no drugs. Can you seize the currency?

A) No—currency isn't illegal and no drugs were found B) Yes—currency combined with scales and packaging materials suggests drug proceeds; seize as evidence and for potential forfeiture proceedings C) No—warrant must specifically list currency D) Only if you also find drugs

Answer: B **Explanation:** The totality suggests drug proceeds: large amounts of cash in small denominations, bundled with rubber bands (consistent with drug sales), scales and packaging (drug paraphernalia), even without drugs present. Cash can be seized as evidence of drug trafficking and for potential civil forfeiture. Warrant allows seizure of evidence of drug crimes, which currency combined with these other factors represents.

Question 23: You're investigating a robbery. The victim provides detailed description of suspect and stolen items. You locate someone matching description two miles away an hour later. Can you stop and frisk this person?

A) No—description match isn't reasonable suspicion B) Yes for stop based on reasonable suspicion (detailed description, proximity, timing); frisk only if reasonable suspicion person is armed C) Yes for stop and automatic frisk D) No—too much time has passed

Answer: B **Explanation:** Detailed description, proximity to recent robbery (two miles, one hour is reasonably close in time and space), and matching description create reasonable suspicion for Terry stop. However, frisk requires additional reasonable suspicion that person is armed and dangerous. Robbery involves weapons typically, so you can likely frisk for officer safety, but articulate specific reasons (robbery often involves weapons, nature of crime suggests dangerousness, bulges in clothing, etc.).

Question 24: You're called to a home where parents report their 16-year-old daughter is "out of control," staying out late, refusing to follow rules, and being "disrespectful." The daughter hasn't committed any crimes. What's your appropriate role?

A) Arrest the daughter for disrespect B) Explain you cannot arrest juveniles for being disrespectful to parents; offer referrals to counseling, youth services, truancy services if applicable; mediate if possible C) Force the daughter to apologize D) Arrest the parents for calling police for non-criminal matters

Answer: B **Explanation:** "Disrespect" and "out of control" behavior that doesn't violate law isn't criminal. Police cannot enforce parental authority for non-criminal behavior. Your role: explain limitations of police authority, provide referrals to appropriate services (family counseling, youth services, school truancy officers), mediate if appropriate and both parties willing. Document call and your actions. Many parents don't understand police can't enforce household rules that aren't laws.

Question 25: You're transporting a prisoner to jail. He spontaneously says, "I shouldn't have killed that guy. I just lost my temper." You haven't given Miranda warnings, as you weren't questioning him. Is this statement admissible?

A) No—Miranda warnings required before any custodial statement B) Yes—spontaneous statements not in response to interrogation don't require Miranda warnings C) No—transport means custody, so everything said needs Miranda D) Only if you immediately give Miranda warnings after he speaks

Answer: B **Explanation:** Miranda requires both custody AND interrogation. This statement is custodial (he's under arrest in police vehicle) but not interrogated (spontaneous, not in response to your questions or actions designed to elicit response). Spontaneous statements are admissible without Miranda. Document that you said nothing to prompt the statement and weren't conducting interrogation.

Question 26: During a traffic stop, you smell what might be marijuana but you're not certain—it's faint and could be hemp or skunk smell. Can you search based on this odor alone?

A) Yes—any marijuana-like odor creates probable cause B) Questionable—with legal hemp and changing marijuana laws, faint ambiguous odor may not create probable cause; look for additional corroborating factors C) No—marijuana odor never creates probable cause anymore D) Yes—odor always justifies search

Answer: B **Explanation:** This tests understanding of evolving marijuana law. Legal hemp smells identical to marijuana. Small marijuana amounts are decriminalized in many Texas jurisdictions. Courts increasingly question whether odor alone, especially faint or ambiguous odor, creates probable cause. Best practice: look for corroborating factors (visible marijuana, paraphernalia, admission of possession, behavior suggesting intoxication). Faint ambiguous odor alone may not suffice. Strong, unambiguous fresh marijuana odor remains stronger basis for probable cause.

Question 27: You're investigating a cold burglary. The victim gives you surveillance video showing the suspect's face clearly. You recognize the suspect as someone you've arrested before. Do you have probable cause to arrest this person for the burglary?

A) No—recognition isn't probable cause B) Yes—victim's video evidence combined with your identification of suspect creates probable cause C) No—victim must identify suspect in person D) Only if victim also recognizes suspect

Answer: B **Explanation:** Video evidence showing suspect committing burglary combined with your reliable identification of suspect from the video creates probable cause. Your prior contact makes your identification reliable. You don't need victim to recognize suspect—video is objective evidence, and your identification based on prior knowledge is legitimate. Document your basis for identification (prior arrests, reports, booking photos) in report.

Question 28: You respond to a domestic violence call where the male subject has active misdemeanor warrant for criminal trespass from another jurisdiction. When you arrive, you determine the domestic violence allegation is unfounded. Can you arrest him on the outstanding warrant?

A) No—warrant is from another jurisdiction B) Yes—valid warrants from Texas jurisdictions can be executed anywhere in Texas C) No—warrant is for misdemeanor D) Only if the issuing jurisdiction agrees to accept him

Answer: B **Explanation:** Valid warrants from any Texas jurisdiction can be executed anywhere in Texas. You're authorized to arrest on warrant regardless of how you encountered the suspect. Misdemeanor warrants are as valid as felony warrants. Most departments require confirming warrant is still active (hasn't been recalled), but valid Texas warrants are executable statewide. Document warrant information (issuing agency, cause number, offense, bond amount).

Question 29: During a vehicle search, you find what appears to be methamphetamine. The driver and passenger both claim the drugs aren't theirs and they don't know how they got there. No other evidence suggests who possesses the drugs. Who do you arrest?

A) Both driver and passenger—joint constructive possession B) Driver only—driver has control of vehicle and constructive possession C) Neither—can't prove possession beyond reasonable doubt at arrest stage D) Passenger only—drugs are usually passenger's

Answer: B **Explanation:** Constructive possession doesn't require physical possession—it requires knowledge of presence and control over the area. Driver has control over vehicle and everything in it, creating constructive possession of contraband in vehicle. While passenger may also have constructive possession depending on circumstances (location of drugs, passenger's behavior, other evidence), driver is most clearly responsible. At arrest stage, you need probable cause (not proof beyond reasonable doubt). Driver's control of vehicle creates probable cause for constructive possession.

Question 30: You're conducting a DWI investigation. The subject refuses all field sobriety tests and refuses to answer questions. Can this refusal be used against him?

A) No—he has right to refuse tests and remain silent B) Yes—refusal to perform FSTs (voluntary tests) can be noted and considered; refusal to answer questions after Miranda is protected C) Yes—all refusals prove guilt D) No—nothing about refusal can be mentioned

Answer: B **Explanation:** Field sobriety tests are voluntary and not protected by Fifth Amendment (they're physical tests, not testimonial). Refusing FSTs can be noted and considered (though some courts limit how prosecutors can reference refusals). However, refusal to answer questions after Miranda warnings is protected and cannot be used against defendant at trial. Distinguish between refusing voluntary FSTs versus invoking Fifth Amendment rights.

Question 31: You observe a vehicle swerving within its lane at 1 AM. You initiate a stop. The driver appears extremely nervous, sweating, and avoiding eye contact. You smell strong cologne/air freshener but no alcohol or drugs. The driver provides valid license and insurance. Do you have reasonable suspicion to extend the stop beyond the traffic violation?

A) Yes—nervousness always indicates criminal activity B) No—nervousness, cologne, and legal documents don't create reasonable suspicion of additional criminal activity beyond initial traffic violation; complete stop and release C) Yes—any nervousness justifies extended detention D) Search the vehicle based on air freshener smell

Answer: B **Explanation:** Nervousness alone doesn't create reasonable suspicion. Air freshener/cologne use is common and legal. Valid documents support lawful activity. Without articulable facts suggesting criminal activity beyond traffic violation, you cannot extend detention. Issue citation/warning for traffic violation and release driver. Rodriguez requires reasonable suspicion for extending stops beyond their original purpose.

Question 32: During a pursuit, the suspect vehicle strikes and kills a pedestrian. You continue pursuing. The suspect crashes and is injured. What are your immediate priorities?

A) Arrest the suspect first B) Check both pedestrian and suspect for injuries; render aid to both; request multiple ambulances; this is now vehicular homicide investigation C) Only help the pedestrian—suspect doesn't deserve aid D) Secure evidence before checking injuries

Answer: B **Explanation:** Life safety is paramount regardless of fault. Check both pedestrian and suspect for injuries, render immediate aid, request multiple ambulances with priority dispatch, preserve scene as homicide investigation, and document thoroughly. Your duty to preserve life extends to suspects. The suspect will face serious charges (intoxication manslaughter, murder if intoxicated), but ensuring he doesn't die from injuries is your immediate duty.

Question 33: You respond to a burglary alarm at 3 AM. The front door is ajar. You announce your presence loudly and hear running footsteps going away from you inside the building. What's your best tactical response?

A) Rush in alone to catch the burglar B) Establish perimeter, request backup, announce presence and orders to exit, wait for sufficient units before entry unless exigent circumstances (injured person, ongoing danger) require immediate entry C) Leave and wait for owner D) Enter alone without announcing

Answer: B **Explanation:** Tactical patience saves lives. Burglar is fleeing (not threatening), building is insured (property not worth officer life), and suspect may be armed/waiting in ambush. Establish perimeter preventing escape, request backup, announce presence ("Police! Exit with hands visible!"), and wait for sufficient units for safe entry. If someone's injured inside or ongoing danger exists, entry may be necessary, but property crime alone doesn't justify solo entry into potentially deadly situation.

Question 34: During a traffic stop, the driver states, "I know my rights. I don't have to answer your questions." How should you respond?

A) Arrest him for obstruction B) "That's correct. I still need your license, registration, and insurance for the traffic violation. You don't have to answer questions, but I need those documents." C) Force him to answer questions D) Let him drive away without documents

Answer: B **Explanation:** He's correct—he doesn't have to answer questions. However, providing driver's license, registration, and proof of insurance during traffic stops is required by law, not optional. Acknowledge his right to remain silent while explaining document requirement. His refusal to chat doesn't eliminate document obligation or your authority to complete the traffic stop's purpose (verify documents, issue citation/warning).

Question 35: You're executing a search warrant for stolen electronics. In the suspect's bedroom, you find child pornography on a computer monitor that's turned on and displaying images. The warrant doesn't mention child pornography. Can you seize the computer?

A) No—warrant doesn't cover child pornography B) Yes—child pornography is contraband observed in plain view during lawful search; immediately apparent incriminating nature permits seizure under plain view doctrine C) No—need separate warrant for each crime D) Only if electronics are stolen

Answer: B **Explanation:** Plain view doctrine permits seizing evidence of crimes not listed in warrant when: you're lawfully present (executing valid warrant), item's incriminating nature is immediately apparent (child pornography is obviously illegal to trained officer), and you have lawful access. Seize computer immediately, document where found and what was visible, photograph screen if possible, secure as evidence, pursue additional charges for possession of child pornography, and possibly contact federal authorities (child exploitation often involves federal jurisdiction).

Question 36: You stop a vehicle for speeding. During the stop, you learn the driver has a suspended license. You arrest him for driving while license invalid. Can you impound his vehicle?

A) No—must release to anyone driver designates B) Yes if no licensed driver available to take possession; follow department impound policy and conduct inventory search per standardized procedures C) No—vehicle must stay where stopped D) Only if vehicle is stolen

Answer: B **Explanation:** When arresting driver who cannot legally drive, vehicle cannot remain illegally parked or be driven by another unlicensed person. If licensed passenger or person driver designates can take possession, release vehicle to them. If no one available, impound vehicle per department policy. Conduct inventory search following standardized procedures (protect owner's property, protect department from false claims). Any contraband found during proper inventory is admissible.

Question 37: During a domestic violence investigation, you determine the male subject is primary aggressor and place him under arrest. His 8-year-old child witnessed the assault. What additional considerations apply?

A) None—focus only on arrest B) Child witnessing family violence may require CPS notification in some circumstances; provide victim with resources including counseling for child; document child's presence and what child witnessed; consider child's welfare in safety planning C) Remove child immediately from home D) Ignore child's presence

Answer: B **Explanation:** Children witnessing family violence suffer trauma. Documenting child's presence and what child saw is important for prosecution and child welfare. Some jurisdictions require CPS notification when children witness family violence. Provide victim with information about counseling services for traumatized children, discuss safety planning including child's safety, and consider whether child is safe remaining in home. Child's welfare is part of comprehensive domestic violence response.

Question 38: You're interviewing a suspect who just invoked his right to counsel. He then says, "Wait, let me just tell you one thing..." and starts to provide information. Can you listen?

A) No—once counsel invoked, no communication allowed B) Yes—if he initiates further communication after invoking counsel and voluntarily waives rights again (after being re-advised), statements may be admissible; but best practice is clarify: "You just asked for a lawyer. Are you sure you want to talk without a lawyer present?" C) Yes—always listen to anything suspect says D) Arrest him for changing his mind

Answer: B **Explanation:** Maryland v. Shatzer and subsequent cases recognize suspect can re-initiate communication after invoking counsel. However, you must: ensure he truly understands he invoked counsel and can refuse to talk, re-advise Miranda rights, obtain clear waiver of right to counsel he just invoked, and document the entire exchange showing his initiation and voluntary waiver. Best practice: "You just asked for an attorney. You don't have to talk to me. Do you want to waive that right and talk without an attorney?" Get clear, unambiguous waiver before proceeding.

Question 39: You respond to a shoplifting call. Store security detained a juvenile (age 15) who stole $50 worth of merchandise. The juvenile admits taking the items. What procedures apply?

A) Same as adult arrest B) Take into custody (not "arrest" terminology for juveniles); notify parents/guardians promptly; consider release to parents vs. detention; different processing than adults; focus on rehabilitation C) Release immediately—juveniles can't be detained D) Treat exactly like adult shoplifter

Answer: B **Explanation:** Juvenile procedures differ from adult procedures: terminology is "taking into custody" not "arrest," parents/guardians must be notified promptly, release to parents is often appropriate for non-violent offenses, processing occurs through juvenile justice system (not adult criminal justice), focus is rehabilitation not punishment, and special protections apply. For minor theft by first-time juvenile offender, release to parents with citation to juvenile court is often appropriate. Document thoroughly, notify parents, and explain juvenile court process.

Question 40: During a consent search of a vehicle, you open the trunk and find a locked toolbox. Can you open the toolbox under the consent given?

A) Yes—consent to search vehicle includes all containers B) Depends on scope of consent; if consent was to search "entire vehicle," locked containers generally included; if consent was limited or person objects to opening locked container, you may not have authority without separate consent or probable cause C) No—locked containers always require separate consent D) Force it open without asking

Answer: B **Explanation:** Consent scope determines search authority. General consent to search vehicle typically includes closed and locked containers within vehicle. However, when you encounter locked container, best practice is clarify: "I'd like to open this toolbox. Do I have your permission?" This avoids later claims consent didn't extend to locked containers. If person withdraws consent or objects to locked container, stop and obtain warrant if probable cause exists. Document scope of consent and any limitations discussed.

Question 41: You're dispatched to a call of a suicidal person with a knife threatening to harm himself. He's alone in his apartment, door locked, and you hear him inside stating he's going to "end it." Can you make forced entry?

A) No—suicide threats don't justify entry B) Yes—emergency aid exception permits entry to prevent imminent harm to person, including self-harm; force entry, secure the person, take knife, request mental health evaluation or emergency detention C) No—let him make his own choice D) Only if he threatens others

Answer: B **Explanation:** Emergency aid exception permits warrantless entry when imminent danger to person exists, including danger to self. Suicidal person with weapon stating intent to harm himself creates emergency justifying forced entry to prevent death. Make entry, secure person (using only force necessary), remove weapon, request mental health professional or initiate emergency detention for psychiatric evaluation under Texas Health & Safety Code Chapter 573. Document specific facts justifying emergency entry (suicide threats, weapon, immediacy).

Question 42: During a vehicle search, you find a purse under the passenger seat. The driver is male; female passenger claims purse is hers. You find drugs in the purse. Who possesses the drugs?

A) Both driver and passenger—joint possession B) Likely passenger who claims ownership of purse (constructive possession through control of container); however, if evidence shows driver knew drugs were in purse, both could have constructive possession C) Driver only—vehicle owner is always responsible D) Neither—can't prove possession

Answer: B **Explanation:** Possession analysis requires knowledge and control. Passenger claiming purse has constructive possession of purse's contents (including drugs). Driver may also have constructive possession if he knew drugs were in purse, but that requires additional evidence (statements, behavior, text messages showing knowledge). Start with arresting passenger (admitted control of container). Investigate whether driver knew about drugs. Document passenger's claim of purse ownership—it helps prove her possession but may shield driver unless knowledge proven.

Question 43: You're investigating a robbery. The victim describes suspect as "Hispanic male, 20s, wearing white tank top and blue jeans." This description matches hundreds of people in your city. You see someone matching description two blocks from robbery scene 5 minutes later. Do you have reasonable suspicion for a stop?

A) No—description too generic B) Yes, marginally—generic description plus proximity to recent crime plus timing creates minimal reasonable suspicion for brief stop; ask about presence in area, observe behavior; but weak reasonable suspicion requires releasing quickly unless additional factors develop C) Yes—always stop people matching any description D) Arrest immediately

Answer: B **Explanation:** This tests minimal reasonable suspicion. Generic description (Hispanic male, 20s, common clothing) plus proximity (2 blocks, 5 minutes) creates bare minimum reasonable suspicion for brief stop. But generic description is weak—you must have compelling reason beyond description. Ask brief questions about presence, observe for injury, stolen property, or nervousness suggesting involvement. Without additional factors quickly emerging, release. Document encounter in case later evidence connects him to robbery.

Question 44: You arrest a suspect for burglary. During transport, without any prompting, he says "The homeowner should have locked his back door better." Is this admissible?

A) No—Miranda required for all statements in custody B) Yes—spontaneous statement showing knowledge of how entry was made (unlocked back door) not in response to interrogation; admissible without Miranda C) No—transport means interrogation D) Only if you immediately Mirandize him

Answer: B **Explanation:** Spontaneous statement without interrogation doesn't require Miranda. His unsolicited comment reveals knowledge of entry method (back door was unlocked), suggesting involvement. Document: you said nothing prompting the statement, statement was spontaneous, and exact words used. If you want to ask follow-up questions about the statement, then Miranda becomes necessary. But spontaneous admission is admissible without warnings.

Question 45: During a traffic stop, you ask driver to step out. He refuses, stating "I don't have to get out unless you're arresting me." What's the legal standard?

A) He's correct—can't order people out without arrest B) He's wrong—Pennsylvania v. Mimms permits ordering driver out during lawful traffic stop for officer safety without additional justification; you can order him out and use reasonable force if he refuses C) He's correct—need reasonable suspicion to order people out D) Only passenger must exit

Answer: B **Explanation:** Pennsylvania v. Mimms (driver) and Maryland v. Wilson (passenger) permit ordering occupants out of vehicle during lawful traffic stops for officer safety without additional reasonable suspicion. If driver refuses, issue clear command: "Sir, you are required to exit the vehicle. If you refuse, you'll be removed and may face additional charges." If continued refusal, you can use reasonable force to remove him and potentially charge with resisting. Document refusal and force used.

Question 46: You're executing a search warrant at a suspected drug house. Inside, you find 5 people present. Can you detain all of them during the search?

A) No—only detain named suspects B) Yes—Michigan v. Summers permits detaining anyone present during search warrant execution without individual reasonable suspicion; all 5 can be detained for duration of search C) No—need reasonable suspicion for each person D) Only people who look suspicious

Answer: B **Explanation:** Michigan v. Summers allows detention of everyone present during warrant execution for officer safety, evidence preservation, and search integrity. You don't need individualized reasonable suspicion for each person. Detain all occupants, identify them, document who was present, observe behavior (may create probable cause for arrests), and release after search unless probable cause develops. If people try to leave during search, you can stop them.

Question 47: You stop a vehicle for broken taillight. The driver provides an ID card (not driver's license) showing he's 16 years old. He states he doesn't have a driver's license. What's your response?

A) Let him drive home—he provided ID B) He's committing offense of driving without valid license; cannot allow him to continue driving; arrest or cite depending on policy; vehicle must be legally parked or released to licensed driver C) Just give warning D) Follow him home to ensure safety

Answer: B **Explanation:** Driving without valid license is a criminal offense. You cannot allow him to continue driving illegally. Options: cite and release to licensed driver (parent, friend called to scene), arrest and impound vehicle (if no licensed driver available), or have parents pick up both driver and vehicle. Check if he has learner's permit (requires licensed adult in vehicle). Document why he didn't have license. Never allow unlicensed driver to continue operating vehicle.

Question 48: During a DWI investigation, the suspect performs poorly on FSTs. Before you can ask for chemical testing, he says "I'm not taking any tests. I know my rights." What's the legal consequence?

A) No consequences—it's his right to refuse B) Refusal to submit to chemical testing results in administrative license suspension (180 days first refusal, 2 years subsequent); refusal can be used as evidence of consciousness of guilt; but it is his right to refuse C) You can force testing without consequences D) Refusal means he must be released

Answer: B **Explanation:** Under implied consent, refusal to submit to chemical testing has consequences: administrative license suspension (180 days first refusal, 2 years subsequent refusals) and refusal can be mentioned at trial as evidence suggesting consciousness of guilt. However, you cannot physically force testing absent exigent circumstances or warrant. Read DIC-24 statutory warning explaining consequences of refusal, document his refusal and exact words, request breath or blood test, document refusal again, and proceed with arrest based on other evidence (FSTs, observations, driving). Many DWI convictions occur without chemical test results.

Question 49: You're investigating a theft at a retail store. Video surveillance shows suspect's face clearly. You recognize the suspect as someone you've encountered before but never arrested. Can you identify him in your report and pursue charges?

A) No—victim must identify suspect B) Yes—your recognition of suspect based on prior law enforcement contact is valid basis for identification; document how you know suspect and basis for recognition C) No—only eyewitness victim identification counts D) Yes—but don't document how you know him

Answer: B **Explanation:** Law enforcement identification based on prior contact is legitimate identification method. Document: "I recognized the suspect in surveillance video as John Doe, who I encountered during [describe prior contact—call for service, prior arrest, field interview]. I am certain of identification based on distinctive features [describe features that aided recognition]." This establishes foundation for your identification. Suspect can be charged based on your identification from video even without victim identifying him in person.

Question 50: During a domestic violence call, you determine probable cause exists to arrest the male subject. His 2-year-old child is present and the victim (mother) is being transported to hospital for injuries. There are no family members available to care for the child. What should you do?

A) Leave child alone in home B) Take child into protective custody, notify CPS immediately, arrange temporary placement; child cannot be left without care C) Take child to jail with father D) Leave with any neighbor

Answer: B **Explanation:** You cannot leave young child without appropriate care. Options: contact family members suspect or victim identify who can take custody, contact CPS for emergency placement, or take child into protective custody and transport to CPS office or emergency shelter. Document efforts to find family placement, why those efforts failed, decision to involve CPS, and where child was placed. Child's safety takes priority over convenience. Never leave young children unsupervised.

Question 51: You observe a vehicle driving 60 mph in a 60 mph zone at 2 AM. The vehicle is driving legally. You decide to follow it to "see where it goes." After 5 minutes of following, you activate your lights to stop it for "investigation." Do you have legal authority to stop?

A) Yes—officers can stop anyone at any time B) No—absent reasonable suspicion or probable cause of violation, you cannot stop vehicle; merely following legal driver hoping to develop suspicion doesn't create authority to stop C) Yes—2 AM is suspicious time D) Yes—you can always investigate

Answer: B **Explanation:** Fourth Amendment requires reasonable suspicion or probable cause for stops. Following legally-operating vehicle hoping to develop suspicion doesn't create authority to stop. Late hour alone isn't reasonable suspicion. If during your following you observe traffic violation, equipment issue, or driving behavior suggesting impairment, then you have basis for stop. But stopping driver who has operated legally throughout your observation violates Fourth Amendment. Suppress any evidence from illegal stop.

Question 52: You're dispatched to a mental health facility for an escaped patient described as "not dangerous, just confused." You locate the person walking on the sidewalk, talking to himself but not bothering anyone. He ignores your commands. Can you forcibly detain him?

A) Yes—he escaped from facility B) Depends on whether he meets emergency detention criteria; if he's not dangerous to self/others and can meet basic needs, forcible detention may not be justified; contact facility, request mental health professional, use verbal engagement rather than force C) Yes—always use force on mentally ill people D) No—let him go

Answer: B **Explanation:** Emergency detention requires danger to self/others or inability to meet basic needs due to mental illness. "Not dangerous" suggests force may not be justified. Better approach: maintain visual contact, use calm verbal engagement (CIT techniques), request mental health professional or facility representative to come to scene, avoid physical confrontation unless safety requires it, and document observations. Facility staff may be better equipped to gain voluntary cooperation. If he's truly not dangerous, patience and de-escalation work better than force.

Question 53: During a vehicle search based on probable cause of drugs, you search the passenger compartment and find nothing. Can you search the trunk?

A) No—passenger compartment search exhausted your authority B) Yes—if probable cause exists that contraband is in vehicle, automobile exception permits searching entire vehicle including trunk and all containers that could contain the contraband C) No—trunk requires separate warrant always D) Only with consent

Answer: B **Explanation:** Automobile exception based on probable cause permits searching entire vehicle and all containers that could hold the contraband you're seeking. If searching for drugs, you can search trunk and small containers. Finding nothing in passenger compartment doesn't exhaust your authority—probable cause extends to entire vehicle. Search trunk, document results (whether evidence found or not), and note probable cause extended throughout vehicle search.

Question 54: You arrest a suspect for aggravated assault. While handcuffing him, he makes spontaneous statements about the assault without any questioning from you. Later at jail, after

Miranda warnings, you ask about the assault and he refuses to answer. Which statements are admissible?

A) Neither—both need Miranda B) Spontaneous statements during arrest are admissible (no interrogation); jail refusal to answer after Miranda is his right and cannot be used against him C) Both are admissible D) Only jail statements count

Answer: B **Explanation:** Spontaneous statements during arrest (without interrogation) don't require Miranda and are admissible. Post-Miranda refusal to answer questions is invoking Fifth Amendment rights and cannot be used against defendant at trial. You have spontaneous admissions from arrest scene (admissible). His later refusal means you got no additional statements, but his refusal cannot be mentioned as evidence of guilt. Use spontaneous statements in prosecution; respect Fifth Amendment regarding his refusal.

Question 55: You conduct a traffic stop and determine the driver has an outstanding misdemeanor warrant from another county. Before transporting him to jail, he asks to smoke a cigarette and walks toward his vehicle. You follow and observe him reach into the vehicle. Can you search the vehicle?

A) No—warrant arrest doesn't authorize vehicle search B) Under Arizona v. Gant, you can search if you reasonably believe evidence of the offense of arrest might be in vehicle; misdemeanor warrant offense (need to know what offense) determines whether evidence might be present C) Yes—all warrant arrests allow vehicle searches D) No—he wasn't driving when arrested

Answer: B **Explanation:** Gant permits vehicle search when arrestee is unsecured and could access vehicle (he just walked to it) OR when evidence of arrest offense might be in vehicle. Determine what the warrant is for: if warrant is for theft, evidence might be in vehicle; if warrant is for failure to appear, evidence wouldn't be in vehicle. His reaching into vehicle while unsecured creates Gant's first scenario (access to vehicle). Search vehicle for weapons and evidence, document his movement toward vehicle, secure him immediately, and document what you found.

Question 56: During a pursuit, you're approaching an intersection with red light. Traffic is crossing perpendicular to you. What's required before proceeding through the red light?

A) Nothing—emergency lights give automatic right of way B) Slow substantially, ensure all lanes are clear and vehicles have yielded, proceed with caution; emergency vehicles must proceed with due regard for safety C) Accelerate through quickly D) Stop completely at every red light

Answer: B **Explanation:** Emergency vehicles have right of way when using lights and sirens, but must proceed with "due regard" for safety. Most crashes involving emergency vehicles occur at intersections. Slow substantially, ensure all lanes clear (don't assume vehicles see or hear you), make eye contact with drivers when possible, and proceed carefully. Arriving slightly slower but alive is better than crashing. Document any intersection crashes—failure to ensure clear intersection may result in liability.

Question 57: You respond to a burglary. The victim describes seeing the burglar inside his home on security camera and provides excellent description. You locate someone matching description 3 blocks away 15 minutes later, walking away from the scene. He's carrying a backpack. Do you have probable cause to arrest?

A) No—matching description isn't enough B) Yes—specific description, very close proximity to fresh crime, short time interval, direction of travel away from scene, and possession of bag possibly containing stolen property create probable cause for arrest C) No—need eyewitness identification first D) Only reasonable suspicion for stop

Answer: B **Explanation:** Totality creates probable cause: specific detailed description (not generic), very close to fresh burglary (3 blocks, 15 minutes), walking away from scene (fleeing direction), carrying bag (could contain stolen property). This isn't mere presence in high-crime area—it's specific facts creating reasonable belief this person just burglarized that home. Arrest based on probable cause, search backpack incident to arrest for stolen property and burglary tools, get victim identification, and document all factors supporting probable cause.

Question 58: You stop a vehicle for speeding. The driver seems extremely intoxicated (strong alcohol odor, slurred speech, bloodshot eyes). Before you can conduct FSTs, he says "Yes, I've been drinking heavily. I know I'm drunk. Just arrest me." Do you still need to conduct FSTs?

A) Yes—FSTs always required before DWI arrest B) No—his admission to drinking heavily plus your observations create probable cause; FSTs would add evidence but aren't legally required when probable cause exists through admission and observations C) Yes—never skip FSTs D) No—let him drive home since he admitted it

Answer: B **Explanation:** FSTs help develop probable cause but aren't legally required when probable cause already exists through other means. His admission to drinking heavily combined with your observations (strong odor, slurred speech, bloodshot eyes) create probable cause for DWI arrest. FSTs would strengthen the case but aren't mandatory. However, consider conducting FSTs anyway to document level of impairment and support prosecution. If he refuses FSTs, you still have probable cause from admission and observations. Document why you arrested without FSTs if you choose that route.

Question 59: During a search warrant execution, you find a subject hiding in a closet. He's not named in the warrant. Can you detain him?

A) No—not named in warrant B) Yes—Michigan v. Summers permits detaining anyone present during search warrant execution; person hiding in closet is "present" and can be detained for duration of search C) No—only people in open areas can be detained D) Only with probable cause for arrest

Answer: B **Explanation:** "Present" during search warrant execution includes people found anywhere on the premises during the search, including hiding in closets. Hiding creates additional suspicion (why hide from police executing search warrant?). Detain him, identify him, check for warrants, observe behavior (nervousness, knowledge of layout, possessing contraband). His presence and hiding behavior may create probable cause for charges (harboring fugitive if that's why he hid, possession of contraband found in closet he was hiding in). Document where found and circumstances.

Question 60: You're interviewing a domestic violence victim at the hospital. She's reluctant to provide details, keeps minimizing injuries, and says "I just want to forget this happened." How should you proceed?

A) Accept her statement and close the case B) Acknowledge her feelings while explaining importance of documentation; gather evidence independently of her cooperation (photos of injuries, statements from medical staff, evidence from scene); pursue evidence-based prosecution even if she's uncooperative C) Force her to cooperate D) Leave without documenting anything

Answer: B **Explanation:** Victim reluctance is common in domestic violence due to fear, trauma bonding, financial dependence, or hoping abuser will change. Your response: acknowledge her feelings ("I understand this is difficult"), explain your role ("I need to document what happened for your safety"), gather evidence that doesn't depend on her testimony (photograph all injuries from multiple angles, get medical records, obtain statements from medical staff about what she told them, document evidence from scene), and provide resources about protective orders and victim services. Evidence-based prosecution uses your documentation, photos, 911 calls, and medical records rather than relying on victim testimony that may become unavailable. Document her reluctance but continue thorough investigation.

Question 61: You observe a parked vehicle with engine running and occupants inside at 3 AM in business parking lot. You approach for welfare check. Through window you see what appears to be drug paraphernalia on the center console. What's your next step?

A) Leave—no crime observed B) Contraband visible in plain view creates probable cause; you can order occupants out, secure them, and search vehicle under automobile exception C) Need warrant first D) Walk away and pretend you didn't see it

Answer: B **Explanation:** During lawful welfare check approach, you observe contraband in plain view through vehicle windows. All plain view elements met: lawfully positioned (welfare check at parked vehicle), incriminating nature immediately apparent (drug paraphernalia clearly visible), and ability to develop lawful access (order occupants out, secure them, search vehicle). Order occupants out for officer safety, secure them, search vehicle under automobile exception (probable cause from plain view of paraphernalia), seize contraband, arrest for possession of drug paraphernalia and any drugs found, and document exactly what you saw in plain view before ordering occupants out.

Question 62: During booking, you search an arrestee and find a cell phone. Can you search the phone's contents without a warrant?

A) Yes—search incident to arrest covers phones B) No—Riley v. California requires warrant for cell phone searches except in exigent circumstances (imminent threat, evidence about to be destroyed) C) Yes—phones are always searchable incident to arrest D) Only if phone is unlocked

Answer: B **Explanation:** Riley v. California held cell phones require warrants despite arrest. Digital information's sensitive nature and vast storage capacity demand stronger protection. Exception: exigent circumstances (specific belief phone contains information about imminent threat, kidnap victim location, bomb about to detonate, or evidence being remotely wiped). Without exigency, secure phone to prevent remote wiping (Faraday bag or airplane mode), obtain search warrant for phone contents, and document phone's make/model/condition. If you need immediate information due to true exigency, document specific facts justifying exception.

Question 63: You arrest someone for public intoxication. At booking, he provides a false name. You discover the false name through fingerprint comparison. What additional charges apply?

A) None—public intoxication is the only charge B) Failure to identify to peace officer (providing false information), potentially additional charges if false name leads to discovering he's wanted fugitive or has other reasons for false identity C) Only if he eventually admits the false name D) Not criminal to lie about name

Answer: B **Explanation:** Providing false name to peace officer violates failure to identify statute. When fingerprints reveal true identity, you have evidence he intentionally provided false information. Additional considerations: why did he lie? Outstanding warrants under real name? Immigration status? Prior felony conviction affecting current charge? Each factor may add charges or enhance current charges. Document when false name was given, how true identity was discovered, and any additional crimes or warrants revealed by true identity. Add failure to identify charge and pursue any additional charges revealed.

Question 64: You respond to a noise complaint at 2 AM. You knock on apartment door. A female answers, appears intoxicated, and invites you inside to "see there's no problem." Can you enter based on her consent?

A) No—need warrant for all entries B) Yes—resident's consent permits entry; once inside, any contraband or evidence in plain view can be seized C) No—she's intoxicated so consent is invalid D) Only if landlord approves

Answer: B **Explanation:** Resident's consent authorizes entry for legitimate purpose (investigating noise complaint). Her intoxication doesn't automatically invalidate consent unless she's so intoxicated she can't understand what she's consenting to. Once inside with valid consent, any contraband or evidence in plain view can be seized. Document: she appeared to understand she was allowing entry, she voluntarily invited you inside, your purpose was investigating noise complaint, and what you observed in plain view. If you observe evidence suggesting she needs medical attention due to intoxication, render appropriate aid.

Question 65: During a traffic stop, you ask the driver's name. He provides a name but seems uncertain and nervous. You check and find no records under that name. What's your next step?

A) Let him go—no record means no problem B) Ask additional identifying questions (date of birth, address, middle name) to verify identity; his uncertainty and lack of records create reasonable suspicion he's providing false information C) Arrest immediately D) Accept whatever he says

Answer: B **Explanation:** Nervous provision of name that returns no records creates reasonable suspicion of false identification. Ask follow-up questions: "What's your date of birth? Social security number? Current address? Do you have any other ID?" Watch for signs he's fabricating answers (hesitation, inconsistent information, wrong details). No records could mean: he provided false name, his information was entered wrong in system, he's never been stopped before (possible but combined with nervousness suggests false ID). If you can't confirm identity and he can't produce ID, you may not be able to complete traffic stop (need to identify driver to issue citation). Consider detaining while investigating identity, checking DMV photo against person, or arresting for failure to identify if statute applies.

Question 66: You respond to a suicide attempt where the subject has overdosed on pills. He's conscious but lethargic. While waiting for EMS, he says, "I killed my girlfriend. She's in the bedroom." You haven't given Miranda warnings. Is this statement admissible?

A) No—Miranda required before any statement B) Yes—spontaneous statement made without interrogation; rescue situations don't require Miranda for volunteered information C) No—medical emergency means no statements allowed D) Only if he signs a waiver

Answer: B **Explanation:** Spontaneous statements made without police questioning don't require Miranda warnings, even in custody. You're providing emergency medical assistance, not conducting interrogation. He voluntarily provided information without prompting. Document that statement was spontaneous, what you were doing when he spoke (providing medical care), and that you asked no questions prompting this admission. After EMS transports him and he's medically stable, give Miranda before any questioning.

Question 67: During a traffic stop, you ask the driver to step out. As he exits, a bag of white powder falls from his lap onto the ground. What is your legal basis for seizing this evidence?

A) No legal basis—it was inside the vehicle B) Plain view—item fell into plain view during lawful traffic stop; incriminating nature immediately apparent C) Search incident to arrest only D) Need consent to seize it

Answer: B **Explanation:** The bag fell into plain view during a lawful traffic stop (you can order drivers out under Pennsylvania v. Mimms). Once in plain view and recognizable as likely contraband (white powder in bag suggests drugs), you can seize it. You don't need to wait for it to "fall"—the dropping occurred during lawful police-citizen encounter. Seize evidence, field test if appropriate, arrest if probable cause develops that it's controlled substance.

Question 68: You're investigating a burglary. A confidential informant tells you that "John Smith" committed the burglary and the stolen property is in his garage. The informant has provided accurate information twice before. Do you have probable cause for a search warrant?

A) No—informant information alone never creates probable cause B) Yes—reliable informant with track record of accuracy providing specific information about crime and evidence location creates probable cause for warrant C) No—need to see the property yourself first D) Only if informant testifies in court

Answer: B **Explanation:** Reliable informants can provide basis for probable cause. Your affidavit should include: informant's reliability (provided accurate information previously resulting in arrests/convictions), basis of informant's knowledge (how does informant know this information?), specificity of information (exact person, exact location, specific property), and corroboration if available (does victim description match informant information?). This combination creates probable cause sufficient for warrant. Courts evaluate totality of circumstances regarding informant reliability.

Question 69: During a DWI investigation, the suspect agrees to field sobriety tests but performs poorly. Before you can arrest him, he says, "I'm invoking my right to remain silent." Can you still arrest him for DWI?

A) No—he invoked his rights so arrest is not permitted B) Yes—invoking right to remain silent doesn't prevent arrest based on probable cause already developed; it only stops questioning C) No—must let him go D) Only if he changes his mind

Answer: B **Explanation:** Invoking Miranda rights stops questioning but doesn't prevent arrest when you already have probable cause. Your probable cause for DWI arrest is based on: driving observation, physical signs of intoxication, odor of alcohol, admission to drinking, and poor FST performance. These observations occurred before invocation and independently support arrest. Invoking rights doesn't erase probable cause already established. Arrest based on evidence you've gathered, don't question further without Miranda waiver.

Question 70: You're dispatched to a home where parents report their 15-year-old son ran away. They provide his description and say he might be at a friend's house. You locate him at the friend's house. He says he doesn't want to go home. What's your authority?

A) Arrest him for running away B) Texas allows parental custody of juveniles who run away; return juvenile to parents unless abuse/neglect is suspected C) Let him stay—he's almost 16 D) Arrest the friend's parents for harboring a runaway

Answer: B **Explanation:** Running away isn't a crime in Texas, but parents have legal custody of minor children. You have authority to take juvenile into temporary custody and return to parents under Texas Family Code. However, if juvenile alleges abuse or neglect at home, or you observe signs of abuse, don't automatically return him. Investigate claims, document carefully, and consider involving CPS if abuse allegations have merit. Interview juvenile separately from parents about reasons for running away.

Question 71: During a search warrant execution, you find documents written in Spanish that appear to be drug distribution records. You don't read Spanish. Can you seize them?

A) No—you can't read them so can't establish probable cause B) Yes—documents appearing to be records relevant to drug investigation can be seized even if you can't read the language; have them translated later C) No—need translator present during search D) Only if warrant specifically mentions Spanish documents

Answer: B **Explanation:** You don't need to read every word to recognize documents as potentially relevant evidence. Factors suggesting these are drug records: found during drug investigation, format appears to be ledgers/lists, names and numbers visible, location where found (with drugs or money). Seize documents, note in report that they appear to be distribution records in Spanish, and arrange for translation. Evidence doesn't need to be in English to be seized when circumstances suggest relevance to investigation.

Question 72: You stop a vehicle for a traffic violation. The driver appears nervous and you smell air freshener. You ask for consent to search and driver says, "I'd really prefer you didn't, but I guess you're going to anyway, right?" Is this valid consent?

A) Yes—he ultimately consented B) No—statement indicates he believes consent isn't voluntary; this doesn't meet voluntary consent standard C) Yes—he didn't explicitly say no D) Yes—nervousness equals guilt

Answer: B **Explanation:** "I'd really prefer you didn't, but I guess you're going to anyway" demonstrates he doesn't believe he has a real choice. Valid consent must be voluntary—freely given without coercion or belief that refusal is futile. This statement suggests resignation, not voluntary permission. Best practice when someone expresses reluctance: clarify their rights ("You can refuse. I'm asking permission, not telling you I'm searching. Do you voluntarily consent?"). If they refuse, respect that unless you have probable cause for warrantless search.

Question 73: During a domestic violence call, you determine the male is the primary aggressor and place him under arrest. As you're handcuffing him, the female victim attacks you, striking you in the back. What's your response?

A) Ignore it—she's the victim B) Arrest her for assault on a public servant—being a victim doesn't authorize attacking officers C) Let her go with a warning D) Release the male and arrest her instead

Answer: B **Explanation:** Being a crime victim doesn't authorize attacking peace officers. While you understand her emotional state and stress of situation, assault on public servant is a third degree felony that you cannot ignore. Use appropriate force to protect yourself, arrest her for assault on public servant, request additional officers for assistance managing both arrests, document circumstances (she was upset about boyfriend's arrest, struck you while you were arresting him), and ensure both are transported safely. Separate them during transport and booking.

Question 74: You're investigating a burglary and obtain security video showing the suspect's face clearly. You create a photo lineup including the suspect's photo and five fillers. You show the lineup to the victim. What's the proper procedure?

A) Tell victim which photo is the suspect B) Use double-blind procedure if possible; ensure fillers reasonably resemble suspect; tell victim suspect may or may not be present; avoid suggesting which photo to choose; document victim's certainty level C) Only show suspect's photo D) Show photos one at a time starting with suspect

Answer: B **Explanation:** Proper lineup procedure minimizes suggestion and false identification: use double-blind administration (administrator doesn't know which photo is suspect), ensure fillers reasonably match suspect's description, tell witness the suspect may or may not be present (reduces pressure to choose someone), present all photos simultaneously, don't suggest which photo to select, document victim's confidence level in their selection, and avoid confirming or denying accuracy until after identification is made. This protects both defendant's rights and identification reliability.

Question 75: You stop a vehicle for speeding. The driver is a judge from a neighboring jurisdiction. She identifies herself and asks you to "extend professional courtesy." What should you do?

A) Always let judges go—professional courtesy B) Treat the stop the same as any other; professional courtesy doesn't override fair and impartial enforcement; use same discretion you'd use for any driver C) Automatically issue citation to avoid appearance of favoritism D) Call your supervisor to decide

Answer: B **Explanation:** Fair and impartial policing means enforcing laws based on conduct and circumstances, not status or profession. While many officers extend "professional courtesy" to other criminal justice professionals, this can't become automatic favoritism. Use the same discretion you'd use for any driver: consider speed, traffic conditions, safety, explanation, and driving record. Make enforcement decisions based on facts and circumstances, not profession or requests for special treatment. Document your decision-making to show it was based on appropriate factors, not status.

Question 76: During a vehicle pursuit, the suspect crashes and you observe him flee on foot into a residential area. You lose sight of him. Residents report seeing someone matching his description run behind a house. Can you enter the property to search for him?

A) No—need warrant for all property entries B) Yes—hot pursuit of fleeing felon creates exigent circumstances justifying entry to apprehend suspect C) No—pursuit ended when you lost sight D) Only if property owner gives consent

Answer: B **Explanation:** Hot pursuit exception permits warrantless entry to apprehend fleeing felon. You don't lose this authority when suspect temporarily moves out of sight if you're in continuous pursuit. Factors supporting lawful entry: pursuit began with serious offense (depends on what he was fleeing from), pursuit is continuous without significant gaps, you have credible information about suspect's location (witness reports), and delay for warrant would allow escape. Search property systematically, announce your presence and purpose when practical, and clear safely with backup if available.

Question 77: You're interviewing a sexual assault victim. She becomes emotional and has difficulty describing the assault. What's your best approach?

A) Pressure her to give details immediately B) Use trauma-informed approach; allow her to tell story at her own pace; take breaks when needed; explain that while you need information, her wellbeing is important; consider forensic interviewer for detailed questioning C) Tell her to stop crying and just give facts D) Cancel the interview—she's too emotional

Answer: B **Explanation:** Sexual assault victims have experienced trauma requiring sensitive approach. Use trauma-informed techniques: allow her to control pacing, take breaks when she needs them, explain why you need information but prioritize her comfort, avoid victim-blaming language or questions, offer victim advocate presence, and consider having a specially trained sexual assault investigator or forensic interviewer conduct detailed interview. Don't minimize her emotional state—it's normal trauma response. Document what she reports but recognize re-traumatization risk from repeated detailed questioning. Balance investigation needs with victim wellbeing.

Question 78: During a traffic stop, you run the driver's information and discover an active protective order prohibiting him from possessing firearms. You see a rifle case in the back seat. Can you seize the rifle?

A) No—need warrant for items in vehicles B) Yes—protective order violation (possessing firearm while subject to order) creates probable cause; rifle case in plain view during lawful stop allows seizure C) No—rifle cases are legal D) Only if he admits there's a gun inside

Answer: B **Explanation:** Protective orders typically prohibit firearm possession (both federal law 18 USC 922(g)(8) and Texas law). Rifle case in plain view + knowledge that person is subject to protective order = probable cause that case contains firearm illegally possessed. Seize case, verify it contains firearm, arrest for protective order violation and unlawful firearm possession, document the protective order information, and note where case was visible. Even if case is empty, person's possession of it combined with protective order creates reasonable basis for investigating further.

Question 79: You respond to a call of a disturbance at a bar. Multiple intoxicated people are arguing but no physical violence has occurred. The bar owner asks you to remove certain individuals. What's your authority?

A) Automatically remove everyone the owner identifies B) Evaluate whether individuals are committing criminal offenses (public intoxication, disorderly conduct, trespass); business owner can refuse service and ask people to leave; if they refuse after being asked to leave by owner and you, arrest for criminal trespass C) Remove no one—no crime occurred D) Remove only the most intoxicated person

Answer: B **Explanation:** Business owners have right to refuse service and ask people to leave for any non-discriminatory reason. If someone refuses to leave after owner requests and you inform them they must leave, they're criminally trespassing (entering or remaining without consent after notice). Evaluate each person individually: are they committing criminal offenses (public intoxication, disorderly conduct)? Did owner specifically ask them to leave? Did they refuse? Give clear verbal notice that they must leave or face arrest for trespass. If they comply, no arrest. If they refuse, arrest for criminal trespass. Document owner's request and individuals' responses.

Question 80: You're investigating a theft and have probable cause to arrest a suspect. When you contact him, he immediately says, "I need to tell you something—my brother forced me to help him steal that stuff. He threatened me." You haven't given Miranda warnings. Is this admissible?

A) No—Miranda required before all statements B) Yes—spontaneous statement made before any interrogation; document that he initiated the statement voluntarily when you contacted him C) No—he's making an excuse so it's not reliable D) Only if you immediately Mirandize him

Answer: B **Explanation:** He spontaneously provided information without your questioning. You can listen to spontaneous statements without Miranda warnings. However, if you want to ask follow-up questions about his statement, give Miranda warnings first. Document carefully: what you said when you contacted him (just that you needed to speak with him? Told him he was under arrest?), his immediate voluntary statement, that you didn't ask questions prompting this response, and exact words he used. This becomes important because his statement suggests duress defense—he claims he was forced to participate by threats from his brother.

Question 81: During a traffic stop, you notice the passenger is very nervous and sweating. Can you order the passenger out of the vehicle based solely on nervousness?

A) No—need reasonable suspicion specific to the passenger B) Yes—Maryland v. Wilson allows officers to order passengers out during lawful traffic stops for officer safety without additional justification C) No—only drivers can be ordered out D) Only if passenger matches a wanted person description

Answer: B **Explanation:** Maryland v. Wilson extends Pennsylvania v. Mimms to passengers—you can order passengers out of vehicle during traffic stop for officer safety without needing additional reasonable suspicion. Once passenger is out, if you have reasonable suspicion he's armed and dangerous, you can conduct Terry frisk. Nervousness alone doesn't create reasonable suspicion for frisk, but combined with other factors (suspicious movements, bulges in clothing, known gang member, high-crime area) might justify protective pat-down for weapons.

Question 82: You're executing a search warrant at a residence. Inside, you encounter a person who says she's just visiting and doesn't live there. Can you search her purse?

A) Yes—warrant covers everyone and everything inside B) No—warrant authorizes searching the premises, not personal belongings of visitors who aren't named in warrant; need separate probable cause or consent to search her purse C) Yes—she's present so you can search anything D) Only if she acts suspiciously

Answer: B **Explanation:** Search warrants authorize searching the premises and items/areas where evidence described in warrant might be located. They don't automatically authorize searching personal belongings of visitors unless those items could contain evidence described in warrant. If warrant describes small drugs that could fit in purse, you might be able to search it. If warrant describes stolen televisions, you can't search purse. If you have separate probable cause she's involved in the crime or purse contains evidence, you can search. Otherwise, you can detain her during warrant execution (Michigan v. Summers) but can't search her personal property without additional justification.

Question 83: During a DWI investigation, the suspect refuses all testing including FSTs and chemical testing. Can you obtain a warrant for blood draw?

A) No—his refusal means you can't test B) Yes—when probable cause exists for DWI and suspect refuses testing, you can seek warrant for blood draw; refusal doesn't eliminate your authority to seek warrant C) No—warrants can't be used for blood draws D) Only if he's been in an accident

Answer: B **Explanation:** Missouri v. McNeely held that natural dissipation of alcohol alone doesn't create exigency justifying warrantless blood draw. However, it doesn't prohibit warranted blood draws. If you have probable cause for DWI (based on driving behavior, physical indicators, odor, failed or refused FSTs), you can seek warrant for blood draw. Texas Transportation Code also requires blood draw in certain circumstances (accidents causing death or serious injury, child passenger). Present probable cause to magistrate, obtain warrant, and execute blood draw by qualified medical personnel. Document refusal and warrant process.

Question 84: You respond to a shoplifting call. Store security has detained a juvenile (age 15) who concealed merchandise. The juvenile's parents aren't present. Can you question the juvenile about the theft?

A) Yes—same as adults B) No—juveniles cannot be questioned without parents present; take juvenile into custody, notify parents, and wait for parents or attorney before questioning C) Yes—but only if he waives rights D) Only about basic identifying information

Answer: B **Explanation:** Texas Family Code provides enhanced protections for juveniles. While you can ask basic identifying information, custodial interrogation of juveniles requires additional safeguards beyond Miranda: parent or guardian must be present, attorney may be required depending on circumstances, and juvenile must understand rights given their age and maturity. Don't question juvenile about offense details without parents present and proper advisement. Take juvenile into custody (not "arrest"—different terminology for juveniles), notify parents immediately, document circumstances, and defer detailed questioning until parents arrive and proper procedures are followed.

Question 85: During a vehicle search, you find a small amount of marijuana and a large amount of cash ($15,000). The driver claims the money is from his legitimate business and has no connection to drugs. Can you seize the cash?

A) No—cash is legal and you can't prove it's drug-related B) Yes—large amount of cash found with drugs creates reasonable inference of drug proceeds; seize cash for evidence and potential forfeiture, though driver can challenge seizure in civil proceedings C) No—need to prove beyond reasonable doubt it's drug money D) Only if driver admits it's drug money

Answer: B **Explanation:** Large amounts of cash found with drugs, drug paraphernalia, or in circumstances suggesting drug activity can be seized as evidence of drug trafficking and for potential civil forfeiture. At seizure stage, you need reasonable basis to believe cash is connected to drug activity, not proof beyond reasonable doubt. Factors supporting seizure: cash found with drugs, large amount for someone to carry, denominations typical of drug sales (small bills), no documentation of legitimate source. Driver can challenge seizure through civil forfeiture proceedings where government must prove connection to illegal activity. Document everything: exact amount, denominations, where found, proximity to drugs, and any explanations driver provides.

Question 86: You're dispatched to a mental health facility for an escaped patient. The patient is described as "non-violent but confused." You locate him walking down the street, not bothering anyone. Can you take him into custody?

A) No—he's not committing a crime B) Yes—Texas Health & Safety Code Chapter 573 authorizes emergency detention when person appears to be mentally ill and presents danger to self/others or is unable to care for basic needs; coordinate with mental health professionals C) Yes—but only with facility administrator permission D) No—only mental health workers can detain mental patients

Answer: B **Explanation:** Emergency detention under Texas Health & Safety Code allows peace officers to take persons into custody for mental health evaluation when they appear to be mentally ill and meet certain criteria: present danger to themselves or others, or unable to provide for basic needs due to mental illness. "Escaped patient" status combined with facility information that he's "confused" suggests he may meet criteria. Take him to designated mental health facility (not jail), complete required paperwork, coordinate with mental health professionals, and don't treat this as criminal arrest. This is medical intervention, not law enforcement action. Document observations supporting belief he needed emergency detention.

Question 87: During a traffic stop, the driver provides a passport showing he's in the country legally. However, the vehicle is registered to someone else and driver provides evasive answers about vehicle ownership. What additional investigation is appropriate?

A) None—he has legal status so ignore vehicle issues B) Investigate vehicle ownership; ask about relationship to registered owner, permission to drive vehicle, where he's going and coming from; check for stolen vehicle; evasive answers about vehicle create reasonable suspicion C) Let him go—passports are sufficient D) Arrest him immediately for vehicle theft

Answer: B **Explanation:** Legal immigration status doesn't affect your authority to investigate potential vehicle crimes. Discrepancy between driver and vehicle registration plus evasive answers creates reasonable suspicion warranting further investigation. Ask clarifying questions: relationship to owner, permission to use vehicle, contact information for owner, where he's going. Run vehicle for stolen status. If answers remain evasive or inconsistent, your suspicion increases. If he can verify legitimate possession (calls owner who confirms permission), complete traffic stop normally. If he can't verify or vehicle is stolen, arrest for unauthorized use of vehicle or theft. Document everything supporting your investigation and decisions.

Question 88: You're investigating a robbery where the victim was injured. At the hospital, the victim makes a statement identifying the suspect and describing the robbery. The victim then goes into surgery and dies from their injuries. Is the victim's statement admissible?

A) No—hearsay that can't be used B) Yes—dying declarations and excited utterances can be admissible; victim's statement made shortly after traumatic event, before opportunity to fabricate, may qualify as excited utterance; document thoroughly C) No—victim must testify in person D) Only if recorded on video

Answer: B **Explanation:** Several hearsay exceptions may apply: excited utterance (statement made while under stress of startling event, before opportunity to fabricate), dying declaration (in limited circumstances), or statement for medical diagnosis/treatment. For excited utterance, factors include: timing (how soon after event?), victim's condition (still under stress?), spontaneity (volunteered or in response to questioning?). Document meticulously: exact words victim used, victim's demeanor and condition, who was present, circumstances of statement, your observations showing victim was still under stress of event. This documentation helps prosecutors establish foundation for admissibility. The fact victim later died makes this statement critical evidence and increases importance of thorough documentation.

Question 89: During a search incident to arrest, you handcuff the suspect and place him in your patrol car. Your partner is securing the scene. Can you search the suspect's cell phone found in his pocket?

A) Yes—search incident to arrest covers cell phones B) No—Riley v. California requires warrant to search cell phone contents even incident to arrest; you can secure phone to prevent remote wiping, but need warrant to search contents C) Yes—cell phones are just like any other item D) Only if you see illegal content on the screen

Answer: B **Explanation:** Riley v. California (2014) held that cell phones require warrants to search contents, even when found during search incident to lawful arrest. Cell phones contain massive amounts of personal information requiring greater privacy protection than physical items. You can seize phone to prevent destruction of evidence (put in airplane mode, turn off, or use Faraday bag to prevent remote wiping), but need warrant to search through calls, texts, photos, apps, etc. Document phone's make/model, where found, and your actions to preserve evidence. Obtain warrant based on probable cause that phone contains evidence of the crime. Exception: exigent circumstances like kidnapping victim whose life is in danger and phone might reveal location.

Question 90: You respond to a domestic violence call. When you arrive, the door is slightly open and you hear sounds of a struggle inside. Can you enter without a warrant?

A) No—need warrant for all home entries B) Yes—emergency aid exception and exigent circumstances (sounds of ongoing violence, open door suggesting emergency) justify immediate entry to protect victim C) No—knock first and wait for answer D) Only if neighbor confirms violence

Answer: B **Explanation:** Sounds of struggle, partially open door, and domestic violence call create exigent circumstances and emergency aid exception justifying immediate warrantless entry. Someone inside is in danger requiring immediate assistance. Announce your presence if practical ("Police! We're coming in!"), but don't delay entry if violence is ongoing. Once inside, separate parties, assess for injuries, determine what occurred, identify primary aggressor, make arrests if probable cause exists, and document circumstances justifying entry (sounds heard, door position, victim's injuries and statements). Your duty to preserve life outweighs need for warrant in emergency situations.

Question 91: During a vehicle pursuit, you observe the suspect drive through a crowded pedestrian area at high speed, narrowly missing several people. The pursuit continues and you lose sight of the vehicle. Later, you locate the vehicle (unoccupied) in a parking lot. Can you search the vehicle?

A) No—pursuit ended when you lost sight B) Yes—probable cause exists that vehicle was used in commission of crimes (evading, reckless endangerment) and contains evidence; automobile exception permits warrantless search C) No—need warrant for all vehicle searches D) Only if you find the driver

Answer: B **Explanation:** Probable cause that vehicle was used in crimes (evading arrest, reckless endangerment by driving through pedestrian area) creates authority to search for evidence under automobile exception. Potential evidence includes: driver identification information, items connecting specific person to vehicle during pursuit, evidence of ownership, drugs/alcohol suggesting impairment, weapons. You don't need to locate driver before searching vehicle—the vehicle itself contains evidence of crimes committed. Document: pursuit details, dangerous driving observed, vehicle location when found, items seized during search. Pursue driver identification through vehicle registration, fingerprints on steering wheel, or security video if available.

Question 92: You're investigating child abuse allegations. The child (age 7) describes abuse but uses anatomically correct terminology and sophisticated descriptions that seem unusual for that age. What should you consider?

A) Child is lying—kids don't talk like that B) Possible prior forensic interview, coaching, or exposure to adult discussions; document exact language, note sophistication, and strongly recommend forensic interview specialist evaluation C) Accept it at face value—smart kid D) Ignore the terminology

Answer: B **Explanation:** Unusual sophistication in child's language warrants careful consideration of several possibilities: previous forensic interviews where child learned correct terminology, coaching by parent or other adult (suggesting possible false allegation), exposure to adult conversations about the abuse, or advanced child who learned terminology from school/books. This doesn't mean abuse didn't occur—it means the case needs expert evaluation. Document child's exact words, note any unusually sophisticated terminology or descriptions, avoid asking leading questions, and request forensic interview by specially trained child abuse interviewer. Forensic interviewers are trained to distinguish coached responses from genuine disclosures and can evaluate reliability of child's statements using proper techniques.

Question 93: During a traffic stop, you discover the driver has multiple prior DWI convictions. You smell alcohol but driver performs adequately on field sobriety tests. Do you have probable cause for DWI arrest?

A) Yes—prior DWIs mean he's guilty now B) No—adequate FST performance suggests he's not currently impaired; prior convictions don't create current probable cause; need evidence of present intoxication C) Yes—smell of alcohol is always probable cause D) Arrest him based on prior record only

Answer: B **Explanation:** Prior convictions are relevant for charging and sentencing but don't create probable cause for current offense. You need evidence of present intoxication: loss of normal use of faculties OR BAC .08+. Factors to evaluate: How was driving? How strong was alcohol odor? What's his appearance and behavior? FST performance? Admission to drinking? If FSTs were performed adequately, driving was normal, and only indicator is slight alcohol odor, you may not have probable cause. Consider: some people can drink small amounts without impairment; odor alone isn't illegal. Document all observations. If probable cause doesn't exist, complete traffic stop and release. His prior history means future encounters will be scrutinized carefully, but don't arrest without current probable cause.

Question 94: You're executing a search warrant for drugs. Inside, you find a locked safe. The warrant describes drugs, money, and drug records. Can you force open the safe?

A) No—warrant doesn't specifically mention safe B) Yes—safe could contain items described in warrant (drugs, money, records all fit in safes); forcing entry is within warrant's scope, though documenting efforts to obtain combination first is best practice C) No—need separate warrant for safe D) Only if suspect volunteers the combination

Answer: B **Explanation:** Search warrant scope is determined by items sought, not specific containers. If safe could reasonably contain items described in warrant (drugs, money, records), you can open it. Best practice: ask for combination first, document refusal if any, then force entry if necessary. Photograph safe before and after opening. Document what's found inside. Note safe's location. If suspect later claims you damaged safe unnecessarily without asking for combination, your documentation shows you acted reasonably. Some departments require supervisor approval before forcing entry to safes or using specialized tools—follow your policy.

Question 95: During a domestic violence call, the female victim has visible injuries but insists she "fell down stairs." The male subject has no injuries and supports her story. No witnesses. You suspect domestic violence but victim denies it. What should you do?

A) Accept her explanation and leave B) Document thoroughly; photograph injuries; note inconsistencies between injuries and explanation; check for prior domestic calls to this address; explain why you're concerned; provide victim resources; make arrest if evidence contradicts "fall" story despite her denial C) Force her to admit the truth D) Arrest the male automatically

Answer: B **Explanation:** Victims often deny domestic violence due to fear, financial dependence, or emotional attachment. Your role is documenting evidence, not accepting denials at face value. Thoroughly photograph all injuries from multiple angles. Document: injury locations (defensive wounds on forearms? injuries inconsistent with falls?), victim's exact explanation, subject's demeanor, prior calls to this address, your observations, and reasons for suspicion. If injuries are clearly inconsistent with fall explanation (facial injuries, defensive wounds, pattern suggesting intentional infliction), you may have probable cause for arrest despite denials. Provide victim resources and safety planning. Explain that false reporting wastes resources, but acknowledge that fear is understandable. Create detailed documentation for potential future prosecution when victim is ready to cooperate.

Question 96: You're investigating a robbery where video shows suspect's face clearly, but you don't recognize him. Can you publish the video on social media asking public for identification assistance?

A) Yes—always post everything publicly B) Depends on department policy and legal guidance; many departments now use social media for suspect identification, but consider: privacy concerns, accuracy of identification, potential for vigilante action, and proper procedures for publishing images C) No—never publish suspect images D) Only if suspect consents

Answer: B **Explanation:** Social media has become valuable investigative tool for identifying suspects, but requires careful consideration. Factors to consider: Does your department have social media policy? Does legal counsel approve? Is video quality sufficient for reliable identification? Are you requesting identification only or asking public to contact/apprehend (latter is dangerous)? Include disclaimers about not taking action against suspects. Monitor responses and verify identifications through proper investigation. Document source of identification. Use this to develop probable cause, not as sole basis for arrest. Social media identifications can be unreliable—confirm through traditional investigation before acting.

Question 97: During a search incident to arrest, you find a piece of paper with what appears to be a name, phone number, and dollar amount. The arrest is for possession of marijuana. Is this paper relevant evidence?

A) No—just a paper with numbers B) Yes—could be evidence of drug sales; seize as potential evidence of distribution, document where found, photograph it, include in evidence inventory C) No—throw it away D) Only if amounts match drugs found

Answer: B **Explanation:** Any documentation found during drug arrests could be evidence of distribution: customer lists, debt records, sales records, supplier contacts. Name + phone number + dollar amount suggests transaction record. Even if arrest is for simple possession, this paper might support enhanced charge of possession with intent to deliver or sale of controlled substance. Seize as evidence, photograph it, document exact location found (pocket? wallet?), include in property inventory, and note in report as potential evidence of drug sales. Investigators can follow up on name and phone number. Dollar amount might correspond to typical drug sale prices. This seemingly minor piece of paper could transform simple possession into more serious distribution charges.

Question 98: You're investigating a suspicious death. The body shows signs of trauma, but the spouse claims the person "fell down the stairs." The scene appears staged—furniture is positioned oddly, and the injuries don't match a simple fall. What's your immediate responsibility?

A) Accept the spouse's explanation and document it as accidental death B) Treat as potential homicide: preserve scene, separate spouse from scene, request detectives and crime scene investigators, document inconsistencies, obtain detailed statement from spouse C) Arrest spouse immediately D) Clean up the scene to help the family

Answer: B **Explanation:** Suspicious circumstances (injuries inconsistent with explanation, staged scene appearance, unusual positioning) require treating this as potential homicide until investigation proves otherwise. Preserve scene integrity, prevent contamination, separate potential suspect from scene, request specialized units (homicide detectives, CSI), document all observations about inconsistencies, and obtain detailed statement from spouse documenting their account. Better to investigate thoroughly and determine it was accidental than to accept explanation and miss homicide evidence.

Question 99: During a traffic stop, you ask the driver to step out of the vehicle for officer safety. The driver refuses, stating "I know my rights. I don't have to get out." What's legally accurate?

A) Driver is correct—cannot be ordered out without probable cause B) Pennsylvania v. Mimms allows officers to order drivers out of vehicles during lawful traffic stops for officer safety without additional justification C) Only passengers can be ordered out D) Need supervisor permission to order driver out

Answer: B **Explanation:** Pennsylvania v. Mimms (1977) and Maryland v. Wilson (1997) authorize officers to order drivers and passengers out of vehicles during lawful traffic stops for officer safety, without needing additional reasonable suspicion or probable cause. The traffic stop itself provides sufficient justification. Driver's refusal after lawful order can constitute obstruction. Explain the law calmly, issue lawful command again, and if continued refusal, consider appropriate enforcement action for obstruction while maintaining professional demeanor.

Question 100: You arrest a suspect for aggravated assault. During booking, he asks "What's going to happen to me?" Before you can respond, he continues, "I didn't mean to hurt him that bad. I just wanted to scare him." You haven't given Miranda warnings. Is his statement admissible?

A) No—all statements by arrested persons require Miranda B) His question was procedural, not interrogation; his follow-up statement was spontaneous elaboration not prompted by your questioning; likely admissible as spontaneous statement C) No—you should have stopped him from talking D) Yes—but only the question, not the admission

Answer: B **Explanation:** His initial question sought procedural information. Before you responded or asked anything, he voluntarily continued with incriminating statement. You didn't interrogate him or say/do anything designed to elicit this response. This spontaneous elaboration following his own question, not police interrogation, doesn't require Miranda warnings. Document precisely: his question, that you didn't respond before his admission, and that statement was unprompted. If you had asked follow-up questions after his admission without Miranda, those responses would be inadmissible, but this initial spontaneous statement is admissible.

Scenario-Based Questions Section (50 Questions)

These 50 questions exclusively test your ability to apply knowledge to realistic field situations. Unlike simple recall questions, scenarios require analysis, priority-setting, and practical decision-making under pressure. This section mirrors the TCOLE exam's emphasis on real-world application. Read each scenario completely before reviewing answer options. Consider all factors presented. Choose the BEST answer that demonstrates sound judgment, legal compliance, and officer safety. Some scenarios have multiple reasonable responses—choose the most complete or most appropriate option.

Scenario 1: You're dispatched to a residence for a welfare check on an elderly female. Neighbors haven't seen her in three days, and she's not answering the door despite her vehicle being present. You knock repeatedly with no response. You look through windows and see what appears to be someone lying on the floor motionless. What is your best course of action?

A) Leave and advise neighbors to call family members B) Make forced entry based on exigent circumstances (emergency aid exception); someone appears injured and in need of immediate assistance C) Wait for supervisor to arrive and make decision D) Get a warrant first

Answer: B **Explanation:** Emergency aid exception permits warrantless entry when someone inside appears to need immediate assistance. Motionless person visible through window combined with failure to respond to door knocks and three-day absence creates reasonable belief emergency exists. Every minute delayed could cost a life. Make entry, check on person, render aid, and document circumstances justifying entry. Waiting for supervisor or warrant could result in death if person needs immediate medical attention.

Scenario 2: During a traffic stop, you ask for consent to search. The driver says, "No, I don't consent." His passenger immediately says, "It's fine, officer, go ahead and search." Can you search based on passenger's consent?

A) Yes—passenger gave consent B) No—passenger doesn't have authority to consent to search of vehicle he doesn't own or control; driver (who has control) explicitly refused consent C) Yes—either occupant can consent D) Search anyway without consent

Answer: B **Explanation:** Vehicle searches require consent from someone with actual or apparent authority—typically owner or driver in control. Passengers generally lack authority to consent to vehicle searches unless they have ownership or control. Driver explicitly refused, which is controlling. Passenger's subsequent "consent" doesn't override driver's refusal. Without consent, you need probable cause or warrant to search.

Scenario 3: You arrest a suspect for aggravated assault. During transport, before Miranda warnings, he asks, "What's going to happen to me?" How should you respond?

A) "You're going to prison for a long time" B) "I can't discuss that with you right now. When we get to jail, you'll be booked and taken before a magistrate who will explain the charges and process" (basic information about procedure without eliciting incriminating statements) C) "Tell me what happened and I'll see what I can do" D) Ignore him completely

Answer: B **Explanation:** His question seeks procedural information, not trying to confess or make statements. You can provide basic information about booking process without Miranda because you're not interrogating. However, be careful not to turn this into interrogation. Don't ask questions or make statements designed to elicit incriminating responses. If he voluntarily makes spontaneous statements, listen and document, but don't prompt or encourage them before Miranda.

Scenario 4: You're on patrol at 2 AM and observe a vehicle parked in a closed business parking lot with engine running and lights on. You approach for a welfare check and see someone slumped over the steering wheel. When you knock on the window, the person startles awake. You detect strong alcohol odor when he rolls down the window. What probable cause issues might you face for DWI?

A) No issues—he's clearly intoxicated B) Must establish he "operated" the vehicle—being found in parked vehicle with engine running while intoxicated creates inference of operation, but he might claim he wasn't driving, vehicle was already there when he fell asleep C) No probable cause exists D) Arrest him immediately without question

Answer: B **Explanation:** Texas courts recognize that being found in driver's seat of running vehicle while intoxicated creates inference of operation. However, defendants can argue they weren't driving—someone else drove, they fell asleep after parking, etc. Strengthen your case by: asking where he came from (admission of driving), checking hood for warmth (indicates recent operation), looking for witnesses, noting key location (in ignition suggests operation). Document all observations supporting operation. While you likely have probable cause, anticipate defense arguments.

Scenario 5: During a search warrant execution for drugs, you find no drugs but discover extensive firearms collection including what appear to be illegal suppressors and short-barrel rifles. The warrant only authorizes searching for drugs. Can you seize the firearms?

A) No—warrant doesn't cover firearms B) Yes—if firearms are in plain view during lawful search for drugs and you recognize them as illegal, plain view doctrine permits seizure C) No—need separate warrant for firearms D) Only if drugs are also found

Answer: B **Explanation:** While executing warrant for drugs, if you observe items in plain view that you immediately recognize as contraband or evidence of different crime (illegal firearms), plain view doctrine permits seizure. You're lawfully present executing valid warrant, firearms' incriminating nature is immediately apparent to someone with your training (suppressors require federal registration, short barrels typically illegal), and you have lawful access. Seize firearms, document where found, note they were observed during lawful drug search, and include in supplemental report.

Scenario 6: You stop a vehicle for speeding. The driver appears extremely nervous, gives inconsistent answers, and you smell air freshener. You request consent to search. Driver says, "I'd rather you didn't." You respond, "Well, if you have nothing to hide, why not let me search?" Driver then says, "Fine, go ahead." Can you search?

A) Yes—he consented B) Questionable—your response suggesting refusal implies guilt may have coerced consent; best practice is accept refusal and complete traffic stop C) Yes—you asked politely D) No—first response was refusal

Answer: B **Explanation:** When someone declines consent ("I'd rather you didn't"), best practice is accept that response and complete the traffic stop. Continuing to pressure them by suggesting refusal implies guilt ("if you have nothing to hide") may coerce consent, making it involuntary. While technically he then consented, a court might find your continued pressure after initial refusal invalidated voluntariness. When someone declines, accept it. If you have probable cause, search anyway. If not, complete stop and release driver.

Scenario 7: You're dispatched to a domestic disturbance. Upon arrival, the female victim has visible injuries and states her boyfriend "beat her up." Before you can arrest the boyfriend, he says, "I want to tell you what really happened. She attacked me first." You haven't given Miranda warnings. Can you listen to his explanation?

A) No—must give Miranda first before he can speak B) Yes—he initiated conversation voluntarily; listen to his statement, but don't ask follow-up questions without Miranda C) No—arrest him immediately and ignore anything he says D) Only if you give Miranda first

Answer: B **Explanation:** He voluntarily initiated the conversation without your questioning. You can listen to his spontaneous statement. However, once he starts talking, don't ask follow-up questions or engage in interrogation without Miranda warnings. If you want to question him about details, give Miranda first. Document that he voluntarily initiated the statement without prompting from you. Spontaneous statements don't require Miranda, but interrogation does.

Scenario 8: During a vehicle search, you find suspected methamphetamine. The driver says it's "just meth for personal use—I'm not a dealer." You're holding the drugs when he says this. Must you give Miranda before he makes this statement?

A) Yes—he's in custody B) No—you didn't question him; his statement was spontaneous response to your discovery of drugs C) Yes—all statements by arrested persons need Miranda D) Only if you arrest him

Answer: B **Explanation:** Finding drugs isn't interrogation—it's investigative action. His spontaneous response to your discovery doesn't require Miranda. You didn't ask questions or do anything designed to elicit incriminating response. If you want to ask follow-up questions about the statement, then Miranda becomes necessary. Document that statement was spontaneous, what prompted it (finding drugs), and that you didn't question him before the statement.

Scenario 9: You respond to a burglary alarm at a jewelry store at 3 AM. You observe the front door has been forced open. You hear noises inside. Can you enter without a warrant?

A) No—need warrant even for businesses B) Yes—exigent circumstances (crime in progress, possible suspect still inside, evidence may be destroyed) and hot pursuit of burglary in progress justify warrantless entry C) No—wait for owner to arrive D) Only with supervisor approval

Answer: B **Explanation:** Burglary in progress with forced entry and sounds of movement inside create exigent circumstances justifying immediate warrantless entry. Waiting for warrant risks: suspect escaping with stolen property, evidence destruction, danger to other officers arriving (suspect could ambush them). You have both hot pursuit of felony in progress and exigent circumstances. Enter tactically, clear building, apprehend any suspects, secure scene, then obtain warrant if further searching needed beyond plain view.

Scenario 10: You're investigating a sexual assault. The victim provides detailed account and identifies suspect. When you interview the suspect, he says, "I want to cooperate and clear this up. Yes, we had sex, but it was consensual." You haven't given Miranda warnings yet. Is his statement admissible?

A) No—Miranda required before discussing the case B) Depends—is he in custody? If this is non-custodial interview and he's free to leave, Miranda not required. If he's under arrest or not free to leave (custody), Miranda required C) Yes—he volunteered information D) No—all suspect statements need Miranda

Answer: B **Explanation:** Admissibility depends on custody status. If you contacted him, he voluntarily came to station for interview, and reasonable person would feel free to leave, this is non-custodial and Miranda isn't required. If he's under arrest or wouldn't feel free to leave (surrounded by officers, told not to leave, etc.), it's custodial and requires Miranda. Document circumstances showing whether encounter was custodial: was he told he could leave? Was he restrained? How did interview begin?

Scenario 11: During a traffic stop, the driver produces a medical marijuana card from another state showing authorization to possess marijuana. You find marijuana in his vehicle. Can you seize it and arrest him?

A) No—medical marijuana card makes possession legal B) Yes—Texas doesn't recognize out-of-state medical marijuana authorization; possession remains illegal in Texas regardless of other states' laws C) No—federal law permits medical marijuana D) Only if amount exceeds his prescription

Answer: B **Explanation:** Texas law controls what's legal in Texas. Out-of-state medical marijuana authorizations don't provide legal defense for marijuana possession in Texas. Federal law still classifies marijuana as Schedule I controlled substance with no accepted medical use. Even if his home state authorized medical marijuana, possessing it in Texas violates Texas law. Seize marijuana, arrest for possession, document his out-of-state card (shows knowing possession), and note that Texas doesn't recognize the authorization.

Scenario 12: You're conducting a welfare check on an elderly person. A family member opens the door and gives consent for you to enter and check on the person. Inside, you observe in plain view on kitchen table what appears to be cocaine and a scale. Can you seize these items?

A) No—you're there for welfare check, not drug investigation B) Yes—you're lawfully present with consent, items are in plain view, and incriminating nature is immediately apparent; plain view doctrine permits seizure C) No—need warrant for drug seizure D) Only if the person you're checking on is harmed

Answer: B **Explanation:** Plain view requirements met: lawfully present (consent from resident for welfare check), immediately apparent incriminating nature (cocaine and scale visible), and lawful access. You don't need separate warrant or investigation authority. Seize evidence, complete welfare check, document observations, explain to family member that you discovered evidence requiring action, and pursue drug charges separately from welfare check results.

Scenario 13: You arrest someone for DWI. At booking, he refuses to provide fingerprints, stating "I don't consent to anything." Can you force fingerprinting?

A) No—he refused consent B) Yes—fingerprinting arrested persons doesn't require consent; it's standard booking procedure for identification and criminal history purposes C) No—need warrant for fingerprints D) Only if he's convicted

Answer: B **Explanation:** Fingerprinting isn't a search requiring consent or warrant—it's administrative booking procedure for identifying arrestees and checking criminal history. Supreme Court has upheld fingerprinting as minimally intrusive identification procedure. Use reasonable force if necessary to obtain fingerprints. Document refusal, force used if any, and that fingerprinting is standard procedure not requiring consent. This differs from searches for evidence, which do require legal justification.

Scenario 14: During pursuit, the suspect crashes into a pole. You approach and find him unconscious with visible injuries. What are your immediate priorities?

A) Search his vehicle for evidence while he's unconscious B) Render medical aid immediately, request ambulance, ensure scene safety, then investigate crash and pursuit C) Complete arrest paperwork first D) Question him about the pursuit

Answer: B **Explanation:** Life safety is paramount. Render immediate medical aid (ABCs—airway, breathing, circulation), request ambulance with priority dispatch, ensure scene safety (traffic control, fire hazards), and stay with injured person until medical arrives. After medical needs addressed, investigate crash and pursuit. Evidence collection, arrest procedures, and questioning come after ensuring person doesn't die. Your duty to preserve life applies even to suspects who fled from you. Document medical aid provided.

Scenario 15: You're interviewing a witness to a robbery. The witness is extremely nervous and gives vague descriptions. You suspect he might be involved but isn't admitting it. What's your best approach?

A) Arrest him immediately for the robbery B) Continue interview, note his nervous behavior and vague responses, ask detailed questions to assess whether nervousness is from being witness or participant, potentially convert to suspect interview with Miranda if evidence develops C) Let him go without documenting anything D) Threaten him with arrest to get better information

Answer: B **Explanation:** Nervousness doesn't equal guilt—many honest witnesses are nervous. Continue professional interview, ask detailed questions (where exactly were you standing? What did you see first? Describe suspect's clothing. What happened next?). Detailed questions reveal whether person actually witnessed events or is fabricating. If evidence suggests he's suspect rather than witness (can't answer details, knows too much about suspect's actions, contradictions), consider stopping witness interview and converting to suspect interview with Miranda. Document nervous behavior and reasons for concern without assuming guilt.

Scenario 16: You stop a vehicle with three occupants. You smell marijuana and see roach in ashtray. Driver, front passenger, and rear passenger all deny ownership. Can you arrest all three?

A) Yes—all have constructive possession based on presence in vehicle with marijuana B) Driver has strongest case for arrest (control of vehicle and contents); passengers more difficult to prove knowing possession unless additional evidence C) No—can't prove who possessed it D) Arrest only the person sitting closest to the marijuana

Answer: B **Explanation:** Driver has control of vehicle and everything in it, creating strongest case for constructive possession. Passengers are more difficult—mere presence isn't enough for constructive possession; need knowledge of presence plus control or access. Consider additional factors: whose vehicle? Who appears nervous? Body language? Prior statements? If marijuana easily accessible to all, all might have constructive possession. If only driver could access it, only driver has possession. Document observations about each person's behavior and relationship to contraband location.

Scenario 17: During a domestic violence call, the victim begs you not to arrest her boyfriend, stating "He'll lose his job and we can't pay rent." You have probable cause for assault. What should you do?

A) Don't arrest—respect victim's wishes B) Arrest based on probable cause; victim cooperation preferences don't control enforcement decisions when probable cause exists C) Wait and see if it happens again D) Arrest only if supervisor approves

Answer: B **Explanation:** Your duty is enforcing law based on probable cause, not victim preferences. Victims often don't want arrest due to financial dependence, fear, emotional attachment, or belief abuser will change. These factors don't eliminate your arrest authority when probable cause exists. Make arrest, document victim's statement about not wanting arrest (important for prosecution understanding of case dynamics), provide victim resources and safety planning, and request emergency protective order. Victim's initial reluctance doesn't mean prosecution won't succeed—evidence-based prosecution uses your documentation, photos, 911 calls, and other evidence.

Scenario 18: You're executing a search warrant for stolen property. In the garage, you find stolen televisions listed in the warrant. Next to them are tools with serial numbers filed off. The warrant doesn't mention tools. Can you seize them?

A) No—warrant doesn't cover tools B) Yes—tools with removed serial numbers are contraband (possessing them is crime) in plain view during lawful search; seize under plain view doctrine C) No—need separate warrant D) Only if tools are also listed as stolen

Answer: B **Explanation:** Tools with filed-off serial numbers are contraband (possession is crime under Texas law—tampering with identification numbers). During lawful search for stolen property, you observe contraband in plain view. All plain view elements met: lawfully present executing warrant, incriminating nature immediately apparent (filed serial numbers indicate stolen property or intent to conceal identity), and lawful access. Seize tools as evidence of separate offense, document where found, photograph serial number areas showing filing/grinding, and pursue additional charges for possession of tools with removed identification.

Scenario 19: You stop a vehicle for speeding. The driver is a uniformed military service member showing military ID and stating he's rushing to base because he's late for formation. He's polite and cooperative. Do you still issue a citation?

A) No—always give military members warnings B) Use discretion based on circumstances, but don't create policy of never citing military members (constitutes bias); consider totality including speed, traffic conditions, safety, prior record C) Yes—always cite everyone regardless of circumstances D) Let supervisor decide

Answer: B **Explanation:** Fair and impartial policing means enforcing laws based on behavior and circumstances, not demographic categories. While military service is commendable, it doesn't create automatic exemption from traffic laws. Use same discretion you'd use for anyone: How excessive was speed? What were traffic/road conditions? Was driving dangerous? What's driver's record? Is explanation reasonable? Being late for formation isn't emergency justifying dangerous speeding. Make enforcement decision based on circumstances, not profession or status. Document your decision-making factors.

Scenario 20: During a traffic stop at night, you notice the driver has dilated pupils, is sweating despite cool weather, is speaking rapidly, and appears agitated. He's not showing signs of alcohol intoxication but behavior suggests drug influence. What's your approach?

A) Let him drive—no alcohol detected B) Investigate further; dilated pupils, sweating, rapid speech, and agitation suggest stimulant influence (cocaine, methamphetamine); conduct DWI investigation for drugs including field sobriety tests and Drug Recognition Expert evaluation if available C) Arrest immediately without investigation D) Search vehicle without probable cause

Answer: B **Explanation:** DWI includes intoxication by drugs, not just alcohol. Symptoms described suggest stimulant intoxication: dilated pupils, sweating, rapid speech, agitation, hyperactivity. Conduct standardized field sobriety tests (HGN may not show impairment with stimulants, but WAT and OLS may), observe driving behavior before stop, note physical symptoms, consider Drug Recognition Expert evaluation if certified DRE available in your agency, and request blood test if probable cause develops (blood testing detects drugs better than breath testing). Document all observations supporting drug intoxication belief.

Scenario 21: You respond to a call of suspicious person looking into car windows in a parking lot. You locate someone matching the description walking through the lot. When you approach, he immediately becomes defensive and refuses to identify himself. Can you detain him?

A) Yes—you have reasonable suspicion based on matching description and suspicious behavior reported B) No—looking into cars isn't illegal C) Yes—but only if someone reports theft D) Arrest him immediately

Answer: A **Explanation:** Call of specific suspicious behavior (looking into car windows—consistent with vehicle burglary) plus matching description creates reasonable suspicion for Terry stop. Detain briefly, ask about his presence and activities, request identification, observe for tools or items suggesting burglary intent. His defensive behavior and refusal to identify don't create guilt but add to suspicion. Many states and local ordinances require providing ID to officers during investigative detention. If he refuses ID, you may arrest in some jurisdictions. Investigate rather than immediately arresting without developing probable cause.

Scenario 22: You're dispatched to a fight at a bar. Multiple people are fighting. You arrive with backup and people scatter. Several people have injuries. Multiple witnesses point to different people as "the one who started it." How do you proceed?

A) Arrest everyone present B) Separate witnesses, obtain individual statements away from each other, identify primary aggressors based on witness consistency, injury patterns, video evidence if available; prioritize arrests based on evidence quality C) Arrest whoever has the most injuries—they must be victim D) Let everyone go—too confusing

Answer: B **Explanation:** Chaotic scenes require methodical investigation. Separate witnesses to prevent collaboration, obtain individual statements (who started fight? What did you see? Who hit whom?), look for consistency across multiple witnesses, examine injuries (defensive versus offensive wounds), request video from bar security, identify people who remained versus those who fled (flight suggests guilt), and determine primary aggressors. Don't assume most injured person is victim—they might have started fight and lost. Build probable cause through investigation, not assumptions. Arrest primary aggressors with strongest evidence.

Scenario 23: During a search incident to arrest, you handcuff the suspect outside his car. Can you search the trunk of his vehicle?

A) Yes—search incident to arrest covers entire vehicle B) No—under Arizona v. Gant, once suspect is secured and cannot access vehicle, search incident to arrest no longer applies to vehicle unless evidence of arrest offense might be in vehicle; trunk is especially problematic as suspect could never access it C) Yes—trunks always can be searched D) Only with consent

Answer: B **Explanation:** Gant dramatically limited vehicle searches incident to arrest. Trunk searches are particularly difficult to justify under Gant because: suspect is secured (can't access vehicle), trunk isn't within grab area even when not secured, and suspect couldn't have accessed trunk anyway. Unless you have probable cause that evidence of arrest offense is in trunk (example: arrested for drug trafficking and believe drugs are in trunk), you can't search trunk as search incident to arrest. Need consent, probable cause for automobile exception, or warrant.

Scenario 24: You're investigating a theft. The suspect's girlfriend calls you and says, "He told me he did it and I want him to get help. Can you come to our apartment? I'll let you in and show you where he hid the stuff." Can you enter and seize evidence based on girlfriend's consent?

A) No—need warrant for all entries B) Yes—girlfriend as resident has authority to consent to entry and show you evidence in common areas; if evidence is in suspect's exclusive area, her consent may not extend there depending on expectation of privacy C) Yes—girlfriend's consent covers entire apartment including suspect's private spaces D) No—only suspect can give consent

Answer: B **Explanation:** This tests third-party consent. Girlfriend as co-resident has authority to consent to your entry and to show you evidence in common areas (living room, kitchen, areas both use). However, if suspect has exclusive control over certain areas (his locked closet, safe, private office he alone uses), girlfriend's consent may not extend to those areas. Courts balance: Does third party have authority over area? Does suspect have reasonable expectation of privacy in that area? If girlfriend shows you stolen property in living room, seizure is lawful. If in suspect's locked safe she can't access, her consent doesn't authorize opening it.

Scenario 25: You stop a vehicle for a traffic violation. The driver is extremely polite, immediately provides license and insurance, and answers all questions cooperatively. Despite cooperation, you detect slight marijuana odor. Do you have probable cause to search?

A) No—cooperation shows he has nothing to hide B) Probable cause depends on strength and clarity of odor; faint marijuana smell is increasingly questionable as probable cause with legal hemp and changing marijuana laws; strong, unambiguous fresh marijuana odor is stronger basis

C) Yes—any marijuana smell always creates probable cause D) No—never search cooperative people

Answer: B **Explanation:** Cooperation is irrelevant to probable cause analysis—Fourth Amendment rights don't depend on politeness. However, marijuana odor as probable cause is evolving. Legal hemp (smells identical to marijuana), CBD products, and changing marijuana laws create challenges. Faint, ambiguous odor may not create probable cause. Strong, unambiguous, fresh marijuana odor combined with other factors (visible marijuana, admission, impairment signs) creates stronger probable cause. Document exact observations: How strong was odor? Fresh or old? Where coming from? Any corroborating factors? Court scrutiny of marijuana odor searches is increasing.

Scenario 26: You're dispatched to a call of "person with a gun." The caller describes the person's location and clothing. You arrive and see someone matching description in that location. Can you conduct a Terry frisk?

A) No—just matching description isn't enough B) Yes—report of person with gun creates reasonable suspicion person is armed; matching description and location allows Terry stop and protective frisk for weapons C) No—need to see gun first D) Only if person acts threateningly

Answer: B **Explanation:** Specific report of person with gun at specific location plus your observation of person matching description at that location creates reasonable suspicion for Terry stop and protective frisk. Person with gun creates officer safety concern justifying frisk. Approach tactically, give commands, conduct pat-down for weapons. If gun is found and person has proper license/permit, return it and document encounter. If unlawfully possessed or threatening behavior observed, develop probable cause for arrest. Document caller's report, dispatch information, and your observations justifying stop and frisk.

Scenario 27: During booking, you search an arrestee and find a small notebook containing what appears to be customer lists with names, phone numbers, and amounts of money. The arrest was for possession of marijuana. Is the notebook relevant evidence?

A) No—notebook not related to marijuana arrest B) Yes—notebook suggests drug sales activity; seize as evidence of drug distribution even though arrest was for possession C) No—return it to suspect D) Only if amounts match money found on suspect

Answer: B **Explanation:** Evidence discovered during lawful search can be seized even if related to different crime than arrest offense. Notebook suggesting drug sales (customer names, phone numbers, amounts suggesting debts or sales) is evidence of drug trafficking. Seize as evidence, document where found (on person during booking search), photograph pages, note contents, and pursue enhanced charges if investigation supports distribution rather than just possession. This could elevate case from simple possession to possession with intent to deliver or drug sales.

Scenario 28: You're executing a search warrant at a residence. Inside, you encounter a person who doesn't match the suspect description but is present in the home. Can you detain this person during the warrant execution?

A) No—warrant doesn't cover this person B) Yes—Michigan v. Summers allows detention of occupants present during search warrant execution for officer safety and investigation integrity, regardless of whether they're suspects C) No—only detain people named in warrant D) Only if they act suspiciously

Answer: B **Explanation:** Michigan v. Summers permits detaining occupants present during search warrant execution without additional reasonable suspicion. Justifications: officer safety (preventing attacks, access to weapons), preventing flight of suspects, preventing destruction of evidence, and facilitating orderly search. Person doesn't need to be named in warrant or match suspect description. You can detain anyone present during execution. Document who was present, where detained, and duration of detention. Release after search completes unless probable cause develops for arrest.

Scenario 29: You respond to a mental health crisis call. The family states their son is "having a breakdown," hasn't slept in days, is talking about government conspiracies, and refusing to take prescribed medication. He's pacing and agitated but hasn't threatened violence. What's your best approach?

A) Arrest him immediately for criminal trespass (in his family's home) B) Use Crisis Intervention Team techniques: maintain distance, speak calmly and non-threateningly, avoid challenging his beliefs, request mental health professional, consider emergency detention for mental health evaluation under Texas Health & Safety Code Ch. 573 C) Force him to take medication D) Leave—no crime occurred

Answer: B **Explanation:** Mental health crisis requires CIT approach, not traditional criminal response. Symptoms suggest possible psychotic episode (no sleep, paranoia, medication non-compliance). Use CIT techniques: maintain safe distance, speak calmly, don't challenge paranoid beliefs (arguing makes it worse), request mental health professional or CIT-trained officer, and consider emergency detention if he meets criteria (danger to self/others or can't provide basic needs due to mental illness). Emergency detention under Chapter 573 allows taking person to mental health facility for evaluation without arrest. This is medical intervention, not criminal process. Document observations supporting emergency detention need.

Scenario 30: During a traffic stop, you smell alcohol. The driver admits drinking "two beers three hours ago." FSTs show minimal impairment (1 clue on HGN, 1 on WAT, 0 on OLS). Do you have probable cause for DWI arrest?

A) Yes—he admitted drinking B) Marginal probable cause; admission to drinking plus minimal FST clues suggests impairment but not clearly meeting .08 standard; consider portable breath test if available, observe driving behavior, note other impairment signs; arrest decision should be based on totality suggesting loss of normal use or likely .08+ BAC C) No—three FST clues minimum required D) Yes—any drinking and driving is DWI

Answer: B **Explanation:** This tests understanding that DWI requires either loss of normal use of faculties OR .08+ BAC. Two beers three hours ago might not produce .08 (depends on weight, gender, food, etc.). Minimal FST clues (2 total across three tests) suggests slight impairment but unclear if meets legal standard. Totality of circumstances matters: How was driving? How strong was odor? Speech pattern? Balance? Eyes? Other signs? Consider PBT if available (not admissible but guides decision). If totality suggests probable cause, arrest. If minimal signs and good driving, consider warning or requiring safe ride. Document all factors supporting your decision.

Scenario 31: You're investigating a burglary and obtain a search warrant for the suspect's residence to search for "stolen electronics including laptops, tablets, gaming systems, and tools used in burglaries." During the search, you open a dresser drawer looking for small electronics and find a handgun. A records check reveals the suspect is a convicted felon prohibited from possessing firearms. Can you seize the gun?

A) No—warrant doesn't mention firearms B) Yes—you're lawfully present executing valid warrant, gun is in plain view during lawful search, and you immediately recognize it as contraband (felon in possession) C) No—you were searching for electronics, not guns D) Only if electronics are also found

Answer: B **Explanation:** Plain view doctrine applies during warrant execution. You're lawfully in the location (valid warrant), searching area that could contain items listed in warrant (dresser drawer could contain tablets, small electronics), and you immediately recognize gun as contraband based on your knowledge that suspect is convicted felon. Seize firearm, document where found, note it was discovered during lawful search for electronics, and pursue separate charges for felon in possession. The scope of your search (drawers that could hold electronics) was appropriate under the warrant.

Scenario 32: You stop a vehicle for broken taillight. The driver appears nervous and gives inconsistent answers about where he's going. You don't smell anything suspicious or see contraband. After issuing a warning for the taillight, you ask, "Mind if I ask you a few more questions?" Driver says, "I guess." You then ask to search the vehicle. He hesitates and says, "Do I have to let you?" What should you tell him?

A) "Yes, if you don't consent I'll get a drug dog" B) "No, you don't have to consent. You're free to refuse. I'm just asking for your permission" (clarifying his rights) C) "If you have nothing to hide, why not let me search?" D) "I'll keep you here until you consent"

Answer: B **Explanation:** When someone asks if they have to consent, they're unclear about their rights. Ethical policing requires clarifying: "No, you don't have to consent. You have the right to refuse. I'm asking for your permission, but you can say no." This ensures any consent given is truly voluntary. Options A, C, and D are coercive and may invalidate consent. If he refuses after your clarification, accept the refusal and complete the stop. If you lack probable cause, release him. Clear voluntary consent is the only kind that withstands legal scrutiny.

Scenario 33: You're called to a school where a 14-year-old student punched another student, breaking his nose. School administrators want you to arrest the offender. The victim's parents are demanding arrest. The offender has no prior record and appears remorseful. What factors should guide your decision?

A) Always arrest juveniles who commit violence B) Consider severity of offense, juvenile's history, school policy, whether juvenile court referral or arrest is more appropriate, whether parents can control juvenile, and whether arrest serves public safety or rehabilitation goals C) Never arrest juveniles on school property D) Let parents decide

Answer: B **Explanation:** Juvenile cases require different analysis than adult cases. Consider: Was this fight mutual combat or assault? Injury severity? Prior history? Is juvenile cooperative? Can parents provide adequate supervision? Will arrest or referral better serve rehabilitation (juvenile justice goal)? School input? Many jurisdictions have diversion programs for first-time juvenile offenders. Serious assault with significant injury may require arrest regardless. Document decision-making thoroughly. Juvenile justice balances accountability with rehabilitation—your discretion plays important role.

Scenario 34: During a traffic stop, you run the driver's information and discover he has an outstanding warrant from another state for failure to appear on a minor traffic violation. Your department policy requires confirming out-of-state warrants before arrest. When you call the issuing state, they say "yes, it's active, but we won't extradite for FTA on traffic warrant." What should you do?

A) Arrest him anyway—warrant is valid B) Don't arrest since issuing state won't extradite; complete traffic stop and document warrant information in report C) Arrest and let jail figure it out D) Pretend you never found the warrant

Answer: B **Explanation:** If issuing jurisdiction won't extradite, arresting serves no purpose—they can't be prosecuted for the warrant offense. Complete your traffic stop appropriately, document the warrant exists but jurisdiction declined prosecution, and notify your records division to possibly flag the warrant as non-extraditable. Some departments still arrest and release on bond, others don't arrest when extradition is declined. Follow your department policy. Document everything so if the person later commits crimes, there's record of the warrant.

Scenario 35: You respond to a domestic violence call. The female victim has visible injuries but insists she "fell down stairs." However, her injuries (defensive wounds on forearms, bruising around throat) are inconsistent with a fall. The male suspect confirms her story. No independent witnesses exist. Do you have probable cause for arrest?

A) No—victim denies assault B) Yes—injuries inconsistent with explanation, location and type suggest assault despite victim's false explanation; your training and experience allow you to recognize injuries consistent with strangulation and defensive wounds C) No—need witness to contradict their stories D) Only if victim admits truth

Answer: B **Explanation:** Probable cause exists when facts and circumstances would lead reasonable officer to believe crime occurred. Victim recantation doesn't eliminate probable cause if evidence contradicts the explanation. Defensive wounds (forearms) suggest she blocked strikes. Neck bruising suggests strangulation. Falls don't typically cause these injury patterns. Your training in recognizing domestic violence injuries creates expertise supporting probable cause despite inconsistent statements. Photograph injuries thoroughly, document exact locations, articulate in report why injuries are inconsistent with fall, note victim's demeanor (fear, minimization), arrest based on physical evidence, and pursue evidence-based prosecution.

Scenario 36: You're executing an arrest warrant at a residence. You knock and announce several times with no response. You hear movement inside and a toilet flushing. Can you make forced entry?

A) No—must keep knocking until someone answers B) Yes—exigent circumstances exist (destruction of evidence suggested by toilet flushing after knock-and-announce); forced entry is justified to prevent evidence destruction C) No—need search warrant, not just arrest warrant D) Only with supervisor approval

Answer: B **Explanation:** You have valid arrest warrant authorizing entry. After proper knock-and-announce, you hear evidence being destroyed (toilet flushing after your announcement suggests drugs being disposed). This creates exigent circumstances justifying immediate forced entry to prevent destruction of evidence and execute valid warrant. Don't create exigency through your own actions (example: aggressive pounding and yelling then claiming evidence destruction), but when executing valid warrant and occupants begin destroying evidence after your lawful announcement, forced entry is justified.

Scenario 37: During a DWI investigation, the suspect performs FSTs adequately—no clues on HGN, one clue on WAT, zero on OLS. However, he admitted drinking, you smell alcohol, and his driving was erratic (weaving, varying speed significantly). Do you have probable cause?

A) No—FST performance too good B) Maybe—totality matters: admission to drinking, odor, and especially poor driving behavior before stop may create probable cause despite good FST performance; some people with high tolerance perform FSTs well despite being legally intoxicated C) No—need more FST clues D) Yes—driving behavior alone is enough

Answer: B **Explanation:** FSTs aren't the only factor. Totality includes: driving behavior (weaving, speed variation—strong indicators), admission to drinking, alcohol odor, and FST performance. Some chronic drinkers perform FSTs reasonably well despite BAC over .08 due to tolerance. Conversely, some sober nervous people perform FSTs poorly. Weigh all factors. Significant driving impairment combined with drinking admission and odor may create probable cause despite limited FST clues. Consider portable breath test if available. Document all factors supporting your decision. If you believe probable cause exists based on totality, arrest. If uncertain and driving wasn't dangerous, consider requiring safe ride home.

Scenario 38: You're called to a business for a theft. The manager shows you surveillance video of an employee stealing money from the register. The employee is still on premises but isn't aware you've been called. Should you advise Miranda before asking him about the theft?

A) Yes—he's a suspect so needs Miranda B) No—not in custody yet; you can interview him without Miranda, but once he's under arrest or not free to leave, Miranda becomes necessary C) Yes—always give Miranda to all suspects D) Only if you plan to arrest him

Answer: B **Explanation:** Miranda requires custody plus interrogation. If you approach him during his shift, tell him you'd like to ask questions, and he reasonably feels free to decline or leave, it's not custodial. You can interview without Miranda. However, if you surround him, tell him not to leave, or make clear he's not free to go, it becomes custodial and requires Miranda. Best practice: conduct interview in manager's office, explain you're investigating theft, ask questions. If he confesses before arrest and interview was non-custodial, confession is admissible. Once you arrest, give Miranda before additional questioning.

Scenario 39: You respond to a vehicle accident with injuries. One driver appears uninjured but shows signs of intoxication. The other driver has serious injuries. What are your priorities?

A) Investigate DWI first—lock down that case B) Ensure injured party receives medical attention first, secure scene for safety, then investigate DWI once life safety needs are addressed C) Interview witnesses before they leave D) Only handle traffic; let someone else handle DWI

Answer: B **Explanation:** Life safety always comes first. Ensure injured person receives immediate medical attention, secure scene (traffic control, prevent secondary crashes), then investigate crash causes including DWI. DWI suspect isn't going anywhere—he's injured party's crash partner. Document his condition and behavior initially (for later DWI case), ensure he's not leaving scene, then prioritize injured victim. After medical needs addressed and scene secured, conduct thorough DWI investigation. Failing to render aid or prioritize life safety violates your duty and reflects poorly on you regardless of DWI prosecution outcome.

Scenario 40: During a search warrant execution, you find $50,000 cash, scales, packaging materials, and a ledger with names and amounts, but no drugs. The suspect claims "I run a cash business, that's my money, you have no right to take it." Can you seize the currency?

A) No—no drugs found so no drug proceeds B) Yes—totality of circumstances (large cash amount, scales, packaging materials, ledger suggesting drug transactions) creates probable cause that currency represents drug proceeds; seize for evidence and potential civil forfeiture C) No—need drugs to prove drug money D) Only if he can't prove legal source

Answer: B **Explanation:** While no drugs were found, the totality suggests drug trafficking: large cash in small denominations, drug paraphernalia (scales, packaging), records suggesting sales (ledger with names/amounts). Currency can be seized as evidence of drug operation and for potential civil forfeiture proceedings. His claim of "cash business" is self-serving and doesn't eliminate your authority when probable cause exists. Document amount precisely, photograph currency, document denomination distribution, photograph scales/packaging/ledger, note lack of any legitimate business records, and file for forfeiture if appropriate. Prosecutor and forfeiture attorney make final decisions on keeping currency, but you have authority to seize based on probable cause.

Scenario 41: You're dispatched to a "welfare check" on an elderly person. Family members called because they haven't heard from her in a week. You arrive, knock, and get no response. You see mail piling up. Neighbors confirm they haven't seen her. Can you enter?

A) No—need warrant for all entries B) Yes—emergency aid exception permits entry when reasonable belief exists that someone inside needs immediate assistance; week-long absence with accumulated mail creates reasonable belief C) No—wait for family to arrive with key D) Only if you see person through window

Answer: B **Explanation:** Emergency aid exception applies when facts create reasonable belief someone inside faces danger or needs immediate medical attention. Week-long absence for elderly person combined with no response and accumulated mail creates reasonable belief she may be injured, ill, or dead. Make entry for welfare check. If you find her deceased, secure scene and notify supervisor/investigators. If alive and needing medical attention, render aid. If alive and fine (went on vacation, forgot to tell family), apologize for entry and document circumstances justifying emergency entry. Courts consistently uphold welfare check entries when facts objectively support belief someone needs help.

Scenario 42: During a traffic stop, the driver becomes argumentative, yells at you, calls you names, but doesn't threaten you or physically resist. He's upset about the ticket but he's sitting in his car complying with commands. Can you arrest him for disorderly conduct?

A) Yes—he's being disorderly B) No—verbal protest and argument, even rude and profane, don't constitute disorderly conduct; absent threats, fighting words, or conduct likely to incite immediate breach of peace, his speech is protected C) Yes—disrespect to officer is always arrestable D) Only if he uses specific profanity

Answer: B **Explanation:** First Amendment protects even offensive speech directed at police. Disorderly conduct requires conduct likely to incite immediate breach of peace, fighting, or disturbing others. One person yelling at officer during traffic stop, while unpleasant, doesn't meet this standard. He's not threatening you, not physically resisting, and not disturbing other people. Remain professional, complete the traffic stop, issue citation, and release him. Your authority doesn't include arresting people for hurting your feelings. If he escalates to threats, attempts to leave without license/vehicle, or physically resists, then you have grounds for arrest on appropriate charges.

Scenario 43: You're investigating a robbery and have detained several people matching the description. You bring the victim to view these individuals for identification. The victim looks at them and says, "I think it's number 3, but I'm not 100% sure." What should you do with this identification?

A) Arrest number 3 immediately—victim identified him B) Note the tentative identification but recognize its weaknesses (only "thinks," not certain); investigate further, look for corroborating evidence, consider other factors before making arrest solely on uncertain identification C) Release everyone—victim wasn't certain D) Have victim look again until certain

Answer: B **Explanation:** Uncertain identifications are weak evidence. "I think" and "not 100% sure" indicate doubt. This identification alone may not create sufficient probable cause for arrest. Look for corroborating evidence: Does suspect have property from robbery? Match detailed description? Have alibi? What does totality show? Document victim's uncertain language exactly. Don't pressure victim to become more certain (coerced identification is inadmissible). If identification is too weak and no corroborating evidence exists, you may lack probable cause for arrest. Strong probable cause requires more than tentative identification. Consider photo lineup later, additional investigation, and building stronger case before arrest.

Scenario 44: You respond to a domestic violence call and determine probable cause exists to arrest the male party. His 3-year-old child is present. The mother (victim) is too injured to care for the child and no other family is immediately available. What are your obligations regarding the child?

A) Arrest father and leave child with injured mother—not your problem B) Ensure child's safety: contact family members to take custody, contact CPS if no family available, don't leave child in dangerous/inadequate situation C) Take child to police station and figure it out later D) Don't arrest so child has parent

Answer: B **Explanation:** Your duty extends to child welfare. Don't arrest father and leave young child with injured mother unable to provide care. Options: contact family members (grandparents, aunts/uncles) to immediately take custody, contact CPS for emergency placement if no family available, have officer stay with child until placement arranged, or delay arrest slightly until child care is arranged (if father isn't immediate danger). Document your efforts to ensure child safety. You can't ignore child welfare because of your law enforcement duties—both responsibilities matter. Most departments have protocols for this situation.

Scenario 45: During a vehicle search, you find a backpack containing drugs. Three people were in the vehicle: driver, front passenger (who owns the backpack), and rear passenger. The backpack owner admits it's his and says the drugs are his. Do you arrest all three or just the backpack owner?

A) Arrest all three—everyone in vehicle has constructive possession B) Arrest backpack owner who admitted ownership; unless evidence suggests others knew about and controlled the drugs, his admission relieves them of constructive possession C) Arrest only driver D) Arrest none—need to determine ownership first

Answer: B **Explanation:** Constructive possession requires knowledge and control. Backpack owner's admission provides clear evidence of his knowledge and control. Unless evidence suggests others knew about drugs and controlled the backpack, the admission limits liability to him. If backpack was under owner's feet and not accessible to others, they may lack constructive possession. However, if drugs were visible and all occupants could access them, everyone might have constructive possession. Consider totality: Where was backpack? Could others see/access contents? Behavior of each person? Statements? Prior relationship? Document reasons for arresting or not arresting each person. Don't reflexively arrest everyone—analyze actual possession and control.

Scenario 46: You're executing a search warrant for drugs. The suspect's 16-year-old son is present but isn't listed in warrant. During the search, you see in plain view in his bedroom what appears to be marijuana and a scale. Can you charge the juvenile?

A) No—he's not named in warrant B) Yes—you're lawfully present executing warrant, items are in plain view in area you're authorized to search, and you recognize them as contraband; juvenile can be charged C) No—need separate juvenile warrant D) Only if parents consent

Answer: B **Explanation:** Warrants authorize searching locations, not just persons. You're lawfully searching residence per warrant, which includes rooms where drugs might be hidden. Finding drugs in plain view in juvenile's room during this lawful search permits seizure and provides probable cause to charge juvenile with possession. Document where found, photograph in place, note it was in plain view during warrant execution, and handle as juvenile case (custody, parental notification, different procedures than adult arrest). Juvenile status doesn't eliminate liability for drug possession—it changes procedures for handling the case.

Scenario 47: You're investigating a sexual assault. The suspect agrees to talk but says, "I want my statement recorded on video so there's no question about what I said." Your department doesn't have video equipment immediately available. Can you interview him without video?

A) No—he requested video so you must provide it B) Yes—Texas requires recording custodial interrogation, but he's not in custody yet; if non-custodial interview, recording isn't required though his request is reasonable C) No—all statements must be video recorded D) Yes—ignore his request

Answer: B **Explanation:** Article 38.22 requires electronic recording of custodial interrogation. If this is non-custodial (he voluntarily came to station, isn't under arrest, free to leave), recording isn't legally required. However, his request is reasonable and smart. Options: obtain video equipment before interview, use audio recording if video unavailable, or explain video isn't immediately available and offer to wait until it is. Recording protects both of you—proves exactly what was said and how interview was conducted. Given the serious nature (sexual assault) and his reasonable request, strongly consider waiting for video capability. Document his request and your response.

Scenario 48: You stop a vehicle for speeding. The driver produces an out-of-state license with address in another state but the vehicle has Texas plates and registration in a different name. Driver says, "I just moved here last month and bought this car." What additional investigation is appropriate?

A) None—speeding is the only issue B) Verify ownership (stolen vehicle check), confirm driver has permission to operate vehicle, determine if driver required to obtain Texas license yet (Texas law requires DL within 90 days of establishing residency) C) Arrest for stolen vehicle D) Search vehicle

Answer: B **Explanation:** Discrepancies warrant investigation to eliminate stolen vehicle possibility and verify compliance with Texas registration laws. Confirm: Who owns vehicle? Does owner know driver has it? If purchased, does he have bill of sale or ownership documents? If established Texas residency, has 90-day period for getting Texas license expired? These questions protect against unauthorized use of vehicle and ensure compliance with registration laws. If explanations are reasonable and vehicle isn't stolen, complete traffic stop appropriately. If suspicious or unable to verify ownership, detain for further investigation.

Scenario 49: During a DWI arrest, the suspect becomes combative during handcuffing, requiring you to use physical force (takedowns, control holds) to complete the arrest. He suffers minor injuries (scrapes, bruising). What documentation is critical?

A) Minimal—just note he resisted B) Detailed documentation: specific resistance encountered (pulled away, struck at you, kicked, etc.), specific force used and why (wrist lock failed due to his strength, used takedown to gain control), injuries resulting, medical attention offered, Graham factors supporting force as objectively reasonable C) Only document injuries D) No documentation needed for minor force

Answer: B **Explanation:** ALL force must be thoroughly documented, even "minor" force. Describe exactly what happened: He tensed up, pulled right arm away when I attempted to cuff him, formed fist with right hand, drew arm back as if to strike, I used wrist lock to regain control, wrist lock failed due to his resistance, I used leg sweep takedown to control him, after takedown he continued thrashing and kicking, I delivered one knee strike to right thigh to overcome resistance, he then complied and was handcuffed. Note injuries (abrasions on right elbow and knee from takedown to pavement, bruising on right thigh from knee strike), medical attention offered, whether accepted, photographs taken. Address Graham factors: serious crime (DWI), immediate threat (active physical resistance), active resistance requiring force to complete lawful arrest.

Scenario 50: You respond to a call of "shots fired" at a residence. Upon arrival, you hear yelling inside but no gunshots. Dispatch updates that caller (neighbor) heard "at least three shots" and yelling before calling 911. Can you enter without a warrant?

A) No—need warrant for residential entry B) Yes—exigent circumstances exist: report of shots fired creates reasonable belief someone inside faces immediate danger or threat; emergency aid exception permits entry to check welfare and investigate reported violence C) No—if shooting stopped, no emergency exists D) Only if you hear more shots

Answer: B **Explanation:** Recent shots fired report creates exigent circumstances justifying immediate entry. Someone inside may be injured, dead, or being held at gunpoint. Continuing yelling suggests ongoing danger. Make tactical entry with backup, announce police presence, clear residence to ensure no victims or ongoing threats, investigate weapons discharge, identify source of yelling. If you find no emergency (TV noise, legal target shooting in backyard, false report), explain your reasonable belief that justified entry. Document caller's specific report (three shots), your observations (yelling heard), and timeline (shots reported minutes before arrival). Courts consistently uphold entries after specific reports of violence creating reasonable belief emergency exists.

Final Scenario Analysis: What These Questions Teach

These 50 scenarios aren't just test questions—they're teaching tools revealing critical concepts for both the TCOLE exam and your career:

Legal Principles Applied: You practiced applying Graham v. Connor to force decisions, search warrant limitations and plain view exceptions, Miranda custody/interrogation analysis, probable cause development from totality of circumstances, and juvenile procedure differences requiring special handling.

Officer Safety Emphasized: Multiple scenarios required tactical decision-making balancing enforcement goals with officer safety. You learned that rushing investigations, entering without backup, or failing to assess threats endangers you and doesn't improve cases.

Community Trust Matters: Scenarios involving consent, cultural competency, mental health crisis response, and ethical decision-making highlight that how you enforce law matters as much as that you enforce it. Community trust depends on procedural justice.

Documentation Critical: Nearly every scenario emphasized thorough documentation. Your reports must withstand scrutiny from supervisors, prosecutors, defense attorneys, and juries. Quality documentation protects you and ensures justice.

Judgment and Discretion: Many scenarios had multiple defensible responses requiring you to choose the BEST option. Law enforcement isn't always black and white. Your judgment, guided by law, policy, training, and ethics, determines outcomes.

Totality Analysis: Successful officers analyze totalities rather than single factors. Marijuana odor alone may not create probable cause. Combined with other observations, it might. Training yourself to consider all factors prevents tunnel vision and strengthens investigations.

Your Rights Matter Too: Scenarios involving custody issues, consent ambiguity, and force documentation remind you that protecting your rights (right to counsel after deadly force, right to reasonable delay before interview, right to union representation) is as important as protecting others' rights.

How to Use These Scenarios for Maximum Benefit

First Pass: Work through all 50 scenarios, choosing your answers and then reading explanations. Focus on understanding WHY answers are correct, not just WHAT the correct answer is.

Identify Patterns: Which scenarios gave you trouble? Use of force decisions? Search and seizure? Juvenile procedures? Your weak areas on scenarios mirror your weak areas on the exam. Review relevant chapters focusing on those topics.

Second Pass (Days Later): Retake scenarios you missed. If you now answer correctly, your review worked. If you still miss them, deeper study of that concept is needed. Don't just memorize the answer—understand the underlying principle.

Apply to Your Life: When reading news about police incidents or watching body camera footage, analyze them using these scenario principles. What would YOU do? What legal principles apply? This active analysis builds judgment skills that serve you on exams and in the field.

Discuss With Study Partners: If you have study partners, work through scenarios together. Explain your reasoning for answers. Teaching concepts to others reinforces your own understanding and exposes gaps in knowledge.

You're Ready

You've completed 50 intensive scenarios requiring you to analyze complex situations, apply legal principles under pressure, balance competing interests, and make sound decisions with incomplete information—exactly what the TCOLE exam and your career demand.

If you scored 80% or higher on these scenarios, you're demonstrating the analytical skills and knowledge application necessary for success. If you scored lower, don't be discouraged.

Scenarios are harder than recall questions. Review your weak areas, understand the principles, and try again.

Remember: The TCOLE exam includes scenario-based questions specifically because memorizing facts isn't enough. They need to know you can apply knowledge to real situations. These 50 scenarios prepared you for exactly that type of testing.

You've invested hundreds of hours in preparation. You've worked through comprehensive content, answered hundreds of practice questions, and analyzed complex scenarios. That's real preparation that translates to exam success.

One final reminder: The night before your exam, don't cram. Get good sleep. Eat a healthy breakfast. Arrive early. Read each question carefully. Trust your preparation. You've got this.

Now go demonstrate everything you've learned. The badge is waiting for you.

Performance Analysis and Final Preparation

How to Interpret Your Scenario Performance:

If you scored 90-100% on scenarios: Outstanding! You're applying knowledge effectively to real situations. You're ready for the TCOLE exam's scenario-based questions.

If you scored 80-89%: Very good! You understand application but missed some nuances. Review explanations for missed questions carefully. Focus on complex scenarios requiring multi-step analysis.

If you scored 70-79%: Adequate but needs improvement. Scenarios require more than knowledge—they require judgment. Review missed questions, understand WHY answers are correct, and practice analyzing situations from multiple angles.

Below 70%: Not ready for scenario-based testing. You may know facts but struggle applying them. Go back to chapter content, work through chapter scenarios again, and focus on understanding principles behind rules rather than memorizing rules themselves.

Common Scenario Question Mistakes:

Overthinking: Sometimes simple answers are correct. If question asks what you should do first at an emergency scene and option includes "render medical aid," that's probably right—it doesn't need complicated analysis.

Ignoring Key Words: Words like "BEST," "FIRST," "MOST appropriate," and "immediate" guide your answer. First priority might be officer safety. Best answer might be most complete option even if others are partially correct.

Missing Nuances: Scenarios often include details that change analysis. "Faint marijuana odor" versus "strong marijuana odor" matters legally. "Subject has gun pointed at victim" versus "subject has gun in holster" creates different threat levels.

Applying Wrong Standards: Use correct legal standard. Reasonable suspicion for Terry stops, probable cause for arrests and searches, objectively reasonable for use of force. Applying wrong standard leads to wrong answers.

Forgetting Officer Safety: When in doubt and multiple answers seem reasonable, choose the option prioritizing officer safety. TCOLE emphasizes that officers who don't go home safely can't serve their communities.

Final Preparation Checklist Before TCOLE Exam:

□ Scored 80%+ on all practice exams and scenarios □ Identified weak content areas and reviewed those chapters thoroughly □ Can articulate Graham v. Connor factors from memory □ Understand search warrant requirements and exceptions □ Know Miranda requirements and when custodial interrogation exists □ Can distinguish between different force levels and when each is appropriate □ Understand Texas Penal Code classification system (Capital, 1st, 2nd, 3rd, State Jail, Class A/B/C) □ Know key Texas statutes and their elements □ Understand vehicle search limitations after Arizona v. Gant □ Can explain chain of custody importance and requirements □ Understand juvenile procedures and how they differ from adult procedures □ Know traffic stop safety procedures and positioning □ Can explain de-escalation techniques and when they're appropriate □ Understand community policing principles □ Know emergency response priorities

You're Ready When:

You consistently score 80%+ on practice questions. You can explain answers, not just select correct options. You understand WHY laws exist, not just what they say. You can analyze scenarios considering multiple factors simultaneously (safety, law, tactics, ethics). You feel confident, not anxious, about the exam. You've completed the entire study plan and reviewed weak areas.

You're Not Ready If:

You're scoring below 75% on practice exams. You're guessing on many questions rather than knowing answers. You can't explain why wrong answers are incorrect. You struggle with scenario-based questions requiring application. You're relying on memorization without understanding principles.

PART VII: FINAL PREPARATION

CHAPTER 12: FINAL REVIEW AND RESOURCES

You're in the home stretch. You've absorbed hundreds of pages covering Texas laws, criminal procedures, patrol operations, traffic enforcement, investigations, use of force, emergency response, ethics, and communication. You've answered practice questions, analyzed scenarios, and taken comprehensive exams. Now it's time to consolidate that knowledge, eliminate last-minute uncertainties, and walk into the testing center with complete confidence. This final chapter serves as your quick reference guide and confidence booster. Use it in your last days of preparation to refresh key concepts, avoid common mistakes, and ensure nothing slips through the cracks. The information here isn't new—it's the essential core you've already learned, distilled into rapid-review format. Think of this as your pre-game warm-up. Athletes don't learn new plays minutes before kickoff; they review fundamentals and get their minds right. You're doing the same. The work is done. The knowledge is in your brain. This chapter helps you access it efficiently when it matters most.

Quick Reference: Essential Law Enforcement Terminology

Actus Reus: The physical act component of a crime; the "guilty act." Criminal law requires both actus reus and mens rea for most offenses.

Affidavit: Written statement made under oath, typically supporting warrant applications. Must establish probable cause through facts and circumstances.

Articulable: Capable of being expressed in words. Reasonable suspicion and probable cause require specific, articulable facts, not hunches or generalized suspicions.

Attendant Circumstances: Additional facts that must exist for certain crimes. Example: victim being peace officer in assault on public servant.

Beyond Reasonable Doubt: Highest burden of proof in criminal law, required for conviction. Not required for arrest (which requires probable cause) or investigative stops (reasonable suspicion).

Booking: Administrative process after arrest including fingerprinting, photographing, recording personal information, and securing personal property.

48-Hour TCOLE Exam Countdown Timeline

You've prepared well. Now execute your final strategy with confidence.

48 — 48 Hours Before Exam

Light Review Organization

- [ ] Review main concepts only (no new material)
- [ ] Gather required documents (ID, confirmation)
- [ ] Confirm exam location and time
- [ ] Stay physically active and hydrated

24 — 24 Hours Before Exam

Final Targeted Review

- [ ] Focus on 2-3 weak areas (1 hour max each)
- [ ] Review quick reference sheets and notes
- [ ] Double-check all exam day documents
- [ ] Plan route to exam location (check traffic)
- [ ] Eat healthy meals, avoid heavy studying

12 — 12 Hours Before Exam

Quick Reference Organization

- [ ] Skim quick reference cards (15 minutes max)
- [ ] Lay out exam day items (ID, pens, confirmation)
- [ ] Pack bag with water, snacks (if allowed)
- [ ] Begin winding down, relaxation activities

Night Before Exam

Rest Final Preparations

- [ ] Light review ONLY if it calms you (10 min max)
- [ ] Prepare comfortable exam outfit (layers)
- [ ] Set 2 alarms with backup wake-up plan
- [ ] Go to bed early (8+ hours before wake time)
- [ ] NO studying - trust your preparation

Morning of Exam - GAME DAY!

Execute Your Plan with Confidence

- [ ] Wake up with time to spare (no rushing)
- [ ] Eat healthy breakfast (protein + complex carbs)
- [ ] Final check: ID, confirmation, pens, layers
- [ ] Arrive 30-45 minutes early (find parking, restroom)
- [ ] Deep breaths, positive mindset - YOU'VE GOT THIS!

Trust your preparation. Stay calm. You are ready!

Burden of Proof: Obligation to prove allegations. In criminal cases, prosecution bears burden to prove defendant guilty beyond reasonable doubt.

Chain of Custody: Documented trail of evidence handling from collection through court presentation. Every transfer must be documented to prove integrity.

Complainant: Person making complaint or reporting crime. May or may not be the victim.

Concurrence: Requirement that criminal act and criminal intent occur simultaneously. You must have required mental state at moment of committing act.

Constructive Possession: Legal theory holding person responsible for items under their control even without physical possession. Driver has constructive possession of contraband in vehicle they control.

Corpus Delicti: "Body of the crime"—proof that crime actually occurred. Must prove crime happened before confessions alone can convict.

Curtilage: Area immediately surrounding dwelling, protected by Fourth Amendment as extension of home. Includes porches, yards, outbuildings closely associated with home.

Custodial Interrogation: Questioning by law enforcement when person is in custody (not free to leave). Requires Miranda warnings.

Deadly Weapon: Item capable of causing death or serious bodily injury, including firearms and items used in manner capable of causing such harm.

De-escalation: Techniques reducing conflict intensity through communication, time, distance, and tactics encouraging voluntary compliance over forced compliance.

Detention: Brief seizure for investigation based on reasonable suspicion. Less intrusive than arrest (which requires probable cause).

Exculpatory Evidence: Evidence favorable to defendant, potentially indicating innocence or reducing culpability. Prosecution must disclose to defense.

Exigent Circumstances: Emergency situations justifying warrantless action: hot pursuit, imminent evidence destruction, emergency aid, preventing escape of dangerous person.

Fruit of the Poisonous Tree: Evidence derived from initial illegality. If original search was unlawful, evidence discovered as result is also tainted and excluded.

Good Faith Exception: Limited exception to exclusionary rule when officers rely in good faith on warrant later determined invalid. Doesn't excuse obvious constitutional violations.

Graham Factors: Three Supreme Court factors evaluating use of force reasonableness: severity of crime, immediate threat to officers/others, active resistance/evasion.

Immediate: Without delay; right now. Deadly force requires imminent (immediate) threat, not future or speculative danger.

Incident to Arrest: Search authority arising from lawful arrest. Allows searching arrestee and immediate grab area without additional warrant or probable cause.

Indictment: Formal charge by grand jury for felony. Required before felony prosecution can proceed to trial.

Information: Formal charge filed by prosecutor without grand jury, used for misdemeanors.

Interrogation: Words or actions by police reasonably likely to elicit incriminating response. Distinguishes from general conversation or spontaneous statements.

Mere Suspicion: Gut feeling or hunch without specific facts. Insufficient for any law enforcement action requiring legal justification.

Mens Rea: Mental state component of crime; the "guilty mind." Four levels in Texas: intentionally, knowingly, recklessly, criminal negligence.

Miranda Rights: Warnings required before custodial interrogation: right to remain silent, statements used against you, right to attorney, appointed attorney if indigent.

Objective Reasonableness: Standard for evaluating police conduct (especially use of force) based on what reasonable officer in same situation would believe, not 20/20 hindsight.

Open Fields: Areas beyond curtilage, even on private property. No Fourth Amendment protection; observation without trespass doesn't constitute search.

Particularity: Fourth Amendment requirement that warrants specifically describe place to be searched and items to be seized. Prevents general warrants.

Pecuniary Loss: Monetary value of damage or theft. Determines many offense classifications (theft, criminal mischief).

Plain View: Warrant exception allowing seizure of evidence when officer is lawfully positioned, incriminating nature immediately apparent, and officer has lawful access.

Preponderance of Evidence: "More likely than not" standard used in civil cases. Lower than beyond reasonable doubt (criminal) or probable cause (arrests/warrants).

Prima Facie Case: Evidence sufficient to establish fact or prove case unless rebutted. Prosecution must present prima facie case before defendant required to present defense.

Probable Cause: Facts and circumstances leading reasonable person to believe crime occurred and particular person committed it. Required for arrests and warrants.

Reasonable Suspicion: Specific articulable facts suggesting criminal activity, less than probable cause. Suffices for Terry stops/brief detentions.

Res Gestae: "Things done"—statements or actions forming part of crime or immediately relating to it. Often admissible even without Miranda.

Seizure (Person): Occurs when reasonable person wouldn't feel free to leave or terminate encounter with police. Arrests and Terry stops are seizures.

Seizure (Property): Meaningful interference with possessory interest in property. Taking evidence, impounding vehicles, or holding property for investigation.

Suppression: Exclusion of evidence from trial because it was obtained illegally. Defense motion to suppress challenges evidence admissibility.

Terry Stop: Brief investigative detention based on reasonable suspicion. Named after Terry v. Ohio.

Voluntariness: Free choice without coercion. Consent searches require voluntary consent; confessions must be voluntary.

Warrant: Court order authorizing arrest or search. Must be based on probable cause, supported by oath, and particularly describing person/place/things.

Important Texas Statutes Summary

TEXAS PENAL CODE - KEY SECTIONS

Title 1: Introductory Provisions §1.07 - Definitions (intentionally, knowingly, recklessly, criminal negligence, bodily injury, serious bodily injury, deadly weapon)

Title 2: General Principles §2.01 - Voluntary Act Requirement §2.02 - Culpable Mental States §7.01-7.02 - Parties to Offenses/Criminal Responsibility

Title 3: Defenses §9.21 - Public Duty Defense §9.22 - Necessity §9.31 - Self-Defense §9.32 - Deadly Force in Defense of Person §9.51-9.53 - Force to Effect Arrest/Prevent Escape

Title 5: Offenses Against Person §19.02 - Murder (1st degree felony) §19.03 - Capital Murder (capital felony) §19.04 - Manslaughter (2nd degree felony) §19.05 - Criminally Negligent Homicide (state jail felony) §22.01 - Assault (Class A misdemeanor, enhanced for certain victims/circumstances) §22.02 - Aggravated Assault (2nd degree felony, 1st degree for certain victims) §22.011 - Sexual Assault (2nd degree felony) §22.021 - Aggravated Sexual Assault (1st degree felony)

Title 7: Offenses Against Property §28.02 - Arson (2nd degree felony, enhanced circumstances) §28.03 - Criminal Mischief (classified by pecuniary loss amount) §29.02 - Robbery (2nd degree felony) §29.03 - Aggravated Robbery (1st degree felony) §30.02 - Burglary (state jail for building; 2nd degree for habitation; 1st degree if habitation with intent to commit felony other than theft) §31.03 - Theft (classified by value: under $100 Class C through $300K+ 1st degree)

Title 8: Offenses Against Public Administration §37.09 - Tampering with Evidence (3rd degree felony) §38.03 - Resisting Arrest (Class A misdemeanor)

Title 9: Public Order Offenses §42.01 - Disorderly Conduct (Class C misdemeanor, Class B for firearm discharge) §46.02 - Unlawful Carrying Weapons §49.04 - Driving While Intoxicated (Class B 1st offense, Class A 2nd, 3rd degree 3rd+) §49.045 - DWI with Child Passenger (state jail felony)

TEXAS CODE OF CRIMINAL PROCEDURE - KEY ARTICLES

Arrest Authority: Art. 14.01 - Arrest Warrant Requirements Art. 14.03 - Warrantless Arrest Authority (presence/view, felonies with probable cause, family violence) Art. 15.17 - Arrest Without Warrant for Failure to Appear Art. 15.24 - Force to Effect Arrest (deadly force limitations)

Search and Seizure: Art. 18.01 - Search Warrant Requirements Art. 18.02 - Grounds for Issuance

Rights Advisement: Art. 27.14 - Magistrate Warning (separate from Miranda) Art. 38.22 - Confessions/Statements (electronic recording requirement for custodial interrogation) Art. 38.23 - Exclusionary Rule

TEXAS TRANSPORTATION CODE - KEY SECTIONS

Driver Licensing: §521.025 - License Required §521.457 - DWLI (Class C 1st, Class B subsequent or DWI-related)

Traffic Laws: §545.060 - Improper Lane Change §545.104 - Failure to Signal §545.351-352 - Speed Regulations §545.401 - Reckless Driving (Class B misdemeanor) §545.420 - Racing on Highway (Class B misdemeanor)

Financial Responsibility: §601.191 - Requirement to Maintain Insurance

Implied Consent: Chapter 724 - Testing for Intoxication

TEXAS FAMILY CODE - KEY SECTIONS

§71.003 - Family or Household Member (defines relationships) §71.004 - Family Violence Definition Chapter 85 - Protective Orders §261.001 - Child Abuse/Neglect Definitions §261.101 - Mandatory Reporting (48-hour requirement)

Must-Know Penal Code Classifications

CAPITAL FELONY Punishment: Death or life without parole Only Offense: Capital Murder (§19.03)

FIRST DEGREE FELONY Punishment: 5-99 years or life, up to $10,000 fine Examples: Murder, Aggravated Robbery, Aggravated Sexual Assault, Burglary of Habitation with intent to commit felony other than theft

SECOND DEGREE FELONY Punishment: 2-20 years, up to $10,000 fine Examples: Manslaughter, Robbery, Sexual Assault, Aggravated Assault, Arson, Burglary of Habitation

THIRD DEGREE FELONY Punishment: 2-10 years, up to $10,000 fine Examples: Stalking, Tampering with Evidence, Deadly Conduct with Firearm, DWI 3rd+

STATE JAIL FELONY Punishment: 180 days-2 years state jail, up to $10,000 fine Examples: Burglary of Building, Theft $2,500-$30,000, Forgery, POCS (certain amounts), DWI with Child Passenger, Unauthorized Use of Vehicle

CLASS A MISDEMEANOR Punishment: Up to 1 year jail, up to $4,000 fine Examples: Assault Causing Bodily Injury, DWI 1st, Resisting Arrest, Theft $750-$2,500

CLASS B MISDEMEANOR Punishment: Up to 180 days jail, up to $2,000 fine Examples: DWI (certain circumstances), POCS 2 oz or less, Terroristic Threat, Criminal Trespass, Theft $100-$750, Reckless Driving

CLASS C MISDEMEANOR Punishment: Fine up to $500 only (no jail) Examples: Theft under $100, Assault by Contact, Disorderly Conduct, Most Traffic Violations, DWLI 1st offense

Common Mistakes to Avoid

Legal/Constitutional Errors:

Mistake: Searching vehicles after arrest without meeting Gant requirements. **Why It's Wrong:** Arizona v. Gant limits vehicle searches incident to arrest to when arrestee is unsecured and can access vehicle, or evidence of arrest offense might be in vehicle. Simply making arrest near vehicle doesn't justify search. **Correct Approach:** After securing arrestee in patrol car, search vehicle only if evidence of arrest offense likely present, or obtain consent/probable cause for automobile exception, or conduct proper inventory if impounding.

Mistake: Continuing interrogation after suspect invokes rights. **Why It's Wrong:** Once suspect invokes right to remain silent or counsel, all questioning must stop immediately. Continuing violates Miranda and results in suppression. **Correct Approach:** Stop all questioning immediately when rights invoked. Document invocation. Don't attempt to persuade suspect to continue talking.

Mistake: Assuming consent is voluntary when person says "I guess so" or "Do I have a choice?" **Why It's Wrong:** These ambiguous, hesitant responses suggest person feels compelled rather than freely consenting. Courts require clear, unequivocal voluntary consent. **Correct Approach:** When consent is ambiguous, clarify: "You have right to refuse. I'm asking for permission. Do you voluntarily consent?" Get clear yes or no. Accept refusals.

Mistake: Making warrantless arrests for misdemeanors not committed in presence. **Why It's Wrong:** Generally, warrantless misdemeanor arrests require offense occur in officer's presence (exceptions: family violence assault, protective order violations). **Correct Approach:** For misdemeanors not in your presence and no exception applies, obtain warrant or issue citation if authorized.

Mistake: Using deadly force to prevent escape of non-dangerous fleeing felon. **Why It's Wrong:** Tennessee v. Garner prohibits deadly force to prevent escape unless suspect poses significant threat of death/serious injury and committed violent crime involving deadly force. **Correct Approach:** Use deadly force only when suspect presents imminent deadly force threat or is escaping after violent crime and poses ongoing danger. Document basis for belief.

Tactical/Safety Errors:

Mistake: Standing directly in front of doors or vehicle windows (the fatal funnel). **Why It's Wrong:** Provides clear line of fire for anyone inside. Limits your ability to see and react to threats. **Correct Approach:** Approach from angles. Position at B-post for traffic stops, not directly at driver window. Minimize time in fatal funnel.

Mistake: Not watching hands during citizen contacts. **Why It's Wrong:** Hands kill, not people. If you can't see hands, you can't see weapons or threatening movements. **Correct Approach:**

Always watch hands. If hands disappear from view, create distance and issue commands to show hands.

Mistake: Rushing into situations without assessment or backup when time permits. **Why It's Wrong:** Creates unnecessary danger when slowing down and waiting for backup would improve safety without compromising mission. **Correct Approach:** Unless immediate life-threatening emergency exists, assess situation, request backup, develop plan, then act. Time and distance are tactical advantages.

Mistake: Ignoring cover or using concealment instead. **Why It's Wrong:** Concealment hides you but doesn't stop bullets. Cover stops bullets. Using concealment when cover available increases risk. **Correct Approach:** Always seek cover (engine blocks, concrete walls, substantial barriers) over concealment when threats exist.

Investigation/Evidence Errors:

Mistake: Breaking chain of custody by failing to document transfers or delaying evidence submission. **Why It's Wrong:** Creates doubt about evidence integrity and authenticity. Defense exploits gaps to suggest tampering, contamination, or substitution. **Correct Approach:** Submit evidence promptly after collection. Document every transfer with who, when, where, why. Never take evidence home or leave in vehicle overnight.

Mistake: Contaminating evidence by improper handling or packaging. **Why It's Wrong:** Cross-contamination destroys evidentiary value, especially for DNA. Improper packaging (wet biological evidence in plastic) causes degradation. **Correct Approach:** Wear gloves. Use separate, clean packaging for each item. Air-dry biological evidence before packaging in paper. Change gloves between items.

Mistake: Inadequate documentation of force incidents. **Why It's Wrong:** Poor documentation makes defending reasonable force difficult even when force was justified. Vague reports ("I used force to gain compliance") provide no useful information. **Correct Approach:** Document specifically: subject actions, commands given, de-escalation attempts, force used (technique, target area, duration), Graham factors, why force necessary. Be detailed and factual.

Mistake: Not photographing injuries (officer and subject) after force. **Why It's Wrong:** Injuries corroborate resistance and need for force. Lack of photos creates defense argument that injuries didn't exist or weren't as described. **Correct Approach:** Photograph all injuries from multiple angles, including close-ups and context shots. Document even minor injuries. Photograph lack of injuries when relevant.

Professional/Ethical Errors:

Mistake: Lying in reports or testimony to help prosecution. **Why It's Wrong:** Destroys your credibility permanently. One lie discovered means every other statement you've made is questioned. You may face criminal charges (perjury, official oppression). **Correct Approach:**

Always tell truth. If you made mistakes, document them honestly. Honesty is defensible; lies are not.

Mistake: Showing bias in enforcement based on race, ethnicity, or demographics. **Why It's Wrong:** Violates constitutional rights, department policy, and professional ethics. Destroys community trust and creates liability. **Correct Approach:** Base all enforcement decisions on behavior and evidence, never on demographics. Document reasons for decisions based on objective factors.

Mistake: Ignoring or covering up partner misconduct. **Why It's Wrong:** Makes you complicit in wrongdoing. Violates oath and ethical obligations. Eventually discovered, ending careers. **Correct Approach:** Report misconduct through proper channels. Document facts. Your integrity matters more than misplaced loyalty.

Test-Taking Pitfalls

Pitfall #1: Not Reading Questions Completely Problem: Jumping to answer before finishing question causes you to miss key words like "EXCEPT," "NOT," "FIRST," or "MOST appropriate." Solution: Read entire question before looking at answers. Circle key words. Identify what's actually being asked.

Pitfall #2: Overthinking Simple Questions Problem: Making simple questions complicated by adding assumptions or "what ifs" not in the question. Solution: Answer based only on information provided. Don't add facts or assumptions. Simple questions often have simple answers.

Pitfall #3: Choosing First "Right" Answer Instead of BEST Answer Problem: TCOLE asks for BEST answer, not just any correct answer. Multiple options may be partially correct. Solution: Read all four options before selecting. Choose the most complete, most accurate, or most appropriate option even if others seem reasonable.

Pitfall #4: Changing Answers Without Good Reason Problem: Second-guessing yourself and changing answers during review often changes correct answers to wrong ones. Solution: Change answers only when you misread the question or realize clear error. First instinct is usually correct if you've studied well.

Pitfall #5: Spending Too Much Time on Difficult Questions Problem: Getting stuck on hard questions wastes time needed for easier questions, creating time pressure and anxiety. Solution: If question takes more than 2 minutes, mark it and move on. Answer easier questions first, return to difficult ones with remaining time.

Pitfall #6: Leaving Questions Blank Problem: Blank answers guarantee zero points. Even random guesses have 25% success rate. Solution: Answer every question. If unsure, eliminate obviously wrong options and make educated guess from remaining choices.

Pitfall #7: Letting One Bad Section Destroy Confidence Problem: Encountering difficult questions or rough section causes panic, affecting performance on remaining questions. Solution: Remember exam covers many topics. Some sections naturally harder for you. Stay calm, keep moving, answer what you know. Bad section doesn't mean failure.

Pitfall #8: Not Managing Time Effectively Problem: Spending equal time on all questions regardless of difficulty, or not tracking pace, leading to incomplete exam. Solution: Average 1.5 minutes per question. Check time periodically. If behind pace, speed up. Save 15-20 minutes for reviewing flagged questions.

Pitfall #9: Ignoring Gut Instinct on Scenarios Problem: Analyzing scenario questions too technically instead of using common sense and officer safety principles. Solution: For scenarios, ask: "What would a reasonable officer do?" Consider safety first, legal requirements second. If multiple answers seem reasonable, choose option prioritizing safety.

Pitfall #10: Test Anxiety Interfering with Performance Problem: Knowing material but unable to access knowledge due to anxiety and stress. Solution: Use deep breathing, positive self-talk ("I prepared well. I know this material."), taking brief mental breaks (close eyes for 10 seconds), and maintaining perspective (one question doesn't determine outcome).

Last-Minute Study Checklist (72 Hours Before Exam)

THREE DAYS BEFORE EXAM (72 Hours Out):

□ Review this chapter's quick reference sections (terminology, statutes, classifications) □ Retake missed questions from practice exams, focusing on patterns in errors □ Review Graham v. Connor factors and use of force decision-making □ Confirm exam appointment details: date, time, location, what to bring □ Visit testing center if you haven't already (know exactly where it is, parking, estimated travel time) □ Prepare outfit for exam day (comfortable, layered clothing) □ Begin adjusting sleep schedule to be well-rested on exam day □ Avoid introducing new study material—focus on reinforcing what you know □ Review weak content areas identified in practice exams one final time

TWO DAYS BEFORE EXAM (48 Hours Out):

□ Light review only—no intensive studying (your brain needs consolidation time) □ Skim chapter summaries and key takeaways □ Review common mistakes list and mentally commit to avoiding them □ Practice stress management techniques (deep breathing, visualization) □ Visualize success: picture yourself confidently answering questions, finishing on time, seeing "PASS" on screen □ Prepare exam day supplies: ID, confirmation number, keys, water bottle for after exam □ Set multiple alarms for exam day (phone alarm, backup alarm, ask someone to ensure you're awake) □ Eat healthy meals, stay hydrated, avoid alcohol or excessive caffeine □

Get to bed early (aim for 8 hours sleep) □ Avoid cramming—it increases anxiety without improving retention

ONE DAY BEFORE EXAM (24 Hours Out):

□ NO NEW STUDYING—today is rest and mental preparation day □ Quick skim of this chapter's quick reference guide only (15-20 minutes max) □ Light physical activity (walk, light workout) to reduce stress and improve sleep □ Eat nutritious meals, stay hydrated □ Prepare everything for tomorrow: lay out clothes, gather ID and confirmation, charge phone □ Review directions to testing center one last time □ Set out breakfast foods for tomorrow morning □ Relaxing evening: no stressful activities, no intense studying □ Avoid caffeine after 2 PM (interferes with sleep) □ Screen-free time before bed (shut off phone, computer, TV 30 minutes before sleep) □ Get to bed early (8+ hours before wake time) □ Use relaxation techniques if needed: deep breathing, progressive muscle relaxation □ Positive self-talk: "I've prepared thoroughly. I'm ready. I'll do my best tomorrow."

48-Hour Countdown: Hour-by-Hour Guide

EXAM DAY MINUS 48 HOURS (Two Days Before):

Morning: Light review of Graham factors, search warrant exceptions, and Miranda requirements (30 minutes). Then close books for rest of day.

Afternoon: Physical activity or relaxation. Take walk, exercise lightly, or engage in hobby. No studying.

Evening: Prepare exam supplies (ID, confirmation). Set alarms. Healthy dinner, hydrate well. Bed by 10 PM.

EXAM DAY MINUS 24 HOURS (One Day Before):

Morning: Quick 15-minute skim of quick reference terminology. That's it for studying. Healthy breakfast.

Midday: Light physical activity. Organize everything for tomorrow. Triple-check you have valid ID.

Afternoon: Relaxing activities only. Watch movie, read (not study material), spend time with family, light exercise.

Evening: Early, nutritious dinner. Hydrate well. Lay out clothes. Charge phone. Set multiple alarms. Screen-free 30 minutes before bed.

Night: In bed by 9-10 PM. Deep breathing or relaxation techniques if needed. Remind yourself you're prepared.

EXAM DAY:

6:00-7:00 AM: Wake up refreshed (at least 2 hours before departure). Shower, dress comfortably in layers.

7:00-7:30 AM: Healthy breakfast (protein and complex carbs—eggs, whole grain toast, fruit). Avoid excess caffeine (normal amount OK, but don't overdo it). Hydrate well.

7:30-8:00 AM: Quick 10-minute review of quick reference guide IF it helps confidence (some people prefer no review at all—do what works for you). Gather ID and confirmation. Use restroom.

8:00 AM: Depart for testing center (assuming 9:00 AM exam time—adjust for your schedule). Arrive 30-45 minutes early.

8:30 AM: Arrive at testing center. Stay in car if early—use restroom, take deep breaths, positive self-talk.

8:45 AM: Enter testing center. Check in. Store belongings in locker. Use restroom again.

9:00 AM: Begin exam. Read tutorial carefully. Start strong. Remember strategies: read completely, eliminate wrong answers, choose BEST option, flag difficult questions, keep moving.

11:30 AM (approximately): Exam complete! You did it! See your preliminary result. Celebrate regardless of outcome—you've accomplished something significant just by preparing and attempting.

Post-Exam: Retrieve belongings. Decompress. Eat something. Hydrate. Rest. Avoid obsessing over questions you think you missed. Wait for official results.

Additional Resources and Study Materials

Official TCOLE Resources:

- Texas Commission on Law Enforcement website: www.tcole.texas.gov (official source for exam information, licensing requirements, and updates)
- TCOLE Basic Peace Officer Course curriculum (check with your academy for materials)

Texas State Law Resources:

- Texas Statutes: statutes.capitol.texas.gov (official state law database)
- Texas Penal Code (complete text available free online)
- Texas Code of Criminal Procedure (complete text available free online)
- Texas Transportation Code (complete text available free online)

Case Law and Legal Research:

- Graham v. Connor, 490 U.S. 386 (1989) - Use of force standard
- Tennessee v. Garner, 471 U.S. 1 (1985) - Deadly force to prevent escape
- Terry v. Ohio, 392 U.S. 1 (1968) - Stop and frisk authority
- Miranda v. Arizona, 384 U.S. 436 (1966) - Custodial interrogation warnings
- Arizona v. Gant, 556 U.S. 332 (2009) - Vehicle searches incident to arrest

Supplemental Study Materials:

- Your academy's study guides and materials
- TCOLE practice exams (if available through your academy or testing vendor)
- Police department ride-alongs (observe actual application of concepts)
- YouTube channels offering law enforcement exam preparation (verify accuracy against official sources)

Apps and Technology:

- Flashcard apps (Quizlet, Anki) for memorizing statutes and terminology
- Note-taking apps for organizing study materials
- Timer apps for practicing exam pacing

Study Groups and Support:

- Fellow academy graduates or current students
- Online forums for Texas peace officers (verify information against official sources)
- Department mentors or training officers

Important: While supplemental materials can be helpful, always verify information against official TCOLE and Texas statutory sources. Laws change, and unofficial sources may contain outdated or incorrect information. When in doubt, consult official sources.

Your Path Forward: After Passing the Exam

The TCOLE exam is a milestone, not the finish line. Passing opens doors to your law enforcement career, but your real education begins when you start working as a peace officer. Here's what to expect and how to prepare for your career ahead.

Immediate Next Steps After Passing

Celebrate Your Achievement: You've passed a challenging exam requiring months of preparation. That's a significant accomplishment worth celebrating. Take a moment to acknowledge your hard work and success. You've earned it.

Wait for Official Results: Preliminary pass/fail results appear on screen immediately after completing the exam, but official score reports take a few business days to process. TCOLE receives results electronically and processes your licensing paperwork accordingly. You can check your status through your TCOLE online account.

Complete Licensing Process: Passing the exam is one requirement for peace officer licensure, but additional steps remain. Your agency or academy will guide you through: verification of background investigation completion, medical evaluation results, psychological evaluation results, oath of office administration, and formal license issuance by TCOLE. Most agencies handle this process for you, but stay engaged and responsive to requests for information or documentation.

Maintain Your License: Texas peace officer licenses must be maintained through: continuing education requirements (required training hours every license period—your agency tracks this), annual firearms qualification (or more frequent per department policy), adherence to professional standards and ethical conduct, compliance with all TCOLE rules and regulations, and avoiding any conduct that could result in license suspension or revocation (criminal convictions, serious policy violations, integrity issues).

Employment Considerations

If You Have Sponsoring Agency: If you attended academy sponsored by a police department or sheriff's office, your employment process is already underway. After passing TCOLE, your department will proceed with: finalizing background investigation (verifying references, criminal history, employment history), completing medical examination to verify physical capability for duties, psychological evaluation to assess suitability for law enforcement work, swearing-in ceremony and badge/equipment issuance, and assignment to Field Training Officer program.

If You Don't Have Sponsoring Agency: If you completed academy as self-sponsored student, now begins your job search. Prepare professional resume highlighting academy performance, test scores, specialized training or certifications, and relevant work or volunteer experience. Research departments aligned with your goals, values, and preferred work environment (urban vs. rural, large vs. small department, municipal vs. county vs. state). Practice interview skills, especially scenario-based questions about how you'd handle specific situations. Be prepared to discuss your motivation for law enforcement career authentically—departments want genuine passion for service, not just job seekers. Apply broadly—getting hired is competitive. Cast a wide net and be willing to relocate if necessary.

Field Training Officer (FTO) Program

Passing TCOLE doesn't mean you're ready for solo patrol. Every new officer, regardless of academy performance, must complete Field Training Officer program under veteran officer supervision. FTO programs typically last 12-16 weeks (3-4 months), though some agencies extend to 6 months depending on performance and complexity.

What FTO Involves: You'll be paired with experienced Field Training Officer who evaluates your performance across all aspects of patrol work. You'll respond to actual calls for service, applying academy knowledge to real situations with immediate feedback. You'll learn department-specific policies, procedures, culture, and expectations. You'll develop practical skills under supervision: report writing using department systems, radio communications with dispatch, evidence processing with department property system, court testimony preparation, and tactical decision-making in fluid situations. You'll gradually assume more independence as you demonstrate competency—starting with FTO handling most tasks while you observe, progressing to you handling tasks with FTO supervision, advancing to you handling calls independently with FTO nearby, and eventually reaching solo patrol readiness.

Approach FTO Program With:

Humility: You don't know everything despite passing the exam. Academy taught fundamentals, but field application is different. Be willing to learn from experienced officers who've handled thousands of calls. Ask questions. Admit when you don't know something rather than pretending you do.

Professionalism: FTOs evaluate you on attitude as much as skills. Show up early, stay late, maintain professional appearance, treat everyone (citizens, coworkers, suspects) with respect, accept criticism gracefully, and demonstrate emotional maturity under stress. Your attitude affects whether FTOs recommend your retention.

Work Ethic: Volunteer for assignments rather than waiting to be told. Take initiative on report writing, follow-up investigation, and evidence processing. Help other officers with tasks during downtime. Demonstrate eagerness to learn and contribute. Work ethic often matters more than raw talent—agencies want officers who work hard and care.

Coachability: Accept criticism and implement feedback. FTOs will critique your performance—that's their job. Don't become defensive. Thank them for feedback, ask clarifying questions if needed, and demonstrate improvement. Officers who resist coaching don't survive FTO programs.

Initiative: Don't wait to be told what to do. Anticipate needs and act. If there's downtime, proactively review reports, organize equipment, study calls from earlier shift, or conduct proactive patrol. Officers who need constant direction struggle in field work requiring independent judgment.

What to Expect: FTO is challenging. You'll make mistakes—everyone does. You'll face situations you don't know how to handle. You'll feel overwhelmed sometimes. That's normal and expected. FTOs understand you're learning. What they're evaluating is your response to challenges: Do you learn from mistakes? Do you seek guidance when unsure? Do you maintain composure under stress? Do you treat people respectfully? Do you demonstrate sound judgment? These qualities matter more than knowing every statute or procedure perfectly.

Continuing Education and Career Development

Your education doesn't end with TCOLE and FTO. Law enforcement is dynamic field requiring continuous learning.

Specialized Training Opportunities:

Crisis Intervention Team (CIT): 40-hour course teaching de-escalation and mental health crisis response. Increasingly valuable as mental health calls grow. CIT officers are resources for entire departments and often experience more satisfying outcomes on difficult calls.

Drug Recognition Expert (DRE): Advanced training in drug impairment detection beyond basic DWI investigation. DREs can testify about drug effects and become department experts on drug investigations. This certification opens doors to specialized DWI enforcement units.

Field Training Officer Certification: After 2-3 years experience, pursue FTO certification to train new officers. This develops leadership skills, enhances your own knowledge (teaching reinforces learning), and positions you for future promotional opportunities.

Supervisor and Leadership Courses: Leadership training prepares you for promotional exams and supervisory roles. Even if you don't plan to promote immediately, leadership skills benefit all officers.

Specialized Unit Training: If interested in K-9, SWAT, investigations, school resource officer, traffic enforcement, or other specialized units, seek relevant training. Certifications and specialized skills make you competitive for these coveted positions.

Professional Organizations: Join professional organizations for networking, advocacy, training opportunities, and support: Texas Police Association, Texas Municipal Police Association, Combined Law Enforcement Associations of Texas (CLEAT), and national organizations like Fraternal Order of Police. These organizations provide legal defense assistance, legislative advocacy, professional development, and connections with officers statewide.

Long-Term Career Paths:

Patrol Officer Foundation: Most officers spend early career years on patrol—the backbone of law enforcement. Don't rush past this. Patrol experience is invaluable foundation for any specialty or promotion. Great detectives, supervisors, and command staff started as great patrol officers.

Specialized Units: After establishing patrol proficiency (typically 2-5 years), consider specialized assignments: Criminal investigations (detectives handling follow-up on serious crimes), Narcotics (undercover and overt drug enforcement), K-9 (handler for police service dog), SWAT/tactical teams (high-risk operations), Traffic enforcement (collision investigation, DWI enforcement), School resource officer (assigned to schools), Training (academy instructor, department trainer), Administrative assignments (records, property, evidence management).

Supervisory Track: If leadership interests you, pursue promotional opportunities: Corporal/Senior Officer (first-line leadership, mentoring newer officers), Sergeant (front-line supervisor, typically supervises 5-10 officers), Lieutenant (watch commander, shift supervision, policy development), Captain/Major (division commander, specialized unit oversight), Assistant Chief/Chief Deputy (second-in-command, administrative oversight), Chief of Police/Sheriff (agency head, policy-making, community liaison).

Federal Opportunities: After gaining municipal or county experience (typically 3-5 years minimum), federal agencies recruit experienced officers: FBI, DEA, ATF, Secret Service, U.S. Marshals Service, Border Patrol, ICE, and others. Federal positions typically offer higher salaries, better benefits, and different investigative focuses than municipal work.

Training and Education: Some officers transition to teaching, becoming academy instructors, college criminal justice professors, or training coordinators. This path allows you to shape future generations of officers while leveraging your field experience.

Maintaining Excellence Throughout Your Career

Law enforcement isn't just a job—it's a career requiring ongoing commitment to excellence.

Never Stop Learning: Laws change through legislation and court decisions. Tactics evolve through research and experience. Technology advances constantly (body cameras, less-lethal options, data systems). Stay current through: attending continuing education training, reading professional publications and legal updates, staying informed on case law affecting your work, seeking feedback from supervisors and peers, learning from mistakes (yours and others'), and remaining intellectually curious about your profession.

Maintain Physical Fitness: Law enforcement is physically demanding. You may need to pursue suspects on foot, control resisting subjects, work long shifts with irregular sleep, and perform physically exhausting tasks under stress. Physical fitness affects: officer safety (fitness enables you to protect yourself and others), career longevity (fit officers have fewer injuries and longer careers), mental health (exercise reduces stress and improves mood), and professional credibility (fitness demonstrates self-discipline and professionalism). Make fitness a lifestyle, not a pre-academy crash course.

Protect Your Mental Health: Law enforcement work is stressful. You'll see humanity at its worst: victims of violence, child abuse, death, suffering, and injustice. You'll work irregular hours disrupting sleep and family life. You'll face criticism from media and public despite doing your job correctly. This stress accumulates over time, affecting relationships, health, and wellbeing if not addressed.

Strategies for Mental Health Protection:

Develop Support Network: Maintain relationships with family, friends outside law enforcement, and trusted colleagues who understand the work. Don't isolate yourself or believe nobody understands. Connection is protective against stress.

Utilize Employee Assistance Programs: Most agencies offer confidential counseling through EAPs. Use these resources preventively, not just during crises. Talking to professional counselor doesn't mean you're weak—it means you're smart enough to maintain your mental health.

Establish Boundaries: Law enforcement can consume your life if you let it. Maintain hobbies and interests outside work. Spend quality time with loved ones. Take vacations and actually disconnect. Work is important, but it's not everything.

Process Difficult Calls: After traumatic calls (child deaths, serious injuries, officer-involved shootings), process your emotions. Talk to peers, supervisors, or counselors. Bottling emotions leads to cumulative trauma over time. Critical Incident Stress Debriefing (CISD) teams help officers process traumatic events—use them.

Monitor Warning Signs: Be aware of symptoms indicating excessive stress: persistent irritability or anger, withdrawal from family and friends, increased alcohol use or other unhealthy coping, sleep problems, hypervigilance off-duty, cynicism and loss of empathy, frequent thoughts about leaving the job. If you notice these signs, seek help proactively.

Remember Why You Started: On difficult days (and there will be many), remember why you chose this career. Most officers enter law enforcement to serve their communities, help people, make a difference, and protect those who can't protect themselves. That purpose doesn't change even when the job is hard. Reconnect with your original motivation.

Maintain Integrity: Your reputation and integrity are your most valuable professional assets. Once damaged, they're nearly impossible to fully restore. Maintain ethical standards even when inconvenient or costly: Be honest in reports and testimony (even when dishonesty might strengthen your case), follow department policies even when nobody's watching, treat all citizens with respect regardless of how they treat you, report misconduct even when it involves friends or partners, maintain professional boundaries with citizens and confidential informants, refuse bribes, gratuities, and inappropriate benefits, and make ethical decisions even when legal decisions might be questionable.

Integrity isn't about being perfect—you'll make mistakes. Integrity is about being honest about mistakes, learning from them, and consistently trying to do what's right even when it's difficult. Officers of integrity have long, fulfilling careers. Officers who compromise integrity face short careers ending in scandal, termination, or worse.

Serve With Pride, But Stay Humble: You've earned the right to wear the badge. That badge represents authority, responsibility, and public trust. Carry it with pride, knowing you've worked hard to earn it. But stay humble. The badge doesn't make you better than anyone—it makes you a servant. You serve the public, not rule them. Police powers are granted by the people to protect the people. Exercise authority with humility, compassion, and respect for human dignity. The best officers are confident in their abilities yet humble in their bearing—firm but fair, professional but personable, authoritative but empathetic.

Conclusion: Your New Beginning

If you're reading this, you're either about to take the TCOLE exam or you've recently passed it. Either way, you're standing at the threshold of your law enforcement career. This study guide has prepared you for the exam, but the exam is just the beginning.

The real test comes every shift when you make split-second decisions affecting people's lives, liberty, and safety. It comes when you're exhausted but someone needs your help. It comes when you face criticism despite doing everything right. It comes when you must balance enforcement with compassion, authority with humanity, and safety with service.

You've chosen one of the most challenging, rewarding, and important careers in society. Law enforcement officers stand between order and chaos, protect the vulnerable, uphold the law, and serve their communities with courage and dedication. That responsibility is enormous, but you're ready for it. You've studied hard, prepared thoroughly, and demonstrated commitment to this profession. Now go prove yourself in the field.

Remember: The citizens you'll serve are your neighbors, your community, your responsibility. Treat them with respect and dignity. The suspects you'll arrest are human beings deserving fair treatment under law. Enforce laws impartially and professionally. The victims you'll help are experiencing their worst days. Show them empathy and provide competent assistance. Your fellow officers are your brothers and sisters in blue. Support them, but also hold them accountable to the highest standards.

Be safe. Be professional. Be ethical. Be the officer your community deserves.

Welcome to law enforcement. Your badge awaits.

Good luck on your exam. You've got this.

Made in United States
North Haven, CT
05 November 2026